The Collected Works of
Marie-Louise von Franz

MLvF

Volume 7

General Editors

Steven Buser

Leonard Cruz

Marie-Louise von Franz
1915-1998

꙳ Volume 7 ꙳

Aurora Consurgens

A Document Attributed to Thomas Aquinas
on the Problem of Opposites in Alchemy

A Companion Work to C.G. Jung's
Mysterium Coniunctionis

Marie-Louise von Franz

Translated by R.F.C. Hull and A.S.B. Glover

Ꮐ CHIRON PUBLICATIONS • ASHEVILLE, NORTH CAROLINA

Logo of the Foundation of Jungian Psychology, Küsnacht Switzerland:
Fons mercurialis from Rosarium Philosophorum 1550 (Fountain of Life).

Current edition originally published by the Bollingen Foundation
Bollingen Foundation, New York, N.Y.

www.ChironPublications.com

Interior update and cover design by Danijela Mijailovic
Cover image by Martina Ott
Printed primarily in the United States of America.
Translated by R.F.C. Hull and A.S.B. Glover

ISBN 978-1-63051-962-9 paperback
ISBN 978-1-63051-963-6 hardcover

"My personal conjecture is that Aurora is indeed this last seminar...significant enough to warrant my submitting them to the judgement of my reader." (Marie-Louise von Franz, *Collected Works,* Volume 7, Paragraph 643)

FOREWORD OF THE FOUNDATION
FOR JUNGIAN PSYCHOLOGY

Since his first encounter with Marie-Louise von Franz, C. G. Jung had the feeling that she "had something to do with alchemy." When she started in analysis with Jung, but had no money as a young woman, she translated alchemical texts for him instead of a payment. She was able to do this as she majored in Latin and Greek at the University of Zurich. Jung first gave her a collection of alchemical treatises published in 1593 from the *Musaeum Hermeticum,* with the order to make translations and excerpts of what she considered symbolically interesting. She felt overwhelmed, but Jung only advised her to use her intuition. One evening she wanted to start and opened a random page. "I saw exactly what I had dreamed a year ago. My dream. The dream I had, was there written in Latin!" This meaningful coincidence had shaken her deeply and at the same time showed her that she was fatefully linked to alchemy. She concludes that one must study alchemy, because "in there is everything that is unconscious to us, and what we actually have to reconcile harmoniously with Christianity in order to come to a holistic view of the world." Marie-Louise von Franz tells all this in an interview she gave in 1982 in her tower in Bollingen.[1]

C. G. Jung wrote in his preface to *Mysterium Coniunctionis,* "The *Aurora Consurgens* tries to reconcile Christian and alchemical views, and I have therefore chosen it as an example of a confrontation of the medieval-Christian zeitgeist with alchemical philosophy and to a certain extent as an illustration for the preceding representation of the alchemical problem of the opposites set at the end of the work. For the first and second part I am responsible, for the third part my colleague Miss Dr. Marie-Louise von Franz. We issue this scripture together because both authors are also involved in each other's works."[2] The prerequisite for the creation of this three-volumes was the complete

---

[1] *Marie-Louise von Franz,* Interview by Françoise Selhofer, Bollingen September 1982, CD with Original sound in German, VoiceOver in English, French, Spanish, Italian, with English subtitles.

[2] C. G. Jung, GW 14 I, Walther-Verlag, Olten und Freiburg im Breisgau, 1971, p. 14.

translation of the Greek and Latin texts by Marie-Louise von Franz. The understanding of the difficult medieval Latin requires special knowledge. In the Collected Works by C. G. Jung published in German, Marie-Louise von Franz is the only author who writes a contribution as her own volume (GW 14/III).[3]

C. G. Jung gave Marie-Louise von Franz from his own library a carefully restored treatise by Heinrich Khunrath (1560-1605) with the immodest title: *AMPHITHEATRUM SAPIENTIAE AETERNAE.*[4] It is the well-preserved complete second and final edition of 1609, published posthumously.[5] On the edge of Jung's ex-libris, which he glued to the first page, Jung wrote by hand: "To thank his faithful collaborator for manifold help. Jan. 1943." This was perhaps the first alchemical treatise out of which Marie-Louise von Franz founded her own historical-alchemical library.

In the Name of the Foundation for Jungian Psychology, Küsnacht
June 21, 2022

PD Dr. Hansueli F. Etter
President

---

[3] Marie-Louise von Franz is only mentioned in a footnote in the English version of the Collected Works of C. G. Jung: «This refers to the Swiss edition, which was published in three parts, each a separate volume, the third being devoted to a contribution by Marie-Louise von Franz. Parts I and II constitute the present volume. Part III has appeared in English under the title *Aurora Consurgens: A Document Attributed to Thomas Aquinas on the Problem of Opposites in Alchemy* (Bollingen Series LXXVII, New York and London, 1966) as a companion volume to *Mysterium Coniunctionis* but outside the Collected Works. –EDITORES. » C. G. Jung, CW, Vol. 14, Foreword, XV, footnote 6.

[4] «Theatre of the eternal alone true wisdom».
[5] Heinrich Khunrath, *AMPHITHEATRUM SAPIENTIAE AETERNAE,* Hanau 1609. A facsimile edited by C. Gilly, A. Hallacker, H.-P Neumann, Wilhelm Schmidt-Biggmann, Stuttgart Bad Canstatt, was published in 2014 as volume 6 of the series: Clavis Pansophiae.

TABLE OF CONTENTS

FOREWORD

1 It was Professor C. G. Jung who discovered the alchemical treatise herewith presented, *Aurora Consurgens,* and brought it to light again. It was at his request that I undertook to prepare the present edition, for which purpose he supplied me with photocopies of the manuscripts and placed at my disposal his copious material on alchemy, which is very difficult to come by even in libraries. For this and for his great help and encouragement during the work I would here like to express my warmest thanks. As to the hypothesis that the text might represent the last words of St. Thomas Aquinas, I must emphasize that my primary concern was with the position of the text in the history of alchemy and with its psychological interpretation. I am fully aware that I lack the knowledge necessary for any kind of excursion into hagio-graphy–but unfortunately the text itself compels one to cut across realms of thought which by their very nature are divided. My concluding chapter, therefore, is nothing but a discussion of an hypothesis, which I put

2 forward in the hope that this question will be clarified by the results of further research.

To me it seemed of greater importance that this valuable text should be made accessible to a wider public, whoever the author might be.

March 1957   MARIE-LOUISE VON FRANZ

EDITORIAL NOTE

The second editions of C. G. Jung's *Psychology and Alchemy* and *The Practice of Psychotherapy* (Vols. 12 and 16 in the Col-lected Works) and the forthcoming edition of *Alchemical Studies* (Vol. 13) are cited in the present work by paragraph numbers.

The translations from Latin and Greek in the Commentary are by A. S. B. Glover unless otherwise indicated. For quotations from the *Summa Theologica* of St. Thomas Aquinas, the trans-lation by the English Dominican Fathers has been used with the permission of the publishers, Benziger Brothers (New York) and Burns, Oates and Washbourne (London).

Paragraph Numbering

Throughout the *Collected Works of Marie-Louise von Franz*, each paragraph has been numbered within the volumes, both in order to assist in locating quotations and to optimize scholarly engagement. In this particular volume, each line of the Latin text was previously numbered, beginning anew with each chapter. While we have left this numbering system, we have also continued our editorial style of numbering each paragraph of English text of von Franz's writing. This is distinct and additional to the numbering of the lines in the Latin text.

FOREWORD TO THE ENGLISH EDITION

3   Although this English edition of *Aurora Consurgens* appears almost ten years after the completion of the German text, the "secret" of alchemy, unlike certain other fields to which Jungian psychology can be applied, has never really lost its fascination for me. The secret has to do with the relation of the unconscious psyche to inorganic matter and to the unitary reality which may be surmised as being their common substrate—that *unus mundus* which Jung describes in the last chapter of *Mysterium Coniunctionis*. It seems to me that with every year the progress of the physical sciences is catching up with the bold results of Jung's pioneer work, and that the time draws nearer when this psychophysical unitary reality will assume a form that may be apprehended by the intellect, even though it cannot be visualized concretely. Here I will mention only two representative examples: the relativists among modern physicists have come up against an "uncertainty relation" of time to events that have not yet entered the field of observation, while for their opponents in quantum physics the principle of causality has been put in question. These difficulties suggest that serious consideration should be given to Jung's proposed introduction of another principle into the explanation of nature, namely synchronicity.

4   In this controversy between the relativists and the quantum physicists over the determinism or indeterminism of events, the German physicist Aloys Wenzl has attempted the role of mediator by proposing that the four-dimensional mathematical continuum which constitutes the Einsteinian model of the universe be regarded *as an only potentially existent model* of reality, whereas the phenomena observed in quantum physics would represent the discontinuous actualizations of these mathematical possibilities.[1] The Einsteinian model would thus become a conceptual parallel of Jung's *unus mundus*, which in Jung's view can be conceived in the form of mathematical structures.

5   Further, a French physicist, Olivier Costa de Beauregard, has

---

[1] *Die philosophischen Grenzfragen der modernen Naturwissenschaft*, pp. 127f.

made the proposal, based on the most recent developments in cybernetic studies, that the physical universe must possess a psychic "underside" as the sphere *par excellence* of "negentropy," [2] and that the unconscious should be conceived as possibly coextensive with the Minkowski-Einsteinian four-dimensional world or "block universe." This would explain the timelessness of the unconscious and certain ESP phenomena. [3]

6   Indeed, Costa de Beauregard goes a step further, arriving independently at a parallel conception of Jung's hypothesis of an "absolute knowledge" (underlying synchronistic phenomena, for instance). The psychic or infrapsychic underside of the universe would have, in Costa de Beauregard's view, to be conceived as a "source of information" which embraces all possible knowledge, a kind of "supraconsciousness" of which the conscious phenomena in animals and men are little crystallizations. The information it contains consists of images that correspond to external situations. [4]

7   I mention this theory because it seems to me that the concept of a *unus mundus* and the hypothesis of an absolute knowledge are no longer so strange today as they were some years ago, seeing that certain branches of modern physics and of information theory have arrived at parallel conceptions. The time may not be too far off when physics and depth psychology will really be able to join hands, [5] and only then will the full significance of Jung's rediscovery of alchemy be appreciated. Perhaps, too, the hypothesis I have put forward, that the *Aurora* text may go back to St. Thomas Aquinas, will then appear less absurd than the reader might think at first sight. Even though I was not able to convince my anonymous critic in the *Bulletin Thomiste*, [6] he nevertheless admits that the idea is "seductive," and Father Victor White recently assured me in a letter that he "likes the

---

[2] Since entropy is the ceaseless running down of the universe by loss of heat, negentropy would be a contrary principle by which "improbable states of order" with higher energy potential are built up.

[3] *Le Second Principe de la science du temps.*

[4] The discovery of a "species memory" in lower organisms (e.g., flatworms), which may be chemically transmitted by the RNA and DNA molecules, also throws a new light on Jung's concept of the collective unconscious. Cf. the studies by James McConnell in *The Worm Runner's Digest,* published at the University of Michigan.

[5] Cf. Ernst Anrich, *Moderne Physik und Tiefenpsychologie.*

[6] Vol. X (1957), I, pp. 33ff.

idea, though there still seem to be a great many difficulties."[7]

The fact that the style and content of *Aurora* differ so widely from St. Thomas's usual manner of writing seems to present, as before, the chief difficulty; but I think two things have to be considered which I would like to repeat here. Firstly, the experience of a breakthrough of the unconscious must necessarily assume a form quite different from that of a text consciously composed by its author, and it will therefore not contain the same clearly defined concepts.[8] Jung himself once said to me jokingly: "When the philologists dig me up again a thousand years hence, they will be a hundred percent certain that the essay on synchronicity and *Answer to Job* cannot have been written by the same author, let alone by the same author in the same year." Often philological criticism, when applied to a creative genius, is too rigid, and St. Thomas was undoubtedly a personality who burst asunder the framework of the conventional scholastic. His sudden breaking off of the *Summa*, together with the reports of his mental disturbance or of some shattering inner experience, seem to me as before to indicate that the approach of death had brought the unconscious uncommonly close.[9]

[7] Father White thinks it odd that St. Thomas did not quote the Moerbeke translation of *De anima* which he himself had put in hand. Against this it must be said that the older Greco-Latin translation differs but slightly from Moerbeke's, so that it is not possible to verify for sure the source of a short passage freely quoted. (Cf. my introduction, infra, pp. 8f.) More to the point, however, is the fact that St. Thomas still used the older translation in his commentary on the first book of Aristotle's *Physics*, and therefore went over to the Moerbeke version only after 1267. (Cf. Pelster, "Die Übersetzungen der Aristotelischen Metaphysik in den Werken des hl. Thomas von Aquin," pp. 377f.; also Grabmann, "Guglielmo di Moerbeke," pp. 41ff., and *Forschungen über die lateinischen Aristoteles-übersetzungen des 13. Jahrh.*, pp. 190ff.; and Verbeke, *Thémistius: Commentaire sur le traité de l'âme d'Aristote, trad. de G. de Moerbeke.*) When, on his deathbed, the unconscious broke through in St. Thomas, it would surely have brought back into his mind the older text which he knew in his youth, together with the alchemical memories from the time of his studies under Albertus Magnus.

[8] The only genuine Aristotle quotation in *Aurora* (infra, p. 37) occurs, how- ever, in a context that fully agrees with St. Thomas's other ideas. Cf. A. C. Pegis ("St. Thomas and the Nicomachaean Ethics," p. 73): "The nature of man is naturally endless since in fact no created good can terminate his intellectual desire short of the vision of the divine essence."

[9] Father White observes in his letter: "Have you noticed that St. Thomas stopped writing the *Summa* just when he had come to deal with the *partes poenitentiae* beginning with the *confessio*? I have often noticed that this presents difficulties

9   So I can still stand today by my proposition—and it is no more than that. On the other hand, in this English edition of the book various errors, incomplete quotations, wrong references, etc. are corrected. And here I would like to express my deepest thanks to Mr. A. S. B. Glover, whose verification of quotations and references when checking the bibliographical data has enabled many improvements to be made in this edition. For his patience and support and for his scholarly translation of the *Aurora* text, I would like to express my lasting gratitude, as well as to Mr. R. F. C. Hull for his careful translation of Parts I, III, and IV.

10   For the present edition I have tried to orient myself with respect to the literature that has appeared in the interim, but working in Switzerland and not having the time to travel abroad I have encountered considerable difficulties in this respect. Thanks to the helpfulness of the public library in Fribourg, I was able to find some of the books I needed, but the collection is limited and some works that I wanted to consult were not obtainable. What particularly surprised me in this connection, however, was the paucity of theological works that concern themselves with comparisons between modern theories of the unconscious and St. Thomas's theory of the soul.[10] I am convinced that a study, by one more qualified than I, of such concepts as the νοῦς ποιητικός, *Sapientia Dei,* and the *rationes aeternae* would bring to light many stimulating points of agreement with Jung's concept of the self, the collective unconscious, and the archetypes. The archetypes, because of their irrepresentable potentiality, seem to correspond by and large to the *intellectus possibilis.* Jung's idea of a potential *unus mundus* seems to me a modern

to those who—with or without analysis—have had a 'drop-through' into the unconscious and so come to realize the inadequacy of conscious *confessio.*"

10 Klingseis ("Moderne Theorien über das Unterbewusstsein und die Thomistische Psychologie") does not once mention either Freud or Jung, and Nolan (*St. Thomas and the Unconscious Mind*), though he mentions Jung, gives an inadequate and partly erroneous account of his views and moreover seems to possess no empirical knowledge of the unconscious. Kelly (*Die neuscholastische und die empirische Psychologie*) does not mention Jung at all. Exceptions must be made of Father Meseguer's very broadminded and intelligent book *The Secret of Dreams,* Father White's *God and the Unconscious,* Father Goldbrunner's *Individuation,* and Joseph Rudin's *Psychotherapie und Religion.* Cf. also the articles in the volume *Neurose und Religion.*

scientific formulation of the archetypal image of *Sapientia Dei*, with, however, the incalculable difference that the *unus mundus* is a concept derived from pure empiricism, whereas that of *Sapientia Dei* is purely metaphysical. Nevertheless, the gulf between the two might, in my opinion, actually have been bridged when, at the end of his life, St. Thomas experienced how the *Sapientia Dei*, which till then had existed for him only as a metaphysical concept in his mind, suddenly revealed its overwhelming psychic reality.

✦

11   At the time when Jung had finished the first draft of *Mysterium Coniunctionis*,[11] in 1944, he had a serious accident followed by the grave illness he describes in his memoirs.[12] During this illness he experienced, on the threshold of death, the great visions of the *coniunctio* reported there. When I saw him again after his illness, he said: "What I wrote in the *Mysterium* is true, I don't need to alter the text. But I only know now how real these things are."

12   Might it not be that St. Thomas Aquinas too, only experienced on his deathbed, when the Song of Songs flooded back into his memory, how real Wisdom and a union with her can be?

Küsnacht-Zurich, June 1964   MARIE-LOUISE VON FRANZ

11 The first draft included "The Psychology of the Transference," published separately in 1946.
12 *Memories, Dreams, Reflections*, pp. 270ff., esp. p. 274 (Amer. edn.; in the U.K. edn., pp. 289ff., p. 294).

ABBREVIATIONS AND SYMBOLS

The MSS denoted by the sigla P, V, etc., are described on pp. 25ff.

P	Codex Parisinus, Bibl. Nat. Latin. No. 14006
P_2	Corrections in P by a second hand
V	Codex Vindobonensis, Österr. Nationalbibliothek No. 5230
V_2	Corrections in V by a second hand
M	Codex Marcianus Venetiarum (Valentinelli, V, 155)
M_2	Corrections in M by a second hand
Rh	Codex Rhenoviensis 172, Zentralbibliothek, Zurich
Rh_2	Corrections in Rh by a second hand
B	Codex in Biblioteca Universitaria, Bologna, No. 747
L	Codex Vossianus Chemicus 520, Leiden, University Library, No. 29
L_2	Corrections in L by a second hand
D	Printed version in Rhenanus, *Harmoniae inperscrutabilis* etc., Frankfort, 1625
[ ]	deleted by editor
< >	added by editor
( )	variants found in single Codices, too good to be consigned only to mid-page apparatus
~	passage of some length omitted
conj.	conjecture
om.	omitted
add.	added
codd.	found in all MSS

I

INTRODUCTION

1. PRELIMINARY

13 As C. G. Jung has shown in *Psychology and Alchemy*, the early
Latin texts of Western alchemy, like the earlier Greek and
Arabic ones, were written in a frame of mind which caused the
alchemist, seeking the divine secret of matter, to project his own
unconscious into the unknown nature of chemical substances.[1]
These early texts have therefore become, for us, documents of
the greatest value in regard to the formation of symbols in general and the individuation process in particular,[2] whereas their
chemical content is of significance only from the historical
point of view. Although they were written before the time when
alchemy split into chemistry on the one hand and hermeneutics
on the other, some of the texts lay more stress on τὰ φυσικά, the
"physical" or "chemical" aspect of the opus, while others give
prominence to τὰ μυστικά, its "mystical" side, and therefore have
a more "psychological" significance.[3] Among those texts whose
significance is almost exclusively psychological we must reckon
the treatise entitled *Aurora Consurgens*, which, both in content
and style, occupies a unique place in the alchemical literature
of its time. Jung was the first to discover the importance of this
treatise, and he discussed it briefly in *Psychology and Alchemy*.[4]
Whereas other texts only occasionally cite conventional passages
from the Holy Scriptures, this treatise is composed almost entirely of Biblical quotations, whose "alchemical" meaning is
hinted at by the interpolation of quotations from classical alchemy. We must therefore suppose that whatever the author
may have understood by "alchemy," he was trying to describe,
or give shape to, a religious experience or—in psychological
terms—an immediate experience of the unconscious. The treatise
was considered "blasphemous" by a later, "enlightened" age,[5]

1 *Psychology and Alchemy*, pars. 346ff., 357ff.   2 Ibid.
3 Par. 342.   4 Pars. 464ff.   5 Par. 464.

but to me it seems beyond doubt that the author was passionately serious and was attempting to express a *mysterium ineffabile*.

14   It is perhaps no accident that the most frequently quoted passages from the Old Testament are those in which the mysterious figure of Sapientia Dei—Wisdom—plays a central role. This Gnostic figure is the chief protagonist, and she is identified with Mary and with the "soul in matter." The anima functions as the mediator in any experience of the unconscious; she is the first content to cross the threshold, and she transmits to consciousness those images from the unconscious which compensate the orthodox Christian ideas that dominate our conscious view of the world.[6] In view of the recent solemn declaration of the dogma of the Assumption of the Virgin, one cannot but regard the glorification of a divine female figure in *Aurora* as a prophetic presentiment of coming events. But behind this figure we catch glimpses of the abyss of the *nigredo*, of the psychological shadow and chthonic man, whose integration has begun to present ethics with some troublesome questions. At all events the problem of darkness, as the text and commentary will show, is touched upon in the *Aurora* though it is not solved.

15   The treatise is traditionally attributed to Thomas Aquinas—an attribution so surprising and, at first sight, so unlikely [7] that hitherto it has never been taken seriously. This is due, among other things, to the fact that the importance of the treatise was not recognized before. The pros and cons of the attribution will not be discussed at this point, but only after we have given the commentary on the text. Whoever the author may have been, he was a man who was vouchsafed an overpowering revelation of the unconscious, which he was unable to describe in the usual ecclesiastical style but only with the help of alchemical symbols. The treatise has about it an air of strangeness and loneliness—which, it may be, touched and isolated the author himself.

[6] *Psychology and Alchemy*, Part I.   [7] Cf. Jung's view, ibid., par. 465.

2. THE TRANSMISSION OF THE TEXT

16 A new edition of the treatise variously entitled *Aurora Consurgens*, "De alchimia," and "Liber Trinitatis" is justified if only because this important work is scarcely known at all, the main reason being that till now it has been available only in a single rare printing in the collection of Johannes Rhenanus, *Harmoniae inperscrutabilis chymico-philosophicae sive Philosophorum antiquorum consentientium Decades duae* (Frankfurt, 1625), and in a few scattered manuscripts.

17 More accessible to posterity was the so-called Part II of *Aurora*, which enjoyed a wide circulation in the compilation entitled *Artis auriferae, quam Chemiam vocant, Volumina duo* (Basel, 1593 and 1610), and in other editions. This second part is, in my view, *a commentary on the first part by another hand*. Evidence for this, aside from its completely different style, is the repetition of quotations from Part I,[1] the naming of Albertus Magnus,[2] who in Part I is never cited by name, and the introductory words typical of a commentary: "In the foregoing it was shown . . ."[3] Also, only Part I is cited in the "Rosarium philosophorum."[4] In contrast to the entirely original, poetico-rhetorical, confessional style of Part I, Part II has a prosaically didactic character which follows the usual style of the contemporary alchemical treatises. The fact that a personified "Mater Alchimia" appears in Part II, that Geber is frequently cited, and that medical considerations occupy a prominent place, seems to me an indication that it was written in the fourteenth or fifteenth

1 For instance the saying: "The mockery of science is the cause of ignorance." *
Also quotations from Avicenna (*Artis auriferae*, 1610, I, p. 147) and Alphidius (p. 140). [For the Latin or Greek of the quotations marked with an asterisk, see Appendix 1, pp. 435ff.]

2 Ibid., p. 153.   3 "In praelibatis ostensum est . . ."

4 *Art. aurif.* (1610), II, pp. 133–252. Ruska assigns the "Rosarium philosophorum" first to the 14th, then to the 15th cent.

5

century. Though this commentary was appended to Part I even in the manuscripts of the fifteenth century, it was published on its own by Conrad Waldkirch in his edition of *Artis auriferae* because, he says,[5] Part I profaned the Christian mysteries by applying them to alchemy. For similar reasons our text may have given offence even earlier and been thrust to one side,[6] although it is without doubt an important document of medieval alchemy.

[5] *Art. aurif.*, I, p. 118.
[6] It is sometimes cited in later works, though the source is not given.

3. THE SOURCES

18 Most of the alchemical quotations in *Aurora,* for which the author almost always gives the source, could be identified. One very general saying ascribed to a certain "Alphonsus," and one source cited in the printed edition as "Liber quintae essentiae," could not be traced, together with a few quotations from Morienus and Calid. The traceable sources are all early works in Latin, the great majority being Latin translations of Arabic treatises. The most important of these is "Lumen luminum," which in *Aurora* is ascribed to the Arabian alchemist Rhazis and later also circulated under the title "Aristotelis de perfecto magisterio." [1] It is cited by Thomas of Cantimpré as a work of Aristotle's, and Thomas of Cantimpré is mentioned in the *Speculum maius* of Vincent of Beauvais,[2] so that it must have been current

1 A "De perfecto magisterio" is attributed to Aristotle in *Bibliotheca chemica curiosa,* I, pp. 638–59, and *Theatrum chemicum* (1659), III, pp. 76–127. The latter volume also contains a "Liber perfecti magisterii" of Arnaldus of Villanova, "qui Lumen luminum nuncupatur" (pp. 128–43). As Arnaldus refers to this treatise as *his* "Lumen luminum," it cannot be identical with the "Lumen luminum" mentioned in *Aurora.* Rather, both he and the author of "De perfecto magisterio" seem to have used "Lumen luminum" as a common source, which in "Consilium coniugii" (*Ars chemica,* p. 50), as in *Aurora,* is ascribed to Rhazis (infra, pp. 48f., n. 9). Cf. Berthelot, *La Chimie au moyen âge,* I, pp. 145, 234, 269, 273, 311ff.; Lippmann, *Entstehung und Ausbreitung der Alchemie,* I, p. 489; Steinschneider, *Die europäischen Übersetzungen aus dem Arabischen bis Mitte des 17. Jahrhunderts,* A, pp. 40f. Ruska (*Tabula Smaragdina,* p. 192, n. 5) doubts, probably wrongly, whether "Lumen luminum" goes back to an Arabic original: "This book, known also by various other names, is supposed to have been translated by Gerhard of Cremona. F. Wuestenfeld [*Die Übersetzungen arabischer Werke in das Lateinische seit dem 11. Jahrhundert,* p. 75] likewise conjectures that it is not based on an Arabic original." But the matter is not as simple as that: Arabic sources do exist. See Thorndike, *History of Magic and Experimental Science,* II, pp. 252ff.
2 Ferckel, "Thomas von Chantimpré über die Metalle," *Studien zur Geschichte der Chemie* (ed. Ruska), p. 76.

7

in Latin form before the middle of the thirteenth century.[3] In
Aurora only a few general sayings are quoted from it.[4] Likewise,
the few sayings from the *Tabula Smaragdina* probably do not
come from an original but from this "Lumen luminum"; one of
them is introduced with exactly the same formula as used there.[5]
For our purpose, therefore, the whole problem of the transmission and dating of the *Tabula Smaragdina* loses its importance.[6]
Again, the sentence at the end of the third chapter, although
cited as a saying of Morienus, presumably comes from "Lumen
luminum." [7]

19   The *Turba philosophorum*,[8] which is cited a few times, was
likewise widely known at the beginning of the twelfth century
and was held as a high authority.[9] For the history of this interesting treatise I must refer the reader to Ruska's works. Of the
various quotations from Aristotle, one comes from a genuine
treatise, *De anima*, II, lectio 8. A partial translation of this from
Greek into Latin existed before 1215 and was used by Alfred of
Sareshel.[10] A translation from the Arabic into Latin was made
(after 1217) by Michael Scotus.[11] The *Aurora* quotation (ch. 1)
runs: "To the size and growth of all things in nature a limit is
appointed, but fire by the addition of combustible matter waxes
without end." This formulates the passage in much the same
way as the older translations—actually it is closer to the version
that was current *before* William of Moerbeke's [12]—so that it is

---

3 Thorndike, II, pp. 458ff. According to Pelster (*Kritische Studien zum Leben und
zu den Schriften Alberts des Grossen*, pp. 98ff.), the *Speculum maius* originated
between 1241 and 1244, and was continuously augmented. The first version was
completed in 1241. Vincent of Beauvais died in 1264. The first part, the "Speculum
naturale," was written before 1241 (ibid., p. 99).

4 Infra, pp. 94–97, nn. 53, 65. Cf. "De perfecto magisterio," *Theatr. chem.*, III
(1659), p. 79.

5 "And Hermes says this in his Secret" (infra, pp. 94f. and n. 54). Cf. ibid., III, p. 80.

6 Ruska, *Tabula Smaragdina*, pp. 186ff.   7 Cf. infra, pp. 48f., n. 9.

8 Lippmann, I, p. 484.   9 Ruska, *Turba Philosophorum*, pp. 13 and 46.

10 Haskins, "A List of Textbooks from the Close of the Twelfth Century," p. 86.

11 Querfeld, *Michael Scotus und seine Schrift De Secretis Naturae*, p. 7; Sarton,
Introduction to the History of Science, II, pp. 561, 579ff., and the literature there
cited. Cf. also Haskins, "The Sicilian Translators of the Twelfth Century . . . ,"
p. 85.

12 *Aurora:* "Omnium natura constantium positus est terminus magnitudinis et
augmenti ignis vero appositione combustibilium crescit in infinitum."

Vetus translatio (Bibl. Mazarinea 3462, Paris, 13th cent., fol. 21vff.): "Ignis
autem augmentum in infinitum est, quousque est combustibile, natura autem

very like the one known to Thomas Aquinas, who, in his commentary on *De anima*,[13] used an older translation, as also did Albertus Magnus.[14] This fact argues definitely in favour of an early dating of *Aurora*, since these older translations fell into disuse soon after 1280.[15]

20 The saying at the end of the eleventh chapter comes from the pseudo-Aristotelian "Secreta secretorum,"[16] an early Latin

---

constantium omnium terminus est ratio magnitudinis et augmenti. Haec autem animae sunt et non ignis et rationis magis quam materiae sunt."

William of Moerbeke (Bibl. Nat. 6296, Paris, 13th cent., fol. 247ᵛ): "Ignis vero augmentum in infinitum est quousque fuit combustibile. Natura autem constantium omnium terminus ratio est et ratio et magnitudinis et augmenti. Haec autem animae sunt, non ignis et id rationis magis quam materiae."

English of the last two: "For the increase of fire is infinite so long as there is anything combustible. But there are limitations to all things that subsist naturally, and some definite principle governs their dimensions and growth. And this belongs to the soul, not to fire, and to a specific principle rather than to matter." (*De anima*, trans. by Foster and Humphries, pp. 218f.) Cf. also Lacombe, *Corpus Philosophorum Medii Aevi: Aristoteles Latinus*, I, pp. 50ff. Later translations (e.g., Sophianus) replace "augmenti" by "actionis" or "accretionis."

13 "There is a limit both to (men's) largeness and their littleness, and whatever determines this limit is the true *principal* cause of growth. But this cannot be fire, because the growth of fire has no naturally fixed limits; it would spread to infinity if an infinite amount of fuel were supplied to it. Clearly, then, fire is not the chief cause of growth and nutrition, but rather the soul. And this is reasonable enough, for the quantitative limits of material things are fixed by form—the specific principle—rather than matter. Now the soul of a living being is to the elements it contains as form is to matter; the soul, then, rather than fire, sets the term and natural limit to size and growth." * (*De anima*, p. 223.)

14 Pelster, pp. 87, 133ff., 150; Sarton, II, pp. 829ff.

15 Pelster, p. 106.

16 I used the edition of 1528, *De proprietatibus originalium et lapidum*, which does not give the place of publication (Paris or Lyons?). Cf. Thorndike, II, p. 267, and Förster, *De Aristotelis quae feruntur Secreta secretorum commentatio*. For MSS and editions of Pseudo-Aristotelian writings see Baeumker, *Der Platonismus im Mittelalter*, p. 42; Förster, "Handschriften und Ausgaben des pseudo-Aristotelischen Secretum Secretorum"; Steinschneider, *Die hebraischen Übersetzungen des Mittelalters und die Juden als Dolmetscher*, pp. 245f. and 248ff.; also his *Die europäischen Übersetzungen*, Part A, pp. 41f., and *Zur pseudepigraphischen Literatur . . . des Mittelalters*, pp. 83f.; Ruska, *Tabula Smaragdina*, p. 186; and Wuestenfeld, *Die Übersetzungen arabischer Werke in das Lateinische seit dem 11. Jahrh.*, p. 81. Cf. further Grabmann, *Forschungen über die lateinischen Aristotelesübersetzungen*, pp. 143f., 175f., 186f., 246f.; Ueberweg and Baumgartner, *Grundriss der Geschichte der Philosophie*, Part II: "Die mittlere oder die patristische und scholastische Zeit," p. 369. The treatise was also called "The

translation of an Arabic treatise of the same name (*Sirr al-asrâr*). The medical part of it was translated by John of Seville during the first half of the twelfth century.[17] Then at the end of the twelfth or beginning of the thirteenth century followed a translation by one Philip (of Tripoli or Salerno),[18] whose exact identity is still disputed. At any rate, the dating of the Latin version must be placed between 1150 and 1220. Roger Bacon regarded the treatise as genuine and wrote a commentary on it.[19] Albertus Magnus, too, cites it as a work of Aristotle.

21   Another Aristotle quotation, "With this stone it is not good to fight" (ch. 10), could not be traced verbatim, but it may be a free rendering of the saying in the "Secreta" about the stone Alchahat: "And no man can fight with one who has this (stone) in his hand." The text of the "Secreta" shows wide variations both in the manuscripts and in the printings. The saying "the (glorified) earth is called the coagulant" (ch. 11), likewise attributed to Aristotle, is probably cited from Senior's *De chemia*, and appears there as a quotation from Maria Prophetissa.[20] It is a saying that frequently occurs in the Arabic literature. Again, the concluding sentence of *Aurora* is attributed not directly to Calid (who elsewhere is cited by name) but to "the author of the Three Words." It is evident that not much reliance could be placed on the names of authors, since often the manuscripts seem to have circulated anonymously or under different names.

22   The Hermes quotation "Sow the gold in the white foliate earth" is another widespread saying that also occurs in Senior (Muhammad ibn Umail at-Tamimi).[21] In two other cases I was able to find the Hermes quotations under a different author. This may be due to errors in transmission or to imprecise ascription of these early Latin texts. There is a Hermes quotation in chapter 1 which I could not trace directly, concerning the lapis as an eternal food that could nourish mankind for many thou-

---

Theology of Aristotle" or "De secretiori Aegyptiorum philosophia." Cf. Jourdain, *Recherches critiques sur l'âge et l'origine des traductions latines d'Aristote,* and Rose, *De Aristotelis librorum ordine et auctoritate,* pp. 183ff.

17 Thorndike, II, p. 269.   18 Ibid., p. 270.

19 Lydgate and Burgh, *Secrees of Old Philosoffres,* ed. Steele, cited in Thorndike, II, p. 268.

20 *De chemia,* pp. 34f. Cf. infra, pp. 122f., n. 6.

21 Ibid.

sands of years.[22] The same saying occurs in "Consilium coniugii" [23] and in "Rosarium," [24] but in the latter it is probably
taken from *Aurora*. A similar thought is expressed in the *Buch
der Alaune und Salze*,[25] namely that Mercurius is sufficient to
grant a man an infinitely long life.

23   The alchemical treatises of Avicenna (ibn Sina, 980–1037),
"De re recta ad Hasen regem epistola," "Declaratio lapidis
physici filio suo Aboali," and "De conglutinatione lapidis," [26]
though not generally regarded as genuine works,[27] were known
in Latin about the middle of the thirteenth century, and are
cited in the *Speculum* of Vincent of Beauvais [28] and in Albertus
Magnus's "De mineralibus."

24   From Calid (reputedly the renowned Omayyad prince,
Calid ibn Yazid, 8th cent.),[29] who according to legend translated Greek treatises on alchemy into Arabic,[30] and who is named
as a source in Senior (10th cent.), *Aurora* cites one work which
is generally regarded as a Latin forgery,[31] "Liber trium verborum," from which the concluding sentence is taken.[32] The
Calid quotations in ch. 9, "Make warm the cold of the one by
the heat of the other" and "Extinguish the fire of the one by the
coolness of the other," can also be traced back, though not verbatim, to "Liber trium verborum" in *Artis auriferae* and the
deviant version in Manget.[33] They are, however, sayings of such

22 Infra, pp. 36f.

23 *Ars chemica*, p. 116: "As Hermes saith, it shall suffice a man for a million years,
and if you shall feed two thousand men daily, you shall not want; for it tingeth
for ever." *

24 *Art. aurif.* (1610), II, p. 149.   25 Ed. Ruska, p. 92.

26 The treatises are printed in *Art. aurif.*, I (1610), pp. 240–45, and *Theatr. chem.*,
IV (1659), pp. 863–86. Cf. Berthelot, I, p. 293. "Epistola ad Hasen" is cited by
Albertus (?) in "De rebus metallicis," Lib. III, cap. 4 (Borgnet, V, p. 63).

27 Lippmann, I, pp. 405f., II, pp. 15 and 28, III, "Avicenna." Cf. also Ruska, "Die
Alchemie des Avicenna," pp. 14 and 45.

28 Supra, p. 8, n. 3.

29 Lippmann, I, pp. 357ff., II, p. 122; Ruska, "Arabische Alchemisten," I, pp. 11f.,
and *Tabula Smaragdina*, p. 49.

30 Ruska ("Arabische Alchemisten," II) has shown that this is probably only a
legend.

31 Lippmann, I, p. 357, n. 6.

32 *Art. aurif.* (1610), I, p. 228ff. Cf. Lippmann, II, pp. 148f., and Holmyard, "A
Romance of Chemistry," pp. 75f.

33 *Art. aurif.* (1610), I, pp. 226f. (cf. infra, pp. 88f., n. 30), and *Bibliotheca chemica*
(1702), II, p. 189.

general import that they might have come from anywhere.[34] The idea that the embryo is nourished in the womb by the elements, also in ch. 9, derives ultimately from Calid and is cited in Senior,[35] so it undoubtedly belongs to the stock of Arabic thought. Another Calid quotation, "Three things are necessary, namely: patience, deliberation, and skill with the instruments" (ch. 10), cannot be traced in the two printed treatises of Calid that have been preserved. It is, however, cited in "Secreta alchimiae," a treatise wrongly ascribed to Thomas Aquinas, as a quotation from Avicenna: "But that at last there may come into being the one substance, as Avicenna says, you must have patience, deliberation, and the instrument." [36] In *Aurora* "instrument" is replaced by "skill with the instruments," and this expression recurs in "Liber sextus naturalium," a genuine treatise of Avicenna.[37] *Aurora* seems to have been known to the author of "Secreta alchimiae." [38]

25   Ruska may be right in thinking that the extant printed treatises of Calid are late compilations. What the author of *Aurora* used were probably scattered treatises circulating under various other names.

26   A similar situation prevails in regard to the quotation "He who hath not patience, let him hold back his hand from the work" (ch. 10), which *Aurora* puts into the mouth of Morienus. It is to be found in the Morienus treatise, "De transmutatione metallorum," [39] but as a saying of Calid, so that the misattribution in *Aurora* is due to the fact that at this point in the dialogue

---

[34] They may derive from the treatise "Khalid Rex et Morienus Romanus," 2nd version, which D. W. Singer cites in her *Catalogue of Latin and Vernacular Alchemical MSS in Great Britain and Ireland dating from before the 16th Century*, I, p. 64, no. 67. Unfortunately I had no access to this version.

[35] Calid, "Liber trium verborum," *Art. aurif.*, I, pp. 228f. (cf. infra, pp. 86f., n. 27), and Senior, *De chemia*, p. 88.

[36] *Theatr. chem.*, III (1659), p. 278 [see biblio.]. Concerning the authenticity of this treatise, cf. infra, p. 408, n. 3.

[37] *Avicennae perhypatetici philosophi ac medicorum*, etc., I, ch. 1, fol. 3: "That power of the soul has other powers . . . which all work for this end, that the skill with the instruments may attain to the second perfections of the soul itself . . ." •

[38] He cites a passage from the last chapter of *Aurora* in *Theatr. chem.*, III (1659), p. 279: "Also in the first days you must rise early, and see if the vineyard flourish . . ." But in that context it makes no sense.

[39] *Art. aurif.* (1610), II, p. 21.

Calid is speaking. There is a similar saying in "Liber de compositione alchimiae,"[40] but there again the speaker is Calid. This is perhaps confirmation of Ruska's view that the treatises mostly circulated under the name of Calid and became associated with Morienus only during the thirteenth and fourteenth centuries.[41] The saying is attributed to Geber in the continuation of the above-mentioned passage from "Secreta alchimiae": "Patience, for according to Geber all haste is of the devil. Therefore he who hath not patience let him hold back his hand from the work." In agreement with "Secreta alchimiae," the saying is to be found in Geber's "Summa perfectionis,"[42] a treatise which Darmstaedter[43] conjectures was written in the twelfth or thirteenth century, in southern Italy or Spain. But it does not seem to have been known under Geber's name to Vincent of Beauvais, Albertus Magnus, or Roger Bacon.[44] I think parts of this treatise must previously have circulated anonymously, or were variously attributed to Avicenna, Calid, and Morienus, and were given Geber's name only later. As Darmstaedter supposes, the author may have been someone who had to be on his guard with the Church, and who therefore remained anonymous.

27   The saying at the end of the third chapter, also attributed in *Aurora* to Morienus, does not occur in his "De transmutatione metallorum," but is preserved in Petrus Bonus[45] and in various other treatises (among them "Consilium coniugii") as a quotation from Rhazis in "Lumen luminum."[46]

28   I was unable to trace in Morienus the sayings (in ch. 10) "Hope and hope, and so shalt thou attain (the goal)," and (in

[40] *Bibl. chem.*, I, p. 512: "And especially the wise man must fear nothing. For if he fear, he will soon despair. And if he despair, his purpose will be unsteady. . . . At this the king [Calid] smiled, and said: Now I know of a truth that unless God give a man patience he shall be cruelly confounded. For haste is of the devil." •
[41] For the literature on this question see Singer, *Catalogue*, I, pp. 62–63.
[42] *De alchemia*, ch. 12, p. 17, and "Testamentum," *Bibl. chem.*, I, p. 562: "He who hath not patience, let him hold back his hand from the work, for credulity will ensnare him if he hasten. . . . For this three things are necessary, patience, deliberation, and skill with the instruments." •
[43] *Die Alchemie des Geber*, p. 5.
[44] Ibid., pp. 6–7 and p. 134, n. 8.
[45] *Pretiosa margarita novella*, ed. Lacinius, p. 42. Perhaps it is in a Morienus treatise to which I had no access, "Secretum maximum ad Flodium," mentioned in Steinschneider, *Die europäischen Übersetzungen*, Part A, pp. 40f.
[46] Not given in the "De perfecto magisterio" version.

ch. 9) "He who shall raise up his soul, shall see its colours." [47]

29   On the other hand, "Already we have taken away the black and made the white" (ch. 9) is to be found in the third section of the Morienus treatise, the part that is based on Arabic sources.[48] Ruska regards the whole treatise as a Latin forgery,[49] but he still thinks this section is of Arabic origin. Certain quotations are found also in Abu'l Qāsim, who evidently had similar sources at his disposal in the thirteenth century.[50] That the third section is of different provenance from the first two seems proved by the further fact that it occurs separately in the manuscripts and agrees only partially with the printed text.[51]

30   Ruska conjectures that the printed version was the work of a monk of the thirteenth or fourteenth century.[52] Accordingly, it is very significant that what was available to the author of *Aurora* as the writings of Morienus cannot be the version known today, but that they were still in the preliminary stages of compilation. Therefore *Aurora* must be dated earlier than the time of compilation conjectured by Ruska (13th to 14th cent.). In these writings, which had not yet been put together to form the text as we know it, may perhaps be found the Morienus sayings I was unable to trace.[53]

[47] But in the "Liber Alphidii," Codex Ashmole 1420, fol. 26 (Bodleian), and in "Cons. coniug." there is the following Alphidius or Assiduus quotation (*Ars chemica*, p. 121): "Unless this vapour riseth up, thou wilt obtain nothing, for it is itself the work, and without it there is nothing." • The soul is described as a vapour also in Senior and in the *Turba*. Cf. "Clangor buccinae," *Art. aurif.* (1610), I, p. 317. It must be emphasized that the printed Morienus treatise differs widely from some of the handwritten versions, e.g., Codex Ashmole 1450, fol. 49, "Questiones Calid Regis ad Morienum Romanum."

[48] "De transmutatione metallorum," *Art. aurif.* (1610), II, p. 22. Cf. Lippmann, II, pp. 148f. Cf. also Holmyard, "A Romance of Chemistry," and Reitzenstein, "Alchemistische Lehrschriften und Märchen bei den Arabern," pp. 63ff.

[49] "Arabische Alchemisten," I, pp. 35ff.

[50] Lippmann, II, p. 149.

[51] As does Codex Ashmole 1450, fol. 49, for instance. (I had a photostat of this MS.) Cf. also Singer, *Catalogue*, I, pp. 61f.

[52] He also thinks that the preface of 1144, by Robert of Chester, is a forgery. In any case it does not belong to *this* compilation.

[53] "He who shall raise up his soul" etc. recalls the saying in the third section of Morienus: "He who shall whiten his soul, and shall make it ascend again, and shall guard his body well, and shall take away from it all obscurity, shall be able to pour it into his body. And in the hour of conjunction great wonders shall appear." • (*Art. aurif.*, 1610, II, p. 24.) Cf. the version in Cod. Ashmole 1450, fol. 53:

14

31   We must certainly be dealing with an Arabic source in the case of Alphidius, whose sayings were widely acclaimed in early medieval literature. His unprinted treatise was available to me in a version contained in Codex Ashmole 1420 (Bodleian Library, fol. 1ff.). It is the same treatise as the one which Thorndike states is available in Codex Riccardianus 1165 (fol. 163a–166b), in Florence.[54] In the latter version four passages are missing which are contained in Codex Ashmole 1420. This Codex also contains all the passages cited in *Aurora*. Unfortunately, to my knowledge no Arabic originals of this interesting treatise have yet been published.[55]

32   Ferguson [56] assigns Alphidius to the twelfth century, but this dating may be true only of the Latin translation of his works. At all events he was known to Albertus Magnus. It is probable that Alphidius is identical with the Alkides or Assiduus cited by Senior.[57] Elsewhere he appears as Asphidus, whom Berthelot

"He who shall whiten his soul, and shall make it ascend upwards, and shall guard his body well from combustion . . . shall be able to extract his soul from his body, and that body will be left obscure and in the hour of conjunction a great wonder will appear." •

54 Thorndike, "Alchemical Writings in Vatican Palatine Manuscripts," p. 378. The Florence codex has the same Incipit: "Scito fili . . ." (I would like to express my thanks to Fr. A. [now Cardinal] Albareda, prefect of the Vatican Library, for his information on this point.) Cf. Thorndike, *A History of Magic*, III, p. 43.

55 Cf. Singer, *Catalogue*, I, p. 127, and Ruska, *Turba*, p. 339.

56 *Bibliotheca Chemica* (1906), I, p. 27.

57 *De chemia*, p. 111. The passage from "Liber Alphidii" (infra, pp. 314f.) on the treasure-house of alchemy that can be opened with four keys (to which the concluding sentence in chapter 10 of *Aurora* probably refers) is cited under the name of Assiduus in "Cons. coniug.," *Ars chemica*, pp. 108f. (Concerning "Cons. coniug." see Berthelot, *La Chimie au moyen âge*, I, p. 249, and Ruska, *Turba*, p. 343.) Another treatise ascribed to Alphidius is cited in Hoghelande, "De alchimiae difficultatibus" (*Bibl. chem.*, I, p. 340) : "Whence Alphidius in Clavis Philosophorum: Thou canst not have this science until thou purifiest thy mind before God and God knoweth thee to have a contrite mind. . . . If thou art humble, its wisdom and knowledge shall be perfected." • Since this version agrees with neither the "Cons. coniug," nor the "Ros. phil." version (infra, pp. 106f., n. 32; see also n. 29), and the source Hoghelande gives is "Clav. Phil.," he may have had before him the treatise on which the *Aurora* passages are based. In Hoghelande may also be found part of the Alphidius quotation in chapter I of *Aurora* (infra, pp. 32f., n. 8): "And Alphidius in Clavis Philosophorum, when he says that our stone is a vile thing in the eyes of men and is loathed as without value, which men trample underfoot in the streets." • It is possible that Ashmole 1420 ("Liber Alphidii") is identical in part with the treatise cited as "Clavis Philosophorum."

interprets as, originally, Asklepios.[58] The idea that the lapis is a house with four walls (ch. 10) occurs as early as Senior and probably goes back to the vision of Zosimos of a temple built of *one* white stone.[59]

33　　We have a clearer picture of the author cited as Senior. He was an Arab by the name of Muhammad ibn Umail at-Tamimi (ca. 900–960), whose "Book of the Silvery Water and Starry Earth" (known in Latin as *De chemia* [60]) was edited by E. Stapleton and M. Hidayat Husain in Vol. XII of the *Memoirs of the Asiatic Society of Bengal.*[61] Stapleton affirms the existence of other works by the same author.[62] In the West he is known by one work only,[63] *De chemia,* printings of which all go back to one version, as, presumably, do the manuscripts.[64] Accordingly, the Senior quotations in *Aurora* must be close to the original version. Since the Latin translation mentions Averroes (ibn Roshd, d. 1098), it may be assigned to the twelfth or beginning of the thirteenth century.[65] Senior also annotated the *Turba,* and seems to have had connections with the Shi'ite sect: one of his friends, Abul Hasan Ali ibn Abdullah,[66] was (according to the *Fihrist*) burned in Baghdad for the sake of his faith.[67] Senior

[58] *La Chimie au moyen âge,* III, p. 16. A "Liber Metheaurorum" or "De lapide philosophico," attributed to Alphidius, is preserved in a MS. at the Bodleian, Digby 1641[13]. Cf. Steinschneider, *Die europäischen Übersetzungen,* Part B, p. 4, and Carini, "Sulle scienze occulte nel medio evo," p. 176, line 4.

[59] Berthelot, *Alchimistes grecs,* III, i, 3.

[60] I used an undated edition of *De chemia,* which Ruska conjectures was printed by Perna in Basel between 1560 and 1570 (cf. Ruska, "Studien zu Muhammad ibn Umail," pp. 320ff.), but which is generally thought to have been printed in Strasbourg in 1566. The treatise is reprinted in *Bibl. chem.,* II, and *Theatr. chem.,* V (1622).

[61] Cf. also Ruska's "Studien" and Singer, *Catalogue,* I, p. 122, No. 136.

[62] He mentions (*Memoirs,* XII, pp. 126f.) a "Combination of the Spirits," "Explanation of the Protected Secret and the Hidden Knowledge," "Book of the Lamp," "Book of the Key of the Greater Wisdom," "The Hidden Book," "Clearing Up of Enigmas," "The Choice Pearl," "Book of Chapters," etc., and various poems rhyming with the letters Dāl, Rā, Mīm, Nūn, Lām, etc.

[63] A second work of Senior's may have been translated under the title "Clavis maioris sapientiae" (*Bibl. chem.,* I, pp. 503–08), if this treatise is identical with the Arabic "Book of the Key of the Greater Wisdom" (Kitâb Mafâtih al-Hikmat al-'Uzmâ), which unfortunately has not yet been investigated (Stapleton, p. 126, n. 1). Otherwise it is cited as a work of Artefius.

[64] Cf. Singer, *Catalogue,* I, p. 122.　　[65] Stapleton, *Memoirs,* p. 126.

[66] Ibid., p. 123.　　[67] Ibid., p. 124.

himself lived a very secluded life and was a decided mystic. He had a considerable influence on the author of *Aurora*, who often quotes him.

I was unable to trace the Alphonsus quotation "This is a true friend, who deserteth thee not when all the world faileth thee" (ch. 10). At any rate in the writings of Alphonsus, King of Castile,[68] I was unable to find anything like this; also, the treatises attributed to him are spurious [69] and late.

Equally untraceable were the quotations which, in the printed version of *Aurora*, are supposed to come from a "Liber quintae essentiae." [70] In the manuscripts the same work is designated as "Liber sextus $\sigma\chi^{ee}$" and "$\sigma c\tilde{\chi}^u$," in the Vienna manuscript as "Liber sexagesimae," [71] and in the second part of *Aurora* as "liber sextarius." [72]

The quotation that appears in the manuscripts as a saying of "Speculator" (ch. 3) raises some difficult problems. With the exception of the opening sentence, "Mockery of science is the cause of ignorance," the passage occurs in three works of Roger Bacon (1214–ca. 1292): *Opus maius*, Part I, ch. IV; "Compendium studii," ch. 3; and "Epistola de secretis artis et naturae et de nullitate magiae," ch. VIII, a work whose genuineness is disputed but which Thorndike regards as a compilation of genuine writings.[73] A. G. Little lists it among the genuine writings, too.[74]

[68] On this question see Lippmann, I, p. 498, and Ferguson, *Bibliotheca Chemica*, I, p. 24.

[69] According to Lippmann, ibid., Alphonsus of Castile was hostile to alchemy.

[70] Infra, pp. 86f., 90f. (possibly based on Albertus Magnus, "De mineralibus," Lib. I, Tract. 2; Borgnet, V, p. 16: ". . . which is truly called a carbuncle, and therefore he who attaineth to its real appearance shineth in the darkness like a lamp" •), 110f.

[71] Once designated in Codex Rhenoviensis as ρ ñh/σo.2 A "Liber sacerdotum" is mentioned in *Aurora* II. Cf. Berthelot, *Moyen âge*, I, pp. 179ff. Or is it the "Liber de septuaginta" cited by Vincent of Beauvais (*Speculum*, Lib. VII, cap. 96)?

[72] *Art. aurif.* (1610), I, pp. 156f.: "Of the third it is written, that it changes stones into precious gems, as is set forth above in the sixth book, where it is said that the stones jacinth, red and white coral, emerald, chrysolite, and sapphire can be formed from that material. And in the charter of the priests it is written, that from crystal can be made by its means carbuncle, or ruby, or topaz, which in colour and substance excel the natural." •

[73] *A History of Magic*, II, p. 630.

[74] *Roger Bacon Essays*, p. 395: "The work consists of ten or eleven chapters, the last five of which Charles considered doubtful (Footnote: "Apparently merely because they are 'enigmatic.' But see the ingenious explanation by Lieut.- Col.

Bacon cites the proverb about "not giving an ass lettuce when thistles are good enough for him" as a saying of Aulus Gellius in *Noctes Atticae*, where, however, it cannot be found.[75] Nor has anyone succeeded in tracing it so far.[76] The proverb appears, among other places, in an inquisitor's report on the Waldensians,[77] and it seems to have been a popular adage.

37   Among the alchemical writings of Roger Bacon there is one that has been preserved under the title "De alchemia," which in Manget's *Bibliotheca chemica curiosa*, Vol. I, is called "Speculum alchimiae." Although the *Aurora* quotation does not occur there, "Speculator" might nevertheless mean "Speculi autor" and thus be a veiled reference to Bacon. The minor treatises of Bacon were nearly all written in his early years,[78] but unfortunately they have not yet been examined for their genuineness and probable date of composition.[79] If the dedication in "Epistola de secretis artis et naturae" is genuine, this treatise would have been written before 1249. It is further to be noted that, when citing the whole passage, the sources Bacon gives are: "Aristotelis secreta secretorum" (which he regarded as genuine),[80] and Aulus Gellius, though this reference, as already mentioned, is not correct. He must therefore have written this quo-

---

Hime, *Gunpowder and Ammunition*, pp. 141–62"), addressed perhaps to William of Auvergne (d. 1248) or to John of London whom Charles identifies with John of Basingstoke (d. 1252)." In *Sanioris medicinae magistri D. Rogeri Baconis Angli de arte chymiae scripta* (Frankfurt, 1603), I could find nothing that referred to *Aurora*. But it is worth noting, on p. 17: "Excerpta de libro Avicennae de anima I," and on p. 86: "Explicit exempla cum laude Dei et eius auxilio, exempla dico Abhuali Principis cognomine Avicennae ad Hasen Regem patrem suum de re recta."

75 Cf. Martin Hertz's edition of Gellius, Introduction to vol. II, pp. xxxviii and xxxix.

76 C. E. Georges (cited by Hertz, p. xxxviii, footnote) refers to Lucilius (St. Jerome, *Selected Letters*, p. 25): "It bears out the proverb which, as Lucilius tells us, made Crassus laugh for the only time in his life: 'When an ass eats thistles, his lips have the lettuce to match them.'" •

77 Hahn, *Geschichte der Ketzer im Mittelalter*, II, p. 257, a report by the inquisitor Walter Map, *De nugis curialium*, I, xxi, who says: "Therefore I have set forth light matters, which no one may ignore knowing that when an ass eats thistles, his lips have the lettuce that suits them." •

78 Thorndike, II, pp. 630ff.

79 Cf. article on Roger Bacon in *Encyc. Brit.*, 11th edn., III, pp. 153–56, by R. Adamson.

80 Thorndike, II, p. 633.

tation down without having the original Gellius text in front of him—he was, as a matter of fact, known for his inexact references, fond as he was of criticizing others in this respect, including Albertus Magnus and Thomas Aquinas![81] The author of *Aurora* avoided this mistake either inadvertently or from better knowledge. Furthermore the Bacon passages are mixed in the *Aurora* version, for in the original they run as follows: *Opus maius*, I, IV: "Where also he [Gellius] says it's silly to offer an ass lettuce when thistles are good enough for him."[82] "Epistola de secretis," ch. VIII: "And Aristotle himself says in the 'Book of Secrets' that he would be a breaker of the heavenly seal who should disclose the secrets of nature and of the art. . . . Also in this regard Aulus Gellius says in his book 'Attic Nights' concerning the conversation of the sages that it would be foolish to offer an ass lettuce when thistles suffice for him."[83] And finally, "Compendium studii," ch. 3: ". . . since the pearls of wisdom are not to be cast before swine, according to Matthew 7 : 6, and it is foolish to give lettuce to an ass, when thistles suffice for him, as Aulus Gellius says in his book 'Attic Nights,' "[84] etc. All these quotations are combined in the *Aurora* version: the Aristotle quotation with the ass proverb and with the passage from Matthew. A possible explanation is that Bacon and the author of *Aurora* worked from a common source (named "Speculi autor"?), from which Bacon arbitrarily quoted now one and now another combination. A further possibility is that the author of *Aurora* knew and combined *all* the passages in Bacon's writings, or that he had the "Epistola de secretis" passage in his head, corrected the attribution to Gellius, and supplemented it with Matthew 7 : 6 in conformity with his style, which is a mixture of Biblical quotations and alchemical sayings.

38   Another knotty problem is raised by a passage which, unfortunately, is based on the uncertain transmission of the manuscripts. It concerns a quotation from Senior in chapter 1, where it is said of Wisdom that "the wise man . . . understandeth her, when his spirits have been enlightened by the *Liber aggregationis*."[85] In the Rhenanus printing and the Leiden manuscript

81 Pelster, *Kritische Studien*, p. 50; Thorndike, II, pp. 642f.

82 *Opus majus*, ed. Bridges, I, p. 10.*

83 *Opera inedita*, ed. Brewer, p. 543. * Cf. variant in *Theatr. chem.*, V (1622), p. 956.   84 Brewer, p. 416.   85 Infra, pp. 38f.

this is replaced by "ex libris agnitionum" (by the Books of Knowledge). The original passage in Senior runs: "by the transmitted books, which the philosophers have hidden." Presumably the later version in the printing and in the Leiden manuscript is a correction which endeavoured to bring the text closer to the Senior quotation, and which was made because the expression "Liber aggregationis" could no longer be understood. But there is in fact a "Liber aggregationis seu secretorum" among the writings of Albertus Magnus, in which the magic of plants, talismans, etc., and also of alchemy, is discussed. This is one of a group of three treatises, "Experimenta Alberti" (also named "Secreta Alberti" or "Liber aggregationis"), "De mirabilibus mundi," and "De secretis mulierum," which were all declared spurious because of their occult or "obscene" content, although they are among his most widely disseminated writings.[86] Manuscripts of the "Liber aggregationis" date from the thirteenth century, and of "De mirabilibus mundi" from the fourteenth century, but both works were brought together even in the earliest printings.[87] The resistance against regarding them as genuine is due mainly to the fact that their content was considered "frivolous" and bad, though Lynn Thorndike rightly stresses that the views they contain in no way contradict those found in the indisputably genuine works of Albertus Magnus.[88] He also emphasizes that we have no valid grounds, either of style or of textual criticism, for cavilling at these works,[89] though in the end he leaves the question open.[90] He remarks only that "De

[86] Thorndike, II, p. 720.
[87] Cf. the *Gesamtkatalog der Wiegendrucke* (ed. Crous), I, no. 617ff. Even in the earliest printings (Ferrara, 1471; Strasbourg, 1478; Bologna, 1478; Reutlingen, 1483; Speyer, 1483; Cologne, 1485), these writings are brought together under the title "Liber Aggregationis." A 15th-cent. biographer of Albertus, Rudolf of Nymwegen (*Legenda litteralis Beati Alberti*, Part III, cap. 7) notes: "Brother Hermann of Mynda, by birth a Saxon, . . . in his book of stories which is entitled *De mirabilibus mundi*, in the fourth book concerning the life of Master Albert, comprehends many things in a few words, which are inserted in their proper place in our own work." • Pelster (p. 33) thinks this treatise of Hermann's is lost, i.e., not identical with the existing one. He conjectures that the author of this lost "De mirabilibus" was Hermann von Lerbecke. But it is not clear to me how this could be connected with the "Secreta Alberti."
[88] Thorndike, II, pp. 724ff.   [89] Ibid., pp. 725ff.
[90] On this question and the literature for and against the authorship of Albertus see Partington, "Albertus Magnus on Alchemy."

mirabilibus mundi" "approaches even more closely to the customary style of Albertus's writings." This treatise contains a theoretical discussion on the nature of magic which is of such outstanding importance that we shall have to go into it more closely in our commentary.

39   The main point to bear in mind is the oldest known manuscripts of *Aurora* really do have "Liber aggregationis" where Senior has "books which the philosophers have hidden," so that the author obviously means that the "Liber aggregationis" was an essential book of this kind which had to be kept secret. The views it propounds on the real nature of alchemy seem to me to fall completely into line with the thinking of *Aurora*, so that I am inclined to retain the reading "aggregationis" or "aggregationum." [91] According to *Aurora*, the purpose of the book was to bring about a preparatory clarification of the mind and to enable one to make subtle distinctions. Now, as we have said, "De mirabilibus mundi," which was always combined with "Liber aggregationis" in the incunabula,[92] contains a fundamental discussion of the nature of all magic including alchemy, and thus does in fact fulfil the role postulated by *Aurora*.

40   To sum up, the sources for *Aurora* yield the following picture: All traceable quotations (including the Biblical ones), such as those from Senior, Alphidius, the *Turba*, Pseudo-Aristotle's "De perfecto magisterio" and "Secreta secretorum," and Gregory the Great, are scrupulously correct. That the Morienus and Calid quotations do not accord with the texts as we have them today may be due to the fact that these works were put into their present form only after *Aurora* was written. I hope other investigators will succeed in locating the passages I was unable to trace, and so complete the picture of the sources which the author of *Aurora* used.

[91] Cf. infra, p. 179, n. 102.
[92] It remains difficult to reconcile this with the fact that "Secreta Alberti" and "De mirabilibus" appear together as "Liber aggregationis" only in late MSS and printed incunabula, whereas in the earlier MSS known to us they appear separately. Yet they must have been brought together earlier under this one title, since the earliest incunabula from a great many different places of printing consistently combine them under the title "Liber aggregationis" (Thorndike, II, p. 721). Thorndike mentions (pp. 569f.), as related "current works," a "Semita recta," "Practica," and a "Speculum secretorum Alberti," MS 138, from the 15th cent., in Bologna.

4. THE PROBLEM OF DATING

41 As I was unable to trace all the sources (especially "Liber quintae essentiae"), no conclusive opinion can be passed on the date of *Aurora*'s composition. All the traceable sources are early Latin treatises or translations of Arabic writings, none of which can be dated later than the middle of the thirteenth century. This argues for a comparatively early date, more particularly as authors like Arnaldus de Villanova (1235–1313) and Raymond Lully (1235–1315), who figure in practically all the later treatises, are not mentioned in *Aurora*.

42 Lynn Thorndike, in his *History of Magic and Experimental Science*, assigns *Aurora* to the fifteenth century.[1] In my view this dating holds only for Part II. Here mention is made of Albertus Magnus (1193–1280) and Geber, who are not named in Part I.[2] The fact that the quotation from Aristotle's *De anima* (II, 8) is based on the old translations argues for an early date. Further conclusions can be drawn from the relation of the Speculator-Gellius quotation to similar passages in Roger Bacon only when the problem of the genuineness and dating of Bacon's minor writings has been cleared up. At all events this relationship points back to Bacon's time, that is, to the thirteenth century.

---

[1] IV, p. 335: "Some anonymous works, distinguishable by their titles, may also probably be assigned to the fifteenth century, such as the 'Soliloquy of Philosophy' or 'The Burst of Dawn.' 25 . . . The latter treatise gives four reasons for its title and then seven parables of which the last is a confabulation of the lover with his beloved. Its second part is in three chapters on astronomy, arithmetic, and the natural process of first doctrine." Note 25: "Vienna 5230, A.D. 1505, fols. 239ʳ–249ᵛ. 'Incipit Aurora consurgens: Venerunt mihi . . . sanguine menstruali per cursum eius.' S. Marco VI, 215 Valentinelli, XVI, 4, A.D. 1475, fols. 65ʳ–101ʳ [Valentinelli, V, pp. 155ff.].With same title and incipit. The latter part of the work was printed in *Art. aurif.* [1593], I, 185[ff]."
[2] For these and other authors see Ruska, *Tabula Smaragdina*, pp. 186ff.

22

43   An upper limit for the dating might be provided by "Rosarium philosophorum," since it quotes from *Aurora*, and moreover only from Part I.[3] Unfortunately the dating of "Rosarium" is much disputed: Berthelot assigns it to the middle of the fourteenth century,[4] and Ruska first agrees with this,[5] but later thinks it should be assigned to the middle of the fifteenth century,[6] though he does not adduce any decisive arguments.[7]

An allusion to Chapter II of *Aurora* is to be found in a treatise which was printed as "Compositum de compositis" under the name of Albertus Magnus.[8] As it is consistent with the whole style of *Aurora* to employ Biblical quotations, and this is true only of the preface to the treatise,[9] which afterwards adopts a prosaic "scientific" tone, we must assume that the first part of it is based on *Aurora* and not the other way round.

44   Further, *Aurora* is cited in the "Aureum vellus sive sacra vatum philosophia" (Antwerp, 1604) of Gulielmus Mennens,[10] whereas Johannes Grasseus, in his "Arca arcani," [11] had only an indirect knowledge of the title [12] but was not acquainted with the text,[13] though it must have been known to his source,

---

[3] *Art. aurif.* (1610), II, pp. 133ff. Though it is no proof, this is further evidence that Part I is by another hand and earlier than Part II. [In sections I and III of the present volume, the "Ros. phil." references are always from *Art. aurif.*, II; but in section II they are from *Bibl. chem.*, II.]

[4] *Moyen âge*, I, p. 234.

[5] *Tabula Smaragdina*, p. 193.

[6] *Turba*, p. 342; Thorndike, III, p. 56.

[7] The citation from *Aurora* in Michael Maier's *Symbola aureae mensae*, p. 65, agrees with "Ros. phil." and probably comes from there.

[8] *Theatr. chem.*, IV (1659), pp. 825ff.

[9] Ibid.: "Therefore the knowledge which I have learned without deceit, I communicate without envy, and if this envy is hidden it is lacking, for such a man shall not be a sharer in God's friendship. All wisdom and knowledge is from the Lord God, but this however it be said is always from the Holy Spirit. . . . Therefore he that hath ears to hear such deifying grace, let him hear a secret bestowed upon me by the grace of God, and let him in no wise reveal it to the unworthy." •

[10] Also in *Theatr. chem.*, V (1622), pp. 267ff.

[11] Ibid., VI, p. 314.

[12] *Bibl. chem.*, II, p. 594: "19: *Aurora consurgens* in *Turba* [!] Ecce," etc. There is no citation from *Aurora*.

[13] Echoes of it may have been transmitted by "Clangor buccinae," the author of which was acquainted with *Aurora*. Cf. *Art. aurif.* (1610), I, p. 348, the same Sextarius quotation; also pp. 309, 311, 325.

the Augustinian monk Degenhardus.[14] The treatise ascribed to Salomon Trismosin, *Splendor solis* (ca. 1490), is full of passages taken from *Aurora*, though the title is not mentioned.[15]

45   I think there can be no doubt that Sir George Ripley (1415–90) knew *Aurora*. Though he does not name it by title, his "Liber duodecim portarum" contains too many of the same combinations of Bible and Senior quotations to be an independent production.[16]

46   The situation is less clear with regard to the "Aquarium sapientum," [17] yet I think it possible that its author was acquainted with *Aurora*. Nor does Boehme's *Aurora* seem to me independent of *Aurora Consurgens*, even though Boehme, as always, remodelled what he had read in a very freehanded way and used it only to amplify his own inner experiences.

47   All in all, *Aurora*, so far as I can see, was little known in the later literature, because it obviously departed too much from the popular alchemical style and was not understood. In conclusion it may be said that the lower limit for *Aurora* must be around 1230, and the upper limit the middle of the fifteenth century ("Rosarium," Ripley). I myself incline to date it to the middle or second half of the thirteenth century.

[14] *Bibl. chem.*, II, p. 593: "Master Degenhardus, a monk of the Augustinian Order, a true possessor of the stone, says in his book of the Universal Way: . . . It is a gift of the Holy Spirit. In it lies hid the mystery of approach to the treasure of the sages. And it is the lead of the philosophers, also called the lead of the air, in which there is a resplendent white dove, called the salt of the metals, wherein consists the magistery of the work. This is that chaste, wise and rich queen of Sheba, clothed in a white veil, who would submit to none but to King Solomon. The heart of no man is able to search deeply enough into these things." •

[15] Ed. J. K., London, 1920. *Aurora* is missing in the anonymous editor's list of sources.

[16] *Bibl. chem.*, II, p. 280, col. 2, or Ripley's *Opera omnia*, Prologus Secundus to "Liber XII Portarum," verse 3: "Make wisdom thy sister and prudence thy friend"; also verses 3, 6, 8 (triune stone), and 9, p. 59: ". . . until it is dried up in the streams (for by this operation the streams have passed into dry land, as the Psalmist saith . . .)"; p. 259, the same Senior quotation; and on p. 300, "For it is written: Thou hast set them bounds which they shall not pass" is referred to the length of human life, as in *Aurora*.

[17] *Musaeum hermeticum* (1683) , pp. 73ff.

5. THE MANUSCRIPTS

⁴⁸ A complete manuscript of the treatise is to be found in the Biblio- **P** thèque Nationale, Paris, Lat. 14006, fol. 1ᵛ–12ᵛ: "Incipit tractatus Aurora consurgens Intitulatus"; fol. 12ᵛ is followed by Part II.[1] The manuscript, which I had at my disposal in photocopy form, dates from the fifteenth century and came from the Bibliotheca Manuscriptorum Coisliniana (earlier Seguenona), which Henri du Campout, Duc de Coislin, Pair de France, bequeathed to the monastery of St. Germain des Prés in 1732.[2] The manuscript is very clean and legible, and a recapitulation of proper names and a short summary of contents are given in the margin of the first two folios. It is cited in the critical apparatus as P, its corrections as P_2.

⁴⁹ Closest to the P readings is a manuscript in Vienna, at the **V** Österreichische Nationalbibliothek, Codex 5230. Our treatise begins on fol. 239ʳ with "Incipit aurora consurgens" and continues to fol. 248ᵛ, where Part II begins, given only in abbreviated form and ending on fol. 249ᵛ. After that come recipes. The preceding treatise ends: "Explicit lapidarius raymundi magici 1467, 16. Junii." The manuscript is mentioned in Thorndike's *History* (IV, p. 335).[3] In the apparatus it is cited as V (Vindobonensis), marginal corrections as V_2.

1 Further alchemical treatises follow, the most important of which are the "Liber secretorum" of Calid, "Correctio fatuorum" of Bernardus Magnus, "Rotatio elementorum" of Alanus, "Collectio ex nobili libro Margaritae pretiosae Novellae" of Petrus Bonus, "Flos Regis," "Propositiones maximae in arte alchimiae" of Albertus Magnus, "Epistola Avicennae ad Hazen philosophum," "Liber intitulatus Lilium evulsum e spinis," "Problema" of Johannes Thonensis, "Colloquium magistri cum discipulo," "Herba incognita ortolana" of Joh. Thonensis, as well as recipes and minor treatises.

2 Cf. the description and examination of the MS in Delisle, *Inventaire des MSS de St. Germain des Prés*, pp. 124ff., and in Corbett, *Catalogue des MSS alchimistiques latins*, I, pp. 178f.

3 Codex 5230 is a collection of MSS on paper, 222 x 159 mm., in brown calf over wooden boards. Besides numerous chemical treatises, our MS contains many illus-

M   50   To the same group as P and V belongs the manuscript in the Biblioteca Marciana, Venice,[4] cited in the apparatus as M, corrections as M_2. This Codex is mentioned (under Class XVI) in J. Valentinelli's *Bibliotheca Manuscripta ad S. Marci Venetiarum* (vol. V, 1872, p. 155), dating from the year 1475. The treatise runs from fol. 65^r to 161^r: "Incipit tractatus Aurora consurgens tract. duo"; it is extraordinarily legible and carefully written.

Rh   51   Likewise of good quality, but unfortunately incomplete, is the manuscript in the Zentralbibliothek, Zurich, Codex Rhenoviensis [5] 172, from the monastery at Rheinau, and assigned by Father C. Mohlberg to the fifteenth century.[6] It is cited in the apparatus as Rh, corrections as Rh_2. It begins towards the end of chapter 9 of *Aurora* with the words: "sitates tollit de corpore . . ." The manuscript contains other alchemical treatises.[7] The *Aurora* fragment is the work of a single hand, has the titles in red and the initial letters in blue and gold, and is illustrated with very beautiful symbolic pictures. The relation of the pictures to the text is, however, somewhat tenuous.

L   52   The same pictures, poorly reproduced, are to be found in the Codex Vossianus Chemicus 520, No. 29 in the University Library at Leiden, dating from the sixteenth century and rather carelessly written. In the apparatus it is cited as L, its corrections

---

trations to the text (chemical symbols, pictures of chemical experiments). The various parts of the MS date from different periods of the 15th and 16th cents. The dates 1465, 1467, 1481, 1516 are mentioned. Cf. *Tabulae Codicum Manuscriptorum . . . in Bibl. Palat. Vindobonensi asservatorum*, ed. Acad. Caes. Vindob., IV, p. 67; also Thorndike and Pearl Kibre, *Catalogue of Incipits of Mediaeval Scientific Writings in Latin*, col. 767, under "Venerunt mihi . . ." Continuations of this publication in *Speculum*, XIV, No. 1: Thorndike, "Additional Incipits of Mediaeval Scientific Writings," and XVII, No. 3: "More Incipits" etc. Thorndike dates the MS 1505 (IV, p. 335, n. 25).

[4] Mentioned in Thorndike, IV, p. 335, n. 25. I am indebted to Fr. A. (now Cardinal) Albareda, prefect of the Vatican Library, for first drawing my attention to this MS. No *Aurora* MS is mentioned in Little, *Initia operum Lat. quae saeculis XIII, XIV, XV attribuuntur.*

[5] Cited earlier in C. G. Jung's publications as Codex Rhenovacensis. The form "Rhenoviensis" was subsequently adopted.

[6] Mohlberg, *Katalog der Handschriften der Zentralbibliothek in Zurich*, I, p. 246.

[7] Albertus Magnus: "Kalistenus unus de antiquioribus . . . dicit," "Questio curiosa de natura solis et lunae"; Petrus de Zolento: "Secreta Hermetis"; Jo. de Garlandia: "Clavis sap. maioris"; excerpts from Geber's writings; "Aurea massa," "Visio Arislei" and other treatises. Further details in Mohlberg.

as L$_2$. The title reads: "Tractatus qui dicitur Thomae Aquinatis de Alchimia modus extrahendi quintam essentiam Liber Alchimiae, qui a nonnullis dicitur Aurora consurgens latine scriptus cum figuris." It is followed by other alchemical treatises.[8] The Codex comes closest to the Rhenanus printing in its readings and is only of occasional importance for establishing the text.

⁵³ Dr. G. Goldschmidt kindly drew my attention to the manuscript in the University Library at Bologna, No. 747, dated 1492, **B** and cited in the apparatus as B. It is unreliable and full of large lacunae. I used a photocopy. The treatise runs from fol. 97ᵛ to 120ʳ, with the title: "Incipit aurea [h]ora quae dicitur Aurora consurgens vel liber trinitatis compositus a Sancto Thoma de aquino." Particularly towards the end, this carelessly written version of the treatise contains so many omissions that I ceased to cite them in the apparatus. For the sake of completeness they are given in Appendix II.

⁵⁴ Finally, cited in the apparatus as D, is the British Museum **D** copy of Johannes Rhenanus, *Harmoniae inperscrutabilis chymico-philosophicae sive Philosophorum antiquorum consentientium decades duae,* apud Conr. Eifridum, Francofurti, 1625, Decas II, pp. 175ff., of which I used a photocopy. Incipit: "Beati Thomae de Aquino Aurora sive Aurea Hora." Chapter headings are missing. This version shows traces of revision by humanist scholars who, shortly before the printing, corrected the Latin and brought the text closer to the Vulgate, which is quoted much more freely in the manuscripts.[9] The text contains repetitions which are probably marginal glosses that have found their way into it.[10] The same is true of M and occasionally of P and Rh.

---

[8] Including a treatise by Albertus Magnus in German, the "Schemata" of Gratus, a treatise "De lapide," recipes, Lully's "Elucidarium testamenti," etc.

[9] Examples are p. 32, l. 11, "ut intelligat" instead of the barely intelligible "et intelligit"; p. 42, l. 5, "vacabit" corrupted into "vocabit" with "te" added; p. 42, l. 9, where the description of alchemy as a "sacramentum," offensive to religious sensibilities, was altered into "sanctuarium"; p. 52, l. 12, "volens" added to the infinitive "videre"; p. 82, l. 14f., the gloss "quod philosophus vult esse," because the equation of the alchemical triad with the Trinity obviously caused offence, and so on.

[10] E.g., p. 76, l. 33, "salvabitur et salvus vocabitur."

6. THE ESTABLISHMENT OF THE TEXT
OF THE PRESENT EDITION

55 As P, M, and V were more or less of equal value, now one and now the other containing the better reading,[1] I could not rely consistently on any one of them but had to take them all into account. For the later chapters, Rh was as important as the others. In the Vulgate quotations the Biblical text could not always be taken as definitive, since the author quotes freely or in deliberately modified form. Certain passages come also from the liturgy of the Mass, for often the same Biblical quotations appear combined in the same way as in the Roman Missal, or less frequently in the Roman Breviary.[2] Because the author is

---

[1] M, for instance, is better on p. 48, l. 21 , p. 50, l. 16, and p. 52, l. 2; P is better on p. 76, l. 33, and p.100, l. 5.

[2] In the preparation of the English edition, Mr. A. S. B. Glover has kindly drawn my attention to a number of other quotations from the Roman Breviary (as well as to some passages which, while not forming part of the Roman Breviary as standardized by Pope Pius V, still appear in the Dominican Breviary), which are included in the footnotes to the *Aurora* text in the next section. These and the quotations I have given may be a sufficient indication of the use of the Breviary in *Aurora*.

Mr. Glover has supplied the following note:

"The text of quotations from the Vulgate given in the footnotes follows *Biblia Sacra juxta Vulgatam Clementinam* . . . , Rome, Tournai, Paris (Typis Societatis S. Joannis Evang.), 1927; and chapter and verse numbers accord with this edition, so that (especially in the case of the Psalms) they will not always agree exactly with references in editions or translations of the Bible not based on the Vulgate. The corresponding English translations are taken from *The Holy Bible, translated from the Latin Vulgate* . . . , London (Burns Oates and Washbourne, Ltd.), 1914, and subsequent (not specifically dated) reprints. In view of the almost numberless slightly differing editions of the *Missale* and *Brevarium Romanum*, particularly of those which give a vernacular text as well as the Latin, references here are given not to the pages of any specific edition, but to the Mass or the Breviary Office in which the passage cited is to be found. The extensive changes and omissions called for in the Masses and other offices by the liturgical reforms of 1955

consciously playing with the meaning of the Biblical quotations, it may be of interest to the reader to compare his wording with the original passages cited in the footnotes to the *Aurora* text and translation. Other, later versions, such as the long quotation from *Aurora* in "Rosarium philosophorum," were consulted only when a conjecture seemed necessary.[3]

56   The apparatus does not indicate the major omissions in B, variations in the spelling of proper names, or single unimportant errors in copying, though these are given in Appendix II for the sake of completeness.[4]

---

and later years, may mean that some of these passages will not be found in editions of the Missal and Breviary published after 1960.

"In the Swiss edition of the book, references to the Roman Missal were given for all those quotations from the Scriptures in the text of *Aurora* which occur in the *Missale Romanum*. In the present edition, such references are given only when the text of the quotation as used in the Missal shows some significant verbal difference from the Vulgate text, and for quotations from the Missal or Breviary of texts which are not borrowed from the Bible."

[3] For instance on p. 34, l. 24, "operationes" for "comparatione."

[4] In the Swiss edition, here followed an account of the editorial principles followed in choosing the Biblical text in German. It is replaced by Mr. Glover's explanation in n. 2, supra. For observations on the literature that has appeared since the Swiss edition went to press (Oct. 1955), see the Foreword to the English Edition, pp. ixff.

II

AURORA CONSURGENS

Text and Translation

BEAT! THOMAE DE AQUINO
AURORA SIVE AUREA HORA. INCIPIT TRACTATUS
AURORA CONSURGENS
INTITULATUS

5 Venerunt mihi omnia bona pariter cum illa[1] sapientia austri,[2] quae foris praedicat, in plateis dat vocem suam, in capite turbarum clamitat, in foribus portarum urbis profert verba sua dicens:[3] Accedite ad me et illuminamini et operationes vestrae non confundentur;[4] omnes qui concupiscitis me divitiis meis 10 adimplemini.[5] Venite (ergo) filii, audite me, scientiam Dei docebo vos.[6] Quis sapiens et intelligit hanc,[7] quam Alphidius dicit homines et pueros in viis et plateis praeterire et cottidie a iumentis et pecoribus in sterquilinio conculcari.[8] Et Senior: Nihil ea aspectu

---

7. orbis *PVM* / 10. ergo *add. D* / 11. ut intelligat *D*, et intelligens *B*, intelliget *V* /

---

[1] Sap. 7 : 11: "Venerunt autem mihi omnia bona pariter cum illa et innumerabilis honestas per manus illius."

[2] Cf. Matth. 12 : 42: "Regina austri surget in iudicio . . ." and Zach. 9 : 14: "Deus in tuba canet et vadet in turbine austri . . ."

[3] Prov. 1 : 20–22: "Sapientia foris praedicat; in plateis dat vocem suam; in capite turbarum clamitat; in foribus portarum urbis profert verba sua, dicens: Usque quo, parvuli, diligitis infantiam?"

[4] Ps. 33 : 6: "Accedite ad eum (sc. Dominum), et illuminamini; et facies vestrae non confundentur."

[5] Ecclus. 24 : 26–30: "Transite ad me, omnes qui concupiscitis me, et a generationibus meis implemini. . . . Qui audit me non confundetur."

[6] Ps. 33 : 12: "Venite, filii, audite me, timorem Domini docebo vos."

[7] Osee 14 : 10: "Quis sapiens, et intelliget ista? intelligens et sciet haec? Quia rectae viae Domini . . ."

[8] "Liber Alphidii," Codex Ashmole 1420, fol. 18: "homines pedibus conculcant in viis . . ." fol. 21: "Thesaurizatum est in viam ejectus vileque et carum . . . quae homines ac pueri in viis praetereunt." Cf. also "Consilium coniugii," *Ars chem.*, p. 88: Assiduus: "Et scito fili quod hunc lapidem de quo hoc archanum extrahitur Deus non emendum praecio posuit quoniam in viis ejectus invenitur ut a paupere et divite haberi possit." Also pp. 62–63: "Quidam (dixerunt lapidem) vile et carum et stercore tectum ad quod vix poterit perveniri quod homines ac pueri in plateis et viis praetereunt." Cf. also "Rosarium philosophorum," *Bibl. chem.*, II, pp.

THE *AURORA* OR *AUREA HORA*
OF BLESSED THOMAS AQUINAS
HERE BEGINNETH THE TREATISE
ENTITLED *AURORA CONSURGENS*

57 All good things came to me together with her,[1] that Wisdom of the south,[2] who preacheth abroad, who uttereth her voice in the streets, crieth out at the head of the multitudes, and in the entrance of the gates of the city uttereth her words, saying:[3] Come ye to me and be enlightened, and your operations shall not be confounded;[4] all ye that desire me shall be filled with my riches.[5] Come (therefore), children, hearken to me; I will teach you the science of God.[6] Who is wise, and understandeth this,[7] of which Alphidius saith, that men and children pass her by daily in the streets and public places, and she is trodden into the mire by beasts of burden and by cattle?[8] And Senior saith: Nought is

---

[1] Wisd. 7 : 11: "Now all good things came to me together with her, and innumerable riches through her hands."

[2] Cf. Matt. 12 : 42: "The queen of the south shall rise in judgment . . ." and Zach. 9 : 14: "God will sound the trumpet and go in the whirlwind of the south . . ."

[3] Prov. 1 : 20–22: "Wisdom preacheth abroad: she uttereth her voice in the streets: At the head of multitudes she crieth out, in the entrance of the gates of the city she uttereth her words, saying: O children, how long will ye love childishness?"

[4] Ps. 33 : 6: "Come ye to him [the Lord] and be enlightened, and your faces shall not be confounded."

[5] Ecclus. 24 : 26–30: "Come over to me, all ye that desire me: and be filled with my fruits. . . . He that hearkeneth to me shall not be confounded."

[6] Ps. 33 : 12: "Come, children, hearken to me: I will teach you the fear of the Lord."

[7] Hos. (Osee) 14 : 10: "Who is wise, and he shall understand these things? prudent, and he shall know these things? For the ways of the Lord are right . . ."

[8] "Liber Alphidii," Codex Ashmole 1420, fol. 18: "men trample it underfoot in the streets . . ." fol. 21: "It is treasured and cast forth in the streets and cheap and dear . . . which men and children pass by in the streets." Cf. also "Consilium coniugii," *Ars chemica*, p. 88: Assiduus: "And know, my son, that this stone, from which this secret thing is extracted, God appointed not to be bought for a price, for it is found cast forth in the streets that it may be possessed by both rich and poor." Also pp. 62–63: "Some (called the stone) vile and dear and covered with filth, to which one could hardly attain, which men and children pass by in

vilius et nihil ea in natura pretiosius, et Deus etiam eam pretio
15 emendam non posuit.⁹ Hanc Salomon pro luce habere proposuit
et super omnem pulchritudinem et salutem; in comparatione
illius lapidis pretiosi virtutem illi non comparavit.¹⁰ Quoniam
omne aurum tamquam arena exigua et velut lutum aestimabitur
argentum in conspectu illius, et sine causa non est. Melior est
20 enim acquisitio eius negociatione argenti et auri purissimi. Et
fructus illius est pretiosior cunctis opibus huius mundi et omnia,
quae desiderantur, huic non valent comparari. Longitudo dierum et sanitas in dextera illius, in sinistra vero eius gloria et
divitiae infinitae. Viae eius operationes pulchrae et laudabiles
25 non despectae neque deformes et semitae illius moderatae et non
festinae, sed cum laboris diuturni instantia.¹¹ Lignum vitae est
his, qui apprehenderint eam et lumen indeficiens, si tenuerint

14. nihil *om. BDLV* / nihil *om. MP* / 15. composuit *B* / 16. operatione *B*, compositione *M*, operationibus *L* / 17. virtutem *om. MPBL* / 18. arenam et exiguum
VPM, arena etiam exigua *D* / 19.–20. causa non melior est enim *DB*, sine causa
non est melior. Est *M* / 20. Et *om. VMP.* / 21. operibus *DLMP* / 22. valeant
MP / 23. illius: eius *DL om. B* / 24. operationes *conj. from Rosarium*, comparatione *codd.* om. *B*, comparatione eius *V* / 26. diurni *VMP* / 27. apprehendunt
MPV, apprehenderunt *L* /

88b–89a: "Scito quod hunc lapidem, de quo hoc arcanum agitur, Deus non posuit
magno pretio emendum, quoniam in via eiectus invenitur, quatenus tam a
paupere quam a divite haberi possit . . ." Braceschius, "De alchemia dialogus,"
ibid., I, p. 594b: "Nam Alphidius dicit hoc secretum pretio non comparari sed
inveniri proiectum in media via . . ." Cf. also "Rosinus ad Sarratantam," *Art.
aurif.* (1610), I, p. 188; Morienus Romanus, "De transmutatione metallorum,"
ibid., II, p. 25; Avicenna, "Declaratio lapidis physici filio suo Aboali," *Theatrum
chem.* (1659), IV, p. 875.
⁹ Cf. Senior, *De chemia* (1566), p. 117: ". . . Philosophus filius Hamuel Zadith
. . . extraxit a fundo eorum margaritas praeciosas, et ostendit tibi manifeste et
aperte hoc secretum celatum quod appropriavit dominus gloriosus, huic lapidi
vili, et inpraeciabili, et est praeciosius in mundo, et vilius." Cf. "Ros. phil.," p.
102. Cf. ibid., p. 106: ". . . de quo dixit Viemon: Proiicitur in sterquiliniis hoc
est, est vile in oculis omnis ignorantis."
¹⁰ Cf. "Ros. phil." p. 100. Cf. Sap. 7 : 7: ". . . venit in me spiritus sapientiae; et
praeposui illam regnis et sedibus, et divitias nihil esse duxi in comparatione illius,
nec comparavi illi lapidem pretiosum, quoniam omne aurum in comparatione
illius arena est exigua, et tanquam lutum aestimabitur argentum in conspectu
illius. Super salutem et speciem dilexi illam, et proposui pro luce habere illam."
¹¹ Cf. Petrus Bonus, *Pret. marg. nov.* (1546), p. 45: ". . . et tu quidem exerciteris
ad illud cum laboris instantia maxima et cum diuturnitate meditationis immensae,
cum illa enim invenies et sine illa non."

more base in appearance than she, and nought is more precious in nature than she, and God also hath not appointed her to be bought for a price.[9] She it is that Solomon chose to have instead of light, and above all beauty and health; in comparison of her he compared not unto her the virtue of any precious stone.[10] For all gold in her sight shall be esteemed as a little sand, and silver shall be counted as clay; and this not without cause, for to gain her is better than the merchandise of silver and the most pure gold. And her fruit is more precious than all the riches of this world, and all the things that are desired are not to be compared with her. Length of days and health are in her right hand, and in her left hand glory and infinite riches. Her ways are beautiful operations and praiseworthy, not unsightly nor ill-favoured, and her paths are measured and not hasty, but are bound up with stubborn and day-long toil.[11] She is a tree of life to them that lay hold on her, and an unfailing light. Blessed shall they be who

the streets and ways." Cf. also "Rosarium philosophorum," in Manget, *Bibliotheca chemica*, II, pp. 88b–89a: "Know that this stone, by which this secret is wrought, God appointed not to be bought for a great price, for it is found cast forth in the streets, so that it may be had both by rich and poor. . . ." Braceschius, "De alchemia dialogus," ibid., I, p. 594b: "For Alphidius saith that this secret thing cannot be bought for a price, but is found cast forth in the midst of the street. . . ." Cf. also "Rosinus ad Sarratantam," *Artis auriferae* (1610), I, p. 188; Morienus Romanus, "De transmutatione metallorum," ibid., II, p. 25; Avicenna, "Declaratio lapidis physici filio suo Aboali," *Theatrum chemicum* (1659), IV, p. 875.

[9] Cf. Senior, *De chemia* (1566), p. 117: ". . . The philosopher Zadith, the son of Hamuel, hath extracted from its fundament precious pearls, and showeth thee openly and covertly this concealed secret which the Lord of glory hath bestowed on this worthless and priceless stone, and it is the most precious thing in the world, and the most despicable." Cf. "Ros. phil.," p. 102. Cf. ibid., p. 106: ". . . whereof Viemon saith: This is cast out upon the dunghills, and in the eyes of everyone that knoweth it not it is of no worth."

[10] Cf. "Ros. phil.," p. 100. Cf. Wisd. 7 : 7: ". . . and the spirit of wisdom came upon me; And I preferred her before kingdoms and thrones, and esteemed riches nothing in comparison of her. Neither did I compare unto her any precious stone; for all gold in comparison of her is as a little sand, and silver in respect to her shall be counted as clay. I loved her above health and beauty, and chose to have her instead of light."

[11] Cf. Petrus Bonus, *Pretiosa margarita novella* (1546), p. 45: ". . . and do thou labour therein with the most urgent instancy, and with long and boundless meditation, for therewith shalt thou find it, but without this not so."

beati,[12] quia scientia Dei numquam peribit, ut Alphidius testatur, ait enim: Qui hanc scientiam invenerit, cibus erit eius legi-
30 timus et sempiternus.[13] Et Hermes atque ceteri (philosophi) inquiunt, quod si viveret homo habens hanc scientiam milibus annis, omnique die deberet septem milia hominum pascere, numquam egeret.[14] Hoc affirmat Senior dicens; quia esset ita dives, sicut ille, qui habet lapidem,[15] de quo elicitur ignis, qui
35 potest dare ignem cui vult et inquantum vult et quando vult sine suo defectu.[16] Hoc idem vult Aristoteles in libro secundo de anima, cum dicit: Omnium natura constantium positus est terminus magnitudinis et augmenti [17] ignis vero appositione combustibilium crescit in infinitum.[18] Beatus homo, qui invenerit

---

28.–29. testatur: dicit *BD, om. L* / 29.–30. legitimus: longaevus *VP*, longus *M* / 30.–31. ceteri: alii *B Geber, Ros.* / philosophi *add. DL* / 31. inquiunt *om. B* / 32. deberet pascere: pasceret *BDL* / 33. numquam: non *BDL* / confirmat *BDL* / Quia esset: Est enim hic *BDL* / 35. sui *BDL* / 38. appositionem *D*, compositione *P* /

---

[12] Prov. 3 : 13–18: "Beatus homo qui invenit sapientiam, et qui affluit prudentia. Melior est acquisitio eius negotiatione argenti et auri primi et purissimi fructus eius. Pretiosior est cunctis opibus, et omnia quae desiderantur huic non valent comparari. Longitudo dierum in dextera eius, et in sinistra illius divitiae et gloria. Viae eius viae pulchrae, et omnes semitae illius pacificae. Lignum vitae est his qui apprehenderint eam, et qui tenuerit eam beatus." Cf. also Bishop Cyrillus, *Speculum sapientiae* (ed. Graesse), pp. 5–7.

[13] "Liber Alphidii," loc. cit.: "Scito fili quod qui hanc invenit scientiam et victum inde habuerit cibus eius legitimus erit." And: "quod thesaurus Dei numquam perit nec deficit." Quoted also in "Ros. phil.," pp. 100b–101a: "Qui hanc scientiam invenerit cibus eius legitimus erit et sempiternus" (also Maier, *Symbola aureae mensae*, p. 65).

[14] Cf. "Cons. coniug.," p. 116: ". . . nec est necesse ut reiteretur, prout dicit Hermes: Sufficiet homini per mille millia annorum, et si quotidie duo milia hominum pasceres non egeres, tingit enim in infinitum." Cf. also *De aluminibus et salibus* (ed. Ruska), p. 59: (Mercurius): "Et si quis junxerit me fratri meo vel sorori meae, vivet et gaudebit, et ero sufficiens ei usque in aeternum et si viveret annos millies millenos."

[15] "Ros. phil.," p. 92a, Hermes et Geber: "Qui hanc artem semel perfecerit, si deberet vivere mille millibus annis et singulis diebus nutrire quatuor milia hominum non egeret. Hoc confirmat Senior dicens: Est ita dives habens lapidem, de quo Elixir fit, sicut qui habet ignem potest dare ignem cui vult et quando vult et quantum vult sine suo defectu et periculo."

[16] Ibid., p. 92a.

[17] Anonymous, in ibid., p. 102a: "positus est certus terminus . . ."

[18] *De anima*, B. 4.416a: ἡ μὲν τοῦ πυρὸς αὔξησις εἰς ἄπειρον, ἕως ἂν ᾖ τὸ καυστόν,

retain her,[12] for the science of God shall never perish, as Alphidius beareth witness, for he saith: He who hath found this science,
it shall be his rightful food for ever.[13] And Hermes and other
(philosophers) say, that if a man who hath this science should
live for a thousand years, and every day must feed seven thousand men, yet should he never lack.[14] This doth Senior confirm,
saying: That such a one is as rich as he that hath a stone [15] from
which fire is struck, who can give fire to whom he will and as
much as he will and when he will without loss to himself.[16] The
same is the intent of Aristotle in his second book *Of the Soul*,
when he saith: To the size and the growth of all things in nature
a limit is appointed,[17] but fire by the addition of combustible
matter waxes without end.[18] Blessed is the man that shall find

[12] Prov. 3 : 13–18: "Blessed is the man that findeth wisdom, and is rich in prudence. The purchasing thereof is better than the merchandise of silver; and her
fruit than the chiefest and purest gold. She is more precious than all riches; and
all the things that are desired are not to be compared with her. Length of days is
in her right hand: and in her left hand riches and glory. Her ways are beautiful
ways; and all her paths are peaceable. She is a tree of life to them that lay hold
on her; and he that shall retain her is blessed." Cf. also Bishop Cyrillus, *Speculum
sapientiae* (ed. Graesse), pp. 5–7.

[13] "Liber Alphidii," loc. cit.: "Know, O son, that he who findeth out this science
and hath his nourishment therefrom, it shall be his lawful food." And: "for the
treasure of God never perisheth nor faileth." Quoted also in "Ros. phil.," pp.
100b–101a: "He who findeth out this science, it shall be his lawful and everlasting
food" (also Maier, *Symbola aureae mensae*, p. 65).

[14] Cf. 'Cons. coniug.," p. 116: ". . . nor need it be repeated, as Hermes saith: It shall
suffice a man for a million years, and if every day thou shalt feed two thousand
men, thou shalt not lack, for it tingeth unto infinity." Cf. also *De aluminibus et
salibus* (ed. Ruska), p. 59: (Mercurius): "And if one shall join me to my brother
or my sister, he shall live and shall rejoice, and I will be sufficient for him for ever,
though he should live for a million years."

[15] "Ros. phil.," p. 92a, Hermes and Geber: "He who shall once have brought this
art to perfection, though he were to live a million years, and every day feed four
thousand men, yet should he not lack. And this doth Senior confirm, saying: He
who hath the stone from which the Elixir is made, is as rich as a man who hath
fire and can give fire to whom he will and when he will and as much as he will,
without loss or danger to himself."

[16] Ibid., p. 92a.

[17] Anonymous author, in ibid., p. 102a: ". . . a certain bound is fixed."

[18] *De anima*, B.4.416a (Foster and Humphries trans., pp. 218–19) : "For the increase
of fire is infinite so long as there is anything combustible. But there are limitations to all things that subsist naturally, and some definite principle governs their

40 hanc scientiam et cui affluit prudentia haec [Saturni];[19] in omnibus viis tuis cogita illam et ipsa ducet gressus tuos.[20] Ut Senior dicit: Intelligit eam autem sapiens et subtilis et ingeniosus arbitrando, quando clarificati fuerint animi ex libro aggregationis.[21] Tunc omnis fluens animus sequitur concupiscentiam

45 suam,[22] beatus qui cogitat in eloquio meo.[23] Et Salomon: Fili, circumda eam gutturi tuo[24] et scribe in tabulis cordis tui et invenies; dic Sapientiae: soror mea es et prudentiam voca amicam tuam;[25] cogitare namque de illa sensus est valde naturalis et subtilis eam perficiens.[26] Et qui vigilaverint constanter propter

50 eam, cito erunt securi.[27] Clara est illis intellectum habentibus et numquam marcescet nec deficiet; facilis videtur his, qui eam

---

40. cui *om. MP* | prudentia haec *MPVB*, haec *om. L*, providentia Saturni *D* | 41. ducit *MPV* | 42. Intelliget *BDL* | 43. animum *P*, cum *M*, om *B* | aggregationis *conj.*, aggregationum *MP*, congregationum *V*, ex libris agnitionum *BDL* | 45. Et: etc. *D*, om. *BL* | 46. tuo *om. MPV* | 51. marcescit *MPVBD* |

τῶν δὲ φύσει συνισταμένων πάντων ἐστὶ πέρας καὶ λόγος μεγέθους τε καὶ αὐξήσεως· ταῦτα δὲ τῆς ψυχῆς ἀλλ᾽ οὐ πυρός, καὶ λόγου μᾶλλον ἢ ὕλης.

[19] Prov. 3 : 13: "Beatus homo qui invenit sapientiam, et cui affluit prudentia."

[20] Prov. 3 : 5–6: "Habe fiduciam in Dominum. . . . In omnibus viis tuis cogita illum, et ipse diriget gressus tuos."

[21] Cf. Senior, *De chemia*, p. 11: ". . . intelligit ipsam ingeniosus, subtiliter arbitrando, quando fuerint clarificati animi ex libris relictis, quos occultaverunt Philosophi . . ." Cf. also Pseudo-Aristoteles, *Secreta secretorum* (1528): "Quoniam illi qui fuerunt velocis apprehensionis et intellectus eorum fuerunt clarificati ad suscipiendam scientiam investigaverunt." Cf. *Liber aggregationis seu secretorum Alberti Magni*, H. Quentell, Cologne, ca. 1485 (incunabulum).

[22] Senior, *De chemia*, p. 12: "Facta ignota (scil. praeparatio), propter hoc ne cognoscat omnis animus concupiscentiam suam: fluit quod videntes dicant."

[23] Ibid., p. 9: "Beatus qui cogitat in eloquio meo, nec dignitas mea ipsi negabitur, nec vilescet per ca[r]nem infirmatus Leo."

[24] Prov. 3 : 3–4: "Misericordia et veritas te non deserant; circumda eas gutturi tuo, et describe in tabulis cordis tui; et invenies gratiam, et disciplinam bonam coram Deo . . ."

[25] Prov. 7 : 3–4: ". . . scribe illam (scil. sapientiam) in tabulis cordis tui. Dic sapientiae: soror mea es, et prudentiam voca amicam tuam; ut custodiat te a muliere extranea . . ."

[26] Cf. Petrus Bonus, *Pret. marg. nov.*, p. 53: "Et quoniam veritas nihil aliud est, quam adaequatio intellectus ad rem," and p. 100: "Et ars eodem modo ut natura operatur."

[27] Sap. 6 : 16: "Cogitare ergo de illa sensus est consummatus, et qui vigilaverit propter illam (scil. sapientiam) cito securus erit."

this science and into whom this prudence [of Saturn] floweth; [19] in all thy ways think on her and she shall direct thy steps.[20] As Senior saith: But the wise man and the discerning and ingenious in judgment understandeth her, when his spirits have been enlightened by the *Liber aggregationis*.[21] For then every spirit bursteth into flood and followeth its desire; [22] blessed is he who meditateth upon my words.[23] And Solomon: My son, put her about thy neck [24] and write in the tables of thy heart and thou shalt find. Say to Wisdom: Thou art my sister, and call Prudence thy friend: [25] for to meditate upon her is a most natural and subtle understanding, which bringeth her to perfection.[26] And they that constantly watch for her shall quickly be secure.[27] For she is clear to them that have understanding, and shall never

dimensions and growth. And this belongs to the soul, not to fire, and to a specific principle rather than to matter."

19 Prov. 3 : 13: "Blessed is the man that findeth wisdom, and is rich in prudence."

20 Prov. 3 : 5–6: "Have confidence in the Lord. . . . In all thy ways think on him: and he will direct thy steps."

21 Cf. Senior, *De chemia*, p. 11: ". . . the ingenious man understandeth it, by subtle reflection, when his spirits have been rendered clear by the books that are left, which the philosophers have hidden. . . ." Cf. also Pseudo-Aristotle, *Secreta secretorum* (1528), cap. "De hora eligendi . . .": "For they who were of quick understanding and whose intellect was enlightened to receive the science have investigated it." Cf. Albert the Great, *Liber aggregationis seu secretorum* (ed. Quentell, ca. 1485; incunabulum).

22 Senior, *De chemia*, p. 12: "It [the tincture] was hidden, lest every spirit should recognize its desire: [for then] it flows, as the seers would say." (My translation. Cf. infra, p. 179, n. 104.—M.L.v.F.)

23 Ibid., p. 9: "Blessed is he who thinketh upon my word, and my dignity shall not be denied to him, and the Lion shall not lose its worth, weakened through the [flesh] (dog)."

24 Prov. 3 : 3–4: "Let not mercy and truth leave thee. Put them about thy neck, and write them in the tables of thy heart: and thou shalt find grace and good understanding before God and man."

25 Prov. 7 : 3–4: ". . . write it (wisdom) upon the tables of thy heart. Say to wisdom: Thou art my sister. And call prudence thy friend: that she may keep thee from the woman that is not thine . . ."

26 Cf. Petrus Bonus, *Pret. marg. nov.*, p. 53: "And because truth is nothing else than the assimilation of the understanding to things as they are," and p. 100: "And the Art worketh in the same way as doth nature."

27 Wisd. 6 : 16: "To think therefore upon her is perfect understanding: and he that watcheth for her (wisdom) shall quickly be secure."

52 sapiunt,[28] quoniam dignos se ipsa circuit et in viis ostendit se hilariter et in omni providentia occurrit; initium namque ipsius verissima est natura,[29] cui non fit fraus.

---

53. prudentia *MP*, scientia *L* / occurret *MPV* / 54. verissima est cui natura *PVB* / sit *B* /

---

[28] Sap. 6: 13: "Clara est, et quae numquam marcescit, sapientia; et facile videtur ab his, qui diligunt eam, et invenitur ab his, qui quaerunt illam."
[29] Sap. 6: 17–18. "Quoniam dignos se ipsa circuit quaerens, et in viis ostendit se illis hilariter, et in omni providentia occurrit illis. Initium enim illius verissima est disciplinae concupiscentia."

fade away nor fail; she seemeth easy to them that have knowledge of her,[28] for she goeth about seeking such as are worthy of her and showeth herself cheerfully to them in the ways and meeteth them with all providence; for her beginning is the most true nature,[29] whereof cometh no deceit.

---

[28] Wisd. 6 : 13: "Wisdom is glorious, and never fadeth away, and is easily seen by them that love her, and is found by them that seek her."
[29] Wisd. 6: 17–18: "For she goeth about seeking such as are worthy of her: and she sheweth herself cheerfully to them in the ways and meeteth them with all providence. For the beginning of her is the most true desire of discipline."

II

QUID SIT SAPIENTIA

Si ergo nunc delectamini sedibus et sceptris regalibus, ut in perpetuum regnetis, diligite lumen scientiae¹ omnes et perquirite,
qui literis naturae estis insigniti, vobis enim sapientiam omnium
5 antiquorum exquir⟨e⟩t sapiens et in prophetis vacabit et in versutias parabolarum si⟨mul⟩ introibit occulta proverbiorum exquiret
et in absconditis parabolarum conversabitur.² Quid scientia sit
et quemadmodum facta sit referam et non abscondam a vobis.
Est namque donum et sacramentum Dei atque res divina, quae
10 maxime et diversimode a sapientum sermonibus typicis est oc-
cultata. Quare pono in lucem scientiam eius et non praeteribo
⟨veritatem⟩ neque cum invidia tabescente³ iter habebo, quoniam ab initio nativitatis hanc investigavi et ignoravi quoniam
mater omnium scientiarum esset illa, quae me antecedebat. Et
15 innumerabiles honestates mihi condonavit, quam sine fictione

---

5. exquiret *conj.*, exquirit *D*, exquerit *L*, requiris *P*, requirit *MV* / vocabit *MPL*,
vocabit te *D*, versutiis vocabit *L* / 6. simul *conj.*, sinum *MP*, suarum *DLVB* / 8.
reseram *DL* / 9.–10. sanctuarium Deitatis res divina est maxime *D*, sanctuarium
Dei atque res divina quia maxime *L* / 11. semitam *MPB* / 12. veritatem *add.*
editor /

---

¹ Sap. 6 : 22–23: "Si ergo delectamini sedibus et sceptris, o reges populi, diligite
sapientiam, ut in perpetuum regnetis. Diligite lumen sapientiae, omnes qui
praeestis populis."
² Ecclus. 39 : 1–3: "Sapientiam omnium antiquorum exquiret sapiens, et in
prophetis vacabit . . . et in versutias parabolarum simul introibit. Occulta proverbiorum exquiret, et in absconditis parabolarum conversabitur."
³ Sap. 6 : 24–25: "Quid est autem sapientia, et quemadmodum facta sit referam,
et non abscondam a vobis sacramenta Dei, sed ab initio nativitatis investigabo, et
ponam in lucem scientiam illius, et non praeteribo veritatem, neque cum invidia
tabescente iter habebo."

II

WHAT WISDOM IS

If therefore now your delight be in thrones and the sceptres of kings, that you may reign for ever, love the light of the science[1] all of you and enquire, ye who are signed with the learning of nature, for the wise man ⟨will⟩ seek out for you the wisdom of all the ancients and will be occupied in the prophets and will enter ⟨withal⟩ into the subtleties of parables and will search out the hidden meaning of proverbs and will be conversant in the secrets of parables.[2] What the science is and how she cometh into being I will lay bare, and will not hide from you. For she is a gift and sacrament of God and a divine matter, which deeply and in divers manners was veiled in images by the wise. Wherefore I bring the knowledge of her to light and will not pass over ⟨the truth⟩, neither will I have to do with consuming envy; [3] for from the beginning of my birth have I sought her out and knew not that she was the mother of all sciences that went before me. And she bestowed on me innumerable riches, which I have

---

1 Wisd. 6 : 22-23: "If then your delight be in thrones and sceptres, O ye kings of the people, love wisdom, that you may reign for ever. Love the light of wisdom, all ye that bear rule over peoples."

2 Ecclus. 39 : 1-3: "The wise man will seek out the wisdom of all the ancients and will be occupied in the prophets. He will keep the sayings of renowned men and will enter withal into the subtilties of parables. He will search out the hidden meaning of proverbs and will be conversant in the secrets of parables."

3 Wisd. 6 : 24-25: "Now what wisdom is, and what was her origin, I will declare. And I will not hide from you the mysteries of God, but will seek her out from the beginning of her birth, and bring the knowledge of her to light, and will not pass over the truth. Neither will I go with consuming envy: for such a man shall not be partaker of wisdom."

didici et absque invidia communicabo et non abscondendo honestatem illius.[4] Est enim thesaurus infinitus omnibus,[5] quem, qui homo invenit, abscondit et prae gaudio illius dicit: [6] Laetare Jerusalem et conventum facite omnes qui diligitis me, gaudete
20 cum laetitia, quia Dominus [Deus] pauperum suorum miseritus est.[7] Etiam Senior dicit: Est enim lapis, quem qui cognoscit ponit super oculos suos qui vero non, in sterquilinium projicit illum,[8] et est medicina, quae fugat inopiam, et post Deum homo non habet meliorem.[9]

16.–17. invidia non abscondendo honestatem illius communicabo L / 16. communico V, communicando BMV / abscondo V / 17. (illius) praeservando add. VP, praesumendo add. M / 20. Deus add. DL / 21. Etiam: Et MBDL / 23. et mediam quam (V: quae) fugat inopia MPV, illum mediamque fugat B /

---

[4] Albertus Magnus, "Compositum de compositis," Theatr. chem. (1659), IV, p. 825: "Et ideo scientiam quam sine fictione didici, sine invidia communico, qua invidia labescente deficit, quoniam talis homo non erit particeps amicitiae Dei. Omnis sapientia et scientia a Domino Deo est, sed hoc quocumque modo dicitur semper a Spiritu Sancto est. . . . Itaque qui habet aures audiendi tantam gratiam Deificam, audiat secretum mihi desponsatum gratiā Dei et indignis nullatenus revelat."

[5] Sap. 7 : 12–14: "(Venerunt autem mihi omnia bona pariter cum illa) . . . et laetatus sum in omnibus, quoniam antecedebat me ista sapientia, et ignorabam quoniam horum omnium mater est. Quam sine fictione didici, et sine invidia communico, et honestatem illius non abscondo. Infinitus enim thesaurus est hominibus; quo qui usi sunt, participes facti sunt amicitiae Dei."

[6] Matth. 13 : 44: "Simile est regnum caelorum thesauro abscondito in agro; quem qui invenit homo, abscondit, et prae gaudio illius vadit, et vendit universa quae habet, et emit agrum illum."

[7] Roman Missal, Introit for Fourth Sunday in Lent: "Laetare Jerusalem, et conventum facite, omnes qui diligitis eam: gaudete cum laetitia, qui in tristitia fuistis . . ." Cf. Isa. 66 : 10: "Laetamini cum Jerusalem, et exsultate in ea omnes, qui diligitis eam; gaudete cum ea gaudio, universi qui lugetis super eam."

[8] Cf. Senior, De chemia, p. 63: ". . . lapidem, quem qui cognoscit ponit illum super oculos suos et qui non cognoscit proiicit illum."

[9] Cf. "Cons. coniug.," p. 119: "Et alibi dicit (Senior): et post Deum non habes aliam medicinam. Ipsa est enim aurum sapientum, quod fugat paupertatem." Cf. also Avicenna, "Declaratio lapidis physici," Theatr. chem. (1659), IV, p. 879: "Et haec est vera hominum et metallorum medicina, laetificans, ac transformans, nec post Deum est alia quae fugat paupertatem."

learned without guile and will communicate without envy, and without hiding her worth.[4] For she is an infinite treasure to all men,[5] which a man having found, hideth it and for joy thereof saith: [6] Rejoice O Jerusalem and gather together all ye that love me; rejoice with gladness, for the Lord [God] hath been merciful unto his poor.[7] Senior likewise saith: For there is a stone, which he that knoweth layeth it upon his eyes, but he that doth not, casteth it upon the dunghill,[8] and it is a medicine which putteth poverty to flight, and after God hath man no better thing.[9]

[4] Cf. Albert the Great, "Compositum de compositis," *Theatr. chem.* (1659), IV, p. 825: "And therefore the science which I learnt without guile, do I communicate without envy, for when envy weakens it faileth, for such a man shall not be a sharer in the friendship of God. All wisdom and science is from the Lord God, but this, in what manner soever it is spoken of, is always of the Holy Ghost. . . . He therefore that hath ears to hear such great and deifying grace, let him hear the secret thing espoused to me by the grace of God, and by no means reveal it unto them that are unworthy."

[5] Wisd. 7 : 12–14: "(Now all good things came to me together with her) . . . And I rejoiced in all these; for this wisdom went before me, and I knew not that she was the mother of them all. Which I have learned without guile, and communicate without envy, and her riches I hide not. For she is an infinite treasure to men: which they that use, become the friends of God."

[6] Matt. 13 : 44: "The kingdom of heaven is like unto a treasure hidden in a field. Which a man having found, hid it: and for joy thereof goeth and selleth all that he hath and buyeth that field."

[7] Roman Missal, Introit for Fourth Sunday in Lent: "Rejoice, O Jerusalem, and come together all you that love her; rejoice with joy, you that have been in sorrow . . ." Cf. Isa. 66 : 10: "Rejoice with Jerusalem and be glad with her, all you that love her: rejoice with joy for her, all you that mourn for her."

[8] Cf. Senior, *De chemia*, p. 63: ". . . the stone, which he that knoweth layeth it upon his eyes, and he that knoweth it not, casteth it away."

[9] Cf. "Cons. coniug.," p. 119: "And elsewhere (Senior) saith: and after God thou hast no other medicine. For it is the gold of the wise, which putteth poverty to flight." Cf. also Avicenna, "Declaratio lapidis physici," *Theatr. chem.* (1659), IV, p. 879: "And this is the true medicine of men and of metals, which maketh glad and transformeth: and after God there is none other that putteth poverty to flight."

DE IGNORANTIBUS ET NEGANTIBUS
HANC SCIENTIAM

Hanc gloriosam scientiam Dei et doctrinam sanctorum et secretum philosophorum ac medicinam medicorum despiciunt
5 stulti[1] cum ignorent quid sit. Hi nolunt benedictionem et
elongabitur ab eis[2] nec decet imperitum scientia talis quia
omnis, qui est eam ignorans, est eius inimicus et non sine causa.
Ait enim Speculator:[3] Derisio scientiae est causa ignorantiae,
nec sunt asinis dandae lactucae, cum eis sufficiant ⟨cardui⟩,[4]
10 neque panis filiorum mittendus est canibus[5] ad manducandum
neque margaritae inter porcos sunt seminandae,[6] nec tales de-
risores sunt participes ⟨inclytae⟩ huius scientiae: hic enim fractor
esset sigilli coelestis qui arcana huius scientiae revelaret indig-

---

6. scientiam talem *MP*, sapientia talis *BD* / 8. Et non sine causa ait *VD* / 9. suffi-
ciunt *MP* / cardui *conj.*, carabe *MVP*, caribe *B*, caules *DL* / 12. inclytae *add. DL* /

---

[1] Prov. 1 : 7: "Sapientiam et doctrinam stulti despiciunt."

[2] Ps. 108 : 18: "Et dilexit maledictionem, et veniet ei; et noluit benedictionem, et
elongabitur ab eo."

[3] An author otherwise unknown. See Introduction, pp. 17ff.

[4] Cf. Roger Bacon, "De mirabili potestate artis et naturae libellus," *Art. aurif.*
(1610), II, pp. 327f. and 340. Also "Epistola Rogerii Bachonis," *Theatr. chem.*
(1622), V, p. 956: "Ipsemet enim dicit in secretis secretorum, quod esset fractor
sigilli coelestis qui communicaret secreta naturae et artis; adjungens quod multa
mala sequuntur eum, qui occulta detegit et arcana revelat. Caeterum in hoc casu
dicit Aulus Gellius in libro Noctium Atticarum de collatione sapientum, quod
stultum est asino praebere lactucas, cum ei sufficiant cardui."

[5] Cf. Roman Missal, Sequence (Lauda Sion) for Corpus Christi, stanza 21, verse 2
(this Sequence was written by St. Thomas Aquinas): "Vere panis filiorum, non
mittendus canibus." Matth. 15 : 26: "Non est bonum sumere panem filiorum, et
mittere canibus."

[6] Matth. 7 : 6: "Nolite dare sanctum canibus, neque mittatis margaritas vestras
ante porcos . . ."

OF THEM WHO KNOW NOT AND
DENY THIS SCIENCE

59   This glorious science of God and doctrine of the saints and secret
of the philosophers and medicine of the physicians fools despise,[1]
for what it is they know not. These will not have the blessing and
it shall be far from them,[2] nor doth such science befit the unskilled, for everyone who is ignorant of it is its enemy, and that
not without cause. For Speculator [3] saith: The mockery of science
is the cause of ignorance, and lettuces are not to be given to asses,
for (thistles) suffice them,[4] nor is the children's bread to be set before the dogs to eat,[5] nor are pearls to be cast before swine,[6] and
such mockers are not partakers in this (noble) science; for he
would be a breaker of the heavenly seal who should make the

---

1 Prov. 1 : 7: "Fools despise wisdom and instruction."
2 Ps. 108 : 18: "And he loved cursing, and it shall come unto him; and he would
not have blessing, and it shall be far from him."
3 An author otherwise unknown. See Introduction, pp. 17ff.
4 Cf. Roger Bacon, "De mirabili potestate artis et naturae," *Art. aurif.* (1610), II,
pp. 327f. and 340. Also "Epistola Rogerii Bachonis," *Theatr. chem.* (1622), V,
p. 956: "For he himself says in the 'Secreta secretorum' that he would be a breaker
of the heavenly seal who should communicate the secrets of nature and of the
Art, and he adds that many evils follow after him who uncovers hidden things
and reveals secrets. Also in this regard Aulus Gellius says in his book *Attic Nights*
concerning the conversation of the sages that it would be foolish to offer lettuces
to an ass when thistles suffice for him."
5 Roman Missal, Sequence (Lauda Sion) for Corpus Christi, stanza 21, verse 2
(this sequence was written by St. Thomas Aquinas): "In truth the bread of the
children, not to be set before dogs." Matt. 15 : 26: "It is not good to take the bread
of the children and to cast it to the dogs."
6 Matt. 7 : 6: "Give not that which is holy to dogs: neither cast ye your pearls
before swine."

nis; [7] neque in grossum corpus introibit spiritus sapientiae huius
15 nec insipiens potest eam percipere propter rationis suae perver-
sitatem; quia non sunt sapientes locuti insipientibus, qui enim
cum insipiente loquitur cum dormiente loquitur.[8] Morienus
(enim) ait: Si omnia vellem enodare prout se habent, nullus
umquam ultra prudentiae locus esset, cum insipiens sapienti
20 aequaretur; neque sub globo lunari aliquis mortalium paupertate noverca ⟨inediarum⟩ angustias defleret,[9] quia stultorum
numerus est infinitus in hac scientia.[10]

15.–16. parvitatem *BDL* | 18. enim *add. L* | enudare *MPV* | 21. inediarum *conj.*,
medias et angustias *B*, medias *PVMBD*, modicis *L* |

---

[7] Pseudo-Aristotle, "Secreta secretorum" (1528), fol. v, 2: "Ego sane transgressor
essem divinae gratiae et fractor coelestis secreti occultae revelationis, quapropter
tibi sub attestatione divine judicii illud detego sacramentum eo modo quo mihi
revelatum . . ."

[8] Ecclus. 22 : 9: "Cum dormiente loquitur, qui enarrat stulto sapientiam . . ."

[9] Cf. Petrus Bonus, *Pret. marg. nov.*, p. 42: "Idem (scil. Rasis) in lumine luminum:
Si enim omnia prout se habent, vellem enodare, nullus ultro prudentiae esset
locus, cum insipiens sapienti aequaretur. Neque sub lunari circulo quisquam
mortalium paupertate noverca inediarum ulterius defleret angustias." Also as
Rhazis quotation in "Cons. coniug.," *Ars chemica*, p. 50; and "De arte chemica,"
Art. aurif. (1610), I, p. 374. The latter is identical with the treatise attributed to
Marsilio Ficino in *Bibl. chem.*, II, pp. 172ff., cap. VII. Cf. Theobaldus de Hoghe-
lande, "De alchimiae difficultatibus," *Bibl. chem.*, I, p. 347.

[10] Eccles. 1 : 15: "Et stultorum infinitus est numerus." cf. Bishop Cyrillus, *Speculum
sapientiae* (ed. Graesse), p. 27.

secrets of this science known to the unworthy;[7] nor shall the spirit of this wisdom enter into a gross body, nor can the fool perceive it on account of the perversity of his reason. For the wise have not spoken to the foolish, seeing that he that speaketh with a fool speaketh with one that is asleep.[8] (For) Morienus saith: If I were to unriddle all things as they are, there would nowhere be any further place for prudence, for the fool would be made equal to the wise; nor would any mortal under the sphere of the moon bewail in stepmotherly poverty the pangs (of hunger),[9] for in this science the number of fools is infinite.[10]

[7] Pseudo-Aristotle, "Secreta secretorum" (1528), fol. v, 2: "But I would surely be a sinner against divine grace and a breaker of the heavenly seal of the hidden revelation, wherefore I uncover this mystery to thee under the sanction of the divine judgment in that wise wherein it was revealed unto me . . .'·

[8] Ecclus. 22 : 9: "He speaketh with one that is asleep, who uttereth wisdom to a fool. . . ."

[9] Cf. Petrus Bonus, *Pret. marg. nov.*, p. 42: "And the same (i.e., Rhazis) in the 'Lumen luminum': For were I to unravel all things as they are, there would be no place found any more for prudence, for the fool would be made equal to the wise. Nor would any mortal under the circle of the moon bewail any more in stepmotherly poverty the bitterness of abstinence." Also as Rhazis quotation in "Cons. coniug," *Ars chemica*, p. 50; and "De arte chemica," *Art. aurif.* (1610), I, p. 374. The latter is identical with the treatise attributed to Marsilio Ficino in *Bibl. chem.*, II, pp. 172ff., cap. VII. Cf. Hoghelande, "De alchimiae difficultatibus," *Bibl. chem.*, I, p. 347.

[10] Eccles. 1 : 15: "And the number of fools is infinite." Cf. Bishop Cyrillus, *Speculum sapientiae* (ed. Graesse), p. 27.

DE NOMINE ET TITULO HUIUS LIBRI

Huius autem voluminis titulus Aurora consurgens baptizatur,
et hoc quatuor de causis: Primo aurora dicitur quasi aurea hora,
sic haec scientia habet horam in finem aureum recte operantibus.
5 Secundo aurora est medium inter noctem et diem rutilans in
colore duplici, scil. rubeo et citrino, sic haec scientia dat colores
citrinos et rubeos, qui sunt medii inter nigrum et album. Tertio
quia in aurora ab omnibus infirmitatibus nocturnalibus patientes allevantur et quiescunt, sic in aurora huius scientiae
10 omnes odores et vapores mali mentem laborantis inficientes de-
ficiunt et senescunt, ut Psalmus ait: Ad vesperum demorabitur
fletus et ad matutinum laetitia.[1] Quarto et ultimo aurora dicitur
finis noctis et principium diei vel mater solis, sic nostra aurora
in rubedine summa est finis totius tenebrositatis et fugatio noc-
15 tis, longiturnitatis hiemalis illius, qui in ea ambulat, si non
caverit, offendetur.[2] De illa namque scriptum est: Et nox nocti
indicat scientiam, dies diei eructat verbum[3] et nox sicut dies
illuminabitur in deliciis suis.[4]

---

4. et scientia haec *V* / horas et finem *MPV*, horam finem *L* / 8.–9. omnes in-
firmitates nocturnales (*M* naturales) patientis (*M* parientes) *BVPM* / 11. vesperam
DL / 16. cavet *P*, caveat *M*, cavit *V* / 18. in deliciis suis *om. MPV*, etc. *B* /

---

[1] Ps. 29 : 6: "Ad vesperum demorabitur fletus, et ad matutinum laetitia."
[2] Joh. 11 : 9–10: "Respondit Jesus: Nonne duodecim sunt horae diei? Si quis
ambulaverit in die, non offendit, quia lucem huius mundi videt; si autem
ambulaverit in nocte, offendit, quia lux non est in eo."
[3] Ps. 18 : 3: "Dies diei eructat verbum, et nox nocti indicat scientiam."
[4] Ps. 138 : 11–12: ". . . et nox illuminatio mea in deliciis meis . . . et nox sicut
dies illuminabitur." Cf. Roman Missal. Exultet of Easter Even: "O vere beata
nox, quae sola meruit scire tempus et horam, in qua Christus ab inferis resurrexit!
Haec nox est, de qua scriptum est: Et nox sicut dies illuminabitur: ex nox
illuminatio mea in deliciis meis."

OF THE NAME AND TITLE OF THIS BOOK

60 Now the title of this book is baptized *Aurora Consurgens*—The Rising Dawn—and that for four reasons: Firstly, it is called Dawn as one should say the Golden Hour, for so hath this science an hour with a golden end for them that rightly perform the Work. Secondly, the dawn is midway between night and day, shining with twofold hues, namely, red and yellow; so likewise doth this science beget the colours yellow and red, which are midway between white and black. Thirdly, because at dawn they that labour under all the infirmities of the night are relieved and have rest; and so at the dawn of this science all evil odours and vapours that infect the mind of the laborant fade away and weaken, as the Psalm saith: In the evening weeping shall have place, and in the morning gladness.[1] Fourthly and lastly, the dawn is called the end of the night and the beginning of the day, or the mother of the sun, and so our dawn at its greatest redness is the end of all darkness and the putting to flight of night, of that long-drawn-out winter wherein he who walketh, if he take not heed, shall stumble.[2] For of this indeed it is written: And night to night showeth knowledge, day to day uttereth speech,[3] and night shall be light as the day in its pleasures.[4]

---

[1] Ps. 29 : 6: "In the evening weeping shall have place: and in the morning gladness."

[2] John 11 : 9–10: "Jesus answered: Are there not twelve hours of the day? If a man walk in the day, he stumbleth not, because he seeth the light of this world: but if he walk in the night he stumbleth, because the light is not in him."

[3] Ps. 18 : 3: "Day to day uttereth speech: and night to night sheweth knowledge."

[4] Ps. 138 : 11–12: ". . . and night shall be my light in my pleasures . . . and night shall be light as the day." Cf. Roman Missal, Exultet of Easter Even: "O truly blessed night, which alone didst merit to know the time and the hour wherein Christ rose from the dead! This is that night, whereof it is written: And the night shall be light as the day: and night shall be my light in my pleasures."

V

DE IRRITATIONE INSIPIENTUM

Numquid sapientia non clamitat in plateis et prudentia dat vocem in libris sapientum dicens: O viri, ad vos clamito et vox mea ad filios intelligentiae: [1] Intelligite insipientes et animad-
5 vertite parabolam et interpretationem verba sapientum et aenigmata eorum; [2] sapientes enim usi sunt diversis locutionibus in assimilatione de omni re, quae est supra terram, et sub globo lunari multiplicaverunt parabolas in hac scientia.[3] Audiens autem sapiens [sapientes] sapientior erit et intelliget, intelligens
10 sapientiam hanc possidebit illam. Haec est sapientia, regina scilicet austri, quae ab Oriente dicitur venisse, ut *aurora consurgens*,[4] audire intelligere nec non videre [volens] sapientiam Salomonis [5] et data est in manu eius potestas honor virtus et

---

2. non *om. PVBLD* | 5. verborum *MPBV* | 9. sapientes *add. D,* sapientem *add. L,* sapientum *M* | 10.–11. quae regina austri . . . dicitur venisse *MPV,* scilicet quae . . . *B* | 12. volens *add. DL* |

---

[1] Prov. 8 : 1–6: "Numquid non sapientia clamitat, et prudentia dat vocem suam? . . . in mediis semitis stans, iuxta portas civitatis . . . dicens: O viri, ad vos clamito, et vox mea ad filios hominum. Intelligite, parvuli, astutiam, et, insipientes, animadvertite. Audite, quoniam de rebus magnis locutura sum . . ."
[2] Prov. 1 : 5–7: "Audiens sapiens, sapientior erit; et intelligens gubernacula possidebit. Animadvertet parabolam et interpretationem, verba sapientum et aenigmata eorum."
[3] Cf. Petrus Bonus, *Pret. marg. nov.,* p. 54: "*Lilium:* Nostri lapidis tot sunt nomina, quot sunt res vel rerum vocabula. Et Alphidius: In hoc opere est parabolarum diversitas et nominum . . . ut ab imperitis celent . . ."
[4] Cant. 6 : 9: "Quae est ista, quae progreditur quasi aurora consurgens, pulchra ut luna, electa ut sol . . . ?"
[5] Matth. 12 : 42: "Regina austri surget in iudicio cum generatione ista, et condemnabit eam: quia venit a finibus terrae audire sapientiam Salomonis, et ecce plus quam Salomon hic." Cf. Luc. 11 : 31.

V

OF THE PROVOCATION OF THE FOOLISH

61 Doth not Wisdom cry aloud in the public places and Prudence put forth her voice in the books of the wise, saying: O ye men, to you I call, and my voice is to the sons of understanding?[1] Understand, ye foolish ones, and mark the parable and the interpretation, the words of the wise and their mysterious sayings;[2] for the wise have used divers manners of speech in making comparison with everything that is upon the earth, and beneath the sphere of the moon they have multiplied parables in this science.[3] For the wise man who heareth [the wise] will grow wiser and understand, and understanding this Wisdom he will lay hold upon her. This is Wisdom, namely the Queen of the South, who is said to have come from the east, like unto the MORNING RISING,[4] [desiring] to hear, to understand, yea and to see the wisdom of Solomon,[5] and there was given into her hand power,

1 Prov. 8: 1–6: "Doth not wisdom cry aloud, and prudence put forth her voice? standing . . . in the midst of the paths, beside the gates of the city . . . saying: O ye men, to you I call, and my voice is to the sons of men. O little ones, understand subtilty, and ye unwise, take notice. Hear, for I will speak of great things . . ."

2 Prov. 1 : 5–7: "A wise man shall hear and shall be wiser: and he that understandeth shall possess governments. He shall understand a parable, and the interpretation: the words of the wise, and their mysterious sayings."

3 Cf. Petrus Bonus, *Pret. marg. nov.*, p. 54: "*Lilium:* There are as many names for our stone as there are things or designations of things. And Alphidius: In this work there is a diversity of parables and significations . . . that they may conceal it from the unskilled . . ."

4 Cant. 6: 9: "Who is she that cometh forth as the morning rising *(aurora consurgens)*, fair as the moon, bright as the sun? . . ."

5 Matt. 12 : 42: "The queen of the south shall rise in judgment with this generation and shall condemn it: because she came from the ends of the earth to hear the wisdom of Solomon, and behold a greater than Solomon here." Cf. Luke 11 : 31.

imperium,[6] ferens regni coronam in capite suo radiis duodecim
15 stellarum rutilantem,[7] tamquam sponsa ornata viro suo [8] ha-
bensque in vestimentis suis scriptum [9] litteris aureis graecis, barbaris et latinis: Regnans regnabo et regnum meum non habebit
finem [10] omnibus invenientibus me et perquirentibus subtiliter
ingeniose et constanter.[11]

---

15. sponsam ornatam *MPVD* / 17.–18. regni mei non est finis *BDL* / 18. et per
alios perquirentibus facientibus *D*, percipientibus *MPVD* / salubriter *MPV* /

---

[6] Roman Missal, Introit for Epiphany: "Ecce advenit Dominator Dominus: et
regnum in manu eius et potestas et imperium." Cf. Mal. 3 : 1.
[7] Apoc. 12 : 1: "(Et signum magnum apparuit in caelo): mulier amicta sole, et luna
sub pedibus eius, et in capite eius corona stellarum duodecim."
[8] Apoc. 21 : 2: "Vidi sanctam civitatem, Jerusalem novam, descendentem de coelo,
. . . sicut sponsam ornatam viro suo."
[9] Apoc. 19 : 16: "Et habet in vestimento suo . . . scriptum: Rex regum et
Dominus dominantium."
[10] Luc. 1 : 32–33: ". . . et regnabit in domo Jacob in aeternum, et regni eius non
erit finis."
[11] Cf. "Ros. phil.," p. 103b: "Salomon Rex: Haec [Sapientia] est filia, ob quam
Regina austri ab Oriente dicitur venisse, ut aurora consurgens audire et intelligere
et videre sapientiam Salomonis posset, et data est in manu eius potestas, honor,
virtus et imperium, et florens regni corona in capite suo radiis septem stellarum
rutilantium, tamquam sponsa ornata viro suo, habens in vestimentis suis scriptum
literis aureis Graecis et Barbaris et Latinis: Ego sum unica filia sapientum, stultis
penitus ignota." On the variations of this text see Jung, *Psychology and Alchemy*,
pars. 467f.

honour, strength, and dominion,[6] bearing upon her head the crown of the kingdom shining with the rays of twelve stars,[7] prepared as a bride adorned for her husband,[8] and having on her garments written[9] in golden letters in Greek, in barbarian (Arabic) script, and in Latin: Reigning I will reign, and my kingdom shall have no end [10] for all them that find me and subtly and ingeniously and constantly seek me out.[11]

---

[6] Roman Missal, Introit for Epiphany: "Behold the Lord the Ruler is come: and a kingdom in his hand, and power and dominion." Cf. Mal. 3 : 1.

[7] Apoc. 12 : 1: "(And a great sign appeared in heaven;) a woman clothed with the sun, and the moon under her feet, and on her head a crown of twelve stars."

[8] Apoc. 21 : 2: "I saw the holy city, the new Jerusalem, coming down out of heaven . . . prepared as a bride adorned for her husband."

[9] Apoc. 19 : 16: "And he hath on his garment . . . written: King of kings and Lord of lords."

[10] Luke 1 : 32–33: ". . . and he shall reign in the house of Jacob for ever. And of his kingdom there shall be no end."

[11] Cf. "Ros. phil.," p. 103b: "King Solomon: This [Sapientia] is my daughter, for whose sake men say that the queen of the south came out of the east, like the rising dawn, in order to hear, understand, and behold the wisdom of Solomon; power, honour, strength and dominion are given into her hand; and on her head the resplendent crown of the kingdom with seven gleaming stars for its rays, like a bride adorned for her husband, and on her garment is written in golden letters, in Greek, barbarian (Arabic), and Latin, 'I am the only daughter of the wise, utterly unknown to the foolish.'" On the variations of this text see Jung, *Psychology and Alchemy*, pars. 467f.

PARABOLA PRIMA DE TERRA NIGRA,
IN QUAM SEPTEM PLANETAE RADICAVERUNT

Aspiciens a longe vidi nebulam magnam totam terram deni-
grantem,[1] quae hanc exhauserat meam animam tegentem et
5 ⟨quia⟩ aquae intraverant usque ad eam, quare putruerunt et
corruptae sunt a facie inferni inferioris et umbra mortis, quoniam tempestas dimersit me;[2] tunc coram me procident Aethiopes et inimici mei terram meam lingent.[3] Ideo non est sanitas
in carne mea et a facie iniquitatis meae conturbata sunt omnia
10 ossa mea.[4] Ergo laboravi per singulas noctes clamans, raucae
factae sunt fauces meae:[2] quis est homo, qui vivit sciens et intelligens, eruens animam meam de manu inferi?[5] Qui me elucidant
habebunt vitam (aeternam)[6] daboque ei edere de ligno vitae,

---

4. quae: qui *PVBL*, *q M* / exhausit *B*, exhauserit *MPLV* / anima *M* / regentem
MPV, tingentem *L* / 5. quia *conj.*, q̇ *M*, q̃ *B*, et quae aquae intraverint *P*, intra-
verunt *MVB*, aquae quae intraverant *D*, aquae quae intraverunt *L* / quare: quae
D, quia *VL* / 13. aeternam *add. DL* /

---

[1] Cf. Roman Breviary, First Responsory at Mattins for First Sunday in Advent:
"Aspiciens a longe, ecce video Dei potentiam venientem, et nubem totam terram
tegentem."
[2] Ps. 68 : 2–4: "Salvum me fac, Deus: quoniam intraverunt aquae usque ad
animam meam. Infixus sum in limo profundi, et non est substantia. Veni in altitudinem maris, et tempestas dimersit me. Laboravi clamans, raucae factae sunt
fauces meae . . ."
[3] Ps. 71 : 9: "Coram illo procident Aethiopes, et inimici eius terram lingent."
[4] Ps. 37 : 4–6: "Non est sanitas in carne mea, a facie irae tuae; non est pax ossibus
meis, a facie peccatorum meorum. . . . Putruerunt et corruptae sunt cicatrices
meae, a facie insipientiae meae . . ." Ps. 6 : 3–4: "Sana me, Domine, quoniam
conturbata sunt ossa mea, et anima mea turbata est valde."
[5] Ps. 88 : 49: "Quis est homo qui vivet et non videbit mortem: eruet animam
suam de manu inferi?"
[6] Ecclus. 24 : 30–31: ". . . qui operantur in me non peccabunt; qui elucidant me
vitam aeternam habebunt."

THE FIRST PARABLE: OF THE BLACK EARTH, WHEREIN THE SEVEN PLANETS TOOK ROOT

₆₂ Beholding from afar off I saw a great cloud looming black over the whole earth,[1] which had absorbed the earth and covered my soul, (because) the waters had come in even unto her, wherefore they were putrefied and corrupted before the face of the lower hell and the shadow of death, for a tempest hath overwhelmed me;[2] then before me shall the Ethiopians fall down and my enemies shall lick my earth.[3] Therefore there is no health in my flesh and all my bones are troubled before the face of my iniquity.[4] For this cause have I laboured night by night with crying, my jaws are become hoarse;[2] who is the man that liveth, knowing and understanding, delivering my soul from the hand of hell?[5] They that explain me shall have (eternal) life,[6] and to him I will give

---

[1] Cf. Roman Breviary, First Responsory at Mattins for First Sunday in Advent: "Beholding from afar off, lo, I see the power of God approaching, and a cloud covering the whole earth."

[2] Ps. 68 : 2–4: "Save me, O God, for the waters are come in even unto my soul. I stick fast in the mire of the deep: and there is no sure standing. I am come into the depth of the sea; and a tempest hath overwhelmed me. I have laboured with crying; my jaws are become hoarse . . ."

[3] Ps. 71 : 9: "Before him the Ethiopians shall fall down: and his enemies shall lick the ground."

[4] Ps. 37 : 4–6: "There is no health in my flesh, because of thy wrath: there is no peace for my bones, because of my sins. . . . My sores are putrified and corrupted, because of my foolishness." Ps. 6: 3–4: "Have mercy on me, O Lord, for I am weak; heal me, O Lord, for my bones are troubled. And my soul is troubled exceedingly."

[5] Ps. 88 : 49: "Who is the man that shall live, and shall not see death: that shall deliver his soul from the hand of hell?"

[6] Ecclus. 24 : 30–31: "He that hearkeneth to me shall not be confounded, and they that work by me shall not sin. They that explain me shall have life everlasting."

quod est in paradiso et sedere mecum in solio regni mei.[7] Qui
15 me effoderit sicut pecuniam et acquisierit sicut thesaurum [8] et
lacrimas oculorum meorum non turbaverit vestimentumque
meum non arriserit,[9] cibum et potum meum non intoxicaverit,
atque cubiculum requiei meae stupro non foedaverit, necnon
totum corpus meum, quod est valde delicatum non violaverit
20 atque supra omnia animam meam [sive columbam], quae est
sine felle tota pulchra ⟨et⟩ decora, in qua macula non est,[10] qui
mihi sedes et thronos non laeserit, cuius amore langueo, ardore
liquesco, odore vivo, sapore convalesco, cuius lacte nutrimentum
suscipio, amplexu iuvenesco, osculo spiraculum vitae recipio,
25 cuius condormitione totum corpus meum exinanitur, illi vero
ero in patrem et ipse mihi in filium,[11] sapiens, qui laetificat patrem,[12] hunc quem primum pono et excelsum prae regibus terrae

---

20. sive columbam *add. MPV* / 24. amplexo *MPDL*, amplexus et oscula investigio
spiraculum *L*, investigo *D* / osculum *MPVDL* / spiritum *MPB*, spiritui *V* / 25. exinanitur *conj.*, exinanito *DL*, exitañito *MP*, excitamento *V* /

---

[7] Apoc. 2 : 7: "Vincenti dabo edere de ligno vitae, quod est in paradiso Dei mei."
Ibid., 3 : 21: "Qui vicerit, dabo ei sedere mecum in throno meo."

[8] Prov. 2 : 3–5: "Si enim sapientiam invocaveris, et inclinaveris cor tuum prudentiae; si quaesieris eam quasi pecuniam, et sicut thesauros effoderis illam;
tunc intelliges timorem Domini, et scientiam Dei invenies."

[9] Cf. *Turba Philosophorum* (ed. Ruska), p. 132: "Omnes huius scientiae inves-
tigatores, operis nummi et auri arcanum est tenebrosa vestis, et nemo novit, quae
philosophi in libris suis narraverunt absque lectionum et tentationum frequenta-
tione ac sapientum inquisitione."

[10] Cant. 4 : 7: "Tota pulchra es, amica mea, et macula non est in te." Cf. Roman
Missal, Gradual for the Immaculate Conception: "Tota pulchra es, Maria: et
macula originalis non est in te."

[11] Hebr. 1 : 5: "Ego ero illi in patrem, et ipse erit mihi in filium," also I Chron.
17 : 13. Cf. also Apoc. 21 : 7: "Qui vicerit, possidebit haec, et ero illi Deus, et erit
mihi filius." Cf. Alphidius in Petrus Bonus, *Pret. marg. nov.*, p. 40: "Adhuc etiam
noverunt quod Deus fieri debebat homo, quia in die novissima huius artis in qua
est operis complementum generans et generatum fiunt omnino unum: et senex
et puer et pater et filius fiunt omnino unum." Cf. also *Turba*, p. 161: "Dico
quod ille senex de fructibus arboris comedere non cessat . . . quousque senex
ille iuvenis fiat . . . ac pater filius factus est."

[12] Prov. 29 : 3: "Vir qui amat sapientiam laetificat patrem suum."

to eat of the tree of life which is in paradise, and to sit with me
on the throne of my kingdom.[7] He that shall dig for me as money
and obtain me as a treasure[8] and shall not disturb the tears of
my eyes and shall not deride my garment,[9] shall not poison my
meat and my drink and shall not defile with fornication the
couch of my rest, and shall not violate my whole body which is
exceeding delicate and above all my soul [or dove] which without gall is wholly beauteous ⟨and⟩ comely, in which there is no
spot,[10] who shall do no hurt to my seats and thrones, he for whose
love I languish, in whose ardour I melt, in whose odour I
live, by whose sweetness I regain my health, from whose milk
I take nourishment, in whose embrace I am made young, from
whose kiss I receive the breath of life, in whose loving embrace
my whole body is lost, to him indeed I will be a father and he
shall be to me a son;[11] wise is he who rejoiceth his father,[12] him
whom I place first and highest among the kings of the earth, and

[7] Apoc. 2 : 7: "To him that overcometh I will give to eat of the tree of life, which
is in the paradise of my God." Ibid. 3 : 21: "To him that shall overcome, I will
give to sit with me in my throne."

[8] Prov. 2 : 3–5: "For if thou shalt call for wisdom and incline thy heart to prudence: If thou shalt seek her as money, and dig for her as for a treasure; then
shalt thou understand the fear of the Lord, and shalt find the knowledge of God."

[9] Cf. *Turba Philosophorum* (ed. Ruska), p. 132: "All ye seekers out of this
science, the secret of the silver and the gold is a dark garment, and no man
cometh to know what the philosophers have written in their books, without
abundant reading and experiment and enquiry of the wise."

[10] Cant. 4 : 7: "Thou art all fair, O my love, and there is not a spot in thee." Cf.
Roman Missal, Gradual for the Immaculate Conception: "Thou art all fair, O
Mary, and there is in thee no stain of original sin."

[11] Hebr. 1 : 5: "I will be to him a father, and he shall be to me a son." Also,
I Chron. 17 : 13. Cf. also Apoc. 21 : 7: "He that shall overcome shall possess these
things, and I will be his God: and he shall be my son." Cf. Alphidius in Petrus
Bonus, *Pret. marg. nov.*, p. 40: "They (of old) knew also that God was to be made
man, because on the last day of this Art, on which is the completion of the work,
the begetter and the begotten become altogether one; and old man and child,
father and son, become altogether one." Cf. also *Turba*, p. 161: "I say, that
that old man ceaseth not to eat of the fruits of the tree . . . until that old man
become a youth . . . and the father hath become the son."

[12] Prov. 29 : 3: "A man that loveth wisdom rejoiceth his father."

et in aeternum servabo illi testamentum meum fidele.[13] Si autem
dereliquerit legem meam [14] et in viis meis non ambulaverit et
30 mandata praedicta non custodiverit. [nil] proficiet inimicus in
eo et filius iniquitatis [non] apponet nocere illi,[15] si autem in
viis meis ambulaverit, tunc non timebit a frigoribus nivis. Omnibus enim domesticis suis erit indumentum, byssus et purpura [16]
et ridebit in die illa dum satiabor et apparuerit gloria mea,[17]
35 quia consideravit semitas meas et panem otiosum non comedit.[18]
Ideo aperti sunt coeli super eum et vox intonuit [19] illius, qui
habet septem stellas in manu sua, qui sunt septem spiritus [20]
missi in omnem terram praedicare et testificari. Qui crediderit
et bene baptizatus fuerit salvus erit, qui vero non crediderit,
40 condemnabitur. Signa autem eorum, qui crediderint et bene
baptizati fuerint sunt haec: [21] dum discernit coelestis rex super

---

27.-28. terrae in aeternum. Servabo *MP*, terrae et *om. V* | 29. dereliquerit legem
meam et *om. MPV*, dereliquerunt *L* | 29.-30. et mandata . . . in viis meis am-
bulaverit *om. MPV* | ambulaverint *L* | 32. nivis: o nobis *MP*, o vobis *V*, nimis *L*,
om. B. | 35. quia: qui *PV* | 38. testificare *MPL*, *om. B* | 40. eos *PL* | 41. sunt *om.*
L | discurit *MP*, cernit *L* |

---

13 Ps. 88 : 27-28: "Ipse invocabit me: Pater meus es tu: Deus meus, et susceptor
salutis meae. Et ego primogenitum ponam illum, excelsum prae regibus terrae.
In aeternum servabo illi misericordiam meam; et testamentum meum fidele ipsi."
14 Ps. 88 : 31-33: "Si autem dereliquerint filii eius legem meam, et in iudiciis meis
non ambulaverint; si iustitias meas profanaverint, et mandata mea non cus-
todierint; visitabo in virga iniquitates eorum . . ."
15 Ps. 88 : 22-23: "Manus enim mea auxiliabitur ei, et bracchium meum con-
fortabit eum. Nihil proficiet inimicus in eo, et filius iniquitatis non apponet
nocere ei."
16 Prov. 31 : 21-22: "Non timebit domui suae a frigoribus nivis; omnes enim
domestici eius vestiti sunt duplicibus. Stragulatam vestem fecit sibi; byssus et
purpura indumentum eius."
17 Cf. Ps. 16 : 15: "Satiabor cum apparuerit gloria tua."
18 Prov. 31 : 25-27: ". . . et ridebit in die novissimo. Os suum aperiet sapientiae,
et lex clementiae in lingua eius. Consideravit semitas domus suae, et panem
otiosa non comedit."
19 Apoc. 4 : 1: ". . . ecce ostium apertum in caelo, et vox prima, quam audivi,
tamquam tubae loquentis mecum, dicens . . ." Cf. Ps. 17 : 14: "Intonuit de coelo
Dominus, et Altissimus dedit vocem suam, . . . et apparuerunt fontes aquarum."
20 Apoc. 1 : 4: ". . . et a septem spiritibus, qui in conspectu throni eius sunt."
1 : 16: ". . . et habebat in dextera sua stellas septem . . ." 2 : 1: "Haec dicit, qui
tenet septem stellas in dextera sua . . ." 3 : 1: "Haec dicit, qui habet septem
Spiritus Dei et septem stellas . . ."
21 Marc. 16 : 16-17: "Qui crediderit, et baptizatus fuerit, salvus erit; qui vero non
crediderit, condemnabitur. Signa autem eos, qui crediderint, haec sequentur: In
nomine meo daemonia eiicient . . ."

I will keep my covenant faithful to him for ever.[13] But if he shall forsake my law [14] and walk not in my ways and keep not my commandments aforesaid, the enemy shall have [no] advantage over him and the son of iniquity shall [not] have power to hurt him; [15] but if he shall walk in my ways, then shall he not fear in the cold of snow. And for all his household there shall be covering, fine linen and purple,[16] and he shall laugh in that day when I shall be satisfied and my glory shall appear,[17] for he hath looked well to my paths and hath not eaten his bread idle.[18] Therefore were the heavens opened above him and there thundered the voice [19] of him who holdeth the seven stars in his hand, which are the seven spirits [20] sent forth into all the earth to preach and to bear witness. He that believeth and is well baptized shall be saved, but he that believeth not shall be condemned. And the signs of those who believe and are well baptized are these: [21] When the

---

[13] Ps. 88 : 27–28: "He shall cry out to me: Thou art my father, my God, and the support of my salvation. And I will make him my firstborn, high above the kings of the earth. I will keep my mercy for him for ever: and my covenant faithful to him."

[14] Ps. 88 : 31–33: "And if his children forsake my law, and walk not in my judgments: if they profane my justices, and keep not my commandments, I will visit their iniquities with a rod . . ."

[15] Ps. 88 : 22–23: "For my hand shall help him: and my arm shall strengthen him. The enemy shall have no advantage over him: nor the son of iniquity have power to hurt him."

[16] Prov. 31 : 21–22: "She shall not fear for her house in the cold of snow: for all her domestics are clothed with double garments. She hath made for herself clothing of tapestry: fine linen, and purple is her covering."

[17] Ps. 16 : 15: "I shall be satisfied when thy glory shall appear."

[18] Prov. 31 : 25–27: "(Strength and beauty are her clothing;) and she shall laugh in the latter day. She hath opened her mouth to wisdom: and the law of clemency is on her tongue. She hath looked well to the paths of her house, and hath not eaten her bread idle."

[19] Apoc. 4 : 1: "(After these things, I looked: and) behold, a door was opened in heaven. And the first voice which I heard, as it were, of a trumpet speaking with me, said: . . ." Cf. Ps. 17 : 14: "And the Lord thundered from heaven, and the Highest gave his voice: . . . and the fountains of waters appeared."

[20] Apoc. 1 : 4: ". . . and from the seven spirits, which are before his throne." 1 : 16: ". . . and he had in his right hand seven stars." 2 : 1: "These things saith he, who holdeth the seven stars in his right hand . . ." 3 : 1: "These things saith he who hath the seven spirits of God and the seven stars . . ."

[21] Mark 16 : 16–17: "He that believeth and is baptized shall be saved: but he that believeth not shall be condemned. And these signs shall follow them that believe: In my name they shall cast out devils . . ."

eos,[22] nive dealbabuntur in Selmon et pennae columbae deargentatae et posteriora dorsi eius in pallore auri.[23] Talis erit mihi
filius dilectus [24] ipsum videte, speciosum forma prae filiis homi-
45 num,[25] cuius pulchritudinem Sol et Luna mirantur.[26] Ipse vero
est privilegium amoris et heres in quem confidunt homines [27]
et sine quo nihil possunt facere.[28] Qui autem aures habet audiendi audiat, quid dicat spiritus doctrinae filiis disciplinae [29]
de septem stellis, quibus opus divinum peragitur. Quas Senior
50 tradit in libro suo, capitulo Solis et Lunae, dicens: Postquam

---

42. eos *conj.*, eam *DL*, eum *MPV* / dealbuntur *L*, dealbantur *M* / Salomon *D*,
Selomen *M* / 43. mihi: noster *D* / 44. spectaculum fore *M. om. B* / pro *D* / 45.
admiratur *D* / 46. amoris: amborum *P*, amborum amorum *M* / 47. sine quo nihil
potest fieri sine quo nihil possunt (*V:* potes) facere *MPV* / 49. percipitur *L*, tradidit
BV, om. MP /

---

22 "Eos" (plural) is necessary here, since a plural is presupposed in both the preceding and succeeding clauses. The idea is probably that of a post-mortal, transfigured state, in which those who are saved follow the Lamb, as virgins (dove).
(Cf. Apoc. 7 : 14: ". . . et laverunt stolas suas, et dealbaverunt eas in sanguine
Agni," —and 14 : 4: "Virgines enim sunt. Hi sequuntur Agnum . . .")
23 Ps. 67 : 14–15: "Si dormiatis inter medios cleros, pennae columbae deargentatae,
et posteriora dorsi eius in pallore auri. Dum discernit coelestis reges super eam,
nive dealbabuntur in Selmon: Mons Dei mons pinguis . . ." Perhaps an allusion
to the "columba deargentata" of Hugh of St. Victor, Migne, *P.L.*, vol. 177, cols.
15ff.: "De Bestiis. Incipit de tribus columbis: Si dormiatis inter medios
cleros . . ."
24 Cant. 5 : 16: ". . . talis est dilectus meus, et ipse est amicus meus, filiae Jerusalem."
25 Ps. 44 : 3 (considered as a Christian epithalamium, with Christ as the bridegroom): "Speciosus forma prae filiis hominum."
26 Cf. Honorius of Autun, *Expos. in Cant.*, *P.L.*, vol. 172, col. 380: "mirantur."
Cf. Roman Breviary, Feast of St. Agnes, Ninth Antiphon at Mattins: "Ipsi sum
desponsata . . . cujus pulchritudinem sol et luna mirantur."
27 Baruch 3 : 18: . . . "et aurum, in quo confidunt homines."
28 Cf. Joh. 15 : 5: "Quia sine me nihil potestis facere."
29 Apoc. 2 : 7: "Qui habet aurem, audiat quid Spiritus dicat Ecclesiis: . . ." Cf.
Matth. 11 : 15: "Qui habet aures audiendi, audiat . . ."

king that is in heaven judgeth over them,[22] they shall be whited with snow in Selmon and shall be as the wings of a dove covered with silver, and the hinder parts of her back with the paleness of gold.[23] Such shall be to me a beloved son,[24] behold ye him, beautiful above the sons of men,[25] at whose beauty the sun and moon wonder.[26] For he is the privilege of love and the heir, in whom men trust [27] and without whom they can do nothing.[28] But he that hath ears to hear, let him hear what the spirit of the doctrine saith to the sons of the discipline [29] concerning the seven stars, by which the divine work is wrought. And of these Senior treateth in his book in the chapter of the Sun and Moon, saying:

[22] " Eos" (plural) is necessary here, since a plural is presupposed in both the preceding and succeeding clauses. The idea is probably that of a post-mortal, transfigured state, in which those who are saved follow the Lamb, as virgins (dove). (Cf. Apoc. 7 : 14: ". . . and (they) have washed their robes and made them white in the blood of the Lamb." And 14 : 4: ". . . for they are virgins. These follow the Lamb whithersoever he goeth.' ')

[23] Ps. 67 : 14-15: "If you sleep among the midst of lots, you shall be as the wings of a dove covered with silver, and the hinder parts of her back with the paleness of gold. When he that is in heaven appointeth kings over her, they shall be whited with snow in Selmon. The mountain of God is a fat mountain . . ." [Cf. RSV, Ps. 68 : 12-15: "The women at home divide the spoil, though they stay among the sheepfolds—the wings of a dove covered with silver, its pinions with green gold. When the Almighty scattered kings there, snow fell on Zalmon. O mighty mountain, mountain of Bashan . . ."] Perhaps an allusion to the "dove covered with silver" of Hugh of St. Victor, Migne, P.L., vol. 177, cols. 15ff.: "De Bestiis. Incipit, Of the three doves: if you sleep among the midst of lots . . ."

[24] Cant. 5 : 16: ". . . Such is my beloved, and he is my friend, O ye daughters of Jerusalem."

[25] Ps. 44 : 3 (considered as a Christian epithalamium, with Christ as the bridegroom). "Thou art beautiful above the sons of men."

[26] Cf. Honorius of Autun, Expos. in Cant., P.L. vol. 172, col. 380: "admire." Cf. Roman Breviary, Feast of St. Agnes, Ninth Antiphon at Mattins: "To him am I espoused . . . whose beauty the sun and the moon admire."

[27] Baruch 3 : 18: ". . . and gold, wherein men trust."

[28] Cf. John 15 : 5: "For without me you can do nothing.' '

[29] Apoc. 2 : 7: "He that hath an ear let him hear what the Spirit saith to the churches." Cf. Matt. 11 : 15: "He that hath ears to hear, let him hear . . ."

51 feceris illa septem quae divisisti per septem stellas (et dedisti septem stellis) ⟨et⟩ novies purgasti donec videantur margaritae (in similitudine) haec est dealbatio.[30]

51. feras illas *P*, feras illa *M* / divisisti *conj.*, dividisti *D*, dimisisti *MPVBL* / et dedisti opem stellis *M*, et septem dedisti septem stellis *D*, *om.* *B* / 52. novem *D* (*arab.* *Text:* novem in *place of* septem) / purgati *M*, compurgasti *L*, purgasti eas *B* / 53. in similitudinem *D*, *om.* *MPV* / dealbo *M*, dealbationem *D* /

[30] Cf. Senior, *De chemia*, pp. 10–11: "Posteaquam feceris illa septem, quae divisisti per septem stellas, purgasti, et hoc tritum minute; donec videantur sicut margaritae in similitudine, haec est dealbatio." Cf. Stapleton, "Muhammad bin Umail," pp. 149–50.

After thou hast made those seven (metals) which thou hast distributed through the seven stars (and hast appointed to the seven stars) (and) hast purged them nine times until they appear as pearls (in likeness)—this is the Whitening.[30]

---

[30] Cf. Senior, *De chemia*, pp. 10–11: "After thou hast made those seven (metals), which thou hast divided among the seven stars, and hast purged them, and hast ground them up carefully, until they appear like to pearls in appearance, that is the whitening." Cf. Stapleton, "Muhammad bin Umail," pp. 149–50.

PARABOLA SECUNDA DE DILUVIO
AQUARUM ET MORTE,
QUAM FEMINA INTULIT ET FUGAVIT

Quando conversa fuerit ad me multitudo maris [1] et torrentes in-
5 undaverunt [2] super faciem meam et sagittae pharetrae meae
sanguine inebriatae fuerint [3] et torcularia mea optimo vino frag-
raverint et horrea mea frumento tritici repleta fuerint [4] et sponsus cum decem virginibus sapientibus in thalamum meum
introierit [5] et postea venter meus a tactu dilecti mei intumuerit
10 et pessulum ostii mei dilecto apertum fuerit,[6] et postquam iratus
Herodes multos pueros in Bethlehem Judaeae occiderit et
Rachel omnes filios suos ploraverit [7] et lumen in tenebris exor-

---

5. et pharetrae *MP*, *om. L* / 6. sanguineae *MPV* / inebriati *D* / fuerint *om.*
MPV / fragraverunt *MPL* / 7. frumenti *MPV*, frumentis *B* / repletum fuerit *L*,
repleta fuerit *M* / sponsum *MP* / 8. in *om. BDL* / 9. introiverit *DL* / tacta *MP* /
intimuerit *P* / 10. iratus fuerit *add. L* / 11. Judaeae: iude *MPV* / occidit *P* /

---

[1] Isa. 60 : 5: "Tunc videbis, et afflues, mirabitur et dilatabitur cor tuum, quando
conversa fuerit ad te multitudo maris, fortitudo Gentium venerit tibi . . ."
[2] Ps. 77 : 20: "Quoniam percussit petram, et fluxerunt aquae, et torrentes in-
undaverunt." Cf. Jonas 2 : 3–6: ". . . de ventre inferi clamavi, et exaudisti vocem
meam. Et proiecisti me in profundum, in corde maris, et flumen circumdedit
me; . . . Omnes . . . fluctus tui super me transierunt . . . circumdederunt me
aquae usque ad animam; abyssus vallavit me, pelagus operuit caput meum . . ."
[3] Deut. 32 : 42: "Inebriabo sagittas meas sanguine . . ."
[4] Prov. 3 : 10: ". . . et implebuntur horrea tua saturitate, et vino torcularia tua
redundabunt." Cf. Joel 2 : 24.
[5] Cf. Matth. 25 : 1ff.
[6] Cant. 5 : 6: "Pessulum ostii mei aperui dilecto meo, at ille declinaverat, atque
transierat . . ."
[7] Cf. Matth. 2 : 16–18 and Roman Missal, Communion Antiphon for Holy Innocents (Dec. 28).

VII

THE SECOND PARABLE: OF THE FLOOD OF WATERS AND OF DEATH, WHICH THE WOMAN BOTH BROUGHT IN AND PUT TO FLIGHT

When the multitude of the sea shall be converted to me [1] and the streams have flowed [2] over my face and the arrows of my quiver are drunk with blood [3] and my presses are fragrant with the best wine and my barns are filled with the corn of wheat [4] and the bridegroom with the ten wise virgins hath entered into my chamber [5] and thereafter my belly hath swelled from the touch of my beloved and the bolt of my door hath been opened to my beloved, [6] and after Herod being angry hath slain many children in Bethlehem of Juda and Rachel hath bewailed all her children [7]

[1] Isa. 60 : 5: "Then thou shalt see and abound, and thy heart shall wonder and be enlarged, when the multitude of the sea shall be converted to thee, the strength of the Gentiles shall come to thee . . ."

[2] Ps. 77 : 20: "Because he struck the rock, and the waters gushed out, and the streams overflowed." Cf. Jonah 2 : 3–6: "I cried out of the belly of hell: and thou hast heard my voice. And thou hast cast me forth into the deep in the heart of the sea, and a flood hath compassed me: all thy billows and thy waves have passed over me. . . . The waters compassed me about even to the soul: the deep hath closed me round about: the sea hath covered my head."

[3] Deut. 32 : 42: "I will make my arrows drunk with blood . . ."

[4] Prov. 3 : 10: ". . . and thy barns shall be filled with abundance, and thy presses shall run over with wine." Cf. Joel 2 : 24.

[5] Cf. Matt. 25 : 1 ff.

[6] Cant. 5 : 6: "I opened the bolt of my door to my beloved, but he had turned aside, and was gone."

[7] Cf. Matt. 2 : 16–18 and Roman Missal, Communion Antiphon for Holy Innocents (Dec. 28).

tum fuerit [8] et Sol justitiae de coelo apparuerit,[9] tunc veniet
plenitudo temporis, in qua Deus mittet filium suum,[10] sicut
15 locutus est, quem constituit heredem universorum, per quem
fecit et saecula,[11] cui dixit olim: Filius meus es tu, ego hodie
genui te: [12] cui magi ab oriente tria munera pretiosa obtulerunt [13] in die illa, quam fecit Dominus, exultemus et laetemur
in ea,[14] quia hodie afflictionem meam Dominus [15] respexit et
20 redemptionem misit,[16] quia regnaturus est in Israel. Hodie
mortem quam foemina intulit foemina fugavit et claustra inferni fracta sunt; mors enim ultra non dominabitur [17] nec portae
inferi amplius praevalebunt adversus eam,[18] quia drachma
decima, quae perdita fuerat est inventa et ovis decima ultra
25 nonaginta in deserto est restaurata et numerus fratrum nostro-

---

13. tunc: dunc *MP* / venierit *M* / 14. quo *DL* / quem *om. L* / 16. cui: qui *PDLV* /
20. Hodie: Homini *D* / 22. confracta *BD* / dominabitur illi *add. L* / 23. inferni vel
inferi *VP*, vel inferni *M₂*, inferni *D* / 24. ultra: atque *MPV* / 25. nonaginta: nona
MPV, de qua *L* /

---

[8] Ps. 111 : 4: "Exortum est in tenebris lumen rectis . . ." Cf. Roman Missal,
Gradual for the Visitation of Mary (July 2): "Felix es sacra Virgo Maria . . .
quia ex te ortus est sol iustitiae Christus Deus."
[9] Mal. 4 : 2: ". . . et orietur vobis timentibus nomen meum Sol iustitiae."
[10] Gal. 4 : 4: "At ubi venit plenitudo temporis, misit Deus Filium suum."
[11] Hebr. 1 : 2: "Novissime diebus istis locutus est nobis in Filio, quem constituit
heredem universorum, per quem fecit et saecula . . ."
[12] Hebr. 1 : 5: "Cui enim dixit aliquando Angelorum: Filius meus es tu, ego hodie
genui te."
[13] Cf. Matth. 2 : 11, and Roman Breviary, First Responsory at Mattins on days
after (formerly within the Octave of) the Epiphany: "Tria sunt munera pretiosa,
quae obtulerunt Magi Domino in die ista."
[14] Ps. 117 : 24: "Haec est dies, quam fecit Dominus; exultemus et laetemur in
ea . . ."
[15] Cf. Gen. 31 : 42: "afflictionem meam . . . respexit Deus."
[16] Ps. 110 : 9: "Redemptionem misit populo suo . . ."
[17] Rom. 6 : 9: "Scientes quod Christus resurgens ex mortuis iam non moritur,
mors illi ultra non dominabitur."
[18] Matth. 16 : 18: "(Tu es Petrus,) et super hanc petram aedificabo ecclesiam meam,
et portae inferi non praevalebunt adversus eam . . ."

and a light hath risen up in darkness [8] and the Sun of Justice hath appeared from heaven,[9] then the fulness of the time shall come when God shall send his Son,[10] as he hath said, whom he hath appointed heir of all things, by whom also he made the world,[11] to whom he said of old time: Thou art my Son, today have I begotten thee: [12] to whom the wise men from the East brought three precious gifts; [13] in that day, which the Lord hath made, let us be glad and rejoice therein,[14] for this day hath the Lord beheld my affliction [15] and sent redemption,[16] for he shall reign in Israel. That death which a woman brought into the world, this day hath a woman put to flight, and the barriers of hell are broken down; for death shall no more have dominion,[17] nor shall the gates of hell prevail against her,[18] for the tenth groat, which was lost, is found, and the hundredth sheep is restored in the wilder-

[8] Ps. 111 : 4: "To the righteous a light is risen up in darkness . . ." Cf. Roman Missal, Gradual for the Visitation of Mary (July 2): "Happy art thou, O sacred Virgin Mary . . . for out of thee hath risen the Sun of justice, Christ our God."
[9] Mal. 4 : 2: "But unto you that fear my name the Sun of justice shall arise . . ."
[10] Gal. 4 : 4: "But when the fulness of the time was come, God sent his Son . . ."
[11] Hebr. 1 : 2: "Last of all in these days (God) hath spoken to us by his Son, whom he hath appointed heir of all things, by whom also he made the world . . ."
[12] Hebr. 1 : 5: "For to which of the angels hath he said at any time: Thou art my son, today have I begotten thee?"
[13] Cf. Matt. 2 : 11, and Roman Breviary, First Responsory at Mattins on days after (formerly within the Octave of) the Epiphany: "Three are the precious gifts, which the Magi offered to the Lord on this day."
[14] Ps. 117 : 24: "This is the day which the Lord hath made: let us be glad and rejoice therein."
[15] Cf. Gen. 31 : 42: "God beheld my affliction . . ."
[16] Ps. 110 : 9: "He hath sent redemption to his people . . ."
[17] Rom. 6 : 9: "Knowing that Christ, rising again from the dead, dieth now no more. Death shall no more have dominion over him."
[18] Matt. 16 : 18: "(Thou art Peter,) and upon this rock I will build my church, and the gates of hell shall not prevail against it . . ."

rum de lapsu angelorum est plenarie integratus.[19] Oportet te ergo hodie fili gaudere,[20] quia amplius non erit clamor neque ullus dolor, quoniam priora transierunt.[21] Qui habet aures audiendi audiat quid dicat spiritus doctrinae filiis disciplinae de
30 foemina quae mortem intulit et fugavit, quod philosophi innuunt his verbis: Aufer ei animam et redde ei animam, quia corruptio unius est generatio alterius[22] hoc est: priva ipsum humore corrumpente et augmenta humore connaturali, per quod erit ipsius perfectio et vita.

---

31. Infer *L* / 32. hoc est priva ipsum: hoc primo cum *L, corr. L₂* / 33. humorem corrumpentem *MPV* / cum (humore) *add. L* / cum naturali *MP* /

---

19 Cf. Apoc. 6 : 11: "Et dictum est illis ut requiescerent adhuc tempus modicum, donec compleantur conservi eorum et fratres eorum." Also cf. Luc. 15 : 1–10.
20 Cf. Luc. 15 : 32: "Fili, . . . epulari autem et gaudere oportebat."
21 Apoc. 21 : 4: ". . . et mors ultra non erit, neque luctus, neque clamor, neque dolor erit ultra, quia prima abierunt."
22 Cf. "Cons. coniug.," p. 259: "Quia corruptio unius est generatio alterius secundum Philosophos." This passage comes from the Arabic treatise "Le Livre de la terre et de la pierre" (Berthelot, *Chimie au moyen âge*, III, p. 223). It is also cited by Thomas Aquinas, *Summa*, I, q. 118, art. II ad 2, and Albertus Magnus, "De lapide philos.," *Theatr. chem.* (1659), IV, p. 855. Cf. Avicenna, "Declaratio lapidis physici," ibid., p. 876.

ness, and the number of our brethren from the fall of the angels is fully made up.[19] It is meet therefore, my son, to make merry this day,[20] for there shall be no more crying nor any sorrow, for the former things are passed away.[21] He that hath ears to hear, let him hear what the spirit of the doctrine saith to the sons of the discipline concerning the woman who brought in death and put it to flight, which the philosophers declare in these words: Take away his soul and give him back his soul, for the corruption of one is the generation of another,[22] that is: Take from him the corrupting humour and add to him the connatural humour, through which shall come to pass his perfecting and life.

19 Cf. Apoc. 6 : 11: "And it was said to them that they should rest for a little time, till their fellow servants and their brethren . . . should be filled up." Also cf. Luke 15 : 1-10.

20 Cf. Luke 15 : 32: "Son . . . it was fit that we should make merry."

21 Apoc. 21 : 4: ". . . and death shall be no more, nor mourning, nor crying, nor sorrow shall be any more, for the former things are passed away."

22 Cf. "Cons. coniug.," p. 259: "For the corruption of one thing is the generation of another, according to the philosophers.' 'This passage comes from the Arabic treatise "The Book of Earth and Stone" (Berthelot, Chimie au moyen âge, III, p. 223). It is also cited by Thomas Aquinas, Summa, I, q. 118, art. II ad 2, and Albert the Great, "De lapide philos., "Theatr. chem. (1659), IV, p. 855. Cf. Avicenna, "Declaratio lapidis physici," ibid., p. 876.

PARABOLA TERTIA
DE PORTA AEREA ET VECTE FERREO
CAPTIVITATIS BABYLONICAE

Qui portas aereas et vectes meos ferreos confregit [1] candelabrum
quoque meum de loco suo moverit [2] nec non vincula carceris
tenebrositatis dirupuerit atque animam meam esurientem, quae
cucurrit in siti oris sui adipe frumenti et (de) petra melle
cibaverit [3] ac peregrinationi meae grande coenaculum praepara-
verit,[4] ut in pace dormiam et requiescant [5] super me septem
dona spiritus sancti [miseritus]. Quia congregabunt me de universis terris, ut effundant super me aquam mundam,[6] et munda-
bor a delicto maximo [7] et a daemonio meridiano,[8] quia a planta
pedis usque ad verticem [capitis] non est (inventa) sanitas.[9]

---

2. ferrae *L* | 4. meas ferreas *DL* | 6. disrumpit *MPB* | 7. in siti: in sit *M* | de
conj. | 8. cibavit *MPV* | atque *DL* | 8.–9. praeparavit *MPV* | 9. quiescam *MVD*,
quiescunt *L*, requiescam *P* | super me septem *om. DL* | 10. miseritus *add. D* | 11.
ut: et *MPV* | 11.–12. emundabor *MVBDL* | 12. a (daemonio) *om. BDL* |

---

[1] Isa. 45 : 2–3: "Ego ante te ibo, et gloriosos terrae humiliabo; portas aereas con-
teram, et vectes ferreos confringam; et dabo tibi thesauros absconditos, et arcana
secretorum . . ."
[2] Apoc. 2 : 5: "Venio tibi, et movebo candelabrum tuum de loco suo, nisi poenitentiam egeris."
[3] Ps. 80 : 17: "Et cibavit eos ex adipe frumenti, et de petra melle saturavit eos."
[4] Luc. 22 : 12 (Last Supper): "Et ipse ostendet vobis coenaculum magnum stratum,
et ibi parate . . .' '
[5] Cf. Ps. 4 : 9: "In pace in idipsum dormiam et requiescam."
[6] Ezech. 36 : 24–25: "Congregabo vos de universis terris, et adducam vos in terram
vestram. Et effundam super vos aquam mundam, et mundabimini ab omnibus
iniquamentis vestris . . ."
[7] Cf. Ps. 18 : 14: ". . . et emundabor a delicto maximo."
[8] Ps. 90 : 5–6: ". . . non timebis . . . ab incursu, et daemonio meridiano . . ."
[9] Isa. 1 : 6: "A planta pedis usque ad verticem non est in eo sanitas . . ."

VIII

THE THIRD PARABLE: OF THE GATE OF BRASS AND BAR OF IRON OF THE BABYLONISH CAPTIVITY

64 He who brake in pieces my gates of brass and my bars of iron[1] shall also move my candlestick out of its place,[2] and shall break asunder the chains of the prison of darkness and feed my hungry soul, which hasted in thirst for his face, with the fat of wheat and with honey (out of) the rock,[3] and shall prepare a large dining room for my pilgrimage,[4] that I may sleep in peace,[5] and the seven gifts of the Holy Spirit may rest upon me, [who hath had mercy upon me]. For they shall gather me together out of all the countries, that they may pour upon me clean water,[6] and I shall be cleansed from the greatest sin,[7] and from the noonday devil,[8] for from the sole of my foot unto the crown [of my head] there is no soundness (found) in me.[9] Therefore they shall cleanse me

---

[1] Isa. 45 : 2-3: "I will go before thee and will humble the great ones of the earth. I will break in pieces the gates of brass and will burst the bars of iron. And I will give thee hidden treasures and the concealed riches of secret places . . ."

[2] Apoc. 2 : 5: "Or else I come to thee and will move thy candlestick out of its place, except thou do penance."

[3] Ps. 80 : 17: "And he fed them with the fat of wheat and filled them with honey out of the rock."

[4] Luke 22 : 12 (Last Supper): "And he will show you a large dining room furnished. And there prepare."

[5] Cf. Ps. 4 : 9: "In peace in the selfsame I will sleep and I will rest."

[6] Ezek. 36 : 24-25: "I . . . will gather you together out of all the countries and will bring you into your own land. And I will pour upon you clean water and you shall be cleansed from all your filthiness . . ."

[7] Ps. 18 : 14: ". . . and I shall be cleansed from the greatest sin."

[8] Ps. 90 : 5-6: ". . . thou shalt not be afraid . . . of invasion, or of the noonday devil."

[9] Isa. 1 : 6: "From the sole of the foot unto the top of the head there is no soundness therein . . ."

Ideo ab occultis et ab alienis sordibus meis me mundabunt,[10]
15 postea omnium iniquitatum mearum non recordabor, quia
unxit me Deus oleo laetitiae [11] ut inhabitet in me virtus pene-
trationis et liquefactionis in die resurrectionis meae,[12] quando
(a) Deo gloriabor.[13] Quia generatio haec advenit et praeterit [14]
donec veniat qui mittendus est [15] qui et aufert iugum capti-
20 vitatis nostrae, in qua sedebamus septuaginta annis super flumina
Babylonis; [16] ibi flevimus et suspendimus organa nostra, pro eo,
quod elevatae sunt filiae Sion et ambulaverunt extento collo et
nutibus oculorum ibant et plaudebant et pedibus suis composito
gradu incedebant. Decalvabit ergo Dominus verticem filiarum

---

13. capitis add. B / inventa om. MPVB / 17. refectionis MPV / quando: quantum
MPDL, cum B / 18. a add. D, cum V / Domino DL / 23. nutibus: mittibus P, miti-
bus M / oculis V /

---

10 Ps. 18 : 13–14: "Ab occultis meis munda me et ab alienis parce servo tuo."

11 Ps. 44 : 8: "Propterea unxit te Deus, Deus tuus, oleo laetitiae, prae consortibus
tuis . . ."

12 Cf. Roman Missal, Alleluia-verse for First Sunday after Easter (Low Sunday):
"Alleluia, Alleluia. [Cf. Matth. 28:] In die resurrectionis meae, dicit Dominus,
praecedam vos in Galileam. [Cf. Joh. 20:] Post dies octo, ianuis clausis, stetit
Jesus in medio discipulorum suorum et dixit: Pax vobis. Alleluia."

13 Cf. Pret. marg. nov., p. 39: "Unde dicit Rasis in quadam epistola: Cum hoc
autem, scilicet lapide rubeo, magnificaverunt se philosophi super omnes alios et
vaticinati sunt futura. . . . Ita quod cognoverunt diem iudicii et consumma-
tionis saeculi debere venire et mortuorum resurrectionem in ipsa, in qua
unaquaeque anima suo primo corpori coniungetur, et de caetero ab invicem non
separabuntur in perpetuum. Et erit tunc, omne corpus glorificatum ad incor-
ruptibilitatem translatum et ad luciditatem et subtilitatem fere incredibilem, et
penetrabit omne solidum, quia eius natura tunc erit natura spiritus sicut et
corporis."

14 Eccles. 1 : 4: "Generatio praeterit et generatio advenit; terra autem in aeternum
stat."

15 Gen. 49 : 10: "Non auferetur sceptrum de Juda, et dux de femore eius, donec
veniat qui mittendus est; et ipse erit expectatio gentium . . ."

16 Ps. 136 : 1–2: "Super flumina Babylonis, illic sedimus et flevimus, cum recorda-
remur Sion. In salicibus in medio eius suspendimus organa nostra . . ." Cf. "Liber
quartorum Platonis," Theatr. chem. (1622), V, p. 144: "Sedentes super flumina
Eufrates sunt Caldaei . . . priores, qui adinvenerunt extrahere cogitationem."

from my secret faults and from those of others,[10] and thereafter
I shall not remember all my iniquities, for God hath anointed
me with the oil of gladness[11] that there may dwell in me the
virtue of penetration and of liquefaction in the day of my resurrection,[12] when I shall be glorified (by) God.[13] For this generation
cometh and passeth away,[14] until he come that is to be sent,[15]
who also taketh away the yoke of our captivity, wherein we sate
seventy years by the rivers of Babylon;[16] there we wept and
hung up our instruments, because the daughters of Sion were
haughty and walked with stretched-out necks and winkings of
their eyes and made a noise and went at a measured pace. Therefore the Lord will make bald the crown of the head of the daugh-

[10] Ps. 18 : 13–14: "From my secret [sins] cleanse me. O Lord, and from those of
others spare thy servant."

[11] Ps. 44 : 8: "Therefore God, thy God, hath anointed thee with the oil of gladness above thy fellows."

[12] Cf. Roman Missal, Alleluia-verse for First Sunday after Easter (Low Sunday):
"Alleluia, alleluia. [Cf. Matt. 28:] On the day of my resurrection, saith the Lord,
I will go before you into Galilee. Alleluia. [Cf. John 20:] After eight days, the
doors being shut, Jesus stood in the midst of his disciples, and said: Peace be
with you. Alleluia."

[13] Cf. *Pret. marg. nov.*, p. 39: "Wherefore Rasis saith in a certain epistle: With
this red stone have the philosophers magnified themselves above others and have
prophesied of future things . . . so that they knew that the day of judgment
and of the consummation of the world must come, and the resurrection of the
dead therewith, wherein every soul will be united with its original body, and
thenceforth they shall not be separated for ever. And then shall every body be
glorified and translated into incorruptibility, and to an incredible brightness and
subtlety, and shall penetrate every solid thing, for its nature shall then be the
nature of spirit as well as of body."

[14] Eccles. 1 : 4: "One generation passeth away, and another generation cometh:
but the earth standeth for ever."

[15] Gen. 49 : 10: "The sceptre shall not be taken away from Juda, nor a ruler from
his thigh, till he come that is to be sent: and he shall be the expectation of
nations. . . ."

[16] Ps. 136 : 1–2: "Upon the rivers of Babylon, there we sat and wept: when we
remembered Sion. On the willows in the midst thereof we hung up our instruments." Cf. "Liber quartorum Platonis." *Theatr. chem.* (1622), V, p. 144: "Those
who sit by the river Euphrates are the Chaldees . . . the first who discovered how
man draws forth thought."

25 Sion et crines earum nudabit,[17] quia de Sion exibit lex et verbum Domini de Jerusalem.[18] In die illa quando apprehenderunt septem mulieres virum unum dicentes: Panem nostrum comedimus et vestimentis nostris cooperimur,[19] quare non defendis sanguinem nostrum,[20] qui effusus est tamquam aqua in circuitu
30 Jerusalem? [21] et divinum receperunt responsum: Adhuc sustinete modicum tempus, donec numerus fratrum nostrorum impletus sit,[22] qui scriptus est in libro hoc; tunc omnis, qui relictus fuerit in Sion salvus vocabitur,[23] cum abluerit Dominus sordem filiarum suarum Sion spiritu sapientiae et intellectus; [24] tunc decem iugera
35 vinearum faciunt lagunculam et triginta modii sementis faciunt

---

25. rex *L* / 26. apprehendent *D* / 27.–28. comedemus *MP* / 31. temporis *L* / 33. abluit *MD* / 34. suarum *om. VDL* / spiritus *MPV* / et *om. P* / 35. et: sed *P* / tres triginta *MP* / faciunt (at end of line) *om. MP* /

---

[17] Isa. 3 : 16–17: "Et dixit Dominus: Pro eo quod elevatae sunt filiae Sion, et ambulaverunt extento collo, et nutibus oculorum ibant, et plaudebant, ambulabant pedibus suis, et composito gradu incedebant; decalvabit Dominus verticem filiarum Sion, et Dominus crinem earum nudabit."

[18] Isa. 2 : 3: "Quia de Sion exibit lex, et verbum Domini de Jerusalem.'

[19] Isa. 4 : 1–2: "Et apprehendent septem mulieres virum unum in die illa, dicentes: Panem nostrum comedemus, et vestimentis nostris operiemur; aufer opprobrium nostrum."

[20] Cf. Roman Breviary, Second Responsory at Mattins for the Feast of the Holy Innocents: "Sub altare Dei audivi voces occisorum dicentium, Quare non defendis sanguinem nostrum? Et acceperunt divinum responsum: Adhuc sustinete modicum tempus, donec impleatur numerus fratrum vestrorum."

[21] Ps. 78 : 3: "Effuderunt sanguinem eorum tamquam aquam in circuitu Jerusalem."

[22] Cf. Apoc. 6 : 9–11: "Vidi . . . animas interfectorum propter verbum Dei . . . dicentes: Usquequo, Domine, sanctus et verus, non iudicas, et non vindicas sanguinem nostrum de iis qui habitant in terra? Et datae sunt illis singulae stolae albae; et dictum est illis ut requiescerent adhuc tempus modicum, donec compleantur conservi eorum et fratres eorum, qui interficiendi sunt sicut et illi."

[23] Isa. 4 : 3–4: "Et erit: Omnis qui relictus fuerit in Sion, et residuus in Jerusalem, sanctus vocabitur, omnis qui scriptus est in vita in Jerusalem. Si abluerit Dominus sordes filiarum Sion, et sanguinem Jerusalem laverit de medio eius, in spiritu iudicii, et spiritu ardoris . . ."

[24] Ecclus. 15 : 5: "   et adimplebit illum spiritu sapientiae et intellectus."

76

ters of Sion, and will discover their hair,[17] for the law shall come forth from Sion and the word of the Lord from Jerusalem.[18] In that day when seven women took hold of one man, saying: We eat our own bread and wear our own apparel,[19] why dost thou not defend our blood,[20] which is poured out as water round about Jerusalem?[21] And they received the divine reply: Rest ye still for a little time, until the number of our brethren is filled up,[22] which is written in this book: then every one that shall be left in Sion shall be called saved, when the Lord shall have washed away the filth of his daughters of Sion [23] with the spirit of wisdom and understanding;[24] then will ten acres of vineyard yield one

17 Isa. 3 : 16–17: "And the Lord said: Because the daughters of Sion are haughty, and have walked with stretched-out necks and wanton glances of their eyes, and made a noise as they walked with their feet, and moved at a set pace: the Lord will make bald the crown of the head of the daughters of Sion, and the Lord will discover their hair."

18 Isa. 2 : 3: "For the law shall come forth from Sion: and the word of the Lord from Jerusalem."

19 Isa. 4 : 1–2: "And in that day seven women shall take hold of one man, saying: We will eat our own bread, and wear our own apparel: only let us be called by thy name. Take away our reproach."

20 Cf. Roman Breviary, Second Responsory at Mattins for the Feast of the Holy Innocents: "Under the altar of God I heard the voices of them that were slain, saying: Why dost thou not defend our blood? And they received the divine reply: Be patient still for a little time, until the number of your brethren be filled up."

21 Ps. 78 : 3: "They have poured out their blood as water round about Jerusalem."

22 Cf. Apoc. 6 : 9–11: "I saw under the altar the souls of them that were slain for the word of God and for the testimony which they held. And they cried with a loud voice, saying: How long, O Lord, holy and true, dost thou not judge and revenge our blood on them that dwell on the earth? And white robes were given, to every one of them one. And it was said to them that they should rest for a little time, till their fellow servants and their brethren, who are to be slain even as they, should be filled up."

23 Isa. 4 : 3–4: "And it shall come to pass, that every one that shall be left in Sion, and that shall remain in Jerusalem, shall be called Holy: every one that is written among the living in Jerusalem. If the Lord shall wash away the filth of the daughters of Sion, and shall wash away the blood of Jerusalem out of the midst thereof, by the spirit of judgment and by the spirit of burning."

24 Ecclus. 15 : 5: ". . . and (she) shall fill him with the spirit of wisdom and understanding . . ."

modios tres.[25] Qui intelligit hoc, non commovebitur in aeternum.[26] Qui habet aures audiendi audiat, quid dicat spiritus doctrinae filiis disciplinae de captivitate Babylonica, quae septuaginta durabat annos, quam philosophi insinuant his verbis:
40 Multiplices sunt septuaginta praeceptorum alternationes.[27]

---

39. durabit *M* / 40. sunt *om. MPV* / altercationes *P*, operationes *V*, *om. M* /

---

[25] Isa. 5 : 10–11: "Decem enim iugera vinearum facient lagunculam unam, et triginta modii sementis facient modios tres."

[26] Prov. 10 : 30: Justus in aeternum non commovebitur," and Ps. 124 : 1: "Qui confidunt in Domino, sicut mons Sion: non commovebitur in aeternum . . ."

[27] Cf. *Pret. marg. nov.*, p. 45: "Rasis in libro septuaginta praeceptorum. . . ." In the Middle Ages there existed a work attributed to Rhazis, the *Liber divinitatis* or *Septuaginta*, also known under the title *Liber alternationum praeceptorum Rasis philosophi in Alchimiam* etc. It had as its source a work of Geber. Cf. M. Steinschneider, *Die europäischen Übersetzungen aus dem Arabischen bis Mitte des 17. Jahrhunderts*, B, p. 28, and Berthelot, *Moyen âge*, III, p. 34.

little measure and thirty bushels of seed yield three bushels.[25] He that understandeth this shall not be moved for ever.[26] He that hath ears to hear, let him hear what the spirit of the doctrine saith to the sons of the discipline concerning the Babylonish captivity, which endured seventy years, of which the philosophers tell in these words: Manifold are the alternations of the seventy precepts.[27]

---

[25] Isa. 5 : 10–11: "For ten acres of vineyard shall yield one little measure: and thirty bushels of seed shall yield three bushels."

[26] Prov. 10 : 30: "The just shall never be moved," and Ps. 124 : 1: They that trust in the Lord shall be as Mount Sion: he shall not be moved for ever that dwelleth in Jerusalem."

[27] Cf. *Pret. marg. nov.*, p. 45: "Rasis in the Book of the Seventy Precepts . . ." In the Middle Ages there existed a work attributed to Rhazis, the *Liber divinitatis* or *Septuaginta*, also known under the title *Liber alternationum praeceptorum Rasis philosophi in Alchimiam* etc. It had as its source a work of Geber. Cf. M. Steinschneider, *Die europäischen Übersetzungen aus dem Arabischen bis Mitte des 17. Jahrhunderts*, B, p. 28, and Berthelot, *Moyen âge*, III, p. 34.

PARABOLA QUARTA DE FIDE PHILOSOPHICA, QUAE NUMERO TERNARIO CONSISTIT

Qui fecerit voluntatem patris mei et eiecerit hunc mundum in
mundum, dabo illi sedem mecum in throno regni mei [1] super
solium David et super sedes tribus Israel. [2] Haec est voluntas patris
mei, [3] ut cognoscant ipsum esse verum (Deum) [4] et non alium, qui
dat affluenter et non improperat [5] in omnibus gentibus in veritate, et filium eius unigenitum, Deum de Deo, lumen de lumine,
et Spiritum Sanctum ab utroque procedentem, [6] qui aequalis est
patri et filio in Deitate, nam in patre manet aeternitas, in filio

---

4.– 5. in hunc modum *D*, *om. L* | 5. mecum *om. MP* | 7. Deum *add. D* | 8. dat:
ditat *DL* | effluenter *PL*, affirentur *M* | 9. in veritate: unitate *P*, *om. B* |

---

[1] Matth. 12 : 50: "Quicumque enim fecerit voluntatem Patris mei . . . ipse meus
frater, et soror, et mater est." Apoc. 3 : 21: "Qui vicerit, dabo ei sedere mecum in
throno meo . . ."
[2] Isa. 9 : 7: "Super solium David, et super regnum eius sedebit . . ." Matth.
19 : 28: "Vos qui secuti estis me . . . sedebitis . . . super sedes duodecim, iudi-
cantes duodecim tribus Israel."
[3] Cf. Joh. 6 : 39: "Haec est autem voluntas ejus qui misit me, Patris."
[4] Cf. Joh. 17 : 3: "Ut cognoscant te solum verum Deum."
[5] Jac. 1 : 5: "Si quis autem vestrum indiget sapientia, postulet a Deo, qui dat
omnibus affluenter, et non improperat."
[6] Nicene Creed: "Credo in unum Deum, Patrem omnipotentem, factorem coeli
et terrae, visibilium omnium et invisibilium. Et in unum Dominum Jesum
Christum, Filium Dei unigenitum. Et ex Patre natum ante omnia saecula. Deum
de Deo, lumen de lumine, Deum verum de Deo vero. Genitum, non factum, con-
substantialem Patri: per quem omnia facta sunt. Qui propter nos homines et
propter nostram salutem descendit de coelis. Et incarnatus est de Spiritu Sancto
ex Maria Virgine: et homo factus est. Crucifixus etiam pro nobis . . . Et in
Spiritum Sanctum Dominum, et vivificantem, qui ex Patre Filioque procedit. Qui
cum Patre et Filio simul adoratur et conglorificatur . . ."

THE FOURTH PARABLE: OF THE PHILOSOPHIC FAITH, WHICH CONSISTETH IN THE NUMBER THREE

65 Whosoever shall do the will of my Father and shall cast out this world into the world, I will give him to sit with me upon the throne of my kingdom [1] and upon the throne of David and upon the seats of the tribes of Israel.[2] This is the will of my Father,[3] that they may know him to be the true (God) [4] and no other, who giveth abundantly and upbraideth not,[5] unto all peoples in truth, and his only begotten Son, God of God, light of light, and the Holy Spirit who proceedeth from both,[6] who is equal in Godhead to the Father and the Son, for in the Father inhereth eter-

[1] Matt. 12 : 50: "For whosoever shall do the will of my Father in heaven, he is my brother, and sister, and mother." Apoc. 3 : 21: "To him that shall overcome I will give to sit with me in my throne . . ."

[2] Isa. 9 : 7: "He shall sit upon the throne of David, and upon his kingdom . . ." Matt. 19 : 28: "You who have followed me . . . shall sit on twelve seats judging the twelve tribes of Israel."

[3] Cf. John 6 : 39: "This is the will of my Father who hath sent me."

[4] Cf. John 17 : 3: "That they may know Thee the only true God."

[5] James 1 : 5: "If any of you want wisdom, let him ask of God, who giveth to all men abundantly and upbraideth not."

[6] Nicene Creed: "I believe in one God, the Father Almighty, maker of heaven and earth, and of all things visible and invisible. And in one Lord Jesus Christ, the only-begotten Son of God, and born of the Father before all ages. God of God, light of light, true God of true God. Begotten, not made, consubstantial with the Father, by whom all things were made. Who for us men and for our salvation descended from heaven. And was incarnate by the Holy Ghost of the Virgin Mary: and was made man. He was crucified also for us: . . . and in the Holy Ghost, the Lord and life-giver, who proceedeth from the Father and the Son, who together with the Father and the Son is adored and glorified . . ."

aequalitas, in Spiritu sancto (est) aeternitatis aequalitatisque connexio; quia sicut dicitur qualis pater, talis filius, talis et Spiritus Sanctus [7] et hi tres unum sunt [8] [quod philosophus vult
15 esse] corpus spiritus et anima,[9] quia omnis perfectio in numero ternario consistit, hoc est mensura, numero et pondere.[10] Nam pater a nullo est, filius a patre est, Spiritus Sanctus ab utroque est procedens, quoniam patri attribuitur sapientia, qua omnia regit et disponsit suaviter, cuius viae investigabiles sunt et incompre-
20 hensibilia iudicia.[11] Filio attribuitur veritas, ipse enim apparens id quod non erat assumpsit,[12] perfectus Deus et homo existens ex humana carne et anima rationali,[13] qui praecepto patris cooper-ante Spiritu Sancto [14] mundum peccato [parentum] perditum

---

1 **2.** est *add.* M | 14.–15. quod philosophus vult esse *add.* BDL | 15. spiritum et animam BDL | 16. trinario VP | 19. quae D | 20. ipso DLV | apparens *conj.*, enim apparente DL, *om.* B, omnia operante illud MPV | 21. non *om.* PB | absumpsit M | **22.** humana natura rationae subsistens B | quae VP | **23.** parentum *add.* DL |

---

7 Athanasian Creed (see Roman Breviary, Trinity Sunday at Prime): "Qualis Pater, talis Filius, talis Spiritus Sanctus."

8 Roman Missal, Preface of the Trinity: "Domine sancte, Pater omnipotens, aeterne Deus. Qui cum unigenito Filio tuo, et Spiritu Sancto, unus es Deus, unus es Dominus: non in unius singularitate personae, sed in unius Trinitate substantiae. Quod enim de tua gloria, revelante te, credimus, hoc de Filio tuo, hoc de Spiritu Sancto, sine differentia discretionis sentimus. Ut in confessione verae sempiternaeque Deitatis, et in personis proprietas, et in essentia unitas, et in maiestate adoretur aequalitas." Cf. I Joh. 5 : 7–8: "Tres sunt qui testimonium dant in coelo: Pater, Verbum, et Spiritus Sanctus; et hi tres unum sunt. Et tres sunt qui testimonium dant in terra: Spiritus, et aqua, et sanguis; et hi tres unum sunt."

9 Senior, *De chemia*, p. 45: "Aes nostrum est sicut homo habens spiritum, animam et corpus. Propterea dicunt sapientes: Tria et tria sunt unum. Deinde dixerunt in uno sunt tria, et spiritus, anima, et corpus sunt unum, et omnia sunt ex uno."

10 Sap. 11 : 21. "Omnia in mensura, et numero, et pondere disposuisti."

11 Rom. 11 : 33: "O altitudo divitiarum sapientiae et scientiae Dei: quam incomprehensibilia sunt iudicia eius, et investigabiles viae eius." Cf. Isa. 45 : 15.

12 Cf. Roman Missal, Preface for Christmas: ". . . quo Unigenitus tuus in tua tecum gloria coaeternus in veritate carnis nostrae visibiliter corporalis apparuit . . ."

13 Athanasian Creed: "Perfectus Deus, perfectus homo, ex anima rationali et humana carne subsistens."

14 Cf. Roman Missal, Ordinary of the Mass, Prayer after the Kiss of Peace: "Domine Jesus . . . qui ex voluntate Patris, cooperante Spiritu Sancto, per mortem tuam mundum vivificasti . . ."

nity, in the Son equality, in the Holy Spirit (is) the bond of eternity and equality; for as it is said, Like as the Father is, so is the Son, and so also is the Holy Spirit,[7] and these three are One,[8] [which the Philosopher would have to be] body, spirit, and soul,[9] for all perfection consisteth in the number three, that is, in measure, number, and weight.[10] For the Father is of none, the Son is of the Father, the Holy Spirit proceedeth from both; for to the Father is attributed wisdom, by which he ruleth and sweetly disposeth all things, whose ways are unsearchable and his judgments incomprehensible.[11] To the Son is attributed Truth, for he in his appearing took upon him that which he was not,[12] subsisting perfect God and man of human flesh and reasonable soul,[13] who at the behest of the Father with the co-operation of the Holy Spirit restored to the world [14] lost by the sin [of the first

[7] Athanasian Creed (see Roman Breviary, Trinity Sunday at Prime): "As is the Father, so is the Son, so is the Holy Ghost."

[8] Roman Missal, Preface of the Trinity: "O Lord, holy Father, almighty, everlasting God. Who together with thine only-begotten Son and the Holy Ghost art one God, one Lord, not in the singleness of one person but in the Trinity of one substance. For what, revealed by Thee, we believe of thy glory, the same we believe of the Son, the same of the Holy Ghost, without difference or distinction; so that in the confession of one true and eternal Godhead there is adored distinction in Persons, oneness in Essence, and equality in Majesty." Cf. I John 5 : 7–8: "There are Three who give testimony in heaven: the Father, the Word, and the Holy Ghost; and these three are one. And there are three that give testimony on earth: the spirit, the water, and the blood; and these three are one."

[9] Cf. Senior, *De chemia*, p. 45. "Our ore is like to a man, having spirit, soul, and body. Wherefore do the wise say: Three and three are one. They say also: In one are three, and: Spirit, soul and body are one and all things are of one."

[10] Wisd. 11 : 21: "(God hath) ordered all things in measure, and number, and weight."

[11] Rom. 11 : 33: "O the depth of the riches of the wisdom and of the knowledge of God! How incomprehensible are his judgments, and how unsearchable his ways!" Cf. Isa. 45 : 15.

[12] Cf. Roman Missal, Preface for Christmas: ". . . on which thine only-begotten Son, coeternal with thee in thy glory, in very truth visibly appeared in our bodily flesh . . ."

[13] Cf. Athanasian Creed: "Perfect God, perfect man, subsisting of rational soul and human flesh."

[14] Cf. Roman Missal, Ordinary of the Mass, Prayer after the Kiss of Peace: "O Lord Jesus . . . who, fulfilling the Father's will, by the cooperation of the Holy Ghost, by thy death hast given life to the world . . ."

restauravit. Spiritui Sancto datur bonitas, quo terrena fiunt
25 coelestia et hoc tripliciter: baptizando flumine sanguine et
flammis: flumine vegetando et abluendo, quando squalores
omnes abluit expellendo fumositates de animabus, sicut dicitur:
Tu animabus vivificandis aquas foecundas.[15] Nam omnium
vegetabilium nutrimentum est aqua,[16] unde cum aqua de coelo
30 descendit inebriat terram [17] et terra per eam vim suscipit omni
metallo imminentem,[18] ob hoc postulat eam dicens: Emitte spiritum tuum, hoc est aquam et creabuntur et renovabis faciem
terrae, quoniam inspirat terram quando facit eam tremere et
tangit montes et fumigant.[19] Cum autem sanguine baptizat, tunc
35 nutrit, ut dicitur: Aqua sapientiae salutaris potavit me,[20] et
iterum: Sanguis eius vere est potus,[21] quia sedes animae est in
sanguine, ut Senior dicit: Mansit autem ipsa anima in aqua,[22]
(quae [hodie] sibi similis est in caliditate et humiditate),[23] in

---

24. qua *DL* / 25. haec *MD* / flumine flaminee et sanguine *MPVB* / 26.–27. et
flammis *add. MV*, flamen *L* / 27. expellit *P* / atque (fum.) *MP* / de: ab *MPB* /
31. ob: ab *PV*, ad *M* / 33. Et (quoniam) *PV* / 34. fumigabunt *DL* / 36. verus *D*,
om. P / 38. (quae hodie ∼ humiditate) *add. DL* /

---

15 Cf. Notkerus Balbulus, *Hymnus in die Pentecostes* (Migne, P.L., vol. 131, col.
1013.) "Tu animabus Vivificandis Aquas foecundas, Tu aspirando Da spiritales Esse
homines." Cf. also Roman Missal, Blessing of the Font on Easter Even.
16 Cf. Senior, *De chemia*, p. 70: ". . . et dixit Hermes: . . . vita cuiuslibet rei est
aqua, et aqua suscipit nutrimentum hominum et aliorum . . ."
17 Isa. 55 : 10: "Et quomodo . . . imber . . . non revertitur, sed inebriat terram,
et infundit eam . . ." Ps. 64 : 10: "Visitasti terram et inebriasti eam."
18 Cf. *Turba*, p. 140: ". . . quousque lapis fiat, quem tunc invidi nuncupant
lapidem omni metallo imminentem."
19 Ps. 103 : 30–32: "Emittes spiritum tuum, et creabuntur; et renovabis faciem
terrae. Sit gloria Domini in saeculum; laetabitur Dominus in operibus suis. Qui
respicit terram, et facit eam tremere; qui tangit montes, et fumigant."
20 Ecclus. 15 : 3: "Cibabit illum pane vitae et intellectus, et aqua sapientiae
salutaris potabit illum."
21 Joh. 6 : 56: "Caro enim mea vere est cibus, et sanguis meus vere est potus."
22 Senior, *De chemia*, p. 44: ". . . mansit ipsa (scil. anima) in aqua sibi simili
quem est pater eius in praeparatione . . . tunc nominaverunt animam, et sanguinem aeris . ."
23 Ibid., p. 58: "Anima . . . facta calida et humida in natura sanguinis et
aeris . . ."

parents]. To the Holy Spirit is attributed Goodness, through whom earthly things become heavenly, and this in threefold wise: by baptizing in water, in blood, and in fire; in water by quickening and cleansing, when he washeth away all defilements and driveth out murkiness from souls, as it is said: Thou dost fecundate the waters to give life to souls.[15] For water is the nourishment of all living things,[16] whence when water cometh down from heaven it plentifully watereth the earth,[17] and the earth by it receiveth strength which can dissolve every metal,[18] wherefore it beseecheth him saying: Send forth thy Spirit, that is water, and they shall be created, and thou shalt renew the face of the earth, for he breatheth upon the earth when he maketh it to tremble, and he toucheth the mountains and they smoke.[19] And when he baptizeth with blood, then he nourisheth, as it is said: He gave me to drink of the saving water of wisdom,[20] and again: His blood is drink indeed,[21] for the seat of the soul is in the blood, as Senior saith: But the soul itself remained in water,[22] (which [today] is like to it in warmth and humidity,)[23] and therein con-

---

[15] Cf. Notker Balbulus, *Hymn for Pentecost* (Migne, *P.L.*, vol. 131, col. 1013; trans. Neale, p. 20): "Thou givest to the waters virtue to quicken souls: thou, by thine inspiration, grantest to men to be living spirits." Cf. also Roman Missal, Blessing of the Font on Easter Even.

[16] Cf. Senior, *De chemia*, p. 70: ". . . and Hermes hath said: . . . the life of all things is in water, and water receiveth the nourishment of men and other beings."

[17] Isa. 55 : 10: "And as the rain . . . return(s) no more (to heaven) but soak(s) the earth and waters it . . . so shall my word be . . ." Ps. 64 : 10: "Thou hast visited the earth and hast plentifully watered it."

[18] Cf. *Turba*, p. 140: ". . . until it becometh a stone, which then the envious call the stone which dissolveth every metal." (I translate *imminere*, threaten, here as 'dissolve.' —M.L.v.F.)

[19] Ps. 103 : 30–32: "Thou shalt send forth thy spirit and they shall be created: and thou shalt renew the face of the earth. May the glory of the Lord endure for ever: the Lord shall rejoice in his works. He looketh upon the earth, and maketh it tremble: he toucheth the mountains, and they smoke."

[20] Ecclus. 15 : 3: "With the bread of life and understanding did she feed him: and gave him the water of wholesome wisdom to drink."

[21] John 6 : 56: "For my flesh is meat indeed: and my blood is drink indeed."

[22] Senior, *De chemia*, p. 44: "For it (the soul) remaineth in the water, which is like unto it and is its father in the preparation . . . wherefore they call the soul also 'Blood of the air.'"

[23] Ibid., p. 58: "The soul becometh warm and damp, after the nature of blood and air. . . ."

qua consistit omnis vita.[24] Cum autem flammis baptizat, tunc
40 infundit animam et dat perfectionem vitae,[25] quia ignis dat formam et complet totum, ut dicitur: Inspiravit in faciem eius
spiraculum vitae et factus est homo, qui prius erat mortuus in
animam viventem.[26] De primo, secundo et tertio testantur philosophi dicentes: [27] aqua tribus mensibus foetum in matrice
45 [conservat] fovet, aer tribus secundis nutrit, ignis tribus tertiis
[et] custodit. Infanti numquam patebit ortus, donec hi menses
consumantur, tunc nascitur et a sole vivificatur, quoniam ipse
vivificator est omnium mortuorum. Unde praedictus spiritus
propter excellentiam sui septiformis muneris [28] dicitur habere
50 septem virtutes operando in terram: Primo calefacit terram (ut
patet in calce) frigiditate mortuam et aridam. Unde propheta:
Concaluit cor meum intra me et operatione mea exardescit
ignis.[29] Et in libro Quintae essentiae: Ignis suo calore pene-
trando et subtiliando omnes pares terrestres multum materiales
55 et minime formales consumit; quamdiu enim ignis materiam
habet, non cessat agere volens rei passivae imprimere suam formam. Et Calet Minor: Calefacite frigiditatem unius caliditate

---

39. Cum: Quando *MPD* / flumine *P*, flamine *MV*, flumen *L* / 43. et secundum *D* /
45. conservat *add. DL* / 46. et *add. DL* / Infans *MPV* / exitus vel ortus *L* / 47. con-
sumentur *BDL* / 48. mortuorum *om. DL* / 51. ut in calce *V*, ut patet in tale *M*,
om. DL / 55.–56. ignis in materiam non cessat agere *DL* / 56. volens *om. LV*,
vultus *P* / passae *MPV*, posse *L* / 57. Et (Cal.) *om. MPVB* / Ut (Sen.) *D* /

---

24 Ibid., p. 31: "Et sicut aer est vita uniuscuiusque rei, similiter aqua eorum est
caput operis. . . . Et sicut aer est calidus et humidus, similiter aqua eorum est
calida et humida, et est ignis lapidis . . ." Ibid., p. 33: "Aer vero ex aqua est . . .
et ex ambobus consistit vita uniuscuique rei." Cf. also "Cons. coniug.," p. 60.
25 Senior, p. 44: ". . . cum spiritu humido . . . Et ipse est reductor ad corpus
suum, quod vivificabit post mortem suam, per hanc vitam. Postea nulla erit mors.
Propterea quod vita infunditur, sicut spiritus corpori."
26 Gen. 2 : 7: "(Formavit igitur Dominus Deus hominem de limo terrae,) et inspiravit in faciem eius spiraculum vitae, et factus est homo in animam viventem."
27 "Scala philosophorum," *Bibl. chem.*, II, p. 135b: "Igitur sciendum quod tribus
mensibus aqua foetum in matrice conservat. Aer quoque tribus mensibus fovet:
ignis vero totidem custodit. . . . Igitur infanti numquam patebit egressus,
quousque aeris flatus exhauriat." Cf. also Calid, "Liber trium verborum," *Art.
aurif.* (1610), I, pp. 228–29. Cf. also "Cons. coniug.," pp. 203, 233.
28 Roman Breviary, Hymn at Vespers for Pentecost (Veni Creator Spiritus): "Tu
septiformis munere . . ."
29 Ps. 38 : 4: "Concaluit cor meum intra me; et in meditatione mea exardescet
ignis."

sisteth all life.[24] But when he baptizeth in flame, then he infuseth the soul and giveth perfection of life,[25] for fire giveth form and completeth the whole, as it is said: He breathed into his face the breath of life, and man, who was aforetime dead, became a living soul.[26] Of the first, second, and third the philosophers bear witness, saying: [27] For three months water [preserveth] nourisheth the foetus in the womb, air nourisheth it for the second three, fire [also] guardeth it for the third three. The infant will never come to birth until these months are expired, then it is born and quickened by the sun, for that is the quickener of all things that are dead. Wherefore the aforesaid Spirit by reason of the excellence of his sevenfold gift [28] is said to have seven virtues in his operation on earth: Firstly, he warmeth the earth (as is to be seen in lime), which by coldness is dead and dry. Wherefore the prophet saith: My heart grew hot within me and in mine operation a fire flames out.[29] And in the *Book of the Quintessence:* Fire, penetrating and subtilizing by its warmth, consumeth all earthly parts which are wholly material and not formal; for as long as fire hath matter, it ceaseth not to act, seeking to imprint its form on the passive substance. And Calet the Less: Make

24 Ibid., p. 31: "And as air is the life of every single thing, so their (the philosophers') water is the head of the work . . . and as air is warm and damp, so is their water warm and damp, and it is the fire of the stone. . . ." Ibid., p. 33: "But the air is from the water . . . and of these two consisteth the life of every living thing." Cf. "Cons. coniug.," p. 60.

25 Senior, p. 44: ". . . with the damp spirit . . . And this it is, which bringeth it (the soul) back to its body, which it shall quicken after death through this life. Thereafter death shall be no more, for life is infused into it, as the spirit into the body."

26 Gen. 2 : 7: "(And the Lord God formed man of the slime of the earth,) and breathed into his face the breath of life; and man became a living soul."

27 "Scala philosophorum," *Bibl. chem.,* II, p. 135b: "Know therefore that water preserveth the foetus for three months in the womb. Air also nourisheth it for three months; and fire guardeth it for as many. . . . Therefore there shall be no issue for the child, until it shall draw in currents of air." Cf. also Calid, "Liber trium verborum," *Art. aurif.* (1610), I, pp. 228–29. Cf. also "Cons. coniug.," pp. 203, 233.

28 Roman Breviary, Hymn at Vespers for Pentecost (Veni Creator Spiritus): "Thou who art sevenfold in thy gifts. . . ."

29 Ps. 38 : 4: "My heart grew hot within me: and in my meditation a fire shall flame out."

alterius.[80] Et Senior: Facite masculum super foeminam, hoc est calidum super frigidum.[31] Secundo extinguit intensum ignem
60 impressum in adustione,[32] de qua Propheta: Exarsit ignis in synagoga eorum et flamma combussit peccatores in terra,[33] hunc ignem extinguit suo temperamento unde subditur: In aestu temperies.[34] Et Calet Minor: Extinguite ignem unius frigiditate alterius.[30] Et Avicenna: Res, in qua est adustio, primum quod
65 resolvitur, ex ea est virtus ignea, quae lenior et dignior est, quam virtutes aliorum elementorum.[35] Tertio mollificat, id est liquefacit duritiem terrae et resolvit partes eius condensas et

---

58. et (hoc) *DL* / 59. in tersum *M*, intensivum *D*, extensum *V*, extensivum *L* impressum: in ipsum *P* / 65. ex: in *D* / 66. alterum *MPV* / liquescit *MPV* /

---

30 Cf. Calid, "Liber trium verborum," in *Art. aurif.* (1610), I, pp. 226-27: "Oportet ergo quod frigidum et humidum recipiant caliditatem et siccitatem quod erat in occulto et fiant una substantia." "Hic est liber Trium verborum, liber lapidis pretiosum, qui est corpus aereum, et volatile, frigidum et humidum . . . et in eo est caliditas, siccitas, frigiditas, et humiditas: alia virtus est in occulto, et alia in manifesto. Quod ut illud quod est in occulto fiat manifestum: et illud quod est manifestum fiat occultum per virtutem Dei, et caliditatem, ut siccitas . . . caliditas et siccitas destruit frigidum et humidum aquosum et adustivum virtute divina . . ." pp. 227-28: ". . . sed virtute Dei fieri potest cum molli temperamento et moderativo termino ignis." Cf. also *Turba*, p. 110.

31 Senior, *De chemia*, p. 38: "Proiicite foeminam super masculum, et ascendet masculus super foeminam," and p. 96: "Commisce humidum cum sicco . . . Masculus est calidus et siccus, foemina autem, est frigida et humida." Cf. also *Pret. marg. nov.*, p. 123, and "Cons. coniug," p. 86: "Facite foeminam super masculum et ascendet masculus super foeminam."

32 Cf. "Aurora consurgens II," *Art. aurif.* (1610), I, p. 148: "Dicitur etiam occisio sive mortificatio, ratione vitae vegetabilis, et ordinatae, et accidentis, hoc est, caloris impressi."

33 Ps. 105 : 17-19: "Aperta est terra, et deglutivit Dathan, et operuit super congregationem Abiron. Et exarsit ignis in synagoga eorum, flamma combussit peccatores. Et fecerunt vitulum in Horeb . . ."

34 Roman Missal, Sequence for Pentecost (Veni sancte Spiritus): "In labore requies, in aestu temperies, in fletu solacium."

35 Avicenna, "De re recta ad Hasen regem epistola," *Theatr. chem.* (1659), IV, p. 866: "Et scivimus quod res in qua est adustio, cum decoquitur, primum quod de ea resolvitur, est virtus ignea, quae est in ipsa, quoniam est levior et dignior vaporatione et separatione, quam virtus reliquorum elementorum."

warm the cold of the one by the heat of the other.[30] And Senior: Set the male upon the female, that is, the warm upon the cold.[31] In the second place he extinguisheth the intense imprinted fire by ignition,[32] of which saith the Prophet: A fire was kindled in their congregation, and a flame burned the wicked upon earth; [33] he extinguisheth this fire by its own temperament, whence it is added: Thou art coolness in the heat.[34] And Calet the Less: Extinguish the fire of the one by the coolness of the other.[30] And Avicenna: A thing in which there is burning, the first thing that is released from it is a fiery virtue, which is milder and more worthy than the virtues of the other elements.[35] In the third place he maketh soft, that is, he liquefieth the hardness of the earth and

---

30 Cf. Calid, "Liber trium verborum," *Art. aurif.* (1610), I, pp. 226–27: "Needs must the cold and damp therefore receive the warmth and dryness, which was in the secret thing, and become one substance." "This is the book of the Three Words, the book of the precious stone, which is a body aerial and volatile, cold and damp . . . and in it is heat, dryness, coldness and dampness; it hath one virtue in secret, and one virtue openly. And that which is in secret must be made manifest, and that which is manifest be hidden by the power of God, and the heat (become) as dryness . . . the heat and dryness hath destroyed the cold and damp, the watery and the burnt, by the power of God. . . ." Pp. 227–28: "but by the power of God it can be done with a gentle temperament and a moderate quantity of fire." Cf. also *Turba*, p. 110.

31 Senior, *De chemia*, p. 38: "Cast the female upon the male, and the male will ascend upon the female," and p. 96: "Mix the warm with the cold, the damp with the dry; the male is warm and dry, but the female is cold and damp." Cf. also *Pret. marg. nov.*, p. 123, and "Cons. coniug.," p. 86: "Place the female upon the male and the male will ascend upon the female."

32 Cf. "Aurora consurgens II," *Art. aurif.* (1610), I, p. 148: "It is also called slaying or mortification by reason of the vegetable life both ordained and accidental, that is, of the impressed heat.' '

33 Ps. 105 : 17–19: "The earth opened and swallowed up Dathan: and covered the congregation of Abiram. And a fire was kindled in their congregation: the flame burned the wicked. They made also a calf in Horeb . . .' '

34 Roman Missal, Sequence for Pentecost (Veni sancte Spiritus): "Thou in labour rest most sweet, thou art coolness in the heat, solace in the midst of woe.' '

35 Avicenna, "De re recta ad Hasen regem epistola," *Theatr. chem.* (1659), IV, p. 866: "And we know that the matter in which there is burning, when it is cooked, the first thing to be released from it is the fiery virtue which is in it: for it is lighter and more worthy, by vaporization and separation, than the virtue of the other elements."

multum compactas, de quo scribitur: Imber sancti spiritus liquefacit.[36] Et Propheta: Emittet verbum suum et liquefaciet eam,
70 flabit spiritus eius et fluent aquae.[37] Et in libro Quintae
essentiae scribitur, quia aer poros partium terrae adaperiet ad
suscipiendam virtutem ignis et aquae. Et alibi scribitur: Mulier
solvit virum et ipse figit eam, hoc est spiritus solvit corpus (et
mollificat) et corpus spiritum indurat. Quarto illuminat, quando
75 omnes tenebrositates tollit de corpore, de quo canitur: Horridas
nostrae mentis purga tenebras,[38] accende lumen sensibus,[39] et
Propheta: fuit eis dux tota nocte in illuminatione ignis[40] et
tunc nox sicut dies illuminabitur.[41] Et Senior: Et facit omne
nigrum album et omne album rubeum, quia aqua dealbat et
80 ignis illuminat.[42] Nam lucet in colore ut rubinus per animam
tingentem, quam acquisivit ex virtute ignis; propter hoc ignis
dicitur tinctor.[43] Et in libro Quintae essentiae: Vides mirabile
lumen in tenebris.[44] Et in libro Turbae philosophorum scribi-

---

68. Imber: Geber *P*, in libro *B* / liquefecit me *MP* / 69. Emittit *DL*, emitte *M* /
ea *DBLV* / 70. flavit *BDLV* / 73. solvit: mollificat *MBV* / 73.–74. (et mollificat)
add. DL / 75.–sitates: Incipit *Rh* / 74.–75. quod omnis tenebrositas tollitur *MP* /
76. ei *MPV* / lux *D* / 81. quas *MPV*, aquam *B* / 82. (essentiae) dicit *add. MP* /
Videns *PV* /

---

[36] Cf. Ecclus. 39 : 9: ". . . et ipse tamquam imbres mittet eloquia sapientiae suae."
[37] Ps. 147 : 18: "Emittet verbum suum, et liquefaciet ea; flabit spiritus eius, et
fluent aquae."
[38] Cf. Notkerus Balbulus, *Hymnus in die Pentecostes* (Migne, *P.L.*, vol. 131, cols.
1012–13): "Spiritus alme, Illustrator hominum, Horridas nostrae mentis Purga
tenebras."
[39] Roman Breviary, Hymn at Vespers for Pentecost (Veni Creator Spiritus):
"Accende lumen sensibus, Infunde amorem cordibus . . ."
[40] Ps. 77 : 14: "Et deduxit eos in nube diei, et tota nocte in illuminatione ignis."
Cf. Sap. 10 : 17: ". . . et fuit illis in velamento diei, et in luce stellarum per
noctem."
[41] Ps. 138 : 11: "Et nox sicut dies illuminabitur."
[42] Senior, *De chemia*, p. 68: "et tingit omne nigrum, et facit album, et tingit omne
album, et facit rubeum. Et ideo res magnificatur . . ."
[43] Ibid., p. 66: "Et quod dixit Rubinus, per hoc vult Animam tingentem propter
quod acquisivit virtutem ex igne . . ." Cf. p. 35: "Anima tingens latet in aqua
. . . alba."
[44] Cf. (not verbatim). Albertus Magnus, "De rebus metall." (ed. Borgnet, V, p. 16):
"Carbunculus . . . lucet in tenebris sicut noctiluca," also p. 32: "Carbunculus
lucet in tenebris sicut carbo, et talem vidi ego."

dissolveth its condensed and exceedingly compact parts, of which it is written: The rain of the Holy Spirit melteth.[36] And the Prophet: He shall send out his word and shall melt it, his wind shall blow and the waters shall run.[37] And in the *Book of the Quintessence* it is written, that the air shall open the pores of the earthly parts to receive the virtue of fire and water. And elsewhere it is written: Woman dissolveth man and he fixeth her, that is, the Spirit dissolveth the body (and softeneth it) and the body hardeneth the spirit. In the fourth place he enlighteneth, when he taketh away all darknesses from the body, of which the hymn singeth: Purge the horrible darknesses of our mind,[38] enkindle a light in our senses,[39] and the Prophet: He conducted them all the night with a light of fire,[40] and night shall be light as the day.[41] And Senior: And he maketh all that is black white and all that is white red, for water whiteneth and fire enlighteneth.[42] For he shineth through the tincturing soul like a ruby in colour, which it hath acquired by virtue of the fire, wherefore fire is called the Dyer.[43] And in the *Book of the Quintessence:* Thou seest a wondrous light in the darkness.[44] And in the *Turba philosophorum*

[36] Cf. Ecclus. 39 : 9: "And he will pour forth the words of his wisdom as showers."
[37] Ps. 147 : 18: "He shall send out his word, and shall melt them; his wind shall blow, and the waters shall run."
[38] Cf. Notker Balbulus, *Hymn for Pentecost* (Migne, *P.L.*, vol. 131, cols. 1012–13; trans. Neale, p. 19): "Merciful Spirit, enlightener of men, purge the fearful shadows of our mind."
[39] Roman Breviary, Hymn at Vespers for Pentecost (Veni Creator Spiritus): "Our minds enkindle with thy light; within our hearts thy love excite."
[40] Ps. 77 : 14: "And he conducted them with a cloud by day: and all the night with a light of fire." Cf. Wisd. 10 : 17: ". . . and she was to them for a covert by day and for the light of stars by night."
[41] Ps. 138 : 11: "And night shall be light as the day."
[42] Senior, *De chemia*, p. 68: "And it tingeth every black thing, and maketh it white, and tingeth every white thing, and maketh it red, and so is the matter glorified."
[43] Ibid., p. 66: And when he saith "ruby," he meaneth it of the tincturing soul, because it hath received virtue from the fire. Cf. p. 35: "The tincturing soul lieth hidden in the white . . . water."
[44] Cf. (not verbatim) Albert the Great, "De rebus metall." (ed. Borgnet, V, p. 16): "The carbuncle . . . shineth in the darkness like the moon," also p. 32: "The carbuncle shineth in the darkness like a coal, and so have I myself seen."

tur, quod si nubes superficiem dealbaverint, procul dubio eorum
85 intima dealbabuntur.[45] Et Morienus ait: Jam abstulimus nigrum et fecimus album, cum sale [et] [a]natron,[46] id est cum
spiritu. Quinto separat purum ab impuro, quando omnia acci-
dentia animae removet, quae sunt vapores scil. odores mali
sicut dicitur: quod ignis separat heterogenea et cumulat homo-
90 genea.[47] Ob hoc Propheta: Igne me examinasti, et non est inventa in me iniquitas,[48] et idem: Transivimus per ignem et
aquam, eduxisti nos in requiem et refrigerium.[49] Et Hermes:
Separabis spissum a subtili, terram ab igne.[50] Alphidius: Terra
liquefit et in aquam vertitur, aqua liquefit et in aerem vertitur,
95 aer liquefit et in ignem vertitur (ignis liquescit et in terram
vertitur glorificatam).[51] Super hoc dicit Rasis, quod perfectae

---

84. superfaciem *ML* / dealbaverit *MD* / 85. Et *om. MPVB* / 86. et (an.) *add.*
MPVRhLB / 88. malos *MPVBD* / 90. exanimasti *L* / 92. in requiem et *om. MPB* /
94. liquescit *MPVB* / aer liq. etc. *om. P* / 95. liquefit et in ignem vertitur *om. P*,
ignis liq. ～ glorificatam *om. DLRhB* /

---

45 *Turba*, p. 120: Parmenides: ". . . et scitote quod si superficies dealbetur,
intima eius dealbabuntur. Et si (Ruska: aeris) superficiem nubes dealbaverunt,
procul dubio intima dealbabuntur."
46 Morienus Romanus, "De transmutatione metallorum," *Art. aurif.*, II (1610),
p. 221: (Datin dicit ad Euthicen . . .): "Jam abstulimus nigredinem et cum
sale [a]natron, id est sale nitri, et almizadir, cuius complexio est frigida et sicca,
fiximus albedinem."
47 Cf. *Pret. marg. nov.* p. 86: "quia calor homogenea congregat et segregat
heterogenea," and "Cons. coniug," p. 252: "Ignis enim heterogenea separat et
homogenea congregat." Cf. Albertus Magnus, "De rebus metall." (ed. Borgnet, V,
p. 25) ". . . calorem ignis, et quod congregat homogenia et disgregat heterogenia,
sicut dictum est in II. meteorum."
48 Ps. 16 : 3: "Igne me examinasti, et non est inventa in me iniquitas."
49 Ps. 65 : 12: "Transivimus per ignem et aquam, et eduxisti nos in refrigerium."
50 *Tabula Smaragdina* (ed. Ruska), p. 2: "Separabis terram ab igne, subtile a
spisso, suaviter cum magno ingenio."
51 The version in brackets is found in P in place of the preceding clause. Cf.
"Clangor buccinae," *Art. aurif.* (1610), I, p. 317: "Dicit Assiduus philosophus:
Ignis coagulatur et fit aer, aer vero coagulatur et fit aqua, aqua vero coagulatur et fit
terra. Ecce in unam naturam inimici convenerunt." Cf. also "Cons. coniug.," pp.
28 and 29, and Flamel, "Excerpta ex Democrito," *Theatr. chem.* (1602), I, p. 891:
". . . elementa . . . transmutantur . . . ignis fit terra, et terra fit aqua, et aqua
aer, et rursus."

it is written, that if the clouds have whitened the surface, without a doubt their inner parts shall be whitened also.[45] And Morienus saith: Already we have taken away the black and have made the white, with the salt [and] [a]natron,[46] that is with the spirit. Fifthly, he separateth the pure from the impure when he removeth all accidents from the soul, which are vapours, that is, evil odours, as it is written: That fire separateth those things that are unlike and bringeth together those things that are like.[47] Wherefore the Prophet: Thou hast tried me by fire, and iniquity shall not be found in me.[48] And again: We have passed through fire and water, and thou hast brought us forth into rest and refreshment.[49] And Hermes: Thou shalt separate the dense from the subtle, the earth from the fire.[50] Alphidius: Earth is liquefied and turned into water, water is liquefied and turned into air, air is liquefied and turned into fire, fire is liquefied and turned into glorified earth.[51] On this saith Rasis, that a certain purifi-

[45] *Turba*, p. 120: Parmenides: ". . . and know that if the surface is whitened, its innermost parts are whitened. And if clouds have whitened the surface [Ruska: of the bronze], without doubt the innermost parts shall be whitened."

[46] Morienus Romanus, "De transmutatione metallorum," *Art. aurif.*, II (1610), p. 221: (Datin to Euthice): ". . . Now we have taken away the blackness (*nigredo*), and with the salt [a]natron, that is the salt of nitre, and *almizadir*, whose nature is cold and dry, we have fixed the whiteness (*albedo*)." *Anatron = An-natron =* Arab. "the natron."

[47] Cf. *Pret. marg. nov.*, p. 86: "For heat gathereth like things together, and setteth unlike things apart," and "Cons. coniug.," p. 252: "For fire separateth unlike things and gathereth together like things." Cf. Albert the Great, "De rebus metall." (ed. Borgnet, V, p. 25): ". . . heat of fire, and that which gathereth together like things and separateth unlike things, as it is written in II. Meteorum."

[48] Ps. 16 : 3: "Thou hast tried me by fire, and iniquity hath not been found in me."

[49] Ps. 65 : 12: "We have passed through fire and water, and thou hast brought us forth into a refreshment."

[50] *Tabula Smaragdina* (ed. Ruska), p. 2: "Thou shalt separate the earth from the fire, the subtle from the dense, gently and with great skill."

[51] The version in brackets is found in P in place of the preceding clause. Cf. "Clangor buccinae," *Art. aurif.* (1610), I, p. 317: "Assiduus the philosopher saith: Fire is coagulated and becometh air, air is coagulated and becometh water, water is coagulated and becometh earth. Lo, the enemies come together in one nature." Cf. also "Cons. coniug.," pp. 28 and 29, and Flamel, "Excerpta ex Democrito," *Theatr. chem.* (1602), I, p. 891: ". . . the elements are transmuted . . . fire becometh earth, and earth water, and water air, and the reverse."

praeparationis operationem praecedit quaedam rerum purificatio, quae a quibusdam administratio vel mundificatio nuncupatur, a quibusdam rectificatio et a quibusdam ablutio vel
100 separatio nuncupatur. Ipse enim spiritus, qui est septiformis
munere [52] puriores partes separat ab impuris, ut abiectis impuris
partibus opus cum puris compleatur.[53] Et hanc quintam virtutem innuit Hermes in suo secreto, cum dicit: Separabis terram
ab igne, subtile a spisso suaviter (etc.).[54] Sexto infima exaltat,
105 quando profundam animam et occultam in visceribus terrae ad
faciem ducit, de quo Propheta: Qui educit vinctos in fortitudine sua.[55] Iterum: Eduxisti animam meam ex inferno inferiori.[56] Et Jesaias: Spiritus Domini levavit me.[57] Et philosophi:
Quicumque occultum fecerit manifestum [58] totum opus novit
110 et qui novit nostrum cambar (i.e. ignem) hic (noster) philosophus est.[59] Morienus: Qui animam (suam) sursum levaverit, eius
colores videbit. Et Alphidius: Nisi (hic) vapor ascenderit, nil

---

102. quartam v. *MP*, virtutem *om. M* / 103. cum: et *MP* / 104. a grosso a spisso
V / etc. *add. DRh* / 110. i.e., ignem *add. MP* / noster *add. DRhLV* / philosophus:
filius *DRh₂* / 111. suam *add. D* /

---

[52] Roman Breviary, Hymn at Vespers for Pentecost (Veni Creator Spiritus): "Tu
septiformis munere, Digitus paternae dexterae . . ."
[53] Cf. Pseudo-Aristotle, "De perfecto magisterio," *Theatr. chem.* (1659), III, p. 79:
"Praecedit autem operationem perfectae operationis quaedam rerum purificatio
quae a quibusdam mundificatio, et a quibusdam administratio, a quibusdam
rectificatio, et a quibusdam ablutio, et a quibusdam separatio nuncupatur. Ipsa
enim puriores rerum partes disgregat ab impuris ut gravioribus abiectis partibus
cum levioribus opus compleatur." Cf. also "Scala philosophorum," *Bibl. chem.*,
II, p. 134a, also in part "Aristotelis Tractatulus," *Art. aurif.*, I (1610), p. 232, and
" Rosarium Arnaldi," ibid., II, p. 271, and Albertus Magnus, "De lapide philos.,"
Theatr. chem. (1659), IV, p. 847.
[54] *Tabula Smaragdina* (ed. Ruska), p. 2.
[55] Ps. 67 : 7: "Qui educit vinctos in fortitudine."
[56] Ps. 85 : 13: ". . . eruisti animam meam ex inferno inferiori."
[57] Isa. 61 : 1 and Luc. 4 : 18: "Spiritus Domini super me . . .' 'Cf. Ezechiel 3 : 14:
"Spiritus quoque levavit me . . ."
[58] Cf. Avicenna, "Declaratio lapidis physici," *Theatr. chem.* (1659), IV, p. 878.
[59] *Turba*, p. 130: "Qui ergo scit cambar philosophorum occultum, iam ei est
notum arcanum." Cambar is frequently mentioned in the *Turba*, and is the
Arabic transcription of the Greek *kinnabaris*, 'cinnabar.' Cf. Ruska, *Turba*, p. 28.
Cf. "Cons. coniug.," p. 198.

cation of things precedeth the work of perfect preparation, which
by some is called administration or cleansing, by others rectification, and by some it is called washing or separation. For the
spirit himself, who is sevenfold in his operation,[52] separateth the
purer parts from the impure, that the impure parts being cast
away, the work may be fulfilled with the pure.[53] And this fifth
virtue doth Hermes refer to in his *Secret,* when he saith: Thou
shalt separate the earth from the fire, the subtle from the dense
gently (etc.).[54] In the sixth place he exalteth the lowly, when he
bringeth to the surface the soul deep and hidden in the bowels
of the earth, of which saith the Prophet: Who bringeth out them
that were bound in his strength.[55] Again: Thou hast delivered
my soul out of the lower hell.[56] And Isaias: The Spirit of the
Lord lifted me up.[57] And the philosophers: Whosoever shall
make the hidden manifest[58] knoweth the whole work, and he
who knoweth our cambar (i.e., fire), he is (our) philosopher.[59]
Morienus: He who shall raise up (his) soul, shall see its colours.
And Alphidius: If this vapour shall not ascend, thou shalt have

---

[52] Roman Breviary, Hymn at Vespers for Pentecost (Veni Creator Spiritus): "Thou
who art sevenfold in thy gifts, finger of the Father's right hand."
[53] Cf. Pseudo-Aristotle, "De perfecto magisterio," *Theatr. chem.* (1659), III, p. 79:
"But a certain purification of things precedeth the work of perfect preparation,
which by some is called cleansing, by some administration, by some rectification,
by some ablution, and by some separation. For it separateth the purer parts of the
materials from the impure, that the heavier parts may be cast away and the work
fulfilled with the lighter." Cf. also "Scala philosophorum," *Bibl. chem.,* II, p. 134a,
also in part "Aristotelis Tractatulus," *Art. aurif.* (1610), I, p. 232, and "Rosarium
Arnaldi," ibid., II, p. 271, and Albert the Great, "De lapide philos," *Theatr. chem.*
(1659), IV, p. 847.
[54] *Tabula Smaragdina* (ed. Ruska), p. 2.
[55] Ps. 67 : 7: "Who bringeth out them that were bound in strength."
[56] Ps. 85 : 13: ". . . thou hast delivered my soul out of the lower hell."
[57] Isa. 61 : 1 and Luke 4 : 18: "The spirit of the Lord is upon me . . ." Cf. Ezek.
3 : 14: "The spirit also lifted me and took me up."
[58] Cf. Avicenna, "Declaratio lapidis physici," *Theatr. chem.* (1659), IV, p. 878.
[59] *Turba,* p. 130: "He therefore who knoweth the hidden cambar of the philosophers, to him is the secret already known." Cambar is frequently mentioned in
the *Turba,* and is the Arabic transcription of the Greek *kinnabaris,* 'cinnabar.'
Cf. Ruska, *Turba,* p. 28; "Cons. coniug.," p. 198.

habebis eo,[60] quod per ipsum et cum ipso et in ipso totum [61]
opus fit. Septimo et ultimo inspirat, quando suo flatu corpus
115 terrenum spirituale facit, de quo canitur: Tu aspirando das
spiritales esse homines.[62] Salomon: Spiritus Domini replevit
orbem terrarum.[63] Et Propheta: Et spiritu oris eius omnis virtus
eorum.[64] Et Rasis in lumine luminum: Non possunt gravia nisi
levium consortio levigari (nec levia nisi combinatione gravium
120 ad ima detrudi).[65] Et [in] Turba: Facite corpora incorporea [66]
et fixum volatile; haec autem omnia nostro spiritu peraguntur
et adimplentur, quia ipse solus est, qui potest facere mundum
de immundo conceptum semine.[67] Nonne dicit scriptura: Lavamini in eo et mundi estote.[68] Et ad Naaman (Syrum) dictum
125 est: Vade et lavare septies in Jordane et mundaberis.[69] Nam ipse

---

115. dicitur vel (canitur) add. MPV, dicitur B / 118. Rasis in om. MPVB, et Rasis
om. B / 119.–120. (nec levia ~ detrudi) add. RhLD / 120. in add. RhLB / 124.
Syrum add. Rh₂ /

---

60 Cf. "Ros. phil., 'p. 118a: Albertus: "Nisi anima corpus suum exierit et in coelum
sursum ascenderit, nihil proficies in hac arte."
61 Alphidius, Codex Ashmole 1420, fol. 26: "Nisi hic vapor ascendat, nihil habetis
eo. quod ipse est opus et per ipsum et in ipso absque quo nihil fit." cf. Roman
Missal, Canon of the Mass: "Nobis quoque peccatoribus . . . Per ipsum et cum
ipso et in ipso est tibi Deo Patri omnipotenti in unitate Spiritus Sancti omnis
honor et gloria." Cf. Rom. 11 : 36: "Quoniam ex ipso et per ipsum et in ipso
sunt omnia. Ipsi gloria in saecula. Amen."
62 Notkerus Balbulus, *Hymnus in die Pentecostes* (supra, p. 84, n. 15).
63 Sap. 1 : 7: "Quoniam spiritus Domini replevit orbem terrarum .
64 Ps. 32 : 6: "Verbo Domini caeli firmati sunt et spiritu oris eius omnis virtus
eorum."
65 Pseudo-Aristotle, "De perfecto magisterio," *Theatr. chem.* (1659), III, p. 79: "Et
hoc dedit Hermes intelligere in suo secreto . . . dicens: Separabis terram ab igne,
et subtile a spisso. Quia non possunt gravia nisi cum levium superius, nec gravia
[?levia] nisi cum gravium inferius consortio detrudi." Cf. also Avicenna, "Declaratio
lapidis physici," *Theatr. chem.* (1659), IV, p. 880, and "Ros. phil.," pp. 129a and
133b.
66 Cf. *Turba,* pp. 141, 155, 151.
67 Job 14 : 4: "Quis potest facere mundum de immundo conceptum semine?
Nonne tu, qui solus es?" Cf. Roman Missal, Prayers to be said before Mass: "Sed
scio veraciter et credo ex toto corde . . . quia potes me facere dignum, qui solus
potes mundum facere de immundo conceptum semine et de peccatoribus iustos
facis et sanctos."
68 Isa. 1 : 16: "Lavamini, mundi estote . . ."
69 IV Reg. 5 : 10: "Vade, et lavare septies in Jordane, et recipiet sanitatem caro
tua, atque mundaberis."

nothing from it,[60] because through it and with it and in it all [61] the work is done. In the seventh and last place he inspireth, when by his breathing he maketh the earthly body spiritual, of which it is sung: Thou by thy breathing makest men to be spir itual.[62] Solomon: The Spirit of the Lord hath filled the whole world.[63] And the Prophet: And all the power of them by the spirit of his mouth.[64] And Rasis in the *Light of Lights:* Heavy things cannot be made to ascend save by alliance with light things (nor can light things be brought down to the depths save by combination with the heavy).[65] And [in] the *Turba:* Make bodies incorporeal [66] and the fixed volatile; but all these things are brought about and fulfilled by our spirit, for he alone it is who can make clean that which is conceived of unclean seed.[67] Doth not the Scripture say: Wash yourselves in it and be clean.[68] And to Naaman (the Syrian) was it said: Go and wash seven times in the Jordan and thou shalt be clean.[69] For there is one

60 Cf. "Ros. phil.," p. 118a: Albertus: "Unless the soul go forth from its body, and rise up into heaven, thou makest no progress in this art."
61 Alphidius, Codex Ashmole 1420, fol. 26: "Unless this smoke ariseth, thou shalt have nothing, for it is itself the work and through it and in it, without which there is nothing." Cf. Roman Missal, Canon of the Mass: "On ourselves too who are sinners . . . through him and with him and in him is to thee, God the Father Almighty, in the unity of the Holy Ghost, all honour and glory." Cf. Rom. 11 : 36: "For of him, and in him, and by him, are all things; to him be glory for ever. Amen."
62 Notker Balbulus. *Hymn for Pentecost* (supra, p. 85, n. 15).
63 Wisd. 1 : 7: "For the spirit of the Lord hath filled the whole world."
64 Ps. 32 : 6: "By the word of the Lord the heavens were established, and all the power of them by the spirit of his mouth."
65 Pseudo-Aristotle, "De perfecto magisterio," *Theatr. chem.* (1659), III, p. 79: "And this did Hermes give to be understood in his Secret . . . saying: Thou shalt sepa-rate the earth from the fire, and the subtle from the gross. For heavy things cannot be lightened save by the consort of light things from above, nor light things brought down save by the consort of heavy things from below." Cf. also Avicenna, "Declaratio lapidis physici," *Theatr. chem.* (1659), IV, p. 880, and "Ros. phil.," pp. 129a and 133b.   66 Cf. *Turba*, pp. 141, 155, 151.
67 Job 14 : 4: "Who can make him clean that is conceived of unclean seed? Is it not thou who only art?" Cf. Roman Missal, Prayers to be said before Mass: "[But] I also know, and with all my heart firmly believe . . . that thou art able to make me worthy, thou who alone canst make that clean which was born un-clean, thou who alone canst out of sinners make just and holy men."
68 Isa. 1 : 16: "Wash yourselves, be clean. . . ."
69 IV (II) Kings 5 : 10: "Go, and wash seven times in the Jordan, and thy flesh shall recover health; and thou shalt be clean."

est unum baptisma in ablutionem peccatorum, ut fides et Propheta testantur.[70] Qui habet aures audiendi audiat, quid dicat spiritus (sanctus) doctrinae filiis disciplinae de spiritus septiformis virtute, quo omnis impletur scriptura, quod phi-

130 losophi insinuant his verbis: Distilla septies et separasti ab humiditate corrumpente.

---

126. absolutionem *D* / 128. sanctus *add. D* / spiritu *MRhL* / virtutis *D* / 130. septies: semel *RH$_2$*/

---

[70] Credo: ". . . unum baptisma in remissionem peccatorum . . ." Cf. Marc. 1 : 4; Luc. 3 : 3; Acta Ap. 2 : 38; Eph. 4 : 5.

baptism for the remission of sins, as the Creed and the Prophet bear witness.[70] He that hath ears to hear, let him hear what the (holy) spirit of the doctrine saith to the sons of the discipline concerning the virtues of the sevenfold spirit, whereby all the scripture is fulfilled, which the philosophers set forth in these words: Distil seven times and thou hast set it apart from the corrupting humidity.

[70] Apostles' Creed: "And I believe . . . in one baptism for the remission of sins." Cf. Mark 1 : 4; Luke 3 : 3; Acts 2 : 38; Eph. 4 : 5.

PARABOLA QUINTA DE DOMO
THESAURARIA, QUAM SAPIENTIA FUNDAVIT
SUPRA PETRAM

Sapientia aedificavit sibi domum,[1] quam quis introierit salvabitur et pascua inveniet[2] teste propheta: Inebriabuntur ab
5 ubertate domus tuae,[3] quia melior est dies una in atriis tuis
super millia.[4] O quam beati, qui habitant in domo hac: [5] in ea
namque qui petit, accipit et qui quaerit invenit et pulsanti
aperietur.[6] Nam Sapientia stat ad ostium dicens: Ecce sto ad
ostium et pulso, si quis audierit vocem meam et aperuerit

---

1. thesaurizaria *MP* / 2. firmam (petr.) *add. L*, supra petram *om. MPV* / 4. testante *MPV* / 5. tuis: eius *RhDML*, tuis *corr.* eius *V* / 8. Ecce: Ego *VP* /

---

[1] Prov. 9 : 1–5: "Sapientia aedificavit sibi domum, excidit columnas septem. Im-
molavit victimas suas, miscuit vinum, et proposuit mensam suam. Misit ancillas
suas, ut vocarent ad arcem et ad moenia civitatis: Si quis est parvulus, veniat ad
me. Et insipientibus locuta est: Venite, comedite panem meum, et bibite vinum
quod miscui vobis . . ." Cf. Senior, *De chemia*, p. 21: "Dixit filius Hamuel, author
huius operis: Feci inimicos in carmine figurarum . . . quas praedixi fuisse . . .
in gremio sapientis . . . sedentis iuxta hostium thalami, in domo quam sibi
aedificaverat . . ." p. 107: "Lapis . . . est sicut domus cum suis 4 parietibus et
tecto . . ."

[2] Joh. 10 : 9: "Ego sum ostium. Per me si quis introierit, salvabitur, et ingredietur
et egredietur, et pascua inveniet."

[3] Ps. 35 : 9: "Inebriabuntur ab ubertate domus tuae, et torrente voluptatis tuae
potabis eos."

[4] Ps. 83 : 11: ". . . quia melior est dies una in atriis tuis super millia . . ."

[5] Ps. 83 : 5: "Beati qui habitant in domo tua, Domine, in saecula saeculorum
laudabunt te."

[6] Matth. 7 : 7–8: "Petite, et dabitur vobis; quaerite, et invenietis; pulsate, et
aperietur vobis. Omnis enim qui petit, accipit; et qui quaerit, invenit; et pulsanti
aperietur . . ."

X

THE FIFTH PARABLE: OF THE TREASURE-HOUSE
WHICH WISDOM BUILT UPON A ROCK

⁶⁶ Wisdom hath built herself a house,[1] which if any man enter in he shall be saved and find pastures,[2] as the prophet beareth witness: They shall be inebriated with the plenty of thy house,[3] for better is one day in thy courts above thousands.[4] O how blessed are they that dwell in this house;[5] for therein everyone that asketh receiveth and he that seeketh findeth and to him that knocketh it shall be opened.[6] For Wisdom standeth at the door and saith: Behold, I stand at the gate and knock: if any man shall

---

1 Prov. 9 : 1–5: "Wisdom hath built herself a house: she hath hewn her out seven pillars. She hath slain her victims, mingled her wine, and set forth her table. She hath sent her maids to invite to the tower, and to the walls of the city: whosoever is a little one, let him come to me. And to the unwise she said: Come, eat my bread, and drink the wine which I have mingled for you. . . ." Cf. Senior, *De chemia*, p. 21: "The son of Hamuel, the author of this book, saith: I have made enemies in the song of the figures, of which I said that they were in the bosom of the wise man . . . who sat by the door of the room, in the house which he had built for himself. . . ." P. 107: "The stone . . . is like unto a house with its four walls and its roof . . ."

2 John 10 : 9: "I am the door. By me, if any man enter in, he shall be saved: and he shall go in and go out, and shall find pasture."

3 Ps. 35 : 9: "They shall be inebriated with the plenty of thy house: and thou shalt make them drink of the torrent of thy pleasures."

4 Ps. 83 : 11: "For better is one day in thy courts above thousands."

5 Ps. 83 : 5: "Blessed are they that dwell in thy house, O Lord; they shall praise thee for ever and ever."

6 Matt. 7 : 7–8: "Ask, and it shall be given you; seek, and you shall find; knock, and it shall be opened to you. For every one that asketh, receiveth; and he that seeketh, findeth; and to him that knocketh it shall be opened."

10 ianuam, introibo ad illum et ipse ad me et satiabor cum illo et ipse mecum.[7] O quam magna multitudo dulcedinis tuae, quam abscondisti introeuntibus domum hanc,[8] quam oculus non vidit nec auris audivit nec in cor hominis ascendit.[9] Domum hanc reserantibus erit ea quae decet sanctitudo et utique longitudo
15 dierum,[10] quia fundata est supra firmam petram,[11] quae non potest scindi nisi ungatur optimo sanguine hircino [12] vel percutiatur virga mosaica ter, ut aquae effluant largissimae, ita ut omnis populus virorum ac mulierum bibat; [13] et amplius non sitient neque esurient.[14] Quicumque domum hanc aperuerit
20 sua scientia, in ea inveniet fontem vivum indeficientem et iuvenescentem,[15] in quo quis baptizatus fuerit, [hic] salvus erit [16] nec amodo senescere potest. Prochdolor pauci [tamen eam]

---

12. ab (introeunt.) *add. L* / quae *VP*, quem *M* / 14. erit ea *om. MPVB* / 17. fluant *MPVD* / 21. hic *add. MPV* / 22. tamen eam *add. D* / 22.–23. eis reseratur *D* /

---

[7] Apoc. 3 : 20: (Angelus Laodiceae ecclesiae:) "Ecce sto ad ostium, et pulso: si quis audierit vocem meam, et aperuerit mihi ianuam, intrabo ad illum, et coenabo cum illo, et ipse mecum . . ."

[8] Ps. 30 : 20: "Quam magna multitudo dulcedinis tuae, Domine, quam abscondisti timentibus te."

[9] I Cor. 2 : 9: ". . . quod oculus non vidit, nec auris audivit, nec in cor hominis ascendit, quae praeparavit Dominus iis, qui diligunt illum."

[10] Ps. 92 : 5: "Domum tuam decet sanctitudo, Domine, in longitudinem dierum." Cf. Ps. 22 : 6: ". . . ut inhabitem in domo Domini in longitudinem dierum."

[11] Matth. 7 : 24: "Assimilabitur viro sapienti, qui aedificavit domum suam supra petram . . ." Cf. Roman Breviary, Fourth Antiphon at Lauds for Dedication of a Church: "Bene fundata est domus Domini supra firmam petram."

[12] Levit. 16 : 18: "Cum autem exierit ad altare quod coram Domino est . . . sumptum sanguinem vituli atque hirci fundat super cornua eius per gyrum . . ." Cf. Senior, *De chemia*, p. 9: "Igitur desinet lux mea, . . . quoniam capient . . . a pinguedine . . . absque sanguine hircorum et discernit verum a falso." Cf. also pp. 78–79.

[13] Num. 20 : 11: "Cumque elevasset Moyses manum, percutiens virga bis silicem, egressae sunt aquae largissimae . . ." Exod. 17 : 6: "Percuties petram, et exibit ex ea aqua, ut bibat populus."

[14] Apoc. 7 : 16: ". . . non esurient, neque sitient amplius, nec cadet super illos sol." Cf. also Isa. 49 : 10 and Joh. 4 : 13–14: "Omnis qui bibit ex aqua hac, sitiet iterum; qui autem biberit ex aqua quam ego dabo ei, non sitiet in aeternum. Sed aqua quam ego dabo ei fiet in eo fons aquae salientis in vitam aeternam."

[15] Cf. Zach. 13 : 1: "In die illa erit fons patens domui David . . . in ablutionem peccatoris . . ."

[16] Marc. 16 : 16: "Qui crediderit et baptizatus fuerit salvus erit."

hear my voice and open the door, I will come in to him and he to me, and I will be satisfied with him and he with me.[7] O how great is the multitude of thy sweetness which thou hast hidden for them that enter this house; [8] which eye hath not seen nor ear heard, neither hath it entered into the heart of man.[9] To them that unlock this house shall be befitting holiness and also length of days,[10] for it is founded upon a sure rock,[11] which cannot be split unless it be anointed with the blood of a most fine buck-goat [12] or be smitten three times with the rod of Moses, that waters may flow forth in great abundance, that all the people both men and women drink thereof,[13] and they shall neither hunger nor thirst any more.[14] Whosoever by his science shall open this house shall find therein an unfailing living fount that maketh young,[15] wherein whoever is baptized, [he] shall be saved [16] and can no more grow old. [Yet], alas, but few open [it] who are chil-

---

[7] Apoc. 3 : 20: (Angel of the church of Laodicea:) "Behold, I stand at the gate and knock. If any man shall hear my voice and open to me the door, I will come in to him and will sup with him: and he with me."

[8] Ps. 30 : 20: "O how great is the multitude of thy sweetness, O Lord, which thou hast hidden for them that fear thee!"

[9] I Cor. 2 : 9: ". . . That eye hath not seen, nor ear heard: neither hath it entered into the heart of man, what things God hath prepared for them that love him."

[10] Ps. 92 : 5: "Holiness becometh thy house, O Lord, unto length of days." Cf. Ps. 22 : 6: "And that I may dwell in the house of the Lord unto length of days."

[11] Matt. 7 : 24: "(He) shall be likened to a wise man that built his house upon a rock." Cf. Roman Breviary, Fourth Antiphon at Lauds for Dedication of a Church: "The house of the Lord is well founded, upon a sure rock."

[12] Levit. 16 : 18: "And when he is come out to the altar that is before the Lord . . . taking the blood of the calf, and of the buck-goat, let him pour it upon the horns thereof round about." Cf. Senior, *De chemia*, p. 9: "Therefore let my light fail, for they take . . . of the fatness . . . without the blood of a goat, and it discerneth the true from the false."

[13] Num. 20 : 11: "And when Moses had lifted up his hand, and struck the rock twice with the rod, there came forth water in great abundance, so that the people and their cattle drank." Exod. 17 : 6: "Thou shalt strike the rock, and water shall come out of it that the people may drink."

[14] Apoc. 7 : 16: ". . . they shall no more hunger nor thirst: neither shall the sun fall on them. . . ." Cf. also Isa. 49 : 10 and John 4 : 13–14: "Whosoever drinketh of this water shall thirst again; but he that shall drink of the water that I shall give him shall not thirst for ever. But the water that I will give him shall become in him a fountain of water, springing up into life everlasting."

[15] Cf. Zech. 13 : 1: "In that day there shall be a fountain open to the house of David . . . for the washing of the sinner . . ."

[16] Mark 16 :16: "He that believeth and is baptized shall be saved."

reserant, qui parvuli sunt et ut parvuli sapiunt; [17] si autem enarraverint illa qui parvuli sunt et sedilia viginti quatuor senio-
25 rum ipsis usurpaverint, procul dubio dignitate eorum et gradu
domum aperient [18] ita ut facie ad faciem [19] oculo ad oculum
omnem claritatem solis et lunae speculabuntur, absque autem
ipsis minime valebunt. Qui enim habent claves regni coelorum
quodcumque ligaverint et solverint;[20] fiet ita. Nam ipsi sequ-
30 untur agnum quocumque ierit.[21] Huius autem domus decor est
inenarrabilis, plateae et muri eius ex auro purissimo, portae
vero eius nitent margaritis [22] atque gemmis pretiosis [23] lapides

---

23. quae *MPVL* / 23.–24. si autem ipsis qui parvuli sunt enarraverint illa . . . *D* /
sedecim *MPV*, seniorem *M* / 25.–26. gradus ipsius domus *MPV* / 26. aperirent *P*,
aperuerunt *M* / 27.–28. absque hoc autem ipsi *RhL* / 29. quaecumque *P*, quem-
cumque *M*, quidcumque *Rh* /

---

17 Ps. 118 : 130: "Declaratio sermonum tuorum illuminat, et intellectum dat
parvulis." I Cor. 13 : 11: "Cum essem parvulus, loquebar ut parvulus, sapiebam
ut parvulus . . ."

18 Cf. Ps. 106 : 32: "Exaltent eum . . . et in cathedra seniorum laudent eum."
Cf. Apoc. 4 : 4ff.: "Et in circuitu sedis sedilia vigintiquattuor: et super thronos
vigintiquattuor seniores sedentes, circumamicti vestimentis albis, et in capitibus
eorum coronae aureae. . . . [v. 10:] . . . procidebant vigintiquattuor seniores
ante sedentem in throno, et adorabant viventem. . . . [5 : 6:] Et vidi, et ecce in
medio . . . seniorum agnum stantem tamquam occisum, habentem cornua septem
et oculos septem, qui sunt septem spiritus Dei missi in omnem terram . . . [5 : 8:]
. . . seniores . . . habentes . . . phialas aureas plenas odoramentorum . . ." Cf.
Senior, *De chemia* ("Epistola Solis ad Lunam crescentem"), p. 8: (Luna dicit:)
". . . exaltabimur, . . . quando ascend(er)imus ordinem seniorum. Lucerna lucis
infundetur lucernae meae et (ex) te et (ex) me (fit) sicut commixtio vini et aquae
dulcis . . . Cum intraverimus domum amoris, coagulabitur corpus meum . . ."

19 I Cor. 13 : 12: "Videmus nunc per speculum in aenigmate: tunc autem facie ad
faciem . . ."

20 Matth. 16 : 19: "Et tibi dabo claves regni coelorum. Et quodcumque ligaveris
super terram, erit ligatum et in coelis, et quodcumque solveris super terram, erit
solutum et in coelis."

21 Apoc. 14 : 4: "Hi sunt qui cum mulieribus non sunt coinquinati, virgines enim
sunt. Hi sequuntur Agnum quocumque ierit."

22 Cf. Dominican Breviary, Hymn for Vespers on the Dedication of a Church: (of
the celestial city) "Plateae et muri ejus ex auro purissimo. Portae nitent margaritis . . ."

23 Apoc. 21 : 10ff.: ". . . et ostendit mihi civitatem sanctam Jerusalem . . .
habentem portas duodecim . . . Et murus civitatis habens fundamenta duodecim
. . . [18:] Et erat structura muri eius ex lapide iaspide; ipsa vero civitas, aurum
mundum simile vitro mundo . . . Et duodecim portae duodecim margaritae
sunt . . . et platea civitatis aurum mundum

dren and are as wise as children; [17] but if they who are children shall tell of these things and shall usurp to themselves the seats of the four and twenty elders, doubtless they shall by their dignity and rank open the house,[18] so that face to face [19] and eye to eye they shall look upon all the brightness of the sun and moon; but without these (elders) they shall not prevail. For they who have the keys of the kingdom of heaven, whatsoever they shall bind or loose,[20] so shall it be. For these follow the Lamb whithersoever he goeth.[21] But the beauty of this house cannot be told; its walls and streets are of the purest gold, and its gates gleam with pearls [22] and precious stones,[23] and its cornerstones are fourteen, containing

---

[17] Ps. 118 : 130: "The declaration of thy words giveth light: and giveth understanding to little ones." I Cor. 13 : 11: "When I was a child I spoke as a child, I understood as a child . . ."

[18] Cf. Ps. 106 : 32: "Let them exalt him . . . and praise him in the chair of the ancients." Cf. Apoc. 4 : 4ff.: "And round about the throne were four and twenty seats: and upon the seats, four and twenty ancients sitting, clothed in white garments. And on their heads were crowns of gold . . . [v. 10:] The four and twenty ancients fell down before him that sitteth on the throne and adored him that liveth for ever . . . [5 : 6:] And I saw, and behold in the midst . . . of the ancients, a Lamb standing, as it were slain, having seven horns and seven eyes; which are the seven Spirits of God, sent forth into all the earth . . . [5 : 8] . . . the four and twenty ancients . . . having . . . golden vials of odours . . ." Cf. Senior, De chemia ("Epistola Solis ad Lunam crescentem"), p. 8: (The Moon saith:) "we shall be exalted . . . when we shall ascend unto the order of the elders. The lamp of light will be poured into my lamp, and of thee and of me there will be a mixture, as of wine and sweet water . . . When we shall enter the house of love, my body will be coagulated. . . ."

[19] I Cor. 13 : 12: "We see now through a glass in a dark manner: but then face to face."

[20] Matt. 16 : 19: "And I will give to thee the keys of the kingdom of heaven, and whatsoever thou shalt bind on earth, it shall be bound also in heaven: and whatsoever thou shalt loose on earth, it shall be loosed also in heaven."

[21] Apoc. 14 : 4: "These are they who were not defiled with women: for they are virgins. These follow the Lamb whithersoever he goeth."

[22] Cf. Dominican Breviary, Hymn for Vespers on the Dedication of a Church: (of the celestial city) "Its streets and its walls are of the purest gold. Its gates gleam with pearls . . ."

[23] Apoc. 21 : 10ff.: ". . . and he shewed me the holy city Jerusalem. . . . having twelve gates, . . . and the wall of the city had twelve foundations . . . and the building of the wall thereof was of jasper stone; but the city itself pure gold, like to clear glass. . . . and the twelve gates were twelve pearls . . . And the street of the city was pure gold . . ."

vero eius angulares sunt quatuordecim tenentes virtutes princi-
pales totius fundamenti. Primus est sanitas, de qua Propheta:
35 Qui sanat contritos corde et alligat contritiones eorum,[24] et
philosophi: Qui utitur eo hominem vigoroso corpore conservat.[25] Secundus est humilitas de qua scribitur: Quia respexit
humilitatem ancillae suae,[26] ecce enim ex hoc beatam me dicent
omnes generationes. Et Propheta: Dominus erigit elisos.[27] Et
40 Aristoteles ad Alexandrum: Cum isto lapide non est bonum
pugnare.[28] Alphidius dicit: Si humilis fuerit, eius sapientia perficietur.[29] Tertius est sanctitas, de qua Propheta: Cum sancto
sanctus eris.[30] Et iterum: sanctitas et magnificentia in sanctificatione eius.[31] Et Alphidius: Scito, quod hanc scientiam habere
45 non poteris, nisi mentem tuam Deo purifices, hoc est in corde
omnem corruptionem deleas.[32] Et Turba: Voluptates reliqui

---

36. hominem *om. RhLD* / 36.–37. conservatur *RhLD* / 41. purgare *RhLDB* /
42.–43. Cum sanctis *MP* / 45. sanctifices *D* /

---

[24] Ps. 146 : 3: "Qui sanat contritos corde et alligat contritiones eorum."
[25] Cf. "Aurora consurgens II," *Art. aurif.* (1610), I, p. 141: "Illa (tinctura) hominem
laetificat et cor hominis sanat, ut Senior dicit, et reddit hominem hilarem, et
juvenilem facit et vigorose corpus conservat."
[26] Luc. 1 : 48: "Quia respexit humilitatem ancillae suae; ecce enim ex hoc beatam
me dicent omnes generationes."
[27] Ps. 144 : 14: "Allevat Dominus omnes qui corruunt, et erigit omnes elisos."
[28] Cf. Pseudo-Aristotle, "Secreta secretorum," fol. xxix: De lapide alchahat: "Et
non potest homo proeliari cum habente ipsum in manu." And fol. xxx: ". . . est
alia arbor, qui istam secum portaverit, erit laetus probus et audax, cum isto non est
bonum luctari vel litigare vel pugnare . . ."
[29] Cf. Hoghelande, "De alchimiae difficultatibus," *Bibl. chem.*, I, p. 340: "Et
Alphidius (in "Clav. phil."): Si humilis fueris eius Sophia et Sapientia perficietur,
sin autem, eius dispositio penitus te latebit."
[30] Ps. 17 : 26: "Cum sancto sanctus eris, et cum viro innocente innocens eris."
[31] Ps. 95 : 6: "Confessio et pulchritudo in conspectu eius; sanctimonia et magnificentia in sanctificatione eius."
[32] Alphidius, Codex Ashmole 1420, fol. 15: "Inspice Fili in libro meo et mandatum
meum respice atque monitionem meam. Et scito quod sapientiam istam habere
non potes quousque mentem tuam Deo purifices, et sciat te Deus habere certum
animum et creatori tuo fidelitatem, quod thesaurus Dei numquam perit nec
deficit." "Cons. coniug," p. 56: "Hanc etenim scientiam inquirentibus necessarium
est habere mentes purificatos a Deo, cum sit donum et secretum secretorum Dei."
Cf. also "Ros. phil.," *Bibl. chem.*, II, p. 91b: "Scito fili quod istam scientiam habere
non potes, quousque mentem tuam Deo purifices, et sciat Deus te habere certum
animum ac rectum et tunc mundo dominari te faciet." Cf. Hoghelande, "De alch.

the principal virtues of the whole foundation. The first is health, of which the Prophet: Who healeth the broken in heart and bindeth up their bruises,[24] and the philosophers: He who useth it ⟨the stone⟩ preserveth manhood in full vigour of body.[25] The second is humility, whereof it is written: Because he hath regarded the humility of his handmaid,[26] for behold from henceforth all generations shall call me blessed. And the Prophet: The Lord setteth up them that are cast down.[27] And Aristotle to Alexander: With this stone it is not good to fight.[28] Alphidius saith: If he shall be humble, his wisdom shall be perfected.[29] The third is holiness, of which the Prophet: With the holy thou shalt be holy.[30] And again: Holiness and magnificence are in his sanctuary.[31] And Alphidius: Know, that thou canst not have this science, unless thou shalt purify thy mind before God, that is, wipe away all corruption from thy heart.[32] And the *Turba:* I have put

24 Ps. 146 : 3: "Who healeth the broken in heart: and bindeth up their bruises."
25 Cf. "Aurora consurgens II." *Art. aurif.* (1610), I, p. 141: "This (the tincture) maketh man glad and healeth his heart, as Senior saith, and maketh man gladsome and young, and preserveth his body in vigour."
26 Luke 1 : 48: "Because he hath regarded the humility of his handmaid: for behold from henceforth all generations shall call me blessed."
27 Ps. 144 : 14: "The Lord lifteth up all that fall: and setteth up all that are cast down."
28 Cf. Pseudo-Aristotle, "Secreta secretorum," fol. xxix: Of the stone Alchahat: "And a man cannot fight with one who hath this stone in his hand." Also fol. xxx: "There is another tree, which shall bear this with it; it shall be joyful and honest and bold, it is not good to struggle or to argue or to fight therewith."
29 Cf. Hoghelande, "De alchimiae difficultatibus," *Bibl. chem.,* I, p. 340: "And Alphidius (in "Clav. phil."): If thou art humble, its wisdom and knowledge shall be perfected, but if not, its disposition will be wholly hidden from thee."
30 Ps. 17 : 26: "With the holy thou wilt be holy: and with the innocent man thou wilt be innocent."
31 Ps. 95 : 6: "Praise and beauty are before him: holiness and majesty in his sanctuary."
32 Alphidius, Codex Ashmole 1420, fol. 15: "Look, son, in my book, and have regard to my command and my admonition. And know that thou canst not have this wisdom until thou dost purify thy mind before God, and God knoweth thee to have a steadfast spirit, and faithfulness to thy creator, because the treasure of God perisheth never nor faileth." "Cons. coniug.," p. 56: "For it is needful that those who seek this knowledge have their minds purified by God, for it is God's gift and his secret of secrets." "Ros. phil.," p. 91b: "Know, my son, that thou canst not have this science until thou purifiest thy mind before God, and God knoweth thee to have a steadfast and right spirit, and then will he make thee to rule over the world." Cf. Hoghelande, "De alch. diff.," in *Bibl.*

et Deum exoravi, ut aquam mihi mundam ostenderet, quam novi esse merum acetum.[33] Quartus est castitas, de qua legitur: Quem cum amavero munda sum, (cum tetigero casta sum).[34]
50 Cuius mater virgo est et pater non concubuit,[35] quia lacte virgineo pastus est [36] etc.[37] Unde Avicenna in mineralibus dicit: Quidam ingeniosi utuntur aqua, quae lac virginis dicitur.[38] Quintus est virtus, de qua dicitur: Virtus ornat animam. Et Hermes: Et recipit virtutem superiorum et inferiorum planetarum et sua
55 virtute penetrat omnem rem solidam.[39] Et in libro Quintae

---

49. (cum tetigero casta sum) *add. MPV* / 50. Cuius mater ∼ pater non *om. MPV* / concumbit *MPB* / 54. recepit *D*, recipiet *RhL* /

---

diff.," in *Bibl. chem.*, I, p. 340: "Unde Alphidius (in "Clav. phil."): Hanc scientiam habere non potes, quousque mentem tuam Deo purifices et sciat te Deus mentem habere contritam."

33 *Turba*, p. 125, Floritis: "Acetum est acerrimum, quod facit aurum esse merum spiritum . . . Et iuro vobis per Deum, quod multo tempore in libris investigavi . . . et Deum oravi ut, quid est, me doceret. Exaudita autem oratione mundam aquam mihi demonstravit, quam novi merum esse acetum."

34 Cf. Matth. 9, 21-22. Roman Breviary, Feast of St. Agnes, Second (before 1961, Third) Responsory at Mattins: "Quem cum amavero, casta sum; cum tetigero, munda sum."

35 Cf. Roman Breviary, ibid.: "cujus mater virgo est, cujus pater feminam nescit."

36 Cf. Dominican Breviary, Sunday within Octave of Christmas, Hymn at Lauds: "Parvoque lacte pastus est, per quem nec ales esurit."

37 Alphidius, Codex Ashmole 1420, fol. 26: "Cuius mater virgo est et pater non concubuit." Cf. the Alphidius quotation in Petrus Bonus, *Pret. marg. nov.*, p. 40: "Hic lapis in viis projectus, est in nubibus exaltatus, in aere habitat, in flumine pascitur et in cacumine montium quiescit, cuius mater virgo est, cuius pater foeminam nescit." Ibid.: ". . . indicaverunt Deum cum homine fieri debere unum, et hoc factum fuit in Christo Jesu et virgine, matre eius. . . . Et ostendit Deus hoc exemplum miraculosum philosophis in hoc lapide." Also as a quotation from Assiduus in "Cons. coniug.," pp. 205, 64, 150.

38 Avicenna, "De congelatione . . ." in *Art. aurif.* (1610), I, p. 240: "Est autem res quaedam, qua utuntur quidam ingeniosi cum volunt rem siccam coagulare, quae componitur ex duabus aquis, et dicitur lac virginis." Also in "De congelatione et conglutinatione lapidis," *Theatr. chem.* (1659), IV, p. 883, and Pseudo-Aristotle, "Secreta secretorum," cap. "De mineralibus." Also as Alphidius quotation in "Liber de magni lapidis compositione et operatione," *Theatr. chem.* (1659), III, pp. 37 and 44.

39 Cf. *Tabula Smaragdina*, ed. Ruska, p. 2: "Ascendit a terra in coelum, iterumque descendit in terram, et recipit vim superiorum et inferiorum. Sic habebis gloriam totius mundi. Ideo fugiat [fugiet] a te omnis obscuritas. Hic est totius fortitudinis fortitudo fortis: quia vincet omnem rem subtilem, omnemque solidam penetrabit."

pleasures aside and prayed to God, that he would show me the pure water, which I know to be pure vinegar.[33] The fourth is chastity, of which it is written: Whom when I love I am pure, (when I touch I am chaste); [34] whose mother is a virgin and whose father hath not cohabited with her,[35] for he is fed upon virgin's milk,[36] etc.[37] Wherefore Avicenna saith in the *Mineralia:* Certain learned ones use a water, which is called virgin's milk.[38] The fifth is virtue, of which it is said: Virtue adorneth the soul. And Hermes: And it receiveth the virtue of the upper and lower planets and by its virtue penetrateth every solid thing.[39] And in

chem., I, p. 340: "Wherefore Alphidius (in "Clav. phil."):Thou canst not have this science, until thou purifiest thy mind before God and God knoweth thee to have a contrite mind."

33 *Turba*, p. 125, Floritis (Socrates): "The vinegar is very sharp, which maketh gold to be pure spirit. . . . And I swear to you by God, that I have sought for long in the books, to arrive at the knowledge of this single thing, and I have besought God in prayer to teach me what it is. And when he had heard my prayer, he showed me the pure water, which I know to be pure vinegar.' '

34 Cf. Matt. 9 : 21–22. Roman Breviary, Feast of St. Agnes, Second (before 1961, Third) Responsory at Mattins: "Whom when I love, I am chaste; when I touch, I am clean."

35 Cf. Roman Breviary, ibid.: "whose mother is a maiden, whose father hath not known woman."

36 Cf. Dominican Breviary, Sunday within Octave of Christmas, Hymn at Lauds: "And He is fed with a little milk, through whom not even a bird goes hungry."

37 Alphidius, Codex Ashmole 1420, fol. 26: "Whose mother is a virgin and whose father hath not cohabited with her." Cf. the Alphidius quotation in Petrus Bonus, *Pret. marg. nov.*, p. 40: "This stone, cast forth into the streets, is exalted to the clouds, dwelleth in the air, and is nourished in the rivers and resteth on the summits of the mountains, whose mother is a maid, whose father knoweth not woman." Ibid.: . . . "it was their judgment, that God must become one with man and that this came to pass in Christ Jesus and his maiden mother. . . . And God made this plain as a wonderful example to the philosophers in this stone.' ' Also as a quotation from Assiduus in "Cons. coniug.," pp. 205, 64, 150.

38 Avicenna, "De congelatione . . . ," in *Art. aurif.* (1610), I, p. 240: "For there is a certain thing, which some men of skill use when they wish to coagulate something which is dry: and it is composed of two waters, and is called virgin's milk." The same in "De congelatione et conglutinatione lapidis," *Theatr. chem.* (1659), IV, p. 883, and Pseudo-Aristotle, "Secreta secretorum," cap. "De mineralibus." Also as Alphidius quotation in "Liber de magni lapidis compositione et operatione," *Theatr. chem.* (1659), III, pp. 37 and 44.

39 Cf. *Tabula Smaragdina* (ed. Ruska), p. 2: "It goeth up from earth to heaven, and cometh down again to earth, and receiveth the virtue of the things above and of the things below. So shalt thou have the glory of the whole world. Let all darkness therefore flee from thee. This is the strong strength of all strength; for it shall overcome every subtle thing, and penetrate every solid thing."

essentiae dicitur: Cum non suffecissem mirari de tanta rei virtute sibi coelitus indita et infusa.[40] Sextus est victoria, de qua
Hermes: Et vincet omnem rem solidam et lapidem pretiosum.[39]
Et Johannes in Apocalypsi: Vincenti subtile dabo manna ab-
60 sconditum et nomen novum quod os Domini nominavit.[41,42]
Et in libro Quintae essentiae: Cum autem operatus fuerit lapis
victoriae, smaragdos jaspides et veros chrysolithos cum lapide
ex ea materia facere informabo, qui in colore, substantia et
virtute naturales praecellunt et excedunt etc.[43] Septimus est
65 fides, de qua legitur: Fides salvat hominem,[44] quam nisi quisque
habuerit, salvus esse non poterit.[45] Fides est intelligere, quod
non vides.[46] Et Turba: Est invisibilis quemadmodum anima in
humano corpore.[47] Et in eodem dicitur: Duo videntur, terra

---

56. mirari: amanti *PV, om. M* /57. sibi: soli *MP* /induta *MP* /58. vincit *MPLRh* /
solidam *om. MPB* / (pretiosum) et subtilem *add. V* / 59. subtilem *M, om. PVB* |
62. veros: achites *MPV* /Crisoliton *MPV* /63. materia *conj.,* manante *DRh,* manente
MPLV, om. B | informabo: Rubinos *MPV* / 64. etc. *om. MPL* / 66. intelligentia
DV / intra *P,* intus *M* / 67. Et *om. MPV* /

---

40 Cf. "Aurora consurgens II," *Art. aurif.* (1610), I, p. 151: "Quod non sit [n]atus,
neque nascitur in futurum, qui hanc scientiam posset complere sine natura,
natura quidem quae coelitus est indita rebus et infusa." Cf. Pseudo-Aristotle,
"Secreta secretorum," fol. xxvi, 2.
41 Apoc. 2 : 17: "Vincenti dabo manna absconditum, et dabo illi calculum can-
didum, et in calculo nomen novum scriptum, quod nemo scit, nisi qui accipit."
42 Cf. Isa. 62 : 2: "Et vocabitur tibi nomen novum, quod os Domini nominabit."
43 Cf. "Aurora consurgens II," cap. 22, *Art. aurif.* (1610), I, pp. 156–57: "ut superius
allegatum est in libro Sextario, ubi dicitur: quod lapides Jacincti, Coralli rubei et
albi, Smaragdi, Chrysoliti, Saphyri, ex ipsa materia formari possunt: Et in charta
Sacerdotum traditur, quod ex chrystallo, carbunculus, sive rubinus, aut topazius
per eam fieri potest, qui in colore et substantia excellunt naturales."
44 Cf. *inter alia* Matth. 9 : 22: "Fides tua te salvam fecit."
45 Athanasian Creed: "Haec est fides catholica, quam nisi quisque fideliter
firmiterque crediderit, salvus esse non poterit."
46 Joh. 20 : 29: "Beati qui non viderunt et crediderunt." Cf. Thomas Aquinas,
Summa theol., I–II, q. 62, art. 3 ad 2: "quia fides est de his, quae non videntur."
47 *Turba,* p. 141: "Hic enim spiritus, quem quaeritis, ut eo quodlibet tingatis,
in corpore occultus est et absconditus, invisibilis quemadmodum anima in humano
corpore." (This does not accord with the Vadiana MS.)

the *Book of the Quintessence* it is said: For I could not wonder enough at the great virtue of the thing, which is bestowed upon and infused into it from heaven.[40] The sixth is victory, whereof Hermes: And it (the stone) shall be victorious over every solid thing and precious stone.[39] And John in the Apocalypse: To him that overcometh I will give the subtle hidden manna and a new name which the mouth of the Lord hath named.[41, 42] And in the *Book of the Quintessence:* But when the stone of victory shall have been wrought, I shall teach how to make with the stone of that material emeralds, jaspers, and true chrysolites, which in colour, substance, and virtue excel and surpass the natural, etc.[43] The seventh is faith, of which we read: Faith saveth a man,[44] and he who hath it not, cannot be saved.[45] Faith is to understand what thou seest not.[46] And the *Turba:* It is invisible like unto the soul in man's body.[47] And in the same it is said: Two things are seen,

---

[40] Cf. "Aurora consurgens II," *Art. aurif.* (1610), I, p. 151: "For there is not nor shall there be in the future any man born who can fulfil this science without nature—the nature, that is to say, which is bestowed upon things and infused into them from heaven." Cf. Pseudo-Aristotle, "Secreta secretorum," fol. xxvi, 2.

[41] Apoc. 2 : 17: "To him that overcometh I will give the hidden manna and will give him a white counter (stone), and in the counter a new name written, which no man knoweth but he that receiveth it."

[42] Cf. Isa. 62 : 2: "And thou shalt be called by a new name which the mouth of the Lord shall name."

[43] Cf. "Aurora consurgens II," cap. 22, *Art. aurif.* (1610), I, pp. 156–67: ". . . as is set forth above in the sixth book, where it is said that the stones jacinth, red and white coral, emerald, chrysolite, and sapphire, can be formed from that material. And in the charter of the priests it is written, that from crystal can be made by its means carbuncle, or ruby, or topaz, which in colour and substance excel the natural."

[44] Cf. *inter alia* Matt. 9 : 22: (Jesus says) "Thy faith hath made thee whole."

[45] Athanasian Creed: "This is the catholic faith, which except a man believe faithfully and firmly, he cannot be saved."

[46] John 20 : 29: "Blessed are they that have not seen and have believed." Cf. Thomas Aquinas, *Summa theol.,* I–II, q. 62, art. 3 ad 2: "For faith concerns those things that are not seen."

[47] *Turba,* p. 141: "For this spirit, which you seek, that you may tinge somewhat therewith, is hidden and concealed in the body, like unto the soul in a man's body." (This does not accord with the Vadiana MS.)

scilicet et aqua, alia vero non, scilicet aer et ignis.[48] Et Paulus:
70 Qui crediderit in eum, non confundetur, nam non credentibus
est lapis offensio et petra scandali.[49] Et Evangelium: Qui non
crediderit, iam iudicatus est.[50] Octavus est spes, de qua dicitur:
Firma spes laetificat res, spes promittit semper finem bonum.
Et Moriens: Spera et spera et sic consequeris. Et Propheta:
75 Sperate in eum omnis congregatio populi,[51] in eum speraverunt
patres nostri et liberati sunt.[52] Nonus est caritas, de qua Apostolus: Caritas omnia suffert. Caritas non agit perperam.[53] Et
Evangelista: Ego diligentes me diligo.[54] Qui omni tempore
diligit, hic amicus est.[55] Et Alphonsus (rex): Hic est vere amicus,
80 qui te non deserit, cum omne saeculum tibi deficit. Et Gregorius: [56] Probatio dilectionis est exhibitio operis. Et Job:
Omnia, quae homo habet dabit pro anima sua,[57] hoc est pro

---

70. in eum *om. PV,* omnino *M* / non (both) *om. MP* / 71. ostensio *P,* offensionis
DV / 73. Firma fides *RhDL* / 79. (amicus est) meus *add. D* / rex *add. M* /

---

48 *Turba,* p. 117: "In his (scil. elementis) est arcanum absconditum, quorum duo
tactum habent (et) aspectum apud visum largiuntur, quorum opus et vi[rtu]s
sciuntur, quae sunt terra et aqua, alia autem duo elementa nec videntur nec
tanguntur . . ."
49 Rom. 9 : 33: "Ecce pono in Sion lapidem offensionis, et petram scandali, et
omnis qui credit in eum non confundetur."
50 Joh. 3 : 18: "Qui credit in eum, non iudicatur; qui autem non credit, iam
iudicatus est."
51 Ps. 61 : 9: "Sperate in eo, omnis congregatio populi; effundite coram illo corda
vestra."
52 Ps. 21 : 5: "In te speraverunt patres nostri; speraverunt, et liberasti eos."
53 I Cor. 13 : 7: "Charitas . . . omnia suffert, omnia credit, omnia sperat . . ."
I Cor. 13 : 4: "Charitas . . . non aemulatur, non agit perperam . . ."
54 Joh. 14 : 21: "Qui autem diligit me, diligetur a Patre meo; et ego diligam eum,
et manifestabo ei meipsum." Prov. 8 : 17: "Ego diligentes me diligo."
55 Prov. 17 : 17: "Omni tempore diligit, qui amicus est."
56 Gregorius Magnus. *Hom. XXX in Evang.* (Migne, *P.L.,* vol. 76, col. 1220): "Probatio dilectionis est exhibitio operis."
57 Job 2 : 4: Satan ait: "Pellem pro pelle, et cuncta quae habet homo dabit pro
anima sua." Cf. Matth. 16 : 26: "Aut quam dabit homo commutationem pro
anima sua?"

namely water and earth, but two are not seen, namely air and fire.[48] And Paul: Whosoever believeth therein shall not be confounded, for to them that believe not the stone is a stumbling stone and a rock of scandal.[49] And the Gospel: He that believeth not is already judged.[50] The eighth is hope, whereof it is said: Firm hope maketh the work glad, hope always promiseth a good end. And Morienus: Hope and hope, and so shalt thou attain (the goal). And the Prophet: Hope in him all ye congregation of people,[51] in him have our fathers hoped and they were delivered.[52] The ninth is charity, of which the Apostle: Charity beareth all things, Charity dealeth not perversely.[53] And the Evangelist: I love them that love me.[54] He is a friend that loveth at all times.[55] And (king) Alphonsus: This is a true friend, who deserteth thee not when all the world faileth thee. And Gregory: [56] The proof of love is the display of the work. And Job: All that a man hath will he give for his soul,[57] that is for this stone. For he

<hr>

[48] *Turba*, p. 117: "In these (elements) is a secret concealed, in that two of them are tangible and display an appearance to the eye, of which the operation and virtue are known, namely earth and water, but the other two elements are neither to be seen nor touched."

[49] Rom. 9 : 33: "Behold I lay in Sion a stumbling-stone and a rock of scandal, and whosoever believeth in him shall not be confounded."

[50] John 3 : 18: "He that believeth in him is not judged: but he that doth not believe is already judged . . ."

[51] Ps. 61 : 9: "Trust in him, all ye congregation of people: pour out your hearts before him."

[52] Ps. 21 : 5: "In thee have our fathers hoped: they have hoped, and thou hast delivered them."

[53] I Cor. 13 : 7: "Charity . . . beareth all things, believeth all things, hopeth all things . . ." I Cor. 13 : 4: "Charity envieth not, dealeth not perversely, is not puffed up."

[54] John 14 : 21: "He that loveth me shall be loved of my Father: and I will love him and will manifest myself to him." Prov. 8 : 17: "I love them that love me."

[55] Prov. 17 : 17: "He that is a friend loveth at all times . . ."

[56] Gregory the Great, *Hom. XXX in Evang.* (Migne, *P.L.*, vol. 76, col. 1220): "The proof of love is the showing forth of the work."

[57] Job 2 : 4: "And Satan answered, and said: Skin for skin, and all that a man hath will he give for his life." Cf. Matt. 16 : 26: "Or what exchange shall a man give for his soul?"

lapide isto. Nam qui parce seminat parce et metet;[58] et qui non fuerit socius passionis non erit consolationis.[59] Decimus est
85 benignitas, de qua dicitur: Nescis, quod benignitas (Dei) te ad poenitentiam ducit. Benignus est iudex, reddere unicuique iuxta opera sua.[60] Nam benignitas reddit bonum pro malo maximum pro pauco, sed bonitas pro bono reddit bonum, parvum pro parvo. Undecimus est patientia, de qua dicitur: Si vis vin-
90 cere, disce pati. Et Apostolus: Per patientiam et consolationem scripturarum spem habeamus.[61] Et Morienes: Qui patientiam non habet manum ab opere suspendat.[62] Et Calet Minor: Tria sunt necessaria, videlicet patientia, mora et aptitudo instru-mentorum.[63] Et Apostolus: Patientes estote, quia adventus
95 Domini appropinquabit etc.[64] Duodecimus est temperantia, de qua scribitur, quod omnia nutrit et fovet et in sanitate conservat. Quamdiu enim elementa sunt in temperantia, anima in corpore delectatur, cum autem discordant, anima in eo abhorret habi-tare. Nam temperantia est elementorum mixtio adinvicem, ut

---

84. compassionis *D* / (cons.) socius *add. D* / est *om. PL* / 85. Dci *add. L*, Divini-tatis *MP* / te *om. M*, Dei est quac te *L* / 86, poenitentiam: praemium *MPV₂* / 91. Et: etc. *DRh*, *om. L* / 92. suspendit *MPVL* / 93. videlicet *om. BPVD* / 95. etc. *om. MPVL* / 98. discordant in eo abhorret anima *DBP* /

---

[58] II Cor. 9 : 6: "Hoc autem dico: qui parce seminat, parce et metet." Cf. Albertus Magnus, "De lapide philos.," *Theatr. chem.* (1659), IV, p. 845: "Nam quaecunque seminaverit homo, haec et metet."
[59] II Cor. 1 : 7: "Ut spes nostra firma sit pro vobis: scientes quod sicut socii passionum estis, sic eritis et consolationis."
[60] Rom. 2 : 4-6: ". . . ignoras, quoniam benignitas Dei ad poenitentiam te ad-ducit? . . . Dei, qui reddet unicuique secundum opera eius." Cf. Ps. 61 : 13.
[61] Rom. 15 : 4: "Quaecumque scripta sunt, ad nostram doctrinam scripta sunt, ut per patientiam et consolationem Scripturarum spem habeamus."
[62] Morienus, "De transmut. metall.," *Art. aurif.* (1610), II, p. 21. Cf. "Ros. phil.," *Bibl. chem.*, II, p. 114a. Cf. also Pseudo-Thomas, "Secreta alchimiae," *Theatr. chem.* (1659), III, p. 278: ". . . quia secundum Gebrum festinantia a Diabolo est. Ideo qui patientiam non habet, ab operatione manum suspendat."
[63] "Ros. phil.," *Bibl. chem.*, II, p. 114a: "Ad hanc tria necessaria sunt, scilicet patientia, mora, et instrumentorum aptatio." Cf. Pseudo-Thomas, "Secreta al-chimiae," p. 278: "Quomodo tandem fit substantia una, ut dicit Avicenna: habere oportet patientiam, moram, et instrumentum." See also Geber, "Summa perfec-tionis," cap. 12, in *De alchemia* (1541), p. 17. Supra, p. 13, n. 42.
[64] Jac. 5 : 8: "Patientes igitur estote et vos, et confirmate corda vestra, quoniam adventus Domini appropinquavit."

who soweth sparingly shall also reap sparingly; [58] and he who is not a partaker of the sufferings shall not be of the consolation.[59] The tenth is goodness, of which it is said: Knowest thou not that the goodness (of God) leadeth thee to penance? Good is the judge, to render to every man according to his works.[60] For goodness returneth good for evil, much for little, but good nature returneth good for good, little for little. The eleventh is patience, of which it is said: If thou wilt conquer, learn to suffer (be patient). And the Apostle: Through patience and comfort of the Scriptures we may have hope.[61] And Morienus: He who hath not patience, let him hold back his hand from the work.[62] And Calet the Less: Three things are necessary, namely patience, deliberation, and skill with the instruments.[63] And the Apostle: Be you patient, for the coming of the Lord is at hand, etc.[64] The twelfth is temperance, of which it is written that it nourisheth and cherisheth all things and keepeth them in health. For as long as the elements are in temperance, the soul delighteth in the body, but when they are in discord, the soul abhorreth to dwell in it. For temperance is a mixture of the elements one with another, such

[58] II Cor. 9 : 6: "Now this I say: He who soweth sparingly shall also reap sparingly." Cf. Albert the Great, "De lapide philos.," *Theatr. chem.* (1659), IV, p. 845: "For what things soever a man sow, these also shall he reap."

[59] II Cor. 1 : 7: "That our hope for you may be steadfast: knowing that as you are partakers of the sufferings, so shall you be also of the consolation."

[60] Rom. 2 : 4–6: "Knowest thou not, that the benignity of God leadeth thee to penance? . . . the just judgment of God, who will render to every man according to his works." Cf. Ps. 61 : 13.

[61] Rom. 15 : 4: "For what things soever were written were written for our learning, that through patience and the comfort of the scriptures we might have hope."

[62] Morienus, "De transmut. metall.," *Art. aurif.* (1610), II, p. 21. Cf. "Ros. phil.," in *Bibl. chem.*, II, p. 114a. Cf. also Pseudo-Thomas, "Secreta alchimiae," *Theatr. chem.* (1659), III, p. 278: ". . . for according to Geber, all haste is of the devil. Therefore he who hath not patience, let him hold back his hand from the work."

[63] "Ros. phil.," p. 114a: "For this three things are necessary, namely: patience, deliberation, and skill with the instruments." Cf. Pseudo-Thomas, "Secreta alchimiae," p. 278: "But that at last there may come into being the one substance, as Avicenna says, you must have patience, deliberation, and the instrument." See also Geber, "Summa perfectionis," cap. 12, in *De alchemia* (1541), p. 17. Supra, p. 13, n. 42.

[64] James 5 : 8: "Be you therefore patient and strengthen your hearts; for the coming of the Lord is at hand."

100 calidum cum frigido, siccum cum humido temperetur; et ne unum excedat aliud philosophi summo studio prohibuerunt dicentes: Cavete, ne arcanum fugiat,[65] cavete, ne acetum in fumum vertatur,[66] cavete, ne regem et uxorem suam fugetis nimio igne,[67] cavete omne, quod est extra modum, sed super

105 ignem putredinis hoc est temperantiae ponite quousque sponte iungantur.[68] Tredecimus est spiritualis disciplina sive intellectus, de quo Apostolus: Littera occidit, spiritus autem vivificat.[69] Renovamini spiritu mentis vestrae et induite (novum) hominem,[70] hoc est intellectum subtilem.[71] Si spiritualiter intel-

110 lexeritis, spiritum utique cognoscetis. Unusquisque vestrum opus suum probet,[72] utrum sit perficiens an deficiens. Quae enim homo seminat eadem et metet.[73] O quam multi non intelligunt dicta sapientum, hi perierunt propter eorum insipientiam, quia caruerunt intellectu spirituali et nihil invenerunt

---

102. Cavete *om.* MP / fugiet *BLRh,* fuget P, fumiget *M* / 103. cavete *om.* PM / fugietis *MPVLRh* / 108. spiritu: spiritus *MPD* / novum *add. BV* / 112. O *om.* *MPVD* / 114. quia: qui *PV* / caruerunt: non curaverunt *V* / intellectum spiritualem *LV* /

---

65 *Turba* (ed. Ruska), p. 126: ". . . et cavete, ne arcanum fumiget . . ." (Codex N. Vadiana 390: fugiet). Cf. ibid., p. 128: "Observate ergo vas, ne compositum fugiat . . ."

66 Ibid., p. 126: ". . . et cavete ne acetum in fumum vertatur et pereat."

67 Ibid., p. 138: ". . . requiem eis constituite et cavete ne fugetis eos comburendo nimio igne. Veneramini regem et suam uxorem et nolite eos comburere."

68 "Liber Alphidii," Codex Ashmole 1420, fol. 10: "Deinde super ignem pone putredinis quousque sponte iungantur et omne corruptum emendatur."

69 II Cor. 3 : 6: "Littera enim occidit, Spiritus autem vivificat."—This is cited by Olympiodorus (Berthelot, *Alch. grecs,* II, iv, 41; Textes, p. 94).

70 Ephes. 4 : 23–24: "Renovamini autem spiritu mentis vestrae, et induite novum hominem . . ."

71 Cf. *Pret. marg. nov.,* p. 38: ". . . et hoc (fixio et permanentia animae et spiritus) fit per adiectionem lapidis occulti, qui sensu non comprehenditur, sed intellectu solum per inspirationem vel revelationem divinam aut per doctrinam scientis . . . et dixit Alexander: duo sunt in hac arte ordines, scilicet aspectus oculo intellectusque corde, et hic lapis occultus est qui proprie dicitur donum Dei, et hic est lapis divinus occultus sine cuius commixtione lapidi annihilatur alchemia, cum ipse sit ipsa alchemia . . . Et hic lapis divinus est cor et tinctura auri quaesita a philosophis."

72 Gal. 6 : 4: "Opus autem suum probet unusquisque, et sic in semetipso tantum gloriam habebit . . ."

73 Gal. 6 : 8: "Quae enim seminaverit homo, haec et metet." Cf. also "Ros. phil., " p. 107b, Pseudo-Aristotle. Also *Pret. marg. nov.,* pp. 116–17.

that the warm is tempered with the cold, the dry with the humid; and the philosophers have been most careful to insist that one may not exceed another, saying: Beware lest the secret escape,[65] beware lest the vinegar be changed into smoke,[66] beware lest ye put to flight the king and his consort with too much fire,[67] beware of all that is beyond the mean, but place it on the fire of corruption, that is of temperance, until they are joined of their own accord.[68] The thirteenth is spiritual discipline or understanding, of which the Apostle: The letter killeth, but the spirit quickeneth.[69] Be renewed in the spirit of your mind and put on the new man,[70] that is, a subtle understanding. If ye understand in the spirit, ye shall also know the spirit.[71] Let every one of you prove his own work,[72] whether it be perfect or defective. For what things a man shall sow, those also shall he reap.[73] O how many understand not the sayings of the wise; these have perished because of their foolishness, for they lacked spiritual under-

[65] *Turba* (ed. Ruska), p. 126: ". . . and beware, lest the secret thing give forth smoke." (Codex N. Vadiana 390: "fugiet": escape.) Cf. ibid., p. 128: "Watch therefore over the vessel, lest the compound escape. . ."

[66] Ibid., p. 126: ". . . and beware lest the vinegar be changed into smoke, and perish."

[67] Ibid., p. 138: ". . . provide rest for them and take care that ye put them not to flight by burning them with excess of fire. Venerate the king and his consort and burn them not."

[68] "Liber Alphidii," Codex Ashmole 1420, fol. 10: "Then place it upon the fire of corruption until the spouses are conjoined and everything that is corrupt is purified."

[69] II Cor. 3 : 6: "For the letter killeth, but the spirit quickeneth." This is cited by Olympiodorus (Berthelot, *Alch. grecs*, II, iv, 41; Textes, p. 94).

[70] Ephes. 4 : 23–24: "And be renewed in the spirit of your mind; and put on the new man . . ."

[71] Cf. *Pret. marg. nov.*, p. 38: ". . . and this (the fixing and permanence of soul and spirit) cometh to pass through the addition of the secret stone, which is not to be comprehended by the senses, but solely through understanding by divine inspiration or revelation or by the teaching of one that knoweth . . . and Alexander saith: There are two orders in this art, that is, beholding by the eye and understanding by the heart, and this is the secret stone which is rightly called a gift of God, and is the divine, secret stone which unless it be commingled with the stone alchemy is annihilated, since it is itself alchemy . . . and this divine stone is the heart and the tincture of the gold, which is sought by the philosophers."

[72] Gal. 6 : 4: "But let everyone prove his own work: and so shall he have glory in himself only . . ."

[73] Gal. 6 : 8: "For what things a man shall sow, those also shall he reap." Cf. also "Ros. phil.," p. 107b, Pseudo-Aristotle. Also *Pret. marg. nov.*, pp. 116–17.

¹¹⁵ praeter laborem. Quartusdecimus lapis est oboedientia, de qua scribitur: Oboedientes estote vestris superioribus ⁷⁴ sicut Christus factus fuit oboediens patri usque ad mortem.⁷⁵ Sic oboedite praeceptis et dictis sapientum, tunc omnia promissa eorum vobis oboediunt et proveniunt Deo Domino annuente.

¹²⁰ Qui habet aures audiendi audiat, quid dicat spiritus doctrinae filiis disciplinae de domo, quam fundavit sapientia super quattuordecim lapides angulares,⁷⁶ quam vigintiquattuor seniores clavibus regni coelorum reserant et quam Senior in prologo libri sui declaravit: Ubi ponit quod ⟨est⟩ aquila in tecto et

¹²⁵ diversarum in lateribus imagines proprietatum.⁷⁷ Et Alphidius in libro suo dicit de domo thesaurizaria, quam docet quattuor clavibus posse reserari, quae sunt quattuor elementa.⁷⁸

---

123. reservant *MP* / 124. dicit seu ponit *L* / est *conj.* / 125. et etc. Alph. *MPB*, Et om. *V* / 126. thesaurorum *M*, thesaurariorum *PBV*, thesaurisariaram *L*, thesaur-archa *D* / dicit *BDLRh* /

---

⁷⁴ Hebr. 13 : 17: "Oboedite praepositis vestris et subiacete eis .   ″

⁷⁵ Phil. 2 : 8: "Humiliavit semetipsum, factus oboediens usque ad mortem, mortem autem crucis . . ."

⁷⁶ Roman Missal, Epistle for 14th Sunday after Pentecost: "Duodecim fructus Spiritus." (Gal. 5 : 16–24.)

⁷⁷ Cf. Senior, *De chemia*, pp. 3–4: "Intravi . . . in domum quandam subterraneam . . . et vidi in tecto imagines novem aquilarum pictas . . . Et in pariete domus, a dextris et a sinistris intrantis, imagines hominum, stantium, pro ut possent esse perfectiores, et pulchriores, induti diversis vestimentis et coloribus . . ." Cf. p. 109: "Est enim lapis Aquilae . . ."

⁷⁸ Codex Ashmole 1420, fol. 22–24. Larger fragments of the teachings of Alphidius concerning the treasure-house are also to be found in "Cons. coniug.," *Ars. chem.*, pp. 108ff.

standing and found nothing but toil. The fourteenth stone is obedience, of which it is written: Obey your superiors,[74] as Christ was made obedient to the Father even unto death.[75] So obey the precepts and sayings of the wise, then all things promised by them will obey you and come to fruition, God the Lord willing. He that hath ears to hear, let him hear what the spirit of the doctrine saith to the sons of the discipline concerning the house which wisdom hath founded on fourteen cornerstones,[76] which the four and twenty elders open with the keys of the kingdom of heaven, and of which Senior in the prologue of his book declared: Where he placed what ⟨is⟩ the eagle on the roof and the images of the various properties on the sides.[77] And Alphidius in his book speaketh of the treasure house, which he teacheth can be opened by four keys, which are the four elements.[78]

[74] Hebr. 13 : 17: "Obey your prelates and be subject to them."
[75] Phil. 2 : 8: "He humbled himself, becoming obedient unto death, even to the death of the cross."
[76] Cf. Roman Missal, Epistle for 14th Sunday after Pentecost: "The twelve fruits of the spirit: (charity, joy, peace, patience, benignity, goodness, longanimity, mildness, faith, modesty, continency, chastity)" (Gal. 5 : 16–24).
[77] Cf. Senior, *De chemia*, pp. 3–4: "I entered . . . into a certain house under the earth . . . and I saw on its roof pictures of nine eagles . . . and on the wall of the house, both on the right and on the left of the entrance, images of men, standing, that they might be more perfect and more beautiful, clothed in garments of divers colours . . ." Cf. p. 109: "For it is the stone of the eagle . . ."
[78] Codex Ashmole 1420, fol. 22–24. Larger fragments of the teaching of Alphidius concerning the treasure-house are also to be found in "Cons. coniug.," *Ars chem.*, pp. 108ff.

XI

PARABOLA SEXTA DE COELO ET MUNDO
ET SITIBUS ELEMENTORUM

Qui de terra est, de terra loquitur, qui de coelo venit super omnes est.[1] Hic iam etiam locatur terra pro principio elemen-
5 torum, coeli vero pro tribus superioribus denotantur (princi-piis), quare libet pauca de terra et de coelo perorare, cum ipsum sit principium et mater aliorum elementorum testante Propheta: Initio tu Domine terram fundasti et opera manuum tuarum sunt coeli,[2] id est aqua, aer et ignis. Nam a terra elementa mori-
10 endo separantur et ad eam vivificando revertuntur, quia a quo res habet componi, in illud habet resolvi [3] testante sacro eloquio: Homo cinis est et in cinerem revertetur.[4] Talem cinerem prae-ceperunt philosophi commisceri aqua permanente, quae est fer-mentum auri, et aurum eorum est corpus scilicet terra, quod
15 vocavit Aristoteles coagulum, cum sit coagulans aquam, quae est terra sanctae promissionis,[5] in quam iussit Hermes filium suum

---

4. pro primum *P*, corr. *P₂* / 5. principiis *add.* *D* / 6. libent *P*, libentur *V* / procreare *PV*, parare *M* / 7. principium: primum, *L, om. B* / 9. et *om. LBRh* / 11. compositionem *P*, composi *M* /

---

[1] Joh. 3 : 31: "Qui desursum venit, super omnes est. Qui est de terra, de terra est, et de terra loquitur. Qui de caelo venit, super omnes est."
[2] Ps. 101 : 26–27: "Initio tu, Domine, terram fundasti, et opera manuum tuarum sunt coeli; ipsi peribunt, tu autem permanes."
[3] Cf. Morienus Romanus: "De transmut. metall.," *Art. aurif.* (1610), II, p. 19: "Hermes quoque ait: Terra est mater elementorum: de terra procedunt et ad ter-ram revertuntur." Cf. also *Pret. marg. nov.*, p. 107: "Hermes: terra est elementum et de terra omnia facta sunt et ad terram convertuntur. Moyses: terra est mater elementorum, omnia de terra procedunt et ad terram convertuntur. Sic recitat Morienus: Haec autem terra est, corpus et fermentum . . . ."
[4] Gen. 3 : 19: ". . . quia pulvis es, et in pulverem reverteris . . ." Ecclus. 17 : 31: ". . . et omnes homines terra et cinis . . ." Job 34, 15: "Deficiet omnis caro simul, et homo in cinerem revertetur."
[5] Cf. Exod. 13 : 5. Cf. Roman Missal, Offertory for Thursday in Easter Week.

THE SIXTH PARABLE: OF HEAVEN AND EARTH
AND THE ARRANGEMENT OF THE ELEMENTS

67   He that is of the earth, of the earth he speaketh, he that cometh
from heaven is above all.[1] Now here also is the earth represented
as the principle of the elements, but the heavens stand for the
three higher (principles), wherefore a little ought to be said of
earth and heaven, for earth is the principle and mother of the
other elements, as the Prophet beareth witness: In the beginning,
O Lord, thou didst found the earth, and the heavens are the
works of thy hands,[2] that is, water, air, and fire. For from the earth
are the elements separated by dying, and to it do they return by
quickening, for what a thing is composed of, into that must it
be resolved,[3] as the holy word testifieth: Man is ashes and to
their ashes shall he return.[4] Such ashes did the philosophers ordain to be mixed with the permanent water, which is the ferment
of gold, and their gold is the body, that is the earth, which Aristotle called the coagulant, since it coagulateth water. It is the earth
of the Promised Land,[5] wherein Hermes commanded his son to

---

1 John 3 : 31: "He that cometh from above is above all. He that is of the earth,
of the earth he is, and of the earth he speaketh. He that cometh from heaven is
above all."
2 Ps. 101 : 26–27: "In the beginning, O Lord, thou foundedst the earth, and the
heavens are the works of thy hands. They shall perish but thou remainest."
3 Cf. Morienus Romanus. "De transmut. metall., "Art. aurif. (1610), II, p. 19:
"Hermes also saith: Earth is the mother of the elements; from earth they come and
to earth they return." Cf. also Pret. marg. nov., p. 107: "Hermes: The earth is an
element, and of the earth are all things made, and into earth are they converted.
Moses: The earth is the mother of the elements, all things came forth from earth
and are turned again to earth. So doth Morienus say: But this earth is a body and a
ferment . . ."
4 Gen. 3 : 19: "Dust thou art, and into dust shalt thou return." Ecclus. 17 : 31:
". . . and all men are earth and ashes." Job 34 : 15: "All flesh shall perish together; and man shall return into ashes."
5 Cf. Exod. 13 : 5. Cf. Roman Missal, Offertory for Thursday in Easter Week.

seminare aurum,[6] ut pluvia viva ascenderet de eo [7] et aqua ipsum calefaciens, ut Senior dicit: Cumque voluerint extrahere hanc aquam divinam, quae est ignis, calefaciunt igne suo, qui est
20 aqua, quem mensurati sunt usque in finem et occultaverunt propter insipientiam fatuorum.[8] Et super hoc iuraverunt omnes philosophi, ne in aliquo loco scriptotenus ponerent lucide, sed attribuerunt glorioso Deo, ut revelaret cui vult et prohiberet a quo vult,[9] quia in ipso est magnum sophisma et obscuritas
25 sapientum. Cumque calor illius ignis ipsi terrae advenerit, solvitur et fit aqua torrens id est vaporans, deinde revertitur ad formam suam priorem terrestrem.[10] Ideo per aquam terra mota est

---

14. est: in M /17. ut: et VD / de eo et aqua: de ipsa aqua MPV / ut: et etc. MP, om. V / 19. quam DML, quem M_2 / 21. propter insipientes MPV / 22. in aliquo loco om. MPV / 23. tribuunt BDLRh / revelet DLRh / voluerit . . . velit DLRh / prohibeat MB / 25. solvetur LRh /

---

[6] Cf. Senior, De chemia, pp. 34–35: "Secundo quod vocat terram benedictam, sitientem, et cinerem, qui est fermentum. Auri aqua est fermentum, et corpora sunt terra eorum, et fermentum huius aquae divinae, est cinis, qui est fermentum fermenti. Quod vocavit Maria sapiens, in quodam loco librorum suorum, Coagulum, cum sit coagulans aquam illorum, in terra eorum, quae est corpus secundum . . . Et de hoc cinere, et de hoc corpore . . . dixit Hermes filio suo: Semina aurum in terra alba foliata." P. 40: "Nominaverunt . . . cinerem . . . et aquam mundam, quia mundata est a tenebris animae." Cf. Pseudo-Aristotle, "Tractatulus," Art. aurif. (1610), I, p. 238: "Terram dealbate, et igne cito sublimate, quousque exeat ex ipsa spiritus quem in ea invenies, qui dicitur avis Hermetis. Hunc cinerem ne vilipendas, quoniam ipse est diadema cordis tui, et permanentium cinis, corona victoriae et coagulum lactis. . . . Hic est ergo cinis extractus a cinere et genitum philosophorum, terra alba foliata in qua seminandum est aurum. Unde dicit Hermes: Extrahe a radio suam umbram et faecem, quae ipsum interficit, et seminate aurum in terra alba foliata . . ." See infra, p. 344, n. 13.
[7] Cf. Senior, De chemia, p. 108: "Et de illo cinere ascendit pluvia viva, et vivificans, quae descendit de coelo . . ." Cf. also pp. 65–66 and p. 38.
[8] Senior, De chemia, pp. 67–68: "Cumque volunt illa(m) extrahere, calefaciunt cum igne suo, quem mensurati sunt illi, et occultaverunt . . ."
[9] Ibid., p. 92: ". . . et hoc est secretum super quo iuraverunt, quod non indicarent in aliquo libro. Nec aliquis eorum declaravit hoc, et attribuerunt illud deo glorioso, ut inspiraret illud cui vellet, et prohibeatur a quo vellet . . ." Cf. also "Cons. coniug.," Ars chem., p. 49 and "De arte chem.," Art. aurif. (1610), I, p. 374.
[10] Cf. "Cons. coniug.," p. 68: ". . . cum invenit illam (scil. aquam congelatam) calor illius ignis, solvitur, et fit aqua currens. Cum autem praeparata fuerit revertitur ad formam suam priorem, et congelatur. . ."

sow gold,[6] that living rains might ascend from it,[7] and water which warmeth it, as Senior saith: And when they desire to extract this divine water, which is fire, they warm it with their fire, which is water, which they have measured unto the end and have hidden on account of the unwisdom of fools.[8] And of this have all the philosophers sworn, that they would nowhere set it forth clearly in writing, but they have left it to the glorious God, to reveal it to whom he will and withhold it from whom he will,[9] for in him is great cunning and the secrecy of the wise. And when the heat of that fire reacheth the earth itself, the earth is dissolved and becometh a boiling, that is an evaporated water, and afterwards returneth to its own former earthly form.[10] Therefore by water is

[6] Cf. Senior, *De chemia*, pp. 34–35: "Secondly, because he calls the blessed and thirsty earth the ash, which is the ferment. The water of gold is the ferment, and the bodies [minerals] are their earth, and the ferment of this divine water is the ash, which is the ferment of the ferment. And Maria the Wise, in a certain place in her books, calls this the Coagulant, since it coagulates the water of those [bodies], in their earth, which is the second body. And of this ash and of this body . . . said Hermes to his son: Sow the gold in the white foliated earth." P. 40: "They named . . . the ash . . . also clear water, for it is purified from the darknesses of the soul." Cf. Pseudo-Aristotle, "Tractatulus," *Art. aurif.* (1610), I, p. 238: "Whiten the earth, and sublime it forthwith with fire, until a spirit go forth from it which thou shalt find in it, which is called Hermes' bird. Despise not this ash, for it is the diadem of thy heart, and the ash of things that endure, the crown of victory and the coagulant of milk. . . . This therefore is the ash extracted from ashes and the thing begotten of the philosophers, the white foliated earth in which the gold is to be sown. Wherefore saith Hermes: Extract from the ray its shadow and the sediment which slayeth it, and sow the gold in the white foliated earth . . ." See infra, p. 344, n. 13.

[7] Senior, *De chemia*, p. 108: "And from the ash there goeth up a living and quickening rain, which cometh down from heaven . . ." See also pp. 65–66 and p. 38.

[8] Senior, *De chemia*, pp. 67–68: "When they desire to extract that [congealed water], they warm it with their [or its] fire, which they have measured out and have hidden . . ."

[9] Ibid., p. 92: ". . . and this is the secret concerning which they swore that they would not reveal it in any book, and none of them has made it known, and they left it to the glorious God to inspire it into whom he would and to withhold it from whom he would . . ." See also "Cons. coniug.," *Ars chem.*, p. 49, and "De arte chem.," *Art. aurif.* (1610), I, p. 374.

[10] Cf. "Cons. coniug.," p. 68: ". . . when the heat of that fire reacheth it [the congealed water], it is loosened and becometh running water. But when it hath been prepared, it returneth to its previous form, and is congealed. . . ."

et coeli distillaverunt super eam [11] et melliflui facti sunt per totum mundum [12] et enarrant gloriam eius.[13] Haec enim gloria
30 soli intelligenti est cognita, quomodo de terra facti sunt coeli,[14] pro eo terra in aeternum permanet et coeli fundantur supra eam, testante Propheta: Qui fundasti terram super stabilitatem suam, non inclinabitur in saeculum saeculi. Abyssus vestimentum eius, super ipsam stabunt aqua, aer, ignis,[15] nec non volucres
35 coeli habitabunt in ea, rigantes ipsam de superioribus elementis, ut de fructu operum ipsorum satiaretur, ut quia in centrum terrae septem planetae radicaverunt et virtutes ibi reliquerunt, unde in terra est aqua germinans diversa genera colorum et fructuum et educens panem et vinum laetificans cor hominis
40 nec non producens foenum iumentis et herbam servituti hominum.[16] Haec inquam terra fecit lunam in tempore suo,[17] deinde ortus est sol [18] valde mane una sabbatorum [19] post tenebras, quas

---

29. et: ut *BDLRh* / 30. quomodo Qño *MP*, quoniam *DL* / 33. declinabitur *MPV* / 34. ipsum *RhL* / et (ignis) *add. DL* / 36. ut: et *BV* / ipsorum: suorum *DLRh* / satiaretur *conj.*, satiabitur *Codd.* / ut quia: utique *B* / 41. In quam terram *MPV* / facit *MPVL* / 42. uno *RhD* /

---

11 Ps. 67 : 9: "Terra mota est, etenim caeli distillaverunt a facie Dei Sinai, a facie Dei Israel." Ps. 96 : 4–5: ". . . vidit et commota est terra. Montes sicut cera fluxerunt a facie Domini . . ." Cf. Isa. 64 : 1.
12 Roman Breviary, Christmas Day, Second Responsory at Mattins: ". . . hodie per totum mundum melliflui facti sunt caeli."
13 Ps. 18 : 2: "Caeli enarrant gloriam Dei . . ."
14 Cf. Prov. 8 : 22–35.
15 Ps. 103 : 5–6: "Qui fundasti terram super stabilitatem suam, non inclinabitur in saeculum saeculi. Abyssus sicut vestimentum amictus eius, super montes stabunt aquae."
16 Ps. 103 : 12–14: "Super ea volucres coeli habitabunt; de medio petrarum dabunt voces. Rigans montes de superioribus suis: de fructu operum tuorum satiabitur terra, producens foenum iumentis, et herbam servituti hominum. Ut educas panem de terra, et vinum laetificet cor hominis."
17 Ps. 103 : 19: "Fecit lunam in tempora, sol cognovit occasum suum."
18 Ps. 103 : 22: "Ortus est sol, et congregati sunt (scil. bestiae), et in cubilibus suis collocabuntur." Cf. *Pret. marg. nov.*, p. 112: "Ex quibus omnibus liquide patet quomodo sol et luna sunt eiusdem naturae et quod luna praecedit solem et ordinatur ad ipsum et quomodo sol est occultus in luna et quomodo de ventre lunae sol extrahitur. Ideo dixit Senior quod sol est oriens in luna crescente."
19 Marc. 16 : 1–2: "Maria Magdalene et Maria Jacobi et Salome emerunt aromata. . . . Et valde mane una sabbatorum veniunt ad monumentum, orto iam sole."

the earth moved and the heavens are poured out upon it,[11] and they flow as if with honey throughout all the world [12] and tell its glory.[13] For this glory is known only to him who hath understanding, how of the earth the heavens were made,[14] and therefore the earth remaineth for ever and the heavens are founded upon it, as the Prophet beareth witness: For thou hast founded the earth upon its own bases, it shall not be moved for ever and ever. The deep is its clothing, above it shall stand water, air, fire,[15] and the birds of the air shall dwell therein, watering it from the upper elements, that it may be filled with the fruit of their works, because in the centre of the earth the seven planets took root, and left their virtues there, wherefore in the earth is water germinating divers kinds of colours and fruits and producing bread and wine that cheereth the heart of man, and also bringing forth grass for cattle and herb for the service of men.[16] This earth, I say, made the moon in its season,[17] then the sun arose,[18] very early in the morning the first day of the week,[19] after the dark-

---

11 Ps. 67 : 9: "The earth was moved, and the heavens dropped at the presence of the God of Sina, at the presence of the God of Israel." Ps. 96 : 4–5: ". . . the earth saw and trembled. The mountains melted like wax, at the presence of the Lord . . ." Cf. Isa. 64 : 1.

12 Roman Breviary, Christmas Day, Second Responsory at Mattins: "Today throughout the whole world the heavens shed down honey."

18 Ps. 18 : 2: "The heavens show forth the glory of God . . ."

14 Cf. Prov. 8 : 22–35.

15 Ps. 103 : 5–6: "Who hast founded the earth upon its own bases, it shall not be moved for ever and ever. The deep like a garment is its clothing; above the mountains shall the waters stand.' '

16 Ps. 103 : 12–14: "Over them [the waters] the birds of the air shall dwell: from the midst of the rocks they shall give forth their voice. Thou waterest the hills from thy upper rooms: the earth shall be filled with the fruit of thy works, bringing forth grass for cattle, and herb for the service of men. That thou mayst bring bread out of the earth and that wine may cheer the heart of man."

17 Ps. 103 : 19: "He made the moon for seasons: the sun knoweth his going down."

18 Ps. 103 : 22: "The sun ariseth, and they (the beasts) are gathered together: and they shall lie down in their dens." Cf. Pret. marg. nov., p. 112: "From all this it appeareth clearly how the sun and the moon are of the same nature and that the moon goeth before the sun and is ordered towards it, and how the sun is hidden in the moon and how the sun is extracted from the body of the moon. Therefore saith Senior, that the sun riseth in the waxing moon."

19 Mark 16 : 1–2: "Mary Magdalen and Mary the mother of James and Salome brought sweet spices. . . . And very early in the morning the first day of the week they came to the sepulchre, the sun being now risen."

posuisti ante ortum solis in ipsa et facta est ⟨nox⟩. In ipsa enim
pertransibunt omnes bestiae silvae,[20] quia terminum posuisti
45 eis, quem non transgredientur [21] usque ad album, sed ordinatione sua perseverant [dies] usque ad rubeum, quia omnia serviunt terrae [22] et dies annorum eius sunt septuaginta anni [23] in-
gredientes super ipsam, quia est portans omnia verbo divinitatis
suae [24] ut in libro Turbae philosophorum scribitur: Terra, cum
50 sit ponderosa, omnia suffert,[25] quoniam est fundamentum totius
coeli, pro eo quod ipsa apparuit arida in elementorum separatione. Deinde via est in mari rubro sine impedimento,[26] quoniam hoc mare magnum et spatiosum [27] percussit petram et
effluxerunt aquae (metallinae), deinde abierunt in sicco flu-
55 mina,[28] quae laetificant civitatem Dei,[29] cum hoc mortale induerit immortalitatem et corruptio vivorum incorruptelam.
Tunc fiet sermo utique qui scriptus est: Absorpta est mors in
victoria, ubi est o mors victoria tua? [30] Ubi abundavit delictum

---

43. nox *conj.* / 44. quia: qua *MPB* / 46. dies *add.* BDLRh / rubrum *P*, album
B / 48. verba *MP* / 51.–52. praeparatione *PV* / 54. fluxerunt *BPV* / metallinae *add.*
RhDL / 57. Abscondita *MPV* / in *om.* MPVRhDL / 58. mortis victoria *D*, haec
mors victoria *L* / o *om.* MPVD / tua *om.* MP /

---

20 Ps. 103 : 20: "Posuisti tenebras, et facta est nox; in ipsa pertransibunt omnes
bestiae silvae . . ."
21 Ps. 103 : 9: ". . . terminum posuisti, quem non transgredientur . . ."
22 Ps. 118 : 91: "Ordinatione tua perseverat dies, quoniam omnia serviunt tibi."
23 Ps. 89 : 10: "Dies annorum nostrorum in ipsis septuaginta anni."
24 Hebr. 1 : 3: "Filio . . . qui cum sit splendor gloriae, et figura substantiae eius,
portansque omnia verbo virtutis suae . . ."
25 *Turba* (ed. Ruska), p. 112: ". . . terra autem cum sit ponderosa et spissa, fert
omnia, quae regit ignis."
26 Sap. 19 : 7: "Nam nubes castra eorum obumbrabat, et ex aqua, quae ante erat,
terra arida apparuit, et in mari rubro via sine impedimento, et campus germinans
de profundo nimio."
27 Ps. 103 : 25: "Hoc mare magnum et spatiosum manibus."
28 Ps. 104 : 41: "Dirupit petram, et fluxerunt aquae, abierunt in sicco flumina
Isa. 48 : 21: "et scidit petram, et fluxerunt aquae."
29 Ps. 45 : 5: "Fluminis impetus laetificat civitatem Dei."
30 I Cor. 15 : 53–55: "Oportet enim corruptibile hoc induere incorruptionem, et
mortale hoc induere immortalitatem. Cum autem mortale hoc induerit immortalitatem, tunc fiet sermo, qui scriptus est: Absorpta est mors in victoria. Ubi
est, mors, victoria tua?"

ness, which thou hast appointed therein before sunrise, and it is (night). For in it shall all the beasts of the wood go about,[20] for thou hast set them a bound which they shall not pass [21] until the whitening, but in their order [the days] go on even until the reddening, for all things serve the earth,[22] and the days of its years are threescore and ten years [23] passing over it, because it upholdeth all things by the word of its godhead,[24] as in the *Turba philosophorum* it is written: The earth, since it is heavy, beareth all things,[25] for it is the foundation of the whole heaven, because it appeared dry at the separation of the elements. Therefore in the Red Sea there was a way without hindrance,[26] since this great and wide sea [27] smote the rock and the (metallic) waters flowed forth. Then the rivers disappeared in dry land,[28] which make the city of God joyful; [29] when this mortal shall put on immortality, and the corruption of the living shall put on incorruption, then indeed shall that word come to pass which is written, Death is swallowed up in victory. O death, where is thy victory? [30] Where

[20] Ps. 103 : 20: "Thou hast appointed darkness, and it is night: in it shall all the beasts of the woods go about . . ."
[21] Ps. 103 : 9: ". . . thou hast set a bound which they shall not pass over . . ."
[22] Ps. 118 : 91: "By thy ordinance the day goeth on: for all things serve thee."
[23] Ps. 89 : 10: "The days of our years in them are three score and ten years."
[24] Hebr. 1 : 3: "By his Son . . . who being the brightness of his glory and the figure of his substance and upholding all things by the word of his power . . ."
[25] *Turba* (ed. Ruska), p. 112: ". . . but the earth, since it is heavy and dense, beareth all things which the fire ruleth."
[26] Wisd. 19 : 7: "For a cloud overshadowed their camp, and where water was before, dry land appeared, and in the Red Sea a way without hindrance, and out of the great deep a springing field."
[27] Ps. 103 : 25: "This great sea which stretcheth wide its arms."
[28] Ps. 104 : 41: "He opened the rock, and waters flowed; rivers ran down in the dry land." Isa. 48 : 21: ". . . and he clove a rock, and the waters gushed out."
[29] Ps. 45 : 5: "The stream of the river maketh the city of God joyful."
[30] I Cor. 15 : 53-55: "For this corruptible must put on incorruption: and this mortal must put on immortality. And when this mortal hath put on immortality, then shall come to pass the saying that is written: Death is swallowed up in victory. O death, where is thy victory? O death, where is thy sting?"

tuum, ibi (nunc) superabundat et gratia.[31] Nam sicut in Adam
60 omnes moriuntur, ita et in Christo omnes [homines] vivificabuntur,[32] quoniam quidem per hominem mors et per [Jesum]
ipsum resurrectio mortuorum advenit.[33] Nam primus Adam et
filii eius de elementis corruptibilibus exordium sumpserunt,
ideo necesse fuit compositum corrumpi, secundus vero Adam,
65 qui dicitur homo philosophicus de puris elementis in aeterni-
tatem transmeavit. Ideo quod ex simplici et pura essentia constat, in aeternum manet.[34] Ut Senior dicit: Est unum, quod
numquam moritur, quoniam augmentatione perpetua perseverat,[35] cum corpus glorificatum fuerit in resurrectione novissima
70 mortuorum, unde fides testatur carnis resurrectionem et vitam
aeternam post mortem.[36] Tunc Adam secundus dicit priori et
filiis suis: Venite benedicti patris mei, percipite regnum aeternum, quod vobis paratum est ab origine operationis,[37] et come-

---

59. nunc *add. MP* / abundat *RhL* / et *om. MPV* / 60. et *om. PL* / et in: de *M* /
homines *add. MP* / 61. ipsum: Jesum *MPVRh* / 66. quod: quia *D, om. M* / 67.
unum: vivum *RhL* / 68. augmentatio *MPV* / 70. unde: ut *RhLD* / 73. reparationis
VPD, temperationis *M,* mundi *scil.* operationis *B* /

---

[31] Rom. 5 : 20: ". . . Ubi autem abundavit delictum, superabundavit gratia."

[32] I Cor. 15 : 22: "Et sicut in Adam omnes moriuntur, ita et in Christo omnes
vivificabuntur."

[33] I Cor. 15 : 21: "Quoniam quidem per hominem mors, et per hominem resurrectio mortuorum."

[34] Cf. I Cor. 15 : 45–47: "Factus est primus homo Adam in animam viventem,
novissimus Adam in spiritum vivificantem. . . . Primus homo de terra, terrenus:
secundus homo de coelo, coelestis." Cf. *Turba,* pp. 115–16: "Ex quatuor autem
elementis pater noster Adam et filii eius, (scil.) ex igne, aere, aqua simul et terra
creati sunt. Intelligite, omnes sapientes, quod omne, quod ex una creavit Deus
essentia, non moritur usque in diem iudicii. Mortis enim definitio est compositi
disiunctio . . . ex duobus autem, tribus vel quatuor unumquodque compositum
separari necesse est, quod est mors."

[35] Senior, *De chemia,* pp. 71–72: "Item unum quod non moritur, quam diu fuerit
mundus, et vivificat quodlibet mortuum." Cf. also "Cons. coniug.," p. 66.

[36] Apost. Creed: "Et exspecto resurrectionem mortuorum. Et vitam venturi
saeculi. Amen."

[37] Matth. 25 : 34: "Tunc dicet rex his, qui a dextris eius erunt: Venite benedicti
Patris mei, possidete paratum vobis regnum a constitutione mundi." Cited as
concluding sentence in Pseudo-Aristotle, "De perfecto magisterio," *Theatr. chem.*
(1659), III, p. 127.

thy sin abounded, there (now) grace doth more abound.[31] For as in Adam all die, so also in Christ all [men] shall be made alive.[32] For by a man indeed came death, and by [Jesus] himself the resurrection of the dead.[33] For the first Adam and his sons took their beginning from the corruptible elements, and therefore it was needful that the composed should be corrupted, but the second Adam, who is called the philosophic man, from pure elements entered into eternity. Therefore what is composed of simple and pure essence, remaineth for ever.[34] As Senior saith: There is One thing, that never dieth, for it continueth by perpetual increase,[35] when the body shall be glorified in the final resurrection of the dead, wherefore the Creed beareth witness to the resurrection of the flesh and eternal life after death.[36] Then saith the second Adam to the first and to his sons: Come, ye blessed of my Father, possess you the eternal kingdom prepared for you from the beginning of the Work,[37] and eat my bread and

31 Rom. 5 : 20: "And where sin abounded, grace did more abound."

32 I Cor. 15 : 22: "And as in Adam all die, so also in Christ shall all be made alive."

33 I Cor. 15 : 21: "For by a man came death, and by a man the resurrection of the dead."

34 I Cor. 15 : 45–47: "The first man Adam was made into a living soul: the last Adam into a quickening spirit . . . The first man was of the earth, earthly; the second man from heaven, heavenly." Cf. *Turba*, pp. 115–16: "But out of the four elements was our father Adam and his sons created, that is, out of fire, air, water, and earth. Understand, all ye who are wise, that all which God created from one essence dieth not until doomsday. For death is defined as the disjunction of the composite . . . each thing that is composed out of two, three, or four must needs be separated, and that is death."

35 Senior, *De chemia*, pp. 71–72: "Moreover there is one thing which dieth not, so long as the world endureth, and it bringeth to life all that is dead." Cf. also "Cons. coniug.," p. 66.

36 Apostles' Creed: "And I expect the resurrection of the dead, and the life of the world to come. Amen."

37 Matt. 25 : 34: "Then shall the king say to them that be on his right hand: Come, ye blessed of my Father, possess you the kingdom prepared for you from the foundation of the world." Cited as concluding sentence in Pseudo-Aristotle, "De perfecto magisterio," *Theatr. chem.* (1659), III, p. 127.

dite panem meum et bibite vinum, quod miscui vobis,[38] quia
75 parata sunt vobis omnia. Qui habet aures audiendi audiat, quid
dicat spiritus doctrinae filiis disciplinae de Adam terreno et
Adam coelesti, quod philosophi insinuant his verbis: Quando
habueris aquam de terra, aerem de aqua, ignem de aere, terram
de igne, tunc plene habes artem (nostram) et perfecte (etc.).[39]

---

74. vobis *om. RhL* / 76. de *om. MPV* / 77. innuunt *MP* / 79. nostram *add. DLRh* /
et perfecte *om. MPVDB* / etc. *add. Rh.* /

---

[38] Prov. 9 : 4–5: "Et insipientibus locuta est (Sapientia): Venite, comedite panem
meum, et bibite vinum, quod miscui vobis."
[39] Cf. Pseudo-Aristotle, *Secreta secretorum* (1528), fol. xxvii, "De proprietatibus originalium lapidum": "Quum igitur habueris aquam de aere et aerem ex igne et
ignem ex terra, tunc habebis plene artem." Cf. "Ros. phil.," p. 101b: "De istis
quatuor elementis dicit Aristoteles in libro de regimine principiorum: Cum
habueris aquam ex aere, et aerem ex igne, et ignem ex terra, tunc plenam
habebis artem Philosophiae: et hic est finis primae compositionis."

drink the wine which I have mingled for you,[38] for all things are made ready for you. He that hath ears to hear, let him hear what the spirit of the doctrine saith to the sons of the discipline concerning the earthly and the heavenly Adam, which the philosophers treat of in these words: When thou hast water from earth, air from water, fire from air, earth from fire, then shalt thou fully and perfectly possess (our) art (etc.).[39]

[38] Prov. 9 : 4–5: "And to the unwise she (Wisdom) saith: Come, eat of my bread, and drink the wine which I have mingled for you."

[39] Cf. Pseudo-Aristotle, *Secreta secretorum* (1528): fol. xxvii: "De proprietatibus originalium lapidum": "Thus when you have water from air and air from fire and fire from earth, then you have the fulness of the art." Cf. "Ros. phil.," p. 101b: "Of these four elements saith Aristotle in his book of the Regimen of the Principles: When you have water from air, and air from fire, and fire from earth, then you have the whole art of philosophy; and this is the end of the first composition."

PARABOLA SEPTIMA DE CONFABULATIONE
DILECTI CUM DILECTA

"Convertimini ad me in toto corde vestro [1] et nolite abiicere me, eo quod nigra sum et fusca, quia decoloravit me sol [2] et abyssi operuerunt faciem meam [3] et terra infecta et contaminata est in operibus meis; [4] quia tenebrae factae sunt super eam [5] pro eo, quod infixa sum in limo profundi et substantia mea non est aperta.[6] Propterea de profundis clamavi [7] et de abysso terrae voce mea ad vos omnes, qui transitis per viam. Attendite et videte me, si quis similem mihi invenerit,[8] dabo in manu sua stellam matutinam.[9] Ecce enim in lectulo meo per noctem

---

5. in *om. MP* / 6. operationibus *D* / 9. vos: eos *MP* /

---

[1] Joel 2 : 12: "Nunc ergo, dicit Dominus: Convertimini ad me in toto corde vestro, in ieiunio et in fletu et in planctu."

[2] Cant. 1 : 4–5: "Nigra sum, sed formosa, filiae Jerusalem, sicut tabernacula Cedar, sicut pelles Salomonis. Nolite me considerare, quod fusca sim, quia decoloravit me sol; filii matris meae pugnaverunt contra me . . ."

[3] Cf. Jona 2 : 6: "Circumdederunt me aquae usque ad animam; abyssus vallavit me, pelagus operuit caput meum . . ."

[4] Ps. 105 : 38: "Et infecta est terra in sanguinibus; et contaminata est in operibus eorum . . ."

[5] Luc. 23 : 44: ". . . et tenebrae factae sunt in universam terram . . ." Cf. Marc. 15 : 33.

[6] Ps. 68 : 3: "Infixus sum in limo profundi et non est substantia. Veni in altitudinem maris, et tempestas demersit me."

[7] Ps. 129 : 1: "De profundis clamavi ad te, Domine; Domine, exaudi vocem meam."

[8] Thren. 1 : 12: "O vos omnes qui transitis per viam, attendite, et videte si est dolor sicut dolor meus . . ."

[9] Apoc. 2 : 28: ". . . dabo illi stellam matutinam . . ."

XII

THE SEVENTH PARABLE: OF THE CONFABULATION
OF THE LOVER WITH THE BELOVED

⁶⁸ "Be turned to me with all your heart [1] and do not cast me aside because I am black and swarthy, because the sun hath changed my colour [2] and the waters have covered my face [3] and the earth hath been polluted and defiled in my works; [4] for there was darkness over it, [5] because I stick fast in the mire of the deep and my substance is not disclosed. [6] Wherefore out of the depths have I cried, [7] and from the abyss of the earth with my voice to all you that pass by the way. Attend and see me, if any shall find one like unto me, [8] I will give into his hand the morning star. [9] For behold

---

1 Joel 2 : 12: "Now therefore saith the Lord: Be converted to me with all your heart, in fasting and in weeping and in mourning."

2 Cant. 1 : 4–5: "I am black but beautiful, O ye daughters of Jerusalem, as the tents of Cedar, as the curtains of Solomon. Do not consider me that I am brown, because the sun hath altered my colour; the sons of my mother have fought against me."

3 Cf. Jonah 2 : 6: "The waters compassed me about even to the soul; the deep hath closed me round about, the sea hath covered my head."

4 Ps. 105 : 38: "And the land was polluted with blood, and was defiled with their works."

5 Luke 23 : 44: ". . . and there was darkness over all the earth." Cf. Mark 15 : 33.

6 Ps. 68 : 3: "I stick fast in the mire of the deep: and there is no sure standing. I am come into the depth of the sea, and the tempest hath overwhelmed me."

7 Ps. 129 : 1: "Out of the depths have I cried to thee, O Lord: Lord, hear my voice."

8 Lam. 1 : 12: "O all ye that pass by the way, attend, and see if there is any sorrow like to my sorrow."

9 Apoc. 2 : 28: ". . . and I will give him the morning star."

quaesivi consolantem et non inveni,[10] vocavi et nemo respondit mihi."—"Surgam ergo et introibo civitatem; per vicos et plateas quaerens [11] mihi unam desponsare virginem castam,[12] pulchram
15 facie, pulchriorem corpore, pulcherrimam veste,[13] ut revolvat lapidem ab ostio monumenti mei [14] et dabit mihi pennas sicut columbae et volabo cum ea in coelo [15] et dicam tunc: Vivo ego in aeternum [16] et requiescam in ea, quia astitit [regina] a dextris meis in vestitu deaurato circumdata varietate. Audi ergo filia
20 et vide et inclina aurem tuam ad preces meas, quia concupivi toto cordis desiderio speciem tuam.[17] O locutus sum in lingua mea, notum fac mihi finem meum et numerum dierum meorum quis est, ut sciam quid desit mihi, quoniam mensurabiles posuisti omnes dies meos et substantia mea tamquam nihilum ante
25 te.[18] Tu es enim ipsa, quae introibit per aurem, per regionem

---

12. non: neminem *MP* / 15. facie pulchriorem corpore pulcherrimam *om.* *MP* / revolvet *PVRhL* / 16. dabo *MPV* / 18. regina *add.* *BD* / 24. meos: tuos *RhBDL* / 25. aurem: auream portam *D* /

---

[10] Ps. 68 : 21: "Et sustinui, qui simul contristaretur, et non fuit, et qui consolaretur, et non inveni . . ."
[11] Cant. 3 : 1–2: "In lectulo meo per noctes quaesivi quem diligit anima mea; quaesivi illum et non inveni. Surgam, et circuibo civitatem, per vicos et plateas quaeram quem diligit anima mea; quaesivi illum, et non inveni."
[12] II Cor. 11 : 2: "Despondi enim vos uni viro virginem castam exhibere Christo."
[13] Cf. Dominican Breviary (pre-1961), Feast of St. Agnes, Eighth Responsory at Mattins: "Pulchra facie, sed pulchrior fide, beata es, virgo."
[14] Marc. 16 : 3: "Et dicebant ad invicem: Quis revolvet nobis lapidem ab ostio monumenti? . . ."
[15] Ps. 54 : 7: "Et dixi: Quis dabit mihi pennas sicut columbae, et volabo et requiescam?" Cf. *Pret. marg. nov.*, p. 123: "Et quia foemina est alba fugiens . . . masculus vero est rubeus persequens foeminam fugientem et ipsam rapiens et retinens . . . dixerunt: Foemina habet alas, masculus vero non." Cf. also Senior, *De chemia,* p. 33.
[16] Deut. 32 : 40: "Levabo ad coelum manum meam, et dicam: Vivo ego in aeternum . . ."
[17] Ps. 44 : 10–11: "Astitit regina a dextris tuis in vestitu deaurato, circumdata varietate. Audi, filia, et vide, et inclina aurem tuam . . . et concupiscet rex decorem tuum, (quia concupivit Rex speciem tuam)." Cf. Roman Missal, Tract for First Mass (*Dilexisti*) of a Virgin not a Martyr.
[18] Ps. 38 : 5–6: "Locutus sum in lingua mea: Notum fac mihi, Domine, finem meum, et numerum dierum meorum quis est, ut sciam quid desit mihi. Ecce mensurabiles posuisti dies meos, et substantia mea tamquam nihilum est ante te."

in my bed by night I sought one to comfort me and I found none,[10] I called and there was none to answer me."—"Therefore will I arise and go into the city, seeking in the streets and broad ways [11] a chaste virgin to espouse,[12] comely in face, more comely in body, most comely in her garments,[13] that she may roll back the stone from the door of my sepulchre [14] and give me wings like a dove, and I will fly with her into heaven [15] and then say: I live for ever,[16] and will rest in her, for she [the queen] stood on my right hand in gilded clothing, surrounded with variety. Hearken therefore O daughter and see and incline thine ear to my prayers, for I have desired thy beauty with all the desire of my heart.[17] O I spoke with my tongue: Make known to me my end and what is the number of my days, that I may know what is wanting to me, for thou hast made all my days measurable and my substance is as nothing before thee.[18] For thou art she who shall enter through the ear, through my domain, and I shall be clothed with a purple

---

[10] Ps. 68 : 21: "And I looked for one that would grieve together with me, and there was none: and for one that would comfort me, and I found none."

[11] Cant. 3 : 1–2: "In my bed by night I sought him whom my soul loveth: I sought him, and found him not. I will rise and go about the city. In the streets and the broad ways I will seek him whom my soul loveth. I sought him, and I found him not."

[12] II Cor. 11 : 2: "I have espoused you to one husband, that I may present you as a chaste virgin to Christ."

[13] Cf. Dominican Breviary (pre-1961), Feast of St. Agnes, Eighth Responsory at Mattins: "Comely in face, yet more comely in faith, blessed art thou, O maiden."

[14] Mark 16 : 3: "And they said one to another: Who shall roll us back the stone from the door of the sepulchre?"

[15] Ps. 54 : 7: "And I said: Who will give me wings like a dove, and I will fly and be at rest?" Cf. *Pret. marg. nov.*, p. 123: "And because the white woman escapeth . . . but the red male followeth after the woman and holdeth her . . . they (the philosophers) said: The woman hath wings, but the man not." Cf. also Senior, *De chemia*, p. 33.

[16] Deut. 32 : 40: "I will lift up my hand to heaven: and I will say: I live for ever . . ."

[17] Ps. 44 : 10–11: "The queen stood on thy right hand, in gilded clothing: surrounded with variety. Hearken, O daughter, and see, and incline thy ear. . . . And the king shall greatly desire thy beauty" (Lit.: "for the king hath greatly desired thy appearance"). Cf. Roman Missal, Tract for First Mass (*Dilexisti*) of a Virgin not a Martyr.

[18] Ps. 38 : 5–6: "I spoke with my tongue: O Lord, make me know my end, and what is the number of my days, that I may know what is wanting to me. Behold, thou hast made my days measurable: and my substance is as nothing before thee."

meam, et ero indutus stola purpurea [19] ex te et ex me procedam tamquam sponsus de thalamo suo,[20] quia circumdabis me vernantibus atque coruscantibus gemmis et indues me vestimentis salutis et laetitiae [21] ad expugnandas gentes et omnes inimicos,
30 nec non corona aurea expressa signo sanctitatis me ornabis et stola iustitiae circumdabis me [22] atque annulo tuo subarrabis me [23] nec non calceamentis aureis calceabis me. Haec omnia faciet amica mea perfecta, pulchra nimis et decora in deliciis suis,[24] quia viderunt eam filiae Sion et reginae atque concu-
35 binae eam laudaverunt.[25] O regina supernorum, surge propera (amica mea) sponsa mea,[26] dic [dilecta] dilecto tuo, quae qualis vel quanta es, propter Sion non tacebis nec propter Jerusalem quiescas [27] loquere mihi, audit (te) enim dilectus tuus."—"Audite

---

27. quae circumdabit *MPV*, circumdas *L* / 28. induens *B*, indueris *V* / vestimento *RhD* / 29. ex purgandas *RhD*, pugnandas *L* / gentes et omnium gentium et nationum (*D:* hoc loco) inimicos nec non corona *RhLD*, om. *P* / et (inimicos) add. *M* / 31. iustitiae om. *MPV* / 31.–32.atque annulo ∼ calceabis me om. *MPV* / concubinae *V₂*, columbinae *MPV*, columbae *RhDL*, om. *B* / 36. amica mea add. *D* / dilecta add. *RhL* / 38. te add. *D* / loquere quae audit dilecto tuo *MPV*, cetera om. *MP* / (Audite) haec add. *VL* /

---

[19] Cf. infra, p. 371, nn. 45 and 47.

[20] Ps. 18 : 6: "In sole posuit tabernaculum suum; et ipse tamquam sponsus procedens de thalamo suo."

[21] Cf. Roman Breviary (pre-1961), Feast of St. Agnes, Fourth Responsory at Mattins: "Induit me Dominus vestimento salutis, et indumento laetitiae circumdedit me . . . circumdedit me vernantibus atque coruscantibus gemmis." Isa. 61 : 10: "Gaudens gaudebo in Domino . . . quia induit me vestimentis salutis, et indumento iustitiae circumdedit me, quasi sponsum decoratum corona, et quasi sponsam ornatam monilibus suis."

[22] Ecclus. 45 : 14: "Corona aurea super mitram eius expressa signo sanctitatis, et gloria honoris . . ."

[23] Cf. Roman Breviary, Feast of St. Agnes, Third Antiphon at Lauds: "Anulo suo subarrhavit me Dominus meus Jesus Christus."

[24] Cant. 7 : 6: "Quam pulchra es et quam decora, charissima, in deliciis!"

[25] Cant. 6 : 8: ". . . Viderunt eam filiae et beatissimam praedicaverunt, reginae et concubinae, et laudaverunt eam."

[26] Cant. 2 : 10: "En dilectus meus loquitur mihi: Surge, propera, amica mea, columba mea . . ."

[27] Isa. 62 : 1: "Propter Sion non tacebo, et propter Jerusalem non quiescam, donec egrediatur ut splendor iustus eius . . ."

garment [19] from thee and from me, I will come forth as a bride-groom out of his bride-chamber,[20] for thou shalt adorn me round about with shining and glittering gems and shalt clothe me with the garments of salvation and joy [21] to overthrow the nations and all mine enemies, and shalt adorn me with a crown of gold engraved with the sign of holiness and shalt clothe me with a robe of righteousness [22] and shalt betroth me to thee with thy ring [23] and clothe my feet in sandals of gold. All this shall my perfect beloved do, exceeding beautiful and comely in her delights,[24] for the daughters of Sion saw her and the queens and concubines praised her.[25] O queen of the heights, arise, make haste, (my love), my spouse,[26] speak [beloved] to thy lover, who and of what kind and how great thou art, for Sion's sake thou shalt not hold thy peace and for the sake of Jerusalem thou shalt not rest [27] from speaking to me, for thy beloved heareth (thee)."—"Hear all ye

---

[19] Cf. infra, p. 371, nn. 45 and 47.

[20] Ps. 18 : 6: "He hath set his tabernacle in the sun: and he, as a bridegroom coming out of his bridechamber. . . ."

[21] Cf. Roman Breviary (pre-1961), Feast of St. Agnes, Fourth Responsory at Mattins: "The Lord hath clothed me with the garment of salvation, and hath vested me with the robe of gladness; . . . he hath surrounded me with shining and glittering gems." Isa. 61 : 10: "I will greatly rejoice in the Lord, and my soul shall be joyful in my God. For he hath clothed me with the garments of salvation and with the robe of justice he hath covered me: as a bridegroom decked with a crown and as a bride adorned with her jewels."

[22] Ecclus. 45 : 14: "And a crown of gold upon his mitre, wherein was engraved Holiness, an ornament of honour . . ."

[23] Roman Breviary, Feast of St. Agnes, Third Antiphon at Lauds: "With the ring of his faith hath he betrothed me."

[24] Cant. 7 : 6: "How beautiful art thou, and how comely, my dearest, in delights!"

[25] Cant. 6 : 8: ". . . The daughters of Sion saw her and declared her most blessed; the queens and concubines, and they praised her.''

[26] Cant. 2 : 10: "Behold, my beloved speaketh to me: Arise, make haste, my love, my dove . . .''

[27] Isa. 62 : 1: "For Sion's sake I will not hold my peace, and for the sake of Jerusalem I will not rest till her just one come forth as brightness."

omnes gentes, auribus percipite, qui habitatis orbem: [28] dilectus
40 meus rubicundus locutus est [29] mihi, petiit et impetravit. Ego
sum flos campi et lilium convallium,[30] ego mater pulchrae dilectionis et [timoris et] agnitionis et sanctae spei.[31] Ego vitis fructi-
ficans suavitatem odoris, et flores mei fructus honoris et honestatis.[32] Ego lectulus dilecti mei, quem sexaginta fortissimi am-
45 bierunt, omnes tenentes gladios suos super femur suum propter
timores nocturnales.[33] Ego tota pulchra et absque macula [34] respiciens per fenestras prospiciens per cancellos dilecti mei,[35] vulner-
ans cor suum in uno oculorum meorum et uno crine colli mei.[36]
Ego odor unguentorum super omnia aromata [37] aromatizans et si-
50 cut cinnamomum et balsamum et myrrha electa.[38] Ego virgo pru-
dentissima [39] progrediens quasi aurora valde rutilans electa ut sol
et pulchra ut Luna [40] absque quod intrinsecus latet.[41] Ego cedrus

---

42. timoris add. V / 44. Sexaginta: se MP, om. B / 48. uno: ictu RhDL / meo MP /

---

[28] Ps. 48 : 2: "Audite haec, omnes Gentes; auribus percipite, omnes qui habitatis orbem . . ."

[29] Cant. 5 : 10: "Dilectus meus candidus et rubicundus, electus ex millibus."

[30] Cant. 2 : 1: "Ego flos campi et lilium convallium, sicut lilium inter spinas . . ."

[31] Ecclus. 24 : 24: (Sapientia loquitur): "Ego mater pulchrae dilectionis, et timoris, et agnitionis, et sanctae spei . . ."

[32] Ecclus. 24 : 23: "Ego quasi vitis fructificavi suavitatem odoris, et flores mei fructus honoris et honestatis." Cf. Joh. 15 : 1: "Ego sum vitis vera . . ."

[33] Cant. 3 : 7-8: "En lectulum Salomonis sexaginta fortes ambiunt ex fortissimis Israel, omnes tenentes gladios, uniuscuiusque ensis super femur suum propter timores nocturnos . . ."

[34] Cant. 4 : 7: "Tota pulchra es, amica mea, et macula non est in te." Cf. Roman Missal, Gradual for the Immaculate Conception: "Tota pulchra es, Maria, et macula originalis non est in te."

[35] Cant. 2 : 9: ". . . en ipse stat post parietem nostrum, respiciens per fenestras, prospiciens per cancellos."

[36] Cant. 4 : 9: Vulnerasti cor meum, soror mea, sponsa . . . in uno oculorum tuorum et in uno crine colli tui."

[37] Cf. Cant. 4 : 10: "Odor unguentorum tuorum super omnia aromata."

[38] Ecclus. 24 : 20: "Sicut cinnamomum et balsamum aromatizans odorem dedi, quasi myrrha electa dedi suavitatem odoris."

[39] Cf. Matth. 25 : 1-13.

[40] Cant. 6 : 9: "Quae est ista quae progreditur quasi aurora consurgens, pulchra ut luna, electa ut sol . . ."

[41] Cant. 4 : 1: ". . . Oculi tui columbarum, absque eo quod intrinsecus latet."

nations, give ear all ye inhabitants of the world; [28] my beloved, who is ruddy, hath spoken to me,[29] he hath sought and besought. I am the flower of the field and the lily of the valleys,[30] I am the mother of fair love and [of fear and] of knowledge and of holy hope.[31] As the fruitful vine I have brought forth a pleasant odour, and my flowers are the fruit of honour and riches.[32] I am the bed of my beloved, which threescore of the most valiant ones surrounded, all holding swords upon their thigh because of fears in the night.[33] I am all fair and there is no spot in me; [34] looking through the windows, looking through the lattices of my beloved,[35] wounding his heart with one of my eyes and with one hair of my neck.[36] I am the sweet smell of ointments giving an odour above all aromatical spices [37] and like unto cinnamon and balsam and chosen myrrh.[38] I am the most prudent virgin [39] coming forth as the Dawn, shining exceedingly, elect as the sun, fair as the moon,[40] besides what is hid within.[41] I am exalted as a cedar

[28] Ps. 48 : 2: "Hear these things, all ye nations: give ear, all ye inhabitants of the world."

[29] Cant. 5 : 10: "My beloved is white and ruddy, chosen out of thousands."

[30] Cant. 2 : 1: "I am the flower of the field, and the lily of the valleys. As the lily among thorns . . ."

[31] Ecclus. 24 : 24: (Wisdom speaks): "I am the mother of fair love, and of fear, and of knowledge, and of holy hope."

[32] Ecclus. 24 : 23: "As the vine I have brought forth a pleasant odour: and my flowers are the fruit of honour and riches." Cf. John 15 : 1: "I am the true vine . . ."

[33] Cant. 3 : 7–8: "Behold three score valiant ones of the most valiant of Israel surrounded the bed of Solomon: all holding swords, and most expert in war: every man's sword upon his thigh, because of fears in the night. . . ."

[34] Cant. 4 : 7: "Thou art all fair, O my love, and there is not a spot in thee." Cf. Roman Missal, Gradual for the Immaculate Conception: "Thou art all fair, O Mary, and there is in thee no stain of original sin."

[35] Cant. 2 : 9: "Behold he standeth behind our wall, looking through the windows, looking through the lattices."

[36] Cant. 4 : 9: "Thou hast wounded my heart, my sister, my spouse . . . with one of thine eyes and with one hair of thy neck."

[37] Cant. 4 : 10: "The sweet smell of thy ointments (is) above all aromatical spices."

[38] Ecclus. 24 : 20: "I gave a sweet smell like cinnamon and aromatical balm; I yielded a sweet odour like the best myrrh."

[39] Cf. Matt. 25 : 1–13.

[40] Cant. 6 : 9: "Who is she that cometh forth as the morning rising, fair as the moon, bright as the sun?"

[41] Cant. 4 : 1: "Thy eyes are doves' eyes, besides what is hid within."

exaltata et cypressus in monte Sion,[42] ego corona, qua coronatur dilectus meus in die desponsationis ipsius et laetitiae,[43] quia
55 unguentum effusum est nomen meum.[44] Ego funda David, cuius lapis Goliae magnum oculum (eruit) et caput eius demum abstulit.[45] Ego sceptrum domus Israel[46] et clavis Jesse,[47] qui aperit et nemo claudit, claudit et nemo aperit.[48] Ego sum illa vinea electa, in quam pater familias misit hora prima, secunda, tertia,
60 sexta et nona operarios suos dicens: Ite et vos in vineam meam et quod iustum fuerit dabo vobis hora duodecima.[49] Ego sum illa terra sanctae promissionis, quae fluit lacte et melle[50] et faciens fructus suavissimos temporibus suis; quare omnes philosophi me commendaverunt et seminaverunt in me aurum
65 eorum et argentum et granum ipsorum incombustibile. Et nisi granum illud cadens in me mortuum fuerit, ipsum solum mane-

---

54. meus *om. MP* / quia sicut *add. BD* / 55.–56. cuius lapis Goliae: quare *MP*, quia *V* / 56. eruit *add. D* / demum: denique *P*, demumque *M, om. V* / de domo *MPV* / 59. qua *PRhLM* / 61. duodecima *conj.*, secunda *DRhL*, nona *MPV, om. B* / 62. sancta *RhDL* / 63. (fructus) suos *add. MP* / quare: quia *RhDL* / 64. in me *om. LV* / 66.–67. ipsum solum ∼ fuerit *om. VLBM, corr. M₂* /

---

[42] Ecclus. 24 : 17: "Quasi cedrus exaltata sum in Libano, et quasi cypressus in monte Sion."

[43] Cant. 3 : 11: "Egredimini et videte, filiae Sion, regem Salomonem in diademate quo coronavit illum mater sua . . . in die desponsationis illius, et in die laetitiae cordis eius." ("Parans crucem Salvatori suo.") Appendix (pre-1961) to Roman Missal, Mass of the Crown of Thorns.

[44] Cant. 1 : 2: "Oleum effusum nomen tuum . . ."

[45] Cf. I Samuel 17 : 49–51.

[46] Cf. Roman Breviary, Antiphon at Magnificat for December 20: "O clavis David, et sceptrum domus Israel, qui aperis et nemo claudit, claudis et nemo aperit."

[47] Cf. Isa. 11 : 1: "Et egredietur virga de radice Jesse, et flos de radice eius . . ." Cf. Rom. 15 : 4–13. Cf. Senior, *De chemia*, p. 10: "Sol est clavis cuiuslibet ianuae . . ." Cf. also p. 17.

[48] Apoc. 3 : 7: ". . . Qui habet clavem David, qui aperit et nemo claudit, claudit et nemo aperit."

[49] Cf. Matth. 20 : 1ff.

[50] Exod. 13 : 5: "Cumque introduxerit te Dominus in terram . . . fluentem lacte et melle." Cf. Exod. 3 : 8: ". . . et educam in terram, quae fluit lacte et melle . . ," Cf. Deut. 26 : 1–11.

and a cypress tree on Mount Sion,[42] I am the crown wherewith my beloved is crowned in the day of his espousals and of his joy,[43] for my name is as ointment poured forth.[44] I am the sling of David, the stone wherefrom (tore out) the great eye of Goliath and finally took off his head.[45] I am the sceptre of the house of Israel [46] and the key of Jesse,[47] which openeth and no man shutteth, shutteth and no man openeth.[48] I am that chosen vineyard, into which the householder sent his labourers at the first, second, third, sixth, and ninth hours, saying: Go you also into my vineyard, and at the twelfth hour I will give you what shall be just.[49] I am that land of the holy promise, which floweth with milk and honey [50] and bringeth forth sweetest fruit in due season; wherefore have all the philosophers commended me and sowed in me their gold and silver and incombustible grain. And unless that grain falling into me die, itself shall remain alone, but if it die,

[42] Ecclus. 24 : 17: "I was exalted like a cedar in Libanus, and as a cypress tree on mount Sion."

[43] Cant. 3 : 11: "Go forth, ye daughters of Sion, and see King Solomon in the diadem wherewith his mother crowned him in the day of his espousals, and in the day of the joy of his heart." ("Preparing a cross for her Saviour.") Appendix (pre-1961) to Roman Missal, Mass of the Crown of Thorns.

[44] Cant. 1 : 2: "Thy name is as oil poured forth . . ."

[45] Cf. I Samuel 17 : 49–51.

[46] Roman Breviary, Antiphon at Magnificat for December 20: "O key of David and sceptre of the house of Israel, who openest and no man shutteth, shuttest and no man openeth."

[47] Cf. Isa. 11 : 1: "And there shall come forth a rod out of the root of Jesse: and a flower shall rise up out of his root . . ." Cf. Rom. 15 : 4–13. Cf. Senior, *De chemia*, p. 10: "The Sun is the key to every door. . . ." Cf. also p. 17.

[48] Apoc. 3 : 7: ". . . he that hath the key of David, he that openeth and no man shutteth, shutteth and no man openeth . . ."

[49] Cf. Matt. 20 : 1ff.

[50] Exod. 13 : 5: "And when the Lord shall have brought thee into . . . a land that floweth with milk and honey." Cf. Exod. 3 : 8: "to bring them . . . into a land that floweth with milk and honey . . ." Cf. Deut. 26 : 1–11.

bit, si autem mortuum fuerit affert fructum triplicem: [51] primum quidem faciet bonum in terram bonam, scilicet margaritarum, secundum bonum quia in meliorem scilicet foliorum, 70 tertium in millecuplum quia in terram optimam scilicet auri.[52] Ex his enim fructibus grani (huius) cibus vitae conficitur, qui de coelo descendit. Si quis ex eo manducaverit, vivet sine fame.[53] De illo namque pane edent pauperes et saturabuntur et laudabunt Dominum, qui requirunt eum et vivent corda eorum in 75 saeculum.[54] Ergo do et non resumo, ego pasco et non deficio, ego securo et non paveo, quid plus referam dilecto meo? Ego sum mediatrix elementorum, concordans unum alteri: illud, quod calidum est frigesco et viceversa, et illud, quod siccum est humecto et viceversa, et illud, quod est durum mollifico et 80 viceversa. Ego finis et dilectus meus principium,[55] ego totum opus et tota scientia in me occultatur,[56] ego lex in sacerdote et sermo in propheta et consilium in sapiente.[57] Ego occidam et vivere faciam et non est, qui de manu mea possit eruere.[58] Ego

---

71. huius *add. RhB* / 72. et (sine) *add. MP* / 73. illa *PL* / 74. requirent *RhL* / 74.–75. in saeculum *om. MPV* / 76. saturo *MP* / 79. durum mollifico: asperum lenifico *MPV* / 81. ego: et *MP* /

---

[51] Joh. 12 : 24–25: "Amen, amen, dico vobis: nisi granum frumenti cadens in terram mortuum fuerit, ipsum solum manet; si autem mortuum fuerit, multum fructum affert."

[52] Cf. Senior, *De chemia*, p. 51: "Quidam vero eorum nomina variant, ut hoc, Ex tribus terris, Quarum prima est margaritarum, secunda terra foliorum, tertia terra est terra auri." Cf. also p. 106.

[53] Joh. 6 : 33: "Panis enim Dei est, qui de coelo descendit et dat vitam mundo." Joh. 6 : 51–52: "Ego sum panis vivus, qui de caelo descendi. Si quis manducaverit ex hoc pane, vivet in aeternum." Cf. Ps. 77 : 24–25.

[54] Ps. 21 : 27: "Edent pauperes, et saturabuntur, et laudabunt Dominum qui requirunt eum; vivent corda eorum in saeculum saeculi."

[55] Apoc. 1 : 8: "Ego sum Alpha et Omega, principium et finis, dicit Dominus Deus . . ."

[56] Cf. Mercurius in Rhazis, *De alum. et salibus* (ed. Ruska), p. 59: "Et ego sum totum ipsum absconditum et in me sapientia latet abscondita."

[57] Jer. 18 : 18: ". . . non enim peribit lex a sacerdote, neque consilium a sapiente, neque sermo a propheta."

[58] Deut. 32 : 39: "Videte quod ego sim solus, et non sit alius Deus praeter me; Ego occidam, et ego vivere faciam; percutiam, et ego sanabo; et non est qui de manu mea possit eruere."

it bringeth forth threefold fruit: [51] for the first it shall bring forth shall be good because it was sown in good earth, namely of pearls; the second likewise good because it was sown in better earth, namely of leaves (silver); the third shall bring forth a thousand-fold because it was sown in the best earth, namely of gold.[52] For from the fruits of (this) grain is made the food of life, which cometh down from heaven. If any man shall eat of it, he shall live without hunger.[53] For of that bread the poor shall eat and shall be filled, and they shall praise the Lord that seek him, and their hearts shall live for ever.[54] I give and take not back, I feed and fail not, I make secure and fear not; what more shall I say to my beloved? I am the mediatrix of the elements, making one to agree with another; that which is warm I make cold, and the reverse; that which is dry I make moist, and the reverse; that which is hard I soften, and the reverse. I am the end and my beloved is the beginning,[55] I am the whole work and all science is hidden in me,[56] I am the law in the priest and the word in the prophet and counsel in the wise.[57] I will kill and I will make to live and there is none that can deliver out of my hand.[58]

[51] John 12 : 24-25: "Amen, amen, I say unto you: unless the grain of wheat falling into the ground die, itself remaineth alone. But if it die, it bringeth forth much fruit."

[52] Cf. Senior, *De chemia*, p. 51. "But some of them use different names, as for example, of the three earths, of which the first is of pearls, the second is the earth of leaves [silver], the third earth is the earth of gold." Cf. also p. 106.

[53] John 6 : 33: "For the bread of God is that which cometh down from heaven and giveth life to the world." John 6 : 51-52: "I am the living bread which came down from heaven. If any man eat of this bread, he shall live for ever." Cf. Ps. 77 : 24-25.

[54] Ps. 21 : 27: "The poor shall eat and shall be filled: and they shall praise the Lord that seek him: their hearts shall live for ever and ever."

[55] Apoc. 1 : 8: "I am Alpha and Omega, the beginning and the end, saith the Lord God . . ."

[56] Cf. Mercurius in Rhazis, *De alum. et salibus* (ed. Ruska), p. 59: "And I am the whole of that hidden thing and in me lieth hid the hidden wisdom."

[57] Jer. 18 : 18: ". . . for the Law shall not perish from the priest, nor counsel from the wise, nor the word from the prophet."

[58] Deut. 32 : 39: "See ye that I alone am, and there is no other God besides me; I will kill and I will make to live, I will strike and I will heal, and there is none that can deliver out of my hand . . .' '

porrigo os dilecto meo et compressit ipsius ad me,[59] ego et ipse
85 unum sumus,[60] quis nos separabit a caritate?[61] Nullus et nemo,
quia fortis est ut mors dilectio nostra."[62]—"O dilecta, immo
perdilecta, vox tua sonuit in auribus meis, quae dulcis est,[63] et
odor tuus super cuncta unguenta preciosa.[64] O quam pulchra
es facie,[65] pulchriora ubera tua vino, soror sponsa,[66] oculi tui
90 piscinae in Esebon,[67] capilli tui aurei, genae tuae eburneae,
venter tuus sicut crater tornatilis non indigens poculis,[68] vestes
tuae candidiores nive, nitidiores lacte, rubicundiores ebore antiquo,[69] totumque corpus tuum cunctis est delectabile atque desiderabile. Filiae Jerusalem, venite et videte et ea, quae vidistis
95 narrate, dicite, quid faciemus sorori nostrae, quae parvula est
et ubera non habet in die allocutionis?[70] Ponam super eam
fortitudinem meam et apprehendam fructus illius et erunt eius
ubera sicut botri vineae.[71] Veni mi dilecta et egrediamur in

---

84. porrigo os *om. MPV* / 86. immo *om. MPDB* / 87. insonuit *MP* / in *om.*
RhDL / 89. a facie *P*, in facie *V* / pulchriora: pulchra *PVD* / vino: unica *PV* /
91. crater tornatilis: tractus cortelis *MP*, tornalis *D*/ 96. In die allocutionis ∼
ponam *MP*, ablactationis *V*, allocutionis V_2 /

---

59 Cf. Cant. 1 : 1: "Osculetur me osculo oris sui . . ."
60 Joh. 10 : 30: "Ego et pater unum sumus."
61 Rom. 8 : 35–39: "Quis ergo nos separabit a charitate Christi? . . . Certus sum
quia neque mors neque vita . . . poterit nos separare a charitate Dei, quae est
in Christo Jesu Domino nostro."
62 Cant. 8 : 6: ". . . quia fortis est ut mors dilectio, dura sicut infernus aemulatio."
63 Cant. 2 : 14: "Ostende mihi faciem tuam, sonet vox tua in auribus meis; vox
enim tua dulcis, et facies tua decora."
64 Cant. 4 : 10: ". . . odor unguentorum tuorum super omnia aromata . . ."
65 Cant. 4 : 1: "Quam pulchra es, amica mea, quam pulchra es!"
66 Cant. 4 : 10: "Quam pulchrae sunt mammae tuae, soror mea sponsa, pulchriora
sunt ubera tua vino."
67 Cant. 7 : 4: "Oculi tui sicut piscinae in Hesebon . . ."
68 Cant. 7 : 2: "Umbilicus tuus crater tornatilis, numquam indigens poculis.
Venter tuus sicut acervus tritici, vallatus liliis."
69 Thren. 4 : 7: "Candidiores Nazaraei eius nive, nitidiores lacte, rubicundiores
ebore antiquo, sapphiro pulchriores . . ."
70 Cant. 8 : 8–9: "Soror nostra parva, et ubera non habet: quid faciemus sorori
nostrae in die quando alloquenda est? . . . Si murus est, aedificemus super
eum . . ."
71 Cant. 7 : 8: Dixi: ascendam in palmam, et apprehendam fructus eius; et erunt
ubera tua sicut botri vineae . . ."

I stretch forth my mouth to my beloved and he presseth his to me; [59] he and I are one; [60] who shall separate us from love? [61] None and no man, for our love is strong as death." [62]—"O beloved, yea supremely beloved, thy voice hath sounded in my ears, for it is sweet, [63] and thine odour is above all aromatical spices. [64] O how comely is thy face, [65] thy breasts more beautiful than wine, my sister, my spouse, [66] thy eyes are like the fishpools in Heshbon, [67] thy hairs are golden, thy cheeks are ivory, thy belly is as a round bowl never wanting cups, [68] thy garments are whiter than snow, purer than milk, more ruddy than old ivory, [69] and all thy body is delightful and desirable unto all. Come forth, daughters of Jerusalem, and see, and tell and declare what ye have seen; say, what shall we do for our sister, who is little and hath no breasts, in the day when she shall be wooed? [70] I will set my strength upon her and will take hold of her fruits, and her breasts shall be as the clusters of the vine. [71] Come, my beloved, and let us go into thy

---

[59] Cf. Cant. 1 : 1: "Let him kiss me with the kiss of his mouth . . ."

[60] John 10 : 30: "I and the Father are one."

[61] Rom. 8 : 35–39: "Who then shall separate us from the love of Christ? . . . I am sure that neither death, nor life, . . . shall be able to separate us from the love of God, which is in Christ Jesus our Lord."

[62] Cant. 8 : 6: ". . . for love is strong as death, jealousy is hard as hell."

[63] Cant. 2 : 14: ". . . shew me thy face. Let thy voice sound in my ears; for thy voice is sweet, and thy face comely."

[64] Cant. 4 : 10: ". . . the sweet smell of thy ointments (is) above all aromatical spices."

[65] Cant. 4 : 1: "How beautiful art thou, my love, how beautiful art thou!"

[66] Cant. 4 : 10: "How beautiful are thy breasts, my sister, my spouse! thy breasts are more beautiful than wine . . ."

[67] Cant. 7 : 4: "Thy eyes like the fishpools in Hesebon . . ."

[68] Cant. 7 : 2: "Thy navel is like a round bowl never wanting cups. Thy belly is like a heap of wheat, set about with lilies."

[69] Lam. 4 : 7: "Her Nazarites [princes] were whiter than snow, purer than milk, more ruddy than the old ivory, fairer than the sapphire."

[70] Cant. 8 : 8–9: "Our sister is little and hath no breasts. What shall we do to our sister in the day when she is to be spoken to? . . . If she be a wall, let us build upon it. . . ."

[71] Cant. 7 : 8: "I said: I will go up into the palm tree and will take hold of the fruit thereof, and thy breasts shall be as the clusters of the vine . . ."

agrum tuum, moremur in villis, mane surgamus ad vineam,
100 quia nox praecessit et dies appropinquabit; [72] videamus si floruit
vinea tua,[73] si flores tui fructus parturierunt. Ibi dabis ori meo
ubera tua et ego omnia poma nova et vetera tibi servavi,[74] fruamur ergo ipsis et utamur bonis tamquam in iuventute celeriter,
vino pretioso et unguentis nos impleamus et non praetereat flos,
105 quin ipsis nos coronemus, primo liliis, deinde rosis, antequam
marcescant. Nullum pratum sit, quod non pertranseat luxuria
nostra. Nemo nostrum exsors sit luxuriae nostrae, ubique relinquamus signa laetitiae, quia haec est pars nostra,[75] ut vivamus
in coitus nostri amore cum gaudio et tripudio dicentes: Ecce,
110 quam bonum et quam iucundum est habitare duobus in unum.[76]
Faciamus ergo nobis tria tabernacula, tibi unum, mihi secundum, filiis nostris tertium,[77] quia funiculus triplex difficile

---

99. surgemus *MP* / 101. flores fructus tui *MPD* / 102. servam *MP*, servabo *D* /
104.–105. praetereat nos floribus ipsis convenimus nos *MP* / 105. deinde: demum
DRhL / 106. marcescunt *ML* / Nullum: non *MPV* / pc̄tum *MPL*, peccum *Rh* /
107. expers *RhDL*, exosus *MP*, exsors *Rh„V* / 109. coitus: interitus *MP*, terris
interitus *V* / nostri *om. DRhL* / 110. est *om. MRhD* / 111. nobis *om. DL* / 112.
nostris: meis *D. om. MPV* /

---

72 Rom. 13 : 12: "Nox praecessit, dies autem appropinquavit. Abiiciamus ergo
opera tenebrarum, et induamur arma lucis."
73 Cf. Pseudo-Thomas, "Secreta alchimiae," *Theatr. chem.* (1659), III, p. 279:
"In primis etiam diebus oportet mane surgere, et videre si vinea floruit . . ."
74 Cant. 7 : 11–13: "Veni, dilecte mi, egrediamur in agrum, commoremur in villis;
mane surgamus ad vineas, videamus si floruerit vinea, si flores fructus parturiunt,
si floruerunt mala punica. . . . Ibi dabo tibi ubera mea. . . . In portis nostris
omnia poma, nova et vetera, dilecte mi, servavi tibi . . ." Cf. *Pret. marg. nov.*,
p. 101: ". . . et terra quae dicitur mater elementorum . . . et haec est arbor
aurea, de cuius fructu, qui comederit, non esuriet umquam."
75 Sap. 2 : 5 ff.: (Dixerunt luxuriantes): "Umbrae enim transitus est tempus
nostrum, et non est reversio finis nostri; quoniam consignata est, et nemo revertitur. Venite ergo, et fruamur bonis quae sunt, et utamur creatura tamquam
in iuventute, celeriter: Vino pretioso et unguentis nos impleamus, et non
praetereat nos flos temporis. Coronemus nos rosis antequam marcescant; nullum
pratum sit, quod non pertranseat luxuria nostra. Nemo nostrum exsors sit
luxuriae nostrae, ubique relinquamus signa laetitiae, quoniam haec est pars
nostra, et haec est sors."
76 Ps. 132 : 1: "Ecce quam bonum et quam iucundum habitare fratres in unum."
77 Matth. 17 : 4: ". . . Si vis, faciamus hic tria tabernacula, tibi unum, Moysi
unum, et Eliae unum." Cf. also Apoc. 21 : 2–3: "Et ego Johannes vidi sanctam
civitatem Jerusalem novam descendentem de coelo . . . et audivi vocem magnam
de throno dicentem: Ecce tabernaculum Dei cum hominibus, et habitabit cum eis."

field, let us abide in the villages, let us go up early to the vineyard, for the night is past and the day is at hand; [72] let us see if
thy vineyard flourisheth, [73] if thy flowers have brought forth
fruits. There shalt thou give thy breasts to my mouth, and I have
kept for thee all fruits new and old; [74] let us therefore enjoy them
and use the good things speedily as in youth, let us fill ourselves
with costly wine and ointments, and let no flower pass by us save
we crown ourselves therewith, first with lilies, then with roses,
before they be withered. Let no meadow escape our riot. Let
none of us go without his part in our luxury, let us leave everywhere tokens of joy, for this is our portion, [75] that we should live
in the union of love with joy and merriment, saying: Behold how
good and pleasant it is for two to dwell together in unity. [76] Let
us make therefore three tabernacles, one for thee, a second for
me, and a third for our sons, [77] for a threefold cord is not easily

[72] Rom. 13 : 12: "The night is passed and the day is at hand. Let us therefore cast
off the works of darkness and put on the armour of light."
[73] Cf. Pseudo-Thomas, "Secreta alchimiae," *Theatr. chem.* (1659), III, p. 279:
"Also in the first days one must rise up early, and see if the vineyard hath
flourished . . ."
[74] Cant. 7 : 11–13: "Come, my beloved, let us go forth into the field, let us abide in
the villages. Let us get up early to the vineyards, let us see if the vineyard flourish,
if the flowers be ready to bring forth fruits, if the pomegranates flourish; . . .
there will I give thee my breasts. . . . In our gates are all fruits; the new and the
old, my beloved, I have kept for thee." Cf. *Pret. marg. nov.*, p. 101: ". . . and the
earth which is called the mother of the elements . . . and this is the golden tree,
of whose fruit he who eateth shall never hunger."
[75] Wisd. 2 : 5ff.: (The wicked said): ". . . For our time is as the passing of a
shadow, and there is no going back of our end; for it is fast sealed, and no man
returneth. Come therefore, and let us enjoy the good things that are present; and
let us speedily use the creatures as in youth. Let us fill ourselves with costly wine
and ointments; and let not the flower of the time pass by us. Let us crown ourselves with roses, before they be withered; let no meadow escape our riot. Let
none of us go without his part in luxury; let us everywhere leave tokens of joy;
for this is our portion, and this our lot."
[76] Ps. 132 : 1: "Behold how good and how pleasant it is for brethren to dwell
together in unity."
[77] Matt. 17 : 4: "Lord, it is good for us to be here: if thou wilt, let us make here
three tabernacles, one for thee, and one for Moses, and one for Elias." Cf. Apoc.
21 : 2–3: "And I John saw the holy city, the new Jerusalem, coming down out of
heaven from God . . . and I heard a great voice from the throne, saying: Behold,
the tabernacle of God with men, and he will dwell with them."

rumpitur.[78] Qui habet aures audiendi audiat, quid dicat spiritus doctrinae filiis disciplinae de desponsatione dilecti ad dilectam.
115 Nam semen suum seminaverat, quod maturescat per eum triplex fructus, quod auctor trium verborum dicit esse tria verba pretiosa, in quibus tota occultatur scientia, quae danda est piis videlicet pauperibus a primo homine usque ad ultimum."[79]

---

114. cum dilecta *MP* / 115. seminat qui *MPV* / 116. esse: ecce *MP* / 117. est: sunt *DRh* / piis *om. MPV* / videlicet *om. M* / 118. (ultimum) hominem *add. RhDL* /

---

[78] Eccles. 4 : 10–12: "Vae soli, quia cum ceciderit, non habet sublevantem se. Et si dormierint duo, fovebuntur mutuo: unus quomodo calefiet? Et si quispiam praevaluerit contra unum, duo resistunt ei: funiculus triplex difficile rumpitur."
[79] Calid, "Liber trium verborum," *Art. aurif.* (1610), I, p. 228: "Et haec sunt tria verba preciosa occulta, et aperta, data non pravis, non impiis, non infidelibus, sed fidelibus et pauperibus a primo homine usque ad ultimum."

broken.[78] He that hath ears to hear, let him hear what the spirit of the doctrine saith to the sons of the discipline concerning the espousal of the lover to the beloved. For he had sowed his seed, that there might ripen thereof threefold fruit, which the author of the Three Words saith to be three precious words, wherein is hidden all the science, which is to be given to the pious, that is to the poor, from the first man even unto the last." [79]

[78] Eccles. 4 : 10–12: "Woe to him that is alone: for when he falleth he hath none to lift him up. And if two lie together, they shall warm one another: How shall one alone be warmed? And if a man prevail against one, two shall withstand him: a threefold cord is not easily broken."

[79] Calid, "Liber trium verborum," *Art. aurif.* (1610), I, p. 228: "And these are the three precious words, concealed and open, to be imparted not to the wicked nor to the impious nor to the unbelievers, but to the faithful and to the poor from the first man even unto the last."

III

COMMENTARY

INTRODUCTORY

69   If the reader allows this text to work directly upon his feelings, he will be struck first of all by the high-sounding poetic language, which is completely different from the usual style of medieval alchemical treatises. A flood of loosely connected Biblical and alchemical quotations pours forth in an uninterrupted spate of rhetoric. What the author is getting at, what his "theoria" might be, cannot be discerned at first, although one senses that he is struggling to express a meaningful experience. Is he an alchemist usurping the language of the Bible, or a cleric using the symbolic language of alchemy in order to formulate something extraordinary? What, indeed, can impel a man to pen such a production? If *Aurora* is not to sink back, as being totally unintelligible, into the oblivion in which it has lain hitherto, there is only one path to follow: to assume that the author did not express himself in clearly understandable concepts *for the simple reason that he did not possess them,* and that he was giving a stammering description of an *unconscious content which had irrupted into his consciousness.*

70   If this is so, the question as to whether he was an alchemist or a cleric is incorrectly posed, for, as Jung has shown in *Psychology and Alchemy,* the alchemist was a man who was seeking to discover the "divine secret"—the secret of the unconscious which he projected into matter. In this sense everyone is an alchemist who struggles to give individual, immediate form to an experience of the unconscious. The complete lack of any "technical" passages in the text leads me to believe that the author was not a practising alchemist and that he had no practical intentions in writing this treatise. He did not "see" the symbols as projected into matter, he experienced their content *in himself,* as inner intuitions, but their nature was such that only the existing alchemical symbolism was of any avail in

153

formulating the inexpressible. The figurative language of the mystics and of ecclesiastical symbolism obviously did not suffice, for reasons which will become apparent. The exalted, poetico-rhetorical style and the logical discontinuities indicate a strong excitement that accompanies an unmistakably numinous experience. Quotations and thoughts tumble over one another, giving one the impression of a *flight of ideas*. It does not, however, get out of hand, but always returns to its theme. Also, there are no signs of schizophrenic breaks in the meaning. On the other hand, the existence of a hypomanic state cannot be ruled out. Unfortunately, nothing certain is known about the author, and so we cannot tell whether this hypomanic state was a phase of manic-depressive psychosis or whether the excitement was of a psychogenic nature and could be traced back to some unconscious religious problem.

71   Faced with such a document, we have no other course than to approach the whole thing as a product of the unconscious, to examine it as methodically as though it were a dream, and to find out the meaning of the context by amplifying the images. It might then prove that the seemingly loose chain of symbolic allusions has, like a dream, a logical continuity of meaning, and that it even reflects a psychic drama of the utmost consistency.

I. HERE BEGINNETH THE TREATISE . . .

⁷² The first chapter introduces a mystical female figure who appears at first as the personified Sapientia Dei or Scientia Dei.[1] This feminine divine hypostasis is painted on a broad canvas, and is amplified by numerous Biblical sayings and comparisons. At first the figure of Sapientia appears in the same personification which we see in Proverbs, Ecclesiasticus, and the Wisdom of Solomon. In patristic literature she was mostly interpreted as Christ, the pre-existent Logos,[2] or as the sum of the *rationes aeternae* (eternal forms), of the "self-knowing primordial causes," exemplars, ideas, and prototypes in the mind of God.[3] She was also considered the *archetypus mundus*, "that archetypal world after whose likeness this sensible world was made,"[4] and through which God becomes conscious of himself.[5] Sapientia Dei is thus

[1] Concerning this concept see Jung, *Psychology and Alchemy*, pars. 464ff. Parallels are Mater Alchimia in *Aurora* II (*Artis auriferae*, I, pp. 126ff.) and Mater Naturae in "Novum lumen," *Musaeum Hermeticum*, pp. 598ff.

[2] E.g., Honorius of Autun, *Quaest. et respons. in Prov. et Eccles.* (Migne, *P.L.*, vol. 172, col. 313): "Wisdom uttereth her voice in the streets . . . Christ Jesus who is the power of God and the wisdom of God . . . in the openings of the gates of the city of Holy Church," etc.• Cf. Thery, "Le Commentaire de Maître Eckhart sur le livre de la Sagesse," *Archives d'histoire doctrinale*, IV, p. 364.

[3] Scotus Erigena, *De divis. nat.*, II, 18 (Migne, *P.L.*, vol. 122, col. 553): "The primordial causes know themselves, since they were created in wisdom and subsist therein eternally." • II, 20 (col. 557): "For the Father simultaneously begat his Wisdom and created all things therein." •

[4] Hugh of St. Victor, *Annot. elucid. in Evang. Joannis* (Migne, *P.L.*, vol. 175, col. 834): "Whence also all things have their life and being from the wisdom of God . . . for according to the wisdom of God, which is the life of all things, was made all that was made. For this was God's exemplar, after the likeness whereof all the world was made, and this is that archetypal world, after whose likeness this sensible world was made." • Similar views are expressed by Alan of Lille.

[5] Scotus Erigena, *De divis. nat.*, II, 31 (Migne, *P.L.*, vol. 122, col. 603): ". . . after the likeness of God and the Father, who begat of himself his Son, who is his Wisdom, whereby he knows himself." •

the sum of archetypal images in the mind of God.[6] Other patristic interpretations equate her with the soul of Christ or, more frequently, with Mary.[7]

73 In modern psychology she would be interpreted as a feminine personification of the collective unconscious. The beginning of the text would accordingly describe a numinous encounter with the anima, whose irruption into the sphere of consciousness the author endeavours to control. From the sublime, almost divine significance here attributed to the anima we must conclude that previously she had been devalued in the author's consciousness, and that this devaluation is here compensated by the sublimity of the image.

74 The beginning of this chapter reminds us almost word for word of the introduction to a youthful work of Albertus Magnus, "Mariale, sive CCXXX quaestiones super Evangelium Missus Est," [8] in which he puts together in praise of Mary the same Biblical passages cited in *Aurora*.[9] It seems to me that in this respect *Aurora* cannot be independent of this supposedly genuine work of Albertus Magnus,[10] though the difference is that our author

---

[6] Thomas Aquinas, *Summa*, I, q. 44, art. 3 (Eng. edn., I, p. 231); also I, q. 56, art. 2 resp. (I, p. 281): "Now in the Word of God from eternity there existed not only the forms of corporeal things, but likewise the forms of all spiritual creatures." • (These "forms"—*rationes*—are also impressed upon the mind of the angels.) *Summa*, I–II, q. 62, art. 2, ad 2 (I, p. 852): "The wisdom which the philosopher reckons as an intellectual virtue, considers divine things so far as they are open to the research of human reason." • Q. 62, art. 3 resp. (I, pp. 852f.): "First, as regards the intellect, man receives certain supernatural principles, which are held by means of a divine light; these are the articles of faith, about which is faith." •

[7] Hugh of St. Victor, *De sapientia animae Christi* (Migne, *P.L.*, vol. 176, col. 848).

[8] *Opera*, ed. Borgnet, XXXVII, p. 3ff. Concerning the authenticity of this work see Pelster, *Kritische Studien*, pp. 108ff. Others attribute it to Richard of St. Laurent. Cf. Daehnert, *Die Erkenntnislehre des Albertus Magnus*, p. 233.

[9] *Mariale*, q. CLXIV, p. 244: "In the house of Wisdom there is medicine against the wounds of sin, and this medicine is the Virgin Mary, who made herself into a house for Solomon." Mary is the mother who crowned Solomon with the crown, the Woman of the Apocalypse crowned with twelve stars, the City of God, and the "woman who will encompass the man" (Jeremiah 31 : 22) (p. 246). She is also the "dawn of illumination" (p. 369).

[10] In Parable IV of *Aurora*, "Of the Philosophic Faith," there are also quotations similar to those in Albertus's "Libellus de Alchemia." The latter says: " 'All wisdom is from the Lord God, and has been always with Him, and is before all time' (Ecclus. 1 : 1). Let whoever loves wisdom seek it in Him and ask it of Him, 'who gives abundantly to all men, and does not reproach' (James 1 : 5). For He is the height

goes on to equate his feminine figure with the "soul in matter" and with the "filius philosophorum" or *lapis*, thus lifting her out of her purely ecclesiastical framework into the empirical sphere of scientifically based alchemy and bringing her closer to individual human experience.

75   It is important to remember that the thirteenth century, to which *Aurora* presumably belongs, was a time when the worship of Mary was on the increase. Psychologically, this would point to a need, rising from the collective unconscious, for a feminine figure to be given a place in the purely masculine, patriarchal Trinity, as the representative of the anima of a man and the self of a woman. But in contrast to the dogmatic development we have before our eyes in this alchemical treatise a direct, individual manifestation of this archetypal image of a divine feminine figure.

76   All good things came to me together with her, that Wisdom of the south, who preacheth abroad, who uttereth her voice in the streets, crieth out at the head of the multitudes, and in the entrance of the gates of the city uttereth her words, saying: Come ye to me and be enlightened, and your operations shall not be confounded; all ye that desire me shall be filled with my riches. Come therefore, children, hearken to me; I will teach you the science of God.

77   Wisdom calls men to her with seductive words,[11] promising

---

and the depth of all knowledge and the treasure house of all wisdom, 'since from Him and through Him and unto Him are all things' (Rom. 11 : 36); without Him nothing can be done; to Him be honour and glory forever. Amen. Therefore, at the beginning of my discourse I shall invoke the aid of Him Who is the Fount and Source of all good to deign, in His goodness and love, to fill up by the grace of His Holy Spirit my small knowledge so that I may be able by my teaching to show forth the light which lies hidden in the darkness and to lead those who are in error to the pathway of truth. . . . Though I have laboriously travelled to many regions and numerous provinces, likewise to cities and castles, in the interest of the science called Alchemy, though I have diligently consulted learned men and sages concerning this art in order to investigate it more fully, and though I took down their writings and toiled again and again over their works, I have not found in them what their books assert. . . . Yet I have not despaired . . . until finally I found what I was seeking, not by my own knowledge, but by the grace of the Holy Spirit. Therefore, since I knew and understood what conquered nature, I began to watch more diligently in decoctions . . ." * (*Libellus de Alchemia*, trans. Heines, pp. 1f.)

11 Cf. Meister Eckhart's commentary on this passage (Thery, III, p. 425): "Wisdom is the one perfection, in which all other good is included."

them health and great riches, the Biblical background of her words indicating that her treasures are of a spiritual nature.[12] Hence it is emphasized a little later that she is more precious than "merchandise of silver and the most pure gold."

78   She is called, further, the "Wisdom of the south" or of the "south wind" *(austri)*, and is thus equated with the Biblical "Queen of the south," the Queen of Sheba,[13] who in alchemical tradition was, like Solomon,[14] the author of alchemical works,[15] and was identified with Maria the Jewess, "sister of Moses."[16] In patristic literature the Queen of Sheba was a prefiguration of Mary. On the other hand, in the hermeneutics of the Church Fathers the Queen of the south was also an image for the Church as the "queen" and "concubine" of Christ,[17] who was called the "King of the south."[18] Indeed, this feminine figure was even identified with God himself, who "shall go with the whirlwinds of the south."[19] The south wind is also a symbol of the Holy Spirit, causing the minds of the elect to seethe, "that they may bring about whatsoever good things they desire."[20] The equa-

[12] This agrees with the oft-cited saying, "Our gold is not the common gold." Cf. Senior, *De chemia,* p. 39. Origen (*In Cant. Cant.,* Lib. II: Migne, *P.G.,* vol. 13, col. 135) likewise distinguishes between common gold and a gold that represents "the invisible and incorporeal nature."

[13] Cf. Matt. 12 : 42.

[14] Cf. the sayings of Suleiman in the *Sefer ha-Tamar* ("Book of the Palm") by Abu Aflah (ed. Scholem), and Lippmann, I, pp. 12, 111, 156, 265, 309.

[15] Ruska, *Turba,* p. 272. She is mentioned as "Bilqis," Queen of Egypt, and is said to have written, among others, a book beginning: "After I had ascended the mountain . . ." Cf. Holmyard, "Abu'l Qāsim al-'Irāqī," p. 407.

[16] Berthelot, *Chimie au moyen âge,* I, p. 242, III, pp. 28 and 125; Lippmann, I, p. 46.

[17] Honorius, *Expositio in Cant. Cant.* (Migne, *P.L.,* vol. 172, cols. 352–54).

[18] Cf. the final struggle between the good "King of the south" and the wicked "King of the north" in the *Concordia* of Joachim of Flora, V, cap. 93 (Hahn, *Geschichte der Ketzer,* III, pp. 311f.). In what follows, my quotations from Joachim are nearly always taken from Hahn, as I was unable to obtain a reliable edition of Joachim's works.

[19] Zech. 9 : 14.

[20] St. Gregory the Great, *Moralia,* Lib. 27 in cap. 37 Job, sec. 63 (Migne, *P.L.,* vol. 76, col. 436; Eng. edn., III, pt. 1, p. 247), and *Super Cant. Cant. expositio,* cap. 4, v. 16 (Migne, *P.L.,* vol. 79, col. 516): "By the south is signified a hot wind, namely, the wind of the Holy Spirit, who toucheth the minds of the elect, relieving them of all sloth and making them fervent, that they may bring about whatsoever good things they desire." •

tion of the Holy Spirit with the south wind is presumably due, as Jung points out,[21] to the hot and dry quality of this wind. The Holy Spirit is fiery and causes exaltation. He warms all things with the fire of love.[22] According to Gregory the Great, the "south" signifies "those unfathomed depths of the heavenly country, which are filled with the heat of the Holy Spirit." [23] In Arabian alchemy the sublimation process is called "the great south wind," by which is meant the heating of the retort and its contents.[24] These amplifications make it clear that in our text Wisdom is a feminine pneuma who enkindles and inspires the author at his work. She is a "spirit of truth," bringing him enlightenment. Thus the anima appears here not as a personal content but in her transpersonal collective significance as a feminine complement of the God-image itself.[25] Her fiery nature accounts for the agitated state of the author.

[21] *Psychology and Alchemy*, par. 473.

[22] Joachim of Flora, *Concordia*, V, cap. 93 (Hahn, III, p. 312): "The daughter of the King of the south (who reigns in heaven and in spirits warmed by love)." • Hahn, p. 321: "Cease [not] to enkindle us with the fire of charity to love . . . [that] we may be able to work in the warmth of the Holy Spirit." •

[23] *Moralia*, Lib. 9 in cap. 9 Job, sec. 17 (Migne, *P.L.*, vol. 75, col. 868; Eng. edn., I, p. 507): "And thus 'the South' are those unseen orders of the Angels, and those unfathomed depths of the heavenly country, which are filled with the heat of the Holy Spirit. . . . There all the day, as at midday, the fire of the sun burns with a brighter lustre, in that the brightness of our Creator, which is now overlaid with the mists of our mortal state, is rendered more clearly visible; and the beam of the orb seems to raise itself to higher regions, in that 'Truth' from Its own Self enlightens us more completely through and through. There the light of interior contemplation is seen without the intervening shadow of mutability." • Cf. Knorr von Rosenroth, *Kabbala denudata*, I, p. 260: "The south is Chesed, wherefore our elders said: Whoso would be wise, let him turn himself to the south." •

[24] Holmyard, *Kitāb al-'ilm al-muktasab*, p. 43: ". . . but what of the speech of Hermes in which he says: 'The great South wind when it acts makes the clouds to rise and raises the cloud of the sea'? He said, if the powdering is not successful the compound will not ascend into the top of the retort, and even if it do ascend it will not pour into the receiver. It is necessary to mix with it the first and second waters before it will ascend to the top of the retort. 'That,' he said, 'is the Great South Wind?' He said: 'Yea, O King,' " etc. Cf. also Holmyard, "Abu'l Qāsim al-'Irāqī," pp. 403ff.

[25] According to Wisd. 7 : 25f., Wisdom is a "vapour of the power of God and a certain pure emanation of the glory of almighty God . . . the brightness of eternal light, and the unspotted mirror of God's majesty, and the image of his goodness."

79 Who is wise, and understandeth this, of which Alphidius saith, that men and children pass her by daily in the streets and public places, and she is trodden into the mire by beasts of burden and by cattle?

80 The Alphidius quotation says of this figure that she is trodden into the mire by the ignorant, which means psychologically that the feminine personification of the unconscious is rejected by the prevailing collective views, with the result that the lapis, the germ of the individuation process, is stifled.[26] The saying is quoted with extraordinary frequency by the alchemists, and almost always it refers to the stone of the wise,[27] so that our author obviously identifies Wisdom with the lapis. The same identification can be found in a quotation from Alexander in Petrus Bonus, who says in his *Pretiosa margarita novella* [28] that the work comes about "by the addition of the secret stone, which is not to be apprehended by the senses, but by the intellect alone, through inspiration or divine revelation, or the teaching of a sage. . . . And Alexander saith, There are two categories in this art, namely, seeing with the eye and understanding with the heart, and this is the hidden stone, which is fitly called a gift of God . . . and this is the divine hidden stone, and unless it be admixed with this stone alchemy would be brought to nought, for it is itself very alchemy. . . . And this divine stone is the heart and tincture of gold which the philosophers seek." Here the stone is described as something invisible, as the God-given gift of understanding, and alchemy is nothing other than this. It is "gnosis." Hence we can understand why the author of *Aurora* makes Wisdom not only the guide but also the goal of the alchemical opus.

81 And Senior saith: Nought is more base in appearance than she, and nought is more precious in nature than she, and God also hath not appointed her to be bought for a price. She it is that Solomon chose to have instead of light, and above all beauty and health; in com-

26 The (Latin) translation, by Rufinus and Jerome, of Origen's *In Cant. Cant.*, III (Migne, *P.G.*, vol. 13, col. 180) runs: "For the Word of God and the Word of Knowledge appears not openly and in public, nor is to be trampled underfoot, but when it is sought, it is found." * Possibly this passage was known to the author of *Aurora*.
27 *Bibliotheca chemica*, II, p. 88b. Cf. Ruska, *Turba*, pp. 122, 142, 165, and *Das Buch der Alaune und Salze* (ed. Ruska), p. 56.
28 *Theatrum chemicum*, V, p. 580.*

parison of her he compared not unto her the virtue of any precious stone. For all gold in her sight shall be esteemed as a little sand, and silver shall be counted as clay; and this not without cause, for to gain her is better than the merchandise of silver and the most pure gold.

82   This passage gives expression to the well-known paradox that the science or the lapis is utterly worthless and yet at the same time a value that exceeds all earthly goods, though it is stressed anew that the stone is an *aurum non vulgi*. The paradoxical formulation that the stone is cheap and precious at once occurs already in the oldest Greek texts. Zosimos says that the stone is "contemned and much esteemed, not given yet given by God." [29] Similar paradoxes were made by the Church Fathers in their sayings about Christ; for instance, Ephraem Syrus says that Christ slept on a dunghill, and that dunghill then became the Church pouring out men's prayers to God,[30] and the allegories (*figurae et typi*) of Christ are his "treasury hidden and of no worth, but when it is opened it is wonderful to behold." [31] Psychologically, this means nothing less than that the symbolical images in the Church's teachings about Christ, by which he was assimilated into the psychic matrix,[32] are the despised though extremely valuable "prima materia" of our faith.[33] It is also significant that

29 Berthelot, *Alch. grecs*, III, ii, 1 and III, vi, 6. Cf. *Turba*, p. 122: "A thing . . . which is found everywhere, which is a stone and no stone, contemptible and precious, hidden, concealed, and yet known to everyone." • P. 165: "How marvellous is the diversity of the philosophers . . . and their agreement about this most worthless little thing, by which the precious is governed. And if the multitude . . . knew that most worthless little thing, they would hold it for a deceit; but if they knew its power, they would not hold it as of no account." • Cf. p. 142 and *Das Buch der Alaune und Salze*, p. 56. "And others have said that arsenic itself is the stone of the nations, of little worth, and rejected and cast out of doors and into the dunghills and sewers." • The same sentences occur in "Le Livre d'Ostanes": Berthelot, *Moyen âge*, III, p. 116.
30 *Hymni et sermones* (ed. Lamy), II, col. 508: "If thou [Christ] restest thy head upon a stone, they divide it and snatch it away; if thou sleepest upon a dunghill, it becometh the Church for the pouring out of prayers." •
31 Ibid., col. 770. •   32 Jung, *Aion*, pp. 181f.
33 Cf. Honorius of Autun's comment on Ps. 112 : 7 ("He lifts up the poor man out of the dunghill"): "That which is rejected by men, is pleasant to our Lord. . . . Behold, thus is the precious stone that lies hidden in the dunghill lifted out of the cloaca of the stench of the world and set in the kingly diadem, which sparkles with fiery gems, in a shining place." *Speculum Ecclesiae* (Migne, *P.L.*, vol. 172, col. 1062).

Thomas Aquinas, in his commentary (I. 1. 9) to the Epistle to the Hebrews, points out that the "corpora vilia" are particularly apt as a representation of the deity.[34]

83   These "materiae viles" are, psychologically speaking, the images and symbols that rise up directly from the unconscious and have not been judged, interpreted, or changed into anything else by the discriminative activity of the collective consciousness. They are the real prima materia of every religious experience, but the tragedy is that they are always "trodden into the mire" by the prevailing collective opinions.

84   Length of days and health are in her right hand, and in her left hand glory and infinite riches. Her ways are beautiful operation and praise-worthy, not unsightly nor ill-favoured, and her paths are measured and not hasty, but are bound up with stubborn and day-long toil. She is a tree of life to them that lay hold on her, and an unfailing light. Blessed shall they be who retain her, for the science of God shall never perish, as Alphidius beareth witness, for he saith: He who hath found this science, it shall be his rightful food for ever. And Hermes . . . saith, that if a man who hath this science should live for a thousand years, and every day must feed seven thousand men, yet should he never lack.

85   Wisdom is described further in terms of her Biblical personi-fication: she is praised as the source of long life and health, as a tree of life, as the everlasting and inexhaustible food of mankind, and as an unfailing light. All these images are archetypal and play a great role in alchemical and patristic literature.[35]

[34] Cf. White, "St. Thomas' Conception of Revelation," p. 11. Also St. Bonaventure, *In I Sent.*, Dist. III, art. 1, q. 3, ad 2 (I, p. 75): "Creatures may be considered as things or as symbols." • Thomas's teacher, Albertus Magnus, was also fond of illustrating his Biblical exegesis with alchemical images: "They believed that [Christ] was not God, and he who was the purest gold they believed to be cop-per." • *Mariale* (Borgnet, XXXVII, p. 242; cf. also p. 243).

[35] The quotations in this part of the text show a striking affinity with the intro-duction to *Mariale*, attributed to Albertus. We must bear this in mind when con-sidering whether Thomas was the author of *Aurora*. *Mariale*, Prooemium (Borgnet, XXXVII, p. 1) runs: "Wisdom is glorious and never fadeth away, as it is written (Wisd. 6 : 13–17) and is easily seen by them that love her, and is found by them that seek her. She preventeth them that covet her, so that she first sheweth herself unto them. He that waketh early to seek her shall not labour: for he shall find her sitting at his door. To think therefore upon her is perfect understanding; and he that watcheth for her shall quickly be secure. For she goeth about seeking such as are worthy of her; and she sheweth herself to them cheerfully in the

86   In alchemy the tree [36] is primarily an image for the prima materia which gradually unfolds during the transformation process and is "sufficient unto itself." For its interpretation the reader is referred to Jung's essay "The Philosophical Tree." [37] The tree symbolizes the individuation process in the sense of living one's own life and thereby becoming conscious of the self, i.e., gnosis.[38]

87   The images which liken Wisdom to "unfailing light" and "rightful food" require no further explanation.[39] They symbolize the stream of contents that flows like a spiritual substance from the unconscious or, as the alchemists would say, from the "lumen naturae," [40] which the adept felt as divine illumination. Being

ways and meeteth them with all providence. Also it is written Ecclus. 24 : 29ff.: 'They that eat me shall yet hunger; and they that drink me shall yet thirst. He that hearkeneth to me shall not be confounded: and they that work by me shall not sin. They that explain me shall have life everlasting.' " •
[36] In the Greek "Oracles of Apollo" (Berthelot, *Alch. grecs*, IV, vii, 2) it is said that the divine water "rises like a virginal laurel to the cover of the vessel," and Zosimos describes how the water in the bowl-shaped altar of the cosmos unfolds like a tree and hears flowers and fruit (IV, i). The tree also plays a large role in Arabic literature. Thus the *Kitāb al-'ilm al-muktasab* (Holmyard, p. 23) says: "This prime matter . . . is taken from a single tree which grows in the lands of the West . . . and this tree grows on the surface of the ocean as plants grow on the surface of the earth. This is the tree of which whosoever eats, man and jinn obey him; it is also the tree of which Adam (peace be upon him!) was forbidden to eat, and when he ate he was transformed from his angelic form to human form. And this tree may be changed into every animal shape." Among the Arabs is also to be found the Platonic and Orphic idea of man as an inverted tree growing down from heaven. Cf. Kern, *Orphicorum fragmenta*, p. 244, no. 228a: "The soul takes root in men from heaven" (or: "the soul in men is rooted in heaven"). • Also Senior, *De chemia*, pp. 75f.: "The stone of the wise is produced in itself and from it come the roots, branches, leaves, flowers, and fruits; for it is like a tree whose branches, leaves, flowers, and fruits spring from itself, that exist through it and belong to it, and it is the whole and the whole springs from it." Cf. also Ephraem Syrus, *Hymni et sermones*, II, col. 538: "Mary and the tree are one. The Lamb hung on its branches . . ." • The cross is the tree of life (col. 612).   [37] Also *Psychology and Alchemy*, index, s.v. "Arbor philosophica."
[38] For a similar conception of the word "gnosis" see Quispel, *Gnosis als Weltreligion*, p. 17: "Gnosis is a mythical projection of experience of the self," i.e., of the individuation process.
[39] Cf. Ruska, *Das Buch der Alaune und Salze*, p. 92, where Mercurius says: "If anyone should unite me with my brother and my sister, he will live and rejoice, and I shall suffice for him for ever, even though he live for a million years."
[40] For the history of this concept see Jung, "On the Nature of the Psyche," pp. 190ff.

inexhaustible, Wisdom also acts like a fire which burns without end.

88   This doth Senior confirm, saying: That such a one is as rich as he that hath a stone from which fire is struck, who can give fire to whom he will and as much as he will and when he will without loss to himself. The same is the intent of Aristotle in his second book *Of the Soul,* when he saith: To the size and growth of all things in nature a limit is appointed, but fire by the addition of combustible matter waxes without end.

89   The quotation is from a genuine work of Aristotle's, *De anima.* Aristotle emphasizes there, in refutation of other theories, that the soul or reason is the cause of all limitation of growth, and not fire. The soul sets limits, and thereby gives the body its form.[41] This conception was further elaborated during the Middle Ages. Thomas Aquinas, for instance, regarded the soul not only as the "form"[42] of the body, but as a form which possesses its own substantiality and also imparts it.[43] It can act creatively on its own account and is thus an "ens in actu" (actual being). Matter, in itself formless, becomes invested with its actual properties only in so far as it receives form from the soul.[44]

[41] Supra, p. 9, n. 13.

[42] "Form" is used here in the Aristotelian or Thomist sense. Cf. Sertillanges, *Der Hl. Thomas von Aquin*, pp. 124ff.

[43] For a full discussion of this question see Gilson, *The Spirit of Medieval Philosophy*, p. 183 and notes. It is the soul or "intellect," an incorporeal substance, that organizes and forms its own material body by co-operating with the elements. Cf. St. Thomas, *De anima*, II, lect. 8 (Eng. edn., p. 223): "The soul of a living being is to the elements it contains as form is to matter." * *Summa*, I, q. 75, art. 2 resp. (Eng. edn., I, p. 364): "Now only that which subsists can have an operation *per se*. For nothing can operate but what is actual; . . . we must conclude, therefore, that the human soul, which is called the intellect or the mind, is something incorporeal and subsistent." * *Summa*, I, q. 76, art. 1 resp. (Eng. edn., I, p. 372): "Thus from the very operation of the intellect it is made clear that the intellectual principle is united to the body as its form." *

[44] "And hence [the soul] is united to the body in order that it may have an existence and an operation suitable to its nature." * (*Summa*, I, q. 89, art. 1 resp.; Eng. edn., I, p. 452.) In all these definitions Thomas, like Albertus, is to a large extent dependent on Avicenna. Cf. the latter's *De anima*, cap. I: "Now we will say then, that the soul can be called a *power or potentiality* in relation to the affections which issue from it. . . . It can also be called a perfection inasmuch as the genus is perfected by it and the species has its being through it," etc. * The soul is the "end and perfection" of everything: "Therefore it is a power of the soul which hath other powers, of which this is one, which all strive to this end,

90   In the light of these conceptions it is clear that Wisdom is not a personification of the individual soul, for the author likens her to a firestone from which inexhaustible fire can be struck,[45] and emphasizes that though all natural things have a limit to their extension, and thus have form, fire does not. The firestone is therefore an image for Wisdom in respect of her *difference* from all forms and formed things, the difference being that she can bestow unending life without ever exhausting herself.[46] Her action, unlike that of the soul, does not aim at individual form but is capable of infinite extension. She gives the prime impulse towards all being and all knowing in their endlessly diverse forms, and as an inexhaustible vitalizing principle her range of action is unlimited. She therefore acts transpersonally, beyond and outside the individual, as an ordering principle showing him the way, "directing the steps" of the alchemist, as the next sentence says. This only confirms that psychologically she is not the personal aspect of the man's anima (in medieval language, not the *anima humana* as the "form of the body"),[47] but is a

that the skill with the instruments may attain to the second perfection of the soul itself." • Incidentally, the same *De anima* passage as the one in *Aurora* (pp. 36f.) is cited in the commentary on the Wisdom of Solomon by Meister Eckhart, who took over a good deal from St. Thomas. (Cf. Thery, "Le Commentaire de Maître Eckhart," pp. 237f.) Meister Eckhart comments on this passage as follows: "Therefore the ideas of motion and magnitude or dimension, considered as a prior form in matter, as the Commentator [Averroes] so well says in *De substantia Orbis*, are infinite, and for this reason there can be something that is more mobile than any mobile thing. God, therefore, since he is infinite, and not restricted by any other motion or operation, can operate or move more swiftly. Therefore the Wise Man, wishing to point out in a hidden and subtle manner the infinity of God and of his wisdom, well says: Wisdom is more mobile [D.V. active] than all mobile [D.V. active] things. Again the imagination in dealing with magnitude is able to imagine something greater than any great thing, even heaven. Thus Augustine in his work *De quantitate animae* proves that the soul is greater than the whole world." •

[45] This is also an allegory of Christ. Cf. *Psychology and Alchemy*, par. 451.

[46] St. Thomas, *Summa*, I, q. 25, art. 3 resp. (Eng. edn., I, p. 138): "The divine existence, however, upon which the nature of power in God is founded, is infinite, and is not limited to any genus of being, but possesses within itself the perfection of all being." •

[47] Albertus, *De anima*, II, ii, 4, refutes the view of certain contemporaries that the soul is a "virtue of fire": "because fire alone of all bodies is nourished and increased by its own virtue . . . by the addition of combustible things." • Cf. supra, p. 9, n. 13.

purely archetypal anima figure, the feminine aspect of the God-image.[48] As an archetype, she is in fact form without limitation, eternal and yet manifest and repeatable in an infinite number of individuals.

91   The comparison of Wisdom with fire is in this context no accident. as it is an allusion to the *ignis occultus* or *ignis noster* of the alchemists.[49] This is a symbolic fire, whose meaning could best be rendered by the modern conception of psychic energy.[50] Flame or fire is a widespread symbol for the soul,[51] and as an image for psychic energy it seems to have been venerated in many primitive religions as something divine. It plays as central a role in the religious life of those communities as the God-image does in ours. (God showed himself to Moses in the burning bush, and Christ is named eternal fire.) [52] Later in the text we shall come upon the fire symbolism of the Holy Ghost.

92   The archetypal idea of a cosmic, divine energy capable of consciousness was not confined in the Middle Ages to certain symbols of the Holy Ghost, but was resuscitated, sometimes in modified form, in the concept of the *intellectus agens* or νοῦς ποιητικός (active intellect). This concept and the discussions that grew up around it seem to me psychologically so important that I would like to go into this question more closely.

93   The main source for the medieval conception of the *intellectus agens* is Ibn Sina (Avicenna).[53] In his view, cognition arises because man is open to the influence of the *intelligentia agens* (active intelligence). which is a cosmic [54] reality whose rays can

---

[48] According to Albertus (ibid.) fire is "the most incorporeal and spiritual of all the elements." Honorius in his *Elucidarium* (Migne, *P.L.*, vol. 172, col. 1113) says that the nature of the angels is a "spiritual fire" (Hebr. 1 : 7). "Eternal fire" is a symbol of Christ (Ephraem Syrus, I, col. 350).

[49] *Psychology and Alchemy*, pars. 157, 336f.

[50] Jung, "On Psychic Energy," pp. 28ff.

[51] *Psychology and Alchemy*, par. 370, n. 57.

[52] "He that is near to me is near to the fire. He that is far from me is far from the kingdom." Uncanonical saying from Origen, *In Jer. hom.*, XX, 3 (Migne, *P.G.*, vol. 13, col. 532), cited in James, *Apocryphal New Testament*, p. 35. For the dark aspect of this fire see *Psychology and Alchemy*, par. 215. The Holy Ghost likewise is a fire (miracle of Pentecost).

[53] I shall not go deeper here into the Aristotelian νοῦς ποιητικός, because Avicenna was the chief transmitter at the time *Aurora* was written. Cf. Gilson, "Pourquoi St. Thomas a critiqué St. Augustin," pp. 5ff., esp. p. 7.

[54] That is, present in nature.

166

be likened to rays of light.[55] This intelligence dwells in the planetary spheres and is an extra-psychic force present in nature, and the root of all human cognition [56] (for which reason Avicenna's theory of knowledge, according to peripatetic tradition, pertains to physics). When the soul comes into contact with the *intellectus agens* she becomes "reflective"; and when she soars up to it "in inspired surmise," a holy power streams into her which causes prophecy. Albertus Magnus and Maimonides took over this conception practically unaltered,[57] whereas William of Auvergne [58] and others rejected it completely. From a psychological point of view it seems to me a very significant one. For Avicenna, the cosmic *intellectus agens* corresponded to the idea of a quasiconscious meaning inherent in the objective physical processes of nature,[59] and thus it corresponds to Jung's concept of an "absolute knowledge." [60]

94   According to Avicenna, man's ego is receptive to the *intel-*

[55] Haneberg, "Zur Erkenntnislehre von Ibn Sina und Albertus Magnus," p. 197.
[56] According to Avicenna there are many such intelligences ruling the individual planetary spheres; the one that influences man is the sublunar intelligence. (Gilson, "Pourquoi St. Thomas," pp. 38–49). Cf. also Grabmann, "Mittelalterliche Deutung und Umbildung der aristot. Lehre vom νοῦς ποιητικός."
[57] Haneberg, p. 247. Cf. the Avicenna quotation in Petrus Hispanus, afterwards Pope John XXI, cited in Gilson, "Les Sources gréco-arabes de l'augustinisme avicennisant," p. 106: "The fifth mode [of knowing] is to know a thing by the uplifting and withdrawal of the mind itself. And of this kind of uplifting the Philosopher [sc., of course, Aristotle] never speaks, but Avicenna speaks thus of it in his book *De anima,* where he says that there are two aspects of the intellect. One is that which the intellect has towards the lower powers, according as the active intellect receives from the possible intellect. The other is that which the intellect has by withdrawal and uplifting from all material conditions, and this it has through relation to the inflowing Intelligence. And when the soul is thus uplifted, the Intelligence uncovers to it many things. Thus Avicenna says that it remembers past things and foretells future things, and can command rain to fall and thunder to sound, and can do harm through the evil eye. Hence Avicenna says that the bewitching eye causes the dog [or possibly the old woman] to fall into the ditch, and thus are those upraised who are in ecstasy, such as religious, contemplatives, and maniacs and phrenetics, and in this way the soul knows the First Being and itself in its essence by its own reflection upon itself." •
[58] Gilson, "Pourquoi St. Thomas," p. 58.
[59] *Intellectus agens* might be translated "creative meaning."
[60] "Synchronicity: An Acausal Connecting Principle," pp. 481, 493, 506. *Nous poietikos* seems to me the Occidental concept that comes closest to the Chinese *tao.* (A classical parallel would be the Heraclitan fire.)

lectus agens.[61] We know today that all thinking which takes place in our ego-consciousness obscures that "absolute knowledge," and that an *abaissement du niveau mental* is required before one can approach it.

95   Thomas Aquinas modified the idea of the *intellectus agens* as a cosmic principle outside the psyche by attributing the capacity for abstract thought to an *intellectus agens* within the human soul (as we would say, in the unconscious), calling it a "natural light." Its other aspect, that of a source of illumination external to man, he identified with God or with Sapientia Dei.[62] For the subtler details I must refer the reader to the work of Gilson. He writes: [63] "God enlightens our souls in so far as he has bestowed upon them the natural light thanks to which they know, and which is that of the active intellect. . . . This active intellect is indeed always *in actu,* but the soul possesses also a possible intellect, and actually knows itself only through the cooperation of its possible intellect [64] with its active intellect." [65]

96   In the act of contemplation the *intellectus agens* brings about contact with Sapientia Dei, whereby an assimilation of the human mind to God can take place.[66] In this theory of St.

[61] In his view, the ego would be the "intelligentia in potentia" and "consideratio vel cogitatio." Gilson, "Pourquoi St. Thomas," pp. 41f.

[62] Ibid., pp. 61ff. Cf. Grabmann, "Die Aristotelesübersetzungen," pp. 112f., and Gilson, "Les Sources gréco-arabes," p. 107. Subsequently, Albertus sided with St. Thomas (Haneberg, p. 219). Roger Bacon also distinguished between an intellect that worked actively upon the soul and a passive-receptive intellect within the soul. "Opus tertium," cap. XXIII (Brewer, p. 74): "For all the moderns say that the active intellect in our souls, enlightening them, is part of the soul, so that in the soul there are two parts: that is to say, the active and the possible; and that is called the possible intellect which is in a state of potentiality to knowledge, and has it not of itself; but when it receives the forms of things, and the agent influences and illuminates it, then knowledge comes to birth in it. . . . And all the ancient sages, and those who have remained unto our own times, have said that this was God." • Cf. Grabmann, "Die mittelalterliche Lehre," p. 10.

[63] "Pourquoi St. Thomas," pp. 62f.

[64] The *intellectus possibilis* would correspond with our modern concept of consciousness.

[65] Cf. Siewerth, "Die Apriorität der menschlichen Erkenntnis nach Thomas von Aquin," pp. 105f.

[66] *Summa,* I–II, q. 3, art. 5 resp. (Eng. edn., I, p. 599): "Thirdly it should again be evident from this that in the contemplative life man has something in common with the things above him, viz., with God and the angels, to whom he is made like by happiness. . . . The likeness of the speculative intellect to God is one of union and information." • According to Thomas, the intrapsychic *intellectus agens* is a gift of God.

Thomas's the νοῦς ποιητικός, or "absolute knowledge," is partially integrated in man. The Thomist splitting-up of the nous-concept signifies, from the psychological standpoint, an advance of consciousness. Generally when an unconscious content becomes conscious it is first split up, one part entering into association with the field of consciousness centred by the ego, the other remaining in the unconscious or being projected into the extrapsychic realm. Our Western intellect, as it developed at the time of Scholasticism, seems to have arisen in this way: one portion of our "pre-conscious thinking" was asserted to be the operation of the subject, the rest remained pre-conscious and was projected into the non-human realm, in other words, it was personified in the "metaphysical" figure of Sapientia Dei. The important thing is that the part which remained in the non-human realm no longer continued to be, as in Avicenna, a purely masculine concept ("intellectus") but was identified with Sapientia Dei: in psychological language, it entered the sphere of the archetypal anima-image.

97   The intrapsychic part of the *intellectus agens* is, according to Thomas, capable of producing, in conjunction with sense-experience, those first principles upon which man is able to erect a scientific system. He can then formulate his truths because he is in active participation with the original truth of God.[67] "The human soul knows all things in the eternal types, since by participation of these types we know all things. For the intellectual light which is in us is nothing else than a participated likeness of the uncreated light, in which are contained the eternal types." [68] Illumination, therefore, does not come down only "from above" to man, who in himself is blind; according to St. Thomas there is an intellectual light innate in man, which by "participated likeness" is capable of knowing the first principles. Prophecy, for instance, is due to this. In Thomas's view there are two kinds of prophecy,[69] one that refers to "things which are to be believed by all and are matters of faith, and another that is given only to the perfect and concerns the higher mysteries." The latter kind

[67] Gilson, *The Spirit of Medieval Philosophy*, p. 140: "From the time of St. Thomas, we are henceforth in possession of a natural light, that of the active intellect. . . . Like [Aristotle's active intellect] it is capable, on contact with sensible experience, of generating first principles, and with these and of these, it will gradually build up the system of the sciences."

[68] *Summa*, I, q. 84, art. 5 resp. (Eng. edn., I, p. 427).*

[69] *Summa*, II–II, q. 171 prolog. (Eng. edn., II, p. 1889).*

belongs to Wisdom.[70] Equally, there are two ways of knowing the truth: "one which comes of nature, and one which comes of grace. The knowledge which comes of grace is likewise twofold: the first is purely speculative, as when divine secrets are revealed to someone, the second is affective knowledge, which produces love for God and properly belongs to the gift of Wisdom." [71] Wisdom therefore contains higher mysteries than faith.

98   These amplifications may suffice to shed light on the nature of Wisdom in *Aurora* as an entirely trans-personal power.[72]

99   The concept of the *intellectus agens* also coincides psychologically with Jung's conception of the "luminosity" (or twilight consciousness) of archetypal contents in the unconscious. Jung comes to the conclusion that the archetypes, in conformity with the cosmic function of the *nous*, must possess a non-psychic, or "psychoid," aspect which even causes them to appear as ordering factors in the physical space-time continuum.[73] We may recall that what St. Thomas calls the *intellectus divinus* or wisdom of God has in Avicenna the character of a power objectively present in created nature as an *intellectus agens* or *intelligentia influens*. If we try to translate this concept into modern psychological terms, it would mean that there exists in nature and in the collective unconscious, at least potentially, a kind of

---

[70] Elsewhere Thomas also distinguishes a "perfect prophecy": "When a man knows that he is being moved by the Holy Ghost . . . this belongs properly to prophecy: whereas when he is moved without his knowing it, this is not perfect prophecy, but a prophetic instinct." • *Summa*, II–II, q. 173, art. 4 resp. (Eng. edn., II, p. 1905). The latter kind is caused by "a most mysterious instinct to which the human mind is subjected without knowing it." • Q. 171, art. 5 resp. (Eng. edn., II, p. 1894).

[71] *Summa*, I, q. 64, art. 1 resp. (Eng. edn., I, p. 320).• Cf. White, "St. Thomas' Conception of Revelation," p. 5.

[72] Cf. further the interesting definition of *intellectus* in Gundissalinus, *De immortalitate animae*, p. 35: "The power of the intellect does not have its end in its operation, nor does it have its end in time." • (This agrees with the definition of fire in *Aurora*.) And on p. 31: "But if anyone should say that the intellect is in no wise a form nor has a form, and that therefore it is impossible for it to act: we reply, that the intellect is itself, in its being and in its species, a form. As the crystalline humour or visible spirit is in its being a form, and yet in regard to light and colours is after a certain manner material: so likewise is the intellect to all intelligibles which are outside it. Nor does it act, inasmuch as it is material, in this way, that is of its essence, but through its form . . ." •

[73] Jung, "On the Nature of the Psyche," pp. 229ff., and "Synchronicity," pp. 481, 493f.

objective consciousness or mind from which the individual ego-consciousness is derived only secondarily and through which it is expanded by "illumination." This agrees remarkably well with the facts known to us from depth-psychology and presented in Jung's essay "On the Nature of the Psyche." On closer investigation, the contents of the unconscious do not seem to be plunged in complete darkness—nor, indeed, could anything be predicated of such an aspect of the unconscious—but to be only relatively unconscious, just as, conversely, the contents of consciousness are hardly ever perceived in all their aspects but are also partially unconscious.[74] The unconscious state of a psychic content must therefore be conceived as a relative one, and we should not imagine that the light of ego-consciousness is set against the total darkness of the unconscious.[75] Even the light of consciousness has, as Jung points out,[76] many degrees of luminosity, and the

[74] Accordingly, one might be tempted to regard the unconscious as a psychic state that does not differ in principle from consciousness. Experience does show, however, that the state of unconscious contents is not quite the same as that of conscious ones. As Jung explains, feeling-toned complexes, for example, are conserved in their original form; they even acquire the "uninfluenceable and compulsive character of an automatism," and finally they assume, "by self-amplification, an archaic and mythological character and hence a certain numinosity. . . . These peculiarities of the unconscious state contrast very strongly with the way complexes behave in the conscious mind. Here they can be corrected: they lose their automatic character and can be substantially transformed. They slough off their mythological envelope, and, by entering into the adaptive process going forward in consciousness, they personalize and rationalize themselves to the point where a dialectical discussion becomes possible. Evidently the unconscious state is different after all from the conscious." ("On the Nature of the Psyche," pp. 186f.)

[75] "The unconscious is accordingly a different medium from the conscious. In the near-conscious areas there is not much change, because here the alternation of light and shadow is too rapid. But it is just this no man's land which is of the greatest value in supplying the answer to the burning question of whether psyche = consciousness. It shows us how relative the unconscious state is, so relative, indeed, that one feels tempted to make use of a concept like 'the subconscious' in order to define the darker part of the psyche. But consciousness is equally relative, for it embraces not only consciousness as such, but a whole scale of intensities of consciousness. Between 'I do this' and 'I am conscious of doing this' there is a world of difference, amounting sometimes to outright contradiction. Consequently there is a consciousness in which unconsciousness predominates, as well as a consciousness in which self-consciousness predominates. . . . So we come to the paradoxical conclusion that there is no conscious content which is not in some other respect unconscious . . ." (ibid., pp. 187f.).

[76] Ibid., p. 189.

ego-complex many gradations of emphasis. On the animal and primitive level a mere luminosity reigns, just as on the infantile level consciousness is not a unity, since it is not yet centred by a firmly knit ego-complex, but only flickers up here and there when inner and outer events, instincts, and affects call it awake. Even on the higher levels, consciousness is not a fully integrated totality but is still capable of indefinite expansion.[77]

100   For this reason the psychic background of our consciousness is often symbolized, in dreams and visions, by a starry sky, a sea of lights, innumerable eyes shining out of darkness, and suchlike motifs. The motif of multiple luminosities plays an important role in alchemy, too, as the *scintillae* (sparks) and *oculi piscium* (fish-eyes), or—in Paracelsus and Dorn—as the "inner firmament."[78] In *Aurora* this motif appears later in the image of "pearls" or "planets in the earth."

101   The luminosity of the archetypes means, in practice, not only that they represent the forms and the meaning of our instincts but that they develop at the same time a quasi-conscious intelligence of their own, which does not coincide with that of ego-consciousness. Consequently, a constellated archetype conveys to the individual ideas, intuitions, insights, inspired thoughts, and a foreknowledge of things which he "really" could not know.[79]

102   In so far as Wisdom was defined by the scholastics as the sum of the "eternal forms," she is a feminine personification of the collective unconscious; and in so far as all these eternal ideas coalesce in her into one, she is a feminine form of the God-image (i.e., of the self) in the human psyche.[80] This psychic reality is not expounded theoretically in *Aurora* but is immediately experienced. The appearance of Wisdom denotes, psychologically, an overpowering invasion of the unconscious, and the inspiring and illuminating aspect of this event is praised enthusiastically by the author.

---

[77] "Therefore we would do well to think of ego-consciousness as being surrounded by a multitude of little luminosities" (p. 190).

[78] Pp. 195f.

[79] In dreams and other unconscious material there is often found a centre of the "inner firmament," for instance a luminary larger than the others, a central sun or star, which represents the archetype of the self, the regulatory centre of all the psychic processes (p. 199).

[80] Cf. what Jung says about Sapientia Dei in "Answer to Job," s.v. index.

103   Blessed is the man that shall find this science and into whom this prudence (of Saturn) floweth; in all thy ways think on her and she shall direct thy steps.

104   The word "Saturni" is presumably a gloss by a late alchemical author which was taken into the printed text. This Prudentia Saturni has the same meaning as the Sapientia or Scientia that is bestowed on the alchemist. "Saturn" is an indication that wisdom flows into the author from the chemical material itself (Saturn = lead = prima materia).[81]

105   As Senior saith: But the wise man and the discerning and ingenious in judgment understandeth her, when his spirits have been enlightened by the *Liber aggregationis*. For then every spirit bursteth into flood and followeth its desire; blessed is he who meditateth upon my words.

106   Senior calls the same secret that appears personified in *Aurora* as Wisdom, the "tincture," and this he defines as that which can change things from potentality into actuality.[82] According to the philosophical thinking of the Arabs, this would be the creative essence of God and the soul, which, Senior says, becomes "free"—active—only when the alchemist has "cleared" his thought by subtle meditation.

107   For the medieval Christian this typical idea of Islamic mysticism could not be assimilated without difficulty, for in his view God alone was endowed with creative power: only God could change the potential into the actual. Nevertheless St. Thomas holds that a real continuation of God's creative power runs through the human soul.[83] The soul does not of course create things directly, like God, but as a "second cause,"[84] with the

[81] Saturn is correlated with lead, in which arcane substance the alchemical secret lies hidden. In lead, according to Olympiodorus (Berthelot, *Alch. grecs*, II, iv, 38–39), there dwells a demon, or a soul that wants to be set free. In Zosimos this soul is represented as a virgin (ibid., III, xxxiv, 1, and xlii). In Khunrath (*Von hylealischen Chaos*, pp. 194f.) the mid point of the world is "ancient Saturn . . . the lead of the wise, rich in mystery." Mylius (*Philosophia reformata*, p. 142) calls lead the "water of wisdom." Cf. also the quotation from Grasseus (supra, p. 24, n. 14). As Jung has shown (*Psychology and Alchemy*, par. 443, n. 59), Grasseus may have known the *Aurora* text.

[82] *De chemia*, pp. 11f. Cf. Stapleton, p. 150.

[83] The soul is "the first act with a . . . relation to the second act." • *Summa*, I, q. 77, art. 1 resp. (Eng. edn., I, p. 383).

[84] Gilson, "Pourquoi St. Thomas," p. 11.

interposition of special functions (*facultates*) which "flow from the essence of the soul as from their principle" (*fluunt ab essentia animae sicut a principio*).[85] They flow from the soul "by a certain resultance . . . as colour from light."[86] In modern language, this means that the human psyche, like God, can intervene creatively in the physical and chemical processes of nature. So if the author of *Aurora* interprets Senior's "fluens" intrapsychically, as a flowing of the spirit resulting in an alchemical transmutation of metals, it is tempting to assume that he too was thinking of a function flowing from the essence of the soul, which can impart actual being and bring about material changes. According to St. Thomas it is one of the special properties of the soul of one who has been enlightened[87] by Wisdom that, by the virtue of God, even matter outside his body will obey him.[88] His soul can intervene effectively in the physical order.

[85] *Summa*, I, q. 77, art. 5 and art. 6 resp. (Eng. edn., I, pp. 387f.). William of Auvergne's view is in this respect extreme: the soul operates directly through its simple, godlike essence ("De anima," *Opera omnia*, III, pars 6). Cf. Gilson, *Med. Phil.*, p. 246f.

[86] *Summa*, I, q. 77, art. 6 and 7 (Eng. edn., I, pp. 387ff.).

[87] I.e., the prophet.

[88] St. Thomas, "De veritate," q. 12, art 3, 7ff. (trans. Mulligan, II, p. 115): "From natural causes we cannot perceive the meaning of those things which do not take place naturally. But astrologers perceive the meanings of prophecies from the movements of the heavenly bodies; therefore, prophecy is natural. In natural science the philosophers discuss only those things which can happen naturally. But Avicenna discusses prophecy. Therefore prophecy is natural. For prophecy, as Avicenna says, only three things are needed: clearness of intelligence, perfection of the imaginative power, and *power of soul so that external matter obeys it.* But these three things can be had naturally. Therefore, one can naturally be a prophet." • According to the Thomist view, God is the only being who cannot be divided into "actual" and "potential" being, but is *only* actual being and the source of all being. N. del Prado (*De veritate fundamentali philosophiae christianae*, p. xxx): "The fundamental truth of St. Thomas's Christian philosophy, formulated in *De ente et essentia*, can be summed up thus: 'The First Being is pure act, but all other beings are made up of potentiality and act. . . . God alone is His own Being; in all else the essence of the thing is distinct from its being'" • (cited in Gilson, *L'Esprit de la philosophie médiévale*, I, p. 315, n. 34). God is "maximum truth" and "maximum being" (cf. *Compendium of Theology*, ch. 69, p. 64), and hence also the cause of the prima materia, which has its "potential being" from him. "Nothing gives existence except in so far as it is a being in act. Now God preserves all things in existence by his providence." • *Summa contra Gentiles*, III, 66 (Eng. edn., III, part 1, p. 158). "Nor is it superfluous, if God can produce all natural effects by Himself, that they should be produced by certain

An interesting account of this remarkable notion is to be
found in a treatise ascribed to Albertus Magnus, entitled "De
mirabilibus mundi," whose genuineness has, as Thorndike emphasizes,[89] been wrongly disputed. Albertus says there: [90] "I found
an instructive account [of magic] in Avicenna's *Liber sextus
naturalium,* which says that a certain power (*virtus*) to alter
things dwells in the human soul and subordinates the other
things to her, particularly when she is swept into a great excess
of love or hate or the like. When therefore the soul of a man
falls into a great excess of any passion, it can be proved by experiment that the excess binds things magically and alters them
in the way it wants. And for a long time I did not believe this,
but after I had read the nigromantic books and others of the
kind on signs and magic, I found that the affectivity (*affectio*)
of the human soul is the chief cause of all these things, whether
because, on account of her great emotion, she alters her bodily
substance and the other things towards which she strives, or
because, on account of her dignity, the other, lower things are
subject to her, or because the appropriate hour or astrological
situation or another power coincides with so inordinate an
emotion, and we [in consequence] believe that what this power

other causes; because this is not owing to the insufficiency of His power, but to
the immensity of His goodness, wherefore it was His will to consummate His
likeness to things not only in the point of their being, but also in the point of
their being the causes of other things." • Ibid., III, 70 (Eng. edn., III, part 1,
p. 174). "Nothing is a cause of being except in so far as it acts by God's power." •
III, 67 (III, part 1, p. 160). "In all things that operate God is the cause of their
operating." • Ibid. Among the intermediary causes in nature, of which God makes
instrumental use, are the heavenly bodies. (Cf. Thorndike, II, p. 607.) According
to St. Thomas, the human soul also possesses that gift of acting as a "secondary
cause" after God; it endows matter with "esse actuale" and thus creates the individual body-soul phenomenon; as form, it gives the only potentially existent
bodily material the "actum essendi," and for that reason is superior to it, because
"esse in actu" is higher than "esse in potentia." This "esse in actu" arises only
by contact with God and by his grace and illuminative effect. The soul can even
produce material effects in the outside world. Cf. Forest, *La Structure métaphysique du concret selon Saint Thomas d'Aquin,* pp. 267–80; and, for Thomas'
conception of physics, Stanghetti, "Da S. Tommaso a Max Planck," pp. 53ff.
[89] *History of Magic,* II, p. 723.
[90] • I cite here from an undated incunabulum in the Zentralbibliothek, Zurich,
Gal. II, App. 429$_3$: "Liber aggregationis seu secretorum Alberti," etc. The library
also contains the printing of Lyons, 1582, and Cologne, ca. 1485.

does is then done by the soul. . . . Whoso, therefore, would learn the secret of doing and undoing these things must know that everyone can influence everything magically if he falls into a great excess . . . and he must do it in that hour when the excess befalls him, and with the things which the soul then dictates to him. For the soul herself is then so desirous of the matter she would accomplish that of her own accord she will seize on the greater and better astrological hour which rules over the things suited to that matter. . . . And thus it is the soul who desires the thing more intensely, who makes things more active and more like what comes forth. For science is the production of signs (*characteres*). . . . Such is the manner of operation in all things which the soul strongly desires. For everything she does to that end has motive power and efficacy for what the soul desires."

109   Thus Albertus, following Avicenna, comes to the conclusion that all magic and occult techniques, including alchemical transmutation, are ultimately and in principle explicable in terms of the human psyche, and are produced by the psyche when a man falls into a kind of ecstasy or trance (we would say, into a completely unconscious state), and that in such states concomitant material phenomena can be observed, as is known today chiefly through the findings of parapsychological research.[91]

110   As Jung—who cites this Albertus passage—has shown,[92] we are concerned here with a phenomenon which he calls "synchronicity," that is, with the remarkable fact that, particularly when archetypal unconscious contents are constellated, a non-psychic event can coincide *meaningfully* with an intrapsychic event, though no causal connection can be established between them. The "magical" thinking of primitives seems to be based partly on the observation of such occurrences. It is worth noting that a man like Albertus Magnus, the teacher of Thomas Aquinas, took an experimental interest in these phenomena and, like Avicenna before him, brought them into connection with the human psyche, or as we should say, with the unconscious. The "production of signs" would correspond to the creation of suitable symbols through which the unconscious is both con-

[91] Rhine, *The Reach of the Mind* and other works.
[92] "Synchronicity," pp. 448f.

stellated and expressed. What distinguishes Jung's interpretation from the medieval one is that the medieval philosophers still interpreted these connections as "magical causality," as primitives do today, whereas Jung considers the same class of events to be acausal and synchronistic. In that way he avoids a regressive amalgamation of the scientific concept of causality with the old, pre-scientific "magical causality," setting up instead, in the concept of synchronicity, a new and fundamental category for the explanation of nature.

111   Unfortunately, Albertus's source, Avicenna's treatise "De anima," which in those days was usually cited as "Liber sextus naturalium," was available to me only in the Venice edition of 1508,[93] in which the sections on magic, alchemy, and the occult sciences had been partially deleted by the Augustinian monks of the monastery of St. John of Viridario. Nevertheless, it was clear from the portions that have been preserved that Avicenna saw in the human soul not only that factor which, "as form, aggregates and builds up the fundamental forces and matter into a body of their own,"[94] but also one which produces material effects outside that body, thus explaining many so-called miracles—the healing of the sick, etc.[95] "And thus it is not to be wondered at, that a strong and noble soul in her workings should go even beyond her own body, so that (if she be not sunk in the body's passions) she can heal the sick and make evil men weak, and that it is even possible for her to render the natures of things compliant, and to change the elements in her interests, so that what is not fire becomes for her fire, and what is not earth becomes for her earth, and that rain and fruitfulness

[93] *Avicennae perhypatetici philosophi . . . opera,* etc. Concerning this treatise see Haneberg, "Zur Erkenntnislehre von Ibn Sina."

[94] Fol. 3: "For it gathers together the principles and matter of its body . . . preserving the body," etc.● Cf. the passage in the Prooemium, fol. 1ʳ: "For the knowledge of the soul is a very great help to knowing the dispositions of the body," etc.● "Now we will say then, that the soul can be called a power or potentiality in relation to the *affections which issue from it.* Likewise it can be called a power on another ground: namely in relation to the sensible and intelligible forms which it receives: it can likewise be called a form in relation to the matter in which it exists: from both of which it is constituted a vegetable or animal substance," etc.●

[95] He also emphasizes that the *idea* of sickness and health in the soul affects the state of the body. As the soul is not imprisoned [*impressa*] in the body's matter, it can alter it at will.

appear at her behest . . ." [96] "And all these things come to pass according to the intelligible virtue, for it is altogether possible that even living beings will follow her wishes, since matter is wont to change into opposites. For matter by nature obeys her and becomes the matter she wills, for it obeys the soul utterly, and obeys her still more than when [only] the opposites work upon it." According to Avicenna, this is one of the basic factors underlying prophecy, for there is in the soul a property that depends on imagination and can act upon matter.[97] This property is conditioned by the *virtus sensibilis motiva desiderativa* in the soul of the prophet.[98] Further, the stars too are an operative factor since they affect the soul in this lower world.[99]

[112]   In psychological terms the constellations in the sky are where the archetypes of the collective unconscious appear in projection, in such a way that, in contrast to myths, fairytales, and other elaborations of the archetype, its time-quality is also taken into account. The individual psyche also (Avicenna is right in this) is instrumentally the place of realization for the archetype, which in itself is transpersonal and, in its lower reaches, even non-psychic.[100] An archetype is constellated, i.e., becomes a realizable power having real effects, only when a specific attitude of consciousness prevails. Avicenna formulates this by saying that the constellation is brought about by "science," that is, by the "right" understanding. Science is the production of the right "imagination," the right symbols. As is clear from the account in "De mirabilibus mundi," Albertus took over in principle Avicenna's hypotheses.[101]

---

96 Cap. IV.

97 Cap. IV, fol. 20ᵛ. *

98 In Tract. 10, cap. 1 of his "De philosophia prima" or "Metaphysica" (1508, fol. 107ᵛ) Avicenna says that the prophet is one "whose soul becomes the intelligence in effect," i.e., is identical with the *intellectus agens.*

99 Ibid., cap. V, Tract. 9 (fol. 105ᵛ): ". . . et a corporibus celestibus fiunt impressiones in corpore huius mundi propter qualitates, quae sunt ei propriae: et ab illis fluit in hunc mundum et ab animabus etiam illorum fiunt impressiones in animas huius mundi et ex his intentionibus scimus quod natura, quae est gubernatrix istorum corporum, est quasi perfectio; et formae fiunt ab anima diffusa vel adjutorio eius."

100 Jung, "On the Nature of the Psyche," p. 230.

101 They enabled him to explain and justify "good" magic, which could operate without the influence of demons and was really a kind of higher science. It was

113   These amplifications seemed to me necessary in order to elucidate the obscure passage in *Aurora* about the flowing of the spirit. They also seem to justify my conjecture "Liber aggregationis," [102] for Albertus's "De mirabilibus mundi" was circulated under this title. The flowing of the spirit means that it was seized by Wisdom, so that the soul of the alchemist not only attained to gnosis but could exert magical effects in the material realm. By a reading of the "Liber aggregationis," the text says, the spirit bursts into flood and follows its desire. The word "desire" seems strange at first, because *concupiscentia* in ecclesiastical language generally meant sinful desire, "the flesh, which lusteth against the spirit" (Gal. 5 : 17).[103]

114   The sentence in *Aurora* is based on a mistranslation of Senior's Arabic text. In the original,[104] Senior says that by the

---

based—as we should say—on correct knowledge of unconscious phenomena and their constellation, thanks to a conscious attitude that enabled the unconscious to co-operate. In this sense the magician does what "the soul dictates to him," and in the hour which "the soul appoints." Observance of the "virtus desiderativa" amounts to following the gradient of psychic energy.

102 The Latin text shows the following variants: M and P, the best MSS, have "ex libro aggregationum"; V has "congregationem"; B, D, and L have "ex libris agnitionum." I take it that M and P come closest to the original text, and I conjecture the singular ending aggregation*is* instead of aggregation*um* only because I assume that the *Aurora* text is referring to the treatise of this title, especially as the author is here concerned with a thorough clarification of the problem of alchemy.

103 Cf. St. Thomas, *De malo*, q. 4, art. 2, where *concupiscentia* is defined as "evil desires, which a man feels without the consent of his will." Cf. also St. Augustine, Sermo CLII, 4 (Migne, *P.L.*, vol. 38, col. 821), and Rom. 7 : 14; Irenaeus, *Adv. haer.*, I, 2, cap. 2 (Migne, *P.G.*, vol. 7, col. 454; Eng. edn., I, p. 7), and St. John Chrysostom, *Gen. homil.*, XV, 4 (Migne, *P.G.*, vol. 53, col. 123). *Concupiscentia* is "something material." See article on "Concupiscence" by Chollet in *Dictionnaire de théologie catholique*, III, cols. 803–14.

104 Cf. Stapleton's discussion of the Arabic original in *Memoirs*, p. 150. The Latin translation of Senior (*De chemia*, p. 12) reads: "But since [the preparation] is difficult, delicate, light, moderate, and without force, the ingenious man understands it by subtle reflection, when his spirits have been rendered clear by the books that are left, which the philosophers have hidden on account of the preparation, which is a matter of difficulty. But it [the preparation or tincture] was hidden lest every spirit should recognize its desire: [for then] it flows, as the seers would say." (Latin: . . . Facta ignota, propter hoc ne cognoscat. Omnis animus concupiscentiam suam fluit: quod videntes dicant.) The punctuation in the Latin is quite arbitrary. I therefore read "cognoscat omnis" and put the colon before "fluit."

inspiration of Allah he discovered the secret of the preparation and thereby the tincture which changes things from potentiality into actuality. In this process the spirit is *freed* from its desire.[105] But the Latin translation says that the tincture was hidden lest the spirit should *recognize* its desire and *flow*.[106] And in *Aurora* this is again reinterpreted to mean that the spirit, when lique-fied, *follows* its desire.

115   The author of *Aurora* evidently took this obscure sentence of Senior's to mean that spirit can accomplish the difficult and hidden preparation when it recognizes the root of its own striv-ing, namely *concupiscentia*, and begins to follow it. This would mean, psychologically, that the spirit begins to follow the nat-ural gradient of psychic energy.

116   The preceding sentence in *Aurora*, "and she shall direct thy steps," shows that during this process Wisdom is at work, exer-cising a seductive fascination. This does not depart too far from the contemporary scholastic views, since many philosophers sup-posed that every act of cognition was preceded by a kind of "love" or "natural appetition" of the knower for the object.[107] According to Bernard of Clairvaux, all higher love and even our love of God begins first with *concupiscentia*, for this is the natural impulse of every creature for its own perfection. St. Thomas, too, holds that the innermost instinct of every creature

---

[105] Cf. Dorn, "Speculativae philosophiae," *Theatr. chem.* (1602), I, p. 298, cited in *Psychology and Alchemy*, par. 377: "In this [truth] lies the whole art of freeing the spirit from its fetters, in the same way that, as we have said, the mind can be freed from the body."

[106] A later Latin treatise, the "Consilium coniugii" (*Ars chemica*, p. 153), gives a negative interpretation of this Senior passage: "Every spirit that follows its yearn-ing, that is, its own vain opinion, is in a state of flux [*fluit*], that is, it wanders and strays by divers wrong paths." •

[107] Witelo, *Liber de intelligentiis*, XVIII, 2 (ed. Baeumker, *Beiträge zur Gesch. d. Philosophie des Mittelalters*, III, part 2, p. 23): "Love or delight naturally . . . goes before knowledge. For unless some appetite of the knowing substance were directed towards the thing that is to be known, there would never be any ordering of the one towards the other, nor would the one be perfected by the other." • St. Thomas also took some such inclination, love or natural appetite, to be the cause of all knowing. (*Summa*, I, q. 60, art. 1; Eng. edn., I, p. 297.) Cf. St. Bernard, *De diligendo Deo ad Haimericum* (Migne, *P.L.*, vol. 182, col. 973): "Since we are carnal, and are born of fleshly concupiscence, needs must that our desire or love begin from the flesh; and if it be governed by right order, going forward by degrees under the guidance of grace, it will at last be consummated in the spirit." •

strives for "perfection" and thus for a "divine likeness." [108] He calls his *amor boni* the "root" of all the other motions of the soul.[109] *Concupiscentia* or *desiderium* is for him a movement towards goodness.[110] It is a movement that arises from knowledge of the desired, or from contemplation of the good and beautiful.[111] The movement of loving is thus circular, and love is the real unitive force.[112] The striving for perfection is even inherent in matter.[113] All this would explain the allusion in

[108] *Summa Contra Gentiles*, III, 21 (Eng. edn., III, part 1, p. 43).* Cf. "De veritate," XIV, 10 resp.: "The ultimate perfection towards which man is directed consists in the perfect knowledge of God." *

[109] *In II Sent.*, Dist. 1, q. 2, art. 2 resp., and *Contra Gent.*, III, 19 and 20 (Eng. edn., III, part 1, pp. 37ff.). *Summa*, I, q. 20, art. 1 resp. (I, p. 114): "Hence love is naturally the first act." Cf. Steinbuechel, *Der Zweckgedanke in der Philosophie des Thomas von Aquino.*

[110] *Summa*, I-II, q. 25, art. 2 (Eng. edn., I, p. 701): "Love is . . . the first of the concupiscible passions. . . . This very aptitude or proportion of the appetite to good is love. . . . Movement towards good is desire or concupiscence, and rest in good is joy or pleasure." * Q. 27, art. 1 (Eng. edn., I, pp. 706f.) and q. 36 art. 2 resp. (I, p. 748): "But since concupiscence or desire is the first effect of love, which gives rise to the greatest pleasure, as stated above: hence it is that Augustine often speaks of desire or concupiscence in the sense of love." * Art. 3: "Love strives towards unity in the sense of perfection of nature." A psychologist might object that the soul also seems to be endowed with a natural "love of evil."

[111] Q. 27, art. 2 ad 2 (Eng. edn., I, p. 707): "The contemplation of spiritual beauty or goodness is the beginning of spiritual love. Accordingly knowledge is the cause of love for the same reason as good is, which can be loved only if known." *

[112] Q. 26, art. 2 resp. (Eng. edn., I, p. 704): "For the appetitive movement is circular, as stated in *De anima* iii, 10 . . . hence, too, Dionysius says that love is a unitive force (*Div. nom.* iv) and the Philosopher says (*Polit.* ii, 1) that union is the work of love." *

[113] *Quaest. disp., De malo*, q. I., art. 2, resp. (pp. 326ff.): "And this matter is not to be called evil." *Summa*, I, q. 44, art. 4 resp. (Eng. edn., I, p. 232): "While every creature intends to acquire its own perfection, which is the likeness of the divine perfection and goodness. Therefore the divine goodness is the end of all things." * (Cf. Gilson, *Med. Phil.*, pp. 279f.) Cf. the Avicenna quotation in Meister Eckhart's commentary on the Book of Wisdom (Thery, part II, p. 348): "But that which every thing desires is being, and the perfection of being in so far as it is being. But privation, inasmuch as it is privation, is not desired." * (Avicenna, *Metaphysica*, Lib. VIII.) Evil is only a privation of good and only by accident real. (*Summa*, I, q. 63, art. 4; Eng. edn., I, pp. 314f.) There is no natural inclination to evil, even among the demons. Cf. *Summa*, I, q. 48, art. 1 ad 1 (I, pp. 248ff.) and *De malo* (q. I, art. 1, resp.; p. 322): Even an evil act, in so far as it is an act, is of God. That is to say, what first sets the will and intellect in motion is something higher than the will and intellect, i.e., God. Cf. Jung's criticism of the *privatio boni* in *Aion*, pp. 41ff.

Aurora that at the touch of Wisdom the human spirit "flows" [114] and begins to follow its most natural desire, namely, for its own perfection and the knowledge of God.

117 And Solomon: My son, put her about thy neck and write in the tables of thy heart and thou shalt find. Say to Wisdom: Thou art my sister, and call Prudence thy friend.

118 The description of Wisdom as sister and friend is probably an allusion to the classic alchemical motif of brother/sister incest.[115] The brother and sister here would be the alchemist and Wisdom. Usually the Biblical quotation was referred to Mary.

119 For to meditate upon her is a most natural and subtle understanding, which bringeth her to perfection. And they that constantly watch for her shall quickly be secure. For she is clear to them that have understanding, and shall never fade away nor fail; she is easily seen by them that have knowledge of her, for she goeth about seeking such as are worthy of her and showeth herself cheerfully to them in the ways and meeteth them with all providence; for her beginning is the most true nature, whereof cometh no deceit.

120 Not only is the alchemist enlightened by Wisdom, but his meditation simultaneously brings her to perfection, by "a most natural and subtle understanding." This idea may go back to the *sensus naturae* of William of Auvergne (who took it over from Avicenna).[116] Albertus Magnus may have had a similar

---

114 In Thomist terms, becomes effective as "actus."

115 Concerning this motif see *Mysterium*, pp. 91f., 149f., 299. The allusion to the incest motif gives the Biblical quotations used by Wisdom as she cries out and walks the streets a peculiar colouring: she appears in the role of a *meretrix* (whore). This is not a fanciful formulation since, as we have seen, she is also the *prima materia*, which the alchemists called, among other things, *meretrix*.

116 According to William of Auvergne ("De legibus," *Opera omnia*, I, pp. 86ff.; cf. Thorndike, II, p. 348), the *sensus naturae* is something higher than any human cognitive capacity and comes close to the gift of prophecy. (Cf. *Avicennae perhypatetici philosophi*, "De anima," I, fol. 4.) Its functioning is similar to that of a dog finding a thief, or a vulture anticipating a battle, or a sheep sensing the presence of a wolf, in all of which cases there is an assimilation of sense to object. (William of Auvergne, "De universo," I, pp. 821ff.) The *sensus naturae* thus coincides partly with what we today call "instinct" and partly with "unconscious perception." Cf. Jung, "On the Nature of the Psyche," pp. 195f.: "Paracelsus was directly influenced by Agrippa von Nettesheim, who supposes a 'luminositas

idea with regard to alchemy, for in his "Libellus de alchemia" [117] (regarded by Thorndike as genuine) he calls upon Wisdom for enlightenment and help and beseeches God "through the grace of the Holy Spirit to increase his little knowledge," that, by his teachings, he may show forth "the light that is hidden in the darkness" [118] and lead the wayward into the path of truth.[119] The spirit of God thereupon helps him to find itself (the spirit of God); in other words, man's enlightenment is brought about by the Holy Spirit leading him to the discovery of the light hidden in the darkness. This idea of the circular workings of truth occurs also in St. Thomas. According to him we know nature through the "speculative intellect," which is passive and receptive towards things and receives from them the first impulse and

---

sensus naturae.' From this 'gleams of prophecy came down to the four-footed beasts, the birds, and other living creatures,' and enabled them to foretell future things. He bases the *sensus naturae* on the authority of Gulielmus Parisiensis, who is none other than William of Auvergne (G. Alvernus; d. 1249), bishop of Paris from about 1228, author of many works, which influenced Albertus Magnus among others. Alvernus says that the *sensus naturae* is superior to the perceptive faculty in man, and he insists that animals also possess it. The doctrine of the *sensus naturae* is developed from the idea of the all-pervading world-soul with which another Gulielmus Parisiensis was much concerned, a predecessor of Alvernus by name of Guillaume de Conches (1080-1154), a Platonist scholastic who taught in Paris. He identified the *anima mundi*, this same *sensus naturae*, with the Holy Ghost, just as Abelard did. The world-soul is a natural force which is responsible for all the phenomena of life and the psyche."

117 *Opera*, ed. Borgnet, XXXVII, pp. 545ff. It was cited as a work of Albertus as far back as 1320. (Cf. Thorndike, II p. 571.) Paneth ("Über die Schrift Alberts des Grossen 'De Alchemia,'" pp. 408ff.) has misgivings about its authenticity, but, on the basis of *De mineralibus* and the "Tractatus de metallis et alchemia" (which he holds to be genuine), he admits that Albertus was an alchemist. Ruska (*Tabula Smaragdina*, p. 186) declares it spurious without substantiating this charge, and so does Sarton, *Introduction to the History of Science*, II, pp. 937ff. Cf. also Daehnert, *Die Erkenntnislehre des Albertus Magnus*, pp. 228f.

118 John 1:5.

119 Cf. Albertus, *De mineralibus et rebus metallicis*, Lib. II (Cologne, 1569), p. 119, where the same story occurs as in *Aurora* (infra, pp. 323f.), that the rock Adamas is softened by goat's blood, and pp. 99, 201, 241, 253, 257, 274-76, 351, on the influence of astrology. Later in the same treatise he emphasizes that after long wanderings and researches he found what he was seeking, "not by my own knowledge, but by the grace of the Holy Spirit," so that when he "knew and understood what conquered nature," he began to "watch more diligently in decoctions."

order, but the things themselves are ordered by the divine intellect.[120]

121   This approximates closely to the view in *Aurora*, according to which Wisdom enlightens man so that with the help of "subtle understanding" he can then find the truth in nature, the innermost essence ("most true nature") of which is Wisdom herself.[121] According to the medieval view the divine likeness (*similitudo*) reaches down even into the physical structure of natural things.[122] That is why *Aurora* says that to meditate on Wisdom is a "most natural understanding." [123] Nevertheless, the entire cognitive process is not simply a circular one in which man is included passively: the intervention of human consciousness has a perfecting influence on Wisdom herself, making her whole, even though her capacities far surpass man's.[124]

122   The idea that the process of cognition is circular plays a central role in alchemy. Petrus Bonus says: ". . . truth is nothing other than the correspondence of the intellect to the thing." [125] Again: "And the art works in the same way as nature." [126] And in one of the sources for *Aurora*, the "Declaratio lapidis physici

120 *Quaestiones disputatae*, "De veritate," I, 2, resp. (Eng. edn., I, p. 77). Cf. "De potentia," VII, 10, ad 5: "But things themselves are the cause and measure of our knowledge, wherefore, as our knowledge refers to things really and not the reverse, so things are referred really to the knowledge of God and not the reverse." • *Summa*, I, q. 16, art. 6 ad 2 (Eng. edn., I, p. 93): "Things are said to be true by comparison with the divine intellect." • Cf. Forest, *La Structure métaphysique*, p. 21.

121 I follow Gilson's formulation, *Med. Phil.*, p. 141. Cf. Bacon, *Opera inedita*, "Opus tertium," p. 82: "That I may show that philosophy is useless and pointless, except in so far as it is raised to the wisdom of God." •

122 Robert de Grosseteste, "De unica forma omnium" (Baur, *Beiträge*, p. 110): "In that manner therefore in which the form of this thing in the mind of such an architect is the form of a house, the art, or wisdom, or Word of almighty God is the form of all creatures. For it is at the same time both the exemplar and the efficient and formal cause preserving things in the form given them, until created things are directed and recalled to it." •

123 This idea occurs among other scholastic philosophers. Thus Alcuin says (Migne, *P.L.*, vol. 100, col. 271) that the truth was implanted by God in nature, where the wiser among men might find it. William of Auvergne identifies the truth of a thing with its being: "For the truth of any thing is nothing else than its substance, or being, or essence." • ("De universo," II, *Opera*, I, p. 836.)

124 Cf. the interpretation of wisdom in Gundissalinus, *De divisione philosophiae* (Baur, *Beiträge*, p. 8): "Wisdom is the truth of the knowledge of primary eternal things." •

125 *Theatr. chem.* (1622), V, p. 667. •   126 Ibid., p. 745. •

filio suo Aboali" of pseudo-Avicenna, it is said: "It is nature that brings about the work with the help of the artifex." [127] This "natural" knowledge is attained through intensive meditation on the substances and has a reactive effect on the alchemist, perfecting his insight. The intellect is a "generative power," [128] so that already in Greek alchemy Petesis, a pupil of Ostanes, could say: "The work is perfected by reflection." [129] "Make the nature come out, and you will find what is sought," [130] the "hidden nature" being the mysterium of the philosophers.[131] This produces the "golden point" in matter.[132]

123   Here we have an allusion to that psychological form of inner experience which Jung calls "active imagination," whereby the conscious mind perceives the contents of the unconscious, and transforms and integrates them by coming to terms with them.[133] In alchemical language, this would be the extraction of the "truth" from matter by means of the right "theoria"—that central preoccupation of the alchemists which Jung has discussed at length in *Aion* [134] and *Mysterium Coniunctionis*. From the passages cited, particularly those from the works of Dorn, it is clear that the arcane substance is nothing other than the unconscious, which in meditation is "attracted" by the "right

127 *Theatr. chem.* (1659), IV, p. 879.• During the process sulphur acts as a *lumen luminum:* "And it illuminates all bodies, for it is a light and a tincture, enlightening and perfecting every substance. And if the artifex of this magistery knows not this light, he strays by many devious ways, as if walking in darkness, because he is far from the truth and unity of this science." • Sulphur, as Jung has shown (*Mysterium*, pp. 126f.), is in late alchemical literature a widespread image for the "natural light" hidden in matter, the source of natural knowledge as opposed to revelation.

128 William of Auvergne, "De trinitate," cap. 15; II, Suppl., p. 27: "Our intellect, that is, the intellective power, is a generative power, and as it were the womb of science or wisdom." •

129 Lippmann, *Alchemie*, I, p. 68, and Berthelot, *Moyen âge*, I, p. 246.

130 Zosimos, Berthelot, *Alch. grecs*, III, xxi, 22.• Cf. ibid., xlvi, 2. The hidden nature corresponds to the "most true nature" in *Aurora*.

131 Ibid., V, ii, 8. Cf. IV, iii, 2 and II, iv.

132 Ibid., III, vi. This nature hidden in matter is really the "divine soul bound in the elements, or the divine pneuma mingled with the flesh." (Cf. the Book of Sophe, Berthelot, III, xlii.) The Neoplatonist Celsus (Bousset, *Hauptprobleme der Gnosis*, p. 11) calls the world soul a fluid force (δύναμις ῥέουσα), and Zosimos (Berthelot, III, ii, 2) a feminine power.

133 *Mysterium*, pp. 494ff. Also Jung's commentary on *The Secret of the Golden Flower*, pars. 20ff.   134 Pp. 155ff.

magnet" [135]—the effective symbol—so that a synthesis is prepared between the conscious and unconscious components of the personality. The essence to be extracted is personified in our text by Wisdom, who, as is expressly emphasized, is at the same the "most true nature, whereof cometh no deceit." Dorn speaks in much the same way of a "truth" which is hidden in natural things.[136] This "truth" is a "metaphysical substance," hidden not only in things but in the human body. "In the human body is concealed a certain metaphysical substance known to very few, which . . . needeth no medicament, being itself the incorrupt medicament." [137] Jung interprets as follows: [138] "Thus the doctrine, which may be consciously acquired 'through a kind of divine inspiration,' is at the same time the instrument whereby the object of the doctrine or theory can be freed from its imprisonment in the 'body,' [139] because the symbol for the doctrine—the 'magnet'—is at the same time the mysterious 'truth' of which the doctrine speaks. The doctrine enters the consciousness of the adept as a gift of the Holy Ghost. It is a thesaurus of knowledge about the secret of the art, of the treasure hidden in the prima materia, which was thought to be outside man. The treasure of the doctrine and the precious secret concealed in the darkness of matter are one and the same thing." [140]

124   To my knowledge, *Aurora* is one of the earliest medieval treatises in which we find the nascent idea that the alchemical opus involves an *inner experience,* and that a numinous content, Wisdom (the anima), is the secret which the adept was looking for in the chemical substances.

125   Jung has discussed the great significance which attaches to this projection of the unconscious into matter [141] in *Psychology*

135 Ibid., p. 159ff.

136 It is the "medicine, improving and transforming that which *is no longer* into that which it *was before* its corruption, and that which *is not* into that which it *ought to be." Aion,* p. 161.   137 Ibid. Cf. *Mysterium,* pp. 478f.

138 *Aion,* p. 162. Cf. *Mysterium,* pp. 480ff.   139 Cf. *Mysterium,* pp. 482ff., 489ff.

140 For a more detailed psychological explanation of these extremely significant ideas of Dorn, see *Mysterium,* p. 494f.

141 Similar ideas to those of the alchemists are found in the *Corpus Hermeticum* (ed. Scott, I, p. 158). God created all visible things through imagination (φαντασία) and manifests himself in everything. He is present in everything and is the visible and the invisible, in that which is and that which is not. Thus the cre-

and Alchemy.[142] The tendency of the alchemists, as he says, was "not only to locate the mystery of psychic transformation in matter, but at the same time to use it as a theoria for effecting chemical changes." [143] That is why Wisdom appears in *Aurora* as a guide ("she shall direct thy steps") during the opus: the psychic content projected into matter has the effect of inspiring the adept. In the pagan texts the same content was personified as the "anima mundi" or as Physis,[144] while in *Aurora* it is equated with Wisdom and the Holy Spirit. It is probably no accident that the author cites just those Biblical passages which come from the latest portions of the Old and New Testaments, and which derived from Hellenized Jewish sources [145] and may safely be regarded as "Gnostic."

---

ative fantasy of God is contained in the visible world and can reveal itself to the elect. God is the dynamic energy (δύναμις ἐνεργής) in all things (p. 210), and everything is full of psyche and moves in perfect order (p. 212). Similarly in the treatise "Asclepius" (pp. 310f.): "In the beginning were God and matter [which in Greek is the cosmos. And a breath hovered over the matter, and was within it. But as yet the elements were not]." Later in the same treatise, matter is identified with the *spiritus mundi* or *natura mundi,* and possesses a self-subsistent *vis procreandi.* In "Kore Kosmou" (p. 462; cf. IV, pp. 450f.), Physis is a beautiful feminine being who arose from the word of the First Father. Her daughter is Heuresis ("finding" or "discovering"), who has power over the cosmic mysteries. Thus here too the "spirit of finding the truth" resides as it were in Nature herself, in the form of a divine feminine being who must reveal herself if Nature is to be known. In another Hermetic fragment (I, p. 382) it is said that although human imagination is a prey to illusion, it can nevertheless attain to a reflection of the truth through an "influence" from above.

142 Pars. 405ff.　　143 Par. 406.　　144 Par. 413.

145 According to Sellin (*Introduction to the Old Testament*), Ecclesiastes cannot be dated prior to 300 B.C. because of the Graecisms it contains (p. 228), the Canticles (Song of Songs) in its present version belongs to the 4th or 5th cent. B.C. (p. 224), Proverbs are post-exilic and belong to the 4th cent. (p. 208), Jesus Sirach (Ecclesiasticus) to about 200 B.C. (p. 294), and the Wisdom of Solomon to the 1st cent. B.C. with demonstrable Greek influences. In this connection it is especially interesting to consider the conception of Sapientia Dei in Philo of Alexandria, since towards the end of the 1st cent. B.C. this Hellenistic philosopher undertook, as a Jew, the attempt to connect the Greek, pre-Christian idea of a world-ordering pneuma with the Old Testament teachings, making special use of the Wisdom of Solomon. (Cf. Leisegang, *Der heilige Geist,* pp. 69ff.) In his interpretation of the Bible there is a mixture of Stoic elements and Greek ideas and mystery wisdom, from which sphere the alchemical philosophers derived their basic concepts and which in turn was applied by our author to the Bible. As Leisegang points out (p. 69), alike in Philo and in the Wisdom of

126   The projection of the anima-image into Physis is in fact an event that left its mark on practically all the Gnostic systems, where it can be found in the motif of the "fallen Sophia." The latter is a feminine hypostasis of the deity, sunk in matter. Thus the followers of Simon Magus revered Helen, his companion, as the "Ennoia" of the Primordial Father, as the "virgin Pneuma" and the "All-Mother" (Prunikos, Holy Spirit, etc.), and taught that she had descended into the lower world and there produced the angels and archons by whom she was afterwards devoured. After many incarnations and much suffering she even sank so low as to become a whore in a brothel in Tyre, from which she was rescued by Simon.[146] In Barbelo-Gnosis a similar goddess sunk in the world and in matter was worshipped as the "Mother of All Living," and was also named the "Holy Spirit." [147] The Sophia of the Ophites was not only a "virgin Pneuma" but had even sunk down into the intermediate realm

---

Solomon Sophia either is or possesses a pneuma, and in the latter case this is a spiritual or psychic faculty which penetrated like a "breath" into man and filled him with "wisdom, reverence, any virtue or any passion" (pp. 71f.). (The same distinction as between Sophia and Pneuma is made in *Aurora* between Scientia and Sapientia. Sapientia either is or had Scientia and passes it on to man.) Sophia is "not only an hypostasis of a quality of God, she is a spiritual being who co-exists independently with God" (p. 73). It is expressly mentioned that she was there when God created the world, and that she knows his works. In the *Corpus Hermeticum*, too (I, p. 145), Sophia is an independent *arche* (uncreated principle) co-existing with God, Nous, Physis, and Hyle. Thus in Philo ("That the Worse is Wont to Attack the Better," Loeb edn., II, p. 239) Sophia becomes the "Mother, by whose agency the universe was brought to completion." (Cf. Scott, III, p. 137.) She is also identical with the spirit of God which brooded over the waters (and which in Hebrew is feminine) because she represents God's ἐπιστήμη (knowledge). (Cf. Scott, I, p. 296, where the body of every living thing is nourished on water and earth, whereas the soul has its roots up above and receives eternal nourishment from the movement of the heavens, "but the spirit with which everything is filled mingles with everything and animates everything.") She is also the nurse and nourisher of those who "demand eternal food" (Leisegang, p. 73). Indeed, in Philo as in *Aurora* the teaching of Wisdom is a mystery. She is initiated into God's knowledge and contains in herself the gnosis of the saints (p. 75). In the Acts of Thomas (James, *Apocryphal New Testament*, pp. 376, 388) the "Mother" is praised as the "revealer of hidden mysteries." Similarly, in *Aurora*, Scientia or Sapientia is called a sacrament and gift of God.

146 Leisegang, *Die Gnosis*, pp. 65ff.

147 Bousset, *Hauptprobleme*, pp. 1, 5, 13, 59–65, and 326, n. 1. (Irenaeus, *Adv. haer.*, I, 29, 4). She is God's "Ennoia," a virginal pneuma, eternal and indestructible. Cf. Eisler, "Angelos," concerning Pistis Sophia and Barbelo.

between God and the world. She signified "Life," or, in Leisegang's interpretation, the "soul embodied in earthly things."
She was also considered to be the mother of the seven planets,[148]
and hence of Heimarmene ("compulsion of the stars") and the
earthly world. The Syrian Gnostic Bardesanes knew this same
goddess in a similar double form, as a heavenly mother-goddess
and as the fallen Sophia, and among the Valentinians the
heavenly Aletheia ("Truth"), the "Mother of All Things," was
contrasted with the lower Achamoth.[149] Similarly, in the so-
called *Books of Jeú* and in *Pistis Sophia,* Barbelo as the Ennoia
of God is contrasted with the fallen Sophia. Among the Mandaeans she appears as Ruhâ d'Qudsâ (Holy Spirit),[150] though in
demonic form, and was also called Namrus, which means midday, the south. Thus she is a demon of the south and the noonday heat (cf. the Queen of the south in *Aurora*).[151] Namrus was
also considered the mother of the planets.[152] The Church Fathers
interpreted the "midday" negatively, as the heat of worldly
ambition (*fervor mundanae gloriae*), from which the Queen of
the south was supposed to have turned away.[153]

127   On a psychological view the Gnostic fall of Sophia, the Wisdom of God, into matter is the self-representation of an unconscious process, of that moment when the "pleromatic" anima
—the anima as an archetype of the collective unconscious—is projected into matter with the result that, although not yet recognized as a psychic content, she is nevertheless brought con-
siderably nearer to the sphere of human understanding.[154] An

148 Bousset, *Hauptprobleme,* p. 11 and 66; Leisegang, *Gnosis,* pp. 169ff. (Origen,
Contra Celsum, VI, 38; Eng. edn., p. 353.) Cf. the prayer to the Mother, who was
thought of as the Holy Ghost, in the Acts of Thomas: "Come, mother of the
seven houses, that thy rest may be in the eighth house" (James, p. 376).
149 Bousset, pp. 58, 63, n. 2.   150 Ibid., pp. 28, 29, 33.
151 The Ruhâ d'Qudsâ combines the qualities of the "noonday devil" (Psalm
90 : 6, D.V.) with those of the Holy Spirit.
152 Brandt, *Die mandäische Religion,* pp. 131 and 182.
153 Honorius, *Expositio in Cant. Cant.* (Migne, *P.L.,* vol. 172, col. 352).
154 Cf. *Psychology and Alchemy,* par. 410: "The idea of the Pneuma as the Son
of God, who descends into matter and then frees himself from it in order to
bring healing and salvation to all souls, bears the traits of a projected unconscious content. Such a content is an autonomous complex divorced from consciousness, leading a life of its own in the psychic non-ego and instantly projecting itself whenever it is constellated in any way—that is, whenever attracted by
something analogous to it in the outside world." "In such visionary images . . .

account of this process can be found, for instance, in the late classical tale of Amor and Psyche, related in the *Metamorphoses* of Apuleius. There the anima appears first as Venus, as a purely divine, i.e., archetypal figure with a strong admixture of the mother-imago. The king's daughter Psyche, who is persecuted by Venus, is on the other hand an anima figure who is already humanized, yet in so far as she is a fairytale princess she is to a large extent still a collective content. Nor is she the bride of a human being, but of Eros, a "daemon." Only her daughter Voluptas (Pleasure), to whom Psyche gives birth at the end of the tale, can be regarded as the individual anima of the hero Lucius.[155]

128   Likewise the tragic love-story of Aeneas and Dido in Virgil's *Aeneid* is a phase in the process of humanizing the anima (making her more accessible to the consciousness of man) that goes on in the unconscious. The mother-goddesses Juno and Venus are the instigators of the love-affair between Aeneas and Dido, but in the end they destroy her, just as Venus persecutes Psyche. This process of realizing the anima, beginning in late antiquity and probably traceable in other texts as well, was then broken off or superseded by the humanization of the Logos in Christ. Only in alchemy was the classical tradition preserved, and not

there is expressed the whole phenomenon of the unconscious projection of autonomous contents. These myth-pictures are like dreams, telling us that a projection has taken place and also what has been projected" (p. 290). What Jung says here about the projection of the Anthropos-image is naturally true also of his feminine counterpart, Sophia.

[155] This interpretation is borne out when one places the Amor and Psyche story in the context of the *Metamorphoses* as a whole. In his fine psychological commentary on the tale (*Amor and Psyche,* esp. p. 141), Neumann takes Psyche more as the exponent of feminine psychology in general, and this is justified in so far as the anima of a man does in fact reflect the psychology of a woman. Seen in the total context of the novel, however, Psyche should be taken as an anima-figure. Her sufferings lead to the birth of "Voluptas," for it is in this childish form that the humanized anima first impinges on a man's consciousness. The novel itself presents the anima as she is experienced by the consciousness of a man: it is through the pursuit of pleasure that Lucius finally comes to a realization of the goddess Isis. The interpolated story, on the other hand, presents the same process "from behind the scenes," as seen from the unconscious, and it is an apt touch that the story is told by an old woman, a personification of the unconscious. It tells how the Queen (anima) strays down into the sufferings of human existence, spurred on by her love for Eros, the mediator between the world of the gods and of men.

until the Renaissance did the problem of humanizing the anima emerge again, as in Francesco Colonna's tale of Poliphilo.[156]

129   In *Aurora* the anima appears as she does in the Gnostic texts, on the one hand as the Biblical Wisdom, on the other hand as the *anima mundi* sunk in matter and calling for help. The need for redemption is sounded already in the first chapter, where she goes about seeking the artifex and exposing herself to the scorn of the multitude, and needs human thought for her perfection. Also, the fact that she arouses "concupiscentia" may be an indication that a natural imperfection clings to her.

130   In most of the Gnostic myths I have mentioned, Sophia before her fall or because of it was a suffering creature like man, searching for God. Though in the doctrine of Simon Magus she incarnates as a whore in Tyre, in other systems she does not sink down to such human misery but is imprisoned in matter, whence she cries out for deliverance. In the myth of Simon she takes on human and personal features too soon, as it were, because he identified himself with the "power of God" and his beloved with "Ennoia" (God's self-knowledge). He thus overstepped the boundary between the limited, personal ego-consciousness and the archetype, which amounts to inflation.[157] This may well have been responsible for the legend of Simon's tragic end.[158] The inflation presumably occurred because, although the need for the projection of the God-image to be taken back into the psyche was present, the contemporary consciousness lacked any concepts which would have enabled Simon to understand the anima as an intrapsychic factor not coincident with the ego. The modern concept of the unconscious alone makes such an integration possible. In the classical alchemical writings the danger of inflation (as distinct from gnosis) was avoided because the anima was largely conceived as a suprapersonal entity, but then everything got projected into matter and stuck there. Sophia remained something mystical and quasipsychic which apparently showed itself in the behaviour of chemical substances.

131   If we bear this fact in mind we shall perhaps understand more easily how shattered the author of *Aurora* must have been

---

156 *The Dream of Poliphilo*, ed. Fierz-David.
157 Leisegang, *Die Gnosis*, pp. 82ff. He appeared as God and world-redeemer. Cf. p. 65.   158 Ibid., pp. 65f.

when Wisdom suddenly appeared to him in personal form. Doubtless he did not know before how *real* an archetypal figure like Wisdom is, and he had taken her merely as an abstract idea. For an intellectual it is a shattering experience when he discovers that what he was seeking "from the beginning of his birth" is not just an idea, but is psychically real in a far deeper sense and can come upon him like a thunderclap. What I mean by "psychically real" is expressed by the author when he says that Wisdom is "most true nature." He is saying that she is not merely an intellectual concept but is devastatingly real, actual, and palpably present in matter. We see here how the symbolic language of alchemy fulfils a saving function: it enabled the author to describe the *numinosum* in all its individual actuality. In this way he could relate to it directly and establish personal contact with it. This personal contact consists in extracting the "most true nature" in the encounter with the anima. In the *Turba* [159] the extraction of the *spiritus occultus, anima occulta, natura abscondita, tinctura veritatis*, etc. is of fundamental importance. This Arabic treatise was probably—apart from Senior —the main source for the author's views concerning a divine truth, itself like a substance, hidden in matter. We read that the "truth of the philosophers" is "nature fused with her bodies," [160] i.e., the metals, which proves that the philosophers sought the "spirit of truth" in matter itself. The same treatise says: [161] "I maintain that the beginning of all things which God hath created is faith and reason. For faith ruleth all things, and in reason also faith appeareth, and the denseness of the earth.[162] But faith is perceived only in a body. And know, all ye assembly, that the denseness of the four elements resteth upon the earth . . ."

---

[159] Ruska, p. 131: "The hidden thing in which is the tincture of the truth." • P. 119: "Therefore order it by cooking it in liquid until its hidden nature appear." • Cf. pp. 134, 141, 149, 309, also *Das Buch der Alaune und Salze* (Ruska, p. 59), where Mercurius says: "I am the whole arcanum, and in me the secret wisdom is hidden." Wisdom is therefore given to man by God in order to accelerate by art the work of nature (p. 62).

[160] *Turba*, p. 190.

[161] Sermo of Anaxagoras, ibid., p. 176 (German), p. 111 (Latin). I have made the (German) translation rather more literal, and have restored one of Ruska's deletions.

[162] "and the denseness of the earth" is deleted by Ruska.

132   Faith (*dín*), according to Ruska, was held to be the source of all religious, supernatural, revealed knowledge, while reason (*áql*) was the source of natural knowledge. In natural knowledge faith (the Transcendental) assumes a real, manifest form ("apparuit"), and so likewise does the denseness of the earth, for it is only in a concrete manifestation that faith can be perceived. Just as the four elements, sinking down, condense into earth, so (and this process is thought of not as running parallel with the first, but as coinciding with it) revealed knowledge receives form in natural knowledge. "Truth" was, in fact, conceived as a substance.[163] This *Turba* text is actually (like all creation myths) describing the coming of consciousness: *áql*, the source of natural knowledge, symbolizes the unconscious archetypal background of the psyche. It is here that transcendental knowledge of God attains empirically graspable form; [164] for example, we can observe the effects which the archetype of the self, the God-image, has upon the individual. From *áql*, so the text says, is produced the "denseness of the earth," composed of the four elements, or, in psychological language, the individual field of consciousness centered in the ego-complex with its four-function structure, which corresponds to the quaternary structure of the self.[165]

133   Such a psychological interpretation was naturally never

163 Cf. "truth" as a "substance of celestial nature" in Dorn, discussed in *Mysterium*, p. 487.

164 *Dín*, being "the Transcendental," is in itself empirically and psychologically inapprehensible.

165 The distinction between a natural and a supernatural source of knowledge is the subject of a subtle discussion in the Sermo of Locustor in the *Turba* (Ruska, pp. 113–79). According to him there are two "creations," one of which is seen only by faith and cannot be described. This faith is called "piety," and is the equivalent of the above-mentioned revelatory knowledge. The invisible creation is heaven. What lies below is a second creation, and this can be known only by reason and with the help of the five senses. This lower creation receives its light from the sun. (Among the Stoics and in the *Corpus Hermeticum* the sun, according to a view widely held in antiquity, is an image of the mind [*mens*], the source of human intelligence.) The light of the sun is of a particularly "subtle" nature. The upper creation does not need the light of the sun, because it is itself of a still subtler nature and receives its light from God. Thus the capacity to cognize sensible things is dependent on the light of the sun, while suprasensible things can be known only by the light of God. Cf. *Mysterium*, pp. 533ff., concerning the "potential world" in Dorn, to which the invisible creation corresponds. It is ruled by the diffuse luminosity of "absolute knowledge."

formulated in alchemy because the psychic processes were projected into matter. Hence the "denseness of the earth" remained the mystical end-result of the process, whereas actually it was a projection of the pre-conscious growth of a new level of consciousness.

134   I have cited the *Turba* passage only to show that an interpretation of Wisdom as the *lumen naturale* and at the same time as a concrete substance is not out of place, since the author must have known this passage. It sheds light on the nature of Wisdom, who appears on the one hand as the divine truth inspiring the alchemist, and on the other as a datum of physical nature which needs to be processed and perfected by the opus.[166] She contains all the attributes of divinity and is the highest and lowest at once; a bringer of enlightenment, the psychopomp to God, and a secret hidden in matter (the unconscious), which can be freed only by extraction (conscious realization).

135   The effect which the invasion of this archetypal image had upon the author seems at first to have been one bordering on exaltation. Placing himself in the background, he utters a beautiful paean of praise to this experience. Only towards the end of the chapter does he hint that man's own attitude is important in such a situation and demands subtle thought.

---

[166] Cf. Avicenna (*Theatr. chem.*, 1659, IV, p. 879): "Its intrinsic virtue is the light of lights, the enlightening tincture." • Also Holmyard, "Abu'l Qàsim al-'Iràqì," pp. 421f., concerning the synonyms for the lapis: dog, eagle, poison of the metals, light, mercury of the east, son of the fire, venom of the lion, son of the philosophers, Satan.

II. WHAT WISDOM IS

136   The second chapter also is devoted to a description of Wisdom, but a slight alteration of tone is perceptible:

137   If therefore now your delight be in thrones and the sceptres of kings, that you may reign for ever, love the light of the science all of you and enquire, ye who are signed with the learning of nature, for the wise man will seek out for you the wisdom of all the ancients and will be occupied in the prophets and will enter into the subtleties of parables and will search out the hidden meaning of proverbs and will be conversant in the secrets of parables.

138   As we shall see later, the author identifies himself with that "wise man" who reveals the secrets of symbols to the elect. An ego-toned trait even appears: *I* will reveal the truth, and he addresses himself only to kings and learned men. Obviously the invasion of consciousness has been followed by a *volte face*, an attempt of the ego to reassert itself—unfortunately by partially identifying with Wisdom.

139   This chapter, too, is given over to an amplification of Sapientia. But whereas the first, particularly towards the end, lays stress on her quality as a natural source of knowledge, the main accent here is on her divine and mysterious nature, which can be grasped only by meditation and inspiration. Hers is the secret of "reigning for ever," that is, of eternal life, and for this reason she can be expressed only in symbolic language. This alchemical text therefore requires as much detailed study and elucidation as the "typi" of Holy Writ.

140   It was a widespread idea among the scholastics, accepted for instance by Joannes Scotus Erigena,[1] Albertus Magnus,[2] and St.

---

[1] *Expositiones super ierarchiam caelestem Sancti Dionysii* (Migne, *P.L.*, vol. 122, col. 146): "As the art of poetry sets forth moral or physical teaching by invented fables and allegorical comparisons . . . so theology like a kind of poetry by fictive imaginations brings Holy Scripture into conformity with the capacities of

Thomas,[3] that Holy Writ had a symbolic content that needed interpreting. This idea permitted the author of *Aurora*, too, to bring the Biblical symbolism into connection with the alchemical.

141   Psychologically, the underlying thought is that the nature of Wisdom can be sketched only by symbolic amplification, that it is something "ineffable"—in other words, akin to an archetype, whose ultimate essence can never be formulated intellectually.

142   The alchemists themselves frequently spoke of the symbolic expressions and "thousand names" for the lapis,[4] justifying them by the need for secrecy. Senior in particular emphasized that he wrote *typice* (symbolically) [5] because the whole matter could be grasped only by divine inspiration.[6] Knowledge came only through the "interior senses," and after lengthy labours God himself had finally revealed that hidden matter to him,[7] "for the perfected science is of the greatest worth and a secret of the glorious God . . . inspired by God himself into his philoso-

---

our mind and with apprehension by the outward bodily senses, as from a kind of imperfect childhood, to the perfect knowledge of intelligible things. For the sake of man's mind Holy Scripture is woven into various symbols and teachings." •

2 "Mariale" (Borgnet, XXXVII, p. 260): "(Naphtali) received the name of 'conversion' because whatever he found written he turned to spiritual understanding." • Mary alone has perfect understanding of Holy Scripture (p. 61). Cf. also Albertus, "Enarrationes in Apocalypsim" (Borgnet, XXXVIII, p. 497), where he says the Apocalypse should be interpreted allegorically lest the book become too clear, be disseminated among the people and thereby become obsolete.

3 According to him, the truth is contained in the Holy Scriptures only "diffusely" (*Summa*, II-II, q. 1, art. 9, ad 1; Eng. edn., II, p. 1177). Revelation is "a kind of shadowy knowledge mingled with obscurity" • ("De veritate," 12, 12). He therefore believes in the "spiritual meaning" of the Scriptures (*Quaestiones quodlibetales*, VII, 16, p. 279). Cf. White, "St. Thomas' Conception of Revelation," pp. 7, 27.

4 Jung, *Psychology and Alchemy*, par. 336. Cf. Zosimos in Berthelot, *Alch. grecs*, II, xxv, 1 and III, xxix, 10, and Democritus, ibid., II, i, 15. "The stone and No-Stone which is called by many names, lest any who is unwise should know it" • (*Turba*, p. 129). The "Aquarium sapientum," which was influenced by *Aurora*, says: "And as the earthly philosophical stone and its substance have a thousand names, so an infinite variety of titles is even more justly predicated of the Chief Good of the Universe." • *Mus. Herm.*, p. 111 (Waite, I, p. 97).

5 *De chemia*, p. 53.

6 Ibid., p. 6; cf. pp. 61 and 82.

7 Pp. 91, 93, 98 and 101f.

phers [8] and into the elect . . . She is sister to Philosophy and hath her being of God by inspiration." [9]

143   What the science is and how she cometh into being I will lay bare, and will not hide from you. For she is a gift and sacrament of God and a divine matter, which deeply and in divers manners was veiled in images by the wise.

144   In this passage the designation of alchemy as a "sacrament" is particularly striking. It comes from the pseudo-Aristotelian treatise "Secreta secretorum," which says: "I therefore reveal to thee, calling divine justice to witness, that sacrament, as it was revealed to me." [10] But on the lips of a Christian writer this word has a far deeper significance, and it cannot be doubted that the author of *Aurora* was thinking of the sacraments of the Church. [11] The paralleling of alchemical symbolism and the Mass is described by Jung in *Psychology and Alchemy*. [12]

145   Wherefore I bring the knowledge of her to light and will not pass over the truth, neither will I have to do with consuming envy; for from the beginning of my birth have I sought her out and knew not that she was the mother of all sciences that went before me. And she bestowed on me innumerable riches, which I have learned without guile and will communicate without envy, and without hiding her worth.

[8] P. 113.
[9] Pp. 120f.: "But thou, O reader, be desirous of learning the fear of God and thou wilt come to see the secret and the visible working of this stone and wilt find it, instructed by the spirit of the All-Highest, that thou mayest know that all wisdom is of God and was always with him, whose name 'Lord' be blessed for ever, who hid this thing from the wise and clever, and revealed it to the poor in spirit (*parvulis*)."
[10] I use the edition of 1528, fol. V.
[11] This becomes obvious when one recalls the words of a later contemporary, Petrus Bonus: "And in this wise Alchemy is supernatural, and is divine. And in this stone is all the difficulty of the Art, nor can any sufficient natural reason be adduced why this should be so. And thus it is when the intellect cannot comprehend this nor satisfy itself, but must yet believe it, as in miraculous divine matters; even as the foundation of the Christian faith, being supernatural, must first be taken as true by unbelievers, because its end is attained miraculously and supernaturally. Therefore God alone is the operator, nature taking no part in the work." ("Pretiosa margarita novella," *Theatr. chem.*, 1622, V, p. 648.) The designation of alchemy as a "sacrament" must be taken in this sense.
[12] Pars. 480ff. See also "Transformation Symbolism in the Mass."

146   Like many other alchemists, the author promises at last to reveal the secret and to do so without "consuming envy"—an allusion to the "invidi" [13] among the philosophers, who grudgingly withheld their knowledge from the world. He then emphasizes that he has sought Wisdom "from the beginning of my birth," [14] a remarkable personal confession which almost makes one think he consciously knew his preoccupation with alchemy meant integrating the innermost essence of his soul, presumably because only in that way could he express his inner processes symbolically. At any rate he suggests that alchemy was a personal concern of his which had interested him from his youth.[15]

147   For she is an infinite treasure to all men, which a man having found, hideth it and for joy thereof saith: Rejoice O Jerusalem and gather together all ye that love me; rejoice with gladness, for the Lord hath been merciful unto his poor.

148   Alchemy is here represented, through the Biblical context, as the Kingdom of Heaven and the treasure hidden in the field,[16] and is thus credited with having the same power of redemption as the work of Christ.[17] It, too, has a healing significance, as is shown by the reference to the liberated Jerusalem and the Lord's mercy. Once again it becomes clear that alchemy is a redeeming or liberating insight, dependent on man's labours on the one hand and God's grace on the other.[18]

---

[13] *Turba*, pp. 122f., 133.

[14] Note that St. Thomas begins his commentary on Boethius with the same quotation from the Bible: "Ab initio nativitatis," etc. (Wisd. 6 : 24f.).

[15] He emphasizes that alchemy is the "mother of all sciences." This is made clearer by a saying of Hermes quoted in "De lapidis physici secreto" (*Theatr. chem.*, 1659, IV, p. 649): "Know, my son, that all the wisdoms which are in the world are subordinate to my wisdom." Such an assertion is valid in so far as alchemy was really concerned with the "divine" mystery of physical creation, so that all other sciences are naturally subordinate to it. Since the alchemists regarded the mystery of creation as divine, they accorded their art a status equal to that of theology, and the author of *Aurora* is no doubt consciously alluding to this when he calls alchemy the mother of all sciences—an epithet which in the Middle Ages was otherwise used only of theology. Cf. St. Bonaventure, "De reductione artium ad theologiam," *Opera*, V, p. 325: "For it is evident how all thinking is the handmaid of theology." •

[16] Matt. 13 : 44.

[17] *Psychology and Alchemy*, pars. 414ff.

[18] Text: "For the Lord hath been merciful unto his poor."

149   Senior likewise saith: For there is a stone, which he that knoweth layeth it upon his eyes, but he that doth not, casteth it upon the dunghill, and it is a medicine which putteth poverty to flight, and after God hath man no better thing.

150   The insight is also the medicine [19] or the stone which, according to Senior, "he that knoweth layeth it upon his eyes." This recalls the "collyrium philosophorum" (eyewash of the philosophers), one of the innumerable synonyms for the "divine water." With the aid of this eyewash one can see the secrets of the philosophers without difficulty.[20] In *Aurora* this eye-opening solution is called the "medicine," just as in general the divine water was often conceived as the $\phi\acute{\alpha}\rho\mu\alpha\kappa\sigma\nu$ $\grave{\alpha}\theta\alpha\nu\alpha\sigma\acute{\iota}\alpha\varsigma$ or $\zeta\omega\tilde{\eta}\varsigma$.[21] The fact that the water appears here in the form of the medicine is directly connected with the "meditation" in the first chapter, which, as it were, produced it.[22] Application of attention to the unconscious produces not only insight ("collyrium"), but also a living afflux of creative contents as well as the feeling of having come into contact with something eternal and suprapersonal. The egocentric tone disappears, and the text once more voices the author's enthusiasm and emotion. The medicine "putteth poverty to flight, and after God hath man no better thing." "Poverty" should be understood here in a general and not merely material sense, and the comparison with God emphasizes afresh the religious value of the eye-opening stone and the healing insight.

151   Thus, on closer analysis, the apparently incoherent and confused text proves to have a consistent meaning and, in its subtle images, sketches a strange but thoroughly comprehensible picture of Wisdom as the primary impulse towards knowledge of the alchemical secret, namely, the unconscious.

[19] For the "medicine" see *Psychology and Alchemy*, par. 418.
[20] "Allegoriae super librum Turbae," *Art. aurif.* (1610), I, p. 90; cf. *Aion*, p. 127. This idea is found in Greek alchemy (Berthelot, *Alch. grecs*, IV, xix, 10). There mention is also made of the "Italic cloud for the eyes." In the Ostanes text the priest promises to make the blind see (IV, ii, 1). Cf. Lippmann, I, p. 68.
[21] *Psychology and Alchemy*, pars. 418, 498.
[22] "Therefore study, meditate, sweat, work. cook . . . so will a healthful flood be opened to you which comes from the heart of the Son of the Great World, a water which the Son of the Great World pours forth from his body and heart, to be for us a true and natural Aqua Vitae." Khunrath, *Von hyleal. Chaos*, p. 274.

III. OF THEM WHO KNOW NOT
AND DENY THIS SCIENCE

152   The third chapter needs little explanation, since in the main it is only a polemic against the fools who know not the art. Its violence and abusiveness are understandable enough if we consider the isolated and sometimes perilous situation of a medieval alchemist, but they must also be regarded as betraying a peculiar uncertainty on the part of the author. The reason for this will be disclosed only too soon—in the sixth chapter, where there follows an abrupt plunge into the realm of the shadow and of darkness. The aggressive tone points even more clearly to a trace of inflation in the author.

153   This glorious science of God and doctrine of the saints and secret of the philosophers and medicine of the physicians fools despise, for what it is they know not. These will not have the blessing and it shall be far from them, nor doth such science befit the unskilled, for everyone who is ignorant of it is its enemy, and that not without cause. For Speculator saith: The mockery of science is the cause of ignorance, and lettuces are not to be given to asses, for thistles suffice them, nor is the children's bread to be set before the dogs to eat, nor are pearls to be cast before swine, and such mockers are not partakers in this noble science; for he would be a breaker of the heavenly seal who should make the secrets of this science known to the unworthy; nor shall the spirit of this wisdom enter into a gross body, nor can the fool perceive it on account of the perversity of his reason.

154   Particular emphasis should be laid on the remark that fools scorn the "blessing," which is another reference to knowledge as an act of God's grace. The quotation of the parable of the pearls that are not to be cast before swine is a pointer in the same direction, for Matt. 7 : 6 says "Give not that which is holy unto the dogs, neither cast ye your pearls before swine." Anyone who does so, says *Aurora,* "would be a breaker of the heavenly seal." This is a clear indication of the divine nature of the

secret. In antiquity the alchemical secret was in fact represented as having been stolen from God.[1] The views expressed by the author are fully in keeping with those of the contemporary investigators of nature, for Roger Bacon, Scotus Erigena,[2] and Averroes[3] repeatedly emphasized that the science was not for the "simple," but only for those who were capable of wise and subtle thought.

155   For the wise have not spoken to the foolish, seeing that he that speaketh with a fool speaketh with one that is asleep. Morienus saith: If I were to unriddle all things as they are, there would be nowhere any further place for prudence, for the fool would be made equal to the wise; nor would any mortal under the sphere of the moon bewail in stepmotherly poverty the pangs of hunger, for in this science the number of fools is infinite.

156   The quotation from Ecclesiasticus 22 : 8 compares those who are ignorant of the art with sleepers, an apt formulation for their unconsciousness. The motif of the "sleepers in Hades," who are awakened to resurrection by the divine water and are reborn, is to be found in the late classical text "Komarios to Cleopatra."[4]

157   The concluding sentence is remarkable in that the author apparently considers the equality of all men and the complete abolition of poverty to be undesirable. We should not take this simply as a "dog-in-the-manger" attitude of wanting to keep for oneself the freedom of consciousness acquired through the secret; it may refer to the knowledge that anything you have not acquired for yourself is injurious.[5] "Bewailing the pangs

---

[1] Cf. how Isis beguiled the secret out of the angel Amnaël (Berthelot, *Alch. grecs,* I, xiii, 1ff.). and the widespread view, derived from the Book of Enoch, that women inveigled God's angels into revealing the secrets of magic, alchemy, and all occult sciences (Charles, *Apocrypha and Pseudepigrapha,* II, p. 192).

[2] *Exposit. super ierarchiam caelestem* (Migne, *P.L.,* vol. 121, col. 146).

[3] "Destructio destructionis," in Aristotle, *Opera latina* (Venice, 1560), tom. X, 1a, 1b; cf. n. 5, 407b: "It is not fitting that this should be so both for fools and for the wise, and both for the multitude and the elect." • Ibid., 344b: "It is for God's honour to keep the thing hidden." • For evidence that St. Thomas recognized the value of symbolic interpretation, see his own interpretations in *Summa,* I, q. 66, art. 1 (Eng. edn., I, pp. 328f.) and q. 68, art. 2 (I, pp. 339f.).

[4] Berthelot, *Alch. grecs,* IV, xx, 15.

[5] Concerning the danger of covetous princes forcibly appropriating the secret, see "Liber Alze," *Mus. Herm.,* p. 331 (Waite, I, p. 266).

of hunger" also seems to be an indispensable condition for undertaking the opus, as elsewhere Morienus emphasizes that one can attain the goal only through the "affliction of the soul." [6]

158   Summing up the psychic events that are expressed in these first three chapters, we are struck most of all by the fact that the author seems to have succumbed to a certain presumptuousness which alienates him from the ordinary man. One would have expected that the encounter with Wisdom would bring about a profound religious upheaval or else a "depression" that drove him back upon himself. This depression does in fact appear in chapter VI. To begin with, however, he tries to override the experience with a kind of intellectual superficiality, to preserve his conscious standpoint by pretending that he knows what it is all about. He even unconsciously identifies with Wisdom in so far as he claims to enlighten the blind by his teachings. This reaction suggests an intellectual inflation in the author. But this attitude does not last long, for he genuinely tries to come to grips with the experience. There is still a trace of the inflationary superficiality in chapters IV and V, as the play on words in the next chapter will show.

[6] *Psychology and Alchemy*, par. 386. Knorr von Rosenroth (*Kabbala denudata*, II, Part 1, p. 251) says that two of God's tears, falling into the sea of wisdom, change its bitterness into sweetness.

IV. OF THE NAME AND TITLE OF THIS BOOK

159   Now the title of this book is baptized "The Rising Dawn," and that for four reasons: Firstly, it is called Dawn as one should say the Golden Hour, for so hath this science an hour with a golden end for them that rightly perform the Work. Secondly, the dawn is midway between night and day, shining with twofold hues, namely, red and yellow; so likewise doth this science beget the colours yellow and red, which are midway between white and black.

160   The chapter is devoted to an explanation of the title, *Aurora Consurgens,* which is explained as a play on the words *aurora* and *aurea hora* (golden hour), and on the other hand by the colour symbolism of the four alchemical stages, for the golden hour of dawn shines yellow and red (*citrinitas* and *rubedo*) midway between night (*nigredo*) and day (*albedo*).

161   Thirdly, because at dawn they that labour under all the infirmities of the night are relieved and have rest; and so at the dawn of this science all evil odours and vapours that infect the mind of the laborant fade away and weaken, as the Psalm saith: In the evening weeping shall have place, and in the morning gladness. Fourthly and lastly, the dawn is called the end of the night and the beginning of the day, or the mother of the sun,

162   The dawn is the "mother of the sun" (sun = gold); it drives away the wintry night and all evil odours that infect the mind of the laborant, "the horrible darknesses of our mind," as is said later in the quotation from the Whitsuntide hymn of Notker Balbulus.[1] In much the same way the Church was praised by the Fathers as the "moon, which hath put all wintry clouds to

---

[1] Cf. Ephraem Syrus, *Hymni et sermones,* I, p. 94: "The union of the two lights comes about through baptism and understanding. These lights shed forth resplendent rays and darkness is lifted from the mind. Then the radiant soul contemplates the hidden Christ of glory." •

flight." [2] And Anastasius the Sinaite says: "Life hitherto was passed in the deep darkness of the night and mists of godlessness, until Christ, the Sun of Justice, rose with his spouse Luna, the Church." [3] According to Honorius of Autun, Satan in his fall swept some of the stars down with his tail and covered them with the mists of sin, until the sun—Christ—rescued them.[4] Senior, too, speaks of the "darkness of the mind" as the *materia nigredinis* and interprets it as *terrestreitas mala*, 'evil earthiness.' [5] These comparisons clearly indicate the "moral" aspect of the "evil odours and vapours" mentioned in the text.

163   No mention is made in this chapter of the passage in the Song of Songs which is the direct source for the designation of Wisdom as "Aurora." There it is said of the Queen of Sheba: [6] "Who is she that looketh forth as the morning, fair as the moon, clear as the sun, and terrible as an army with banners?" But it is alluded to in the next chapter, which says: "This is Wisdom, namely the Queen of the south, who is said to have come from the east, like unto the morning rising." The famous verse from the Song of Songs was interpreted by the Fathers as the earthly Church, "which shall show forth the coming of the divine sun and dispel the darkness of ignorance." [7] St. Gregory says: "For what is the place of dawn but the perfect brightness of the internal vision?" [8] The variant title, "Aurea Hora," as an explanation of "Aurora," is significant inasmuch as the saying

[2] Methodius of Philippi, *Symposion*, VIII, 12.

[3] *Anagogicae contemplationum in Hexaemeron*, 4.

[4] *Speculum Ecclesiae* (Migne, *P.L.*, vol. 172, col. 937).

[5] *De chemia*, p. 40. Cf. Scott, *Hermetica*, I, p. 370: "The Father . . . illuminates man with that knowledge alone which is the property of mind; whereby the darkness of error is dispelled from the soul, and truth is seen in all its brightness, and so man's consciousness is wholly absorbed in the knowledge of God."

[6] Cant. 6 : 9f.

[7] Theodoret of Cyrus, *Explanatio in Cant. Cant.*, IV, 9 (Migne, *P.G.*, vol. 81, cols. 52–53). Cf. St. Gregory, *Moralia*, Lib. 4 in cap. 3 Job, sec. 10 (Migne, *P.L.*, vol. 75, col. 648): "For the *dawn* is the title of the Church, which is changed from the darkness of its sins into the light of righteousness. . . . *Who is she*, etc., for like the Dawn does the Church of the Elect arise, in that she quits the darkness of her former iniquity, and converts herself into the radiance of new light" • (Eng. edn., I, p. 197). Sec. 46: "But the *rising* of the *dawn* is that new birth of the Resurrection, whereby Holy Church, with the flesh too raised up, rises to contemplate the sight of Eternity" • (p. 214). Cf. Honorius, *In Cant. Cant.* (Migne, *P.L.*, vol. 172, col. 454).

[8] *Moralia*, Lib. 29 in cap. 38 Job, sec. 4 (Migne, *P.L.*, vol. 76, col. 479).•

from St. Bernard's commentary on the Song of Songs: "Rara hora et parva mora" [9] was constantly cited by the early medieval mystics as a reference to that "rare and fleeting moment" when human knowledge makes direct contact with the wisdom of God and "tastes" it in ecstasy.[10] Thus the "rising dawn" is really the moment of mystical union with God. St. Augustine's doctrine of a "dawn knowledge" and a "twilight knowledge" in man is of interest in this connection. It is a characteristic of creaturely knowledge to grow dim at evening (because it is sunk in the world and turns to worldly things) and to become morning again when it recognizes itself in the wisdom of God and returns to the love of God.[11]

164   The east from which the dawn comes should also be understood in its alchemical context, for in alchemy the east signified "blood and life." [12] Among the Byzantine-Greek alchemists the

[9] *In Cant. Cant.*, Sermo XXIII, cap. 15 (Eng. edn., I, p. 253): "But all too rare that privilege, and all too short-lived."

[10] Gundissalinus, *De anima:* "For *sapientia* is derived from *sapor* (savour), but the savour of a thing is not experienced until that thing is tasted. But it is tasted when for a moment it is touched by taste: wisdom truly is perfected by intelligence alone, for by that alone indeed is God experienced rarely and for a fleeting moment. . . . Thus God is said to be tasted by the intelligence alone, for by that alone of all the powers of the soul he is touched as if with no intermediary both in the present and in the time to come. Here indeed we are properly said to taste when for a moment and fleetingly we experience through our intelligence something of God. There shall we be satisfied, where we shall enjoy him without end." • Cf. Loewenthal, *Pseudo-Aristoteles über die Seele*, pp. 124f.

[11] *The City of God*, Book XI, ch. 7: "For the creature's knowledge, compared with the Creator's, may be said to be a twilight knowledge; and it grows light, and is morning, when it is applied to the praise and love of the Creator, and it does not turn into night, where the Creator is not abandoned by the creature's love. . . . But the creature's knowledge, considered in itself, is, so to speak, more colourless *than when it is known in the wisdom of God*, as if in the art whereby it was made. And so it may be called evening rather than night, and, as I said, when it is used for the praise and love of the Creator, it becomes morning again. And when it does this *in the knowledge of itself*, it is *one day;* when in the knowledge of the firmament, the second day; when in the knowledge of the land and sea and all things that come into being in them, and continue to have roots in the earth, the third day; . . . and in the knowledge of man himself, the sixth day." • Cf. Jung, "The Spirit Mercurius," pars. 299–301.

[12] "Take the stone that floats on the sea . . . and kill with it the quick and quicken with it the dead, and it has within it death and life. . . . In it are two opposites: water and fire, and the one quickens this, and the other kills that. . . . And afterward will the Oriental redness appear, and the redness of blood." ("Opusculum autoris ignoti," *Art. aurif.* [1610], I, p. 250.)

correlation of the substances and colours with the four directions played a considerable role. The technical treatises of the Greeks and Arabs often speak of an "oriental quicksilver" (ὑδράργυρος ἀνατολική),[13] and Olympiodorus (end of the 6th cent.) [14] says: [15] "To the North they assigned the *nigredo*, to the East the *albedo*, the white substance, which is called silver . . . for Hermes says . . . the white substance is assigned to the East, inasmuch as they [the philosophers] made the beginning of the work equal to the beginning of the day, when the sun rises over the earth.[16] Mark also Apollo, who says, 'Behold, [earth] is taken for the procedure at dawn.' 'At dawn' clearly means 'before sunrise' and is the first beginning of the whole work before the *albedo*." This means, he says later, that the earth should be taken "while it still contains dew," for the sun robs it of its dew in order to nourish itself, and then the earth is "a widow and without husband." [17] From these amplifications it is evident that the east or dawn was correlated not only with the *rubedo* (blood and life) but also with the feminine, white, "dewy" substance fertilized by the spirit.

165   Psychologically this "aurora" symbol denotes a state in which there is a growing awareness of the luminosity of the unconscious.[18] It is not a concentrated light like the sun, but rather a diffused glow on the horizon, i.e., on the threshold of consciousness.[19] The anima is this "feminine" light of the unconscious, bringing illumination, gnosis, or the realization of the self, whose emissary she is.

166   In ecclesiastical symbolism the east is accordingly a symbol for Mary. Ephraem Syrus says: "The east with its stars was a figure of Mary, from whose womb the Lord of the stars was born for us. He by his birth put to flight darkness from the world." [20] A liturgical commentary says: "The dawn shining in the heaven

13 Berthelot, *Alch. grecs*, V, ii, 7, and *La Chimie au moyen âge*, III, pp. 207, 209: "Le livre du Mercure Oriental."
14 Lippmann, II, p. 10.
15 "On the Sacred Art," Berthelot, *Alch. grecs*, II, iv, 31.
16 In the "Kore Kosmou," too, Isis (or Hermes?) received the gnosis of the higher mysteries, later set forth in the "Mysteries of Osiris," at sunrise. (Scott, *Hermetica*, I, p. 460.) (I retain the reading of Patricius: τῆς ἀνατολῆς γενομένης.)
17 *Alch. grecs*, II, iv, 35.   18 *Mysterium*, pp. 148ff., 181ff.
19 For the significance of dawn see Hurwitz, "Archetypische Motive in der chassidischen Mystik," pp. 203f.   20 *Hymni et sermones*, II, col. 584.*

of redemption and grace, from whose womb the sun rises outshining her a thousandfold, is Mary." [21] Among the Fathers "aurora" also signified the Church,[22] and according to Alan of Lille all reason begins in the east.[23] But whereas in these passages the dawn-symbol is merely an allegorical image, in our text it has a far deeper meaning that goes right down into concrete reality. Deliverance from "all the infirmities of the night" [24] is meant in the physical as well as the psychic sense and alludes yet again to the medicinal properties of the lapis. The evil odours and vapours which infect the mind of the laborant are also physical and psychic. Taken psychically, they symbolize soul-destroying collective opinions [25] and the poison of repressed contents.

167 and so our dawn at its greatest redness is the end of all darkness and the putting to flight of night, of that long-drawn-out winter wherein he who walketh, if he take not heed, shall stumble. For of this indeed it is written: And night to night showeth knowledge, day to day uttereth speech, and night shall be light as the day in its pleasures.

168 The allusion to John 11:9–10 points once more to the moral background of the opus: the long, dark winter's night in which the laborant "stumbles" is a reference to the "affliction of the soul" which prevails over the beginning of the work. This hint prepares the way for chapter 6, the parable "Of the Black Earth." In the present chapter, which is devoted to the Aurora image, the author subtly foreshadows the coming peripeteia and at its end refers for the first time to the coming birth of the

---

21 *Messbuch* (Schott edn.), p. 1041.

22 Rahner, "Mysterium Lunae," pp. 342ff., and St. Gregory, *Moralia*, Lib. 4 in cap. 3 Job, sec. 19 (Eng. edn., I, p. 203).

23 *Distinctiones dictionum theologicialium* (Migne, *P.L.*, vol. 210, col. 866): "As in the macrocosm the firmament is moved from east to west and back to the east again, so in man his reason is moved from the contemplation of eastern, that is, heavenly things, first considering God and divine things, then it descends to western things, that is, to consider earthly matters, that through visible things it may contemplate things invisible; then it returns to the east to consider heavenly things again." •

24 "Night" in patristic literature is also an image for Antichrist. Cf. Honorius, *In Cant. Cant.* (Migne, *P.L.*, vol. 172, col. 472). Cf. col. 451: "For as the rising dawn drives away the darkness of night and brings the sun to the world, so the new-born Church drives away the darkness of ignorance and by her teachings and examples brings the sun to the world." •

25 *Mysterium*, pp. 162f.

new sun. The passage from Psalm 138 : 11–12 is also cited in the Missal, where it is sung in the Exultet at the consecration of the Easter candle: [26] "O truly blessed night, which alone didst merit to know the time and the hour wherein Christ rose from the dead! This is that night, whereof it is written: And the night shall be light as the day: and night shall be my light in my pleasures." This is Easter night, the night of Christ's resurrection.[27]

169   By this reference to the Exultet the author gives an almost imperceptible hint that the opus is a real rebirth mystery, and that the new birth is a figure whom he even puts on a par with Christ. The suggested parallelism will become even clearer later. Here, for the first time, the symbolism goes beyond the encounter with the anima (Wisdom) to delineate a masculine figure in a resurrection mystery.

[26] Exultet, in Easter Eve Mass, Roman Missal.

[27] Ibid.: "Let the earth also be filled with joy, illuminated with such resplendent rays; and let men know that the darkness which overspread the whole world is chased away by the splendour of our eternal King. Let our mother the Church also be glad, finding herself adorned with the rays of so great a light."

V. OF THE PROVOCATION OF THE FOOLISH

170   By identifying Aurora at the end of the last chapter with the first light of Easter morning, the author fitted his experience into the framework of ecclesiastical ideas that were familiar to him, thereby weakening its individual value; but by so doing he escaped the danger of inflation. In consequence, the tone of this chapter is no longer so egocentric: the author retires into the background and lets Wisdom herself speak.

171   Doth not Wisdom cry aloud in the public places and Prudence put forth her voice in the books of the wise, saying: O ye men, to you I call, and my voice is to the sons of understanding? Understand, ye foolish ones, and mark the parable and the interpretation, the words of the wise and their mysterious sayings; for the wise have used divers manners of speech in making comparison with everything that is upon the earth, and beneath the sphere of the moon they have multiplied parables in this science.

172   This chapter is a real "Protreptikos"[1] to the study of alchemy. Wisdom again cries publicly in the streets to the "sons of understanding," as in Proverbs. Then follows a new reference to the enigmatic expressions used by the alchemists, and to the thousand names for the stone: they have named it "in making comparison with everything that is upon the earth."[2] Everything "beneath the sphere of the moon," in the world of generation and corruption where conflict, action and passion reign,[3]

_____

[1] "Exhortation."

[2] Cf. the *Lilium* quotation in Petrus Bonus: "The philosophers of old saw that this stone . . . could be compared in parables . . . with all the things that are in the world" (*Theatr. chem.*, V [1622], p. 660).

[3] Gundissalinus, *De immortalitate animae*, p. 23: "For every place under the sphere of the moon is a place of generation and corruption, for it is a place of conflict and action and passion, from which generation and corruption invariably come." •

can become an image for the lapis, since it is itself the light of nature hidden in all things. Psychologically this means that the projection of the psychic content symbolized by the lapis, namely the self, can be found everywhere at any time.[4]

173 This is Wisdom, namely the Queen of the south, who is said to have come from the east, like unto the morning rising, to hear, to understand, yea and to see the wisdom of Solomon, and there was given into her hand power, honour, strength, and dominion, bearing upon her head the crown of the kingdom shining with the rays of twelve stars, prepared as a bride adorned for her husband, and having on her garments written in golden letters in Greek, in barbarian script, and in Latin: Reigning I will reign, and my kingdom shall have no end for all them that find me and subtly and ingeniously and constantly seek me out.

174 Here some kind of goal seems to have been reached. A relatively detached objectivation of the anima has been achieved: the author portrays her with the help of Biblical images and alchemical symbols as a divine figure, very vividly seen. She comes forth "as a bride adorned for her husband." Only one burning question remains: Who is the bridegroom? He cannot be the eschatological Christ of the Apocalypse, for the world is not yet dissolved away, Satan is still unvanquished, the final struggle has still to be fought. According to the text she desires to hear the wisdom of Solomon—human wisdom, so presumably she is also seeking her bridegroom on earth among living men. Certainly the author is seeking *her* in order to be illuminated by her, *but is he not also the one whom she loves and seeks as a bridegroom?* This question does not seem to be answered unequivocally at present, but it is a conjecture that will be confirmed later.

175 This concluding passage sketches a magnificent picture of Wisdom as the personified *anima mundi,* a picture that contains a bewildering assortment of features from figures in the Bible.

First she is again equated with the Queen of the south, who desires to "hear, to understand, and to see" the wisdom of Solomon. This is no doubt an allusion to the concrete results of the opus, for other alchemists assure us that the lapis can be

[4] *Psychology and Alchemy,* par. 433.

"seen and handled." [5] They emphasize this in order to avoid the misunderstanding that it is a mere allegory.

176   From the Queen of Sheba the author's mind switches to the image of the woman in the Apocalypse who was crowned with twelve stars and pursued by the dragon,[6] and then to the heavenly Jerusalem, which comes down from heaven "as a bride adorned for her husband." [7] The "great woman" (γύνη μεγάλη) of the Apocalypse is in patristic allegory an image for the Church; she stands for a "self-subsistent power" (δύναμις καθ' ἑαυτήν), an idealized hypostasis of a "power of illumination pervading nature" (ἡ παρωρμημένη φωτίζεσθαι δύναμις).[8] She is also, because she stands on the moon, a symbol of transcendence over all change, over earthly decay and the "realm of the spirits of the air." An especially important interpretation that comes close to our text by likewise contaminating the bride in the Song of Songs with the woman in the Apocalypse can be found in Lib. V of the *Concordia* of Joachim of Flora (d. 1202).[9] He says that by the radiance of the sun (of the woman in the Apocalypse) is meant the contemplative life of the anchorites, by the radiance of the moon is meant the active life of the cenobites, and by the stars are meant the individual virtues which caused the old monks to live each alone in his own cell. Yet since all heavenly phenomena refer also to the contemplative life, sun, moon and stars signify the "ecclesia contemplativa," that same Church which is represented by the woman, and of whom it is written in the Song of Songs: "Who is she that cometh forth as the morning rising, fair as the moon, clear as the sun?" etc. This Church is formed of the monastic orders, and the closer she stands to God, the more she shuns the darkness of the world and its doings. According to Joachim the stars signify the gifts of the Holy Spirit, and this idea may have led to seven [10] instead of twelve stars being mentioned in the passage from *Aurora* as quoted in the *Rosarium philosophorum*. This interpretation of

[5] "Rosarium philosophorum" (*Art. aurif.*, II, p. 133): ". . . which I have seen with mine own eyes, and touched with my hands."

[6] Rev. 12 : 1.

[7] Rev. 21 : 2.

[8] Methodius of Philippi, *Symposion*, VIII, 4 and 5 (Migne, *P.G.*, vol. 18, col. 145).

[9] As I could not obtain a copy of *Concordia*, I cite from the text given in Hahn, *Geschichte der Ketzer im Mittelalter*, III, p. 297.

[10] In Parable 4, the Holy Spirit has seven gifts (*munera*) or functions.

Joachim's is particularly important because—as we shall see in the course of the commentary—a certain affinity with his ideas is apparent in the author's thought and in the contamination of symbols.

177 In an alchemical context, the astrological significance of the woman should also be considered. Originally she was identical with Virgo (an earth sign), at whose feet stands the constellation of Hydra, and thus far she corresponds to Isis as the Queen of Heaven or "Kore kosmou." Equally, she has a far-reaching correspondence with the numerous Gnostic feminine personifications of the Holy Ghost, such as Barbelo, Achamoth, Sophia, etc.[11] In these figures the pagan background of the image stands out more strongly. But the ecclesiastical interpretation of the woman as a "power of illumination pervading nature" would equally well explain her identification with Wisdom, who in *Aurora* is conceived not only as illumination "from above" but also as a *lumen naturale*.[12] Pope Pius XII gave expression to this collective, unconscious need for a "divine mother" who is closer to nature in his Encyclical *Ad Caeli Reginam,* where he extols the mother of God as "Ruler of the Cosmos," citing those Church Fathers who praised her as the "domina creaturae" and "domina rerum." He goes so far as to say that she is her Son's "partner in the work of Redemption" and attributes to her "a unique part in the work of our eternal salvation." [13]

178 The author of *Aurora* goes beyond the usual medieval symbolism in that his goddess represents not only Mary or Wisdom or the Church, but also a Physis who will bear a child in the future, and whose offspring and son-lover, as will be shown, will be not the historical Christ but the *homo totus* or lapis philosophorum.[14]

179 But now, in contrast to the Apocalypse, something unexpected and momentous happens in *Aurora:* the woman crowned

---

11 Boll, *Aus der Offenbarung Johannis,* pp. 100ff.

12 Alanus de Insulis (Alan of Lille) invokes nature as follows:
> "Peace, love and virtue, principle and power,
> Law, order, way, beginning, end, and leader,
> Life, form and figure, fount of light and splendour,
> Rule of creation." *

De planctu naturae (Migne, *P.L.,* vol. 210, col. 447).

13 *Ad Caeli Reginam,* 1 Nov. 1954 (*Mary, Queen of All Creation,* pp. 15ff.).

14 For the significance of this motif see Jung, "Answer to Job," pp. 438ff.

with stars, who in the Apocalypse was hidden in the desert, descends to the human world, presumably to the author himself,
"prepared as a bride adorned for her husband." This is formulated even more clearly later in the text, and means nothing less
than that the archetypal motif of the coniunctio, which had
always been projected upon divine or royal figures,[15] bursts
through into the realm of mortal man and elevates him to the
Rex Gloriae. For anyone who had not learned to discriminate the
domain of ego-consciousness from that of the collective unconscious [16] this was bound to have a shattering effect,[17] as the beginning of *Aurora* shows. He would be lifted out of his ordinary
human context and would himself acquire symbolic significance; [18] for the coniunctio, as Jung points out, involves a
"transsubjective union of archetypal figures," and its goal is
complete individuation.[19] Although these considerations would
suggest that the identification of the alchemist with the divine
son-lover of Wisdom is a dangerous situation,[20] for medieval
man it was probably a necessary stage on the way to individuation, because otherwise the mysterium coniunctionis would
have remained for ever projected upon Christ and the Church
or Christ and Mary, outside the realm of the individual. The
new, inner birth that is obviously intended by this union, that
is, the birth of the lapis, a new symbol of the self over and above
Christ, would then never have taken place. As Jung has shown
in *Aion*,[21] from a psychological standpoint Christ represents only
the positive, "light" aspect of wholeness, or of the self; he lacks
the shadow, the dark counter-pole, the existence of which had
been anticipated in the prediction of the coming Antichrist.
Consequently, the Christian symbol of the self remains alienated
from the concrete earthly reality of the individual man. The
alchemical symbol of the self, on the other hand, the lapis, paradoxically includes both the light and the dark aspect of man's
wholeness. That is why alchemy forms a compensatory (though
not contradictory) undercurrent to Christian ideas.[22]

[15] "The Psychology of the Transference," pars. 419ff., 438ff.
[16] Ibid., par. 469.
[17] See especially par. 440, concerning the projection of the divine numen into
matter as an approximation to the human level.
[18] Par. 462.   [19] Par. 469.   [20] Pars. 471f.   [21] Pp. 41ff.
[22] *Psychology and Alchemy*, Introduction.

180   It was perhaps for this reason that the author felt impelled to describe his experience not only in a Biblical paraphrase but also by means of alchemical quotations and images. Here we have the first hint that it was not a matter of an ever-repeated "inner" birth of Christ, but of producing the filius philosophorum—a more comprehensive self-symbol that unites the opposites Christ and Antichrist.

181   With the image of the heavenly Jerusalem the author again takes up a Biblical motif which contains a wealth of classical and Hellenistic ideas. The twelve gates of the city, like the twelve stars, are a reference to the signs of the zodiac,[23] and this is also an allusion to the symbolic significance of the twelve chapters of *Aurora*. Further, the heavenly Jerusalem anticipates a motif that becomes of central importance in chapter 10, concerning the treasure-house of Wisdom. The woman in the Apocalypse had "two wings of a great eagle"; [24] this too is not without significance for our text, for later the eagle is mentioned as an emblem of the lapis,[25] and in the final chapter the heavenly bride appears with wings. Thus, in these veiled references to the woman and the city, we already have hints of symbolic representations of the anima that are developed in the

---

[23] Boll, p. 39. The text of this *Aurora* passage is somewhat different in the "Rosarium" (*Art. aurif.*, 1610, II, p. 193). Cf. the translation in *Psychology and Alchemy*, par. 467: "This [Sapientia] is my daughter, for whose sake men say that the Queen of the South came out of the east, like the rising dawn, in order to hear, understand, and behold the wisdom of Solomon; power, honour, strength, and dominion are given into her hand; she wears the royal crown of seven glittering stars, like a bride adorned for her husband, and on her robe is written in golden lettering, in Greek, Arabic, and Latin: 'I am the only daughter of the wise, utterly unknown to the foolish.' " Jung continues (pars. 468f.): "The original text has twelve instead of seven stars, the latter evidently referring to the seven stars in the hand of the apocalyptic 'one like unto the Son of Man' (Rev. 1 : 13). These represent the seven angels of the seven Churches and the seven spirits of God. The historical *sous-entendu* of the seven is the antique company of seven gods who later took up their abode in the seven metals of alchemy. . . . The twelve stars of the original text refer to the twelve disciples and the twelve signs of the zodiac. . . . In Clement's second Homily it is observed that the number of the apostles corresponds to the twelve months. In the Manichaean system the saviour constructs a cosmic wheel with twelve buckets—the zodiac—for the raising of souls. This wheel has a significant connection with the *rota* or *opus circulatorium* of alchemy, which serves the same purpose of sublimation."
[24] Rev. 12 : 14.
[25] See end of Parable 5, infra, p. 337.

later chapters. In the image of the bride coming down from heaven the ultimate goal of the opus, the coniunctio as described in the final chapter, is mentioned for the first time.

182   At this point the first part of *Aurora* comes to an end, and a series of parables begins, with new contents. The division into twelve chapters has, as we have said, a symbolic significance. In alchemy the number twelve plays a role as the number of the months, the hours of the day and of the night, and the signs of the zodiac, with which the phases of the work were often correlated.[26] In medieval symbolism it was important as denoting the number of cornerstones of the heavenly Jerusalem, the twelve tribes of Israel, and the twelve privileges of Mary. Whereas the first five chapters revolve round a central concept, Wisdom as the spirit or soul of alchemy, in the attempt to enrich it with more and more new images, the seven parables that follow portray in dynamic images a progressive process that is intended to illustrate the course of the alchemical opus. This course is represented as a *spiral* procedure, since each of the seven parables describes the whole opus in miniature, at any rate by allusion, always beginning with a *nigredo* and ending with the goal. At the same time the seven parables—one has only to look at their titles!—arrange themselves in a chain that exemplifies the opus as a whole.

183   The seven parables may be understood as alluding to the seven planets and the corresponding metals or spirits of the metals, which are the arcana or pillars [27] of the opus.[28] In ecclesiastical symbolism, seven is significant as the number of days of Creation (indeed, the opus imitates the Creation). They were interpreted by Joachim of Flora and others as the seven ages of the world; in the seventh and last age, according to Joachim,

---

26 Senior, "De chemia," in *Theatr. chem.* (1660), V, p. 212: p. 53: "And this [the Philosophers] meant when they set forth symbolically the seven planets and the twelve signs, and their natures and colours, and all that is in them." • Cf. Ruska, *Tabula Smaragdina*, p. 110.

27 Lippmann, II, p. 44.

28 "Aquarium sapientum," *Mus. Herm.*, p. 94 (Waite, I, p. 85): "There are seven cities, seven metals, seven days, and the number seven; seven letters, seven words in order meet, seven times, and as many places; seven herbs, seven arts, and seven stones . . . in brief, all will proceed favourably in this number." • For the role of the number seven in alchemy see Lippmann, I, p. 187, and II, pp. 192f and 219.

the "ecclesia contemplativa" of the Holy Spirit will appear, and the "Great Sabbath" come upon mankind.[29]

[29] *Concordia*, V (Hahn, III, pp. 291, 305f., 315). It seems to me possible that *Aurora* was directly influenced by the teachings of Joachim. Cf. the following parallels in Hahn, III, p. 141: "The spirit of wisdom will speak all truth to both peoples and will show itself to be one of the seven angels. . . . [Removing] the filth of the letter from the eyes of the mind . . ." • P. 127: ". . . the justice of the religious which is greater and more precious will fail of its worth in those days, in comparison with the spiritual justice which is signified by gold." • P. 127: "The number seven relates to the Holy Spirit, because of the seven gifts of grace." P. 129: "There shall be one day, which is known to the Lord: it shall be neither day nor night, and at eventide there shall be light. And it shall be in that day that living waters shall go forth from Jerusalem, half of them to the east and half of them to the west sea." • P. 309: "The new Jerusalem which is founded at Rome, with apostles, martyrs, confessors, and virgins for its precious stones." •

VI. THE FIRST PARABLE: OF THE
BLACK EARTH ...

184 The sixth chapter is the parable "Of the Black Earth, wherein the Seven Planets took Root."

185 Beholding from afar off I saw a great cloud looming black over the whole earth, which had absorbed the earth and covered my soul,

186 Here the author himself seems to be speaking, as though he were watching what was going on in the retort. The cloud (*nubes* or *nebula*) is a well-known alchemical image for whose interpretation I would refer the reader to Jung.[1] The direct source for this image in *Aurora* is probably the *Turba*.[2] As Ruska points out,[3] "cloud" signifies *pneuma*, or a sublimate,[4] more specifically of evaporated mercury. Perhaps the appearance of the cloud is not without reference to the Queen of the south alluded to in the previous chapter, for the *Turba* says: "Know that most of the wind of noonday, when it is roused up, drives the clouds high and lifts up the vapours of the sea." [5] The cloud (νεφέλη) played a large role in Greek alchemy: it was called "the darkness of the water," the "vapour," the "runner," [6] and in a treatise ascribed to Zosimos [7] it was interpreted as "a black, damp, unmixed pneuma," and of this cloud Maria Prophetissa had said: "The ore doth not tincture, but is tinctured, and only when it hath been tinctured doth it tincture, and when it hath been nourished it nourisheth, and when it hath been perfected

1 *Mysterium*, pp. 170f.
2 Ruska, pp. 190f.
3 Ibid., p. 190, n. 7.
4 Cf. Lippmann, I, p. 37.
5 P. 240. This remark occurs also in Holmyard, *Kitāb al-'ilm al-muktasab*. Cf. Ruska, p. 240, n. 6.
6 *Alch. grecs*, I, iii, 11; II, i, 27; II, iv, 8; III, vi, 6.
7 Ibid., III, xix, 4 and III, xx, 4.

it perfecteth." [8] From this it is clear that the cloud, like the ore, is the arcane substance which is transformed and works transformation, being both active and passive.

187   In our text the cloud, as in Zosimos, is black, because it is mixed with earth. In alchemical terms, the state of *nigredo* has appeared. This reminds us of a similar description in the second poem of the *Carmina Heliodori*,[9] which says that the dragon (arcane substance) should be divided in two in the midst of the sea, until a cloud rises up from it. From this the water pours down again and bathes everything "like a black darkness" (ὡς μέλαν σκότος). According to the *Turba*,[10] the substances must be tormented with an "ancient black spirit" until they change. In most of the alchemical texts the *nigredo* is the result of a preliminary union of opposites and of a first operation, and since there is no mention of this in our parable we must assume that the *nigredo* is the result of what was described in the preceding chapters—in other words, the result of the author's encounter with Wisdom. Psychologically it was the collision of his consciousness with the unconscious, personified as a woman. What distinguishes the present account of the *nigredo* from other alchemical parallels is the fact that the author seems to have been affected by it in a much more personal way: it gave rise to unexpectedly intense suffering and a perception of his own darkness. In the mystical texts of the same period this personal aspect is much less pronounced. The state was described by several other authors, including Hugh of St. Victor, who described his "overshadowing" by the unconscious very beautifully as the "imagination" gaining power over the light of reason. He says [11] that this *imaginatio* is nothing other than an image of the body, perceived from outside by the senses and then con-

---

8 Cf. ibid., V, xxv; III, xxviii, 4; III, xxix, 16; IV, i, 11; III, xii, 9; III, xiii. The cloud is whitened by pure sulphur. Cf. III, xx, 1. Zosimos says (IV, vii, 2): "The quicksilver is fixed in the cloud that is of the same essence." And Hermes (III, xxi, 3): "Triturate the cloud in the sun." Agathodaimon (III, xx, 3): "The potential cloud works upon the potential ore, and they dwell in amity." Cf. ibid., the sayings of Maria about the cloud.

9 Compiled in the 7th–8th cent. (Lippmann, II, pp. 29f.) or in the 4th? (I, p. 95). Edited by Goldschmidt, *Heliodori carmina IV ad Fidem Codicis Casselani*. According to him, they were compiled 716–17.

10 P. 152.

11 *De unione corporis et spiritus* (Migne, *P.L.*, vol. 177, cols. 285f.).

ducted inside to the purer part of the corporeal spirit (vital spirit) and impressed upon it. The *anima rationalis,* he says, is an incorporeal light, but the imagination, being an image of the body, is a shadow (*umbra*). When therefore the imagination ascends to reason like a shadow which approaches the light and overwhelms the light, it—the imagination—becomes manifest and is more sharply outlined, but only if it approaches the light: if it overwhelms the light, it overshadows it and covers it up. This is the result of an "affectio imaginaria," by which the soul is affected through its contact with the body. When God influences reason from above, wisdom arises; when the imagination influences it from below, it produces "scientia."

188   In the process described in *Aurora,* however, the influences from above and below coincide, so that wisdom and science are equated with one another. The descent of Wisdom to the adept is followed by an extinction of consciousness, a "darkening of the light," a state of complete disorientation and depression.[12] The text describes the process as it is directly experienced, as an invasion of the unconscious in which spirit and instinct, good and evil, wisdom and knowledge, are indissolubly mixed.

189   In the passages that follow it is not always clear who is actually speaking. Sometimes it seems to be the author or artifex, sometimes the arcane substance or its indwelling spirit; and often it cannot be made out whether this is its masculine or its feminine personification (sponsus or sponsa). One gets the impression that the author, giving free rein to his "true imagina-

---

[12] The mystical treatise attributed to Albertus, "De adhaerendo Deo" (Borgnet, XXXVII, p. 533), describes how the *caligo* (darkness) forms the first stage of contemplation. There is much in this treatise that reminds us of *Aurora*—for instance, that "as a result of contemplation the soul is enkindled to long after heavenly and divine and eternal good things, and to behold all temporal things from a distance as if they were naught." The soul detaches itself stage by stage from the things perceived by the senses, from the imagined images, and from the "intelligibles" until it contemplates Ultimate Being itself, which dwells in creatures. "And this is the dark cloud (*caligo*) wherein God is said to dwell, into which Moses entered, and therethrough into the inaccessible light." "Howbeit that was not first which is spiritual, but that which is natural, and afterward that which is spiritual" (I Cor. 15 : 46), and therefore one must pass through the usual stages from active effort to rest in contemplation, he adds. The treatise is not by Albertus, but was probably written by a monk at the end of the 14th or beginning of the 15th cent. Cf. Pelster, *Kritische Studien,* p. 172, n. 1, and Daehnert, *Die Erkenntnislehre des Albertus Magnus,* pp. 232f.

tion," [13] has sometimes let the voices of the unconscious speak directly, and that he himself is only occasionally taking part in the conversation with his ego-consciousness.

190 . . . because the waters had come in even unto her, wherefore they were putrefied and corrupted before the face of the lower hell and the shadow of death, for a tempest hath overwhelmed me;

191   Here the text speaks of the waters that had penetrated even to the soul in the lower hell and were putrefied at the sight of the abyss. The preceding passage spoke of the "cloud covering my soul," but suddenly it is not altogether clear whether it is still the author speaking or the prima materia which the "tempest hath overwhelmed." At any rate it is evident that a mixture has taken place and that the author has become one with the material in the retort. The passages from the Psalms make it clear that the *nigredo* corresponds both to the psychic distress of the alchemist and to the distress of the soul imprisoned in matter, which consists in a profound, remorseful feeling of sin. This moral aspect of the *nigredo* occurs also in Senior, who calls the "material of the *nigredo*" the "darkness of the soul" or, still more emphatically, "malitia" (wickedness).[14] In patristic literature *caligo tenebrarum* (mist of darkness), *nebula,* etc. are almost always images for sin, the devil, and death; [15] on the other hand St. Gregory says that the hidden decrees of God are like "a certain kind of darkness." [16] Later in *Aurora* the elements of the *nigredo* are called the "horrible darknesses of our mind" and "accidents of the soul." [17] Already in antiquity the flood had become an image for ἀγνωσία (ignorance of God and of one's self, or unconsciousness). Thus the seventh treatise of the *Corpus Hermeticum* says: [18] "This evil of igno-

13 *Psychology and Alchemy*, pars. 360, 390ff.

14 *De chemia*, p. 40. Cf. the ecclesiastical interpretation of sin in Honorius (Migne, P.L., vol. 172, col. 929): "And to the night of death and misery, which beginning with Adam's sin has involved all men in its darkness, this holy night [of the resurrection] puts an end." •

15 Cf. Boehmer, *Der Neoplatonismus*, pp. 51ff., for a varied collection of passages referring to the words *caligo, nubilum ignorantiae,* etc.

16 *Moralia*, Lib. 4 in cap. 3 Job, sec. 29 (Eng. edn., I, p. 203).• Cf. also the view of St. Augustine (*De Genesi*, III, 10): "The darksome atmosphere is as a prison to the demons until the judgment day," • cited by St. Thomas in *Summa*, I, q. 64, art. 4 (Eng. edn., I, p. 323).

17 Infra, pp. 303, 307.   18 Scott, I, pp. 170ff. Cf. Reitzenstein, *Poimandres*, pp. 9ff.

rance floods all the land; its current sweeps along the soul which is penned up in the body. . . . Suffer not yourselves then to be borne along downstream by the strong current, but avail yourselves of a backflow, those of you who are able to reach the haven, and cast anchor there, and seek a guide to lead you to the door of the House of Knowledge. There you will find the bright light which is pure from darkness; . . . all . . . look up and see with the heart of him whose will it is that with the heart alone He should be seen." Here the flood has the additional moral meaning of unconsciousness, guilt, and alienation from God. In it dwells the devil, the "father of darkness" and prince of this world, who rouses up the "tempests of the fierce and bitter sea." [19]

192　　The encounter with the sublime figure of the anima, which sent the author into an ecstasy but also gave him an inflation, was followed by an enantiodromia, and now the shadow has been constellated.[20] With reference to a similar situation Jung says that it is "a kind of *descensus ad inferos*—a descent into Hades, and a journey to the land of ghosts somewhere beyond this world, beyond consciousness, hence an immersion in the unconscious." It is brought about by the "rising up of the fiery, chthonic Mercurius, presumably the sexual libido which engulfs the pair." [21] In this sense Mercurius would be the chthonic equivalent of Wisdom. It is perhaps not unimportant to remember that the woman in the Apocalypse was pursued by a dragon, who was unable to catch her (wherefore her child was "caught up unto God"). The dragon there symbolized the lower world, matter, reality, etc. The role of the dragon in alchemical imagery, as a symbol of Mercurius, is sufficiently well-known. In the passage from the *Carmina Heliodori* cited earlier, the black cloud rises up from the slain dragon,[22] whereas in our

19 Cf. the impressive collection of illustrative passages from classical and patristic sources in Rahner, "Antenna Crucis II." For the significance of the "sea" see Jung, "The Psychology of the Transference, "ch. 4.

20 Cf. ibid., par. 470.

21 Par. 455. The "pair" refers to the royal pair sitting in the bath, on whom the Holy Ghost had previously descended. (Ibid., fig. 4.)

22 Cf. *Turba*, pp. 162, 247: "Therefore a tomb is dug for that dragon, and the woman is buried with him, and he being securely bound with the woman . . . is with the woman's weapons . . . cut into pieces . . . and turned entirely into blood." • Cf. *Mysterium*, p. 21.

text it seems to be produced by the descent of Wisdom into the human world, or by her encounter with the author. We may perhaps compare this descent with the "fall of Sophia" described in various Gnostic texts. From the standpoint of the Pleroma, of the unconscious world of archetypes, the coming to consciousness of an archetypal content in man would be a kind of fall from the realm of spirit into the darkness of psychophysical life. In other words, the divine Sapientia precipitates herself into the dark confines of human comprehension, while for its part man's ego feels caught in the nebulous vagueness of the archetypal world of spirits, which is why one no longer knows in the text *who* is the observer and *who* is calling for help.

193   then before me shall the Ethiopians fall down and my enemies shall lick my earth. Therefore there is no health in my flesh and all my bones are troubled before the face of my iniquity.

194   In the Biblical context the "Ethiopians" falling down and licking the earth are performing homage or obeisance. But here it looks more like an enemy invasion, especially as the "Ethiopian" occurs elsewhere as an image for the *nigredo* and in most texts has a negative significance.[23] Thus the "Scriptum Alberti super arborem Aristotelis" [24] says that the prima materia should be purified and distilled until the "black head," [25] which is like an Ethiopian, is well washed and begins to turn white. In the *Chymical Wedding* of Christian Rosencreutz a Moor appears as a symbol of the *nigredo*.[26] In patristic literature Ethiopians "black with sin" [27] are the embodiment of the "Gentiles," i.e., they symbolize the pagan spirit. Since we may suppose that the author was quite familiar with these interpretations, it seems possible that he had an inkling of the non-Christian character of the contents now appearing in the work, and this would explain the feeling of guilt manifested in the quotations from the Psalms, which immediately follow. The shadow has come up,

23 Melchior Cibinensis, "Addam et processum sub forma missae," *Theatr. chem.*, III, p. 853. Cf. *Psychology and Alchemy*, par. 484.
24 *Theatr. chem.*, II, p. 526; *Psychology and Alchemy*, par. 484, n. 171.
25 Like the *caput corvi* (raven's head), a symbol for the *nigredo*.
26 *Mysterium*, p. 513.
27 "Denigrati peccato." Epiphanius, *Panarium* 26, 16 (ed. Holl, I, p. 296). Further material in von Franz, "Passio Perpetuae," pp. 467ff. Cf. Rahner, "Antenna Crucis II," pp. 110ff.

bringing with it all those fantasies and impulses which seem so sinful and shocking to the Christian consciousness.[28]

195   The waters, which according to the text penetrate even to the lower hell, symbolize a loosening of the personality structure or a dissociation.[29] The feeling of guilt, however, is due not only to the author's having been overwhelmed [30] by the shadow and by pagan fantasies of the unconscious but also to the previous inflation. The contamination of the psyche with the suprapersonal contents of the collective unconscious, brought about by the encounter with Wisdom, had damaged the personality by producing an "impure" mixture of earth (reality or consciousness of reality) and sea (collective unconscious).[31]

196   For this cause I have laboured night by night with crying, my jaws are become hoarse; who is the man that liveth, knowing and understanding, delivering my soul from the hand of hell? They that explain me shall have eternal life, and to him I will give to eat of the tree of life which is in paradise, and to sit with me on the throne of my kingdom.

197   The *nigredo* is, at the same time, clear evidence of the imperfection of the prima materia, which needs to be worked on in order to become the gold. Hence it cries out for the help of a man who, "knowing and understanding," will save its soul from hell. The rescuer is promised, in the words of God in the Apocalypse, the fruit of the tree of life in paradise, and even

[28] Cf. Avicenna, *De anima*, Part 4, cap. 4, fol. 20ʳ: "Likewise the man of good disposition imagines evil desires, though he does not will them, but another wills them; and these twofold dispositions belong not to man alone, but to all animated beings." •

[29] Corresponding to the dissolution of Gabricus into atoms in the body of Beya, described in the "Visio Arislei." Cf. *Psychology and Alchemy*, par. 439, and "The Psychology of the Transference," par. 455.

[30] It was more than just a confrontation with the shadow: the author was regularly overwhelmed by it.

[31] "The Psychology of the Transference," pars. 472f.: "With the integration of projections—which the merely natural man in his unbounded naïveté can never recognize as such—the personality becomes so vastly enlarged that the normal ego-personality is almost extinguished. In other words, if the individual identifies himself with the contents awaiting integration, a positive or negative inflation results. . . . At all events the integration of contents that were always unconscious and projected involves a serious lesion of the ego. Alchemy expresses this through the symbols of death, mutilation, or poisoning. . . . The alchemists assert that death is at once the conception of the *filius philosophorum* .   "

the throne of the kingdom.[32] It becomes clear that the prima materia crying out in distress, or its hidden spirit or soul, is none other than Wisdom herself, for the words that immediately follow ("He that shall dig for me as money," etc.) refer to her (Prov. 2 : 3–5). Wisdom, therefore, according to our text, has not only come down to man, as in the Bible, but has become sunk in matter and finds herself in distress and darkness. A parallel or coincident event has taken place: the alchemist and Wisdom have become mutually entangled. *He* has sunk down into the darkness of the unconscious; but for the luminosity of the archetype the approach to human reality also denotes a darkening, and thus divine Wisdom loses her way in the depths of materiality.

198   He that shall dig for me as money and obtain me as a treasure and shall not disturb the tears of my eyes and shall not deride my garment, shall not poison my meat and my drink . . .

199   Wisdom now begs the alchemist not to poison her meat and drink and, later, not to defile her couch and violate her body. He is also not to deride her garment; all this clearly emphasizes her imperfection and weakness. The anima's fear of defilement and violation refers in all probability to the danger, often mentioned by the alchemists, of applying too much fire ("nimio igne") or too violent purifying procedures, and thus destroying the prima materia instead of cleansing it.[33] This could be interpreted psychologically as too strong a desire to drag the unconscious contents to light. They have to be handled with a certain amount of tact, and all "either/or" interpretations should be avoided. There are positive values in both the shadow and the anima, undeveloped germs that have to be treated with delicacy and respect.

200   The garment that must not be derided is, in alchemical

---

32 Apoc. 2 : 7, and 3 : 21.

33 *Aurora*, Part II (*Art. aurif.*, I, p. 151). Cf. *Turba*, p. 121: "And beware of increasing the fire, for if you increase the fire before the red ending comes about, that is of no profit to you, for in the beginning of the operation you want the *albedo*." * P. 138: "Beware lest you drive them [bride and bridegroom] to flight by burning them in too hot a fire. Honour the King and his spouse, and do not burn them away, for you know not when you will need those things which ennoble the King and his spouse." Olympiodorus (Berthelot, *Alch. grecs*, II, iv, 8) also warns against excessive ἐκπύρωσις (firing).

terms, the "body of the ore," the darkness whose removal as preparation for the work already played a role in Greek alchemy.[34] In the "Carmen Archelai" from *Carmina Heliodori* [35] the *nigredo* is described as "a wall like the blackness of darkness," as a mist (ἄχλυς) that has to be dispersed by the alchemist. And in the fourth poem from the same work [36] it is said: "The body shall come forth from the darkness, from Hades . . . and cast off the mist of darkness," and put off the "garment of corruption" (χιτῶνα φθορᾶς).[37] This goes back to the originally Orphic view, widespread in antiquity, that the body (σῶμα) was the grave (σῆμα) of the soul.[38] In the above-mentioned treatise from the *Corpus Hermeticum,* where the soul is admonished to save herself from the flood of *agnosia* (unconsciousness), the text goes on to say: [39] "But first you must tear off this garment which you wear,—this cloak of darkness, this web of unconsciousness, this [prop] of evil, this bond of corruption, this living death, this visible corpse, this tomb you carry about with you, this inner robber." [40] Later in *Aurora* there is similar talk of a prison and of the "barriers of hell" that must be broken.[41] The image of the garment or couch must therefore be taken as the "body" of the ore, from which the liquid "metallic soul" or "water" is melted out or distilled.[42] Psychologically, this could be seen as

---

[34] Ibid., IV, i and III, xxiv. The Arabian *Buch der Alaune und Salze* (p. 71) requires as *prima materia* an "ore without shadow." The same idea occurs in the *Turba* (pp. 154, 156, 160), evidently taken over from the Book of Krates (p. 36).

[35] Goldschmidt, p. 55, Carmen IV, verses 170–71.

[36] Verses 214ff.

[37] This expression derives from the mysteries of late antiquity and occurs also in St. Paul. Cf. Reitzenstein, *Hellenistische Mysterienreligionen*, pp. 204ff.

[38] Porphyry, "De antro nympharum," ch. 14, *Opuscula Selecta*, p. 66 (σῶμα = χιτών). Cf. Alfarabi, *Das Buch der Ringsteine*, p. 19: "Thou hast on account of thyself a veil besides the covering of thy body, therefore make haste to put it off, that thou mayest reach the goal [God]." Also St. Ambrose, *Hexaemeron*, VI, 6 (Migne, *P.L.*, vol. 14, col. 256) and St. Gregory, *Moralia* (Eng. edn., I, pp. 295 and 538ff.).

[39] Scott, I, pp. 172f.

[40] The latter corresponds to the "Ethiopians and enemies" in *Aurora*.

[41] Infra, p. 251; supra, p. 69.

[42] A perfect parallel to this is to be found in St. Bernard, *In Cant. Cant.*, XX, 7 (Eng. edn., I, p. 243): "The shadow of Christ, I take it, is that Flesh of His which overshadowed even His Mother, and by its opacity, as by a veil interposed, tempered for her the burning heat and dazzling splendour of the Spirit." * Also Honorius, *Speculum* (Migne, *P.L.*, vol. 172, col. 937). Cf. Daniel, *Thesaurus Hymnologicus*, II, p. 205: "In this place did the Eternal / Human flesh and

a "breakthrough" to one's innermost essence (the self). There-fore a logion of Jesus promises salvation "when ye have trampled on the garment of shame, and when the two shall be one, and the outside as the inside, and the male with the female is neither male nor female." [43]

201   The putting off of garments and of the "garment of darkness," referring to the obnoxious qualities of the prima materia, played an important role in the later alchemical parables, particularly with reference to Song of Songs 5 : 3: "I have put off my coat, how shall I put it on?" In the parable of Henricus Madathanus cited by Jung,[44] "Aureum saeculum redivivum," the filthy, evil-smelling clothes of the "bride" are a symbol for the prima materia.[45] The artifex has a dream of an old woman who warns him not to despise these clothes, and so, although he is unable to understand their significance, he keeps them with him until he finally discovers the *lixivium* with which he is to cleanse them, whereupon he wins the bride, the most beautiful of the "doves" from Solomon's harem. Probably this parable is not un-connected with our text.[46] In the *Zohar*, too, the old attitude to be cast off is often symbolized as a dirty garment.[47]

202   This "dirty garment" may also signify exposure to autoerotic affects and fantasies which threaten to gain the upper hand when consciousness is in the *nigredo* state of dissociation.[48] But these dark components veil like a garment something supra-personal which should not be rejected along with them because of their unpleasant aspect. As the anima figure begs so anxiously for indulgence, we may conjecture that the author was an in-

nature don: / Hidden here the sacred Bridegroom / Put his wedding garment on." * Hugh of St. Victor called the "imagination" (supra, pp. 218f.) a garment or pelt that veils reason. *De unione corporis et spiritus* (Migne, *P.L.*, vol. 177, cols. 285ff.).

[43] Clement of Alexandria, *Stromata*, III, 13, 92 (trans. James, p. 11). Further parallels in Franz, "Passio Perpetuae," p. 473.

[44] *Mysterium*, p. 50, n. 72.

[45] "Filthy and defiled and worn out are her garments, but I will cleanse them and love her with all my heart. And let her be my sister, my spouse, with one of mine eyes." * (*Mus. Herm.*, p. 61.)

[46] Cf. the numerous quotations from the Song of Songs in the "Aureum saeculum redivivum," and especially the allusion to *Aurora* (*Mus. Herm.*, p. 69) and the epilogue (p. 72), where Madathanus declares himself a "frater Aureae crucis."

[47] *Sohar*, ed. Muller, pp. 151f.: the garment is also Kether, the Crown.

[48] "The Psychology of the Transference," ch. 7.

tellectual with a puritanical cast of mind, and that he stood in danger of rejecting the emergent unconscious contents on account of their dubious outer aspect without grasping their underlying meaning.

203 . . . and shall not defile with fornication the couch of my rest, and shall not violate my whole body which is exceeding delicate and above all my soul (or dove) which without gall is wholly beauteous and comely, in which there is no spot, who shall not do hurt to my seats and thrones,

204 The couch that is not to be defiled has much the same meaning as the garment that is not to be derided. The "bed" (*lectulus*) is the place where the coniunctio is consummated, a synonym for the distilling vessel. Rosinus,[49] commenting on the text, says "they wedded themselves in their bed, that is, mingled in their vessel." In alchemy, the vessel had to be sealed with the *lutum Sapientiae* (clay of wisdom) [50] and not cracked by overheating; like the "house" or "temple" it represented the "body." [51] The "seats and thrones" in our text have a similar meaning. In explanation of a figure of Hermes sitting on a cathedra (throne or teacher's chair), Senior says expressly that the cathedra is the vessel, the place of transformation.[52] In the *Turba*, on the other hand, "thrones" signify angelic powers.[53] As such they represent spirits—ministering spirits, companions of the anima or sponsa, and they too should not be destroyed by overheating. They are presumably identical with the twenty-

---

49 *Art. aurif.*, I, p. 191.
50 Cf. Albertus, *De mineralibus*, 4, 1, 7 (Borgnet, V, p. 93).
51 *Mysterium*, pp. 152f.
52 *De chemia*, p. 122: "The cathedra signifies the place of the operation, and the shape of the vessels, [and] what is in them." •
53 Ruska, p. 32: "For of these four elements are all things created, heaven, the throne, angels, sun, moon, stars, earth," etc. • In the Koran God is the "Lord of the sublime throne." After Allah had created heaven and earth, he seated himself on the throne in order to rule the world. "His throne is as vast as the heavens and the earth, and the preservation of both does not weary him." Sura 2, 255 (Dawood trans., p. 349). In versions B and C of the *Turba* passage, *thronus* is changed into *throni*, because the translators did not understand this Islamic concept and referred it to a group of angels who in Christian angelology are called "thrones." The "thrones" were originally a Jewish concept. Cf. Daniel 7 : 9, Matt. 19 : 28, Col. 1 : 16, Rev. 20 : 4. They belong to the same category as the "principalities and powers." Cf. Scott, *Hermetica*, III, p. 512.

four elders of the Apocalypse mentioned later in the text.[54] The "stone" must circulate through them, so that they are, as it were, necessary ingredients in the work. Psychologically they embody autonomous contents of the collective unconscious which are constellated round and by the anima.[55] She appears as if surrounded by a cluster of creative contents pushing into the light of consciousness, and these contents are in danger of being destroyed by the alchemist, presumably because they are incompatible with his conscious attitude or difficult to reconcile with it.

205   It is not only the "body of the ore," the inferior side of man, which should not be destroyed by too drastic a process of purification, but also his "spirits" and above all, as the text says, his "soul." [56]

206   An interpolation (presumably a marginal gloss that got into the text) designates the speaker as the "dove," a typical attribute of Mary, and praises her purity ("without gall," "in which there is no spot").[57] We have already encountered the white dove in the passage quoted from Johannes Grasseus, as an image for the soul hidden in matter, so that in the present context it is quite clear that the soul in matter is speaking. "Without gall" means "without bitterness," a reference to the symbolism of *amaritudo*, fully discussed in Jung.[58] The *amaritudo* is in the nature of an "accident," not pertaining to the innermost soul of matter but

---

[54] Infra, pp. 327ff.; supra, p. 105.

[55] Cf. the fairytale motif of the anima-figure surrounded by dwarfs in "Snow White."

[56] Interestingly enough Meister Eckhart likewise warns against an incorrect, i.e., violent, love for Wisdom. Cf. Thery, "Le Commentaire de Maître Eckhart," III, p. 268. "Note that every action is wearisome and burdensome to the agent, unless the patient also contributes and imparts some force to it, and so cooperates with the agent or effector. 'An act is violent when the agent is external, the patient contributing nothing,' as the Philosopher says in *Ethics* III . . . and that is why a violent movement falls short of its end, but a natural movement is directed to its end. For nature is a force innate in things." • Cf. St. Thomas, "De coelo et mundo," I lect. 17 and II lect. 8 (*Opera omnia*, III, pp. 67–70 and 149–51).

[57] Wolbero, *Commentaria super Cant. Cant.* (Migne, *P.L.*, 195, col. 1086): "It is without gall, which likewise spiritually Christ's spouse should be without, as the apostle hath it: Let all bitterness and anger and indignation and clamour and blasphemy be put away from you, with all malice (Eph. 4 : 31)." • The dove is also the Church (Honorius, *Speculum*, Migne, *P.L.*, 172, col. 379). Christ will return as a dove in a flock of doves (Bousset, *The Antichrist Legend*, p. 90).

[58] *Mysterium*, pp. 192ff.

only to the impurity of the prima materia. According to Meister Eckhart, the bitterness is produced merely by the misunderstanding with which men approach Wisdom; if they surrendered to her, the bitterness of the struggle would no longer prevail, but only the "sweetness" of pure love.[59]

207   he for whose love I languish, in whose ardour I melt, in whose odour I live, by whose sweetness I regain my health, from whose milk I take nourishment, in whose embrace I am made young, from whose kiss I receive the breath of life, in whose loving embrace my whole body is lost,

208   After dwelling on the difficulties of the "praeparatio delicata," as Senior calls it,[60] Wisdom's discourse gradually passes over into a passionate declaration of love. Significantly enough, it remains unclear whether this declaration is addressed to the sponsus, conceived as the arcane substance, or to the alchemist. In other words, here again the indissoluble mingling of alchemical processes with the psyche of the alchemist is the only explanation of the discourse as it glides from figure to figure. The anima yearns for the inner unity or wholeness of the personality through a coniunctio of opposites.

209   The words "in whose embrace I am made young" deserve emphasis, as this is probably a reference to the motif of the king's renewal, so often mentioned in alchemy. It must have been known to the author if only from the passage in the *Turba*,[61] where the old man rejuvenates himself by feeding on a white tree.[62] The interpretation of this motif can be found in Jung.[63] The renewal has as its object a complete alteration of the conscious attitude. The one who is usually renewed and rejuvenated is the *king*, that is, an archetypal figure who can be interpreted as the symbolic dominant of a collective attitude

[59] Cf. Thery, "Le Commentaire de Maître Eckhart," III, pp. 275f.: "Good as good is always sweet. . . . Dregs are bitterness." • P. 278: "Everything that acts seeks to make itself something else, and is in toil until it attains it; and all the unlikeness and imperfection which it displays is hard and bitter. If it gave itself that other thing in the first place, all action would be gentle on both sides, that of the agent and that of the patient: nor would there be the bitterness of struggle between them, but gentleness and sweetness." •

[60] *De chemia*, p. 11.   [61] Ruska, pp. 161f.

[62] Cf. "Rosinus ad Sarratantam," *Art. aurif.*, I, p. 192, and *Carmina Heliodori*, I, pp. 29f., verses 110ff. (father-murder motif).

[63] *Mysterium*, pp. 72ff.

of consciousness.[64] Here it is Wisdom who wants to be rejuvenated, and from this we must conclude that the interpretation of this archetype hitherto—i.e., the Church's conception of Wisdom—was in need of renewal. She became, as we mentioned earlier, something completely abstract, the "sum of ideas in the mind of God," or was interpreted as the "art" by which God created the world, or was simply identified with Christ as the Logos that existed before the world. The feminine element in this personification was, however, overlooked. Too little attention was paid to her anima quality, to her specific nature as a connecting, mediating factor, and to the feeling-values she contains. Now, by being rediscovered through a primordial archetypal experience, she is as it were rejuvenated and comes alive again.

210   It is no accident that about this time Meister Eckhart wrote his commentary to "Sapientia." Sapientia Dei, as a feminine personification of God, is a figure in whose nature the antinomy of Yahweh is abolished, since she stands for his "absolute knowledge" and wisdom.[65] She seems to have been the goal towards which the unconscious of that time was striving; hence the increasing worship of Mary, the rediscovery of Aristotle and his universalist thinking, and the efflorescence of Western alchemy, whose chief concern was the production of the One: "one is the stone, one the vessel, one the procedure, and one the medicine."

211   The words "in whose loving embrace my whole body is lost" allude to an equally far-reaching symbolic context. It seems to me not without reference to the verse of St. Ambrose in which he speaks of the "emptying" of Ecclesia-Luna.[66] The latter embodies the sufferings of unredeemed humanity and of creation in general,[67] and her sufferings assist the "emptying" (*kenosis*) of the Logos made flesh. For the psychological interpretation of this ecclesiastical allegory I must refer the reader

[64] Just as in many fairytales there is an old king who seeks the fountain of life, or the rejuvenating apple, or the water that cures blindness. Cf. the Grimms' fairytale "The Golden Bird."

[65] Jung, "Answer to Job," pp. 386ff.

[66] *Hexaemeron*, IV, 8, 31 (Migne, *P.L.*, vol. 14, col. 203): "[Christ] emptied her [Ecclesia] that he might fill her, as he also emptied himself that he might fill all things. . . . Thus has the moon proclaimed the mystery of Christ." •

[67] Rahner, "Mysterium Lunae."

to Jung.[68] The dissolution and "melting" are also connected with the "flowing of the spirit," mentioned earlier, which then follows its desire. The author of the treatise "De adhaerendo Deo" [69] says: "For love has a unifying and transforming effect, it changes the lover into the beloved, and the reverse. Love draws the lover . . . out of himself and transports him into the beloved. . . . For the soul is more when it loves than when it only animates. . . . Love is the life of the soul itself, her wedding garment [70] and her perfection, upon which depend the whole law and the prophets, and the commandment of the Lord."

212   to him indeed I will be a father and he shall be to me a son; wise is he who rejoiceth his father, him whom I place first and highest among the kings of the earth, and I will keep my covenant faithful to him for ever.

213   The whole ensuing part of the text tells of Wisdom's promise to her lover, but it is *no longer described as the experience of the artifex.* Psychologically this means that the text which now follows, speaking of salvation, redemption, and the consummation of the work, is the intuitive anticipation of a solution not yet realized. It is as though the author had suddenly leapt out of the *nigredo* and into the ecstatic bliss of the coniunctio. Human reality, in which the ego is caught, plays no role any more, and the divine bride celebrates her marriage with the bridegroom, the "knowing" saviour, with whom the author no doubt felt somehow identical.

214   The dark side of the classical alchemical coniunctio was only fleetingly hinted at in the motif of melting in the lover's embrace, for the discourse now passes on to the saying from Hebrews 1 : 5: "I will be to him a Father, and he shall be to me a Son" [71]—which, in view of the fact that a female figure, the anima or Wisdom, is speaking, sounds somewhat remarkable. But in the Church's eyes Wisdom and the Logos do form a unity, since both are creative aspects of God. Also, Jung's view that the unconscious and the conscious stand in a father-

---

68 *Mysterium*, pp. 35ff.
69 Albertus, *Opera* (Borgnet, XXXVII, p. 536).   70 Supra, pp. 224ff.
71 The words "Whoso loveth wisdom rejoiceth his father" (Prov. 29 : 3) were referred to the mystery of baptism. Honorius, *Quaest. et. Resp. in Proverbia,* cap. 10 (Migne, *P.L.*, vol. 172, col. 317).

son relationship [72] makes it easier to understand how Wisdom, or the anima, can describe herself as the father of the alchemist.

215   These words, therefore, indicate the nature of the relationship between Wisdom and the adept. Later the figure of Wisdom appears in passing as the masculine God-image or as the Holy Spirit—for ultimately she represents psychic wholeness in its male-female aspect, more or less paralleling the Gnostic father-mother—and, accordingly, sometimes the feminine side predominates and sometimes the masculine side. Here she suddenly presents the aspect of a protecting father—with the proviso, as we shall see, that man shall "walk in my ways." It seems as if "religio," understood as the "careful consideration" of the unconscious by consciousness, were a conditioning factor for the manifestation of her "fatherly" aspect. That the adept is the son seems proved by the text, for the bridegroom for whom the speaker yearns was defined earlier as he who, "knowing and understanding," shall deliver her from the abyss of the *nigredo* without mocking or injuring her, and that can only be the alchemist, i.e., a human being. Were it not for that cautionary remark about possible defilement, the passage could be interpreted as the soul yearning for her soul-mate Christ; but then there would be no need of this anxious request that he should not injure her. The anima is not calling Christ to her aid, but a human ego. It is important to remember that all this took place in a man who, so far as his conscious attitude was concerned, was probably quite familiar with the conception of Christ as the bridegroom of the soul, and who was inclined to neglect the significance of his own ego. This was a characteristic of the medieval mind which later was amply compensated by the egoism of the Renaissance man.

216   But what does the anima really want, with her extraordinary, urgent courtship? She wants—as the text says—to establish a relationship which is parallel with that of God the Father to his Son. In the text itself it looks as if not just a parallel but an identity were meant, yet this is not possible when we consider the Biblical context. It can only be a parallel: anima-Wisdom relates to the alchemist as God to Christ.

217   The unconscious symbolism thus expresses that progressive Christification of the individual the importance of which is dis-

[72] *Mysterium*, pp. 100f., and "Transformation Symbolism in the Mass," pp. 262ff.

cussed by Jung in *Answer to Job*, together with its religious background. The *ordinary man* is chosen to be the place of God's birth, and in him is incarnated not only (as in Christ) the "light" side of Yahweh: in him God regenerates himself as a totality, in both his light and dark aspects. Thereby the individual man, as *Aurora* says, becomes a son of God and is placed "first and highest among the kings of the earth." [73] Not only does Wisdom promise to exalt the alchemist to the status of a God-man, she also promises to keep her "covenant faithful to him for ever." Accordingly, since she is "friendly to man," [74] she offers him protection against the dangerous and incalculable side of herself,[75] or of God, and causes God to adopt the kindly-father attitude.[76] It is clear from the text that the author fully identifies his mysterious female figure, the anima in matter, with God. She is his feminine aspect, but at the same time, paradoxically, God himself.

218 But if he shall forsake my law and walk not in my ways and keep not my commandments aforesaid, the enemy shall have advantage over him and the son of iniquity shall have power to hurt him; but if he shall walk in my ways, then shall he not fear in the cold of snow. And for all his household there shall be covering, fine linen and purple,

219 The very dangerousness of the alchemical undertaking, whereby the artifex is exalted to the son of God, makes the author speak at this point of the devil: if the alchemist does not heed the ways of Wisdom, he exposes himself to the assaults of the "enemy" and the "son of iniquity." [77] The alchemists often speak of the assaults of the devil,[78] which include haste, arrogance, avarice, etc. The danger in our text is "the cold of snow." This might be a chemical reference to the premature cooling of the substances.[79] As we have said, the danger in the

73 Cf. Psalm 88 : 28.   74 "Answer to Job," pp. 389, 397.
75 See beginning of second parable: "the arrows of my quiver are drunk with blood."
76 Concerning the changes manifested in the unconscious during the individuation process see *Mysterium*, p. 172.
77 The text is corrupt here, and has been reconstructed to the best of my ability.
78 Cf. the "machinations of the thief" in *Mysterium*, pp. 165ff.; also "Liber Alze," *Mus. Herm.*, p. 331 (Waite, I, p. 266).
79 Silberer, *Problems of Mysticism and Its Symbolism*, p. 340.

corresponding psychological situation is that of inflation. In such cases feeling, relatedness to one's fellow-men, perishes and is replaced by an intellectual form of relationship. This is one of the dangers of exalting the alchemist to a state of Godlikeness. Since "fine linen and purple" [80] are mentioned as protection against the cold, this cold is thought of as coming from outside, whereas the texts usually emphasize that no "extraneous things" should be added to the work.[81]

220   The reference to the "enemy" therefore has a background of deep meaning. For if Wisdom elevates the alchemist to the position of her "son," he then becomes an incarnation of God. But this son of God is not, like Christ, the benevolent father-god made flesh in a pure human vessel: this time God the Father incarnates in an ordinary human being begotten in sin, because man's own nature, vacillating between brightness and darkness, better corresponds to God's antinomy and therefore makes a more complete incarnation possible. The chosen one must unite the opposites in himself; that is to say his anima must serve as the birthplace for God's wholeness. Lest this task, or rather God's antinomy, should burst him asunder, he is warned to walk in the ways of divine Wisdom, for the anima is the mediatrix between the irreconcilable opposites in the Godhead, just as the connecting and unifying element pertains more to the nature of woman than of man.

221   In patristic literature snow is a symbol of eternal damnation,[82] and in Dante's *Inferno* Satan stands up to his middle in ice. This is an allusion to the "frigidity of sinners"—Satan reigns in the north, the north wind is one of his symbols.[83] The motif probably refers also to the psychological danger of getting stuck in a conflict. The experience of the dark side of God could freeze all love, and the icy "fear of God" extinguish every vital impulse. Only Wisdom can protect man from this by giving him

---

[80] St. Gregory, *Epistolae*, Book I, indict. ix, Ep. 25 (Migne, *P.L.*, vol. 77, col. 471): "And what is signified by fine linen, if it be not bodily chastity shining with the comeliness of purity?" •

[81] Ripley, "Liber de Mercurio philosophorum," *Opera omnia*, p. 104: "Take heed therefore of all things foreign and strange."

[82] Also in Berthelot, *Alch. grecs*, III, viii, 1–2, Hoghelande, *Theatr. chem.*, IV, p. 150, and Rhabanus Maurus, *Allegoriae in sacr. script.* (Migne, *P.L.*, vol. 112, col. 1006).

[83] Further documentation in *Aion*, pp. 99f.

"fine linen and purple," i.e., by implanting the right attitude.

222   I need not go into the red-white symbolism of the clothing here, as I can refer the reader to Jung's statements.[84] From these it is clear that red and white are the colours of the *filius philosophorum* and his bride. It is evident from what follows that the author is fleetingly identified with these figures, for he is undoubtedly the one who is warned to "walk in my ways," and yet it is not his glorification that ensues, but the appearance of a suprapersonal King of Glory who is distinct from the alchemist. The admonition to conscientiousness and diligence ("he hath not eaten his bread idle") may also be regarded as a compensation against the danger of inflation, for by heeding it the adept suddenly becomes the servant of the work.

223   The mention of other servants or *domestici* ("all his household") may be explained by the fact that the metals, with respect to gold, were often called the servants of the king.[85] It is all the more probable that the metals are meant here, as a few lines later the seven stars or seven spirits of the Apocalypse are mentioned, and these were interpreted alchemically as the seven planetary spirits or metals.[86] They appear here as the servants of Wisdom. There are seven of them, and Wisdom adds herself to them as the eighth, whereby they all attain perfection. Psychologically, this probably expresses the idea of the unification of all the autonomous, collective components of the personality into an inner whole. The servants of the work are protected from the "cold" when the adept heeds the ways of Wisdom: the devil, the destructive principle of evil [87] that threatens the individuation process, would get into the work if the servant is not protected by Wisdom, and she can protect him only if the adept (the human ego) pays heed to her ways (the guiding, symbolic products of the unconscious) and comports himself as a servant. Then he and his unconscious psyche are protected against the disintegrative effect of evil.

---

[84] *Mysterium*, pp. 4, 43.

[85] In the parable of Bernardus Trevisanus (*Bibl. chem.*, II, pp. 388ff.) the planets are the servants of the king. Cf. *Psychology and Alchemy*, fig. 173, where the king is killed by his servants.

[86] The planets were identified with metals since the earliest times.

[87] This probably refers not to the "inferior" shadow, the "Ethiopian," who represents the evil in man that can be integrated, but to that ultimate evil which no man can integrate.

224   and he shall laugh in that day when I shall be satisfied and my glory shall appear, for he hath looked well to my paths and hath not eaten his bread idle.

225   Wisdom says that she will then be "satisfied" and that her "glory shall appear." The same quotation from the Bible (Psalm 16 : 15) is used by the author of "De adhaerendo Deo": he sees in it the moment when the soul fully knows God.[88] In the alchemical texts the prima materia is often described as *terra sitiens*, the thirsting earth, which in the coniunctio is saturated by the rain, "the king descending from heaven." [89] The same image occurs in Ephraem Syrus with reference to Mary: she is the thirsting earth who, "bedewed by the dew of God, bore Christ, the bread of life." [90] Another ecclesiastical interpretation identifies the thirsting earth with the human body: "Rightly is the Church compared to the moon, because she sprinkles us with the dew of the font and quickens the earth of our body with the dew of baptism." [91] (The symbolism of baptism is mentioned in the next passages of our text.) After the "woman," the thirsting earth, is "satisfied" by the king descending from heaven, or by the labours of the alchemist (according to "De adhaerendo Deo" knowledge of God occurs when the soul "reflects on itself" [92]—proof of the significance of the king as consciousness! [93]) her "glory shall appear"—indeed, she becomes God himself! [94] Psychologically this means that the divine, numinous aspect of the anima, which brings healing, becomes visible only when consciousness actively participates and gives her due attention and the right understanding. Then the dry emptiness of the thirsting earth within reveals itself as the place where God himself appears.

[88] Albertus Magnus, *Opera*, XXXVII, p. 533.

[89] Cf. the quotation from Maria Prophetissa in Senior, *De chemia*, p. 80: "And that it is which they have called the King coming forth from the earth and coming down from heaven. And it is the like of this that is said to be in this water." •   [90] *Hymni et sermones*, II, col. 744.

[91] Maximus of Turin, *Homil. 101* (Migne, *P.L.*, vol. 57, col. 488).• Cf. Isidore of Seville, *De natura rerum*, p. 38.

[92] Borgnet, XXXVII, p. 533: "reflectitur in se ipsam."

[93] Concerning the king see *Mysterium*, ch. IV.

[94] The anima could well have this exalted significance, because as a result of the inflation there is an undervaluation of the unconscious. Hence the alchemist is degraded to a servant and the anima acquires a divine status.

226   Therefore were the heavens opened above him and there thundered the voice of him who holdeth the seven stars in his hand, which are the seven spirits sent forth into all the earth to preach and to bear witness. He that believeth and is well baptized shall be saved, but he that believeth not shall be condemned.

227   In these words we recognize the epiphany of God in the Apocalypse,[95] where it is also said that his hair was like white wool, as white as snow, his eyes were as a flame of fire and his voice as the sound of many waters, and his countenance was as the sun—a description that must have involuntarily suggested to an alchemist any number of associations with his *filius philosophorum*. With this apparition, those that believe shall be saved, "when the king that is in heaven judgeth over them," continues the text. They shall be "whited with snow": they are like neophytes or as though transfigured.[96]

228   Behind Wisdom there emerges the face of the "Ancient of Days," [97] the judge who separates the believers from the unbelievers. After a fleeting mention of the "son of iniquity" the text abruptly passes on to optimistic promises for the future. The problem of evil has been touched on, but has obviously not become fully conscious. In its place, the image of the Last Judgment rises up with its final separation of the opposites instead of their union. Although wholeness is there in the God-image— the Ancient of Days holding the seven stars in his hand—man is saved only through the participation of faith. What happens to the condemned ones who have not believed is not mentioned in the text.

229   The heavenly judge who now appears is an alchemical parallel to the filius philosophorum. He is, as it were, the glorified, ultimate manifestation of the prima materia and is thus in a mysterious manner identical with Wisdom. Similarly, in Ripley's "Cantilena," Luna changes into the "splendour of the sun." [98]

230   This transformation of the feminine substance into the

95 Rev. 1 : 14–16.

96 Ephraem Syrus, *Hymni et sermones*, I, col. 110 (Hymn of the Baptized): "Your garments, brethren, are white as snow, and your brightness shines like the brightness of the angels." * The alchemical symbolism of baptism is discussed in the following chapters.

97 Daniel 7 : 9.   98 *Mysterium*, pp. 313ff.

masculine recalls the view of Theodoret of Cyrus that Ecclesia-Luna, who represents a "composition of souls fully initiated into the mysteries," in her final glorification becomes the sun, the image of Christ, whose light calls forth the wonder of men.[99] Throughout this whole passage, therefore, *Aurora* does not really depart from the Christian doctrine of redemption. The author has reverted to his earlier views.

231   The identity of Wisdom with the filius [100] comes out in the following passage:

232   And the signs of those who believe and are well baptized are these: When the king that is in heaven judgeth over them, they shall be whited with snow in Selmon and shall be as the wings of a dove covered with silver, and the hinder parts of her back with the paleness of gold.

233   The last words refer to Psalm 67:14–15: "If you sleep among the midst of lots, you shall be as the wings of a dove covered with silver," etc. Hugh of St. Victor interprets "among the midst of lots" as a place between fear and desire, between left and right.[101] The dove was generally interpreted as the "multitude of the righteous." [102] She thus appears as an image of plurality in a place midway between the opposites. Joachim of Flora interprets the passage as referring to the two orders of monasteries and monks who shall be united "at the great Sabbath." [103]

234   The relation between the author and Wisdom described in the opening chapters has undergone a remarkable change. At first they confronted one another alone in a shattering encounter, after which they both sank into the darkness of the abyss. Then Wisdom promised to make the alchemist her son-lover if he rescued her, "knowing and understanding." Afterwards followed the warning about the "son of iniquity" and the admonition to careful and diligent work. She then appeared

99 *Explanatio in Cant. Cant.*, IV, 9 (Migne, *P.G.*, vol. 81, col. 177). Cf. the transformation of the moon, symbolizing the soul, into the sun (Christ) in St. Gregory, *Expos. in Cant. Cant.*, 6, v. 9 (Migne, *P.L.*, vol. 79, cols. 530f.).
100 "Psychology and Religion," p. 74. Christ is the "man encompassed by a woman" (ibid., p. 92).
101 Cf. his commentary in *De bestiis* (Migne, *P.L.*, vol. 177, cols. 17f.).
102 Ephraem Syrus, II, col. 176.
103 *Concordia*, II (Hahn, III, p. 271).

surrounded by ministering spirits, and finally in masculine form as the divine judge in the midst of the righteous who have been saved, the whole throng having the appearance of a dove covered with silver and gold. The central symbol has become a plurality, and the alchemist is only one among many, secretly included in the image of the dove (a compound of Wisdom and filius). This pluralization may have something to do with the previous reference to evil—that is to say, with the fact that there has been no conscious and individual confrontation with the shadow. The moral problem thus remains a collective one: the "righteous" are saved, the "unbelievers" damned. The reconciliation of the light with the dark can take place only in the individual, so that the avoidance of the encounter with the shadow brings about a pluralization and regression to the dominant collective views: the new "son" is identified with Christ, whose "body" by tradition consists of the multitude of the righteous, and it is only the *belief* in Christ that brings redemption.

235   Such shall be to me a beloved son, behold ye him, beautiful above the sons of men, at whose beauty the sun and moon wonder. For he is the privilege of love and the heir, in whom men trust and without whom they can do nothing.

236   The filius is of one nature with the silver and gold dove.[104] But the dove, as already mentioned, is a symbol for the Holy Spirit, the Church, Mary, and also for Christ.[105]

237   In the Missal, the words from Psalm 44 : 3, "Thou art beautiful above the sons of men," are referred to Christ.[106] In *Aurora,* on the other hand, the "son" is understood alchemically as a product of the union of sun and moon, whose heir he is, and who gaze at him in wonder, like parents. The coniunctio is no longer between Wisdom and the author but between sun and moon, and has thus become an "extra-personal" event projected into the cosmos. Moreover the "son" is the earthly gold, for it is this to which the words from the Book of Baruch ("in

104 Cf. Honorius, *Expos. in Cant. Cant.* (Migne, *P.L.*, vol. 172, col. 380).
105 Bousset, *Hauptprobleme der Gnosis*, p. 266.
106 Roman Missal, Gradual for Sunday within Octave of Christmas. Of Christ's beauty Ephraem Syrus says (II, col. 562): "Thy lips distil the drug of life, balm flows from thy fingers, beauteous are thine eyes . . . all the children of the Church seek eagerly after thee." •

whom men trust") refer,[107] so that once again it is evident that the "son" has changed into a non-Biblical, alchemical figure. Nevertheless, it is difficult to see what the author had in mind. The silver-gold dove would be an alchemical image for the *albedo,* the whitened prima materia, or the gold. In ecclesiastical symbolism it represents Wisdom or the Apocalyptic Christ, or his body ("multitude of the righteous"). Did the author understand the *albedo* in a religious sense, or did he interpret the religious symbolism in an alchemical sense? Presumably both. It is possible that he saw the image in a dream or vision and then tried to interpret it in terms of the imagery familiar to him. The striking thing in this passage is that the individual element takes a back place. The style is once more that of an "annunciation" or hymn of praise, and the end is decidedly didactic. With the disappearance of the dark elements everything personal has vanished from the scene.

238 But he that hath ears to hear, let him hear what the spirit of the doctrine saith to the sons of the discipline concerning the seven stars, by which the divine work is wrought. And of these Senior treateth in his book in the chapter of the Sun and Moon, saying: After thou hast made those seven which thou hast distributed through the seven stars (and hast appointed to the seven stars), and hast purged them nine times until they appear as pearls—this is the Whitening.

239 The concluding sentence has a strong alchemical coloration and shows that the first parable really is concerned with the appearance of the classical *albedo.* The quotation from Senior speaks of the seven powers which are correlated with the seven stars and have to be purified until they look like pearls. The seven stars are the same as those which are mentioned in the Apocalypse as attributes of God. It is evident that the seven metals are meant, for these in their totality are often said to constitute the stone, and are fused in it to form the "crown." [108] The concluding words of the parable allude once more to the title: "Of the Black Earth wherein the Seven Planets took Root." For in the medieval view the seven metals are not only

---

107 Also in *Das Buch der Alaune und Salze* (p. 64) gold is "Lord of the Stones . . . and king . . . and thus gold is among bodies like to the sun among the stars, for the sun is king and light of the stars, and by it are brought to fruition things of the earth and growing things." •

108 *Mysterium,* p. 9.

correlated with the seven planets but, through their *instillatio* or "influence," are in the most literal sense formed in the earth.[109] Evidently in the black cloud mentioned at the beginning of the parable, and in the inundation it produced, heaven and the stars came down to earth and impressed themselves upon it.[110] The bride, who at the end of the previous chapter came down from heaven, was likewise crowned with stars. She is, in a sense, consubstantial with the cloud, in so far as both bring heaven down with them.

240   The union of heaven and earth is a favourite alchemical image for the coniunctio. A Hermes quotation says: "It is needful that heaven and earth be conjoined, which is a philosophic word." [111] Or again: "The male is the heaven of the female and the female is the earth of the male." [112] An anonymous Greek author says: [113] "Heaven above, earth below, through the male and the female is the work accomplished." [114]

[109] Mennens, "Aureum vellus" *Theatr. chem.*, V, p. 307: "Someone will say, How shall the aforesaid influences of the metals . . . make their way into the parent mountains? The royal prophet replies, The mountains like wax have flowed before the face of the Lord." •

[110] Cf. the negative description of this motif in Honorius, *Speculum* (Migne, *P.L.*, vol. 172, col. 937): "The seven-headed dragon, the prince of darkness, drew down from heaven with his tail a part of the stars, and the cloud of sin overshadowed them, and covered them with the darkness of death. Wherefore the eternal sun hid the ray of his brightness beneath the cloud of the flesh. In the sunset of his death he died in place of the stars; bringing them forth from the darkness he the dayspring restored them from the night of death to the calm sky." •

[111] Petrus Bonus, *Theatr. chem.* (1622), V, p. 647. Cf. *Psychology and Alchemy*, par. 192, n. 67.

[112] "Tractatus aureus," *Ars chemica*, p. 12. •   [113] *Alch. grecs*, III, x.

[114] The primordial image of the union of heaven and earth probably entered alchemy via the mystery religions. Aeschylus describes this union in the fragment from his *Danaids:* "The holy heaven yearns to wound the earth, and yearning lays hold on the earth to join in wedlock; the rain, falling from the amorous heaven, impregnates the earth, and it brings forth for mankind the food of flocks and herds and Demeter's gifts; and from the moist marriage-rite the woods put on their bloom." (*Works*, trans. Smyth, II, pp. 394f.) Proclus (*In Timaeum Commentaria*, 40E; Diehl, III, p. 176) interpreted the cry ὖε–κύε at the Eleusinian mysteries in the same sense: "The sacred ordinances of the Athenians . . . provided for the celebration of the marriage of heaven and earth, as a preparation for initiation into the mysteries. Looking up to heaven they cried 'Let it rain,' and looking down to earth, 'Make fruitful,' thus recognizing that all things are born of these as of a father and mother." In Gnosticism this cosmic process was already interpreted psychologically. For instance, in Justin's Book of Baruch

241   The black earth in the title is obviously the receptive element which absorbs the planetary forces. This not only agrees
with the general views of "Mother Earth" in antiquity [115] but
is borne out by the alchemical texts. For instance, to
Euthicia's question "Quis foemina?" Rosinus answers "Terra
nigra." [116] All this suggests very strongly that the earth is identical with the sublime figure of Wisdom at the end of the preceding chapter.[117]

242   On closer examination this is really a tremendous thought.
The "Wisdom of God" in the Bible was the playmate of
Yahweh, who was with him before the beginning of the world.
In patristic literature she was, as we have mentioned, defined as
the "archetypal world" (mundus archetypus) or as the sum of
eternal ideas in the mind of God, the prototypes from which
he created all things. She may also be compared with the Indian
Shakti or Maya and with the Gnostic Sophia. And yet in our
text this figure is equated with the soul of the dark earth, the
impure prima materia! Alchemy, accordingly, lays upon man
the task, and confers upon him the dignity, of rescuing the
hidden, feminine aspect of God from imprisonment in matter
by his opus, and of reuniting her with the manifest, masculine
deity.

243   Through the ablution described at the end of the parable
the earth, or the seven stars or metals within it, become "as
pearls." In Senior the pearl is a synonym for the lapis,[118] which,
as the "subtle pearl," is formed from the divine water. "De adhaerendo Deo" calls Wisdom a "precious pearl." [119] In our text

---

heaven is equated with pneuma, and earth with psyche. Hippolytus, *Elenchos*,
V, 26, 36 (Legge, I, p. 179); cf. also Reitzenstein, *Das iranische Erlösungsmysterium*, p. 104. The same interpretation occurs in Philo, "Allegorical Interpretation of Genesis" (*Works*, I, p. 159), where heaven and earth are νοῦς and αἴσθησις
(sense-perception), and are also interpreted as the heavenly and the earthly man.
These significations are taken up in Parable VI of *Aurora*.

[115] Documentation in Dieterich, *Mutter Erde*.

[116] *Art. aurif.*, I, p. 169.

[117] In Philo, too, the paradisal earth is a "symbol of wisdom." ("Questions and
Answers on Genesis," I, p. 5.) The identity of the earth with Wisdom is clearly
expressed in Parable VI.

[118] *De chemia*, p. 11.

[119] "For this is that hidden heavenly treasure and precious pearl" (Borgnet,
XXXVII, p. 524).

the pearl is split into seven, which points to a dissociation, i.e., the pluralization mentioned earlier. This is probably the reason why the alchemical procedures are repeated in the second parable.

244   In Greek alchemy the pearl is a synonym for the divine water, or its spirits (pneumata, vapours). An anonymous author says: "The philosophers named the waters or spirits 'pearls' and 'precious stones,' as they are full of great power.[120] When thou makest the hidden nature to come out, thou hast the mystery of the philosophers." [121]

245   In our text the pearls are a symbol of the *albedo* and probably also of the female power of the anima or Wisdom. In Christian symbolism the pearl signifies purity and virginity,[122] and this emphasizes the moral aspect of the whitening. The theme of chemical and psychic ablution and the symbolism of baptism are discussed more closely in the following parables.

246   Summing up, we may say that the first parable describes an essentially new psychic event, the sudden emergence of Wisdom from below, from matter, and her demand for succour through man's work and efforts. Not only would she thereby regain her former sublime status, but the final redemption of humanity would also be made possible. Wisdom appears, further, in the form of a male judge, who is, psychologically, the embodiment of a tendency in the unconscious to force the conscious mind to make sharper distinctions. Discrimination (presumably between ego and self, personal and impersonal) has become urgently necessary because of the previous contamination of the author's personality with the archetypal anima image. Therefore the parable ends with a didactic admonition for a ninefold purification of the "pearls." Whereas anima-Wisdom speaks in the middle section of the parable, the author himself speaks again at the end. Evidently the differentiation has been temporarily successful—but it is not definitive, for it is again the anima speaking at the beginning of the next parable.

---

[120] The Arabian mystic Alfarabi uses the term "precious stone" for "all that truly is." Cf. Horten, *Das Buch der Ringsteine*, p. 2.

[121] *Alch. grecs*, V, ii, 8. Zosimos says (III, ii, 2): "I will also explain to you the power of the pearl: cooked in oil, it has within it the feminine power . . . the perfection of the material is wrought by the pearl."

[122] Cf. Ephraem Syrus, I, col. 70, and col. 314n.

VII. THE SECOND PARABLE: OF THE
FLOOD OF WATERS ...

247   The significance of the second parable is already apparent in its title: "Of the Flood of Waters and of Death, which the Woman both brought into the World and put to Flight." As will be seen, the woman is again Wisdom. In commenting on the previous chapter we had deduced only indirectly that Wisdom, or her descent to the adept, was the cause of the *nigredo*, but it was not stated directly in the text. The situation of distress in which both found themselves was simply there, all of a sudden. The author's attempts at discrimination in the last chapter seem, however, to have given him an inkling that it was Wisdom herself who brought about this "death."

248   The parable again begins with the description of a flood. As I have said, it is as though each parable were an abbreviated recapitulation of the whole opus. This time the anima alone speaks, describing the *nigredo* as though it were already in the past.

249   When the multitude of the sea shall be converted to me and the streams have flowed over my face . .

250   Here the *nigredo* state is amplified in a new direction. The flood is not caused only by the cloud penetrating into the earth, but is described as an invasion of the sea. "The multitude of the sea" in Isaiah (60 : 5) means really the pagans dwelling by the sea (AV: "the forces of the Gentiles"), and this is again an allusion to the motif of the Ethiopians, symbolizing an inrush of pagan psychic contents. Significantly, a similar conception is to be found in a Byzantine commentator of alchemical treatises, Christianos. He says in explanation of the "sea-water" that the old philosophers meant the fixing and generative water of the art, "for the sea breaks in not only by reason of the multitude

244

of fishes, but because it is also the dwelling-place of barbarians."
Hugo Rahner, in his compilation of patristic sources for the
symbolical significance of the sea,[1] says that the "diabolical sea"
is a metaphor for the pagan nations which have given themselves to the devil. He cites St. Hilary, who says: [2] "We understand the waters as rightly signifying the peoples. . . . For the
waters of the earth are unquiet, earthly, darksome, seeking to
overwhelm us, their spirits excited with wrath, and moved with
the violence of diabolical rage." Over the sea are the mists and
whirlwinds of the demons.[3] This view probably underlies the
passage from Christianos, which explains why the inrush of barbarians—or, in our text, the multitude of the sea—could destroy
the adept, an allusion to a possible outbreak of insanity. Christianos goes on to say that the ore is a "red thing" which destroys
those who handle it without experience.[4] The ancient authors
pointed out that in lead (a prima materia) there dwelt a daemon
who could induce "mania." [5] In our text this is expressed in
figurative language as an invasion of the sea. The image is understandable psychologically since the sea represents the collective unconscious, which was quite capable of destroying the
senses of the adept not only because of its pagan contents but
because of its overwhelming power. The anonymous author of
the work often cited as "Rhazis Epistula" speaks of the water as
"our sea full of giants." [6]

251   Simultaneously with the flood of waters, a bloody struggle
has broken out.

252   . . . and the arrows of my quiver are drunk with blood . . .

253   Without warning, the same figure, the anima projected into
matter, declares that she had made herself drunk with butchery
and bloodshed. The quotation (Deut. 32 : 42) is evidently an
allusion to that treacherous murder in the *Turba*,[7] when the

---

[1] "Antenna Crucis II."
[2] *Tractatus super Psalmos*, 123, 5 (Migne, *P.L.*, vol. 9, col. 677).*
[3] Peter Chrysologus, Sermo 20 (Migne, *P.L.*, vol. 52, col. 254), and Augustine (?),
Sermo 366, 5 (Migne, *P.L.*, vol. 39, col. 1649).
[4] Berthelot, *Alch. grecs*, VI, xii, 4.
[5] Petasios in Olympiodorus (Berthelot, *Alch. grecs*, II, iv, 43 and 44). Cf. *Mysterium*, p. 351.
[6] *Art. aurif.* (1610), I, p. 251. The treatise is a Latin translation of an Arabic text.
[7] Pp. 229 and 247. Cf. *Alch. grecs*, III, vi, 8, and *Art. aurif.*, I, p. 189.

"woman" slays her lover during the coniunctio with the "weapons hidden in her body." In other texts it is described as the μάχη θηλείη, "female combat." [8] The symbolism and its ecclesiastical parallels are discussed in Jung.[9] In ecclesiastical language, love is something that both kills and makes to live; thus St. Augustine says: [10] "love kills that which we were, in order that we may be that which we were not; love makes as it were a death for us." According to St. Thomas, excess of love causes a "liquefactio" [11] and a "languor." [12]

254   In the Biblical context (Deut. 32 : 42) the arrows drunk with blood signify God's victory over his enemies, and his vengeance.[13] So once again the anima is equated with God. Further, the "woman" does not murder only her lover, as in most of the alchemical texts, but wallows in an indiscriminate blood-bath.[14] Just as the murder of the innocents was a concomitant of Christ's birth, so here this "new birth" is accompanied by mass murder on an Apocalyptic scale.

[8] *Carmina Heliodori*, p. 56, Carmen IV, verse 225.

[9] *Mysterium*, pp. 21ff., 145, 159f.

[10] *Enarr. in Psalm.* 121 (Migne, *P.L.*, vol. 37, col. 1628).•

[11] *Summa*, I–II, q. 28, art. 5 resp. (Eng. edn., I, p. 713): "Consequently love of a suitable good perfects and betters the lover; but love of a good which is unsuitable to the lover wounds and worsens him. Wherefore man is perfected and bettered chiefly by the love of God; but is wounded and worsened by the love of sin. . . . Melting denotes a softening of the heart, whereby the heart shows itself to be ready for the entrance of the beloved." • *In Sent.* III, Dist. xxvii, q. 1a, 1 ad 4: "For the lover is separated from himself, and tends towards the beloved, and on this account love is said to cause ecstasy and to glow, because that which glows outside itself bubbles up and sends forth vapour." •

[12] Meier, *Die Lehre des Thomas von Aquino "De passionibus animae" in quellenanalytischer Darstellung*, p. 55. Cf. Gilbert of Hoyland, *Sermones in Cantica XLVI*, 3 (Migne, *P.L.*, vol. 184, col. 244); William of Thierry, *Expositio altera super Cant. Cant.*, cap. 2 (Migne, *P.L.*, vol. 180, col. 515); Baldwin of Canterbury, *Tractatus XIV* (Migne, *P.L.*, vol. 204, col. 539); William of Auvergne, "De trinitate," cap. XXI, *Opera omnia*, II (Suppl.) , p. 26: "and love is commonly called a wound."

[13] Cf. also Joel 3 : 12ff.

[14] An older mythological parallel would be the Egyptian legend of the goddess Hathor: when the sun-god Ra grew old, men conspired against him, so he sent his eye, the goddess Hathor, down to earth. Hathor created such havoc among mankind that, in order to save the human race from total destruction, Ra caused quantities of red beer to be prepared which she mistook for blood, "and she returned home drunken and knew not men." Cf. Neumann, *Origins and History of Consciousness*, pp. 55f. and 74, and Vandier, *La Religion égyptienne*, p. 38.

255   . . . and my presses are fragrant with the best wine and my barns are filled with the corn of wheat and the bridegroom with the ten wise virgins hath entered into my chamber and thereafter my belly hath swelled from the touch of my beloved and the bolt of my door hath been opened to my beloved,

256   The triumph of the victor, the positive aspect of the slaughter, is celebrated in the passage about the presses and barns.[15] For the *nigredo*, as a saying from Avicenna [16] makes clear, signifies the victory or domination of the female.[17]

257   The blood-bath is evidently an allusion to the "death" which the woman brought about, and this, to judge by parallel ideas in other texts, seems to have been a consequence of the first coniunctio; therefore the text goes on to speak of the ten virgins to whom the bridegroom came, and of the impregnation of the woman. It is as though the blood-bath had had the reactive effect of making the woman pregnant by the heavenly bridegroom. Psychologically this would mean that the hostile, emotional outbreak of the "divine" element, utterly destroying the world of consciousness, has a deeper significance in that it makes the anima pregnant and initiates a new birth, that is, a further and more comprehensive incarnation of God. The parable of the ten virgins hints at a hierosgamos with the deity. It is worth while refreshing our memories with the actual text (Matt. 25 : 1–13, AV): "Then shall the kingdom of heaven be likened unto ten virgins, which took their lamps, and went forth to meet the bridegroom. And five of them were wise, and five were foolish. They that were foolish took their lamps, and took no oil with them; but the wise took oil in their vessels with their lamps. While the bridegroom tarried, they all slumbered and slept. And at midnight there was a cry made, Behold, the bridegroom cometh; go ye out to meet him. Then all those virgins arose, and trimmed their lamps. And the foolish said unto the wise, Give us of your oil, for our lamps are gone out. But the wise answered, saying, Not so, lest there be not enough for us and you; but go ye rather to them that sell, and buy for yourselves. And while they went to buy, the bridegroom came; and they

15 Cf. Joel 2 : 24.
16 *Theatr. chem.*, IV (1613), p. 991: ". . . for until the *albedo* the corruption of humidity and the rule of the female is in force." •
17 In the Biblical context the raging female is, as we have said, identical with God.

that were ready went in with him to the marriage: and the door was shut. Afterward came also the other virgins, saying, Lord, Lord, open to us. But he answered and said, Verily I say unto you, I know you not. Watch therefore, for ye know neither the day nor the hour wherein the Son of man cometh." [18]

258   This motif of a group of women, all waiting for *one* bridegroom who appears in the middle of the night, is strange enough in itself, and probably echoes some pre-Christian tradition. In the cult of Adonis and also in the popular festivities celebrating the death and refinding of Osiris, the death of the god and his hierosgamos with the mother goddess were accompanied by choruses of women, who shared the sufferings of the Great Mother and her feast of joy.[19] The bier and the marriage-bed were one.[20] The festival was celebrated mainly by women.[21] After the finding of the dead Osiris there followed in Busiris the "festival of burning lamps," at which the celebrants conducted the dead god to the island of the dead.[22] If the parable in the Bible should have connections with such ideas, then it would contain echoes of the archetypal motif of the death-marriage, which is the central theme of the final chapter of *Aurora*.

259   The striking thing in our text is the fact that *all ten* virgins enter the bridal chamber with the bridegroom, so that the foolish virgins are included in the work of redemption as described here, whereas in the Bible version the door to the kingdom of Heaven remained shut. This intimation of a more comprehensive redemption, in which even the inadequate human being shares, is presumably due to the irruption of God's shadow into the human psyche. The significance of the number 10 will be gone into later,[23] when the text returns to it in another form. What deserves special emphasis here is the fact that those human beings who in the Christian view were excluded from the heavenly marriage are, in our text, admitted as having equal rights.

The inundation and the blood-bath simultaneously brought about an impregnation which will result in the birth of the

18 Honorius interprets this passage as Christ's entry into the soul. *Expos. in Cant. Cant.* (Migne, *P.L.*, vol. 172, col. 534).
19 Gressmann, *Tod und Auferstehung des Osiris*, ch. "Adonis und Osiris."
20 Ibid., p. 16.
21 P. 25. Cf. the maenads in the Dionysus cult.
22 P. 38.
23 Infra, pp. 253ff.

filius philosophorum.[24] Looking back, we can see that the flood and the cloud in the preceding parable have acquired a new aspect: they are not only destructive but fertilizing factors. In Greek alchemy the cloud bestowed life. The treatise of Komarios says: "See and understand how the clouds rise up from the sea, carrying the blessed waters with them, and they saturate the earth, and there spring up seeds and blossoms." [25] In Senior the divine water is the "cloud which quickens the lower world." [26] In ecclesiastical symbolism Mary is the "freshening cloud." [27] Just as in the last parable the flood had the double aspect of a deadly inundation and a purifying ablution (indicated at the end by the *albedo*), so here have the flood and the *nigredo:* they kill and quicken at once.[28]

260   and after Herod being angry hath slain many children in Bethlehem of Juda and Rachel hath bewailed all her children and a light hath risen up in darkness and the Sun of justice hath appeared from heaven,

261   The interweaving of destruction and new life is further elaborated by the reference to the massacre of the innocents and to Rachel robbed of her children. The threatening of the child-hero is a widespread archetypal motif for the psychological interpretation of which I would refer the reader to Jung's essay "The Psychology of the Child Archetype." In the hermeneutics

24 For the psychological significance of the "soul's pregnancy" see "The Psychology of the Transference," pars. 461ff.

25 Berthelot, *Alch. grecs*, IV, xx, 12.

26 *De chemia*, pp. 24f.: "Likewise they call this water the Cloud which quickens the lower world, and by all these they mean the foliate Water, which is the gold of the Philosophers." • A parallel image occurs in Ephraem Syrus, according to whom the Gospel "spreads over the earth beneficent as a cloud" (*Hymni et sermones*, II, col. 766).

27 Albertus, "Biblia Mariana" (Borgnet, XXXVII, p. 384): "[Mary] is the cloud that cooleth, raineth, and bestoweth." She is also (p. 373) the "cloud of overshadowing and guidance." •

28 Cf. the passage from Komarios in *Alch. grecs*, IV, xx, 10: "The floods and rolling waves wound the substance in Hades, that is, in the grave, wherein it lies; but when the grave is opened, it will rise up therefrom like a child from the womb." The "Aquarium sapientum," *Mus. Herm.*, p. 86 (Waite, I, p. 79), says: "Everything contributes to the formation of this stone. It is conceived in hell, born in the earth, quickened in heaven, dies in time, and at length attains eternal glory." • Origen similarly interpreted the Flood as the κάθαρσις (purification) and διόρθωσις (correction) of the world. *Contra Celsum*, IV, 69 (Chadwick, pp. 238f.).

of the Church Fathers, Rachel was an image for the "dying Church." Cyril of Alexandria says that just as Rachel died at the birth of her last-born, "so the Church in her earthliness dies into the birth of eternal life." [29] It is to be assumed that this symbolical background plays a part in our text: just as in the *nigredo* the woman dominated at first, so she is now robbed of her dominion at the birth of the filius philosophorum; she dies, and her life passes into the new being.

262   The new birth is called "the Sun of justice," an image from Malachi 4 : 2 which the Church has always referred to Christ.[30] Thus the Gradual for September 8, Nativity of the Blessed Virgin Mary, says: "Happy art thou, O Virgin Mary . . . for of thee is born the Sun of Justice, Christ our God." [31] Ephraem Syrus says: [32] "Mary . . . bears in her womb the sun; her mystery affrights all who wish to speak of it." [33] And the "Biblia Mariana" of pseudo-Albertus says of Mary: "She it is whom Solomon compared with the dawn at her birth, with the full moon at the mysterious conception of the son of God, with the sun at her ascension, with the terrible hosts of the Lord for the affrighting of demons." [34] The complex psychological significance of Sol as a primordial image of consciousness and of its source, the self, is fully discussed in Jung.[35]

263   As in the first parable, the initial situation of distress passes over without a break into a hymn of praise, this time in honour of the birth of a saviour; and, as in the first parable, the change goes hand in hand with the Christian interpretation of the

[29] *Glaphyra in Genesin* (Migne, *P.G.*, vol. 69, cols. 223–26).

[30] Doelger, *Die Sonne der Gerechtigkeit und der Schwarze*, pp. 49ff.

[31] Concerning the identification of Christ with the sun see St. Augustine, *Enarr. in Psalm.* 10 (11), 3 (Eng. edn., I, p. 94): "[Christ] in many places of Holy Scripture is allegorically called the Sun." •

[32] *Hymni et sermones*, II, col. 530, also 174.

[33] Cf. ibid., col. 540: "Risen from her [Mary] is the Sun of Justice, who in his rising lit the whole world." Col. 792: "All things become distinct in the light, and all things are declared in Christ." Vol. I, col. 10: "Conquered is the darkness, that the victory over Satan may be known, and the sun was victorious that it might announce the First-Born. Conquered is the darkness and the spirit of darkness, and our Light was victorious with the author of light." (Cf. also I, cols. 8, 16, 130; II, cols. 478, 526, 550, 630, 794, 812.) Elsewhere (II, col. 496) Ephraem Syrus calls Christ a pillar of light, and this recalls the conception of the Redeemer as a pillar of light among the Manichaeans.

[34] Borgnet, XXXVII, p. 399.   [35] *Mysterium*, pp. 106ff.

event: the newborn saviour is identified in nearly all the quotations with Christ. It is as though the author has got himself again and again into the unconscious darkness of pagan and alchemical contents, but as soon as an image of the self is manifest in the chaos, he equates it with Christ and feels safe again, rehabilitated, and delivered from the hand of the "enemy." He pushes the problem of the shadow too far away from him, so that the darkness always comes back.

264   then the fulness of the time shall come when God shall send his Son, as he hath said, whom he hath appointed heir of all things, by whom also he made the world, to whom he said of old time: Thou art my Son, today have I begotten thee: to whom the wise men from the East brought three precious gifts; in that day, which the Lord hath made, let us be glad and rejoice therein, for this day hath the Lord beheld my affliction and sent redemption, for he shall reign in Israel.

265   These sentences all refer to the birth of a figure who each time is paralleled with Christ: "when the fulness of the time shall come," [36] "heir of all things," [37] "thou art my son, today have I begotten thee," [38] "wise men from the East." [39] It is particularly significant that it was this son "by whom God made the world," [40] for the filius philosophorum, like Christ, is here interpreted as the world-creating Logos. The words "in that day, which the Lord hath made, let us be glad," etc.[41] form the Gradual for Easter Sunday and throughout Easter Week, thus indicating that the birth of the filius philosophorum is also a resurrection or rebirth. This is the more significant in that, psychologically considered, it concerns not merely the birth of the "inner man," the self, but at the same time the rebirth of man's ego-consciousness. The birth of the alchemical filius could be interpreted as a resurrection of Christ in compensatory, changed form; for the archetype of the self, as such, is presumably "eternal"—only the archetypal image which represents it in the psyche "dies" and changes in accordance with the changes in individual consciousness.

266   That death which a woman brought into the world, this day hath a woman put to flight, and the barriers of hell are broken down; for

---

36 Gal. 4 : 4.   37 Hebr. 1 : 2.   38 Hebr. 1 : 5.
39 Matt. 2 : 11.   40 Hebr. 1 : 2.   41 Ps. 117 : 24.

death shall no more have dominion, nor shall the gates of hell prevail against her,

267   The statement that on the day when the son appears "death shall have no more dominion" [42] shows that this son is identical with the risen Christ: he is an image of the immortal man.[43] At the same time the author experiences the banishment of his "affliction"; he feels saved, and death is driven out of the world. For since he is inseparably bound up with the wretchedness and despair of the prima materia, its purification and deliverance from all darkness and corruptibility denote his own redemption and give him a feeling of immortality.

268   Thus a typically Christian solution has been found: the alchemist is saved not so much by his own work as by his participation in the birth of the saviour. In the unconscious something becomes complete and whole again, and through it the ego feels pacified. It is as though the vacillations between the extremes of hell and bliss in these parables had gradually brought about an equalization of opposites, without the author's fully realizing what sort of alterations in his conscious view of the world this would entail. Therefore the process remains partially unrecognized, and the author thinks he can equate his experience of the filius—the self—with the Church's conception of Christ, although, as Jung has pointed out,[44] the filius philosophorum is really a compensatory mirror-image of the dogmatic figure of Christ arising out of the unconscious. In comparison with Christ the alchemical image is much the more complete as it contains a light and a dark side—the inferior part of human nature is included in it. As the next passage will show, this is true also of the saviour figure in *Aurora;* yet the author identifies this more complete figure with Christ, because he has not really become conscious of the problem of including the dark side.

[42] Rom. 6 : 9.
[43] Similarly, the author of "De adhaerendo Deo" says: "When our heart and mind . . . is gradually concentrated upon an immutable sufficient Good and has learned to abide with itself . . . and has fully habituated itself to that supreme Good until it is itself made immutable and immutably attains that true life which is God the Lord . . . [then] it inwardly abides in that peaceful and secret place of the Godhead, fully established in itself in Jesus Christ, who is the way, the truth, and the life." (Borgnet, XXXVII, p. 530.)
[44] *Psychology and Alchemy,* pars. 29ff.

for the tenth groat, which was lost, is found, and the hundredth sheep is restored in the wilderness, and the number of our brethren from the fall of the angels is fully made up.

269   This passage indicates what is the nature of the "redemption" or wholeness in the unconscious, by reference to the parables of the lost piece of silver and lost sheep (Luke 15 : 1–10), which in their turn are connected with the "number of our brethren from the fall of the angels." This frame of reference derives from Church hermeneutics, for according to St. Gregory the ten groats signify the nine choirs of angels together with mankind, which are the property of the divine Sophia (!), that is, of God's son, who is diligently seeking for the one that is lost. Elsewhere, the woman is interpreted as the Church, and sinners are represented as unreasoning animals (sheep) and as groats of little worth. A similar interpretation of the parable as the fallen angels or the fallen Sophia occurs in the Gnostic sect of the Marcosians, whose teachings are reported by Irenaeus.[45] It runs as follows: [46] "The creation of the Aeons and the story of the sheep that was lost and found again are for them [the Marcosians] one and the same, and they endeavour to interpret these things mystically . . . maintaining that the universe was formed out of the numbers 1 and 2, and then, counting from 1 to 4, they generate the Decad [the number 10]. For when 1, 2, 3, and 4 are added together, they give rise to the number of the ten Aeons. And again, the number 2 advancing from itself up to six—two, four, and six—produces the Dodecad [the number 12]. . . . They therefore call the Dodecad— because it contains Episemon [= the number 6], and because Episemon waits upon it—the Passion. And for this reason, because an error occurred in connection with the twelfth number, the sheep ran off and went astray: for they assert that a fall took place from the Dodecad. In the same way they oracularly declare that, a power having departed from the Dodecad and perished, this was represented by the woman who lost the drachma and, lighting a lamp, found it again. But of the pieces of money there now remain nine, and of the sheep eleven. These numbers, when multiplied together, produce the number 99. . . .

---

[45] Cf. *Writings*, I, pp. 54ff.
[46] Leisegang. *Die Gnosis*, p. 340.

Wherefore they also maintain that the word AMEN contains this number."

270   According to Marcos, the sum of all the numbers or letters produce the Virgin of Light, Aletheia (Truth).[4] [7]She is a feminine emanation of God, the creative thought by which he "thinks" the world. Marcos, according to Irenaeus,[48] also assumed a decad of ten heavenly circles and a dodecad of twelve zodiacal signs.[49] The dodecad represents evil, earthly fate,[50] but the decad is "soul-producing," and, according to the Pythagoreans,[51] life and light are united in it; it is therefore an image of the world-creating Nous.[52] The monad is descended from the original pneuma and includes the decad, and the decad in its turn includes the monad. This Pythagorean idea, widespread in late antiquity, lived on in alchemy thanks in particular to the *Turba*. A sermon of Pythagoras, the Arabic text of which is still preserved, runs: "Know, therefore, that the root of counting and its beginning is One, male and single, and that from that One the whole of creation proceeded. And as to Two, it comes after One and is female. . . . And Three is male. . . . But when Four came, it was female. . . . The perfection of all counting is therefore Four, for Ten is perfected by Four. . . . Thus did God create all creatures from the four different natures; after they had come to ten in number, they were joined to one another . . . and God brought forth everything from them. . . . Therefore there is no distinction and no separation between Ten and Four . . . Ten cannot be separated from Four, and Ten is perfected only by Four. But beyond this there is no counting and no knowledge." [53]

---

[47] Ibid., pp. 329f.   [48] Bousset, *Hauptprobleme,* p. 341.

[49] There are ten heavens also in Mani's system. Bousset, n. 1.

[50] Similarly, in the 13th treatise of the *Corpus Hermeticum* a dodecad of evil punitive spirits (the signs of the Zodiac) is contrasted with the ten good powers of God. Cf. Scott, *Hermetica,* I, pp. 238ff., especially pp. 247–48. Also Reitzenstein, *Poimandres,* p. 336, Bousset, p. 364, and Reitzenstein, *Mysterienreligionen,* pp. 49f.

[51] Scott, *Hermetica,* II, p. 393.

[52] Proclus, *In Timaeum,* I, 87, line 28 (cited in Scott, IV, p. 388). Lydus, *De mensibus,* 3, 4: "The world-creating Decad, the Nous shining in souls." • (Cf. Proclus, II, 236, line 12.) The decad is also the "head of Kronos" (Iamblichus, *De vita Pythagorae,* 298, Kern, *Orphicorum fragmenta,* 315, 316, Hippolytus, *Elenchos,* 4, 43). Cf. also "The Psychology of the Transference," pars. 525ff., and Hurwitz, "Archetypische Motive," pp. 194ff.

[53] *Turba,* pp. 300ff.

271   This passage from the *Turba* seems to have influenced Senior,[54] whose work contains a good deal of number symbolism. Thus in his "poem" he describes ten figures,[55] five to the left of the Table and five to the right. During the opus the water is divided into nine parts and placed over the "white foliate earth" [56] until one earth and one water arise. Then the earth is saturated with six parts (called "daughters"),[57] and these have ten colours which appear, corresponding to the nine "eagles," but the tenth is the dirty sediment (*faex*) from which they were extracted. From this we can see the alchemical meaning here of nine and ten: nine parts of the substance can be sublimated, and are therefore represented as birds,[58] but the tenth part is the unsublimable residue. This would correspond to the lost groat or sheep in *Aurora* and to the choir of fallen angels. The entire work of the alchemists is an endeavour to reintegrate that unsublimable residue, the sinners on earth and the fallen angels, into a whole. The two parables in Luke 15 come immediately before the parable of the prodigal son, another sinner over whose repentance "there is joy in the presence of the angels of God." [59] The filius—to put it in Senior's language—is the volatile (spiritual) substance and the earthy (bodily) substance which have become one, and, as the end of our parable says, have attained "perfecting and life."

272   Looking back, we can see from such amplifications why the five foolish virgins could enter the bridal chamber with the five wise ones: they were an integral part of the decad, in which that

---

54 Ibid., p. 304, n. 1. These sermons of Pythagoras are the source for Senior's remarks in *Theatr. chem.*, V, p. 203: "Then the second new salting enters into it, which is the second female, and the whole become four, that is, two males and two females, out of which went forth four colours, and these are its number. Understand this principle of number, first and second, and you say two, and they are three in number, and you say three, which are six in number, and then you say four, and they become in number ten manifest numbers, but four of them are hidden. But with these numbers you perfect the Magnesia, which is Abarnahas, existing out of the four. But ten are four, and are extracted from them, and four of them are ten. These are the four of nature, that is, earth, water, air, and fire, of which every created thing consists. But understand this." •

55 *De chemia*, p. 23.   56 Ibid., p. 27.   57 P. 28.

58 P. 122: "By eagles you may understand the volatile substance." •

59 Luke 15 : 10. According to *Pistis Sophia* the evil in the world consists in the mixture of light and darkness, and their final separation will occur only when the perfect number (of just souls) is completed. Bousset, *Hauptprobleme*, p. 102.

unsublimable, rejected residue, dark and earthy, ıs to be included and redeemed.

273 It is meet therefore, my son, to make merry this day, for there shall be no more crying nor any sorrow, for the former things are passed away.

274 In the view of the author, darkness and evil have been finally put to flight, and he even hints at a complete apocatastasis. All separation is over, the lost groat and the lost sheep have been found, and the fallen angels are, as the text says literally, "plenarie integratus"—fully integrated.[60]

275 He that hath ears to hear, let him hear what the spirit of the doctrine saith to the sons of the discipline concerning the woman who brought in death and put it to flight, which the philosophers declare in these words: Take away his soul and give him back his soul, for the corruption of one is the generation of another,

276 Here the text returns to the motif of "the woman who brought in death and put it to flight," but this time it is explained as a taking away of the soul from matter, and its restoration. Although the author did in reality have an experience of death and the overcoming of death, his knowledge of alchemical texts evidently caused him to understand it in alchemical terms, thereby putting a distance between himself and his emotion.

277 In Biblical language the "woman who brought death into the world" would be Eve. Ephraem Syrus,[61] with his love of antithetical formulations, says: "Eve, the mother of all living, became the fount of death to all living." [62] In alchemy we often come across Eve as a name for the feminine arcane substance,[63] probably because of the interpretation of her name as the

[60] Cf. *Mysterium*, pp. 533ff. It is an apocatastasis of everything that exists, when man also will re-experience his original oneness with nature and God. The intuition of this goal momentarily frees the author from his involvement in the unconscious drama; he even sees it as an alchemical process which can be initiated by man, and this accounts for his sudden access of didacticism in the following passages.

[61] *Hymni et sermones*, I, col. 154.*

[62] In his Encyclical Letter, *Mary, Queen of All Creation*, Pius XII calls Mary a "new Eve" (p. 19), citing Albertus, "Sermones de Sanctis," XV. Cf. Cyril of Jerusalem, *Catecheses*, I, xii, 29 (ed. Reischl and Rupp, II, p. 41).

[63] E.g., in Senior, *De chemia*, pp. 95f., the part which is also printed in *Art. aurif.*, I, pp. 158ff. as "Rosinus ad Euthiciam."

"mother of all living" (Gen. 3 : 20).[64] For the Gnostic sect of the Peratics Eve was the embodiment of the *anima mundi*, understood as the "common nature" of gods and angels, mortals and immortals.[65] Even more pointed is the dualistic view of the Mandaeans, who recognized two female principles, a "mother of the living" and a "death" which they thought of as a woman. Death was bound up with the life of the body, which was also the seat of sin.[66] Because of her significance as the mother of all living, Eve became a prefiguration of the Church.[67] If Eve is, paradoxically, the fount of both life and death, "the woman who put death to flight" can be found in another dogmatic figure, that of Mary. Ephraem Syrus says: "From Mary arose the light which scattered the darkness that Eve brought." [68] And: "Mary hath felled the tree that brought death, and hath bestowed the fruit which maketh all to live." [69] From these formulations it is clear that the author of *Aurora* experienced the woman as a unified embodiment of the figure that was otherwise personified separately in Eve and Mary.[70] Once again the unconscious tries to bring together the too widely separated light and dark aspects of the same archetypal figure.

278   This figure is then clearly characterized as the "anima" of the alchemical substance, and hence as the same feminine personification who appeared previously now as Wisdom and now as the soul of matter calling for help.

279   that is: Take from him the corrupting humour and add to him the connatural humour, through which shall come to pass his perfecting and life.

[64] Philo, "On Husbandry," sec. 21, *Works*, III, pp. 118f.

[65] Leisegang, *Die Gnosis*, p. 184, and Bousset, *Hauptprobleme*, p. 59.

[66] Reitzenstein, *Das iranische Erlösungsmysterium*, pp. 137f.

[67] Anastasius the Sinaite, *Anagogicae contemplationes*, 4 (Migne, *P.G.*, vol. 89, cols. 905f.): "Eve is interpreted as Life. But Life is also the Church, showing forth the perpetual regeneration of baptism and the life which is through water and spirit." • The Church arose from the water and blood that flowed from Christ's side, just as Eve arose from Adam's rib (col. 906).

[68] *Hymni et sermones*, II, col. 526.

[69] Ibid., col. 530. Cf. Bruno of Asti, *Sententiae*, Lib. V, cap. 2 (Migne, *P.L.*, vol. 165, col. 1023): "Death came through Eve, life was restored through Mary. The former was overcome by the devil, the latter bound and conquered him." •

[70] Cf. *Mysterium*, pp. 56ff., concerning the paradoxes occasioned by the Aelia Laelia Crispis inscription.

280   It is apparent that this anima is a corrupting and at the same time "connatural" (i.e., vivifying) humour, and, as such, embodies the divine water of the art.

281   As in alchemy, the water has the dual meaning of life and death in many Gnostic systems.[71] As the heavenly ocean it is an image for Sophia.[72] Among the Peratics, on the other hand, Edem or Eve as the world-soul in the Book of Baruch [73] corresponds to the "power of the Abyssal mud" (δύναμις ἀβυσσικοῦ θόλου), also named the "sea." [74] Zosimos mentions "the round element of Kronos" as a profane designation for the mystery of the divine water.[75] Elsewhere [76] he says this water has in itself "life and spirit and the destructive element" (ἀναιρετικόν).[77] In explanation of a saying of Maria Prophetissa: "Touch it not with the hands, for it is a fiery medicine," he says: "Quicksilver is death-dealing, and gold decomposes in it." [78] But this water is also the "seed-bed" (πανσπέρμιον), the round element Ω, the sea-water and the egg,[79] and it has roughly the same mean-

---

[71] Cf. the Naassene idea that when it flowed downwards the Ocean brought forth Creation, and the gods when it flowed upwards (Leisegang, *Gnosis*, pp. 140f.); it is the uroboros, the ring of "genesis and decay." It is the "moist substance, without which nothing in the world can exist, whether mortal or immortal, living or lifeless; the river that flows from Eden and divides into the four streams." Among the Peratics this serpent was Eve, the "mother of all living" (p. 148); opposed to her is the corrupting moisture of Kronos, the "cause of decay in all creatures" (p. 149).

[72] Bousset, *Hauptprobleme*, p. 69, and Irenaeus, I, 30, 3. Concerning the "supracelestial waters" see "Psychology and Religion," pp. 98ff.

[73] Leisegang, *Die Gnosis*, pp. 163ff., 175f., and Hippolytus, *Elenchos*, V, 14.

[74] Bousset, p. 73, n. 1. The "power of the abyssal mud" is said to "receive and carry the dirt of the imperishable, mute, wet element; it is the whole power of the watery state of convulsion, eternally in motion, which supports that which rests, contains that which trembles, liberates that which is to come . . . destroys growing things. . . . This power the ignorant call Kronos, who was flung into chains." (Leisegang, *Die Gnosis*, pp. 149f.; cf. Hippolytus, *Elenchos*, V, 14.) This corresponds to the "shuddersome water of the beginning" (ὕδωρ φοβερόν) among the Sethians, from which came a wind that caused everything to be. (Leisegang, pp. 153f.; Bousset, p. 104.)

[75] "On Equipment and Furnaces," in Berthelot, *Alch. grecs*, III, xlix, 1.

[76] III, ix, 2.

[77] Concerning the "deadly" (θανατῶδες) quality of the water see also the anonymous treatise in *Alch. grecs*, IV, vii, 2.

[78] III, xxix, 13.

[79] I, iii, 4 and 8.

ing as the "bright water of Kronos" among the Peratics.[80]
Ostanes says of the divine water: "This water makes the dead
to rise and slays the living, it lightens the darkness and darkens
the light." [81] Many of these late classical ideas can be found in
Senior [82] and in the *Turba*, and were certainly known to the
author of *Aurora*. In the *Turba* the water is a water of life and
also a poison.[83] "The philosophers spoke the truth when they
called the water living, because that which is mixed with the
water first dies, then lives again and is made young. And it is
the sharpest vinegar, which decomposes everything, or a poison.
But this poison is, as it were, birth and life, because it is a soul
extracted from many things. . . . Its colour is therefore life for
those bodies from which it takes away a defect, and death for
those bodies from which it is extracted." [84] This fully accords
with the passages in *Aurora* about taking away and giving back
the soul, and removing the corrupting humour and adding the
connatural humour.[85] Psychologically considered, this water is
an aspect of Mercurius, whose paradoxical qualities are discussed in Jung.[86] According to St. Thomas Aquinas, the old
and oft-quoted saying "The corruption of one is the generation
of another" is a fundamental law of all change aiming at perfection; "through many generations and corruptions we arrive
at the ultimate substantial form." [87] These, therefore, were

---

[80] Hippolytus, *Elenchos*, V, 16. This water stands for entanglement in the corruptible world.

[81] Berthelot, IV, ii, 3.

[82] *De chemia*, pp. 85, 106f., and for the mysterium of the water in general pp. 17,
21, 34f., 70ff., 87.

[83] P. 130.

[84] *Turba*, p. 162. Cf. pp. 125, 213.

[85] The *Buch der Alaune und Salze* (p. 63) says that the process consists essentially
in "extracting the corrupting humour and infusing the fiery humour." Of Mercurius it is said (pp. 58f.) that he copulates with himself and makes himself pregnant and gives birth in a single day. Cf. Zosimos in *Alch. grecs*, III, ix, 1: There
are two natures and one substance, one nature attracts the other, and one conquers the other, and that is mercury, the male-female, ever-elusive divine water,
which not all know and whose nature is difficult to see.

[86] "The Spirit Mercurius."

[87] *Summa*, I, q. 118, art. 2 ad 2 (Eng. edn., I, p. 575): "We must therefore say that
since the generation of one thing is the corruption of another, it follows of neces-
sity that both in men and in other animals, when a more perfect form supervenes
the previous form is corrupted; yet so that the supervening form contains the
perfection of the previous form, and something in addition. It is in this way that

widely known ideas, but in alluding to them the author introduces a bold innovation when he tries—for the first time with
such clarity—to relate these paradoxical conceptions of the
divine water as the anima in matter to the figures of Eve and
Mary, and to fuse their dual nature in a single figure.[88] Here in
particular we see the role which the alchemical symbols play in
the text: they have the function of uniting the opposites.

through many generations and corruptions we arrive at the ultimate substantial
form, both in man and other animals. . . . We conclude therefore that the intellectual soul is created by God at the end of human generation, and this soul is at
the same time sensitive and nutritive, the pre-existing forms being corrupted." *
[88] It is true not only of this passage, but of alchemy in general, that the same
archetypes which were seen and experienced in their dual aspect as a totality, in
Christian allegory appear split up in a dualism of bright and dark images.

VIII. THE THIRD PARABLE: OF THE
GATE OF BRASS . . .

282   In the course of the preceding parable it became increasingly clear that Wisdom and the "corrupting humour," or the death-dealing woman, represented one and the same thing. But, as in most alchemical texts, the author was not aware that he was projecting his anima into matter. For this reason she remains "unredeemed," i.e., caught in the projected state and not recognized as a psychic factor. Hence, as the title of the present parable states, she still languishes in "Babylonish captivity" and speaks as follows:

283   He who brake in pieces my gates of brass and my bars of iron . . .

284   The quotation from Isaiah (45 : 2-3), "I will go before thee. . . . I will break in pieces the gates of brass and will burst the bars of iron," goes on to say: "And I will give thee hidden treasures and the concealed riches of secret places, that thou mayest know that I am the Lord who called thee by thy name. . . ." Alchemically interpreted, this would be an allusion to the gradual extraction of the "fluid soul" from the mineral body (ore or iron).[1] The simultaneous "moral" or psychological aspect of this process can be seen very clearly in the seventeenth Ode of Solomon,[2] where the "Redeemed," identifying himself with Christ, says: "And from thence he [God] gave

[1] Thus Lucas says in the *Turba* (Sermo 67, pp. 166 and 252): "The definition of the art is the liquefaction of bodies and the separation of the soul from the body, for copper, like man, has a soul as well as a body. You must therefore . . . destroy the body and extract the soul from it; wherefore the philosophers have said that it is not the body that penetrates the body, but the fine nature, namely the soul, which penetrates and tinges the body."

[2] *Odes of Solomon* (trans. Bernard), pp. 81f. Cf. Reitzenstein, *Das iranische Erlösungsmysterium*, p. 87.

me the way of His footsteps and I opened the doors that were closed and brake in pieces the bars of iron; but my iron melted and dissolved before me; nothing appeared closed to me, because I was the door of everything." [3]

285   Psychologically, the alchemical "unlocking of the iron" would mean the emotional release of the ego caught in its prejudices and caprices. Contact with the unconscious opens the prison which we have made for ourselves with our conscious views and ego-bound aims, and at the same time an analogous process takes place in the unconscious psyche: through the application of conscious insight the unconscious is freed from its irreducible, unchanging quality, and is altered by contact with the understanding consciousness. In this phase of the opus the situation of the alchemist coincides with that of the anima in the prison of hell.

286   shall also move my candlestick out of its place, and shall break asunder the chains of the prison of darkness . . .

287   The "Bar of Iron of the Babylonish Captivity" in the title refers to the doors of hell,[4] hence the anima is imprisoned in the centre of the earth and, from the Christian point of view, is actually in hell. This is confirmed by her words in the first parable, where she calls for help from the "lower hell." Such an interpretation would shed light on the somewhat obscure passage that now follows, namely, the anima's request for her "candlestick to be moved out of its place." This is an allusion to Rev. 2 : 5: "Or else I will come unto thee quickly, and will remove thy candlestick out of his place, except thou repent" (AV). It is to be assumed that this had happened before the parable began, and that, as a punishment, her candlestick was removed to hell, for which reason the anima now asks for it to be restored.[5] According to a commentary of Albertus Magnus

---

[3] Cf. the prayer of Gizeh (4th cent.), ibid., p. 265.
[4] Cf. Daniel, *Thesaurus hymnologicus*, IV, p. 117: "Christ the king, the world's Creator, / Thou who ope'st the prison hard, / Thou who break'st the bars of iron, / And releasest those inbarred." *
[5] Cf. the laments of the fallen Sophia in *Pistis Sophia* (Leisegang. *Die Gnosis*, pp. 378ff., and Reitzenstein, *Erlösungsmysterium*, pp. 174ff.). In some respects the anima of our text might also be compared to the "virgin of light" in the Coptic-Gnostic writings. Cf. Bousset, *Hauptprobleme*, p. 61.

on the Apocalypse, the candlestick is an image for the Church,[6] and, in other of his writings, for Mary.[7] Similarly, the golden candelabrum was interpreted as an allegory of Christ,[8] whereas in the Cabala it signifies the Shekinah or Metatron.[9] The soul's sojourn in the interior of the earth and in hell is the consequence of a previous "fall" when she was caught in matter[10]—a portrayal of that age-old projection of the unconscious into nature upon which alchemy is based.[11]

288   The idea of the fallen soul also occurs in scholastic philosophy. Thus William of Auvergne says that through Adam's sin the soul was "cast down from the height of its natural luminosity and nobility."[12]

289   A similar formulation to the one in *Aurora*—and perhaps its source—occurs in a passage from "Rosinus ad Sarratantam,"[13] where the personified "lunar moisture" (a parallel to our figure) says: "And whoso shall remove me, who have the Lunar and Mercurial matter, from my place, i.e., from the body of the metal, by force, i.e., by the force of putrefaction and dissolution, and shall join my beloved, i.e., the solar fatness, with me, i.e., with the humidity of the moon . . . they shall regenerate us unto life, by which death shall be no more."[14]

290   That the soul in the hellish abyss of matter is represented in *Aurora* as a candlestick or a light accords with her interpretation as the *lumen naturale* or *scintilla*, the wider context of which is discussed in Jung.[15] Even in the first chapter Wisdom

---

[6] "Enarr. in Apocalypsim" (Borgnet, XXXVIII, p. 491): "And the Church is called the golden candlestick, because it is illuminated with knowledge, precious in grace, confirmed in patience, ready in obedience, resounding in preaching, enduring in perseverance, firm in the faith of the Trinity, which is filled with the sevenfold grace of the Holy Spirit." • The genuineness of this work is disputed.

[7] "Biblia Mariana" (Borgnet, XXXVII, p. 371): "Mary is the candlestick of enlightenment." •

[8] St. Gregory, *Homil. I in Ezech.* (Migne, *P.L.*, vol. 76, col. 831).

[9] Knorr von Rosenroth, *Kabbala denudata*, I, Part 1, p. 543.

[10] In the Cabala this is the imprisonment of the light in the dark vessel. Ibid., II, Part 1, pp. 261f.   [11] Cf. *Psychology and Alchemy*, pars. 405ff.

[12] "De anima," V, 19, *Opera omnia*, II, p. 144. •   [13] *Art. aurif.*, I, p. 188.•

[14] This is from a commentary on a text part of which is also contained in "Cons. coniug." (*Ars chemica*, pp. 120–29), describing the coniunctio as in Senior's "Epistola Solis ad Lunam crescentem" (*De chemia*, pp. 7–10). Cf. the Christian image of the body as a prison.

[15] "On the Nature of the Psyche," pp. 190ff., and *Mysterium*, pp. 48ff.

calls herself "an unfailing light" which blesses those who find her. But in order to illuminate men she must obviously first be delivered from the depths of hell.[16] Without the understanding participation of consciousness the unconscious cannot exert its illuminating and helpful function.

291 and feed my hungry soul, which hasted in thirst for his face, with the fat of wheat and with honey out of the rock, and shall prepare a large dining-room for my pilgrimage, that I may sleep in peace, and the seven gifts of the Holy Spirit may rest upon me, who hath had mercy upon me.

292   The feeding of the thirsting soul had been hinted at in the "adding of the connatural humour" at the end of the last parable. Joachim of Flora interprets the "honey out of the rock" (Psalm 80 : 17), which was usually considered an image for God, as "spiritual understanding" and the "spiritual joy" bestowed by the Holy Spirit.[17] The alchemical reference here is to the "nourishment of the stone," a definite phase of the work. Thus the "Exercitationes in Turbam XV"[18] says that the material is first embodied in milk, then in blood and in water; then the limbs are formed, "and at last God gives to matter soul, that is, the power by which our medicine is increased and nourished." The second part of *Aurora* (which, as I have said, is probably a commentary on the first[19]) combines the phase of ablution with that of nutrition, and says after describing the former:[20] "The philosophers desire to nourish their grain of seed with the connatural humour until it lives and brings forth fruit, and they desire to quicken that which is dead."[21] In our text the ablution is similarly described as a rebirth, and mention is

16 Cf. Senior, *De chemia*, pp. 5, 6, 26, where a ray of sunlight descended to the lower world, splitting it and at the same time surrounding it.

17 *Concordia*, V (Hahn, *Geschichte der Ketzer*, III, p. 332): "And yet he who believes and fears yet understands not is brought as it were to the knowledge of the Father alone . . . but they who believe and understand are brought to the knowledge of the Father and the Son, for the Son is the wisdom of the Father . . . but they who believe, understand, and enjoy, having knowledge of the Father and the Son, have reached even to the understanding of the Holy Spirit, for he is the delight and love of God, he is honey from the rock and oil from the flinty rock. Verily he is honey from the rock, he is spiritual joy . . ." •

18 *Art. aurif.*, I, p. 117.   19 Supra, p. 5.

20 *Art. aurif.*, I, pp. 148f. Cf. also pp. 150f.

21 Cf. the "Flos florum" of Arnaldus, *Art. aurif.*, II, p. 322.

made of the "seven gifts of the Holy Spirit." This may be an allusion to the words of the priest who, plunging the candle into the water, says at the benediction of the font: "May the virtue of the Holy Spirit descend into all the water of this font, and make the whole substance of this water fruitful, and capable of regenerating." [22] This signifies an "inner quickening," an increase in vitality and psychic strength.[23] According to Paracelsus, honey signifies the "sweetness of the earth"—the anima is joyless and needs the loving attention of the conscious mind.

293 For they shall gather me together out of all the countries, that they may pour upon me clean water, and I shall be cleansed from the greatest sin, and from the noonday devil, for from the sole of my foot unto the crown of my head there is no soundness in me. Therefore they shall cleanse me from my secret faults and from those of others, and thereafter I shall not remember all my iniquities, for God hath anointed me with the oil of gladness,

294 The first thing to be noted here is the motif of "gathering together out of all the countries," an allusion to the gathering of the "light particles" or "soul particles" of God which are scattered throughout matter.[24] The aim is to produce the unitary man (*vir unus*) who is without stain. This stain, according to the text, is not only the chemical impurity of the metal, but is called "the greatest sin" (*maximum delictum*) and the "noonday devil." The noonday, as has been mentioned, is the "heat of worldly ambition," and Artefius says that "since the devil's interior is of the nature of fire, it is manifest that it is contrary and hostile to the nature of the soul, which is a nature of equality." [25] Therefore the anima in our text is cleansed with water and anointed with the oil of gladness in the day of her resurrection. All this is an allusion to the symbolism of Chris-

22 Roman Missal, Blessing of the Font on Easter Eve.
23 Cf. Ephraem Syrus, *Hymni et sermones*, I, col. 54, 58, 80, and Anastasius the Sinaite, *Hexaem.* 4: ". . . that through her [the Church] we may be born and reborn until . . . the night of this world pass away and Christ the sun of justice shall have risen again." • "But the moon has the government and administration of the authority of water and the Holy Spirit . . . that through it we may be born and regenerated." • These symbolisms are elaborated in the following chapters.
24 *Mysterium*, pp. 48ff.
25 "Clavis maioris sapientiae," *Theatr. chem.* (1659), IV, p. 211. •

tian baptism, which was interpreted as a burial and resurrection. The alchemical parallels are discussed in Jung.[26] The oil of gladness is the chrism, the oil used at confirmation and at the consecration of bishops in imitation of the oil with which Christ was anointed at his baptism.[27] In addition, fat or "shining oil" played an important part in alchemy as a symbol of the soul or of the *aqua divina* or *aqua sapientiae*.[28] Accordingly, the anointing in *Aurora* is, in a sense, another designation for "adding the connatural humour." In Church symbolism fat was an image for the manna that fell from heaven,[29] so that again allusion is made to the motif of supernatural nourishment.

295 that there may dwell in me the virtue of penetration and of liquefaction in the day of my resurrection, when I shall be glorified by God.

296   With these words the author subtly reverts to the theme of the "unitary man" or Anthropos which was sounded shortly before, and as in the preceding chapters equates the purified material with the risen Christ: once more it assumes a masculine form. The words "in the day of my resurrection" refer to the Alleluia verse for Low Sunday, where, in a variant of the words spoken by the angel at the sepulchre,[30] the Lord says: "On the day of my resurrection . . . I will go before you into Galilee." The "virtue of penetration" is a reference to the *Tabula Smaragdina:* ". . . it conquers every subtle thing and penetrates all solids." [31] The author compares this virtue with the apparition of the risen Christ in his glorified body.[32] All these statements ultimately refer to the filius philosophorum, risen from the transformed feminine substance. That the filius really

26 *Mysterium*, pp. 235ff.

27 *Pontificale Romanum*, Blessing of the Oils on Maundy Thursday.

28 Senior, *De chemia*, pp. 49, 55, and 57: "By oil he means the Soul." Pp. 75 and 82: "And this that is born is the fatness which they call the soul and the egg." • Cf. "Collectanea ex Rhasi" in the Lacinius edition of *Pret. marg. nov.*, p. 169.

29 Ephraem Syrus, II, col. 676.

30 Matt. 28 : 5ff.

31 P. 2. Cf. Pseudo-Aristotle, "De perfecto magisterio," *Theatr. chem.* (1659), III, p. 79, and Senior, *De chemia*, p. 116: "For Hermes saith: Every subtle thing enters into every gross thing." •

32 Similarly, Petrus Bonus compares the penetrative power of the lapis with man's glorified body. In the same way, the Mercurial spirit was compared with the ubiquitous presence of the Paraclete (*Mysterium*, pp. 16, 30).

is meant is confirmed by the passage that now follows: "For this generation cometh and passeth away, until he come that is to be sent, who also taketh away the yoke of our captivity," etc. The first part is from Ecclesiastes 1 : 4: "One generation passeth away, and another generation cometh: but the earth abideth for ever" (AV). For anyone who knew the Bible, therefore, the author was here giving a plain hint that an "everlasting earth" had been produced, a body endowed with immortality.[33] This theme is taken up again later on. The second part of the passage is from Gen. 49 : 10 (DV): "The sceptre shall not be taken away . . . till he come that is to be sent: and he shall be the expectation of nations." Of this figure it is said: "His eyes shall be red with wine, and his teeth white with milk" (Gen. 49 : 12, AV). For an alchemical reader this is a clear allusion to the *rubedo-albedo* symbolism, and to the fact that the filius is a "unio oppositorum."

297   The text, then, says in sum: if the anima is "gathered together" (withdrawn from projection in matter) and "washed with the spirit of wisdom and understanding" [34] (made conscious by insight), there will arise a spiritual entity which, like the risen Christ, can penetrate and pervade all material things. This new form of the anima is represented as masculine: it is that completer image of the self which is symbolized by the filius philosophorum. At the same time this masculine figure can deliver the anima from the "Babylonish captivity," i.e., from the state of unconsciousness. *The psyche, therefore, redeems itself.* Previously the anima-image and the self were so contaminated that they could hardly be distinguished from one another. Now for the first time the self crystallizes out as an independent content and manifests itself as that more comprehensive centre of the psyche which, as we shall see, guides the anima-impulse towards a definite goal—the individuation process.

298   For this generation cometh and passeth away, until he come that is to be sent, who also taketh away the yoke of our captivity, wherein we sate seventy years by the rivers of Babylon; there we wept and hung up our instruments,

---

[33] For evidence that the opus was concerned with the production of the immortal inner man, see *Mysterium*, pp. 453f., and Parable 7 of *Aurora*.
[34] See infra, p. 273.

299   The unredeemed state of the anima in matter is here expressed figuratively as a captivity.[35] In ecclesiastical allegory the Babylonian exile was interpreted as the "supremacy of the heathen and of sin" and thus forms a parallel to the domination of the "Ethiopians" and the "multitude of the sea" mentioned earlier. In patristic literature Babylon was called *lacus inferior* (the lake below).[36] This interpretation occurs also in the Acts of Cyriac, where Babylon is called a "marshy sea," full of "hippocentaurs," dragons, and the great Uroboros (which for the alchemist symbolized the divine water). It was also called the "centre of hell." [37] It signified confusion [38] ($\sigma\acute{v}\gamma\chi\nu\sigma\iota\varsigma$) and the "evil thoughts which confound the heart." The "rivers of Babylon" mentioned in the text were interpreted by the Church Fathers as the "streams of lust" and the "stream of this world." [39] Here we have another allusion to the theme of *concupiscentia* which was mentioned in the first chapter as a concomitant of Wisdom.[40] These amplifications show that the author's anima is still overpowered or at least oppressed by shadow elements, from which she can be cleansed only by becoming conscious.

300   With the words "there we wept," etc. the discourse suddenly changes from the first person singular into the plural, as though the anima had become a plurality during the Babylonian exile. The captivity was at the same time a dispersion, or, in psychological terms, it involved a dissolution into separate autonomous complexes or a dissociation of the personality.[41] That is why the text spoke of the need for a "gathering together out of all countries."

35 Cf. the *ieiunium* (fast) and the 40-day imprisonment of the gold in the Cabala (Knorr von Rosenroth, I, Part 1, p. 302).
36 Ephraem Syrus, II, col. 226: "And do vengeance upon them, who have led the people into the lake below, i.e., into Babylon." •
37 Reitzenstein, *Erlösungsmysterium*, pp. 77ff.
38 St. Gregory, *Moralia*, Lib. 6 in cap. 5 Job, sec. 25 (Eng. edn., I, p. 330): "Forasmuch as Babylon is rendered 'confusion.' "
39 Honorius, *Speculum* (Migne, *P.L.*, vol. 172, cols. 937ff,): "By the sea is meant this world, which is continually disturbed by the swirling of adversities. The devil swimmeth about in it like Leviathan, and devoureth a multitude of souls." • Concerning this symbolism, see Rahner, "Antenna Crucis."
40 Cf. the Gnostic equation of Babel and Aphrodite, who is the cause of all adultery. Leisegang, *Die Gnosis*, p. 161.
41 One-sided accentuation whether of brightness or of darkness always seems to produce a dissociation.

301   Among the Gnostic sect of the Naassenes the river that flowed
through Babylon was interpreted (in contrast to the symbolism
cited above) as the living water by which the *pneumatikoi* were
made elect.[42] Mesopotamia was the "great stream of Ocean
which flows from the midst of the perfect man." Its water contained the "spirit of God." [43] This positive aspect of the water
will be mentioned later.

302   because the daughters of Sion were haughty and walked with
stretched-out necks and winkings of their eyes and made a noise and
went at a measured pace. Therefore the Lord will make bald the
crown of the head of the daughters of Sion, and will discover their
hair, for the law shall come forth from Sion and the word of the
Lord from Jerusalem.

303   After the self has crystallized out as a separate, central content from the chaos of the initial state, the author recognizes,
as a further aspect of the figure he had previously identified with
Eve, Mary, and Wisdom, yet another plurality—the haughty
daughters of Sion whom God has punished but who, the text goes
on to say, all yearn for *one* husband. Evidently sufficient stability of consciousness had been attained for the author to perceive, in retrospect, this ambiguous aspect of the anima. Consciously he no doubt related these female figures whom God
had humbled to the spirits of the metals or planets imprisoned
in the earth.[44] The captivity is an important concept in the
Turba and there it symbolizes the intentional "fixing" (solidify-
ing) of a volatile spirit or soul for the purpose of transformation. "The soul is held fast like a slave, so that she cannot flee,
and she falleth into sickness and rust and perisheth. But because she fleeth not, she is made free and gaineth her spouse." [45]
The fixing is called κατοχή (imprisonment) in Greek alchemy.[46]
In one of the oldest texts, "Komarios to Cleopatra," the metals
are called "corpses" which lie around in Hades, harassed and
chained up in mist and darkness. Then the elixir, the "blessed
waters," come down to them and rouse them from sleep.[47] The
term κατοχή played an important role in the contemporary

---

42 Bousset, *Hauptprobleme*, pp. 280–81, n. 2.

43 Ibid., p. 81, Cf. *The Clementine Homilies*, II, 24, p. 185.

44 Cf. "Demonstratio naturae," *Mus. Herm.*, p. 167 (Waite, I, p. 138), and *Psychology and Alchemy*, fig. 21.   45 P. 222.

46 Olympiodorus in *Alch. grecs*, II, iv, 9.   47 Ibid., IV, xx, 8.

religious literature, where it meant "seizure by a divinity" (and even frenzy) or the "voluntary seclusion" of a novice.[48]

304   In *Aurora* it is *seven* women who suffer the imprisonment —they are the planetary powers in the earth.[49] These seven captives recall the seven female spirits chained together, who appear in the *Testament of Solomon* [50] as elements of the Lord of Darkness, and to each of whom seven stars were assigned. The idea that the planetary spirits were imprisoned because they were apostate angels is very old and is widely distributed. In the Ethiopic Book of Enoch [51] the spirits of the stars had to atone for their rebellion against God by being locked up in seven burning mountains, and in the late classical treatise "Kore Kosmou" [52] the spirits of the stars, who were once "pure souls," were locked up in human bodies because of their disobedience.[53] In *Aurora,* too, the seven women were punished for their sins and were incarcerated in Babylon, that is, in the centre of hell. These seven souls of the stars thus form another parallel to the Gnostic motif of the fallen Sophia.

305   In that day when seven women took hold of one man, saying: We eat our own bread and wear our own apparel, why dost thou not

---

[48] Reitzenstein, *Mysterienreligionen,* pp. 200ff.; *Erlösungsmysterium,* p. 198.

[49] Cf. Bousset, pp. 25ff.; Lippmann, I, pp. 215ff. Also the influence of the planets on the earth in Philo, "De opificio mundi," 113–14 (Loeb edn., I, pp. 90ff.), and Scott, *Hermetica,* IV, p. 447.

[50] Pp. 31 and 51. Cf. Bousset, p. 21, n. 2. According to Theodor bar Konai, the sect of the Kukaeans had a myth in which seven daughters of the "Great Mother of Life" were abducted by the powers of darkness and await their heavenly bridegrooms in the cities of Matra, Mabug, and Harran. (Bousset, p. 263, n. 2.)

[51] Charles, *Apocrypha and Pseudepigrapha,* II, p. 200. Cf. Bousset, p. 53, and Lippmann, I, p. 221.   [52] Scott, I, p. 464.

[53] Similar conceptions in *Pistis Sophia,* Book 4 (cf. Bousset, p. 51) and among the Mandaeans (pp. 31, 35). There Ruhâ, the feminine Holy Spirit, is the "mother of the seven," who incites them to revolt so that, for punishment, they must burn in their own fire. (Bousset, p. 36; Reitzenstein, *Erlösungsmysterium,* pp. 59ff.) The same motif occurs among the Parsis (Bousset, p. 41) and in the Book of Jeû (ibid., pp. 51f.). Ruhâ, therefore, was regarded as a seven-headed dragon (Reitzenstein, *Erlösungsmysterium,* p. 85). Cf. the serpent of the Ophites (Leisegang, *Gnosis,* p. 179). The Seven were regarded as hermaphroditic demons and as the cause of propagation, and consequently of death and the seven deadly sins. (Lippmann, I, p. 242; Boll, *Sphaera,* p. 13; Scott. *Hermetica,* IV, p. 419.) According to Honorius the heptad is the number of the Old Testament, the octad that of the New, because Christ rose on the eighth day. *Quaest. et resp.* (Migne, *P.L.,* vol. 172, col. 345).

defend our blood, which is poured out as water round about Jerusalem? And they received the divine reply: Rest ye still for a little time, until the number of our brethren is filled up, which is written in this book:

306 According to the passage in Isaiah (4 : 1) the proud daughters of Sion were seven women who were condemned to remain unmarried and unfruitful. At the same time, by an allusion in the text ("why dost thou not defend our blood?"), they are compared to "the souls of them that were slain for the word of God" (Rev. 6 : 9f.), the saints and martyrs, whose blood is "poured out as water round about Jerusalem" (Psalm 78 : 3). *They are thus sinners and martyrs at once!* The reply they received from the Lord on begging to be freed was that they should wait a little time until the number of their brethren was made up (Rev. 6 : 11). This refers to those martyred for the Church. Accordingly, the incarceration of the planetary spirits is represented as the consequence of a sin,[54] but the torment they undergo in the opus is a martyrdom for the sake of redemption.[55]

307 The identification of the proud daughters of Sion with the souls of the martyrs was no doubt suggested to the author by ecclesiastical allegory, which interpreted Sion as the Church oppressed by the devil but later freed, and the daughters of Sion as the souls reborn in Christ.[56] They also signified the souls lost in this world.[57] The unmarried and unfruitful woman was equally a symbol for the Church,[58] for the Church is that once rejected earth (*terra repudiata*) which, chosen by God,

[54] Cf. the removal of the candlestick earlier.
[55] Origen once named the Christian martyrs "rubbish and muck." *Commentaria in Joannis Ev. IV* (Migne, *P.G.*, vol. 14, col. 295).
[56] Thus Ephraem Syrus says (II, col. 172): "A Saviour shall come out of Sion. The spiritual . . . Sion and the hill of visions or revelations is the Church." • Of Zeph. 3 : 14, "Give praise, O Daughter of Sion," he says (cols. 296f.): "This signifies also the mystery of the Church, which is delivered through the Cross from the hand of the devil." • Cf. Honorius: "And the daughters of Sion, that is the souls reborn in Christ, this day rejoice in their King." • *Speculum* (Migne, *P.L.*, vol. 172, cols. 1041 and 930).   [57] Ephraem Syrus, II, col. 346.
[58] Ibid., II, col. 134: "I am barren and solitary. These things concern the Church, for whether they revere or persecute her they greatly magnify and multiply her." • Honorius: "But the Church, long barren, gave birth to a faithful son, that is, the Christian people, for special observances." • *Speculum* (Migne, *P.L.*, vol. 172, col. 1041). Cf. the widow as an image for the soul in St. Gregory, *Moralia*, Lib. XVI in cap. 22 Job, sec. 10 (Eng. edn., II, p. 230).

received the name *voluntas mea* (my pleasure) or *terra maritata* (wedded earth),[59] and her spouse is the clergy and the righteous.[60] (This accords with the symbolism of the "thirsting earth" mentioned earlier as an image for Mary.)[61] We can sum up this part of the text by saying that it refers to the redemption of an anima figure who, as the "body" or "earth," is of seeming material nature, and who, tainted with the stain of sin and ungodliness, languishes in the depths of the earth and in hell. At the same time she is clearly connected with the Church and Mary, and is ultimately identical with Wisdom. Her sufferings are a punishment and at the same time a martyrdom for God's sake.

308   We meet here with the well-known alchemical idea of redemption which occurs in almost all texts. The alchemist, as Jung says, was primarily interested in the "fate and manifest redemption of substances, for in them the divine soul lies captive and awaits . . . release. The captive soul then appears in the form of the 'Son of God.' For the alchemist, the one primarily in need of redemption is not man, but the deity who is lost and sleeping in matter. . . . His attention is not directed to his own salvation through God's grace, but to the liberation of God from the darkness of matter. . . . Since it is not man but matter that must be redeemed, the spirit that manifests itself in the transformation is not the 'Son of Man' but . . . the *filius macrocosmi*." [62]

309   As with the Gnostic figure of Sophia, so in our text the anima in her unconscious state has been unfaithful to the God of Israel and yielded to pride and worldly pleasure. Therefore she sank into wretchedness and loneliness, and now God answers her cries with the promise of his help. But the Biblical passages which are quoted as God's answers continue in a strain quite different from what we would expect: the martyrs are to wait until more of their fellow servants and brethren are slain even as they were (Rev. 6 : 11), and "the Lord shall wash away the filth of the daughters of Sion, and shall wash away the blood of Jerusalem out of the midst thereof, by the spirit of judgment

---

[59] Isa. 62 : 4 (AV).   [60] Ephraem Syrus, II, col. 186.

[61] Ibid., col. 146: "Christ ascended . . . like a root out of the thirsty ground from Mary the Virgin." • Cf. also col. 744.

[62] *Psychology and Alchemy*, par. 420.

and by the spirit of burning" (Isa. 4 : 4). Something decisive must have taken place in the author: he twists the motif of the Apocalyptic blood-bath and fiery judgment into a promise of redemption. In the ensuing text it is not the fiery wrath of God's judgment that shall cleanse the daughters of Sion, but "the spirit of wisdom and understanding." God's wrath and vengeance are not mentioned at all, and the author evidently believes that the spirit of understanding will enable him to endure the suffering caused him by the dark aspect of God. Exactly *who* put the anima in the dark prison and *who* demands her martyrdom remain obscure. Previously we interpreted imprisonment as the state of being projected; but this state cannot be put down to any human sin, for it is not man's conscious mind that makes the projection, but rather an unconscious process. That is why the Gnostics say that Sophia got entangled in matter through the blandishments of the demon Ialdabaoth; the cause of the tragedy is a dark aspect of God himself. This dark aspect remains unmentioned in *Aurora,* so that the guilt seems to devolve on man.

310 then every one that shall be left in Sion shall be called saved, when the Lord shall have washed away the filth of his daughters of Sion with the spirit of wisdom and understanding; then will ten acres of vineyard yield one little measure and thirty bushels of seed yield three bushels. He that understandeth this shall not be moved for ever.

311   The motif of "gathering together out of all countries" is again taken up here, and, as in the earlier passage, the ablution brings about a unification of the scattered elements. The closing words of the parable show that what is unified is a plurality characterized by the number 7 (like the seven daughters of Sion), which alchemically interpreted refers to the seven metals. These, as we have said, are identical with the planets, the lords of Heimarmene. Psychologically they symbolize the collective constituents of the personality. The uniqueness of the individual is expressed in the specific pattern of their constellation. The regulating factor of the constellation is, however, that supraordinate centre which Jung calls the self. The self is something unique and individual, and is therefore the psychic factor which gathers the collective personality components together in a functional unity. A symbolical illustration of this is the

saying of St. Gregory that "our Redeemer coming in the flesh joined together the [seven] Pleiades." [63] As a symbol of the self, Christ is the "one man" for whom the seven women longed (Isaiah 4 : 1). The seven had been mentioned earlier, at the end of the first parable, as the seven stars that are to be purified until they appear as "pearls"; this image, too, referred to the souls of the metals. It is as though the intrapsychic process portrayed in the parables had taken a purely circular course, so that nothing essentially new has been reached in this later phase. This is reflected in the fact that only *seven* stars or pearls are purified and united—the eighth, which here would be the longed-for spouse of the seven women, is missing. For the far-reaching significance of this problem of seven and eight, and of three and four, I must refer the reader to Jung.[64]

312 　　But who—psychologically considered—would be the missing spouse of the seven women? Comparison with other alchemical texts allows of two possibilities: the anima often has an illegitimate lover who personifies the shadow. Thus in *The Chymical Wedding* of Christian Rosencreutz the princess is abducted by a Moor before she wins the king, and in a parable cited by Jung [65] "Sulphur" is the thief who comes between the true lovers. Whereas the illegitimate lover represents the shadow, the "true" spouse is the self, with whom the anima is finally united. In ecclesiastical symbolism this would be the "bridegroom of the soul," Christ.

313 　　In this part of the text it is not clear who the husband of the seven women will be—moreover the author as speaker has vanished at this point, and it often looks as though he were identical with the seven women. This would mean that he had been overpowered by the unconscious, for when the ego, as Jung says,[66] "proves too weak to offer the necessary resistance to the influx of unconscious contents" it is "assimilated by the unconscious, which produces a blurring or darkening of ego-consciousness and its identification with a preconscious wholeness." This seems to me to have happened at times to the author of *Aurora,* so that the text often becomes very obscure. In order

[63] *Moralia*, Lib. XXIX in cap. 38 Job, sec. 74 (Eng. edn., III, Part 1, p. 355). *
[64] *Psychology and Alchemy*, index, s.v. "numbers."
[65] *Mysterium*, pp. 115ff.
[66] "On the Nature of the Psyche," pp. 224f.

to get out of the dissociation, as the text says, "the spirit of understanding" is needed. Then "the filth of the daughters of Sion" will be washed away. Psychologically this would mean an integration of the unconscious contents by a suitable view or interpretation (*aqua doctrinae*).[67] In a certain sense *Aurora* is just such an attempt to understand the influx of archetypal contents by alchemical amplification and to reconcile them with the ruling Christian ideas. The "spirit of understanding" is itself an aspect of Wisdom, which helps the author to grasp her chthonic side. The dissociated components of the personality are thus "gathered together," and a new conscious standpoint is won. That is why the text says that "thirty bushels of seed yield three bushels," and "he that understandeth this shall not be moved for ever." The reduction from thirty to three is a *reduction of the plurality to the essential:* the chaotic contents of the unconscious are reduced to their essential expression. From a concretistic point of view it would certainly be a disappointing harvest if ten acres of vineyard yielded but one little measure and thirty bushels of seed only three bushels. But just as wine is the essence of the whole process of viniculture and is something won by human effort,[68] and as seed contains, *in potentia*, the essence of a whole field of grain, so this reduction must be understood as a concentration upon what is essential. Three and one, moreover, are well-known alchemical formulae for the wholeness of the central symbol.

314   The washing of the daughters of Sion with the spirit of understanding represents not only an attempt to make the anima conscious and to eliminate her dissociative effect, but also to *work out the hidden meaning* of the initial invasion. The "immovability" thereby gained is the acquisition of a higher standpoint which includes both conscious and unconscious.[69] The aim of the unification is to produce the *unus mundus* (one world) or *res simplex*, a theme to which we shall return later on. The ternary symbolism of thirty and three

[67] "The Psychology of the Transference," par. 478.
[68] "Transformation Symbolism in the Mass," p. 221: "The combination of offering and offerer in the single figure of Christ is implicit in the doctrine that just as bread is composed of many grains of wheat, and wine of many grapes, so the mystical body of the Church is made up of a multitude of believers." For bread and wine as cultural achievements of man, cf. ibid., pp. 252ff.
[69] "The Psychology of the Transference," par. 479.

forms the theme of the next parable, where the author tries to regain his conscious, Christian standpoint.[70]

315   He that hath ears to hear, let him hear what the spirit of the doctrine saith to the sons of the discipline concerning the Babylonish captivity, which endured seventy years, of which the philosophers tell in these words: Manifold are the alternations of the seventy precepts.

316   The seventy years of captivity and the seventy precepts are presumably connected with the seven women (souls of the metals) who, psychologically, are the collective constituents of the personality. At the same time, seventy years represent the Biblical length of human life. Consequently it is possible that the process here described corresponds to the living development of the human individual. The "manifold alternations" of the seventy precepts suggest that the working out of the meaning requires a multitude of individual data, and that the symbolic account of the process in alchemical terms stresses only the essential aspects, whereas actually it follows a devious course with many ups and downs.

317   Three and seven (and their multiples by ten) were considered "masculine" numbers, and their appearance in the text may be a hint that the work has now entered a phase in which the masculine consciousness of the author has to reassert itself, as it clearly does in the next parable.

[70] The number 30, as 3 x 10, is assigned by Joachim of Flora to the monastic orders which build the *Ecclesia spiritualis:* "For this reason the number ten would seem to pertain to the married, the number twenty to the clergy: to monks the number thirty, that is, three tens." • *Psalterium decem chordarum* (Hahn, III, p. 331).

IX. THE FOURTH PARABLE: OF THE
PHILOSOPHIC FAITH ...

318   The fourth parable treats "Of the Philosophic Faith, which consisteth in the number Three," and the opening passage leads, as we shall see, into a direct paraphrase of the Creed.[1]

319   Whosoever shall do the will of my Father and shall cast out this world into the world, I will give him to sit with me upon the throne of my kingdom and upon the throne of David and upon the seats of the tribes of Israel. This is the will of my Father, that they may know him to be the true God and no other, who giveth abundantly and upbraideth not, unto all peoples in truth,

320   "Casting out this world into the world" presumably means the alchemical processes of purification by which all "superfluities" and "accidents" are removed.[2] Only after these unclean elements have been eliminated can the alchemist be elevated to the filius Dei who sits upon the throne.

321   Whereas the alchemist, by implication, is here secretly identified with the filius philosophorum as in the earlier chapters, the text now proceeds to give an objective description of the filius as a trinitarian being.

322   But even then it is not altogether clear who is actually speaking. In the opening sentences it appears to be Wisdom, who is identical with Christ; but in the next passage the style becomes didactic and impersonal. It is rather as if the author were speaking, but in that preaching tone which people drop into who

[1] Unfortunately it is not cited literally enough to offer any sure evidence as regards dating. The idea that the Holy Spirit proceeds from the Father and the Son (*filioque*) might be taken as a reference to the Creed of the Lateran Council, 1215, though it was already implicit in the Athanasian, 381.

[2] Mennens, "Aureum vellus," *Theatr. chem.*, V, p. 316: ". . . in that place under the name of David, speaking of Christ, who saith: I have overcome the world, and elsewhere: The prince of this world is cast out." *

think they are announcing a higher metaphysical truth. Obviously the author has identified himself with the Christian interpretation of the process which he is now putting forward, and hopes in this way to gain the upper hand of his emotionality.

323 So I must beg the reader to be patient if the interpretation of the following passage turns out to be somewhat long-winded. He is, nevertheless, taking part in that same wearisome process of elaboration which the author himself attempted in this parable.

324 and his only begotten Son, God of God, light of light, and the Holy Spirit who proceedeth from both, who is equal in Godhead to the Father and the Son, for in the Father inhereth eternity, in the Son equality, in the Holy Spirit the bond of eternity and equality; for as it is said, Like as the Father is, so is the Son, and so also is the Holy Spirit, and these three are One, (which the Philosopher would have to be) body, spirit, and soul, for all perfection consisteth in the number three, that is, in measure, number and weight.

325 The most likely source for the last part of this passage is Senior, who says: [3] "Our metal hath, like man, spirit, soul and body.[4] Therefore the sages say: three and three are one. Further they say: in one are three, and: spirit, soul, and body are one, and all is of One." [5] The divine water, he says, is "one, in which are three, namely, water, air and fire." [6] Similarly Rosinus (Zosimos): [7] "Our stone hath its name in common with the Creator, for it is triune and one" (triunus et unus).[8] The Carmina Heliodori also call the stone triune; [9] it is a "thrice-blessed fount," [10] "one sprout with three faces" (μία φυτλή τριῶν προσώπων), or a "rampart" formed of soul, body and pneuma, this

---

3 De chemia, pp. 45 and 58.

4 This triad could be compared with the "Comma Johanneum," infra, p. 289.

5 Senior calls his upper triad an "image of divine spirituality."

6 De chemia, p. 25; cf. p. 58.

7 Art. aurif., I, p. 192 (quotation from Rhazis).

8 This saying probably does go back to Zosimos, who taught (Alch. grecs, III, vi, 18) that the demiurge created two triads, for which reason he was called Hermes Trismegistos. The upper triad was indivisible and a monad, active, creative, and caused the stone to live; the lower was cosmic, divisible, material, consisting of ore, lead, and the Etesian stone. (Cf. the threefold sonship of Basilides in Mysterium, p. 346, and Aion, pp. 64f.)

9 P. 29, and Carmen II, verse 134, p. 38.

10 Carmen II, 85, p. 45.

last being the "third wreath." [11] Christian influences are noticeable here, and later Petrus Bonus carried the parallel between this alchemical triad and the Christian trinity still further, expressly emphasizing the parallel between the lapis and the "glorified body." [12] The same equation is made in *Aurora.*

326   The author now cites a further triad: "measure, number, and weight." In alchemy this would refer to a subtle "pondering" of spiritual and earthly components during the production of the lapis. Another view worth noting, which may have been not without influence on the quotations in this parable, is put forward in St. Augustine's *City of God,* where he says that a reflection of the Trinity is to be found in every creature, namely essence (Father), knowledge (Son), and love (Holy Spirit).[13] And Albertus Magnus says in his "Paradisus animae" (though its genuineness is disputed): "God's omniscient direction of the world should lead us to observe measure, since he ordered all things in measure, number, and weight. In accordance with this order each of our deeds, our attitude and our life also should be measured, numbered, and weighed; that is, in the power of the Father, to whom is attributed measure, in that of the Son, to whom appertains number, and in that of the Holy Spirit, to whom is ascribed weight." [14] The passage refers to the Wisdom of Solomon 11 : 20 (AV): ". . . thou hast ordered all things in measure, and number, and weight." On this Augustine [15] comments that God created all things in himself, who is number without number, measure without measure, weight without weight.[16] A not uninteresting explanation is given by the

---

[11] "Carm. Archelai," IV, verses 16ff., p. 50. Cf. "On the Names of the Egg" (*Alch. grecs,* I, iii, 13): "If two do not become one, and three do not become one, and the whole composition does not become one, the expectation [of the philosophers] will come to nothing."

[12] *Pret. marg. nov.,* ed. Lacinius, pp. 171ff. Fuller citation infra, pp. 336, 397f. For the correspondence between Mercurius and the triune God see "The Spirit Mercurius," pars. 270ff.

[13] *The City of God,* Book X, ch. 27, Part II, pp. 210ff.: "Of essence, knowledge of essence, and love of both."

[14] Borgnet, XXXVII, p. 466.

[15] *De Genesi ad litteram,* Lib. IV, cap. 3, sec. 8 (Migne, *P.L.,* vol. 34, col. 299).

[16] "He created all things in weight, etc., that is, in himself, who is number without number, measure without measure, weight without weight. Or it is otherwise explained thus: God created all things in number, that is, every number is certain in his sight, so likewise is the measure of all things certain, and of whatever has

alchemist William Mennens, who, like Augustine, interpreted these three principles as instruments, existent and non-existent at once, by means of which God or Wisdom created the world.[17]

327   It is not yet apparent from this part of the text how the author suddenly came to speak of the Christian symbol, and his train of thought will become clearer only in what follows. It is, however, psychologically meaningful that, after having been overwhelmed by the flood of unconscious contents, he should think back to the very foundations of his Christian standpoint, especially as this would support a masculine-spiritual attitude [18] and bring about a reinforcement of consciousness.

328   In what follows the author dwells exclusively on *one* figure in the Trinity, that is, on the Holy Spirit and his workings. This is of great significance not only intrinsically, but also as regards the historical context. *Aurora* belongs, in my view, to the thirteenth century, and this was the century in which numerous sects sprang up, all of them, despite their differences, showing the same tendency to give the Holy Spirit a central place in religious life. The teachings of Joachim of Flora, though somewhat older in time, exerted a noticeable influence everywhere,[19] so that in them we can most easily find traces of what was obviously pushing up from the unconscious and coming to light in that age. This, as we have said, showed itself in a sudden, intense preoccupation with the third hypostasis of the Trinity, the Person of the Holy Spirit, and it is no exaggeration to say that the hallmark of almost all heresies at that time was an attempt to found a new religion or church of the Holy

weight, that weight is most certain before him. Or again: In these three, number, measure, and weight, Holy Writ seeks to show that there is nought equal to God. For number excludes simplicity, measure immensity, weight felicity and stability. He created all things in number, that is, he created nothing of perfect simplicity; in measure, that is, he created nothing that is immeasurable; in weight, that is, he created nothing that can fail of itself or fall from its felicity." •

17 *Theatr. chem.*, V (1622), p. 319: "Therefore in unity, in a point, and a centre, which are the three principles of number, measure, and weight (though this is none of them), are all things created, and though they seem nothing to us, yet before God and in God they are all things: and therefore is God said to have created all things from nothing in the beginning, which is a great mystery, namely, the most holy Trinity and Wisdom itself; for in the centre he sustains all, in the point fulfils all, and in unity perfects all." •

18 "A Psychological Approach to the Dogma of the Trinity," pp. 193ff.

19 Hahn, *Geschichte der Ketzer*, II, pp. 450ff. Cf. *Aion*, pp. 82ff.

Spirit, or a free community in which the main accent lay on the Paraclete and on the individual who was inspired or guided by him, and on that individual's interpretation of the Scriptures. Abbot Joachim of Flora had propounded a doctrine of three great ages or "estates" (*status*) as follows: The first was the age of the Father, when the law of the Old Testament and fear of God prevailed; this age lasted up to the birth of Christ. The second was that of the Son or of Wisdom, when the Church and her sacraments were considered to be the new dispensation; this was to last until the year 1260.[20] But the third age, which would then dawn, is the age of the Holy Spirit, when the "Ecclesia contemplativa" will arise, and the Scriptures will be read anew with "spiritual understanding" and will be taken no longer literally but symbolically. Then there will be no more fear of God and no more servitude, nor any subjection to the letter; but jubilation, love, and liberty shall reign.[21] Then shall come the "Great Sabbath," when the "spirit of truth" teaches men,[22] and the "Third Estate" will hold dominion, the monastic orders and "Poor Men" (Parvuli) who are chosen for the liberty of contemplation.[23] "Then the people of the Gentiles shall be joined with the people of the Hebrews and there shall be one flock and one shepherd, and this conjunction is rightly to be attributed to spiritual men." [24]

[20] Cf. Reuter, *Geschichte der religiösen Aufklärung im Mittelalter*, II, pp. 204ff., 365ff. and notes, concerning the difficult question of authorship. This, however, is of less interest to us because what is said above undoubtedly gives the substance of Joachim's thoughts.

[21] *Expos. in Apocal.* (Hahn, III, p. 111): "It seems however that any work pertains to the Father, reading to the Son, rejoicing to the Holy Spirit: for the fear of God calls for true servitude to him, and the mastery of Christ the subjection of doctrine, and the joy of the Holy Spirit the rejoicing of jubilation. . . . Thus there are three things by which God the Three in One is said to draw near to us: fear, wisdom, and love, and three through which those three remain in us: work, reading, and joy." • Cf. Haupt, "Zur Geschichte des Joachimismus," pp. 372ff., and "Zur Geschichte der Sekte vom Freien Geiste und des Beghardentums," pp. 503ff.

[22] Hahn, III, p. 128: "When that spirit of truth shall come he will teach us all virtue," etc.

[23] *Concordia*, II, tract. 2: "(The third order) which proceeds from both is chosen for the liberty of contemplation, the Scripture bearing witness which says: Where is the Spirit of the Lord, there is liberty." • Hahn, p. 272: "The Holy Spirit manifests liberty, for he is love." •

[24] *Concordia*, V, cap. 51.•

329   This doctrine of Abbot Joachim and others like it, for instance that of Amalric of Bene, who took over much of Joachim's teachings,[25] further state that heaven and hell exist primarily as realities within the soul. Similar views were held by David of Dinant and the Poor Men of Lyons, the Tertiaries or Fratres Minores, the Parvi, Fratres Spirituales, and also by the Lollards, Beguines and Beghards, and the "Friends of God in the Rhineland." Almost all of them turned against the visible Roman Church, and these sects must therefore be regarded as pre-Reformation reform movements. Joachim's doctrine was even taken over officially by a stricter sect of the Franciscan Order, and in 1254 was officially proclaimed in Paris in the form of the "Introductorius in Evangelium Aeternum." [26] A year later it was condemned by Pope Alexander IV.[27] The teachings of these Tertiaries were as follows: [28] the end of the world was coming now, and only the Third Order among the Franciscans, called the Fratres Spirituales or Beguines of the Third Order, would survive it.[29] The secular Church would then be repudiated and a new Church established which would be humble and a true Ecclesia spiritualis.[30]

330   The strong emphasis on the Holy Spirit and on the revelation wrought by him in the individual, and on the symbolic interpretation of the Scriptures, led many other sects to repudiate the existing Church in favour of an Ecclesia spiritualis, which was to consist of individuals whom the Holy Spirit had inspired.[31] The Poor Men of Lyons or "Humiliati" even went

---

25 Caesarius of Heisterbach, *Dialogus miraculorum*, Distinctio V, 22.

26 Hahn, II, pp. 426ff.

27 Ibid., III, pp. 159ff.

28 II, pp. 437ff.   29 II, p. 438.   30 II, p. 438, n.

31 See Hahn, II, pp. 358f. on the "Friends of God," and I, pp. 53f. on the "Ortlibarii." Cf. also an earlier, typical document of a neo-Manichaean sect cited by Hahn (I, p. 36) from D'Achery, *Spicilegium*, II (Mansi, *Sacrorum Conciliorum nova et amplissima collectio*, XIX, cols. 376f.): "Thou shalt be sprinkled with the waters of wisdom, until thou art instructed, and by the sword of God's word art able to dispense with the thorns of vices, and after foolish doctrine hath been driven out of thy breast, thou art able to receive in purity of mind our heavenly teaching handed down from the Holy Spirit . . . indeed they surely open to thee the dregs of their wickedness covered hitherto by the words of the divine books . . . doubtless thou hast lain hitherto in the Charybdis of false opinion with the unlearned; but now, raised up unto the summit of all truth, thou hast begun to open the eyes of thy whole mind to the light of the true faith . . . and thou shalt

so far as to say that the individual soul of every good man was the Holy Spirit himself.[32] The Brethren of the Free Spirit likewise taught that the human soul was of the substance of God,[33] and that man *together with his body* can become God—to the point, indeed, where he does not need God any longer.[34]

331   As Jung has shown in *Aion*,[35] the spiritual assumptions of the alchemists have a great affinity with the ideas current in these movements, for they identified their *lumen naturale* with the hypostasis of the Holy Spirit. The—possibly genuine—treatise "De alchemia" of Albertus Magnus offers one of the earliest examples of this. It is therefore not surprising if we find notable alchemists of that time among the mendicant orders or sects we have mentioned: for instance, Johannes de Rupescissa (Jean de Roquetaillade) among the Poor Men of Lyons,[36] Roger

---

be filled with the gift of the Holy Spirit, who will teach thee without scruple the depth and true dignity of all these scriptures." • Another sect at Montfort taught, like the Ortlibarii (Hahn, I, pp. 39 and 53f.), a mystic interpretation of the Scriptures, and interpreted the mysteries of faith as inner processes: "But then the Son of God is crucified and scourged . . . then does the Son die when any of them falls into mortal sin or returns from the sect: but he rises again through penance." • Or the heretics of Montfort (Hahn, I, p. 42), who held that the Father is God, the Son the human spirit beloved of God, and the Holy Ghost the understanding of the Scriptures.

32 As transmitted by one Stephen of Borbone (Hahn, II, p. 266, n. 3, and pp. 267f.).

33 Preger, *Geschichte der Mystik im Mittelalter*, I, p. 462f. (also pp. 14, 37). Cf. Hahn, II, p. 267: "Likewise, the spirit of man, in so far as he is good, if he die, is the same as the spirit of God, and is itself God." • "Also, this is the Trinity which or in which they believe: that he is the Father who turns another to good; he who is turned, the Son; that by which he is turned and into which he is turned, the Holy Spirit." • They held that the Incarnation was not a proven historical fact, but was an inner process in man (p. 268).

34 The ethical attitude among these sects varied from religious rigorism to complete amorality in accordance with the dictum: "Where the spirit is, there is liberty." Thus the Amalricians said: "If anyone who is in the spirit commits fornication, or is polluted with any other pollution, it is no sin in him, for that spirit, which is God, altogether separated from the flesh, cannot sin." • (Hahn, II, pp. 470ff.; cf. I, p. 403.) The Brethren of the Free Spirit said that a man who was united with God could no longer sin, since he became God or the divine soul itself. (Preger, I, p. 462, nos. 15 and 21.) On the other hand, the utmost moral rigour prevailed among the Brethren of the Free Spirit (Hahn, II, pp. 450ff.).

35 Pp. 86, 150.

36 They, too, favoured a spiritual interpretation of the Bible (Hahn, II, pp. 256f.). They had affinities with the Waldensians of Piedmont.

Bacon among the Franciscans,[37] Raymund Lully [38] among the Franciscan Tertiaries, who at that time had not yet dropped away from the Church, and Albertus Magnus among the Dominicans.[39]

332   We may regard the followers of the Holy Ghost movements, and also these alchemists, as forerunners of our modern psychology of the unconscious in that they went beyond mere *belief* in the contents of religion and sought to obtain individual *experience* of them. What they called the "spirit in matter" or the "Paraclete," we today call the guiding function of the unconscious, which is experienced as "meaning." [40] The psychological significance of this shift of accent to the third Person of the Trinity presents such a deep and far-reaching problem that I must refer the reader to Jung's discussion of it in "A Psychological Approach to the Dogma of the Trinity." If I cite here some of his views, I do so in full awareness that I am tearing them out of their context, so that what follows should be taken as a mere sketch. Jung states that "Father," conceived psychologically as a symbol, "denotes the earlier state of consciousness when one was still a child, still dependent on a definite, ready-made pattern of existence which is habitual and has the character of law. It is a passing, unreflecting condition, a mere awareness of what is given, without intellectual or moral judgment." But "the picture changes when the accent shifts to the son." The situation then calls for "conscious differentiation from the father and from the habitus represented by him. This requires a certain amount of knowledge of one's own individuality, which cannot be acquired without moral discrimination and cannot be held on to unless one has understood its meaning. Habit can only be replaced by a mode of life consciously chosen and acquired. The Christianity symbolized by the 'Son' therefore forces the individual to discriminate and to reflect." "The third step, finally, points beyond the 'Son' into

[37] For his allegorical interpretation of the Bible and his belief in alchemy see his *Opus minus* (ed. Brewer), p. 359.
[38] The extant alchemical writings of Lully have not been examined for their authenticity.
[39] Thorndike, *History of Magic*, II, pp. 522ff. Cf. *Aion*, p. 87.
[40] In his "Liber de spiritu et anima" Joachim of Flora attempted a psychological interpretation of the Trinity symbol, thus clearly expressing the trend of the age. Cf. *Aion*, p. 253.

the future, to a continuing realization of the 'spirit,' i.e., a living activity proceeding from 'Father' and 'Son.' " The "Son" represents a transition stage and a state of conflict; not only is it in opposition to the still-existing earlier state, but freedom from the law brings a sharpening of the moral opposites. In the third stage the patriarchal initial state is, in a sense, re-established, but this is not just a repetition of the first stage, for the values of the second must be held fast. "Though the new level of consciousness acquired through the emancipation of the son continues in the third stage, it must recognize that *it* is not the source of the ultimate decisions and flashes of insight which rightly go by the name of 'gnosis,' but that these are inspired by a higher authority which, in projected form, is known as the 'Holy Ghost.' Psychologically speaking, 'inspiration' comes from an unconscious function. . . . Accordingly, the advance to the third stage means something like a recognition of the unconscious, if not actual subordination to it." The transitions from one stage to another are—as Jung emphasizes—"very fateful transformations indeed. Usually they have a numinous character, and can take the form of conversions, illuminations, emotional shocks, blows of fate, religious or mystical experiences." [41]

333   Just such an experience is described in *Aurora;* moreover, it is a description of the transition from the second to the third stage, which is why the recognition of the Holy Spirit occupies a central place. The author has experienced something that caused him, willy-nilly, to be seized by the Holy Spirit, just as had happened to many other men of his time.

334   A later passage in *Aurora*, where the "parvuli" (little ones, children) are mentioned as those who are chosen for the opus,[42] suggests that the author may have belonged to, or been connected with, one of the mendicant orders. He does not seem to have been hostile to the Church, but to have felt it possible to reconcile his views with tradition. If Thomas Aquinas were to be considered the author, it should be pointed out that though he rejected in part the teachings of Joachim of Flora,[43] he expressly warned against a too rigorous and summary condemnation of his views.[44]

[41] "Dogma of the Trinity," pp. 181ff.   [42] Infra, pp. 327f.; supra, p. 105.
[43] 4 *Sent.*, dist. 43, p. 4, col. II ad 3 (Paris edn., vol. 11, p. 284).
[44] Infra, p. 421, n. 6.

335   From this historical standpoint, therefore, it is well worth while examining the conception of the Holy Spirit in *Aurora* more closely.

336   For the Father is of none, the Son is of the Father, the Holy Spirit proceedeth from both; for to the Father is attributed wisdom, by which he ruleth and sweetly disposeth all things, whose ways are unsearchable and his judgments incomprehensible. To the Son is attributed Truth, for he in his appearing took upon him that which he was not, subsisting perfect God and man of human flesh and reasonable soul, who at the behest of the Father with the co-operation of the Holy Spirit restored the world lost by the sin of the first parents.

337   The Holy Spirit proceeds from the Father and the Son because, according to the text, wisdom is an attribute of the Father, and truth of the Son.[45] The Holy Spirit is therefore a combination of Wisdom with the incarnate Truth, so that once again we can plainly discern his connection with Wisdom who was defined in the beginning as "most true nature." The Holy Spirit, as conceived in dogma, has here acquired a feminine and material character. It should be noted, however, that Scotus Erigena regarded the "mind of God" as a sort of anima mundi, and that, in consequence, even in the realm of ecclesiastical ideas the Holy Spirit, though not actually identified with the anima mundi, was nevertheless compared with it. Thus Honorius of Autun says: [46] "In the view of certain persons, the anima mundi is the Holy Spirit, for through God's goodness and will (which is the Holy Spirit) lives everything that exists in the world. Others name the anima mundi a natural vigour [47] which was implanted in things by God, and by which the many creatures live, feel, and think. . . . Yet others name the anima mundi an incorporeal substance which is entire in all bodies, albeit that, on account of the inertia of many bodies, it does

---

[45] Honorius identifies the Father with the *potentia divina,* the Son with Sapientia Dei, and the Holy Spirit with God's will. *De philosophia mundi* (Migne, *P.L.,* vol. 172, col. 45). Cf. Joachim of Flora, *Psalterium decem chordarum* (Hahn, III, p. 328): "Some . . . attributed power to the Father . . . and wisdom to the Son . . . will or love to the Holy Spirit." • P. 327: "The Holy Ghost enkindles us with the fire of love . . ." • P. 321: "He is that light which enlightens every man coming into this world and proceeds as that warmth which quickens all things." •
[46] Migne, *P.L.,* vol. 172, col. 46.
[47] This view goes back to the Stoics.

286

not work and create equally in all." [48] The conception of the Holy Spirit in *Aurora* comes close to these ideas of an anima mundi immanent in matter.

338   To the Holy Spirit is attributed Goodness, through whom earthly things become heavenly, and this in threefold wise: by baptizing in water, in blood, and in fire;

339   As in Honorius of Autun, so here the Holy Spirit possesses "goodness," and through him "earthly things become heavenly." In the previous passage there was an allusion to the incarnation. In the incarnation something heavenly and spiritual became earthly, and now the text emphasizes that at the same time a bit of earthly humanity became heavenly, i.e., was spiritualized. For an alchemist this was a clear allusion to the oft-repeated saying of Maria Prophetissa that one should make the corporeal incorporeal, the incorporeal corporeal, whereby the two become one.[49] The alchemical background of this part of the text, with its seemingly dogmatic statements, is clearly revealed in the continuation of the parable, where the three workings of the Holy Spirit are described.

340   in water by quickening and cleansing, when he washeth away all defilements and driveth out murkiness from souls, as it is said: Thou dost fecundate the waters to give life to souls. For water is the nourishment of all living things,

341   The whole water symbolism of the preceding parables is recapitulated in this reference to baptism: water quickens and cleanses souls. Even if by "souls" are meant the souls of the metals, the allusion to Notker Balbulus (Hymn for Pentecost) [50] and to the Missal immediately puts the chemical *ablutio* in a religious setting. Once more the artifex has got inextricably involved in the chemical process. The water of the Holy Spirit washes away the "squalores et fumositates," the superfluous dross which in other treatises is called sulphur,

[48] These pantheistic tendencies may be compared with the teachings of David of Dinant. (Preger, *Geschichte der Mystik*, II, pp. 76 and 462.)
[49] Cited in Olympiodorus (*Alch. grecs*, II, iv, 40): "Unless you make the corporeal incorporeal, the incorporeal corporeal, and the two one, your expectation will come to nothing." •
[50] "Thou givest to the waters virtue to quicken souls: thou, by thine inspiration, grantest to men to be living spirits." Neale, *Collected Hymns*, p. 20.

the thief, etc., and whose psychological significance as the shadow Jung discusses.[51] The water has a purifying effect because, the text says, it contains the spirit of God, which moved over the waters at the Creation and fecundated them. As the ensuing quotation from Psalm 103 : 30–32 shows, the water is nothing less than the spirit of God itself, which renews the face of the earth and makes it to tremble. From this it is clear that the author completely identifies the Holy Spirit, personified Wisdom, and the spirit of God indwelling in the baptismal water with the divine water of the alchemical opus. This water is also the nourishing ground-substance of all concrete organic phenomena. At the same time it is the *aqua fortis* which dissolves the metals.[52]

342   whence when water cometh down from heaven it plentifully watereth the earth, and the earth by it receiveth strength which can dissolve every metal, wherefore it beseecheth him saying: Send forth thy Spirit, that is water, and they shall be created, and thou shalt renew the face of the earth, for he breatheth upon the earth when he maketh it to tremble, and he toucheth the mountains and they smoke.

343   These ablutions, dissolutions, and upheavals have, as it were, answered the prayer of the anima when she was imprisoned in the centre of the earth: the breaking of the barriers of hell. In psychological terms, what had solidified into fixed, unshakable convictions—more, the whole personality—is loosened up and opens itself to new realities: the ego makes ready to receive the influences of the self.

344   The *ablutio* and *solutio* are followed by the *nutritio*, which, like them, is described as the action of the Holy Spirit or divine water.

345   And when he baptizeth with blood, then he nourisheth, as it is said: He gave me to drink of the saving water of wisdom, and again: His blood is drink indeed, for the seat of the soul is in the blood, as Senior saith: But the soul itself remained in water, which is like to it in warmth and humidity, and therein consisteth all life.

346   The quotation from Ecclus. 15 : 3, "She gave him the water of wholesome wisdom to drink," shows that blood and water

[51] *Mysterium*, pp. 192ff., 235ff.

[52] *Turba* (p. 218) says that just as man has air in him as a life-principle (breath), so the ore possesses a "humour" which, when it solidifies into the lapis, can dissolve every metal.

are synonyms for the *aqua Sapientiae*. This passage refers to the so-called "comma Johanneum": "For there are three that bear witness in heaven: the Father, the Word, and the Holy Spirit; and these three are one. And there are three that bear witness on earth: the Spirit, and the water, and the blood; and these three are one." [53] Whereas in the Bible a heavenly and an earthly triunity are contrasted with one another, in *Aurora* they are identified—which means that the metaphysical entities have been drawn into the human sphere, into the unconscious psyche (in so far as blood is the seat of the *anima vegetativa*). Thus man himself becomes the psychic carrier of the trinitarian symbol; in other words, the ordinary man, the artifex, is assimilated to God. The author even dares to identify the alchemical blood-water with the blood of Christ, as the quotation from John 6 : 55 shows.[54] The nourishment of the stone therefore has the "human" aspect of a communion with the Godhead, thanks to the mediation óf the soul-containing blood,[55] or as we should say, the unconscious psyche. Just as Christ the exemplar gave his blood for mankind, so also the alchemist gives his blood, not to man but to the stone; and the fact that he can do this he feels is a gift or working of the Holy Spirit. Psychologically it would mean that the "spirit" of the unconscious, that is, its inspiring and guiding function, has led him to give himself with his whole being to the "production" of the self (i.e., its conscious realization), during which process the self is "nourished" by him like a child.[56]

347   The nourishment of the lapis by water (or milk) and blood is then followed by its quickening.

[53] I John 5 : 7–8. This is probably a late interpolation. Cf. "A Psychological Approach to the Dogma of the Trinity," p. 138n.

[54] "For my flesh is meat indeed, and my blood is drink indeed."

[55] In the *Turba* (p. 129) the divine water is interpreted as "spiritual blood," also in the Book Al-Habib (ibid., pp. 42f.), which says: "You must learn the power of the permanent water . . . because its power is a spiritual blood . . . and it changes the body into spirit . . . so that the body which then comes into being is spiritual and coloured like blood, for everything that the soul possesses, the blood possesses also." For the Greek alchemists, too, blood was a synonym for the divine water. Cf. Olympiodorus in *Alch. grecs*, II, iv, 38 and 44, and Zosimos, ibid., III, xliii, 5.

[56] Cf. Jung's commentary on Dorn's text in *Mysterium*, pp. 485f. where the union of mind with body is produced by the admixture, among other things, of human blood.

348   But when he baptizeth in flame, then he infuseth the soul and giveth perfection of life, for fire giveth form and completeth the whole, as it is said: He breathed into his face the breath of life, and man, who was aforetime dead, became a living soul.

349   The same is said in "Exercitationes in Turbam XV": "And in the end of those days God poured out the blessing of the human seed, that is, the soul or life." [57] The three stages are also said to correspond to an addition of milk (= water), blood (= "our salt"), and flesh (= anima or rex), the latter being added over a "moderate fire." The last stage, as we have seen,[58] is an incarnation and a quickening at once. Our text therefore mentions, as the third working of the Holy Spirit, the quickening of Adam in Genesis 2:7, and this is followed by the famous saying from Calid about the nourishing of the foetus by water, air, and fire, each time for three months.[59]

350   Of the first, second, and third the philosophers bear witness, saying: For three months water nourisheth the foetus in the womb, air nourisheth it for the second three, fire also guardeth it for the third three. The infant will never come to birth until these months are expired, then it is born and quickened by the sun, for that is the quickener of all things that are dead.

351   In Greek alchemy this third stage would be that of the ἀναζωπύρωσις, "quickening by fire," and of the resurrection of the dead (τὰ νεκρὰ σώματα ἐμψυχοῦνται).[60] The quickening in our text is effected by the sun, "the quickener of all things." In some authors the quickening by fire is a parallel process to the whitening.[61] Zosimos, for instance, says: "The whitening is a burning, and this is a quickening by fire; for it (the substance) consumes itself in itself and quickens itself by fire and fertilizes

---

[57] *Art. aurif.*, I, p. 117.* Cf. on the other hand the Christian equation of blood, water, and spirit, documented by Rahner in "Flumina de ventre Christi," p. 277 and especially pp. 370–71, 373, 381. Honorius, *Speculum* (Migne, *P.L.*, vol. 172, col. 910) says that the Church was formed from the water and blood that flowed from the wound in Christ's side: "She is redeemed with blood, she is washed with water."   [58] Supra, p. 264.

[59] See supra, pp. 85–87, quotations from Senior in nn. 22–25. Cf. further Senior, *De chemia*, pp. 87f., Berthelot, *La Chimie au moyen âge*, III, pp. 92, 97, 109, Lippmann, *Alchemie*, I, p. 47, and *Tabula Smaragdina*, pp. 3ff., where the lapis is called a "cosmic" child.

[60] *Alch. grecs*, III, lvi, 2 and 3, and III, viii, 2: "Deny not resurrection to the dead."
[61] Ibid., III, xl, 2.

itself and impregnates itself and gives birth to the living being (ζῷον) desired by the philosophers." In the fire of the matrix the organism receives "colour, shape and extension," and is then visibly born.[62] Similarly, Komarios says that the fire brings about a ripening and transfiguration of the elements and "changes the material into a divine being, for it is nourished in the fire as the embryo little by little grows in the womb." [63] The material rises up "with natural life like a child from the womb. . . . For the art imitates the growth of a child, and when it is perfected in all—behold, that is the sealed mystery." [64] In *Aurora* the quickening is effected not by the fire alone but, as in Genesis 2 : 7, by the breath of God, by his pneuma, with which the human soul was held to be consubstantial. The soul was also conceived as a vapour or steam.[65] This agrees with the Stoic conception of the soul as an ἀναθυμίασις, bubbling up or exhalation of the blood,[66] or as air [67] or warm pneuma,[68] which was the very fine substance of God and caused in man "enthusiasm" (lit. inspiration by the god) and the "airy phantoms of dreams." In Simon Magus air is the intermediary between spirit and earth; "in it is the father who sustains, nourishes, and safeguards all things." [69] Similar views are reflected in a Hermetic fragment: the heated material turns to fire and water,

[62] III, xliii, 5. Cf. III, vi, 17, *Moyen âge*, III, p. 98, and Reitzenstein, "Alchemistische Lehrschriften," pp. 75 and 83.

[63] *Alch. grecs*, IV, xx, 10. Cf. *Carmina Heliodori*, pp. 28ff.

[64] *Alch. grecs*, Textes, p. 338, and V, iii. Cf. Senior, *De chemia*, pp. 16, 19, 30, 44, 58f., 77; *Turba*, pp. 137f., 163.   [65] *Turba*, p. 142.

[66] Aristotle, *De anima*, I, 2, 405 (Foster and Humphries trans., p. 77); Areios Didymos, 39, 2 in Diels, *Doxographi*, p. 471; Chrysippus, cited in Galen, *De placitis Hippocratis et Platonis*, Book III, pp. 249ff.; Diogenes Laertius, 7, 156 (Loeb edn.), II, pp. 260f.; Macrobius, *Somn. Scip.*, I, 14, 19; Tertullian, *De anima*, 5 (*Writings*, II, p. 419); Plotinus, 4.7.4 (*Enneads*, p. 344); Alexander of Aphrodisias, *De anima*, 26, 13 (ed. Bruns, p. 3, line 18); Nemesius, *De natura hominis*, cap. 2 (Scott, *Hermetica*, III, p. 612).

[67] Lippmann, I, p. 133.   [68] Leisegang, *Der heilige Geist*, pp. 26ff.

[69] Leisegang, *Gnosis*, p. 81. Cf. Didymus of Alexandria, *De trinitate*, Lib. II, cap. 27 (Migne, *P.G.*, vol. 39, col. 756). (Scott, I, p. 542.) The pneuma is the γόνιμον ἐν ("one thing that is fecund"). In the Latin Asclepius (Scott, ibid.), air is the universal instrument by which all things come into being and which holds everything together, mortal and immortal, since the breath of the spirit moves the whole world. Ephraem Syrus (I, col. 16) praises the air because it is pure enough to penetrate everything and even saw the Lord formed in the womb. (Cf. Calid's words!)

then the fire dries the water, and earth is formed. Steam from fire, earth, and water produces air. All come together "according to the Logos of harmony," and from the combined breath of the opposed qualities arises a pneuma and sperma that corresponds to the divine pneuma. "From this creative pneuma the child is formed in the matrix." [70] A similar description of the formation of a "child" from cosmic elements is found in the Logos vision of the Gnostic Valentinus:

352

> "I behold how all things in the
> aether are mixed with pneuma.
> I see in spirit how all things
> are sustained by pneuma:
> Flesh hangs itself upon soul,
> Soul is upborne by air,
> Air hangs itself upon aether.
> Fruits rise up from the depth,
> A child is lifted from the womb." [71]

353   A further parallel is the vision in II Esdras 13 : 1–4: "And it came to pass after seven days, I dreamed a dream by night. And lo, there arose a wind from the sea, that it moved all the waves thereof. And I beheld, and, lo, that man flew with the clouds of heaven; [72] and when he turned his countenance to look, all things trembled that were seen under him. And whensoever the voice went out of his mouth, all they burned that heard his voice, like as the earth when it feeleth the fire." [73] As Reitzenstein observes, individual features of this description can be found in Manichaeism. [74] Thus, at the ascension of Shitil, it was said that the winds had fetched him away, storms had lifted him up in a cloud of light; and in a poem the Manichaean Original Man says: [75]

[70] Scott, I, p. 438; Stobaeus, *Anthologium*, I. 41. 7.

[71] Cited from Leisegang, *Gnosis*, p. 283. Cf. Hippolytus' interpretation of this passage (ibid.). It is related of Simon Magus that he created a homunculus by letting human pneuma congeal into water and then into blood and then into "flesh." (Lippmann, I, p. 224.)

[72] AV: "waxed strong with the thousands of heaven."

[73] Charles, *Apocrypha and Pseudepigrapha*, II, p. 616.

[74] *Erlösungsmysterium*, pp. 121f.

[75] Ibid., pp. 49f. Cf. the early Christian apocryphon in Solomon of Basra, *The Book of the Bee* (ed. Budge), p. 81: "At the end of time, and at the final dissolu-

354

> "I am a great Mana,
> I who dwelt in the sea;
> I dwelt in the sea
> Until I was given wings,

355

> Until I became a winged one
> And lifted up my wings
> to the place of light."

356   Again, in the *Carmina Heliodori* [76] it is said that the lapis remains "hidden in the womb for a long time and calls for deliverance like a treasure in the depth. . . . He is found wherever men dwell, he rises up from the sea into the clouds and strides over the sea in a garment of clouds . . . and he sits in the cloud like a light smoke lifted up by an inward fire." [77] The same thing is meant by the celebrated saying from the *Tabula Smaragdina:* "The wind hath carried it in his belly."

357   Such was the alchemical background to which the author of *Aurora* alludes when he makes the baptism by the Holy Spirit in water, blood, and fire end with Calid's description of the lapis as a foetus nourished by water, air, and fire. It appears, however, that the three protecting elements are really one, that they form a triunity in accordance with the "Philosophic Faith, which consisteth in the number Three." The triad of elements is not always clearly established in the text, which speaks now of water, blood, and fire and now of water, air, and fire. In both cases earth is missing. This is psychologically significant. Looking back over the inner development which has taken place in the course of the parables, we can observe a gradual *shifting of the centre of gravity towards the conscious side.* The image of Wisdom in her light as well as her chthonic aspect ("the woman

---

tion, a child shall be conceived in the womb of a virgin. . . . And he shall be like a tree . . . laden with fruit . . . then he will come with the armies of light and be borne aloft upon white clouds; for he is a child conceived by the Word which establishes the natures."

[76] P. 28, verses 7off.

[77] Cf. Senior, *De chemia,* pp. 16–19 and 30: "They mean therefore by the mediating air . . . that the son of Wisdom is born in the air, when it is sublimed in the alembic. Wherefore the water quickens their earth and the embryo, which is earth, which is the soul from their bodies." • Cf. p. 44.

who brought in death") has receded, and the contamination of conscious and unconscious which the irruption of her image occasioned has been largely removed by the "gathering together" and ablution, and by the "spirit of understanding." The same numinous factor that was previously designated by the name of "Wisdom" has been superseded by—or has coalesced with—the hypostasis of the Holy Spirit, whose workings the author now praises. Dirt and the world are cast out, and the identity of the alchemist with the filius philosophorum, which had often struck us before, seems no longer to exist. It is as though, through the insight afforded by the traditional alchemical symbolism, the author were able to stand off from his experience. After having been initially overwhelmed by the spate of unconscious contents, he seems gradually to have arrived at a conscious standpoint and found inner peace. In this he was helped by the ternary structure of his philosophic credo; for, as Jung has pointed out, a ternary pattern of order fosters an emancipation of consciousness from mere nature. "The Trinity is an archetype whose dominating power not only fosters spiritual development but may, on occasion, enforce it." [78] But threeness is not a natural expression for wholeness as compared with the quaternity.[79]

358   This is due to the structure of our consciousness, which seems to be made up of four orienting functions,[80] of which on average three at most are at our conscious disposal. The fourth or "inferior" function is usually in an undeveloped state, is contaminated with the unconscious, and shows primitive, archaic features. At the same time, it is the connecting-link with the collective unconscious and with its immense network of symbolic meanings and associations.[81]

359   Thus, if we correlate the alchemical quaternity of elements with the four psychological functions, the absence of the element earth would lead us to conclude that one of the author's four functions has remained in the unconscious. The absence of this particular element would mean specifically that the re-

[78] "A Psychological Approach to the Dogma of the Trinity," p. 193.
[79] Ibid., p. 167.
[80] Psychological Types (1923 edn.), pp. 428ff., and "Dogma of the Trinity," pp. 165f.
[81] "Dogma of the Trinity," p. 121.

lationship to materiality and the concrete world is lacking.[82] We must therefore assume that the solution of the problem as presented in this part of *Aurora* has more the character of a *spiritual intuition,* but that complete individual realization is not yet possible.

360   The difficulty of bringing the alchemical quaternity of elements into harmony with the Christian conception of the Trinity is yet another example of that common vacillation between three and four, of which Jung says: [83] "It must be stressed that side by side with the distinctive leanings of alchemy (and of the unconscious) towards quaternity there is always a vacillation between three and four which comes out over and over again. . . . In alchemy there are three as well as four *regimina* or procedures, three as well as four colours. There are always four elements, but often three of them are grouped together, with the fourth in a special position—sometimes earth, sometimes fire. . . . This uncertainty has a duplex character—in other words, the central ideas are ternary as well as quaternary. The psychologist cannot but mention that a similar puzzle exists in the psychology of the unconscious: the least differentiated or 'inferior' function is so much contaminated with the collective unconscious that, on becoming conscious, it brings up among others the archetype of the self as well. . . . Four signifies the feminine, motherly, physical; three the masculine, fatherly, spiritual. Thus the uncertainty as to three or four amounts to a wavering between the spiritual and the physical." [84]

82 Pp. 122f. Cf. Jung's argument that trinitarian thinking not only corresponded to a patriarchal order of society but enabled the human mind to "think in opposition to nature, thus demonstrating its godlike freedom" (p. 176). The Pythagorean quaternity, on the other hand, was a "purely naturalistic, intuitive idea born of the nature-bound mind" (ibid.). "The quaternity schema . . . [fetters] trinitarian thinking to the reality of this world" (p. 178). The Fourth always brings up the problem of "realization," i.e., worldly materiality (p. 171).

83 *Psychology and Alchemy,* par. 31.

84 As Jung has shown, trinitarian thinking entails a dissociation of the fourth, "inferior" function: "This peculiar dissociation is, it seems, a product of civilization, and it denotes a freeing of consciousness from any excessive attachment to the 'spirit of gravity.' If that function, which is still bound indissolubly to the past and whose roots reach back as far as the animal kingdom, can be left behind and even forgotten, then consciousness has won for itself a new and not entirely illusory freedom. It can leap over abysses on winged feet; it can free itself from bondage to sense-impressions, emotions, fascinating thoughts and presentiments by soaring into abstraction." ("Dogma of the Trinity," pp. 165f.)

361   Turning back to our text, we see that the author's prefer-
ence for a ternary formulation of his credo coincides with the
disappearance of the feminine figure of Wisdom and her re-
placement by the masculine hypostasis of the Holy Spirit. The
identity of the two is evidenced, among other things, by the
fact that both—first Wisdom and now the Holy Spirit—are identified with the saving water of the art.

362   The hypostasis of the Holy Spirit has in the course of history often showed a tendency to become feminine. He was even
interpreted as the mother of Christ, but that, as Jung says,
"would merely have kept him within the archaic family-picture,
within the tritheism and polytheism of the patriarchal world." [85]
On the other hand, in the official tradition of the Church he
represents the breath of life and of love between Father and
Son, and is thus "essentially . . . an hypostatized noumenon
tacked on to the natural family-picture of father and son." [86]
In that form he is "psychologically heterogeneous in that he
cannot be logically derived from the father-son relationship and
can only be understood as an idea introduced by a process of
human reflection." [87] "Not only is he the life common to Father
and Son, he is also the Paraclete whom the Son left behind
him, to procreate in man and bring forth works of divine
parentage." [88] "Just as the Holy Ghost is a legacy left to man,
so, conversely, the concept of the Holy Ghost is something begotten by man and bears the stamp of its human progenitor.
. . . The Trinity, therefore, discloses itself as a symbol that
comprehends the essence of the divine *and* the human." [89]

363   Jung goes on to say that the "Gnostic interpretation of the
Holy Ghost as the Mother contains a core of truth in that
Mary was the instrument of God's birth and so became involved
in the trinitarian drama as a human being. The Mother of
God can, therefore, be regarded as a symbol of mankind's essential participation in the Trinity. The psychological justification
for this assumption lies in the fact that thinking, which originally had its source in the self-revelation of the unconscious,
was felt to be the manifestation of a power external to consciousness. The primitive does not think; the thoughts come to
him. We ourselves still feel certain particularly enlightening

85 "Dogma of the Trinity," p. 159.
86 Ibid.   87 P. 160.   88 P. 159.   89 P. 161.

ideas as 'in-fluences,' 'in-spirations,' etc. Where judgments and flashes of insight are transmitted by unconscious activity, they are often attributed to an archetypal feminine figure, the anima or mother-beloved. It seems as if the inspiration came from the mother or from the beloved, the 'femme inspiratrice.' In view of this, the Holy Ghost would have a tendency to exchange his neuter designation (τὸ πνεῦμα) for a feminine one. . . . Holy Ghost and Logos merge in the Gnostic idea of Sophia, and again in the Sapientia of the medieval natural philosophers, who said of her: 'In gremio matris sedet sapientia patris' (the wisdom of the father lies in the lap of the mother)." [90]

364   These remarks of Jung's shed light on the psychological happenings that found expression in *Aurora*. The fact that the numinosum appeared first as Wisdom, a feminine figure, leads us to suppose that overpowering new insights were approaching the author's consciousness, and that the anima was constellated as a mediatrix. If later she retires from the scene, we must infer that a process of reflection had occurred in the interim, which attempted to incorporate the experience in a spiritual order. This inevitably entailed a retreat from the unconscious, which found symbolical expression in the exclusion of the element earth.[91] But, as we have already seen, earth is an aspect of Wisdom herself, her own chthonic side, as it were.

365   Wherefore the aforesaid Spirit by reason of the excellence of his sevenfold gift is said to have seven virtues in his operation on earth.

366   The element earth is not entirely lacking, as this passage shows; but it is excluded from the triad praised in the author's philosophic credo and is put in parenthesis, so to speak, appearing as something opposed to it, a passive, imperfect element that still has to be worked on.

367   Looking at this part of the text in the light of our earlier remarks on the four-function schema of consciousness, we would have to conclude from the exclusion of the fourth element that the author's consciousness found difficulty in assimilating the

---

[90] Pp. 161f.

[91] Previously I interpreted the missing earth as an incomplete realization, but now as a retreat from the unconscious. For anyone with a knowledge of the psychological facts this is not a contradiction, because a retreat from the unconscious is the same as unconsciousness and hence an incomplete realization.

fourth, "inferior" function. This function, here represented by earth, is in a man always contaminated with the anima and the collective unconscious.[92]

368 Now if the step from three to four appears too difficult, we often find in the unconscious material a doubling of these numbers, and the problematical step is then from seven to eight, so that the inferior function appears to have been reduced by half. The doubling, therefore, represents a process of psychological differentiation.

369 This accords with certain symbolical explanations of the number seven which may be found in Allendy's book *Le Symbolisme des nombres*.[93] In his view, seven is produced by a double division of three:

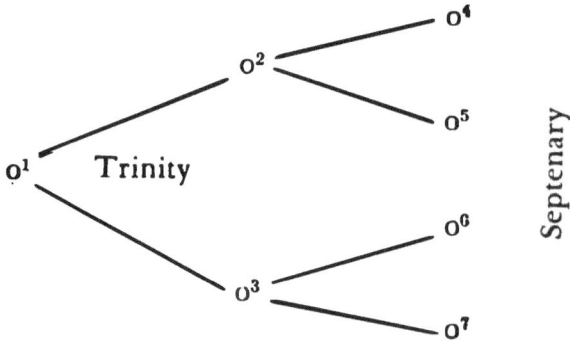

370 This derivation, he remarks, is the rule in progressive series of numbers.[94] Whereas four reflects the continuous, self-con-

[92] *Psychology and Alchemy*, pars. 192f.: "In the psychology of the functions there are two conscious and therefore masculine functions, the differentiated function and its auxiliary. . . . Since the conflict between the two auxiliary functions is not nearly so great as that between the differentiated and the inferior function, it is possible for the third function—that is, the unconscious auxiliary one—to be raised to consciousness and thus be made masculine. It will, however, bring with it traces of its contamination with the inferior function, thus acting as a kind of link with the darkness of the unconscious. It was in keeping with this psychological fact that the Holy Ghost should be interpreted as Sophia. . . . The fourth function is contaminated with the unconscious and, on being made conscious, drags the whole of the unconscious with it. . . . At first a violent conflict breaks out, such as any reasonable man would experience when it became evident that he had to swallow a lot of absurd superstitions."

[93] Pp. 172ff.

[94] By a progressive series is meant a series of numbers so arranged that the ratio of their relationship remains constant, whether they increase or decrease.

tained cycle of natural processes, seven represents the evolving circle of progress in spiral form. According to Jakob Boehme,[95] there are in the cosmos seven organizing spirits who actualize the eternal wisdom. They consist of an upper triad (Desire, Motion, Rest), a lower, natural triad (Love, Word, Body), and a mediator, Lightning or Fire, who establishes the contact between nature and spirit. Also in other systems of number symbolism seven, according to Allendy, stands for the clash between an upper, spiritual triad and a lower, natural quaternity.[96]

371   These amplifications seem to me relevant as throwing light on the sevenfold gifts of the Spirit which are described in the following passages. They also explain how it is that the author suddenly switches from the three workings of the Holy Spirit to his seven gifts or virtues. The seven virtues, we are told, refer specifically to his operation on earth, which represents the excluded fourth (or eighth) element. But this earth, as we know from the earlier parables, is the "black earth" and the woman in the pit of sin and hell. Although the author would hardly have had any conscious doubts about his own Christianity, the inclusion of *this* element in his alchemical and Christian view of the world nevertheless seems to have presented difficulties. In the same way the alchemist William Mennens, borrowing from Cabalistic ideas, called the prima materia "God's shadow" and "God's back parts." [97] In medieval number symbolism it was co-ordinated with the quaternarius.[98] It is no accident that this difficulty should have cropped up in *Aurora* specifically in connection with the Holy Spirit, for, as Jung has shown,[99] this is the very figure in the Trinity who forms the connecting-link with the rejected "fourth," or with evil. Not only is he the "breath common to man, the Son, and the Father," but, as the

[95] *The Signature of All Things*, XIV, 10, p. 178.

[96] *Le Symbolisme des nombres*, pp. 181ff.

[97] *Theatr. chem.*, V, p. 301: "Therefore the four-letter name of God is seen to designate the most holy Trinity and matter, which is also threefold, as we have set forth earlier, and is also called his shadow, and by Moses God's back parts." * Cf. Knorr von Rosenroth, *Kabbala denudata*, I, Part 1, pp. 73 and 581, and II, p. 29, Supplement ("Adumbratio Kabbalae Christianae").

[98] Meister Dietrich, *De miscibilibus in mixto*: "Because that which is the first matter, is in itself many and plural and fourfold in number according to the four elements." * (Krebs, *Die Schriften Meister Dietrichs*, p. 46 * [the asterisk here is a part of the page number].)

[99] "Dogma of the Trinity," p. 178.

Paraclete, the Comforter of man suffering evil, he is the "reconciliation of opposites and hence the answer to the suffering in the Godhead which Christ personifies." [100] The author, as we have seen, was unexpectedly confronted with the problem of evil, with the dark side of God, as a result of his encounter with Wisdom, and so he was in quite particular need of the Holy Spirit, who reconciles the opposites in God. Therefore he equates this hypostasis of the Godhead specifically with the aqua divina and makes him the real operator in the work of bringing about the transformation of the black earth.

372   We could briefly interpret what has happened so far as follows: the initial inrush of the collective unconscious—personified at first in the sublime anima-image of Wisdom—led to an inundation of consciousness. In this "dark night of the soul" all the repressed shadow elements, the heathen Ethiopians and the sinful daughters of Sion, appeared, so that the author fell into a profound depression. To save himself from complete dissolution, he now calls to his aid his conscious Christian views and implores the Holy Spirit to help him purify the black earth (the unconscious that caused the depression). Only one thing remains obscure and is stated in the text only indirectly: *the black earth is itself Wisdom!* He thus, like Job, calls upon God for help against God.[101] A secret enantiodromia has taken place: what first broke through was the bright image of Wisdom, but later this gradually changed into a darkness that had to be "operated" on and worked with. We now see why the author had recourse to the saving language of alchemy, for only in that way could he formulate such a paradoxical experience at all.

373   Firstly, he warmeth the earth (as is to be seen in lime), which by coldness is dead and dry. Wherefore the prophet saith: My heart grew hot within me and in mine operation a fire flames out. And in the *Book of the Quintessence:* Fire, penetrating and subtilizing by its warmth, consumeth all earthly parts which are wholly material and not formal; for as long as fire hath matter, it ceaseth not to act, seeking to imprint its form on the passive substance.

374   The discussion of the seven virtues of the Holy Spirit is really an amplification of the three workings described in the

100 Ibid., pp. 158 and 176.   101 "Answer to Job," p. 369.

first part of the parable. The Spirit is again described as a fire which has a warming and purifying effect on the cold earth. The moral aspect is not overlooked, for the author compares him with the hidden fire of wrath which David sends out against the wicked.[102] The passive and (as we shall see) "compact" earth which is cleansed, subtilized, and "imprinted" by this fire is thus identical with wickedness and sin, and hence with the Ethiopians and sinful daughters of Sion in the earlier parables.

375 And Calet the Less: make warm the cold of the one by the heat of the other. And Senior: Set the male upon the female, that is, the warm upon the cold.

376 The quotations from Calid and Senior show the operation of the Spirit as a balancing of opposites in the well-known image of the coniunctio of man (= active, warm) and woman (= passive, chthonic, cold). Through the warm participation of consciousness the unconscious is changed and "imprinted" —though it should not be overlooked that in the process the upper, Spirit, comes down and enters the lower, Physis.

377 In the second place he extinguisheth the intense imprinted fire by ignition, of which saith the Prophet: A fire was kindled in their congregation, and a flame burned the wicked upon earth; he extinguisheth this fire by its own temperament, whence it is added: Thou art coolness in the heat. And Calet the Less: Extinguish the fire of the one by the coolness of the other.

378 The second operation of the Spirit is represented as the self-consuming and self-quenching of the spiritual fire which at the same time consumes the ungodly like the fire of hell.[103] The underlying alchemical idea is probably that of "nature conquering nature," and that there is in the arcane substance itself (i.e., the unconscious) a "temperament," an inner equability, which removes the destructive elements within it. The psychology of the unconscious has rediscovered this fact in its own field, as when Jung shows that psychic energy, though in itself polaristic (for instance as instinct and spirit), balances out its

102 Ps. 38 : 4.
103 Ps. 105 : 17–19: "The earth opened and swallowed up Dathan, and covered the congregation of Abiram. And a fire was kindled in their congregation: the flame burned the wicked."

own polarities.[104] In the Christian view, on the other hand, the two fires are usually distinct. Thus Ephraem Syrus says: "Baptism extinguishes with its fire the fire which the Evil One has kindled. The pure fire of our Redeemer put out the fire which flamed up in sinners." [105] Once again alchemy unites the separated aspects in one paradoxical idea. The author boldly illustrates the alchemical "fiery virtue" by a verse from the "Veni sancte Spiritus" of Pentecost: "Thou art coolness in the heat," thus uniting the fire-water symbolism of the Holy Ghost in ecclesiastical allegory [106] with the alchemical *ignis noster*.

379 And Avicenna: A thing in which there is burning, the first thing that is released from it is a fiery virtue, which is milder and more worthy than the virtues of the other elements.

380 With this quotation the author hints that this paradoxical fire is really a "fiery virtue" immanent in elemental matter itself, so that the fire of the Holy Spirit acquires a concrete, material aspect. The psychic experience expressed in his statements about the inner "temperament" of the fire seems to me a very important one, for it looks as if it had begun to dawn on the author that he had fallen into the hands of an overwhelming power which, however, contains within itself the capacity to neutralize its own forces, and which thereafter heals as well

---

104 *Symbols of Transformation*, pp. 437ff.

105 *Hymni et sermones*, I, col. 80. Cf. Peter Damian's hymn "In solemnitate S.P. Benedicti" (Blume and Dreves, *Analecta hymnica medii aevi*, XLVIII, p. 42): "The thorns and briers he plungeth in / With wounds make whole the wounds of sin: / His mind aflame with heaven's breath / The fire with fire extinguisheth; / And, with for stone the Cross's sign, / Shatters the cup of poisoned wine." • St. Gregory, *Homiliae in Evangelia*, XXX (Migne, *P.L.*, vol. 76, col. 1223): "Fittingly therefore did the Spirit appear in fire, for he driveth out the deadness of cold from every heart that he filleth." •

106 Cf. Hippolytus' commentary on Song of Songs in Rahner, "Mysterium Lunae," p. 79: the Holy Spirit is fire and at the same time soul-cooling dew. Also Origen, *Comm. in Epist. ad Rom.*, V, 8 (Migne, *P.G.*, vol. 14, col. 1038), Hugh of St. Victor, *De Unione corporis et spiritus* (Migne, *P.L.*, vol. 177, col. 286), and *Eruditionis Didascaliae* (vol. 176, col. 746). Compare the Holy Spirit as fire with the baptism by fire at the end of time in Anastasius the Sinaite, *Anagog. contempl.* 4 (Migne, *P.G.*, vol. 89, col. 900). Also Ephraem Syrus, I, col. 62: "The Spirit anoints his flock with a secret fire." The baptismal water assimilates the opposites to one another "that the hidden and the manifest may be brought together" (ibid., col. 72). Cf. Doelger's "aqua ignita" in *Antike und Christentum*, pp. 175–83.

as wounds. This dawning realization gives him a chance to recover his lost balance at a deeper level of psychic reality.

381 In the third place he maketh soft, that is, he liquefieth the hardness of the earth and dissolveth its condensed and exceedingly compact parts, of which it is written: The rain of the Holy Spirit melteth. And the Prophet: He shall send out his word and shall melt it, his wind shall blow and the waters shall run.

382 The *aqua Sapientiae* is also a rain, and is indirectly equated here with the Word of God, the Logos. Through an influence from above (i.e., consciousness) the compact and impenetrable darkness of the unconscious is gradually broken up, so that the imprisonment of the personality in seemingly immutable facts ceases, and, through "penetrating" understanding, psychic life begins to flow again.[107]

383 And in the *Book of the Quintessence* it is written, that the air shall open the pores of the earthly parts to receive the virtue of fire and water. And elsewhere it is written: Woman dissolveth man and he fixeth her, that is, the Spirit dissolveth the body and softeneth it, and the body hardeneth the spirit.

384 The author here interprets the earth's collision with the spiritual triad (water, air, fire) as the opposition between body and spirit, or woman and man. This is a reference to the coniunctio, which becomes of central importance in the concluding parable. In this passage the author is no longer actively participating; it is as though not he personally were having it out with his shadow, but as though two archetypal spheres—an upper, bright, spirit-triad (spiritual insight) and a dark "fourth" (something not understood)—were clashing together. The author has, as it were, taken refuge in the light part.

385 In the fourth place he enlighteneth, when he taketh away all darknesses from the body, of which the hymn singeth: Purge the horrible darknesses of our mind, enkindle a light in our senses,

386 Now follows a reference to the personal aspect of the process, in the quotation from Notker Balbulus's Hymn for Pentecost and from the "Veni Creator Spiritus." [108] This is an indication

[107] Cf. *Mysterium*, pp. 204ff.
[108] "Our minds enkindle with thy light; within our hearts thy love excite."

that the "operation" of the triune water-air-fire spirit upon the earth was, after all, an encounter with the darkness of the author's own mind, and that this (as the following quotation from Psalm 77 : 14 shows) can come to a good end only by the grace of God and by his guidance.

387 and the Prophet: He conducted them all the night with a light of fire, and night shall be light as the day.

388 The author likens this redemption to the exodus from Egypt, and since in patristic literature Egypt was generally interpreted as sin and "this world," [109] we have here yet another allusion to the captivity, *nigredo,* flood, etc. of the previous parables.

389 The words "and night shall be light as the day" recapitulate the end of Chapter IV, and, as there, are an allusion to the mystic birth of the filius philosophorum, who is later described as "a wondrous light in the darkness." [110] This light is the *lumen luminum,* called by Dorn the "invisible sun." Psychologically it signifies the illumination of the unconscious, in whose chaotic darkness a "meaning" and a regulating centre independent of the ego—the self—gradually become perceptible.[111] An illuminating insight flashes out from a previously incomprehensible content.

390 And Senior: And he maketh all that is black white and all that is white red, for water whiteneth and fire enlighteneth. For he shineth through the tincturing soul like a ruby in colour, which it hath acquired by virtue of the fire, wherefore fire is called the Dyer.

391 The light is described as a ruby, a synonym for the lapis.[112] Senior interprets the ruby as the "tincturing soul" (*anima tin-*

---

[109] Documentation in von Franz, "Passio Perpetuae," pp. 464ff.

[110] In Alphidius also the lapis is described as a resplendent and transparent light (Codex Ashmole 1420, fol. 11). In other texts it is a "secret light," and the "Rosarium" says that it "comes with light and is born with light." Cf. *Turba,* Sermo LXII: "This is the red sulphur that emits light in the darkness and it is the red jacinth . . . and the conquering lion." • In "Abu'l Qāsim al-ʿIrāqī" (Holmyard, pp. 421f.) the lapis is called "dog, eagle, harmless lion, fiery poison, light, son of the fire, Satan."

[111] Cf. "On the Nature of the Psyche," pp. 192ff., and the parallels given there.

[112] Jung, "A Study in the Process of Individuation," p. 331, n. 127: "The carbuncle is a synonym for the *lapis.* 'The king bright as a carbuncle' (Lilius, an old source in the "Ros. phil.," *Art. aurif.,* 1593, II, p. 329). 'A ray . . . in the earth, shining in

gens),[113] which is hidden in the water.[114] From the soul come the colours. Psychologically the red of the ruby denotes feeling, emotion, passion. In alchemy red (and the *rubedo*) was interpreted as masculine, white as feminine. The "king," or the lapis as bridegroom of the white bride (anima), is red. It is as though at this stage of the process active life and emotion had returned after the rigidity and depression of the *nigredo*, and after the phase of objective insight in the *albedo* is over. But this "vita nuova" (of the *rubedo*) no longer proceeds from the ego, but from the self.

392   Senior's remark that the soul produces the colours is an allusion to the motif of the "cauda pavonis," [115] of which Jung says: [116] "The appearance of these colours in the opus represents an intermediate stage preceding the definitive end-result.

---

the darkness after the manner of a carbuncle gathered into itself' * (from Michael Maier's exposition of the theory of Thomas Aquinas, in *Symbola aureae mensae*, p. 377). 'I found a certain stone, red, shining, transparent, and brilliant, and in it I saw all the forms of the elements and also their contraries' * (quotation from Thomas in Mylius, *Philosophia reformata*, p. 42). For heaven, gold, and carbuncle as synonyms for the *rubedo*, see ibid., p. 104. The *lapis* is 'shimmering carbuncle light' (Khunrath, *Von hyleal. Chaos*, p. 237). Ruby or carbuncle is the name for the *corpus glorificatum* (Glauber, *Tractatus de natura salium*, Part 1, p. 42). In Rosencreutz's *Chemical Wedding* the bed-chamber of Venus is lit by carbuncles (p. 97)."
113 *De chemia*, p. 66: "And when he saith 'ruby,' he meaneth it of the tincturing soul, because it hath received its virtue from the fire." *
114 Ibid., p. 35: "The tincturing soul lieth hidden in the white . . . water." * Cf. Knorr von Rosenroth, *Kabbala denudata*, II, Part 2, pp. 21f. for the hyacinthine colour and *rubedo* in the sea; also II, Part 2, p. 12, and Part 1, pp. 461f. for the *albedo* and *rubedo* in the crystal.
115 "A Study in the Process of Individuation," p. 330, n. 124 (mod.): "The *cauda pavonis* is identified by Khunrath with Iris, the 'nuncia Dei.' Dorn ("De transmutat. metallorum," *Theatr. chem.*, I, 1602, p. 599) explains it as follows: 'This is the bird which flies by night without wings, which the first dew of heaven by continual decoction, and by ascent and descent upwards and downwards, turns into the raven's head, and then into the peacock's tail, and afterwards it acquires very brilliant and swanlike feathers, and lastly an extreme redness, an indication of its fiery nature.' * In Basilides (Hippolytus, *Elenchos*, X, 14, 1) the peacock's egg is synonymous with the *sperma mundi*, the κόκκος σινάπεως. It contains the 'fullness of colours,' 365 of them. The golden colour should be produced from peacock's eggs, we are told in the Cyranides (Delatte, *Textes latins et vieux français relatifs aux Cyranides*, p. 171). The light of Mohammed has the form of a peacock, and the angels were made out of peacock's sweat (Aptowitzer, "Arabisch-jüdische Schöpfungstheorien," pp. 209, 233)."
116 "A Study in the Process of Individuation," pp. 330f.

Boehme speaks of a 'love-desire or a Beauty of Colours; and here all Colours arise.' " [117]

393   In "The Earthly and Heavenly Mystery" Boehme says: [118] "And then we are able to recognize an eternal substantiality of Nature, identical with water and fire, which are as it were mixed together; where then this gives a light-blue colour, like the flash of fire; where it hath a form as a ruby mixed with crystal in one substance, or as yellow, white, red, and blue mingled in a dark water; where it is as blue in green, yet each has its lustre, and shines. And the water checks the fire, so that there is no consuming there, but an eternal essence, or substance, in two mysteries united in one another, and yet the distinction of two principles as two kinds of life." The phenomenon of the colours owes its existence to the "Imagination of the great Mystery, where a wondrous essential life is born." [119]

394   Contact with the unconscious causes a world of fantasy and feeling to blossom forth—the world of Eros lights up in the darkness, as the passages that follow will show.

395   And in the *Book of the Quintessence:* Thou seest a wondrous light in the darkness. And in the *Turba philosophorum* it is written, that if the clouds have whitened the surface, without a doubt their inner parts shall be whitened also. And Morienus saith: Already we have taken away the black and have made the white, with the salt [a]natron, that is with the spirit.

396   The transformation of night, sin, and death into a world of light and colour is explained as the *dealbatio*, the whitening. This, says the text, is brought about by the "salt natron" [120] or the spirit. The manifold significance of this new analogue of the Holy Spirit, salt, is discussed in Jung.[121] Even though the author may not have known its significance as Eros,[122] he equates

---

[117] *The Signature of All Things*, p. 178.

[118] "On the Earthly and Heavenly Mystery" (trans. Earle), pp. 147f.

[119] "A Study in the Process of Individuation," p. 331.

[120] "Anatron" is due to transcription of the Arabic *al-natron*. Natron is derived from the Egyptian *ntr*, God. Cf. Steuer, *Über das wohlriechende Natron bei den alten Aegyptern.*   [121] *Mysterium*, ch. III, sec. 5.

[122] Cf. Albertus, "Biblia Mariana" (Borgnet, XXXVII, p. 385), who identifies salt with Christ: "For salt is the son of God. Because when he had put that salt into the fountain of waters, which was done at the Annunciation, he said: Thus saith the Lord, I have healed these waters, that is, inconstant and pestiferous human nature, and death and barrenness shall be no more, but life and fruitfulness." •

salt with the Holy Spirit,[123] who was also interpreted as the fire of love,[124] and for him both are an analogy expressing the paradoxical nature of the arcane substance.

397 Fifthly, he separateth the pure from the impure when he removeth all accidents from the soul, which are vapours, that is, evil odours, as it is written: That fire separateth those things that are unlike and bringeth together those things that are like. Wherefore the Prophet: Thou hast tried me by fire, and iniquity shall not be found in me. And again: We have passed through fire and water, and thou hast brought us forth into rest and refreshment. And Hermes: Thou shalt separate the dense from the subtle, the earth from the fire. Alphidius: Earth is liquefied and turned into water, water is liquefied and turned into air, air is liquefied and turned into fire (fire is liquefied and turned into glorified earth).

398 After what we have said, this passage can be understood without further explanation, but the Alphidius quotation needs stressing, as it raises a problem of transmission. The manuscripts differ in regard to the third clause, for instead of "air is liquefied and turned into fire" the Paris manuscript has "fire is liquefied and turned into glorified earth." It is not mere chance that a textual difficulty presents itself at this point—for once again it is the problem of three and four! [125] Considering his "philosophic faith," the author ought really to enumerate

---

[123] Cf. salt as the mediator and uniter of opposites in *Mus. Herm.*, p. 11 (Waite, I, p. 14): ". . . the true spirit of mercury, and the soul of sulphur, united to spiritual salt." •

[124] Donahoe, *Early Christian Hymns*, p. 107: "Well art thou called the Paraclete, / Thy mercies comfort and condole, / The fount of life, the love, the heat, / The soothing unction of the soul." • Richard of St. Victor, *De tribus appropriatis Personis in Trinitate* (Migne, *P.L.*, vol. 196, col. 993): ". . . in the Holy Scriptures power is more especially attributed to the Father, wisdom to the Son, love or goodness to the Holy Spirit." •

[125] A similar uncertainty occurs in the "Opusculum autoris ignoti," usually cited as "Rhazis Epistula" (*Art. aurif.*, I, p. 251): "This stone is triangular in its being, quadrangular in its quality." • Also in the *Carmina Heliodori*, p. 57 (Carmen 4, verse 260), where the stone is called a "triple bulwark" formed from spirit, soul and body, and a "fortress joined by the four elements." In *Alch. grecs*, I, vi, 3, the lapis is likened to a dragon with four feet (elements) and three ears (vapours). Vacillation between three and four is occasionally found in patristic literature, e.g., Ephraem Syrus, who compares the ecclesiastical oil to the river Eden and says (II, col. 790) that the river had four names and four prophets (the four evangelists), whereas the oil had three names (= trumpets of baptism).

a triad, but the traditional "rota" or circulatory process in alchemy, to which Alphidius is referring, was always performed with the *four* elements, so that the author or a copyist slipped up at this point, and the text is so corrupt that it is hardly possible to reconstruct the original version. Once again the cold, black earth becomes a "stone of scandal" which the Paris version tries to get round by wafting a "glorified earth" up to the realm of the spirit.

399 On this saith Rasis, that a certain purification of things precedeth the work of perfect preparation, which by some is called administration or cleansing, by others rectification, and by some it is called washing or separation. For the Spirit himself, who is sevenfold in his operation, separateth the purer parts from the impure, that the impure parts being cast away, the work may be fulfilled with the pure. And this fifth virtue doth Hermes refer to in his *Secret*, when he saith: Thou shalt separate the earth from the fire, the subtle from the dense gently.

400 The Rhazis quotation shows that the procedures described in this parable, as also in the preceding ones, are still concerned with washing and purification, but the text stresses that these purifications are for the purpose of separating the dense from the subtle. In psychological terms this would be the laborious process of coming to terms with the unconscious and discriminating between its subjective and objective components, whose significance in the individuation process Jung discusses in "The Psychology of the Transference." [126] The wearisome shuttling to and fro between the opposites at this point in the text, or in the psychic process it describes, is not without meaning. If we look back at the events in the previous three parables, we find each time a description of an initial darkness and state of distress (flood, imprisonment, etc.), and then a sudden, momentary swing-over to an ecstatic state of bliss. In this parable, on the other hand, a shuttling movement begins in which the dark is worked upon by the light; and not just *one* swing-over is described, but a gradual illumination and sublimation of the dark element by the repeated operations of the Spirit. It is no accident that this sets in with the credo cited at the beginning of the parable; the collective, conscious religious values and

126 Pars. 502ff.

contents are included in the process and an attempt is made to build up a firm standpoint within the theatre of warring opposites. Nor is the darkness merely "suffered" any more, it is being worked through. The only odd thing is that the struggle is really between two suprapersonal forces, the Holy Spirit and the dark earth, while the author seems to have been banished from the process and to be present only as a spectator.

401 In the sixth place he exalteth the lowly, when he bringeth to the surface the soul deep and hidden in the bowels of the earth, of which saith the Prophet: Who bringeth out them that were bound in his strength. Again: Thou hast delivered my soul out of the lower hell. And Isaias: The Spirit of the Lord lifted me up. And the philosophers: Whosoever shall make the hidden manifest knoweth the whole work, and he who knoweth our cambar [127] (i.e., fire), he is our philosopher.

402 The process of discrimination initiated by the Holy Spirit has the effect of liberating the soul from the bowels of the earth, where she had been languishing—an event which the author compares with the state of exaltation induced by the Spirit of the Lord.[128] The unconscious, hitherto projected into matter, gradually becomes apprehensible to consciousness and is felt as an inner reality that "inspires" new contents. The lifting up of the soul signifies at the same time her deliverance from the lower hell and is described as a display of colours.[129] The psychological significance of this display as the transition stage between the *nigredo* and the *albedo* is discussed in Jung.[130]

403 Morienus: He who shall raise up his soul, shall see its colours. And Alphidius: If this vapour shall not ascend, thou shalt have nothing from it, because through it and with it and in it all the work is done.

404 The Alphidius quotation describes the soul as a vapour,[131]

---

127 Cinnabar.   128 Isa. 61 : 1.

129 Cf. Synesios in *Alch. grecs*, II, iii, 13–14, and *Turba*, p. 123: "When this stone is broken, various colours will appear before you." • Tincturing with the "invariable colour" is the goal of the opus (pp. 123, 141). "Moisten it, until God extract the colours for you and they appear" (p. 136). • Senior, *De chemia*, p. 82: "And when the colours or tinctures shall appear, it will be as when the . . . little chick appears." •   130 *Mysterium*, pp. 285ff.

131 For the antiquity of this idea cf. the saying of Maria Prophetissa in Olympiodorus (*Alch. grecs*, II, iv, 40): "Unless everything is sublimed by the fire and the spiritualized vapour is carried up, the process will not go forward." •

and the allusion to Romans 11 : 36 ("of him, and in him, and by him, are all things") equates this vapour with the Holy Spirit. The Holy Spirit, therefore, is simultaneously *the actor and the acted-upon*, the producer and the product, as Wisdom was before; he is the equivalent of the alchemical uroboros. In Morienus [132] and in the *Turba* the vapour is the "soul of the metals" or the soul herself; it is the "life-breath" of man and all creatures,[133] and "thus our work . . . is nothing but vapour and water." [134] Psychologically it is still a question of "raising" the contents of the unconscious to consciousness and understanding them in a spiritual sense.

405   In the seventh and last place he inspireth, when by his breathing he maketh the earthly body spiritual, of which it is sung: Thou by thy breathing makest men to be spiritual. Solomon: The Spirit of the Lord hath filled the whole world. And the Prophet: And all the power of them by the spirit of his mouth.

406   The description of the seventh virtue makes it clear that the Spirit represents the active and passive arcane substance (the psyche itself as the substrate of consciousness and the unconscious): he spiritualizes the earthly body by breathing into it ("inspirat"), and this breathing is none other than the Spirit of the Lord which fills the whole world [135] and "inspired" enlightenment into men at Pentecost. What is described here is, both psychologically and alchemically, a process of sublimation which takes place in the psyche itself without the interference of the ego. In a state of "inspired" understanding the author experiences the dwindling importance of earthly things, and, by his growing awareness of the self, even the spirit-body antithesis drops away, for the psyche is the link between them.[136]

132 Cited in "Ros. phil., "*Art. aurif.*, II, p. 247.

133 Ibid., p. 154: "Therefore saith the Philosopher, the wind hath carried it in his belly. It is clear therefore that wind is air, and air is life, and life is soul: that is, oil and water." •

134 *Turba*, pp. 142f.: "Then all things become vapour . . . but this and the spirit and the soul the philosophers have called vapour . . . thus our work . . . is nothing but vapour and water." • Cf. pp. 43, 139, 152. Also Wisd. 7 : 25, where Wisdom is called a "vapour of the power of God" (DV; AV: "breath").

135 Wisd. 1 : 7.

136 Cf. "Aquarium sapientum," *Mus. Herm.*, pp. 84f. (Waite, I, p. 78): "It is the Spirit of the Lord who fills the universe, and in the beginning moved upon the face of the waters. They also call it the spirit of truth that is hid in the world,

The author obviously understands this living psychic substrate as the Holy Spirit, with whom his consciousness becomes more and more indistinguishably coalescent.

407 And Rasis in the *Light of Lights:* Heavy things cannot be made to ascend save by alliance with light things, nor can light things be brought down to the depths save by combination with the heavy. And the *Turba:* Make bodies incorporeal and the fixed volatile; but all these things are brought about and fulfilled by our spirit,

408   The Spirit brings about an assimilation of man to God. But, simultaneously and conversely, the higher, heavenly things are made corporeal, that is, are actualized—a process that was hinted at earlier by the reference to the incarnation of God in Christ at the beginning of the parable. The realization of the spirit should probably *not* be understood as a complete inclusion of the common earth—it is, rather, a spiritual realization. Nevertheless it takes place in a particular individual and is no longer just a collective idea. In this individual the self is realized and is then interpreted as the filius philosophorum and Christ.

409 for he alone can make clean that which is conceived of unclean seed. Doth not the Scripture say: Wash yourselves in it and be clean.

410   The earthy darkness is not included, for the spirit helps men on the contrary to rid themselves of the dark stain of original sin.

411 And to Naaman was it said: Go and wash seven times in the Jordan and thou shalt be clean. For there is one baptism for the remission of sins, as the Creed and the Prophet bear witness.

412   As the healing of Naaman shows, the purification is analogous to baptism, the symbolism of which has appeared several times already in the text. The washing of Naaman seven times in the Jordan once more stresses seven as the number of the planets, metals, etc. In ecclesiastical symbolism, on the other hand, the number seven pertains to the doctrine of the sevenfold gifts or functions of the Holy Spirit, and the story of Naaman, as we have said, was regarded as a prefiguration of baptism. Other

---

and cannot be understood without the inspiration of the Holy Spirit. . . . It is found potentially everywhere and in everything, but in all its perfection and fulness only in [this] one thing. In short, it is a spiritual essence which is neither celestial nor infernal, but an aerial, pure, and precious body." •

prefigurations are: [137] the Creation (when the "dry land of faith was divided from the heathen waters"), the Flood, the sacrifice of Isaac, the crossing of the Red Sea, the Song of Isaiah (Isa. 54 : 17–55), the praise of Wisdom (Baruch 3 : 9–37), the valley of dry bones (Ezekiel 37 : 1–14), the paschal lamb (Exod. 12 : 1–13), the conversion of Nineveh (Jonah 3 : 1–10), the Song of Moses (Deut. 31 : 22–30), the fiery furnace (Daniel 3 : 19ff.), the washing of the daughters of Sion (Isa. 4 : 4), cited earlier in *Aurora*, and finally the healing of Naaman (2 Kings 5 : 1ff.), when Naaman dipped himself seven times in the Jordan.[138] The Jordan rises in Mount Lebanon, a name which the Church Fathers interpreted as *candidatio*, "whitening," and so, they said, the Jordan signified the "fount of baptism in which the chosen are made white from the filth of sin." [139] Just as Naaman's leprosy was washed away in the water by the "hidden power" of God, so sin is removed by baptism.[140] The leper was considered an image for the heretic.[141] In alchemy and in the Cabala the story of Naaman was applied to the *leprositas* of the metals.[142] The "Clangor buccinae" [143] says, probably not without reference to *Aurora:* "Our mineral has a dropsical body like Naaman the Syrian . . . wherefore he sought a bath of renewal in the Jordan, that he might be cleansed from his inborn sufferings [or passions: *passionibus*]." [144] In the Arabic

137 Cf. Roman Missal, "Prophecies" read on Easter Eve previously to the simplification of the rite in 1955.

138 Ephraem Syrus, I, col. 6: "The seven purifications of Elisha are a figure of the seven spirits that are cast out by baptism." • Cf. col. 52.

139 Honorius, *Speculum* (Migne, *P.L.*, vol. 172, col. 1099).

140 Ephraem Syrus, I, col. 60: "Elisha consecrated the natural waters, invoking him that is hidden, [and] the leper immersed himself in them, but a hidden power cleansed him. Leprosy is cleansed away in the waters and iniquity in baptism." •

141 Rhabanus Maurus, *Allegoriae in sacram Scripturam* (Migne, *P.L.*, vol. 112, col. 985).

142 Knorr von Rosenroth, *Kabbala denudata*, I, Part 1, p. 151: "[210], which is the number of the word Naaman, that is, of Naeman the Syrian and chief of the army of the king of Aram, 2 Kings 5 : 1, by whom is allegorically understood the matter of the metallic Medicine to be seven times purified in the Jordan, which many students of the metallic art call Gur." •

143 *Art. aurif.*, I, p. 322.

144 For evidence of dependence of this treatise on *Aurora* cf. the Senior quotation, ibid., p. 314. The same idea occurs in "Aquarium sapientum," which was also influenced by *Aurora*. *Mus. Herm.*, p. 122 (Waite, I, p. 106).

Buch der Alaune und Salze [145] it is said that lead is really gold into which a sickness has penetrated, "like as a sickness befalls an unborn child in the womb." And in the *Corpus Hermeticum* the evil in the world is compared with rust (ἰός).[146] In other alchemical allegories the sickness of the material is said to be epilepsy or hydrophobia,[147] or is an "original defect." [148]

413 He that hath ears to hear, let him hear what the spirit of the doctrine saith to the sons of the discipline concerning the virtues of the sevenfold spirit, whereby all the scripture is fulfilled, which the philosophers set forth in these words: Distil seven times and thou hast set it apart from the corrupting humidity.

414 The material is cleansed of its impurity and of original sin by a sevenfold distillation which casts out the "corrupting humidity" or "lethal water." The symbolism of distillation refers psychologically to the realization of unconscious, emotionally charged impulses in the background. When a conglomeration of feeling-toned ideas rises up, it is to begin with something "exceedingly compact" (p. 303)—as the word "complex" itself suggests—a regular "packet" of disquieting contents. But if you penetrate into it with "spiritual understanding," its apparently irreducible qualities are dissolved, and the unconscious, split-off components (the corrupting humidity) evaporate. An understanding of the unconscious thus produces a subtler understanding of psychic processes in general—greater detachment and closer penetration at once. The separation of the dense from the subtle points further to a discrimination between the physical and spiritual components, or between what is visibly going on in the foreground and the subtle meaning lying behind it. The length and intensity of the purifying procedures here described show, indirectly, how dangerous were the inrush of the unconscious and the resulting contamination with its numinous contents, and how hard it will be for the author to recover his inner stability.

[145] Pp. 68–76 and 113.
[146] Tract. 14. Scott. *Hermetica*, I, p. 260.
[147] *Mysterium*, p. 155.
[148] Ripley's *Cantilena*, ibid., p. 276.

X. THE FIFTH PARABLE: OF THE
TREASURE-HOUSE ...

415 The fifth parable takes an important step beyond the liberating, purifying, and distilling procedures described in the first four parables, for it treats "Of the Treasure-House which Wisdom built upon a Rock."

416 Wisdom hath built herself a house, which if any man enter in he shall be saved and find pastures, as the prophet beareth witness: They shall be inebriated with the plenty of thy house, for better is one day in thy courts above thousands.

417 The alchemical basis for this parable is to be found first of all in Senior, who compares the lapis to a house with four walls,[1] and then more particularly in Alphidius. In the eighth chapter of the "Liber Alphidii philosophi"[2] it is said: "I will show thee the place of this stone. . . . Know, my son, that this knowledge is in a certain place and that this place is everywhere. The place is the four elements, and they are four doors, which if thou wouldst know I say firstly that they are four stations, four corners, four ends, and four walls. . . . This is the treasure-house in which are treasured up all the sublime things of science or wisdom or the glorious things which cannot be possessed. . . . The house in which these treasures are is closed with four doors and they are locked with four keys, each door having one. And none can enter this house nor extract anything from it nor find the secret hidden within it unless he knows the key or has it with him or belongs to the servants of the house. Know therefore, my son, that he who knows one key and knows not the rest shall open the doors of the house with his key, but he shall not see the things that are in the

1 *De chemia*, p. 107.
2 Codex Ashmole 1420, Bodleian, fols. 23f.

house, for the house has a surface which stretches far out of sight.[3] Therefore each door must be opened with its own key, until the whole house is filled with light, then anyone may enter and take of the treasure." [4]

418   The Alphidius text goes on to interpret the four keys as the extraction of the water, the softening of the "earthy body" (ore), its saturation and fixation. Each of the four operations leads to the lapis, but *only the combination of all four can reveal its true essence.*

419   These statements seem to point to a psychic process for realizing the self by means of all four functions of consciousness.[5] Naturally this is only one aspect of the process, for the idea of opening the house (self) with four keys can be further related to that remarkable diagram of quaternions which Jung put forward in *Aion* as a model for the inner structure of the self.[6] It refers to certain dynamic processes of transformation *within the self* which lead to a conscious realization of its contents. Jung first shows that these processes take place according to the following formula:

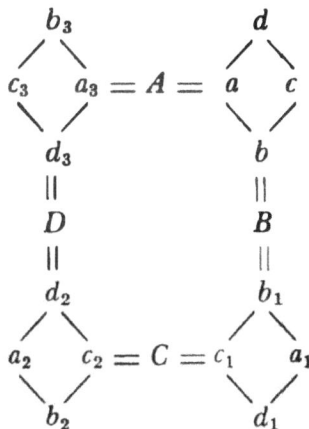

$$
\begin{array}{ccc}
b_3 & & d \\
\diagup\diagdown & & \diagup\diagdown \\
c_3 \quad a_3 = A = & a \quad c \\
\diagdown\diagup & & \diagdown\diagup \\
d_3 & & b \\
\| & & \| \\
D & & B \\
\| & & \| \\
d_2 & & b_1 \\
\diagup\diagdown & & \diagup\diagdown \\
a_2 \quad c_2 = C = c_1 & a_1 \\
\diagdown\diagup & & \diagdown\diagup \\
b_2 & & d_1
\end{array}
$$

[3] "ad infinitum visum tendentem." Or: "leads to endless looking"? The text is corrupt. I read "infinitum" for "infimum."

[4] This passage also occurs in "Cons. coniug.," *Ars chemica*, pp. 108ff.

[5] "The Psychology of the Transference," pars. 488ff. The "superficiem ad infinitum visum tendentem" if the house is opened with only *one* key may refer to the psychological danger of using only *one* function to "unlock" the unconscious. Fascinated by thinking, feeling, intuition, or sensation (fact-collecting), one sees only the "surface" and not the whole house by an inner "fixation."

[6] P. 259; see also pp. 231ff., 247f.

420 He then continues: "The formula repeats the ancient alchemical tetrameria which is implicit in the fourfold structure of

unity: $A = a$ $\begin{array}{c} d \\ \diagup \diagdown \\ \qquad c. \\ \diagdown \diagup \\ b \end{array}$ What the formula can only hint at, however,

is the higher plane that is reached through the process of transformation and integration. The 'sublimination' or progress or qualitative change consists in an unfolding of totality into four parts four times, which means nothing less than its becoming conscious. When psychic contents are split up into four aspects, it means that they have been subjected to discrimination by the four orienting functions of consciousness. Only the production of these four aspects makes a total description possible. The process depicted by our formula changes the originally unconscious totality into a conscious one. The Anthropos A descends from above through his Shadow B into Physis C (= serpent), and, through a kind of crystallization process D (= lapis) that reduces chaos to order, rises again to the original state, which in the meantime has been transformed from an unconscious into a conscious one. Consciousness and understanding arise from discrimination, that is, through analysis (dissolution) followed by synthesis, as stated in symbolical terms by the alchemical dictum: 'Solve et coagula' (dissolve and coagulate)." "The formula presents a symbol of the self, for the self is not just a static quantity or constant form, but is also a dynamic process. . . . The four transformations represent a process of restoration or rejuvenation taking place, as it were, inside the self . . ." [7]

421 As applied to our text, the descent of the Anthropos corresponds to Wisdom's descent to the alchemist. Then follows the phase of imprisonment in Physis through the influence of the shadow (B), which in *Aurora* is represented by the fall into the pit of hell. Phase C, the serpent, is symbolized in *Aurora* by the "woman who brought in death" or by the "corrupting humidity." The fourth phase, D, begins in the present chapter: the crystallization process symbolized by the building of the treasure-house, which represents the coagulation of the lapis.

[7] Pp. 259f.

In Alphidius the fourth stage is also one of fixation, and this is precisely what the parable of the house built on a rock signifies.

422   In our text Wisdom once more appears personified, in accordance with Proverbs 9 : 1–5, on which the whole parable is based, though there is also an allusion to Matthew 7 : 24, concerning the wise man who built his house on a rock. This wise man is the one who not only hears Christ's words but acts upon them—i.e., does not regard Christ's act of redemption passively, as something that has already happened and is sufficient for his own salvation, but himself takes an active part by his own endeavours.

423   The fact that Wisdom—the anima—should appear once again is itself significant, for it is proof that the wearisome operations described in the previous parables have been successful. Through them the author has regained so much stability that he is no longer buffeted about by the opposites, vacillating between despair and ecstasy, but can now confront the anima in person, this time more consciously. Since this state is played out in projection, it seems as if the anima were building herself a house, an indestructible "setting" or temenos in which the author can meet her without falling back into the *nigredo*. In subsequent passages yet another fundamental advance becomes discernible: the anima is no longer the sole and central experience—behind her or in her house something far greater is revealed: the God-image itself.

424   O how blessed are they that dwell in this house; for therein everyone that asketh receiveth and he that seeketh findeth and to him that knocketh it shall be opened. For Wisdom standeth at the door and saith: Behold, I stand at the gate and knock: if any man shall hear my voice and open the door, I will come in to him and he to me, and I will be satisfied with him and he with me.

425   The Biblical treasure-house of Wisdom forms a parallel to the heavenly Jerusalem alluded to in the fifth chapter of *Aurora*, which is a synonym for Wisdom and in patristic literature was identified with the Church.[8] Here it is described as the house

[8] Ephraem Syrus, II, col. 156 (referring to Isa. 54 : 11f.): "Behold, I will make thy stones beryls and will lay thy foundations with sapphires. And I will make thy bulwarks of jasper, and thy gates of stone of crystal. And all who have departed out of my hands shall enter into thee. These things are spiritual and belong today to the Church and heretofore were figured by the precious things of the earth." •

and courts of the Lord (Psalm 35 : 9, 83 : 5, 11), and is equated with Christ as the "door" to salvation (John 10 : 9).[9] Honorius of Autun [10] interpreted Wisdom building herself a house as a prefiguration of Christ: "Wisdom, that is, the Lord Jesus Christ, the Son of God, built himself a house, for he created a man in the womb of the Virgin, and took him up into the unity of his Person." [11] The seven pillars of the house of wisdom Honorius interpreted as the seven gifts of the Holy Spirit.[12] Seen from this standpoint, the alchemical *fixatio* can be understood as an incarnation of God, which had already been alluded to in the previous parable. Also, in *Aurora* as in Honorius, Wisdom is identified with the Holy Spirit. The fixation or incarnation of the spiritual content can be conceived psychologically as an actualization of the archetype of the self. For the self, the centre and totality of the psyche, is only potentially existent so long as it is not perceived by consciousness. But in this phase of development the inner experience of the self becomes "consolidated." Nevertheless, it should be noted that the fixation takes place somewhere in the "beyond," i.e., in the unconscious (as Alphidius says: "in a certain place which is everywhere"); for the treasure-house of Wisdom, like the heavenly Jerusalem and the courts of the Lord, is not of this world.

426   If we try to understand the text psychologically, we find ourselves confronted with a strangely paradoxical situation. On the one hand a realization of the self seems to have taken place, on the other hand the human ego seems to have been in large measure extinguished, so that a genuine, conscious realization of the self is scarcely possible. We must therefore suppose that there was an *intuitive* realization of the self in a delirious or trance-like state, as is in fact suggested by the style of the text. The ego would then have gone a long way towards the infinity of the self, and the self a long way towards man ("I will come in to him and he to me").

[9] Matt. 7 : 7, "Ask, and it shall be given you," etc. is cited also by Christianos (*Alch. grecs*, VI, i, 4).

[10] *Quaest. et Resp. in Prov. et Eccl.* (Migne, *P.L.*, vol. 172, cols. 316ff.).

[11] "Biblia Mariana" (Borgnet, XXXVII, p. 388): "[Mary] is the house and wardrobe from which the Son of God was clothed with flesh." * She is also the "house of all renovation and restoration" (p. 411), and the "ark of salvation" (p. 366).

[12] Cf. also Alcuin, *Grammatica* (Migne, *P.L.*, vol. 101, col. 853), and John the Deacon, *Life of St. Gregory*, 2, 13 (Migne, *P.L.*, vol. 75, col. 92).

427   Wisdom prepares a love-feast for the man who enters her house. Apocalypse 3 : 20, "If any man shall hear my voice and open to me the door, I will come in to him and sup with him, and he with me," was interpreted as an allusion to the Eucharist, which was a *pharmacum vitae* and was called by Ephraem Syrus a "ferment" or "cup of life." [13] In *Aurora* this supper is identical with the "living fount" mentioned later on.

428   O how great is the multitude of thy sweetness which thou hast hidden for them that enter this house; which eye hath not seen nor ear heard, neither hath it entered into the heart of man. To them that unlock this house shall be befitting holiness and also length of days,

429   These images give expression to the hope for a life after death. In consequence of the relative timelessness and non-spatiality of the archetype, the experience of the self does indeed bring with it a sense of immortality.[14] This passage, too, seems to me to confirm that the text was composed when the author was in a semi-conscious, rapturous state—perhaps a state near to death.

430   so that face to face and eye to eye they shall look upon all the brightness of the sun and moon; [15]

431   Here the figure of Wisdom appears as God himself. The previous reference to I Corinthians 2 : 9, "Eye hath not seen nor ear heard, neither has it entered into the heart of man, what things God has prepared for those who love him," and the four-and-twenty elders mentioned later (p. 327), who in the Apocalypse fell down before the Lamb, show that a symbol of the highest numinosity is revealed in the midst of the treasure-house.[16] In our text, significantly enough, it is not actually God that is seen but "all the brightness of the sun and moon," by which must be meant the mystery of their conjunction. It may

---

13 Ephraem Syrus, I, cols. 390 and 340: "Through his wine is union made." •
14 "The Psychology of the Transference," par. 531.
15 In the *Aurora* text this passage comes later, at p. 327 (supra, p. 105). I have moved it here only in the commentary.
16 Cf. the remarkable parallel in the Gnostic Book of Baruch (Bousset, *Hauptprobleme*, p. 293): "After the neophyte has sworn the oath, he goes in to the good [God] and sees what eye hath not seen nor ear heard . . . and drinks of the living water, and that among them is baptism."

also be a veiled allusion to Apocalypse 21 : 23–24: "And the city had no need of the sun, neither of the moon, to shine in it: for the glory of God did lighten it, and the Lamb is the light thereof. And the nations of them which are saved shall walk in the light of it, and the kings of the earth do bring their glory and honour into it." In the Apocalypse, therefore, the place of the sun and moon is taken by a supernatural light, the Lamb of God.[17] According to St. Thomas the highest heaven, the empyrean, "has light, not condensed so as to emit rays, as the sun does, but of a more subtle nature. Or it may have the brightness of glory which differs from mere natural brightness." [18] Obviously some such supernatural light is meant in *Aurora*. But whereas in the Apocalypse it *takes the place* of the sun and moon, here it is *begotten* by the sun and moon in accordance with the classical alchemical formula. That the lapis arises between the sun and moon is mentioned in the earliest Greek texts. Thus the treatise entitled "The Eight Tombs" [19] says that the lapis is a winged being consisting of the four elements and lying between the sun and moon, and that this is the alabaster egg.[20] Zosimos calls the stone a "Mithraic" mystery,[21] perhaps because Mithras was held to be a mediator who connected the sun with the moon.[22] In classical times it was widely believed that the sun was a symbol of the demiurgic power of God and of the "truth" by which he created the world.[23] It was the cosmic Nous, spreading God's power and goodness through the universe.[24] Psychologically, the sun symbolizes the archetypal foundation of consciousness and of its expansion.

[17] Cf. the ecclesiastical interpretation in Cyril of Alexandria, *In Isaiam Commentarium*, cap. 60, v. 19 (Migne, *P.G.*, vol. 70, cols. 1346f.) and Theodoret of Cyrus, *Interpretatio in Isaiam*, 60, 19 (Migne, *P.G.*, vol. 81, cols. 69, 469). Also Honorius, *Elucidarium* (Migne, *P.L.*, vol. 172, col. 1111): "In the fiery substance [of the sun] therefore understand the Father, in the splendour the Son, in the warmth the Holy Spirit." •

[18] *Summa*, I, q. 66, art. 3 (Eng. edn., I, p. 333). •   [19] *Alch. grecs*, IV, xxxiii, 1.

[20] Cf. also Olympiodorus, ibid., II, iv, 49.   [21] III, ii, 1.

[22] Bousset, p. 120. A similar idea occurs in the Gnostic Bardesanes: the sun and moon are the "father and mother of life," and from them proceeds the "hidden son of life." Mani, too, was the "medius Solis et Lunae."

[23] Scott, *Hermetica*, I, pp. 266, 348, 388, 454 (Stobaeus, 1.41.11), and III, p. 464. Cf. *Das Buch der Alaune und Salze*, p. 64, *Turba*, p. 333, and *Pret. marg. nov.*, p. 119.   [24] Scott, I, pp. 187ff., Reitzenstein, *Erlösungsmysterium*, p. 200 n.

432   The coniunctio of sun and moon as the central mystery of the treasure-house occurs also in Senior's "Epistola Solis ad Lunam crescentem," [25] where it symbolizes a unio mystica of two transcendent powers.

433   So far the parable seems to come closer to the generally accepted Christian views than does the earlier part of the text. The reason for this must be that the author has separated himself from the black earth and has passed into a vision of the world beyond. But here, in this passage, he communicates something portentously new: in the Holy of Holies, which the Christian may hope to enter only after death, he beholds not the Godhead but the mysterium coniunctionis of sun and moon. The "woman" in the Apocalypse is "clothed with the sun, and the moon under her feet" (Apoc. 12 : 1), so that this motif had already been foreshadowed in the earlier appearance of the anima.[26] An authentic parallel to the image in *Aurora* would be the vision of the heavenly Jerusalem "as a bride adorned for her husband" in Apocalypse 21 : 2ff., where the city is described as the "Lamb's wife." The light that emanates from the city "was like unto a stone most precious, even like a jasper stone, clear as crystal" (Apoc. 21 : 11).[27] This recalls the λίθος τιμιώτατος, "most costly stone" of the Greek alchemists. The hierosgamos of opposites in the self represents the climax of the alchemist's endeavours, and has its parallel in the Apocalyptic hierosgamos: "And God shall wipe away all tears from their eyes; and there shall be no more death, neither sorrow, nor crying, neither shall there be any more pain . . ." (Apoc. 21 : 4).[28] In the same place occur the words which must have been of great import to an alchemist: "I will give unto him that is athirst of the fountain of the water of life freely. He that overcometh shall inherit all things; and I will be his God, and he shall be my son" (Apoc. 21 : 6f.).[29]

434   It is as though the author in his vision had anticipated the union of the Mother of God with Christ in the "heavenly bridal chambers," which is now promulgated in the Papal

25 *De chemia*, pp. 7–9.
26 Supra, pp. 213ff.
27 Cf. "Answer to Job," p. 447f., 461ff.
28 Cf. the union of God with the Shekinah in the Cabala (ibid., p. 447).
29 Cf. supra, p. 59 and n. 11.

Encyclical.[30] The significance of this symbol for the whole of Christianity is discussed in Jung's *Answer to Job*.[31] The fact that it appeared in the vision of a man living in the thirteenth century shows that these compensatory and conciliatory tendencies had long been constellated in the collective unconscious. Perhaps we may deduce from this vision that the author was one who had penetrated especially deeply into the problem of opposites in Christianity, so that the unconscious broke through with this uniting symbol. Another important parallel to be mentioned is the coniunctio symbolism in the Cabala.[32] According to the Cabala the Original Man was created male-female after the image of God. The *Zohar* says: "Therefore an image (*diokna*) which does not contain male and female is not a higher image. . . . Come and see, the Holy One, blessed be He, will not set up His tabernacle in a place in which male and female are not united." [33] A similar view is expressed in the description of the union of Tifereth and Malchuth, where Yesod, signifying the phallus, effects spiritual procreation.[34] Malchuth is compared also to a "watered garden" (after Isa.

30 *The Assumption of Our Blessed Lady: Munificentissimus Deus*, quoting St. John Damascene, *Homilia II in Dormitionem BMV*, 14 (Migne, *P.G.*, vol. 96, col. 742): "The Bride whom the Father had espoused had to abide in the heavenly bridal chambers." "The intimate union of Mary with her Son." "Similarly, in their treatment of the subject, they describe the Queen triumphantly entering into the royal court and sitting at the right hand of the Divine Redeemer. Again, they adduce the Spouse of the Canticles 'that goeth up by the desert, as a pillar of smoke of aromatical spices, of myrrh and frankincense,' to be adorned with a crown. And these are put forward by the same writers as figures of that heavenly Queen and celestial Spouse who together with the Divine Bridegroom is elevated to the court of heaven." •

31 Pp. 461ff.

32 Hurwitz, "Archetypische Motive in der chassidischen Mystik," pp. 175ff.

33 *Zohar*, I, 55b. Cf. Sperling and Simon, trans., I, p. 177.

34 Hurwitz, "Archetypische Motive," p. 177. The *Idra Suta* says: "But Tifereth is JHWH, whence comes the name JHWH-Zebaoth. The male member is at the extremity of the body and is named Yesod. It is the element [stage] which delights woman." "If therefore only the high priest has permission to enter there [the Holy of Holies] . . . only he may enter that upper place [the Holy of Holies of the Matronita, the upper stage] who is named Love [Chesed, i.e., Tifereth in his Chesed aspect]. When he enters the Holy of Holies the Matronita is delighted, and this Holy of Holies is blest in the place that is named Zion. But Zion and Jerusalem are likewise two stages, one corresponding to Love, the other to stern judgment." Rosenroth, *Kabbala denudata*, II, part I, pp. 593 (sec. 743), 594 (secs. 753f.).

58 : 11), which is a striking reminder of the symbolism of the bride in the last chapter of *Aurora*. Hurwitz interprets these passages to mean that the "generative and creative principle of the unconscious has entered consciousness." [35] In *Aurora* we have the same primordial image of the hierosgamos. The important thing in our text, however, is that this symbol explicitly represents the Godhead.

435   At the sight of the hierosgamos the visionary is seized with a feeling of immortality: he is granted "befitting holiness and also length of days"—obviously because something immutable and eternal has revealed itself to him.

436   for it is founded upon a sure rock, which cannot be split unless it be anointed with the blood of a most fine buck-goat or be smitten three times with the rod of Moses, that waters may flow forth in great abundance, that all the people both men and women drink thereof, and they shall neither hunger nor thirst any more. Whosoever by his science shall open this house shall find therein an unfailing living fount that maketh young, wherein whoever is baptized shall be saved and can no more grow old.

437   Although the unshakability of the rock is praised, the unexpected demand is now made that it should be split by anointing it with the blood of a buck goat or by the rod of Moses, so that the fountain of life shall flow forth. The rock is evidently both the foundation of the house and something found in the house, as well as the house itself. It is the lapis philosophorum. The goat's blood with which it is opened is probably a borrowing from the parable of Marchos in Senior, quoted by Jung; [36] there it signifies the "flowing soul" of the stone, a synonym for the divine water. Picinellus says that the stone Adamas ("unconquerable," "adamant," hence "diamond") could neither be broken by iron nor destroyed by fire. It was "ever the same and ever constant and without flaw." Therefore, he says, it was also an allegory of the soul of Mary. It could be softened only by goat's blood, which signified benevolence, love, and also the "heat of libido." [37] In other texts Adamas symbolizes the morally irreproachable man who could be undone only by "the

[35] Hurwitz, p. 178.
[36] *Mysterium*, pp. 72ff.; Senior, *De chemia*, pp. 78f. In Zosimos (*Alch. grecs*, III, xxv, 3) goat's blood is a synonym for the water and the name of a stone.
[37] Picinellus, *Mundus Symbolicus*, I, p. 677.

goat's blood of lust" (*luxuria*).[38] Goat's blood thus stands for something very like the *concupiscentia* mentioned in the first chapter of *Aurora*. In its dual significance as benevolence and love on the one hand and lust and dissipation on the other it represents an animal and emotional factor in man that has to be included in the process, so that a living effect can stream forth from the "sure rock" of the spiritually stable personality. The unsplit rock and the goat's blood express the paradoxicality of Wisdom (i.e., the unconscious), who confers immutability and vitality at once. There is a similar combination of rock, house, and fountain in Zosimos,[39] who recommends the adept to build a temple from one stone of Prokonnesos marble "without beginning or end." "And in it shall be a fount of purest water and a sunlike light shall flash out. In the fount is the treasure you seek, the metal priest," who is changed to silver and finally to gold. Similarly, the *Carmina Heliodori*[40] say that the lapis is a "light without shadow," a marvellous thing that makes a great golden fountain to gush forth from itself.[41] Again, the *Turba*[42] says that a stone can be made which shines like marble, and from which the "hidden nature" can be extracted, and in the *Buch der Alaune und Salze*[43] Mercurius says that he brings light to substances because he is the living water, the "fount of creatures" (*fons animalium*), and whoever drinks him shall not die for ever.

438   The treasure-house and the fount are found also in the *Corpus Hermeticum,* where in the seventeenth "Treatise to King Ammon" Asclepius says: "You can see that in the earth there gush forth many springs of water and of air in its midmost parts, and that these things, air, water, and earth, are

---

[38] Milo, *De sobrietate*, II, 797–98 (*Poetae Latini aevi Carolini*, ed. Traube, III, p. 668): "He who would be a diamond, let him beware of being tainted with the goat's blood of lust, lest the hammer break him." •

[39] *Alch. grecs*, III, i, 5. Cf. Jung, "The Visions of Zosimos," par. 87, and, concerning the "hieratic house" in Zosimos, *Alch. grecs*, III, xxix, 12.

[40] P. 45.

[41] Cf. Christianos (*Alch. grecs*, IV, i, 2) who says that his teaching is like the fountain of eternally procreative water in the midst of Paradise, and like the sun shining at midday without casting a shadow, and like the moon that illumines the night. Nothing could reach its desired end without the "moisture of the philosophers." Alphidius likewise calls the stone a "light lacking shadow."

[42] P. 145.   [43] Pp. 58f.; cf. p. 91.

found in the same place, being attached to one single root. Hence we believe that the earth is the storehouse of all matter." [44] This source of power is fed by the sun, the universal creative spirit. In the treatise "Asclepius" [45] the house is an image of the hylic man, or body; in it the "divine mind" rests, "fenced in by the body, as it were by a wall." Among the Naassenes the body was the "enclosure" in which the first Adam or Logos dwelt. "This is Adamas, the cornerstone, which is added to the citadel of Zion." [46] According to Simon Magus, man as the microcosm is a "house" which contains the root of the universe, and in this root is sealed and hidden the unbounded fiery power of God.[47]

439   While the alchemical conceptions were drawn partly from late classical images of this kind, it is probable that the author also associated them with patristic symbolism. Thus Honorius of Autun [48] comments on I Corinthians 3 : 17: "The temple of God is holy, and it is within you. O how blessed is he in whom God dwelleth, for as this house is built of four walls, so is the temple of our body made from the four elements." He goes on to say that the sanctuary of this temple [49] is our mind, which thinks spiritual things. The forecourts are the soul, which allows what is necessary to the life of the body to reach it through the senses. The altar of sacrifice is the heart, in which pure thoughts and prayers are offered up to God. The tower is our head, the windows are our eyes, and the images our good works. But the light of the lamp is the *lumen scientiae*. The image of the fount frequently occurs in patristic literature: Christ or his

44 Scott, *Hermetica*, I, pp. 264ff.
45 Ibid., p. 298.
46 Leisegang, *Gnosis*, p. 125.
47 Ibid., p. 68.
48 *Speculum* (Migne, *P.L.*, vol. 172, col. 1105).
49 Cf. *The Zohar* (trans. Sperling and Simon, III, p. 293): "This is a secret entrusted to the keeping of the wise alone, and here is the substance thereof. In the midst of a mighty rock, a most recondite firmament, there is set a Palace which is called the Palace of Love. This is the region wherein the treasures of the King are stored, and all His love-kisses are there. All souls beloved of the Holy One enter into that Palace. And when the King Himself appears, 'Jacob kisses Rachel' (Gen. 29, 11), that is, the Lord discovers each holy soul, and takes each in turn up unto Himself, fondling and caressing her." Cf. in the Cabala the "aedes divitiarum" of the divine name Adonai, whose four letters form the four exits of the rivers of Paradise (Knorr von Rosenroth, *Kabbala denudata*, I, Part 1, p. 32).

body the Church is a fount of life.[50] According to Origen, Christ lives as an "inner rock" in the "kingly inner man," and from this rock the "spiritual senses flow out like living water." [51] These are the "living stones" which Dorn says men must change themselves into. The water from the rock was generally interpreted by the Fathers as knowledge of God, or as the *fons scientiae*.[52] In the Church's view Christ is the rock smitten by the rod of Moses, for just as that rock yielded living water, so water and blood flowed from Christ's side; [53] his body is a "pneumatic rock" from which the water of spirituality flows.[54] Peter, the natural man who accompanied him, became the rock of the Church. Basil interprets the water as the vision of God, which will one day perfectly satisfy our thirst.[55] In *Aurora*, too, it is suggested that nothing less than a vision of God is meant. Gregory of Nyssa calls the mystic who experiences God and the Logos in the depths of his soul a "treasure-house of living water," [56] and St. Ambrose says that the mind of man is the place where the water of the spirit given by Christ gushes up.[57] Ephraem Syrus [58] calls Christ's body a "thesaurarium" from which he gives to the needy heathen. That the author really did have such associations in mind is proved by the reference in the text to Mark 16 : 16, "He that believeth and is baptized shall be saved." Yet, in contrast to the ecclesiastical parallels, there is as we have said an apparent contradiction in the text: on the one hand the treasure-house is founded on a sure rock, on the other the rock must be split so that the saving water can flow out. If an unshakable foundation has been found within, why should it be broken up again? The reason for this is probably—once more—that the "fixation" of the self occurred in an

---

50 Ephraem Syrus, *Hymni et sermones*, II, cols. 130, 790, and 558: "From thee flows life on all sides," and I, col. 166: "Glory to thee, who didst put on the body of mortal man, and made it a fountain of life to all mortals." •

51 *In Numeros hom.*, 12, 2 (Migne, *P.G.*, vol. 12, col. 659).

52 Rahner, "Flumina de ventre Christi," p. 274.

53 Ibid., pp. 278, 385, 390ff.   54 Pp. 372, 377, 379.   55 P. 285.

56 P. 286. Cf. Niklaus von der Flue's vision of the reservoir of water in Lavaud, *La Vie profonde de Nicolas de Flue*, pp. 71 and 73ff., and the image of the tabernacle as the ground of the soul in Meister Eckhart (Evans, I, p. 187), where God eternally gives birth to the son. Cf. also Jundt, *Essai sur le mysticisme spéculatif de Maître Eckhardt*, p. 102.

57 Rahner, pp. 288f. This Nous is also Paradise, where the fourfold river of the Logos rises and waters the whole earth.   58 I, col. 168.

intuitive vision of the world beyond, that is, on a pneumatic plane. Therefore the stone must be softened with goat's blood, because otherwise too much psychic life would be excluded from the process. Certain parts of the personality are, as the next passage shows, not yet integrated. This intuitive vision of the self corresponds to the stage of the *unio mentalis* in Dorn, which has still to be united with the body by means of the art and with the aid of human blood.[59] The goat's blood in our text represents, as it were, the soul of the goat and symbolizes the animal man. The mythological connection of the goat with the Egyptian god Set and the devil, with black magic and the chthonic world, is too well known to need further amplification here. This animal world is the solvent by which the rock, the self, is drawn into a new process of development.

440 Yet, alas, but few open it who are children (*parvuli*) and are as wise as children; but if they who are children shall tell of these things and shall usurp to themselves the seats of the four and twenty elders, doubtless they shall by their dignity and rank open the house, (so that face to face and eye to eye they shall look upon all the brightness of the sun and moon) but without these (elders) they shall not prevail.

441 This passage is textually corrupt, but at least it makes clear that those who enter the treasure-house need the help of the four and twenty elders in order to behold "all the brightness of the sun and moon."

442 As regards the historical position of our text, it should particularly be noted that only the "parvuli" can open the treasure-house with the help of the twenty-four elders. "Parvuli" was the official title of members of the mendicant orders, that is, the Dominicans and Franciscans.[60] Already at the time of Joachim of Flora the chosen ones from the contemplative monastic orders who would build the Ecclesia spiritualis were called "Parvuli." According to him [61] they were the "holy people" of whom God had said: "I will be to him a Father and he shall be to me a son," a saying which also occurs in *Aurora*. The interpretation of "parvuli" as an allusion to the mendicant orders is confirmed by the closing words of *Aurora*, where the

59 *Mysterium*, p. 485.
60 Concordia, V (Hahn, *Geschichte der Ketzer*, III, p. 301).   61 Ibid., p. 300.

chosen are called "the poor," which was another accepted title for these two orders. Since many other points of contact with Joachim's *Concordia* will be revealed in the course of the commentary, it may be assumed on the one hand that the author of *Aurora* was acquainted with his writings, and on the other that he himself was probably a member of one of these orders or at least had close connections with it.

443 For they who have the keys of the kingdom of heaven, whatsoever they shall bind or loose, so shall it be. For these follow the Lamb whithersoever he goeth.

444   The four and twenty elders are now said—like the παρθένοι in the Apocalypse [62]—to follow the Lamb of God and to have the keys that bind and loose (i.e., the power of Peter and the Church).[63] Here this power refers at the same time to the alchemical *solve et coagula*. The image of the twenty-four elders is taken from the Apocalypse, but it is very difficult to determine what they mean alchemically. Part II of *Aurora*, which I regard as a commentary on Part I,[64] interprets them as the "greater humours" (*humores maiores*),[65] and one thinks at once of such pictures as the Ripley "Scrowle," where the gods of the planets and metals are shown pouring liquids into the basin of the arcane substance.[66] There may be an allusion to the "order of the elders" in Senior's "Epistola Solis ad Lunam crescentem," [67] where the moon says to the sun: "We shall be exalted by the spirit when we shall ascend the order of the elders. . . . The lamp of the light will be poured into my lamp, and of thee and of me there will be made a mixture, as of wine and sweet water. . . ." These "elders" are thus assistants at the coniunctio.[68] The word "ascend" (*ascenderimus*) may give a clue to their meaning: they are probably connected with the twenty-four hours of the day, or with the *gradus* (degrees or steps) of the fire, or the πύργοι (divisions) of the sun.[69] Many of the mys-

[62] Apoc. 14 : 4: "These are they which were not defiled with women; for they are virgins."
[63] Matt. 16 : 19.   [64] Supra, p. 5.
[65] *Art. aurif.*, I, p. 123.   [66] *Psychology and Alchemy*, fig. 257.
[67] *De chemia*, pp. 7–9. Cf. Stapleton, "Muhammad bin Umail," p. 149.
[68] Cf. the advice of the "old philosophers" in the *Xenodochium* (hospital) of Dorn ("Spec. phil.," *Theatr. chem.*, I, pp. 256f.).
[69] *Carmina Heliodori*, p. 37.

tery initiations in antiquity were divided into twelve hours. Thus a Mandaean text [70] says that at the "semence de l'homme nouveau" the twelve hours are "douze rois lumineux des transformations successives." [71] These twelve kings are the "signs which symbolize the sun round and complete." Elsewhere they are twelve virgins.[72] In the Mithraic mysteries the celebrant changed his garment (symbolizing his form) twelve times to correspond with the twelve signs of the zodiac,[73] and the twelve hours of day and night played an important role in the Egyptian liturgy for the dead.[74] In some mysteries only the twelve night-hours were considered, in others those of the day as well. In *Aurora* they would be added together, as is obvious since the lapis unites in itself the upper and lower powers. The Cabalistic *sefiroth*, which are shining lights, are called *gradus* in the Latin translations. "And in that light, which is in each step (or degree), is revealed whatever is revealed . . . And therefore all ascend on to one step and all are crowned with one and the same thing. . . . That light which is manifested is called the garment. For the king himself is the innermost Light of all. And all lamps and all lights are lighted by the Most Holy Anointed One." [75] This refers psychologically to the archetypal idea of the personality as a "conglomerate soul." Another such multiple unity is *hiranyagarbha* (golden germ), one of the Indian symbols of the self.[76] Roger Bacon says of Christ: "For Christ is the cornerstone, as being the point in which are gathered together the twelve apostles, and otherwise the twenty-four elders of the Apocalypse; and whosoever would be united to Christ and founded upon Christ must be spiritually of one number or the other." [77]

445   Considered purely arithmetically, 24 can be viewed as $1 \times 2 \times 3 \times 4$, just as 10 represents $1 + 2 + 3 + 4$, and this

---

[70] Reitzenstein, *Erlösungsmysterium*, p. 153.   [71] Ibid., p. 154.

[72] Theodor bar Konai, ibid., p. 156.   [73] P. 168.

[74] Pp. 170f. Cf. pp. 95–98, 155–62, and Moret, *Mystères égyptiens*, pp. 22ff. Also Junker, *Die Stundenwachen in den Osiris-Mysterien*, and the twelve fatherly and twelve motherly angels in the Book of Baruch (Leisegang, *Gnosis*, pp. 170f.). Ephraem Syrus, I, col. 10: "The sun hath overcome, and the number of steps by which he ascended signified a mystery. Lo, it is twelve days since he ascended, and today is the thirteenth, a perfect symbol of the Son and his twelve apostles." *

[75] Knorr von Rosenroth, *Kabbala denudata*, II, Part 1, p. 555.*

[76] *Mysterium*, p. 208.   [77] *Opus tertium* (ed. Brewer), cap. xl, p. 138.*

gives both numbers the significance of a totality. From ancient times 24 was regarded as significant because it was a multiple of 4. Anselm of Laon says of the twenty-four elders: "This [number] is composed of twelve and twelve, and it is also composed of three and four; for the holy preachers announce the name of the holy Trinity through the four quarters of the world."[78] According to the Marcosians, the sum of the letters composing the highest Tetrad[79] gives the number 24. This was also true of the second Tetrad and of the name "Jesus."[80] The *Pistis Sophia* says that Jesus came from the last mystery, the twenty-fourth, and that there were twenty-four "Invisibles" which were emanations of the highest God.[81] We find 24 as a multiple of 4 also in Zosimos. A rather obscure passage says: "From the most general musical lines ABCD twenty-four different lines arise . . . and only with these twenty-four lines can the numberless melodies of hymns be composed . . . including those concerning the sacred knowledge, for instance concerning the solution and dissolution. . . . Herein is found that which has power over the one true material for the genesis of the bird" (bird = lapis).[82] Evidently the twenty-four lines constitute the active and formative principle in matter, and this is in agreement with the contemporary Gnostic speculations about the *stoicheia* (basic elements, letters), which were interpreted as aeons and emanations of light. The twenty-four *stoicheia* were called "symbola," and according to Philo of Alexandria were derived, like the musical signs, from Egypt.[83] Hence, in alchemy, the stars were considered to be the twenty-four letters of a golden alphabet in the heavens, the "heavenly crown" which unites all things.[84]

---

[78] *Enarr. in Apoc.*, cap. IV (Migne, *P.L.*, vol. 162, col. 1517).•

[79] Arrhetos, Sige, Pater, Aletheia.

[80] Leisegang, *Gnosis*, p. 336.

[81] Ibid., pp. 351 and 360ff.

[82] *Alch. grecs*, III, xliv, 1.

[83] "On the Life of Moses" (Loeb edn.), VI, pp. 286f. Cf. Scott, *Hermetica*, III, p. 490.

[84] According to Mennens ("Aureum vellus," *Theatr. chem.*, V, p. 329), the heavens are a parchment, and the inscription on it is the stars. "And the said alphabet or heavenly crown, although it includes various causes of things, yet are they closely conjoined, and conspire together for one species of man and the production of those things which are for his use." •

446   These amplifications enable us to understand the twenty-four elders as elements or powers which work together in the coniunctio and are synthesized into a whole, a motif whose psychological significance is discussed in Jung.[85]

447   But the beauty of this house cannot be told; its walls and streets are of the purest gold, and its gates gleam with pearls and precious stones, and its cornerstones are fourteen, containing the principal virtues of the whole foundation.

448   In our text the treasure-house of Wisdom is built upon fourteen pillars, whereas in Proverbs 9 : 1 it is "hewn out of seven pillars"—no doubt as a reflection of the cosmos with its seven planetary spheres.[86] The heavenly Jerusalem, with which the treasure-house is implicitly compared, stands upon twelve foundations (Apoc. 21 : 14ff.).[87] The number 14 in our text may be regarded as a doubling of 7 or as the sum of 4 and 10 (both, as we have seen, significant numbers). It signifies the "helpers in need"[88] and is the number into which the forbears of Jesus were grouped.[89] This grouping may have been influenced by the ancient Egyptian idea that the Pharaoh had fourteen ancestors or ka's.[90] Remarkably enough, in some texts the fourteen ka's are described as the moral and physical attributes of the Pharaoh,[91] just as "virtues" are attributed to the fourteen cornerstones in Aurora. In Arabic legend Adam had fourteen children—seven pairs of twins who were the "parents of the world."[92] According to Boehme, the number 14 symbolizes

85 Mysterium, "The Journey through the Planetary Houses," pp. 224ff.

86 Reitzenstein, Erlösungsmysterium, § 4: "The Eternal City."

87 Boll (Aus der Offenbarung Johannis, p. 23) interprets them as the twelve signs of the zodiac. Cf. the twelve or fourteen privileges of Mary in Albertus, "Mariale" (Borgnet, XXXVII, p. 239).

88 Type of saint in Catholic folklore.

89 Matt. 1 : 17: "So all the generations from Abraham to David are fourteen generations; and from David until the carrying away into Babylon are fourteen generations; and from the carrying away into Babylon unto Christ are fourteen generations." Cf. Joachim of Flora, Concordia, V (Hahn, III, p. 307).

90 Jacobsohn, Die dogmatische Stellung des Königs in der Theologie der alten Aegypter, pp. 32 and 67.

91 Moret, Mystères égyptiens, p. 209. The ka's are strength, light, intelligence, sight, hearing, wealth, etc.

92 "Le Livre d'Hermès," MS No. 2578 Paris, cited in Blochet, "Études sur le gnosticisme musulman," p. 73.

the Holy Ghost as manifested in the "Liberty" and unconsciously in nature.[93]

449   In the text, the fourteen cornerstones represent the virtues
required of the alchemist if Wisdom is to build her house. Her
house is accordingly the lapis in Senior's sense of a microcosm; [94]
hence the lapis symbolizes the inner structure of the alchemist
himself.[95] Moreover, in many places the cornerstones are described as if each one stood for the *whole* lapis; they are in fact
only single aspects of one and the same thing.

450   The first is health, of which the Prophet: Who healeth the broken
in heart and bindeth up their bruises, and the philosophers: He
who useth it preserveth manhood in full vigour of body. The second
is humility, whereof it is written: Because he hath regarded the humility of his handmaid, for behold from henceforth all generations
shall call me blessed. And the Prophet: The Lord setteth up them
that are cast down. And Aristotle to Alexander: With this stone
it is not good to fight. Alphidius saith: If he shall be humble, his
wisdom shall be perfected. The third is holiness, of which the
Prophet: With the holy thou shalt be holy. And again: Holiness
and magnificence are in his sanctuary. And Alphidius: Know, that
thou canst not have this science, unless thou shalt purify thy mind
before God, that is, wipe away all corruption from thy heart. And
the *Turba:* I have put pleasures aside and prayed to God, that he
would show me the pure water, which I know to be pure vinegar.
The fourth is chastity, of which it is written: Whom when I love
I am pure, when I touch I am chaste; whose mother is a virgin and
whose father hath not cohabited with her, for he is fed upon virgin's
milk. Wherefore Avicenna saith in the *Mineralia:* Certain learned
ones use a water, which is called virgin's milk. The fifth is virtue, of
which it is said: Virtue adorneth the soul. And Hermes: And it
receiveth the virtue of the upper and lower planets and by its virtue

[93] Allendy, *Le Symbolisme des nombres*, p. 361, who also gives the literature on
the number 14. Always the time element is of significance here. Cf. Agrippa von
Nettesheim's view that Christ was sacrificed on the fourteenth day of the moon
(*De philosophia occulta*, II, 15, fol. m ii^v).

[94] *De chemia*, pp. 25 and 83.

[95] Cf. the ecclesiastical interpretation of the twelve cornerstones or precious
stones of the heavenly Jerusalem as virtues, e.g., steadfastness of faith, simplicity
of heart, unquestioning faith, humility, chastity, etc. Cf. Anselm of Laon, *Enarr.
in Apoc.*, XXI (Migne, *P.L.*, vol. 162, cols. 1579–82), who comments on a hymn
entitled "Cives coelestis patriae," by Marbod of Rennes (d. 1125), cited in Neale,
Collected Hymns, p. 28.

penetrateth every solid thing. And in the *Book of the Quintessence* it is said: For I could not wonder enough at the great virtue of the thing, which is bestowed upon and infused into it from heaven.

451   No detailed commentary is needed here. The first and second cornerstones represent health and humility, two virtues which are often demanded as prerequisites of the opus.[96] The third is holiness, defined by Alphidius as purity of mind before God, and by the *Turba* as an ascetic way of life, for only so can one find the "pure vinegar," i.e., the divine water.[97] The fourth, the stone of chastity, is amplified by the well-known alchemical saying, "Whose mother is a virgin," and by a reference to virgin's milk,[98] known already in Greek alchemy.[99] The prima materia was considered to be a virgin who bore the filius philosophorum from her finest substance. Virgin's milk occurs also in a hymn of Ephraem Syrus,[100] which says: "Let the earth praise him [Christ], who with her waters nourishes the fruits and adores the sun, and looks upon the pure child who sucks the virgin's milk." It is probable that the author of *Aurora* was here

---

[96] "Ros. phil.," *Art. aurif.*, II, p. 147: "[The alchemist] should drive far from himself the vice of arrogance and be pious. . . . But the son of the doctrine should be a man adorned with a most subtle mind . . . clear-headed, firm, and constant in his purpose." •

[97] Cf. the chapter on "The Bitterness" in *Mysterium*, pp. 192ff.

[98] Senior, *De chemia*, p. 19; "Rosinus ad Sarrat.," *Art. aurif.*, I, p. 198; Ruska, "Al-Razis Buch Geheimnis der Geheimnisse," p. 67.

[99] *Alch. grecs*, V, ii, 4, and I, iii, 11. The prima materia was considered to be virginal, and the distilling vessel had breastlike openings from which the distillate was poured. (Cf. Synesios, the dialogue with Dioscurus on Democritus, ibid., II, iii, 6.) Cf. the Stephanos quotation in *Carmina Heliodori*, I, p. 32, verses 189–90: "From the sea there rises . . . the shining milk of a bridal virgin, to feed the newborn child." Zosimos (*Alch. grecs*, III, xliii, 6) says that others named the divine water the "water of the amalgam" (μαξυγίου). "But the amalgam is the ore . . . others derive it from the vessel (φάνος), which has breasts." (Cf. also Zosimos, "On Vapours," ibid., III, lvi, 4; IV, vii, 1: "with breast-shaped apparatus," Lippmann, I, pp. 97f.) Since the prima materia was often praised as virginal because it was untouched and unformed, a formless "arche" and hypostasis, the divine water that issued from it was called the "untouched water" or "virgin's milk." The idea that the *filius philosophorum* was the son of the "virginal pneuma" was current in ancient alchemy. Thus the idea (derived from the Eleusinian mysteries) lingered on among the Naassenes of a son of a virgin who was not psychic and not somatic, but the "aeon of aeons" (Hippolytus, *Elenchos*, V, 8, and Scott, III, p. 189).

[100] "Hymnus in Festum Epiphaniae," II, 12, vol. I, col. 18.

making a conscious allusion to the virgin's son [101] in order to emphasize the Christ-lapis parallel.[102] The fifth stone is virtue, which here has the double connotation of moral virtue and power, more particularly the power of penetration. In Komarios the end-result of the opus is described as a "murderous" medicine which penetrates all bodies.[103] Mercurius, as *spiritus mundus,* pure spirit, penetrates, quickens, illuminates and transforms all things.[104]

452 The sixth is victory, whereof Hermes: And it [the stone] shall be victorious over every solid thing and precious stone. And John in the Apocalypse: To him that overcometh I will give the subtle hidden manna and a new name which the mouth of the Lord hath named. And in the *Book of the Quintessence:* But when the stone of victory shall have been wrought, I shall teach how to make with the stone of that material emeralds, jaspers, and true chrysolites, which in colour, substance, and virtue excel and surpass the natural.

453 The sixth stone is the "hidden manna," the "white pebble upon which a new name is written" (Apoc. 2 : 17)—a statement which makes it plainer than ever that this stone has to do with the innermost nature of man. In his commentary on the Apocalypse Albertus Magnus interpreted the hidden manna as the Holy Spirit because of its sweetness, and as Christ because of its fortifying power; but the white pebble (*calculus*) signified "eternal contemplation" or the glorified body. "Because of its whiteness it is called clarity; of its solidity, impassibility; of its moderation, subtlety; of its roundness, agility." [105] Elsewhere he

---

101 Bonus, *Pret. marg. nov.,* p. 40: "They judged that God must become one with man, and this came to pass in Jesus Christ and his virgin Mother, and God has revealed it as a wondrous example to the philosophers in this stone."

102 *Psychology and Alchemy,* pars. 447ff.

103 *Alch. grecs,* IV, xx, 17. Cf. supra, p. 266, concerning the penetrative power of the glorified body.

104 Ruska, *Buch der Alaune und Salze,* pp. 58f. This idea, which seems to have influenced the Arabic alchemists, might be compared with the "perfect nature" of the Manichaeans, who regarded the "perfect body" as the source of revelation and as the "original nature" or "original self." (The Aramaic word *quōmā* means person, matter, body and self at once.) It functions also as the "daemon" or "familiar spirit" in man. (Reitzenstein, *Erlösungsmysterium,* pp. 75f., 112f. Cf. the Arabic "Book of Hermes," ca. 8th cent., there mentioned, which contains the same idea.)

105 Borgnet, XXXVIII, pp. 516f. •

comments: " 'I will give unto him a pebble,' that is, Christ, who is figured by the pebble, for the pebble is a precious stone, which is called carbuncle, and it takes this name from charcoal, taking a likeness therefrom: for it shines when placed in the dark. So did Christ shine forth in the darkness of this world, when 'the Word was made flesh and dwelt among us.' " [106]

454   The psychological significance of the lapis comes out even more plainly in the description of the next four cornerstones: faith, hope,[107] charity,[108] and goodness. These four are the principal Christian virtues and they are also required for the alchemical opus. By his paraphrase of Job 2 : 4, "All that a man hath will he give for his soul, that is, for this stone," the author himself clearly states that the lapis is *man's soul in the sense that it is his life,* his breath or life-principle.

455   The seventh is faith, of which we read: Faith saveth a man, and he who hath it not, cannot be saved. Faith is to understand what thou seest not. And the *Turba:* It is invisible like unto the soul in man's body. And in the same it is said: Two things are seen, namely water and earth, but two are not seen, namely air and fire. And Paul: Whosoever believeth therein shall not be confounded, for to them that believe not the stone is a stumbling stone and a rock of scandal. And the Gospel: He that believeth not is already judged. The eighth is hope, whereof it is said: Firm hope maketh the work glad, hope always promiseth a good end. And Morienus: Hope and hope, and so shalt thou attain [the goal]. And the Prophet: Hope in him all ye congregation of people, in him have our fathers hoped and they were delivered. The ninth is charity, of which the Apostle: Charity beareth all things, Charity dealeth not perversely. And the Evangelist: I love them that love me. He is a friend that loveth at all times. And King Alphonsus: This is a true friend, who deserteth thee not when all the world faileth thee. And Gregory: The proof of love is the display of the work. And Job: All that a man hath will he give for his soul, that is for this stone. For he who soweth sparingly shall also reap sparingly; and he who is not a partaker of the sufferings shall not be of the consolation. The tenth is goodness, of which it is said: Knowest thou not that the goodness (of God) leadeth thee to penance? Good is the judge, to render to every man

[106] Ibid. •

[107] *Summa*, I–II, q. 62, art. 3 ad 2 (Eng. edn., I, p. 853): "Faith is of things unseen, and hope, of things not possessed." •

[108] Cf. Albertus, in Borgnet, XXXVIII, p. 498: "Charity, which is compared to gold because of its worth, colour, and preciousness." •

according to his works. For goodness returneth good for evil, much for little, but good nature returneth good for good, little for little.

456   An allegorical style predominates throughout this part of the text, as if the author were consciously trying to face up to the moral aspect of the opus. Once again his conscious reflections come to the fore. The next stone is patience, a virtue repeatedly described by the alchemists. This is followed by temperance, and it is interesting to see how its psychological aspects gradually merge with the chemical processes in the retort. First it is a question of preserving the health of the soul in the human body, and then of combining the substances in the vessel. This part of the text demonstrates very clearly the peculiar way in which intrapsychic and chemical processes run side by side and coalesce in the opus.

457   The eleventh is patience, of which it is said: If thou wilt conquer, learn to suffer [be patient]. And the Apostle: Through patience and comfort of the Scriptures we may have hope. And Morienus: He who hath not patience, let him hold back his hand from the work. And Calet the Less: Three things are necessary, namely patience, deliberation, and skill with the instruments. And the Apostle: Be you patient, for the coming of the Lord is at hand. The twelfth is temperance, of which it is written, that it nourisheth and cherisheth all things and keepeth them in health. For as long as the elements are in temperance, the soul delighteth in the body, but when they are in discord, the soul abhorreth to dwell in it. For temperance is a mixture of the elements one with another, such that the warm is tempered with the cold, the dry with the humid; and the philosophers have been most careful to insist that one may not exceed another, saying: Beware lest the secret escape, beware lest the vinegar be changed into smoke, beware lest ye put to flight the king and his consort with too much fire, beware of all that is beyond the mean, but place it on the fire of corruption, that is of temperance, until they are joined of their own accord.

458   The next stone, spiritual discipline or understanding, is particularly significant as it brings about an intrapsychic conversion or renewal. This is the "subtle" understanding so frequently stipulated by the texts [109] in order that the adept should not come to grief through a concretistic misunderstanding of the symbols. Similarly, in Joachim of Flora's doctrine of the

109 Supra, p. 333, n. 96.

three ages, it is stressed that in the third age, that of the Holy Spirit, the "subtler mysteries" would be understood.[110] He speaks repeatedly in his *Concordia* of the spiritual and mystic understanding of the Bible which the Holy Spirit will inspire,[111] and he himself tried to interpret it symbolically. This spiritual understanding is particularly the concern of monks.[112]

459   The thirteenth is spiritual discipline or understanding, of which the Apostle: The letter killeth, but the spirit quickeneth. Be renewed in the spirit of your mind and put on the new man, that is, a subtle understanding. If ye understand in the spirit, ye shall also know the spirit. Let every one of you prove his own work, whether it be perfect or defective. For what things a man shall sow, those also shall he reap. O how many understand not the sayings of the wise; these have perished because of their foolishness, for they lacked spiritual understanding and found nothing but toil. The fourteenth stone is obedience, of which it is written: Obey your superiors, as Christ was made obedient to the Father even unto death. So obey the precepts and sayings of the wise, then all things promised by them will obey you and come to fruition, God the Lord willing.

460   The last stone, obedience, signifies submission to the will of God—or, psychologically, renunciation of the ego-attitude and subordination to the self.

461   He that hath ears to hear, let him hear what the spirit of the doctrine saith to the sons of the discipline concerning the house which Wisdom hath founded on fourteen cornerstones, which the four and twenty elders open with the keys of the kingdom of heaven, and of which Senior in the prologue of his book declared: Where he placed the eagle on the roof and the images of the various properties on the sides. And Alphidius in his book speaketh of the treasure-house, which he teacheth can be opened by four keys, which are the four elements.

462   The conclusion of the parable refers to Senior and Alphidius as the two main sources used by the author. It also shows that the fourteen cornerstones of the treasure-house all represent the one lapis in its different aspects. The twenty-four elders, like the eagle, symbolize the volatile substance. The author sees the

110 Hahn, *Geschichte der Ketzer*, III, p. 303.

111 Ibid., p. 273.

112 P. 333: ". . . knowing and revering the letter of the Old and New Testament in the patriarchs and apostles, whom they know to be elect, they [monks] cleave to the spiritual understanding which proceeds from both works," etc. •

whole edifice as comparable to the "kingdom of heaven"; in other words, he beholds in an intuitive vision a crystallization of the self in the world beyond.

463   In conclusion we can sum up as follows: in the opening chapters there is manifest a tremendous tension of opposites accompanied by an almost deliriously excited manner of speaking. The mood alternates between ecstatic joy and profound despair—now the ego seems caught in an inflation, now utterly dissolved. The anima (Wisdom) appears contaminated with shadow elements (black earth, Ethiopians, corrupting humidity, etc.), and behind her looms up the dark, vindictive, destructive side of God. Not until the fourth parable is reached does the author succeed, with the help of the reconciling function of the unconscious, in building up a spiritual standpoint and gaining a spiritual understanding of what is going on within him. The opposites no longer alternate, but begin to influence one another reciprocally, and this assists their reconciliation or union in the unconscious. The union of irreconcilables is experienced in the present parable as a visionary reality and is revealed in the form of an authentic God-image. The vision of the hierosgamos in the treasure-house of Wisdom seems, temporarily at least, to have gripped the author's feelings; for whereas in the preceding parable an attempt was made to integrate the irruption of unconscious contents in a spiritual hierarchy, the present parable goes on to describe the author's emotional and moral confrontation with these inner events. The predominance of feeling is reflected in the reappearance of the anima in the figure of Wisdom as contrasted with the Holy Spirit in the preceding parable. The lapis as treasure-house is now represented primarily as the sum of man's moral qualities, the didactic, allegorical style and the disappearance of the poetic element being particularly striking—for one would hardly expect this after so momentous a vision. Obviously the content of the vision has been grasped only intuitively, and closer contact with the experience is still lacking. Nevertheless, the vision seems to have had a calming effect on the author, which caused him to be mindful of his own attitude and of his situation as a human being. This sense of calm and reassurance was no doubt due very largely to the feeling of immortality which the vision gave him.

XI. THE SIXTH PARABLE:
OF HEAVEN AND EARTH ...

⁴⁶⁴ The sixth parable treats "Of Heaven and Earth and the Arrangement of the Elements," and is concerned mainly with an alchemical world-creating process. It revolves round the image of the "earth," which seems to symbolize a feminine divinity. From this earth a new cosmos blossoms forth.[1] The whole

[1] As was evident from the amplifications, the treasure-house of Wisdom was also a reflection of the cosmos, but there the main emphasis fell on the microcosm of the inner man, who in the medieval view was an image of the macrocosm. Cf. Honorius, *Elucidarium*, I, 11 (Migne, *P.L.*, vol. 172, col. 1116): "Thus the bodily man consists of the four elements, for which reason he is named the microcosm, i.e., little world; for from the earth he has his flesh, from the water his blood, from the air his breath, and from the fire his heat. His head is round after the manner of the heavenly sphere, from which his two eyes shine like the two luminaries in the skies. Seven openings adorn him like the seven harmonies of heaven," etc. The same image occurs in the *Hortus deliciarum* of Herrad of Landsberg and in Hildegard of Bingen (Reitzenstein, *Erlösungsmysterium*, pp. 137ff.). Reitzenstein has there unearthed the classical and Persian sources of this idea. Blochet, who particularly emphasizes the Persian influences on the Arabian Gnostics ("Études sur le gnosticisme musulman," pp. 247ff.), cites a Persian MS, "Medjma el-bahrein," by Shems ed-Din, according to which the human heart corresponds to the sun. There is the "house of salvation," a reflection of the heavenly *Ka'aba*, in which the heavenly spirit dwells. The cosmos, like a μέγας ἄνθρωπος, is formed in the image of man. Among other things the author says that the human heart is a coffin in which the soul is imprisoned; it is midway between the tangible and the intangible world. In the beginning God built a city for his khalifs and officers. This city was formed of man's body as well as of the earth and the real world. The foundations of the city rested on the four elements. The heart was the palace of the khalif, who, after the philosophers, was the spokesman of reason. The place he retired to was the brain. But he was also the spirit that dwelt in the heart. The senses were the gates and watchmen of this city. Similar views are expressed by the author of the *Mersad el-ibad:* Man's body corresponds to the earth, his heart to the sky. The heart has two aspects, called by the mystics *dil* and *kolb,* each with seven parts corresponding to the seven heavenly spheres and seven regions of the earth. The heart also corresponds to the throne of Allah, one

parable appears to depict a kind of apocatastasis. We can easily recognize the "earth" as the anima-Wisdom figure of the earlier chapters, but now she is purified and spiritualized. Psychologically considered, the parable is a description of the stage which Dorn calls the production of the *unus mundus* (unitary world), and for further details I must refer the reader to Jung's interpretation of Dorn's text.[2] Here it is sufficient to say that after the self has been experienced as a divine centre within the psyche, this experience expands into a feeling of oneness with the whole cosmos. An Indian parallel would be the dissolution of the individual *atman* in the universal *atman*. Such an experience is so far removed from the ordinary sphere of ego-consciousness that one wonders in what state the author must have been to have found himself so lost to the world and reality.

465 We saw in the commentary to the fourth parable that the earth was the fourth element, which was so difficult to fit into the alchemical trinity. In the meantime, a further alchemical operation has been performed, the *fixatio,* which was the theme of the fifth parable. This was the production of an unshakable inner core, the well-founded treasure-house of the self, the ego appearing only as a "guest," i.e., a marginal phenomenon. The description of this "interior stone" was bound up with a vision of God, and it is psychologically possible that the vision—the hierosgamos of sun and moon—was itself the "rock," that is, an inalienable experience upon which the whole future man is founded. But this rock or "new world" is not just an "inner" reality which adds itself to the "old world"—it is *total reality.* Therefore the author tries in the present chapter to describe this totality and ultimate reality which is the substrate of his experience.

466 He that is of the earth, of the earth he speaketh, he that cometh from heaven is above all. Now here also is the earth represented as the principle of the elements, but the heavens stand for the three higher principles, wherefore a little ought to be said of earth and heaven, for earth is the principle and mother of the other elements,

---

side of which can be touched, but the other side touches the world beyond. Thus one side of the heart is turned towards the world of the body, the other to that of the spirit. Alphidius' description of the mystic treasure-house has affinities with these conceptions.

2 *Mysterium,* pp. 465ff.

467   By "he that cometh from heaven is above all" is probably meant the filius philosophorum, who, according to the *Tabula Smaragdina*, after ascending to heaven descends again to earth, thereby uniting in himself the upper and lower powers. Similarly, heaven and earth unite in our text. In heaven there are the three elements, fire, air, and water; earth forms the fourth. The unsolved problem of the fourth parable—the integration of the fourth element—is taken up again. On closer analysis it is apparent that the earth described here is not simply the fourth element which is added to the other three, but that it possesses the character of a mystical totality. This earth is the *archē* (first principle) in the sense intended by classical philosophy; [3] indeed, in our text it is praised as the "principle and mother of the other elements," a view borne out by the quotation from Psalm 101 : 26 in the next passage, and also by Morienus, Hermes, and Moses. [4]

468   This earth is really identical with Wisdom, who in Proverbs 8 : 22f. is, if not the "mother," then at least God's helper at the work of Creation: [5] "The Lord possessed me in the beginning of his way, before his works of old. I was set up from everlasting, from the beginning, or ever the earth was" (AV). [6] Thomas

[3] Cf. Olympiodorus (*Alch. grecs*, II, iv): "Understand, thou who hast all wisdom, that the earth was not taken for an element by the philosophers because it was not generative. And this hath a meaning in respect of our problem: for Hermes saith somewhere, that the virgin earth is found in the tail of a virgin."

[4] Morienus, "De transmut. metall.," *Art. aurif.*, II, p. 19: "Hermes also saith: Earth is the mother of the elements; from earth they come and to earth they return." • Bonus, *Pret. marg. nov.*, p. 107: "Hermes: The earth is an element, and of earth are all things made, and into earth are they converted. Moses: The earth is the mother of the elements, all things come from earth and are turned again to earth. So doth Morienus say: But this earth is a body and a ferment." •

[5] She is, as it were, the positive counterpart to Tehom or Tiamat.

[6] According to St. Augustine, she is the "art" by which God created the world. Philo interprets this passage as follows: "With His knowledge God had union. . . . And knowledge having received the divine seed . . . bore the only beloved son who is apprehended by the senses, the world which we see." "De ebrietate," 30 (Loeb edn.), III, pp. 334f. Cf. Leisegang, *Gnosis*, p. 95. The idea of two "archai," God and a mother goddess, Hyle, is found in Asclepius Latinus (Scott, *Hermetica*, I, pp. 310ff.): "In the beginning was God and matter" (ὕλη). Hyle is also the cosmos, the *natura mundi* or *spiritus mundi*; she is the matrix of all things and their receptacle, and at the same time the cause of evil. Cf. the teachings of Hermogenes (Tertullian, *Adv. Hermogenem*, 12). Similar views in Numenius (*Comm. in Timaeum*, 294); cf. Scott, III, pp. 68ff., 77, 84, 272, and the related Gnostic ideas of Simon Magus in Leisegang, *Gnosis*, pp. 74, 81, 95.

Aquinas attempted a symbolical interpretation of the passage in Genesis, "And the earth was without form, and void": it was the invisible, only potentially existent prima materia.[7] This may shed light on the statement that earth is the first principle; it is *materia in potentia*, which receives its form from God.

469   as the Prophet beareth witness: In the beginning, O Lord, thou didst found the earth, and the heavens are the works of thy hands, that is, water, air, and fire. For from the earth are the elements separated by dying, and to it do they return by quickening, for what a thing is composed of, into that must it be resolved,

470   Here the author, besides praising the earth as the mysterious *arche* of the cosmos and the basis of all life, introduces a curious new idea: that the founding of the heavens above the earth, or the creation of the world by a sundering of the upper from the lower, is a *death,* and that, in consequence, the dissolution of the world and its return to the undifferentiated *arche* signifies a renewal of life. Strangely inverting the Genesis story, he presents the Creation as a process of destruction, and the destruction of the world as a reunion—not a dissolution, but a fusion with the original unity. At first this is described as a cosmic process, but its intrapsychic, human aspect is revealed in the continuation of the text.

471   The destruction of the world, when the elements return at death to earth, is, psychologically, a symbol for the complete extinction of consciousness, and accordingly it often appears in dreams at the onset of a psychosis. We know from the earlier parables that the author must have been in a state bordering on complete dissociation, in which his conscious world at least was totally disrupted. But, in contrast to a pathological dissolution, the psychic hierarchy seems to have built itself up again out of the chaos, so that the "destruction of the world," or return of the three higher principles ("the heavens" $=$ spiritual sphere of consciousness) to earth (the unconscious) is an individuation process signifying the birth of a new, transcendental cosmos.

472   as the holy word testifieth: Man is ashes and to ashes shall he return. Such ashes did the philosophers ordain to be mixed with the per-

---

[7] *Summa,* I, q. 66, art 1 ad 1 and 3 (Eng. cdn., I, pp. 329f.): "In this respect, then, the earth is said to be void and empty, or invisible and shapeless, that matter is known by means of form. Whereas matter, as such, is essentially being in potentiality." •

manent water, which is the ferment of gold, and their gold is the body, that is the earth, which Aristotle called the coagulant, since it coagulateth water.

473   As the *archē* of all corporeal things, the earth (in the symbolic sense of prima materia) [8] is the basic substance of the human body, as the text indicates when it says, "Man is ashes." "*Such* ashes," it continues significantly, "did the philosophers ordain to be mixed with the permanent water": which amounts to saying that the prima materia is, among other things, the human body. This primary "body-matter" (which the text by a series of equations again shows to be earth) is the "ferment of gold," and is thus a means for "fermenting" and maturing the inner man, but at the same time it is water,[9] the *aqua permanens* of the alchemical opus. Psychologically, we have to do once again with the unconscious in its somatic aspect—with its "actualizing" function.[10] The body can be understood as a symbol of the personality with its individual limits, so that what the text is saying, in symbolic language, is that the individual human being is the maturing-ground and birthplace of a divine inner man, and that the specific qualities of the individual are the sole basis for the whole process of inner development. This is not a contradiction of ecclesiastical doctrine, but it does show a tendency to shift the accent on to a recognition and acknowledgment of the physical man. Jung says of this shift: "What unconscious nature was ultimately aiming at when she produced the image of the lapis can be seen most clearly in the notion that it originated in matter and in man, that it was to be found everywhere, and that its fabrication lay at least potentially within man's reach. These qualities all reveal what were felt to be the defects in the Christ-image at that time: an air too rarefied for human needs, too great a remoteness, a place left vacant in the human heart. Men felt the absence of the 'inner' Christ who belonged to every man. Christ's spirituality was too high and man's naturalness was too low. In the image of

---

8 Cf. the chapter on "The Increatum" in *Psychology and Alchemy*, pars. 430ff. Certain statements in Paracelsus point to a principle coequal with God and corresponding to a *dea mater* (ibid.).

9 In the *Summa*, I, q. 68, art. 2 (Eng. edn., I, p. 340), water is the "matter of bodies."

10 *Mysterium*, pp. 519ff.

Mercurius and the lapis the 'flesh' glorified itself in its own way; it would not transform itself into spirit but, on the contrary, 'fixed' the spirit in stone. . . . This image of the 'Son of the Great World' tells us from what source it was derived: it came not from the conscious mind of the individual man, but from those border regions of the psyche that open out into the mystery of cosmic matter." [11]

474   The "earth" in our text stands for this mystery, and further on the author calls it the "Promised Land," an image that reappears in the next parable and can be regarded as a symbol of the self. At the same time it is fiery and airy, and it receives the gold or the "honoured soul" into itself like seeds.[12] It is evident that this earth or "second body" is something that unites in itself the qualities of all the other elements: [13] it is an airy earth, a fiery water, a fluid fire, etc., and as such it is a mystery known to God alone. In the Cabala it is compared with Malchuth.[14] It could be said to correspond with the primitive conception of the "subtle body."

475   In other alchemical treatises, too, earth or ash is the most precious thing and a great mystery. The *Turba* calls it a "spiritual dust" which turns into water,[15] and to which all bodies must first be pulverized or burnt.[16] In Senior ash is the feminine arcane substance, and in Greek alchemy it was known as the

---

[11] "The Visions of Zosimos," par. 127.

[12] Senior, *De chemia*, p. 25: "The lower world is the body and the burnt ash to which they reduce the honoured soul. And the burnt ash and the soul are the gold of the wise, which they sow in their white earth." • Cf. supra, pp. 122–23.

[13] Cf. "Ros. phil.," in *Art. aurif.*, II, p. 185: Hermes: "Sow your gold in white foliated earth, which by calcination is made fiery, subtle, aerial." • And p. 200: "Sow the soul therefore in white foliated earth, which retaineth it, for when it ascendeth from earth to heaven and again descendeth to earth it shall receive the virtue of the things below and also of the things above . . ." • For the four elements as constituents of man see "Isis to Horus" (Stobaeus, I, 49, 69); Περὶ ἐμψυχώσεως (Scott, I, pp. 514ff.); Philo, "De sacrificiis Abelis et Caini," 33, 107 (Loeb edn.), II, pp. 172f.

[14] Knorr von Rosenroth, *Kabbala denudata*, I, p. 118: "And Malchuth will be the metallic woman, and the Moon of the sages, and the field into which are cast the seeds of the secret ores, namely Water of gold, as this name occurs in Gen. 36 : 39; but know, my son, that in these things are hidden mysteries so great, that no human tongue can tell them." •

[15] P. 143.

[16] P. 139. Cf. p. 159: "How precious is the ash . . . and how precious is that which is made from it. So, mixing the ash with the water, cook it again . . ." •

"ash of Mary" (σκωρίδια καὶ τέρφαι Μαρίας),[17] which plays an important role in the literature. Zosimos cites a saying of Agathodaimon that "the ash is all." [18] It symbolizes that irreducible and indissoluble substrate of physical and psychic facts which everyone has from birth and out of which individuation is accomplished. This absolute endowment is the raw material of an "objective" ego, i.e., the self.[19]

476   It is the earth of the Promised Land, wherein Hermes commanded his son to sow gold, that living rains might ascend from it, and water which warmeth it, as Senior saith: And when they desire to extract this divine water, which is fire, they warm it with their fire, which is water, which they have measured unto the end and have hidden on account of the unwisdom of fools. And of this have all the philosophers sworn, that they would nowhere set it forth clearly in writing, but they have left it to the glorious God, to reveal it to whom he will and withhold it from whom he will, for in him is great cunning and the secrecy of the wise.

477   The secret earth is thus formed by a union of opposites, by a fiery water or watery fire, since in the self all opposites—conscious and unconscious, psyche and physis, and so on—unite.

478   And when the heat of that fire reacheth the earth itself, the earth is dissolved and becometh a boiling, that is an evaporated water, and afterwards returneth to its own former earthly form. Therefore by water is the earth moved and the heavens are poured out upon it, and they flow as if with honey throughout all the world and tell

---

17 *Alch. grecs*, II, iv, 37; cf. II, iv, 48.

18 Ibid., III, lvi, 2. Especially famous in later times was the saying of Morienus ("Rosinus ad Sarrat.," *Art. aurif.*, I, p. 183f.): "Despise not the ash which is at the bottom of the vessel: it is in the lower place, but it is the earth of thy body, and the ash of things that endure." • "Ros. phil." variant: "Despise not the ashes, for they are the diadem of thy heart." • Cf. "Psychology of the Transference," par. 495.

19 Ibid., p. 199: "[Analysis] must be a genuine process of purification where 'all superfluities are consumed in the fire' and the basic facts emerge. Is there anything more fundamental than the realization, 'This is what I am'? It reveals a unity which nevertheless is—or was—a diversity. No longer the earlier ego with its make-believes and artificial contrivances, but another, 'objective' ego, which for this reason is better called the 'self.' No longer a mere selection of suitable fictions, but a string of hard facts, which together make up the cross we all have to carry or the fate we ourselves are." The "ash" is its prima materia, and it is produced by burning the initial material, i.e., by analysis of the conscious and unconscious contents.

its glory. For this glory is known only to him who hath understanding, how of the earth the heavens were made,

479   This passage shows that the secret earth is produced by a circulatory process: [20] after being liquefied by fire and water, it evaporates and "returns to its own former earthly form." The art, as we know, proceeds like a wheel or vortex.[21] Basing himself on the views of Heraclitus and other early Greek philosophers,[22] Zosimos says that the elements have to be transformed "into themselves" (εἰς ἑαυτά), for, although they are different in quality, they are not so in substance (οὐσία); and just as all things arose from the dissolution of the elements, so the art must proceed likewise.[23] Ever since the time of Aristotle the elements had been divided into two upper ones, air and fire, which were active and "psychic," and two lower ones, water and earth, which were passive and "somatic." [24] A similar view is found in the treatise "Asclepius" and in "Isis to Horus" in the *Corpus Hermeticum:* [25] "[Air] enters into earth and water, and fire enters into air. That only which tends upward is life-giving; and that which tends downward is subservient to it. Moreover, all that descends from on high is generative; and that which issues upward from below is nutritive. Earth, which alone stands fast in its own place, receives all that is generative into itself, and renders back all that it has received. . . . The ele-

---

[20] As will become clear infra, pp. 348ff.

[21] "Komarios to Cleopatra" in *Alch. grecs*, IV, xx, 17. Cf. *Psychology and Alchemy*, pars. 468ff., also 212ff.

[22] Freeman, *Ancilla to the Pre-Socratic Philosophers*, p. 29, fragm. 60: "The way up and the way down is one and the same." Diogenes Laertius, 9, 8 (Loeb edn., II, pp. 416f.), explains that this is the way of "change" (μεταβολή) by which the cosmos came into being; for when fire "condenses," it turns into water, and when this solidifies, it turns into earth, and that is the way down; but when earth liquefics, it turns back into water, and so to fire, and that is the way up. Cf. Cleomedes, *De motu circulari corporum caelestium*, 1.11.61 (ed. Ziegler, pp. 110ff.); Philo, "De aeternitate mundi," 21, 109 (Loeb edn., IX, pp. 260f.); Maximus of Tyre, *Dissertations*, 41, 4 (trans. Taylor), II, pp. 219ff.; Iamblichus, Περὶ ψυχῆς in Stobaeus, 1.49.39. In Plato, rotation characterizes the motion of the Logos (*Timaeus*, 39D). Cf. the circular movement of the life-pneuma in "Isis to Horus" (Stobaeus, 1.49.69), Scott, I, p. 522, III, p. 610, IV, p. xxiii.

[23] *Alch. grecs*, III, xliii, 16. Cf. V, ii, 12.

[24] Olympiodorus, ibid., II, iv, 28; *Carmina Heliodori*, pp. 23, 25, 52; Lippmann, I, pp. 99, 147, 259.

[25] Scott, I, pp. 289ff. and 528ff.

ments through which all matter has been indued with form are four in number—fire, water, earth, and air; but matter is one, soul is one, and God is one . . . Matter has been made ready by God beforehand to be the recipient of individual forms of every shape; and nature, fashioning matter in individual forms by means of the four elements, brings into being, up to the height of heaven, all things that will be pleasing in God's sight." Note that the elements here are by their very nature instruments for actualizing God's ideas in matter. This is also the view of Zosimos; he calls them "limbs of the sacred science" or "pure centres." [26]

480 It is evident from these examples that the classical theory of the four elements was largely symbolical and that it really expressed a projected psychic content—the quaternary structure of the self and its reflection in the four-function structure of ego-consciousness. The quaternary structure is inherent both in the starting-point (the preconscious totality) and in the end-product (the actualized totality). Hence the mystic "earth" in the present parable is a product of the *fixatio* (treasure-house of Wisdom) described in the preceding one and, paradoxically, it is also the prima materia; a cosmic *arche* which is the mother of the other elements.[27]

[26] *Alch. grecs*, III, xliv, 1. Cf. VI, xv, 2–3, and Christianos, ibid., VI, x, 1. This explains why in alchemy generally and also in *Aurora* the elements are described in such a paradoxical way: water is "spiritual blood" and fire; air is pneuma, fire, soul, and water; fire is water, and water is earth, ash, or the human body. In Senior (*De chemia*, p. 25) the secret water is of threefold nature, containing in itself water, fire, and air. Air, in its turn, is the "mediator" between fire and water and thus contains both (p. 30); and water is really the fire of the stone or "corporeal air" (p. 19) or "starry earth" (p. 23): *terra stellata*, γῆ ἀστερίτης. Finally, Senior says that the secret is warm water, motionless air, liquefied earth and circumambient fire (p. 33). And from these four elements everything is made (pp. 30–31): "And even as air is warm and moist, so is their [the philosophers'] water warm and moist and is the fire of the stone and the circumambient fire, and the moisture of their water is the water. And when air is cooked for a long time, it turns to fire, since in the form of air it has the action of fire." Air is also the soul or the blood (pp. 44 and 58). St. Thomas thought it possible the elements could change into one another (*Summa*, I, q. 67, art. 3; Eng. edn., I, pp. 335f.).

[27] The text stresses that one must know the secret of creation in order to under-stand this—a reference to the classical view that the lapis must be produced after the manner of the cosmos. Cf. Zosimos, *Alch. grecs*, III, vi, 22, and Pseudo-Aristotle, "De perfecto magisterio," *Theatr. chem.*, III (1659), p. 79: "As this world was created, so is the Stone created."

and therefore the earth remaineth for ever and the heavens are founded upon it, as the Prophet beareth witness: For thou hast founded the earth upon its own bases, it shall not be moved for ever and ever.

481   The preceding passages described a process of sublimation which was compared to the ascent of a "living rain." Afterwards the product—the distillate—drops down to earth again, "the heavens are poured out upon the earth and tell its glory." But this glory is known only to him who knows "how of the earth the heavens were made," in other words, who knows the alchemical process of sublimation which imitates God's cosmogonic work of creation.[28] During this process the earth, as the text now says, forms the everlasting and immovable foundation of the heavens. And just as the earth is dissolved and transformed by the divine fiery water, so in the Bible "the mountains melted like wax at the presence of the Lord" (Psalm 96 : 5). Once again, therefore, a power equal to God's is attributed to the water.

482   The deep is its clothing, above it shall stand water, air, fire, and the birds of the air shall dwell therein, watering it from the upper elements, that it may be filled with the fruit of their works,

483   "The deep is its clothing": it is surrounded by the abyss of ocean, which in antiquity and the Middle Ages was depicted as the uroboros. Above the earth the lighter elements arrange themselves in layers, and, since these elements will return to it again, the process is symbolized by birds watering the earth.[29] In alchemy birds or, in the singular, the swan, goose, dove, raven, etc. symbolize vapours, sublimated volatile substances, hence also spirits, and the birds watering the earth mean the same thing as the previously mentioned distillation of the heavens and the falling rain. In both cases it is the divine water, "which they call the king rising from the earth and descending

---

28 Senior, *De chemia*, p. 106: "But when it is all coagulated, then it is called the Sea of the sages. And this earth is the mother of wonders, and the mother of the heavens . . . and it is all, and from it all is taken." •
29 According to Joachim of Flora, birds are the prophets, who "with their wings fly up to heaven far in advance of all other mortals." *Concordia*, V (Hahn, III, p. 293).

from heaven." [30] In the *Summa,* Thomas Aquinas cites Origen's view that the "waters above the heavens" are "spiritual substances," [31] and this is borne out by our text.

484   The circulatory distillation continues: the waters are sublimated and rise like birds [32] over the earth, which remains below as if dead, then drop down again like living rain or dew.[33] This stage represents the reunion with the body (following the stage of the *unio mentalis,* which is discussed in Jung).[34] The birds watering the earth symbolize the fertilizing effect which the archetypes in their spiritual aspect have upon the reality-bound consciousness of the individual. The meaning of the process comes out in the next passage: the earth receives the powers of the upper elements.[35]

485   because in the centre of the earth the seven planets took root, and left their virtues there, wherefore in the earth is water germinating divers kinds of colours and fruits and producing bread and wine that cheereth the heart of man, and also bringing forth grass for cattle and herb for the service of men.

486   The earth receives the virtues of heaven, and these are nothing other than the planetary powers, discussed earlier, which have now descended into the centre of the earth.[36] The "mountains that melted like wax at the presence of the Lord" are, in the Book of Enoch,[37] mountains made of celestial metal, and

---

30 Senior, p. 17. Cf. the *Tabula Smaragdina:* "He ascends from earth to heaven and again descends to earth, and receives the power of Above and Below. Thus you have the glory of the whole world." •

31 I, q. 68, art. 2 (Eng. edn., I, p. 339).

32 Cf. Senior, p. 122, and the ecclesiastical interpretation of eagles in Ephraem Syrus, I, col. 86: "In the beginning the spirit of fruitfulness brooded over the waters: and they conceived and bore dragons, fishes, birds. The Holy Spirit brooded over the waters of baptism, which bore mystical eagles, namely, virgins and the directors of the Church." •

33 Cf. the return of the soul in "The Psychology of the Transference," par. 497.

34 *Mysterium,* pp. 475ff., 519ff.

35 Cf. the imitation of the upper stars in the lower heaven in Dorn (ibid., p. 478f.).

36 *Summa,* I, q. 67, art. 3 (Eng. edn., I, pp. 335f.): "The light of the heavenly bodies is a cause of the substantial forms of earthly bodies, and also gives to colours their immaterial being, by making them actually visible. Light, then, is not a sensible quality, but rather a substantial or spiritual form . . . so does light act instrumentally, by virtue of the heavenly bodies, towards producing substantial forms." •

37 Charles, *Apocrypha and Pseudepigrapha,* II, p. 204.

in similar manner the precipitating heavens signify that the planets become earthly in the form of metals.[38] It was widely believed in the Middle Ages that the metals were formed in the earth by the "influences" of the planets. Thus, in our text, they produce in the earth a "germinating water" (evidently identical with the metals),[39] and from this is produced the food of men and animals and spiritual nourishment in the form of wine.[40] In Psalm 103 : 12–14, which is quoted here, this germinating water is identical with the power of God. Similarly, Senior says that the lapis is born of pure seed and is endowed with the power of grace.[41] This generative cosmic principle is the water.[42]

487   After all harmful admixtures coming from the unconscious have been removed from the conscious personality by these purificatory procedures, the unconscious is more and more able to exert an inspiring and vivifying effect. The birds watering the earth suggest mental and spiritual enrichment. It is worth noting that Thomas Aquinas based his inaugural lecture as Magister in Paris on this passage from Psalm 103 : 13: "Thou waterest the hills from thy upper rooms, the earth is sated with the fruit of thy works"—and moreover because of a dream. He was reluctant to accept this new honour, but then an old man appeared to him in a dream who comforted him and suggested that passage as a text for his lecture.[43] The dream was evidently an admonition to St. Thomas to rely more on the creative inspiration of the unconscious and not to torment himself unnecessarily with doubts and misgivings.

488   This earth, I say, made the moon in its season, then the sun arose, very early in the morning the first day of the week, after the darkness, which thou hast appointed therein before sunrise,

489   The germination of colours and the production of a gay, fruitful world would be, in alchemy, comparable to the *cauda*

---

38 In Komarios the water is called the "water on the mountain tops" (*Alch. grecs,* IV, xx, 4): "The earth has been solidified above the waters, and the waters are raised above the mountain tops." •   39 Infra, p. 354.

40 Cf. the role of wine in Dorn (*Mysterium*, pp. 477ff.).   41 Cf. Stapleton, p. 169.

42 *De chemia*, pp. 58, 59. P. 87: "Hermes saith that the secret of every thing is in water alone . . . and the beginning of the generation of man is water." •

43 Grabmann, *Die echten Schriften des heiligen Thomas von Aquin*, p. 25. This lecture has been preserved and is edited by Fr. Salvatore in *Due sermone inediti di San Tommaso d'Aquino.*

pavonis which follows the *nigredo*, and whose psychological significance is discussed in Jung.[44]

490   This stage is usually followed by the *albedo*, here represented by the rising moon, and then by the *rubedo*—the rising sun.[45] With the sun and moon, however, time comes into existence.[46]

491   Before the creation of the sun and moon, and hence of "sidereal time," it is as if the world were outside time, in a kind of dawn-state. In it there was light, but as yet there were no "luminaries." We may recall here Dorn's conception of a *mundus potentialis,* an image for the world of archetypes, in which "luminosity" [47] is present but no discriminating ego-consciousness, and therefore no categories of space and time. Then first the moon rises—a diffuse state of consciousness which is easily extinguished; and this is followed only later by a clear and steady state of consciousness (sun). Seen in the context of *Aurora* as a whole, this re-creation of the world signifies a re-structuring of consciousness from the very depths, after it had been annihilated by the invasion of the unconscious. The new, nascent world of consciousness has, however, a different centre: it is no longer the ego, but a figure which the text later calls Christ and the Second Adam, that is, a symbol of the self.

492   In patristic literature, the words from Psalm 103 : 19, "He made the moon for seasons: the sun knoweth his going down," were generally interpreted as referring to the Church and Christ. Ecclesia-Luna, symbolizing the mortality of this life, dies as she draws nearer to the sun, i.e., is taken up in Christ.[48] That the author knew of such interpretations of this passage and consciously had them in mind is proved by the words that follow

[44] *Mysterium,* pp. 285ff.

[45] Cf. the earth as mother of the sun and moon in the Phœnician cosmology of Sanchuniathon (Eusebius, *Praeparatio evangelica,* i. 10. 2), according to which the world was created in the form of an egg: "and from it came Mot [the mother goddess], then the sun and moon, and then the stars."

[46] According to St. Thomas, time came into existence only with the creation of the sun and moon on the sixth day, but light, having been created earlier by itself, "signified the formation of spiritual creatures." *Summa,* I, q. 67, art. 4 ad 4 (Eng. edn., I, p. 337).

[47] "On the Nature of the Psyche," pp. 190ff.

[48] Augustine, *Enarr. in Psalm.* 103. 19 (Eng. edn., 5, p. 121): "We understand spiritually the Church increasing from the smallest size, and growing old as it were from the mortality of this life, yet so, that she draweth nearer unto the sun." •

("very early in the morning the first day of the week"), which allude to Christ's resurrection.[49] The equivalence of the filius philosophorum and the risen Christ runs through the whole treatise and shows that the author was fully conscious of what he was doing. The mysterious earth or ash which forms the basic stuff of the human body is, accordingly, the substance of the resurrected body or of the Second Adam—a god-man or Anthropos figure who in the text sometimes has a superhuman aspect, but sometimes seems to be identical with the alchemist himself.

493   and it is night. For in it shall all the beasts of the wood go about, for thou hast set them a bound which they shall not pass until the whitening, but in their order go on even until the reddening,

494   This and the previous passage recapitulate the three main stages of the procedure: the *nigredo* (the night that precedes sunrise), *albedo* (moon), *rubedo* (sun).[50] In the night of the *nigredo* the beasts of the wood go about. This is probably an allusion to the wealth of animal symbolism in the opus, characterizing the initial stages in particular; the arcane substance is symbolized by the serpent, uroboros, lion,[51] reptiles,[52] eagle,[53] dog, wolf, and camel.[54] It may be that the author also had in mind the famous passage in Virgil's *Georgics*, II, 336ff., about the springtime of the world: "Springtime it was; the great world was keeping spring . . . when the first cattle drank in the light and man's iron race reared its head from the hard fields, and the wild beasts were let loose into the forests and the stars into heaven."[55] Servius[56] remarks that this meant the spring equinox, when there was a new "unloosing of the planets" in the heavens, like wild beasts let loose in the wood or the stadium

49 Mark 16 : 2.

50 Of importance for the interpretation of this passage is a later amplification of it in Mennens (*Theatr. chem.*, V, p. 364), according to which the sun and moon were created on the fourth day: "For the number four is perfect and contains in itself all number or multitude, for one, two, three, and four added together make the number ten, beyond which you cannot go save by returning to unity." •

51 Parable of Marchos in Senior, *De chemia*, p. 63.

52 Senior, pp. 78 and 108.

53 Zosimos, *Alch. grecs*, III, vi, 5 and III, xxix, 18. Cf. the "eagle-stone" (λίθος ἀετίτης), I, iv, 1.   54 "Opusculum autoris ignoti," *Art. aurif.*, I, p. 251.

55 Virgil (Loeb edn.), I, p. 139.

56 Cf. Norden, *Die Geburt des Kindes*, p. 17 and n.

of a circus. In *Aurora*, too, the author depicts a springtime of the world, a *genitura mundi*, so that the beasts of the wood going about might conceivably be understood as the planets entering their new orbits. This is suggested all the more strongly by the words that follow: "for thou hast set them a bound which they shall not pass over . . . but in their order go on even until the reddening." The beasts going about were usually interpreted as a reference to the coming of Antichrist. Thus Joachim of Flora says that when Antichrist appears, this will be "a night of tribulation and anguish, a night in which all the beasts of the wood shall go about." [57] This, he says, will happen in the sixth age. (The beasts are mentioned in the *sixth* parable!) He adds: "These beasts and reptiles, which God created on the sixth day, signify the reigns of the heathen and sects of pseudo-prophets." [58] It seems to me probable that the author of *Aurora* knew of such interpretations.

495   for all things serve the earth, and the days of its years are threescore and ten years passing over it, because it upholdeth all things by the word of its godhead,

496   The author's idea is that before the final glorification of the substances as described in the seventh parable there will be one last outbreak of all the dark powers, and that this has something to do with the human body. But he goes on to say that the beasts shall not transgress the bound because "all things serve the earth." Earth signifies the body, so the instincts (beasts) are restrained by the body's very nature. Instinct is not boundless; somewhere it runs up against its own limitation. The words "for all things serve the earth" are particularly significant *because the author here puts the earth in the place of God:* Psalm 118 : 91 says "for all things serve *thee*"! This earth itself is the risen Christ and the divine mystery—indeed, it is God himself. But, the text goes on, the life of this earth is "threescore and ten years," [59] so the earth is at the same time the

[57] *Concordia*, V, cap. 92 (Hahn, III, pp. 129f.).*
[58] Ibid., IV, cap. 6 (Hahn, III, pp. 114f.; cf. note on p. 112).
[59] Ripley, who obviously knew *Aurora*, interpreted the "bounds" in this sense ("Medulla philosophiae chemicae," *Opera omnia*, p. 300): "For it is written, Thou hast set them bounds which they shall not pass over" (Ps. 103 : 19). He says this refers to the fact that even with the aid of the "medicine" human life could not be prolonged beyond 70 years.

ordinary mortal man! Yet it also "upholds all things by the word of its godhead" (cf. Hebrews 1 : 3): that is to say, it is the world-creating Logos. For the explanation and interpretation of this tremendous paradox I must refer the reader to Jung; [60] evidently it concerns the production of a divine-human figure, which like Christ is very God and very man and in *Aurora* is at the same time the ordinary mortal individual.

497 as in the *Turba philosophorum* it is written: The earth, since it is heavy, beareth all things, for it is the foundation of the whole heaven, because it appeared dry at the separation of the elements.

498 Here the mysterious end-product of the opus is again something non-human: it is the "earth" which bears all things and is the "foundation of the whole heaven." And yet it is the same primordial earth of Genesis, which appeared at the separation of land from water—the prima materia of the cosmos.

499 Therefore in the Red Sea there was a way without hindrance, since this great and wide sea smote the rock and the metallic waters flowed forth.

500 The emergence of the first bit of dry land in the primordial chaos is compared with the parting of the Red Sea, when "a way without hindrance" appeared for the children of Israel, "and out of the great deep a springing field" (Wisd. 19 : 17). This allusion refers back to the germination of a new world, but as it is a motif that occupies a large place in the final parable, I am deferring the commentary until then. On the other hand, the "Red Sea" is an alchemical synonym for the divine water, and amplifications on this theme will be found in Jung.[61]

501 It is remarkable that "this great and wide sea" is further identified with the rod of Moses, with which he struck water from the rock and with which he also divided the Red Sea. Mercurius, representing the divine water, is often symbolized

---

60 Cf. the Christ-lapis parallel in *Psychology and Alchemy*, pars. 447ff., and *Mysterium*, pp. 452ff.

61 Ibid., ch. III, § 5c. Cf. the designation of the water as the "Egyptian sea" in Komarios, *Alch. grecs*, IV, xx, 11. The *Turba* (p. 249) says that purple is a colour which is "extracted from our red, most pure sea." Cf. also pp. 125, 248 and Senior, *De chemia*, pp. 82, 83. The Gnostics, like the Church Fathers, interpreted the Red Sea as the perishable world (Leisegang, *Gnosis*, pp. 139–40 and 143).

by the caduceus.[62] So here again the water is both the producer and the product. (The "rod of living water" is an idea found among the Mandaeans.) [63] The rod symbolizes an orienting factor which is contained in the "water" of the unconscious and which, like the magic staff of Hermes, causes sleep and waking, rouses to life or leads the way into death. In ecclesiastical symbolism "Mary is that golden rod, the symbol of eternal life." [64]

502   Then the rivers disappeared in dry land, which make the city of God joyful; when this mortal shall put on immortality, and the corruption of the living shall put on incorruption, then indeed shall that word come to pass which is written, Death is swallowed up in victory. O death, where is thy victory?

503   The rivers which make the city of God joyful (Psalm 45 : 5) disappear (abierunt) in dry land (Psalm 104 : 41). These two Biblical quotations seem to contradict one another, but they are probably meant as follows: the corrupting humidity, the divine water in its chaotic, corrosive aspect, disappears, and from it the secret earth grows up as dry land in the fixatio or coagulatio.[65] This firm ground is not only "earth" but also the treasure-house of Wisdom or the heavenly Jerusalem, the "city of God," and in it the water is preserved, now gushing forth as a fountain which grants rejuvenation and eternal life in the spirit. The "rivers which make the city of God joyful" were interpreted by Origen and St. Gregory as Christ and the Holy Ghost,[66] and Joachim of Flora interpreted the dry land between the rivers as the Ecclesia spiritualis.[67] But in our text the "city of God" is the immortal body or immortal inner man, the

---

[62] "The Spirit Mercurius," par. 255. In the Turba (p. 255) the raw material is called the "rod of the metals." Cf. the ecclesiastical interpretation of the rod in Ephraem Syrus, I, col. 54: "The rod of Moses opened the rock and the waters gushed forth. . . . Behold, from the side of Christ gushed forth the fountain of life." *

[63] Bousset, Hauptprobleme, p. 31.

[64] "Biblia Mariana" (Borgnet, XXXVII, p. 389). *

[65] Cf. the interpretation of this passage in Ripley, "Medulla philosophiae chemicae," p. 159, in connection with the appearance of the "fish's eyes."

[66] Rahner, "Flumina de ventre Christi," p. 277. Cf. St. Gregory, Expos. in Cant. 4, verse 15 (Migne, P.L., vol. 79, col. 515): ". . . when through the gift of the Holy Spirit mightily bedewing holy Church with the wisdom of Scripture, or the mind of whosoever receives it, he makes them to rejoice with his outpouring." *

[67] Concordia, V (Hahn, III, pp. 296f.).

second Adam (or, according to Gregory, "the mind of whosoever receives" the gift of the Holy Spirit).

504 Where thy sin abounded, there now grace doth more abound. For as in Adam all die, so also in Christ all shall be made alive. For by a man indeed came death, and by him himself the resurrection of the dead.

505   The text becomes a dithyrambic song of victory over death and corruption, expressed with such passion that we can see at once that for the author the alchemical process in which he was participating meant his own inner rebirth and transformation from corruption into incorruption. Commenting on the words of St. Paul, "Where sin abounded," etc., Joachim of Flora says: "As the Son is like the Father, so he must also act . . . in like manner; but because He who is named the Spirit of truth proceeds from Him who is truth and from the Father also, mercy in the New Testament must be doubled: hence 'where sin abounded, grace did more abound.' " [68] I cite this because the Holy Spirit is the Person of the Trinity on whom the greatest stress is laid in *Aurora*.[69]

506   This part of the text is particularly important psychologically as the description of what seem to be cosmic processes gradually slips into a description of a *human figure,* of an immortal Adam "composed of simple and pure essence." It is as if the author had become conscious of the intrapsychic aspect of the opus. More and more it is understood as the production of a greater, inner man, the self; and in contrast to the beginning of *Aurora,* where the author in his inflation repeatedly identified himself with the filius philosophorum, this same figure now crystallizes out within his psyche, pure and no longer sullied by the "corruption" of unconsciousness. This inner Anthropos is an immortal man who has nothing more to do with the corruptible earthly world.

507 For the first Adam and his sons took their beginning from the corruptible elements, and therefore it was needful that the composed

68 Ibid., IV (III, p. 287).

69 St. Thomas cites the same passage from St. Paul in the *Summa*, III, q. 1, art. 3 ad 3 (Eng. edn., II, p. 2029): "God allows evil in order that something better may come of it, wherefore it is said in Rom. 5 : 20: Where sin abounded, grace did more abound. Hence, too, in the blessing of the Paschal candle, we say: O happy fault, that merited such and so great a redeemer!" •

should be corrupted, but the second Adam, who is called the philosophic man, from pure elements entered into eternity. Therefore what is composed of simple and pure essence, remaineth for ever.

508   For the interpretation of the first and second Adam I would refer the reader to Jung's work,[70] where the significance of these allusions is made quite clear.[71]

509   As Senior saith: There is One thing, that never dieth, for it continueth by perpetual increase, when the body shall be glorified in the final resurrection of the dead, wherefore the Creed beareth witness to the resurrection of the flesh and eternal life after death. Then saith the second Adam to the first and to his sons: Come, ye blessed of my Father, possess you the eternal kingdom prepared for you from the beginning of the Work, and eat my bread and drink the wine which I have mingled for you, for all things are made ready for you.

510   What deserves special emphasis here is that the second Adam proves himself identical with Wisdom, for the words "Come eat my bread and drink the wine which I have mingled for you" are a direct quotation from Proverbs 9 : 5, where Wisdom is the speaker. In this respect the author is following the official view of the Church.[72] The changing form of the Anthropos, appear-

[70] *Mysterium*, ch. V, "Adam and Eve," and *Psychology and Alchemy*, par. 476.
[71] Cf. "Aquarium sapientum," *Mus. Herm.*, pp. 111, 114f. (Waite, I, pp. 98, 100), with reference to this part of the text: Christ has within him the "heavenly Adam." Irenaeus, *Contra haer.*, III, 21 (trans. Roberts and Rambaut, I, p. 358): "And as the protoplast himself, Adam, has his substance from untilled land and as yet virgin soil (for God had not yet sent rain, and man had not tilled the ground), and was formed by the hand of God, that is, by the word of God . . . so did he who is the Word, recapitulating Adam in himself, rightly receive a birth, enabling him to gather up Adam [into himself] from Mary, who was as yet a virgin." •
[72] Hugh of St. Victor, *De Sapientia animae Christi* (Migne, *P.L.*, vol. 176, col. 848): "What is the Word but Wisdom? For the same who by John is called the Word of God, is by Paul called the wisdom of God. For Christ, saith the Apostle Paul, is the power of God and the wisdom of God (I Cor. 1). Christ therefore is himself the Word and himself wisdom. The Word is wisdom, and wisdom is the Word. The Word is wisdom, because 'My heart hath uttered a good word' (Ps. 44). Wisdom is the Word, because 'I Wisdom out of the mouth of the Most High . . .' (Ecclus. 24). Wisdom therefore is the word of the heart. . . . Therefore if the Word giveth light, wisdom giveth light." • Joachim of Flora (Hahn, III, p. 332): "For the son of the Father is wisdom." Scotus Erigena, *De divis. nat.*, III, 9 (Migne, *P.L.*, vol. 122, col. 646): "To be the wisdom of God the Father . . . and the creative cause of all things and to be created and made

ing now as a man and now as a woman, is found also in the teachings of the Mandaeans, where the Redeemer is sometimes called Adakas, or Adam, or the "inner man" (ὁ ἔσω ἄνθρωπος), and sometimes appears as a shining female figure, and also as the "knowledge of God" embodied in Manda d'Hajje.[73] These conceptions are a survival of Manichaean ideas, one of which was that the feminine Daena (the immortal self of every individual) can take the form of a wise old man.[74] Again, the Manichaeans interpreted the Original Man who was sunk in matter as the world-soul (ψυχὴ ἁπάντων), and, according to St. Augustine, as the *anima bona*.[75] According to Clement of Alexandria, this world-soul was "divine in the beginning, but being made effeminate by sensual desire, came here below to generation and destruction." [76] This is significant inasmuch as Wisdom appeared as a feminine spirit of desire at the beginning of the work and in the end has finally become masculine (second Adam).

511   The second Adam, alias Wisdom, now invites the "sons" (presumably the alchemists) to a banquet, using the words spoken by Christ the King of Glory: "Come, ye blessed of my Father, possess you the kingdom prepared for you from the foundation of the world" (Matt. 25 : 34). The rest of the quotation (Prov. 9 : 5) was interpreted by the Church Fathers as a

---

in all things that he creates and to contain all things in which he is created and made." • II, 31 (col. 603): "God, who out of himself gives birth to his Son, who is his wisdom." • II, 18 (col. 552): "The primordial causes know themselves, since they are created in wisdom, and subsist eternally therein." • (Cf. Preger, *Geschichte der Mystik*, I, p. 161.) II, cap. 2 (col. 529): ". . . as those primordial causes of things are called by the Greeks prototypes, that is, primordial exemplars or proorismata." •

73 Reitzenstein, *Erlösungsmysterium*, pp. 22f.

74 Ibid., p. 54. In the Gnostic systems we find more frequently a syzygy, e.g., Protanthropos and Barbelo, Logos and Ennoia, Autogenes and Aletheia, Adam and his companion γνῶσις τελεία (perfect knowledge), or power of the "virginal pneuma." (Schmidt, "Ein voriraenisches gnostisches Originalwerk," p. 843; Bousset, *Hauptprobleme*, pp. 160ff.) According to the heresy of the Jewish Christian Symmachus, Adam is the world-soul. Cf. Reitzenstein, *Erlösungsmysterium*, p. 103, and Marius Victorinus Afer, *In Epistolam Pauli ad Galatas* (Migne, *P.L.*, vol. 8, col. 1155).

75 *De vera religione*, 9 (*Earlier Writings*, p. 234). Cf. Titus of Bostra, *Adv. Manichaeos*, I, 29 (Migne, *P.G.*, vol. 18, col. 1109); Alexander of Lycopolis, "On the Tenets of the Manichaeans" (trans. Clark and Hawkins), pp. 238f.

76 *Stromata*, III, 13, 92; Bousset, p. 178. •

reference to the Eucharist. This passage is particularly important psychologically because, as we saw earlier, the alchemist, as the chosen son of Wisdom, had *himself* been exalted to the King of Glory, and even represented Wisdom's male partner in the mysterium coniunctionis.[77] Since then, and through the exclusion of the fourth element (earth) and the return to a trinitarian faith, the identification has ceased. The coniunctio was glimpsed in the heavenly place, in "all the brightness of the sun and moon," male and female are now united in the second Adam, and the alchemist is only a guest at the banquet. This shows plainly enough how the author has come to terms with the irrupted contents and has found a way back to his Christian faith.

512   The alchemist now partakes of the immortal essence of the filius philosophorum by a true communion. The Eucharistic meal had already been hinted at in the fifth parable, where Wisdom invited the alchemists into her house, and "they shall be inebriated with plenty." She stood at the door and invited them in with the words of the angel of the Apocalypse: "Behold, I stand at the gate and knock. If any man shall hear my voice and open to me the door, I will come in to him and will sup with him, and he with me" (Apoc. 3 : 20). This was the "banquet of Christ" in the Apocalypse, which Ephraem Syrus interpreted as a hierosgamos with God.[78] And Mary was called the "cellar-keeper of the whole Trinity, who giveth of the wine of the Holy Spirit, pouring it out to whom she will and as much as she will." [79]

513   The figure who appears now as the Rex coelestis or the

---

[77] Supra, pp. 213ff.

[78] *Hymni et sermones,* II, cols. 822ff.: "Let the banquet praise thee, for thou hast multiplied its wine. . . . I will give thanks among the guests, for he hath refreshed me with drink. I have invited the heavenly bridegroom, who himself took a lower place, that he might invite all. I will enter as a guest his most pure banquet, I will give thanks among the young men, for he is the bridegroom and none shall knock at his chamber in vain." • The Marcosians celebrated communion with a feminine deity, invoking the Holy Spirit as the "Mother." Cf. Acts of Thomas (James, *Apocryphal New Testament,* p. 388): "Come, O perfect compassion, Come, she that knoweth the mysteries of him that is chosen. . . . Come, she that manifesteth the hidden things and maketh the unspeakable things plain, the holy dove. . . . Come, hidden mother. . . . Come and communicate with us in this eucharist which we celebrate in thy name." •

[79] "Biblia Mariana" (Borgnet, XXXVII, p. 398). •

"heavenly Adam" and now as Wisdom celebrating the communion with the alchemists is, according to the closing words of the parable,[80] the product of the circulatory distillation of the four elements. The first or earthly Adam likewise consisted of four elements, but he was a composite that might easily disintegrate and was therefore corruptible; but the second Adam "is composed of simple and pure essence, and remaineth for ever." This essence has been distilled as the fifth—the "quintessence"—from the circulation of the four. In other texts it is *life*, and it is beyond the opposites since it contains them within itself, male, and female and all contraries.[81] It is a spiritual earth,[82] psychic reality itself.

514 He that hath ears to hear, let him hear what the spirit of the doctrine saith to the sons of the discipline concerning the earthly and the heavenly Adam, which the philosophers treat of in these words: When thou hast water from earth, air from water, fire from air, earth from fire, then shalt thou fully and perfectly possess our art.

[80] This saying from Pseudo-Aristotle (cf. *Art. aurif.*, II, pp. 185 and 163) does in fact reflect the Aristotelian view that the elements could be transformed into one another: "cyclically, upwards and downwards." Cf. Lippmann, I, p. 141.

[81] "Expositio epistolae Alexandri regis," *Art. aurif.*, I, p. 245: "The feminine retentive virtue is cold and dry, and is the earth. The digestive or alterative virtue is male, warm, and damp, and is the air. . . . But the quintessence is life, which is peculiar to itself, and is neither warm nor damp nor cold nor dry, neither male nor female." • Cf. Senior, *De chemia*, p. 96.

[82] The fact that the quintessence is spiritual recalls Philo's view that everything corporeal consists of the four elements, but that the "fifth" is the intelligible soul (ψυχὴ νοερά), which is a "circulating substance" (οὐσία κυκλοφορητική). This is "stronger than the four"; from it are composed the heavens and the stars, and the soul therefore returns to the heavenly aether as to its father. "Quis rerum divinarum heres?" 57, 283 (Loeb edn., IV, pp. 310ff., 428f.); "De plantatione," V, 18 (Loeb edn., III, pp. 222f.); "Legum allegoriae," III, 55 (Loeb edn., I, pp. 336f.). Cf. also Philostratus, *Life of Apollonius of Tyana*, I, pp. 308f.; Iamblichus, *De anima* (Stobaeus, 1. 49. 32); Scott, *Hermetica*, III, p. 40; Bousset, *Hauptprobleme*, p. 196. Epicurus described the soul as a mixture of four things: a fiery, an airy, and a pneumatic quality, and a fourth thing, which was unknown. Plutarch, "Adversus Coloten," 20, 1, 118D, in *Moralia* (ed. Bernardakis) VI, p. 453; Lucretius, *De rerum natura*, 3, 231–45 (Loeb edn., pp. 186f.); Aetius, *De placitis reliquiae*, IV. 3. 11 (Diels, *Doxographi Graeci*, p. 388); Scott, III, p. 506. Not only the earthly man is composed of the four elements, but his immortal divine part also (Scott, I, pp. 304f.; cf. the Latin Asclepius, ibid., p. 298, and "Isis to Horus" on ἐμψύχωσις, p. 522). In patristic literature the regenerated inner man, son of Luna-Ecclesia and of Sol-Christus, is composed of the four elements of the sun and moon (Rahner, "Mysterium Lunae," p. 76).

515   The second Adam, composed of the sublimated and unified elements, combines in himself their qualities—warm and cold, dry and damp, active and passive, etc.—which were divided into the opposites; he is also male and female, appearing now as the heavenly King or risen Christ or alchemical filius philosophorum, and now as Wisdom or the alchemical earth or world-soul. Taken as a whole, the picture is an anticipation of the complete fusion of these two aspects which forms the theme of the seventh and last parable. What the parable of the "Philosophic Faith" did not quite succeed in bringing off—the circulation of the four elements without the exclusion of the fourth—has now become possible: all four elements have become one in the quinta essentia, the immortal essence of the second Adam. But this apocatastasis is realized in the "Beyond," and in a moment which for the ordinary mortal comes close to the moment of death. The former man, the "first Adam and his sons," is still standing on the threshold; but at the next step, the step to which the whole process has been tending, he himself will be received into immortality.

XII. THE SEVENTH PARABLE: OF
THE CONFABULATION ...

516   The last parable, "Of the Confabulation of the Lover with the
Beloved," leans heavily on the Canticles (Song of Songs) both
in its composition and in its wealth of quotations. The Church
traditionally interpreted the Biblical version (originally, perhaps, a Babylonian love-song) [1] as the conversation of Christ with
the soul or with the Church, or as the "delectation of the Holy
Spirit"; [2] and in a sermon Origen says very aptly that one must
first have left Egypt and crossed the Red Sea before one could
interpret the Canticles. He himself had passed through the
"spiritual wilderness" until he came within sight of the Promised Land, where he sang the Song standing upon the banks of
the Jordan.[3] How many voices there were in it he did not know
precisely, but in answer to his prayer God had revealed that
there were *four* of them: the bridegroom and the bride, the
bridegroom's chorus of youths and the bride's chorus of virgins.[4]

517   The author of *Aurora,* who was no doubt familiar with the
Church's interpretation,[5] employs the Canticles for the greater
glorification of *his* coniunctio. As in the Biblical version, the
speakers alternate, and the transition from one to the other is
sometimes not at all clear. It is as if the two figures were speaking directly out of a state of non-differentiation, out of that
mutual contamination which is characteristic of unconscious
contents. Psychologically, it is remarkable that after so many
purificatory procedures the parable still begins as before with a
nigredo. Evidently the appearance of the King of Glory at the

---

[1] Wittekindt, *Das Hohe Lied und seine Beziehungen zum Istarkult.*

[2] Hippolytus, *Commentarium in Cant. Cant.* (ed. Bonwetsch), p. 21.

[3] *In Cant. Cant. homiliae,* I, 1-2 (Migne, *P.G.,* vol. 13, col. 37).

[4] Ibid., col. 38.

[5] For instance, that of Honorius, *Speculum* (Migne, *P.L.,* vol. 172, col. 1065).

end of the preceding parable was so overpowering that the author was flung back into the darkness. Hence the indistinctness of the speaker, which had almost disappeared in the preceding chapters. This renewed darkening of consciousness may have been induced by the communion with the divine "second Adam" at the end of the last parable.

518   Be turned to me with all your heart and do not cast me aside because I am black and swarthy, because the sun hath changed my colour and the waters have covered my face and the earth hath been polluted and defiled in my works;

519   Here the bride, or the prima materia or its soul, is speaking, and she begs for help and deliverance.[6] But, as the quotation from Joel [7] shows, she is at the same time identical with God. This is one of the places where that equation, often dimly hinted at before, is expressed most clearly; where God, or at any rate his feminine aspect, appears as the spirit or soul in matter and awaits redemption by the work of man.[8] Origen identifies the black bride of the Song of Songs with Miriam, the second wife of Moses,[9] and also with Mary in her "overshadowing" by God.[10] In alchemy the black woman is an embodiment of the *nigredo,* or of the *umbra Solis,* or of the new moon darkened by the sun: [11] a motif the psychological significance of which is discussed in Jung.[12]

[6] "Aquarium sapientum," *Mus. Herm.,* p. 117 (Waite, I, p. 102): "The sages have called our compound . . . the Raven's Head, on account of its blackness (Cant. 1, 'I am black')."

[7] Joel 2 : 12: "Now therefore saith the Lord: Be converted to me with all your heart . . ."

[8] *Psychology and Alchemy,* pars. 414ff.   [9] Cf. *Aion,* pp. 209f.

[10] *In Cant. Cant.,* Lib. II (Migne, *P.G.,* vol. 13, col. 103).

[11] The ecclesiastical interpretation is the blackness of sin over the Church (Hippolytus, *Comm. in Cant.,* p. 35). The sun is the "light of the world" (Meister Eckhart, trans. Evans, II, p. 82) or Christ, who convicts the Church of her sins (St. Gregory, *Super Cant. Cant.,* cap. 1: Migne, *P.L.,* vol. 79, col. 486): "The holy soul perceives the foulness of her sins." Cf. Honorius, *Expos. in Cant.* (Migne, *P.L.,* vol. 172, cols. 367–69). Origen, *In Cant. Cant.,* I, 6 (Migne, *P.G.,* vol. 13, col. 360) interprets this passage as meaning that the bride was about to turn white: "For because she is not yet purged of the filth of all her sins . . . and not yet bathed in salvation, she is called black, but she doth not remain black in colour. Therefore she is white when she riseth up to greater things . . . and it is said of her, Who is this that goeth up whitened?" •

[12] *Mysterium,* pp. 24ff., 145ff., 173ff.

for there was darkness over it, because I stick fast in the mire of the deep and my substance is not disclosed. Wherefore out of the depths have I cried, and from the abyss of the earth with my voice to all you that pass by the way.

520 The words "there was darkness over it" (the earth) refer to the Crucifixion, when the sun and moon were darkened. The Crucifixion itself was interpreted as the novilunar conjunction of the sun (Christ) with the moon (Church).

521 Attend and see me, if any shall find one like unto me, I will give into his hand the morning star. For behold in my bed by night I sought one to comfort me and I found none, I called and there was none to answer me.—Therefore will I arise and go into the city,

522 In moving words the anima cries out for help—but in the sentence that immediately follows, "Therefore will I arise," it is the bridegroom speaking, and *he* is the buried one who seeks a virgin to deliver him. The transition from one speaker to the other is barely perceptible, so that one is inclined to think that it is the same figure speaking now as a woman and now as a man, just as so often before Wisdom coalesced with the Holy Spirit, Christ, or God. One has the impression that the author, having achieved direct contact with the unconscious, is letting the voices speak just as he hears them, without bringing his ego into it at all, as if he and the unconscious had again become identical. Later in the text it sometimes seems as if he felt himself to be identical with the bridegroom calling for help from the grave, although, as the next passage makes clear, this buried bridegroom is an impersonal, objective figure.

523 seeking in the streets and broad ways a chaste virgin to espouse, comely in face, more comely in body, most comely in her garments, that she may roll back the stone from the door of my sepulchre . . .

524 The male partner, it now appears, is the alchemical "body" or corpse that has to be reanimated. Thus in the *Carmina Heliodori* [13] the corpse cries out: "Where is the living soul that has separated from me? . . . O wash me that I may become a shining house . . . for the spirit and the purified soul."

and give me wings like a dove, and I will fly with her into heaven and then say: I live for ever, and will rest in her, for the queen stood on my right hand in gilded clothing, surrounded with variety.

[13] Carmen IV, verse 240, p. 57.

384

525   We can now understand why the bride gives her lover "wings like a dove": she endows the body with her own volatility so that it can fly with her into heaven.[14] Senior says: "And because the white woman escapeth . . . but the red man followeth after the woman and holdeth her, they (the philosophers) said: the woman hath wings but the man not."[15]

526   Hearken therefore O daughter and see and incline thine ear to my prayers, for I have desired thy beauty with all the desire of my heart. O I spoke with my tongue, Make known to me my end and what is the number of my days, that I may know what is wanting to me, for thou hast made all my days measurable and my substance is as nothing before thee.

527   It is evident from these words that the man really does represent the body or *corpus glorificatum:* only through the soul can he attain eternal life. In similar wise the Manichaean texts speak of a post-mortal union of body and soul; the heavenly half of the dead man rising to heaven comes down to him in the form of a wise old man or a shining female figure (Daena), and calls him the "body."[16] As Reitzenstein emphasizes,[17] the spirit is, as it were, a lower part of the soul, which serves the true soul as a kind of body.[18]

---

14 Mennens, *Theatr. chem.,* V, p. 280: "Wherefore the prophet exclaims, Who will give me wings like a dove, that is, pure and simple thoughts and contemplations, and I will fly and be at rest? Who but the heavenly Father? Wherefore saith Christ, No man cometh unto me except my Father draw him, and then indeed when he hath completed a whole circle, and God shall be all in all, as he always was." •

15 *Pret. marg. nov.,* p. 123. Cf. *De chemia,* p. 33. Cf. Merculinus in "Ros. phil.," *Art. aurif.,* II, p. 242: "The stone . . . bears wings and is the moon, who by herself shines more than all others." In Senior the volatility is represented by eagles; cf. the allusion in *Aurora* (p. 214) to the woman who has "wings of the great eagle" (Rev. 12 : 14). Augustine likens the transfigured Church to a young eagle that "flies aloft as before" (*Enarr. in Ps.* 102 [103] 9, trans. Tweed, V. p. 46). For the motif of the fledged and unfledged see Zosimos, *Alch. grecs,* III, xxviii: "If two do not become one, that is, if the fledged does not conquer the unfledged, your expectation will come to nothing."

16 Reitzenstein, *Erlösungsmysterium,* pp. 4f.; cf. pp. 28ff.

17 Ibid.

18 A similar view is found among the Mandaeans, ibid., p. 50 (*Ginza,* 1. 111. 24ff.): "I am a great Mana, / I who dwelt in the sea; / I dwelt in the sea / Until I was given wings . . . / Until I became a winged one / And lifted up my wings to the place of light."

528   A Christian interpretation of the same alchemical process is given in Petrus Bonus.[19] "In the magistery and end of the work, when the soul herself arises, it is to be seen that she seeks her body, and is united therewith and receives life and activity; and that union and composition comes about by the mediation of the spirit; and when she is joined to the body she lives forever with her body. But this conjunction takes place at the birth and resurrection of the soul, for though she was created first, the soul with her body could not show forth her own proper and incorruptible activities because of the body's defilement and corruptibility, nay more, she lay useless and as if dead, and as if buried with her body, and when through the magistery she is purified and made white, she rises again separated from her body, and then her body is also purified, and she seeks her body and desires to be joined therewith that she may live for ever, and cannot be conjoined with another body. . . . For our soul arose on the horizon of eternity [20] before she was united with her body . . . and in this conjunction of resurrection the body becomes wholly spiritual, like the soul herself, and they are made one as water is mixed with water, and henceforth they are not separated for ever, since there is no diversity in them, but unity and identity of all three, that is, spirit, soul, and body, without separation for ever."

529   Psychologically this process represents a further stage in the integration of the self. Previously it was essentially concerned with freeing the anima from matter, that is, withdrawing her projection and transforming her into a function of relationship with the unconscious. The self was then manifested as the King of Glory and the "second Adam." But now a new problem is constellated: the freeing of the body itself, in which the "fallen Sophia" was imprisoned. This is the stage of the *unio corporalis* discussed in Dorn.[21] According to him, the "body" must be distilled until it turns into a blue liquid called "heaven" (*caelum*), the parallel action in our text being the volatilization or sublimation of the body, which is accomplished by the bride giving it wings and clothing it in royal garments. The opposition be-

[19] *Pret. marg. nov.*, pp. 119ff.*
[20] This is from the so-called "Liber de causis"; cf. Bardenhewer, *Die pseudo-aristotelische Schrift über das reine Gute: Liber de causis.*
[21] *Mysterium*, pp. 482ff., 487ff.

tween "body" and "spirit" is thus resolved. Joannes Scotus Erigena's conception of resurrection [22] is of significance in this respect. He says that just as iron in the fire becomes fire without losing its essence, so will the substance of the body turn into the substance of the soul—into a "better substance" which is purely spiritual and sexless. After its transfiguration Christ's body was bisexual. The body, after being dissolved into the four elements, arises from them anew.[23] Similar views were held by various neo-Manichaean sects.[24]

530   The "making one" (adunatio) of the two sexes is immediately followed (according to Erigena and the Amalricians) by the unification of earth and paradise.[25]

In the passage we quoted earlier,[26] Jung, interpreting the lapis as a compensatory figure to Christ, continues: "Correctly recognizing the spiritual one-sidedness of the Christ-image, theological speculation had begun very early to concern itself with Christ's body, that is, with his materiality, and had temporarily solved the problem with the hypothesis of the resurrected body. But because this was only a provisional and therefore not an entirely satisfactory answer, the problem logically presented itself again in the Assumption of the Blessed Virgin, leading first to the dogma of the Immaculate Conception and finally to that of the Assumption." [27]

531   Not only does our text contain clear, unconscious anticipations of this development, but certain symbolic allusions even go beyond it and carry the alchemical idea of the "God become physical" [28] still further to include the physical man, so that each individual becomes the vessel for an incarnation of God.

532   Since the body is also a symbol for the individual limitations of the conscious personality, its dissolution in our text could be conceived as the extinction of the conscious individual in

---

[22] De divis. nat., V, 8 (Migne, P.G., vol. 122, col. 879), and I, 10 (col. 451).

[23] Preger, Geschichte der Mystik, I, p. 164.

[24] Hahn, Geschichte der Ketzer, II, pp. 107ff. They believed in an adunatio sexuum.

[25] De divis. nat., II, cap. 8 (Migne, col. 533): "And since after the unification of man, that is, of the two sexes, into the pristine unity of nature, in which there was neither male nor female, but there was simply a human being, forthwith shall follow the unification of earth and paradise." *

[26] Supra, pp. 343f.

[27] "The Visions of Zosimos," par. 127.   [28] Ibid., par. 138.

the unconscious, here described positively as a deliverance from the "sepulchre" of conscious limitations, as the moment of union with the inner totality in which there are no more opposites.[29] In the Christian view this union occurs only after death at the resurrection of the glorified body.

533   The motif of resurrection had been alluded to just before in the text, when the lover begged the chaste virgin to roll the stone from the door of his sepulchre. This allusion parallels the earlier motif of the breaking of the barriers of hell and the "gates of brass and bars of iron" (Isaiah 45 : 2 and Psalm 106 : 16), a passage generally interpreted by the Church Fathers as referring to Christ's stay in limbo.[30] According to Cyril of Jerusalem, the buried Lord was like a "stone within the stone" —a spiritual stone covered by the tomb. By his burial the tree of life was planted in the earth, that the dead be set free.[31] Such formulations could easily be understood alchemically. Not only Christ but Wisdom, too, makes a descent to the centre of the earth. In Ecclesiasticus 24 : 45 she says: [32] "I will penetrate to all the lower parts of the earth, and will behold all that sleep, and will enlighten all that hope in the Lord." [33] A similar image occurs in the *Odes of Solomon,* where the "living, eternal water of the Lord" descends to quicken the dead and carries them up transfigured. They rise up "by the dew of the Lord" to the "cloud of peace." As Lippmann observes,[34] this is strikingly like the alchemical idea of the ἀναζωπύρωσις (quickening by fire) as described by Komarios [35] in connection with the hierosgamos: "Behold, in the midst of the mountain, there beneath the male lies his companion, with whom he unites and upon whom he

---

[29] Cf. Jung's commentary to *The Tibetan Book of the Great Liberation*, pp. 490, 498.

[30] The same motif occurs in Hippolytus, *Comm. in Cant.*, pp. 6off.

[31] Cf. *Katechesis*, 13, cap. 35 (ed. Reischl and Rupp, II, p. 96), where Christ says: "I am the cornerstone, elect, precious, I am hidden within the stone for a short time, a stone of stumbling to the Jews, but of salvation to them that believe. Therefore was the tree of life sown in the earth, that what was accursed might obtain blessing and that the dead might be set free." •

[32] Cf. Bousset, *Hauptprobleme*, pp. 256ff.

[33] The prototype of this is Ishtar's journey to the underworld.

[34] I, p. 222.

[35] *Komar* is the Syriac word for 'priest.' According to Jung the "Book of Komarios" belongs to the 1st cent. A.D. For contrary views see Lippmann, II, p. 33, and Reitzenstein, *Erlösungsmysterium*, p. 167.

rejoices. And nature rejoices in nature and unites with nothing outside herself. . . . See O ye sages and understand: see the consummation of the art, when the bride and bridegroom unite and are made one!" "And then when the soul and spirit unite and are made one . . . you will have the gold which not even the treasuries of kings contain. Behold, this is the mystery of the philosophers." [36] During this process the spirit becomes corporeal, the dead body receives a soul and takes up again the spirit that had been extracted from it, and now they all "rule and let themselves be ruled by one another." "When the dark pneuma [37] is driven away . . . the body will be illuminated, and now soul and spirit rejoice, for the darkness has departed from the body. Wake up from Hades, stand up from the grave and come forth from the darkness. . . . The medicine of life [38] has entered into you. And the spirit rejoices again to dwell in the body, and the soul, too, loves it . . . now that it is illuminated; and they shall be no more divided for ever." [39] In Zosimos the coniunctio is at the same time a "palingenesis" [40] and a resurrection.[41] The alchemist's idea of producing the resurrected body and the elixir of immortality by a chemical procedure is derived from the Egyptian embalming rites and the ceremonies for the dead Osiris. From the very beginning, therefore, the alchemists were preoccupied with the problem of the post-mortal state of the soul, and though the metaphysical validity of their statements is not susceptible of scientific proof they may well be intuitively correct anticipations of the psychological experience of death. At any rate these statements have to do with a reality which is far removed from life as ordinarily lived and from the sphere of ego-consciousness.

534   The conception of the coniunctio as a post-mortal event runs

---

[36] *Alch. grecs*, IV, xx. 13. Cf. Reitzenstein, "Zur Geschichte der Alchemie und des Mystizismus," p. 17, line 123, and *Erlösungsmysterium*, p. 6.

[37] The "horrible darknesses" of our text.

[38] Cf. also the animation of the dead by the φάρμακον ζωῆς in "Ostanes to Petesis" (Lippmann, I, p. 67).

[39] This unity is described as a statue of light, which comes out of the fire (Berthelot, *Alch. grecs*, IV.xx.7). Cf. Bousset, *Hauptprobleme*, pp. 34f. on the parallelism between this statue and the Naassene conception of Adam's body, also the Mandaean parallels.

[40] *Alch. grecs*, III, xxxiv, 2; cf. III, xl, 2.

[41] Ibid., III, lvi, 3; cf. III, viii, 2: "Deny not resurrection to the dead."

through the whole history of alchemical symbolism and is found also among the Arabic alchemists who were the sources for *Aurora*. Thus the *Turba* [42] says that the *res* (thing, matter) is buried like a man, and then God gives it its soul and spirit back again, and after the decomposition it grows stronger and is purified, just as after the resurrection a man becomes stronger and younger than he was upon earth. And Calid says: "This hidden thing is of the nature of sun and fire, and it is the most precious oil of all hidden things, and the living tincture, and the permanent water, which ever liveth and remaineth, and the vinegar of the philosophers and the penetrative spirit: and it is hidden, tincturing, aggregating, and reviving: it rectifieth and enlighteneth all the dead and causeth them to rise again." [43]

535   In *Aurora* the risen bridegroom stands at the left hand of the Queen, who appears to him "in gilded clothing, surrounded with variety." This figure, the Queen of alchemy, is again Wisdom, the anima in her glorified form purged of all super-fluities. She stands to the right of the bridegroom—that is to say, he is more deeply buried in the unconscious than she, and is a figure even stranger to consciousness than the anima. He is also the body, which in Christianity is of lesser worth than the soul.

536   At the Last Judgment and the "coming of the Great Sab-bath," Joachim of Flora says, the glory of the just will appear as a queen in golden robes sitting at the right hand of God. The text is similar to that of *Aurora:* "Then the glory of the just shall appear like unto the sun in the kingdom of their father when the walls of Jerusalem are wholly complete and the whole number of the elect is filled up, and she shall appear glorious and happy, seated like a queen on the right hand of God in gilded raiment, surrounded with variety. And the Lord God will give her a part of his glory and will reign with her even for ever and of his kingdom there shall be no end. Amen." [44]

537   For thou art she who shall enter through the ear, through my do-main, and I shall be clothed with a purple garment from thee and from me, I will come forth as a bridegroom out of his bride-chamber,

538   Here we find a curious detail: the soul enters the resurrected body through the ear. This refers to the ecclesiastical idea of

---

[42] P. 139.   [43] "Liber trium verborum," *Art. aurif.*, I, p. 227.*
[44] *Expositio in Apoc.* (Hahn, III, p. 341).*

"conception through the ear," according to which the Holy Ghost entered Mary's ear as the "Word" and so begot Christ. St. Isaac of Antioch says: "Unless [Christ] were God, how could he enter through the ear? . . . For by the ear the spirit entered and out of the womb issued the flesh." [45] And Ephraem Syrus: "[Christ] entered through the ear and dwelt secretly in the womb." [46] By alluding to these ideas the author of *Aurora* probably wished to indicate that the resurrection coniunctio was simultaneously an incarnation of the Logos or of God,[47] thereby expressing the spiritual and supernatural nature of the coniunctio.

539   When the soul has entered the body and the bride has united with the bridegroom, she adorns him with a purple garment and jewels.

540   for thou shalt adorn me round about with shining and glittering gems and shalt clothe me with the garments of salvation and joy to overthrow the nations and all mine enemies, and shalt adorn me with a crown of gold engraved with the sign of holiness . . .

541   For the significance of the crown I would refer the reader to Jung.[48] As the feminine arcane substance [49] it represents the anima or, in our text, the earth or body, so that here the roles are interchanged—for in the end both opposites always signify both.[50] In the "Tractatus aureus Hermetis" [51] the lapis likewise appears as a crowned king "who cometh forth from the fire . . .

[45] *Opera omnia*, I, p. 60. • John Damascene, *De fide orthodoxa*, IV, 14 (Migne, P.G., vol. 94, col. 1162): "And the conception came about by hearing." • Cf. Euthymius Zigabenos, *Panoplia dogmatica* (Migne, P.G., vol. 130, col. 1302), and Agobardus of Lyons, *De correctione antiphonarii*, 7 (Migne, P.L., vol. 104, col. 332): "The word entered through the Virgin's ear and came out by the golden gate." •

[46] II, col. 570. •

[47] Hence also the motif of clothing with a purple garment. Cf. Daniel, *Thesaurus hymnologicus*, II, p. 205: "In this place did the Eternal / Human flesh and nature don: / Hidden here the sacred bridegroom / Put his wedding garment on." •

[48] *Mysterium*, p. 378.

[49] *Turba*, p. 336: "The body is called earth, ash, chalk, mother . . . Holy Virgin, kingly crown . . . wood, sea, sputum of the moon." Senior, *De chemia*, p. 41: "The white foliated earth is the crown of victory . . . and the second body." Cf. ibid., pp. 16 and 35.

[50] Cf. the interpretation of Honorius, *Expos. in Cant.* (Migne, P.L., vol. 172, col. 440).

[51] *Ars chemica*, pp. 21f. Cf. "Ros. phil., "*Art. aurif.* (1610), II, p. 248.

then is death overcome, and the son reigneth in the red garment, and the purple is put on." [52] At the coronation scene in
our text the bride clothes her lover with a "purple garment
from thee and from me." In alchemy this would mean the
rubedo, already referred to in the Senior quotation in the fourth
parable: "He shineth in colour like a ruby through the tincturing soul, which it hath acquired by virtue of the fire." [53] This
is the much-prized *color invariabilis* (unchanging colour), whose
origin the *Turba* attributes to the soul: "For out of sulphur
mixed with sulphur cometh the most precious colour, which
doth not vary nor flee from the fire, when the soul is introduced
to the innermost parts of the body, and containeth and giveth
colour to the body." [54] "O wonderful nature, which coloureth
the other natures, O heavenly natures, which transform . . .
the elements!" [55] This *anima tingens* is of a spiritual nature [56]
and assimilates the body to itself so that it too becomes spiritual.[57] When the body is pulverized to a "spiritual powder" the
fire tinges it with the "unchanging colour"; and "this spirit
which you seek, that you may tinge somewhat therewith, is
hidden and concealed in the body, like unto the soul in a man's
body." [58] The soul or bride in our text is thus a fiery, tincturing
spirit who gives the bridegroom rising from the grave (i.e., the
spiritualized body) a "garment" (colour).[59] This motif recalls
the ancient idea of the soul as a coloured garment enveloping
the material world. According to the Gnostic Basilides the

[52] Cf. the role of the crown in the Cabala (Bousset, pp. 201f.) and in Manichaeism
(p. 202, n. 1). There the crown of victory is borne ahead of the Primordial Man.
Also the Manichaean "wreath of light" (Reitzenstein, *Erlösungsmysterium*, p. 3).

[53] The same Senior quotation occurs in "Ros. phil.," *Art. aurif.*, II, p. 248.

[54] *Turba*, p. 123. •

[55] Ibid., p. 166. Cf. pp. 251f.: "For it is the soul that penetrates and tinctures the
body."

[56] P. 135: "The soul . . . is a spiritual nature out of which the colours appeared." •

[57] P. 155; cf. pp. 136 and 140.

[58] P. 141; cf. p. 160: "Then they become bodies having tincturing spirits and souls,
because they fertilize one another." •

[59] *Turba*, p. 147: "Saturate and cook, until that arises which he commanded to be
ruled by you, an intangible spirit, and until you see the elixir clothed with the
royal garment (that is, with the Tyrian hue)." P. 127: "When man and woman
are conjoined, the woman is no longer volatile and the compound is spiritualized,
and when this compound is changed into a red, spiritual breath, then arises the
beginning of the world."

world-soul is nothing but an "enphasis" or "colour" of light which has descended into matter.[60] As Philo puts it, it produces the "many-coloured fabric of this world."[61] The same archetypal image played a great role in the ancient mystery cults, when the neophyte was given a new "heavenly garment" as a symbol of his inner transformation and rebirth. The garment represented his final *solificatio*,[62] for which reason it was sometimes described as "light," "seal of light," etc.[63] These ancient ideas were preserved for a long time among the Manichaeans and the Mandaeans,[64] and they penetrated very early on into

[60] Hegemonius, *Acta Archelai*, p. 96, and Bousset, pp. 92, 94.

[61] For the seven aetheric garments of Physis see Hippolytus, *Elenchos*, V, 8, and Scott, *Hermetica*, IV, p. 409.

[62] Apuleius, *The Golden Ass*, pp. 285ff., and Reitzenstein, *Erlösungsmysterium*, p. 164: "The meaning is clear: the neophyte, reborn, becomes God, and the sun-god at that." These ancient ideas are probably based on the primitive equation garment = skin = soul. Cf. Ninck, *Wodan und germanischer Schicksalsglaube*, pp. 43ff.

[63] Bousset, pp. 303ff. Cf. the "Book of the Secrets of Enoch," 22 : 8–9 (Charles, *Apocrypha and Pseudepigrapha*, II, p. 443): "And the Lord said to Michael: 'Go and take Enoch from out of his earthly garments, and anoint him with my sweet ointment, and put him in the garment of my glory.' And Michael did thus, as the Lord had told him: He anointed me, and dressed me, and the appearance of that ointment is more than the great light, and his ointment is like sweet dew.' 'Acts of Philip (James, *Apocryphal New Testament*, p. 450): "Clothe me in thy glorious robe and thy seal of light that ever shineth." In the Ascension of Isaiah (Charles, pp. 52ff.), Isaiah sees in the highest heaven the crowns and robes which are to be given to the believers. In *Pistis Sophia*, his heavenly garment of shining light was sent down to Jesus after his resurrection, so that he might ascend in it. Likewise in the Acts of Thomas (James, pp. 414f.) a shining robe "that was made like unto me as it had been in a mirror" came down from heaven to the king's son. Similar ideas existed among the Mandaeans, and for a long time induced them to wear only white clothes (Bousset, p. 303, n. 2 and 364, n. 2). Cf. the rite of the Sethians, in which the celebrants were given a drink of the living water, then stripped off the likeness of slaves and put on the heavenly garment (Hippolytus, *Elenchos*, V, 19 and 27, and Bousset, p. 293).

[64] Thus the *Fihrist* says of the teachings of Mani (Reitzenstein, *Erlösungsmysterium*, pp. 28f.): "When a truthful man is about to die, the Primordial God sends a god of light in the form of the leading sage, together with three gods, and with them the water vessel, the robe, the head-band, the crown, and the wreath of light. . . . Also the devil appears to him . . . As soon as the truthful man sees them, he calls to his aid the goddess who has assumed the form of the sage . . . But they take him and clothe him with the crown, the wreath and the robe . . . and rise with him . . . to the sphere of the moon." (Cf. ibid., p. 177, and I Cor. 15.) It is worth noting that the helpful figures are *four* gods with *four* objects!

alchemy. Thus, in his visions, Zosimos saw the transformed *anthroparion* clad in a robe of royal purple.[65] He is therefore equated with the sun-god Mithras, who appeared to the neophyte as a king in a scarlet robe.[66] That just such a *solificatio* of the bridegroom is meant here is proved by the reference to Psalm 18 : 5–6, ". . . he hath set his tabernacle for the sun, which is like to the bridegroom coming out from the bridal chamber." [67] In patristic literature Christ was the "new sun," so that once again the Sol-Christus-filius-lapis parallel is taken up in our text. It should be borne in mind that throughout this part of the parable the bride and bridegroom are winged beings, i.e., spirits, and that everything that happens between them takes place in heaven, i.e., in the world beyond, the unconscious. The earth, the body, and earthly reality in general have been left behind like an empty grave. Therefore the author no longer intervenes in the dialogue with interpolated comments; he has, as it were, vanished in the impassioned converse of Wisdom and the glorified king.

542   In general, clothes signify, psychologically, an inner attitude that has become manifest, or one that either acts upon the environment or protects against it. The change of clothing in the mysteries therefore signifies a change of psychic attitude; for instance, the disrobing with which some of them begin means casting off the previous unsuitable attitude or persona (mask), and the *solificatio* robe means the new, religious attitude which has been found on a higher level of consciousness. The robing of the bridegroom by the queen thus indicates that he is not only transformed and has attained illumination, but can manifest it on a higher level of activity. Red or purple signifies healing power, mana, incorruptibility, enhanced power of irradiation.[68]

543   and shalt clothe me with a robe of righteousness and shalt betroth me to thee with thy ring and clothe my feet in sandals of gold. All this shall my perfect beloved do, exceeding beautiful and comely

---

65 "The Visions of Zosimos," par. 86 (III, v, 1), and Lippmann, I, p. 81.

66 Dieterich, *Eine Mithrasliturgie*, p. 10.

67 Ephraem Syrus, I, col. 532: "Light shone out before them, Jesus the bridegroom came forth from his chamber, the tomb remained with the angels in the midst." *

68 Concerning these significations of red, see Wunderlich, *Die Bedeutung der roten Farbe im Kultus der Griechen und Römer*.

in her delights, for the daughters of Sion saw her and the queens and concubines praised her. O queen of the heights, arise, make haste, my love, my spouse, speak beloved to thy lover, who and of what kind and how great thou art, for Sion's sake thou shalt not hold thy peace and for the sake of Jerusalem thou shalt not rest from speaking to me, for thy beloved heareth.

544   This passage continues the motif of the robing and adornment, and it should be noted that the bride is once more identified with God, for Isaiah 61 : 10 says: "I will greatly rejoice in the Lord, and my soul shall be joyful in my God. For he hath clothed me with the garments of salvation, and with the robe of justice he hath covered me: as a bridegroom decked with a crown and as a bride adorned with her jewels." Ephraem Syrus interprets this as the hierosgamos of the neophyte with God or the Church.[69] The author of *Aurora* must therefore have been fully aware that he was describing a *unio mystica* with God, and that the figure he variously calls Wisdom, the woman, the water, and the bride is nothing less than God himself or at any rate some aspect of him. The ring indicates the eternity of the lovers' union in the self, the golden sandals signify an incorruptible standpoint.[70] The bridegroom speaks throughout with such humility that one is inclined to see in him an ordinary mortal, indeed the author himself; but later it becomes increasingly clear that he is a personification of the self with whom the author has become emotionally identified. In contrast to the beginning of the treatise, however, there is no evidence of inflation. This may be because the scene has changed: the material world and the ego are abolished, everything is extinguished in the unconscious, so there can be no more question of an impure

[60] *Commentarius in Jesaiam*, cap. 61 (ed. Lamy, II, col. 184): "Let the Church rejoice in her God, for he hath clothed me with the garment of salvation, that is the stole of glory of baptism; for that is the true garment of salvation and white robe of glory. And he hath made me as a glorious bridegroom by absolution. And as a bride adorned. The bride is the Church, which is adorned with the beauty of all peoples." • I, col. 44, "Hymnus in Festum Epiphaniae," No. 4, verses 2–3: "For from heaven is his divine nature and from earth his garment of flesh. Everyone who puts off his garments mixes them with the garment of Christ for ever. Receive from him in the waters the garment which is not worn out or lost, wherewith he covers for ever those who put it on." • Cf. the real spiritual marriage which the Marcosians, for instance, celebrated in earthly imitation of the marriage of Sophia with the Saviour (Bousset, pp. 267ff., and esp. p. 315).
[70] von Franz, "Passio Perpetuae," p. 480.

mixture of this world and the world beyond, of conscious and unconscious. I must confess that I cannot conceive how this might be possible unless the author were in a state near to death. If it were just a passing delirium, the ego-personality would still be hovering in the background and, one would think, would make itself felt in one way or another.

545   After the bridegroom has praised his glorification by the queen in all humility, he beseeches her to tell him who she is, and the bride now gives answer.

546   Hear all ye nations, give ear all ye inhabitants of the world; my beloved, who is ruddy, hath spoken to me, he hath sought and besought: I am the flower of the field and the lily of the valleys, I am the mother of fair love and of knowledge and of holy hope.

547   All the aspects of the central figure of the opus, which were elucidated separately in the earlier parables, are summed up in this proclamation. She describes herself as the "flower of the field" and the "lily of the valleys," following the bride in the Canticles, in that well-known verse (2 : 1) which the Fathers consistently interpreted as referring to Mary or the Church.[71] Hugo Rahner [72] has comprehensively shown the classical prehistory of this symbol, as well as its patristic interpretations.[73] The flower, particularly the lily, also played an important role in alchemy. It symbolized the arcane substance, and as such was often called Lunatica (honesty), berissa, or moly. The lily was specifically a synonym for the white, feminine substance (as contrasted with the red rose) and for silver (as contrasted with gold).[74] The *succus lunariae* (juice of the moon-plant) was a synonym for the divine water; [75] hence we can understand why the bride, following Ecclesiasticus 24 : 23, immediately after-

71 Honorius, *Expos. in Cant.* (Migne, *P.L.*, vol. 172, col. 382), or "Sequence for the Nativity of the BVM," in *The Liturgical Poetry of Adam of St. Victor*, II, p. 220: "Flower of the field, unique lily of the valleys, from thee did Christ come forth. Thou, heavenly paradise, and unfelled Lebanon, breathing forth sweetness—thou art the throne of Solomon, to which no other throne is like in material or workmanship." • Cf. Hippolytus, *Comm. in Cant.*, pp. 49f., where "the Queen stood" is interpreted as the Church; and Honorius, *Quaest. et Resp. in Prov. et Eccl.*, cap. 31 (Migne, *P.L.*, vol. 172, col. 330).   72 "Die seelenheilende Blume."
73 Cf. also Jung, "The Philosophical Tree," ch. 9.
74 A detailed account is to be found in the treatise *Der kleine Baur* (see Bibliography s.v. Grasshoff). For the symbolism of the Lunaria see *Mysterium*, pp. 133f.
75 "Ros. phil.," *Art. aurif.*, II, p. 137.

wards calls herself the "vine": she is the source or fundamental substance of the red and white "water" (wine), symbolizing the opposites. Lily and vine are also symbols for Mary.[76]

548 As the fruitful vine I have brought forth a pleasant odour, and my flowers are the fruit of honour and riches.

549 Vine and grapes played a large role in classical alchemy. Hermes is there called the "vintner" ($\beta o \tau \rho v \chi i \tau \eta s$), who "reddens the white brands of his vintage with fire." [77] In the *Carmina Heliodori* the lapis is called the "white grape," which, crushed in the hand, gives out a fiery, odorous wine like blood.[78] Zosimos interprets this motif as the "mystery of the washing," or as the rust or poison ($i o s$).[79] In Ruland's *Lexicon* the "grapes of Hermes" are still defined as the philosophical water, distillation, solution, etc.[80]

550 In our text the allusion is also to Christian symbolism, to Christ as the "true vine" of whom Ephraem Syrus says that the souls are his shoots.[81] Mary too was compared with the vine. Ephraem Syrus says of her: "And Mary flourished, a new vine in place of that old vine Eve, and the new life Christ dwelt in her." [82] Or again: "Mary is the vine that grew from the blessed root of David. Her shoots yielded a grape filled with life-giving blood. Of that new wine did Adam drink, and returned resurrected to paradise." [83]

551 Just as the vine in ecclesiastical symbolism can mean Christ or Mary, so the bride in *Aurora* is obviously the producer of

---

[76] "Biblia Mariana" (Borgnet, XXXVII, p. 397): "Mary is the lily of all chastity; as a thorn to the rose, so Jewry gave birth unto Mary." •

[77] *Alch. grecs*, V, iv.

[78] *Carmina Heliodori*, p. 32, verses 180–85. Cf. the Eucharist of the Marcosians, where a cult-transformation of white into red wine took place (Leisegang, *Gnosis*, p. 347).

[79] *Alch. grecs*, III, vi.   [80] Latin edn. (1612), under "uvae."

[81] I, col. 22. Christ is also the grape that let itself be pressed to revivify souls with its wine (II, col. 482).   [82] I, col. 154. •

[83] II, col. 618. Cf. Hymn XX, col. 640: "Simeon bore in his arms the cluster of life gathered from the virginal vine." • Hymn I, col. 524: "The virginal vine gave grapes whose sweet wine brought consolation to them that weep." • Honorius, *Speculum* (Migne, *P.L.*, vol. 172, col. 902): "[Mary] was indeed the paradise of apples, the fount of the gardens, for in her rose up the tree of life, and from her flowed forth the fount of wisdom, and she was enriched with all delights, in whom were hidden all the treasures of wisdom and knowledge." •

the white (lily) and red (wine), a hermaphroditic being who unites the opposites in herself. Not only are they contained in her, she is actually the medium of their conjunction, as the next passage shows.

552   I am the bed of my beloved, which threescore of the most valiant ones surrounded, all holding swords upon their thigh because of fears in the night.

553   The "fears" are comparable with the "horrible darknesses of our mind" mentioned earlier—a last echo of the *nigredo*, now finally overcome. Honorius of Autun [84] interpreted the sixty "valiant ones" as indicating the number of perfection; [85] they symbolize "those perfected in the law of the Church, who wield the sword of the Logos and of discrimination (*discretio*) against heresies." Alchemically they probably refer (despite the multiplication by ten) to the six luminaries—Venus, Mercury, Mars, Jupiter, Saturn, Earth—which are present as servants at the coniunctio of sun and moon. The somewhat remarkable designation of the bride as the "bed" (*lectulus*) may be an allusion to Solomon's "litter" (Song of Songs 3 : 7–8), whose pillars he made of silver, the seat of gold, and the covering of purple—a passage which would invite alchemical interpretations. [86] In patristic literature Solomon's bed was taken as an image of the eternal bliss in which the Church reposes, or a symbol of the Church itself as Christ's couch. It was further interpreted as the "house of the banquet" (cf. supra, pp. 314, 358f.), or as an image for the sanctified soul which has become the resting-place of the inner Christ. [87] Mary, too, was "Solomon's bed, in which God's son

[84] *Expos. in Cant.* (Migne, *P.L.*, vol. 172, cols. 404–6).
[85] According to Augustine (*The City of God*, trans. Healey, Bk. X, ch. 30) the number 6 signifies perfection, because it is composed of 1 + the first even number, 2, + the first odd number, 3.
[86] Cf. the alchemical interpretation of the *lectulus* as the *vas coniunctionis* in "Rosinus ad Sarrat.," *Art. aurif.*, I, p. 192. In Origen (*In Cant. hom.*, Migne, *P.G.*, vol. 13, col. 51) the bed signifies the human body.
[87] Honorius, *Expos. in Cant.* (Migne, *P.L.*, vol. 172, cols. 406–8). Richard of St. Victor, *Explic. in Cant.* (Migne, *P.L.*, vol. 196, col. 410) says that "on my bed" etc. means "the soul, which seeks God." Cols. 410–11: "So peace and tranquillity of mind is the couch on which the bride resteth." ● Cf. the designation of the Church as the "sun-throne of Christ" in Athanasius, *Expos. in Ps. LXXXVIII* (Migne, *P.G.*, vol. 27, cols. 391–92), and Mary as "Solomon's throne" in Adam of St. Victor (n. 71 supra). Cf. Hippolytus, *Comm. in Cant.*, pp. 73f.

rested for nine months." [88] In this sense the bride serves as a *vas coniunctionis* for man with God.[89]

554   I am all fair and there is no spot in me; looking through the windows, looking through the lattices of my beloved, wounding his heart with one of my eyes and with one hair of my neck.

555   For the phrase "wounding his heart with one of my eyes," etc., I would refer the reader to Jung.[90] In patristic literature the hairs are interpreted as "subtle thoughts"; [91] hence this passage indicates a spiritual union. "Looking through the lattices of my beloved" refers to the soul penetrating the "prison of the body" —another coniunctio image.[92] The "window of escape" or "window of illumination" is an attribute of Mary,[93] corresponding to the "spiracle of eternity" in Dorn.[94] The *mysterium fenestrae* plays an important role in the Cabala, where the "window" means the link of light connecting Kether (the Crown) with Wisdom, and Wisdom with Intelligence.[95] Through these windows the highest Sefiroth are connected with the divine Light.

556   I am the sweet smell of ointments giving an odour above all aromatical spices and like unto cinnamon and balsam and chosen myrrh.

557   The bride is a sweet-smelling pneuma and is thus identified with the Holy Spirit.[96] The idea that the divine spirit is a perfume seems to be of Oriental origin; it is found again in late Jewish literature and also in Gnosticism.[97] Thus the Marcosians used an oil of balsam at baptism as a symbol of the "fragrance above all," [98] and the Sethians compared their light-pneuma to

---

88 "Biblia Mariana" (Borgnet, XXXVII, p. 399).

89 Cf. Isis as "throne."   90 *Mysterium*, pp. 31f.

91 Honorius (*Expos. in Cant.*, Migne, *P.L.*, vol. 172, col. 443): "The hairs are subtle thoughts." He interprets "one hair of thy neck" as unity of faith (col. 419).

92 In Origen (*In Cant. hom.*, II, 12, Migne, *P.G.*, vol. 13, col. 57) the window signifies the senses through which impressions go in and out.

93 "Biblia Mariana," p. 385.

94 *Mysterium*, p. 471.

95 Knorr von Rosenroth, *Kabbala denudata*, II, Part I, pp. 281f.

96 Leisegang, *Der heilige Geist*; Bousset, *Hauptprobleme*, p. 120, n. 1; Hippolytus, *Comm. in Cant.*, pp. 26, 32.

97 Lohmeyer, *Vom göttlichen Wohlgeruch*, and Steuer, *Über das wohlriechende Natron bei den alten Aegyptern*.

98 Bousset, p. 301.

the scent of myrrh.[99] Oil (μύρον or *unguentum*) was thought to confer indestructibility (ἀφθαρσία).[100] So this image, when amplified, coincides with that of the anima as a "tincturing" spirit that confers immortality, of which we spoke before.

558 I am the most prudent virgin coming forth as the Dawn, shining exceedingly, elect as the sun, fair as the moon, besides what is hid within.

559 The "most prudent virgin" and the "rising dawn" are images we have met before in the earlier parables, and already interpreted. "Besides what is hid within" [101] refers in the Canticles (4 : 1) to the "doves' eyes" of the beloved, radiating love.[102] Here it takes up again that strange image of the coniunctio as a sort of entry of God into the eye of the woman, which is at the same time the entry of the sun into the moon, as is subtly indicated in the text by the way the words "besides what is hid within" (4 : 1) link up with the immediately preceding "elect as the sun, fair as the moon" (6 : 9). For according to Senior, the goal of the coniunctio is the emergence of the full moon.[103] Hence the hint at that richly developed sun-moon symbolism whose significance is discussed in Jung.[104]

560 I am exalted as a cedar and a cypress tree on Mount Sion, I am the crown wherewith my beloved is crowned in the day of his espousals and of his joy, for my name is as ointment poured forth.

561 The image of the bride as the "crown wherewith my beloved is crowned," etc., is all the more significant because of its Biblical background, for in Canticles (3 : 11) the place of the bride is taken by the mother of Solomon ("see king Solomon in the diadem wherewith his mother crowned him"), who was interpreted as the mother and bride of Christ.[105] Thus the bride

---

99 Ibid., p. 302. Cf. the marriage hymn in Acts of Thomas (James, *Apocryphal New Testament*, p. 367): "Her garments are like the flowers of spring, and from them a waft of fragrance is borne."

100 Bousset, p. 302, n. 3.

101 St. Gregory the Great compares "what is hid within" to the "chambers of the south" that is, the heavenly land where the Holy Spirit dwells. *Moralia*, Lib. 9 in cap. 9 Job, sec. 18 (Eng. edn., I, p. 508).• Concerning the south, see supra, pp. 158 f.

102 Honorius, *Expos. in Cant.* (Migne, *P.L.*, vol. 172, col. 411): "Love in the eyes."

103 *De chemia*, pp. 37f.   104 *Mysterium*, ch. III, § 2 and 4.

105 Honorius, *Expos. in Cant.* (Migne, *P.L.*, vol. 172, col. 409). In the Acts of John (James, *Apocryphal New Testament*, p. 268), the diadem is a designation for the

in our text is the mother as well as the "sister" and "spouse" (p. 388) of the filius philosophorum, with whom he commits the royal incest. The Church interpreted this passage in Canticles as a prefiguration of the incarnation, as suggesting that Christ was clothed by his mother with the "diadem" of his fleshly existence. Ephraem Syrus praises Mary as the mother *and* sister *and* bride of Christ,[106] and according to Honorius of Autun the Canticles are here celebrating Christ's nuptials with his bride the Church in the womb of his virgin mother.[107] An alchemical parallel to our text would be that passage in the "Tractatus aureus Hermetis" where the king says: "I am crowned and adorned with the diadem, and I am clothed with the royal garment and bring joy to the heart; for, being chained to the arms and breast of my mother, and to her substance, I cause my substance to hold together and rest. . . ."[108] And in the "Allegoriae super librum Turbae" Mercurius says: "The mother bore me and was herself begotten by me."[109] Or again, in Aenigma VI: "Lay the red slave . . . over his mother. . . . Kill the mother . . . and marry the two in a glass."

562   That the bride is secretly the mother of the filius philosophorum is borne out by the preceding sentence, where she calls herself a cedar and cypress, for the tree in alchemy has among

---

Saviour (Reitzenstein, *Erlösungsmysterium*, p. xi). Cf. ibid., p. 9, where, among the Mandaeans, the living spirit and the Mother of Life clothe the *chroshtag* (call) and the *padwahtag* (answer) and then send them down as redeemers to the lost primordial man. See also *Mysterium*, p. 9.

106 II, col. 564: "There stands Mary, thy mother, thy sister, thy spouse, thy handmaiden. . . . O Master of thy Mother, God of thy Mother, younger and older than thy Mother . . ." • In some of the Gnostic systems Sophia appears as the sister, mother, and bride of Christ. Cf. Irenaeus, I. 30. 12; I. 11, and I. 3. 3 (*Writings* I, pp. 110, 46, 13); Hippolytus, *Elenchos*, VI, 34; Bousset, pp. 265–68, 272f., 315.

107 *Speculum* (Migne, *P.L.*, vol. 172, col. 1063): "The king who prepared a marriage feast for his son is God the Father, who joined the Church as bride to Jesus Christ, his son. The marriage bed of these nuptials is the holy Virgin's womb." • Col. 1065: "Concerning these nuptials King Solomon wove a comely marriage song when in praise of the bride and bridegroom he composed by the aid of the Holy Spirit the Canticle of Canticles." • The same motif occurs in the myth of Osiris, who was united with his twin sister Isis even in the mother's womb.

108 The same quotation also occurs in "Ros. phil.," *Art. aurif.*, II, pp. 247f.

109 Ruska, *Turba*, p. 329. • Senior, *De chemia*, p. 108: "The lapis is the gold and the mother of the gold, since it generates it; from it comes the dragon who devours his tail . . . and the rain watering the earth that flowers may sprout."

other things a maternal significance.[110] The significance of the crown and the incest motif is discussed in Jung.[111] All this part of the text reveals the anima more and more clearly in her helpful and favourable aspects. At the beginning Wisdom appeared in the role of a sublime psychopomp, but now she becomes more and more the lover. "Eros" and "Gnosis" are fused together in her.

563   In the words "my name is as ointment poured forth" she again describes herself as the unguent, which in alchemy is one of the many synonyms for the divine water, more particularly as connoting the *soul* of matter.[112] The "oil of gladness" mentioned in the third parable (pp. 265f.) is here taken up again.

564   I am the sling of David, the stone wherefrom tore out the great eye of Goliath and finally took off his head.

565   The dangerous side of the anima has not entirely disappeared, but it no longer troubles those who serve her, for in their hands it works like a sling with which they can conquer their enemies. Once it is controlled by conscious understanding, the previously destructive emotionality of the anima becomes an instrument for overcoming blind unconsciousness and one-sidedness. Goliath, like the dragon, is a symbol of the prima materia in the state of sinfulness and *nigredo*,[113] and—though the lapis itself is the ultimate goal—it is at the same time the mysterious means of reaching that goal.[114] The "great eye of Goliath," referred to in the singular, reminds us of Polyphemus: Goliath is blinded like the Cyclops. The significance of the eye (here considered primarily in its nefarious aspect) as the devouring female darkness is discussed in Jung.[115]

---

110 "The Philosophical Tree," ch. 13. Cf. "Answer to Job," pp. 387f.

111 *Mysterium*, ch. IV, *passim*.

112 Senior, *De chemia*, pp. 49, 55, 57, and 69: "By oil he means the Soul . . . which does not enter through the fire, but water extracts it." • Pp. 75 and 82: "And this that is born is the fatness which they call the soul and the egg." • Cf. *Pret. marg. nov.*, p. 169.

113 Mennens, *Theatr. chem.*, V, pp. 316f.: ". . . which overcame Goliath, that is, sin."

114 Honorius, *Speculum* (Migne, *P.L.*, vol. 172, col. 1041): "For the sling [of David] which was hurled is the humanity of Christ, whirled by his passions, [and] the stone which entered the forehead of Goliath was his divinity which pierced the jaw of Leviathan." •   115 *Mysterium*, p. 31ff.

566   I am the sceptre of the house of Israel and the key of Jesse, which openeth and no man shutteth, shutteth and no man openeth.

567   The motif of the sceptre of Israel and key of Jesse "which openeth and no man shutteth" emphasizes the *instrumental* significance of the lapis. The sceptre probably refers to the alchemical "regimen," and the key in other texts (as also in Roger Bacon) is an image for the arcane substance and the lapis. The "Rosarium" [116] says: "For this stone is the key . . . for . . . it is [endowed with] the most mighty spirit," and with it the doors of the metals are opened.[117] The lapis functions as a key inasmuch as the experience of the self (lapis) gives consciousness a "method" for realizing the secrets of the unconscious, namely its symbols. Hence the "Rosarium" says: "The philosophers speak of the salt, and they call it the soap of the sages and the little key which shutteth and openeth, and again shutteth and no man openeth; for without this little key, they say, no one in this world can attain perfection in this science, that is, except he understand the calcining of the salt after its preparation." [118] The manifold significance of salt is discussed in Jung,[119] and its connotations as a principle of Eros, understanding, wit, etc. help to explain why Wisdom refers to herself as the "key" in our text.

568   I am that chosen vineyard, into which the householder sent his labourers at the first, second, third, sixth, and ninth hours, saying: Go you also into my vineyard, and at the twelfth hour I will give you what shall be just. I am that land of the holy promise, which floweth with milk and honey and bringeth forth sweetest fruit in due season;

569   Wisdom compares herself to the vineyard in the parable (Matt. 20 : 1ff.) [120] and to the Promised Land, thus emphasizing her identity with the "spiritual earth" of the previous parable. She is the reality of the psyche as such.

570   wherefore have all the philosophers commended me and sowed in me their gold and silver and incombustible grain. And unless that

---

116 *Art. aurif.*, II, p. 162 (Rosinus quotation).
117 Ibid., p. 181.   118 P. 146.   119 *Mysterium*, ch. III, § 5.
120 Cf. the interpretation of Mennens (*Theatr. chem.*, V, p. 338), who sees in the sum of the 1st, 3rd, 6th, 9th, and 11th hours an allusion to the number 30.

grain falling into me die, itself shall remain alone, but if it die, it bringeth forth threefold fruit: for the first it shall bring forth shall be good because it was sown in good earth, namely of pearls; the second likewise good because it was sown in better earth, namely of leaves; the third shall bring forth a thousandfold because it was sown in the best earth, namely of gold.

571   This motif, too, is taken over from the previous parable, where Hermes commanded his son to sow gold in the earth of the Promised Land. The "earth of leaves" (*terra foliorum*) is the "white foliate earth" (*terra alba foliata*), or silver-earth.[121] In Senior, *granum* (grain) is sometimes the tincture, sometimes gold, and sometimes the soul.[122] The "Rosarium," commenting on this passage, explains the grain as the "grain of the body" and the earth as the prima materia, which absorbs the "fatty vapour" (Mercurius).[123] In Aenigma VII of "Allegoriae super librum Turbae" the "single grain of burgeoning seed" must be joined in mystic marriage to the "primordial vapour of the earth."[124] The primordial earth-vapour, the fatty vapour, and Mercurius are, accordingly, all synonyms for the Promised Land and show that an airy, sublimated earth is meant.[125] This consists of three substances: pearls, silver, and gold; we find the

121 "Clangor buccinae," *Art. aurif.*, I, p. 330.
122 *De chemia*, p. 42: "For in the beginning they dissolve this tincture with the moisture, which is from itself, and in the end with fire, as you see the grain Hospho or Offoto in its stalk, naturally nourished or increased with water and fire, and the tincture comes to birth in it. . . . Turn the gold into leaves . . ." •
P. 115: "The tincture, which Hermes also called gold when he said, Sow the gold in the white foliate earth, signified this tincture, and they called it crocus and Effer." • P. 70: ". . . the true tincture of Calid, that is, fixed and incombustible, whereas its grain was formerly combustible." •
123 *Art. aurif.*, II, p. 146.
124 Ruska, *Turba*, p. 329. Cf. the words of the *filius regis* or lapis in the "Metaphora Belini" (*Art. aurif.*, II, p. 249): "I am the grain sown in pure land, which being born grows and multiplies and brings forth fruit to the sower; for everything which is generated is generated in its own kind, and each individual multiplies the form of its own species and not otherwise." •
125 This recalls the Orphic idea of the "heavenly Earth" (moon), from which souls came. Plutarch, *De facie in orbe lunae*, 21 (Loeb edn., XII, p. 141); Macrobius, *Somn. Scip.*, I. 19. 8; Rahner, "Mysterium Lunae," pp. 68, 124. The "air-earth" or "light-earth" of the Manichaeans is a similar concept (cf. Flügel, *Mani, seine Lehre und seine Schriften*, p. 86: Bousset, p. 135). It corresponds to Sophia or Sapientia.

same classification in Senior, from whom it was taken over.[126] This mystic earth is therefore a kind of lower Trinity.[127] The psychological significance of the "lower triad" is discussed in Jung.[128]

572   The essential thing about this lower Trinity is that it is described as an earth, i.e., as a psychic reality which has to do with the nature of matter. Matter thus acquires an importance of its own and is even raised to divine rank—in complete reversal of the medieval scholastic view, according to which matter, unless it is given form, has only potential reality. The text is, in effect, proclaiming a glorification of the feminine principle, of the body and matter. From this we can see what a shattering breakthrough of unconscious contents was needed before a man of the Middle Ages could hazard such a statement, and it is also clear that it could, as the text shows, be formulated only indirectly, in the language of trance or delirium—for these are the compensatory statements of the unconscious and not the conscious views of a man of that age.

573   For from the fruits of this grain is made the food of life, which cometh down from heaven. If any man shall eat of it, he shall live without hunger. For of that bread the poor shall eat and shall be filled, and they shall praise the Lord that seek him, and their hearts shall live for ever.

574   In this threefold earth is sown the incombustible grain, which dying brings forth a thousandfold and from which is made the bread of life. Alchemically this would refer to the phase of the *multiplicatio,* when, by "projection" of the tincture or of the gold upon base metals, the latter are turned into gold. The author parallels the alchemical *multiplicatio* by a Christian *amplificatio,* for the bread of life is the Host, i.e., Christ's body signifying the *multitudo fidelium* (multitude of the faith-

---

[126] *De chemia,* p. 51. Foliate gold is called "sand" or "washed earth" by Maria Prophetissa (Olympiodorus in *Alch. grecs,* II, iv). Senior's "starry earth" is the γῆ ἀστερίτης of the Greeks (ibid., II, iii, and III, xxv).

[127] Cf. this interpretation in Mennens, *Theatr. chem.,* V, p. 301.

[128] "Phenomenology of the Spirit in Fairytales," pp. 234ff. Cf. "The Visions of Zosimos," par. 127: "In the image of Mercurius and of the lapis the 'flesh' glorified itself in its own way; it would not transform itself into spirit but, on the contrary, 'fixed' the spirit in stone and endowed this with practically all the attributes of the Trinity."

ful). In so far as the *multiplicatio* occurs here in a single individual it would mean—in Indian terms—a dissolution of the
individual in the universal atman. In the self the one is also
the many, and the many are all comprised in the one. This
extraordinary insight seems to indicate a supreme, borderline
state in which the individual ego is extinguished and replaced
by an experience that includes all men. Such a state might well
be conceived as an illumination before death.

575   In alchemy the *multiplicatio* progresses by multiples of ten,
and here I can refer the reader to Jung's statements in
"Psychology of the Transference." [129] According to Rhabanus
Maurus, ten is the number of perfection and of the everlasting
reward.[130] In the teachings of Joachim of Flora the *ecclesia
spiritualis* will arise in the seventh age, the age of the monastic
orders when "Sacerdotium" and "Imperium" will finally be
united like sun and moon.[131] I mention this because clear traces
of the idea of an *ecclesia spiritualis* can be found in this seventh
parable (corresponding to the seventh age); but as this motif is
touched on again in the closing words of the parable and thus
seems to be the real goal of the opus, I shall come back to it
later on.

576   I give and take not back, I feed and fail not, I make secure and fear
not; what more shall I say to my beloved? I am the mediatrix of
the elements, making one to agree with another; that which is warm
I make cold, and the reverse; that which is dry I make moist, and
the reverse; that which is hard I soften, and the reverse. I am the
end and my beloved is the beginning, I am the whole work and all
science is hidden in me,

577   In Senior the "soul" is described as the power which makes
the opposites come together in one.[132] She works miracles and
also reverses them. She is, as our text shows, "the whole work,"
"all science," and—so far as the soul and her spouse are *one*
being—the beginning and the end, alpha and omega, another
token of her divine status. An interesting parallel is the collec-

129 Pars. 525ff.
130 *Alleg. in sacr. script.* (Migne, *P.L.*, vol. 112, col. 907): "The denarius is Christ,
as in the Apocalypse (vi, 6), and they who hold to it in faith and works belong to
Christ." •
131 Hahn, *Geschichte der Ketzer*, III, pp. 289ff.
132 *De chemia*, p. 34.

tion of honorific titles which Albertus Magnus (?) put together in praise of Mary in the "Biblia Mariana": [133] she is the empyrean, the light that scatters the darkness of ignorance, the fruitful earth that bore the green grass, Christ; the fountain of life, "hospitatrix" of wandering souls, bride, mother of grace, "our sister," stairway to heaven, gate of the kingdom, dawn of illumination (*Aurora illuminationis*), dawn that affrights the demons; treasure-house of sanctity which Christ opened, queen of the world, door, year, time of grace, cloud of the overshadowing, cooling mist, ark of the covenant, rock from which water of grace or oil flows, star of enlightenment, shining lamp, "best earth," sister of our poverty, sun, mount of benediction, bridal chamber of God's delight, window of escape or illumination, altar, fleece of the divine dew, "sole eagle." She clothes us with the garment of divinity, she is the Queen of Sheba and the throne of Solomon and of the Trinity, the tabernacle for God's union with human nature. These symbols all describe a feminine numen which closely resembles the bride in our text, save that here the dark and dangerous side is also included.

578 I am the law in the priest and the word in the prophet and counsel in the wise. I will kill and I will make to live and there is none that can deliver out of my hand. I stretch forth my mouth to my beloved and he presseth his to me; he and I are one; who shall separate us from love? None and no man, for our love is strong as death.

579 The identity of the bride with God is beyond all doubt, for the words she speaks are God's own (Deut. 32 : 39: "I kill, and I make alive; I wound, and I heal; neither is there any that can deliver out of my hand"). She *is* God, or his feminine "correspondence" in matter. She is God—but as a loving woman embracing the man in order to draw him into God's own antithetical nature and at the same time into his all-enveloping wholeness. This experience, as the text says, transcends even death.

580 This unio mystica is, compared with the usual medieval texts, something new and completely different, because ordinarily it is the human soul as a feminine being that unites with Christ or God. Man or his anima is the bride. Here, on the contrary, God is the bride, and man or the self the bridegroom.

133 Borgnet, XXXVII, pp. 367ff.

This singular exchange of roles must be understood in the first place as a compensatory phenomenon: the masculine, spiritual God-image has turned into its opposite, into a figure that unites God's "self-reflection"—Sophia or Wisdom—with matter and nature. What is manifest in this figure is an aspect of God which is striving to become conscious of itself—as though the human psyche and matter were the chosen place for God's self-realization. The son-lover of this figure, however, is a human being in a glorified end-state, who has passed through death. In contrast to Wisdom, *he* has cast off the darkness from himself. This situation explains the somewhat uncanny effect of unreality which the concluding part of the text conveys. The "unreal," glorified human being now addresses Wisdom.

581 O beloved, yea supremely beloved, thy voice hath sounded in my ears, for it is sweet, and thine odour is above all aromatical spices. O how comely is thy face, thy breasts are more beautiful than wine, my sister, my spouse, thy eyes are like the fishpools in Heshbon, thy hairs are golden, thy cheeks are ivory, thy belly is as a round bowl never wanting cups, thy garments are whiter than snow, purer than milk, more ruddy than old ivory, and all thy body is delightful and desirable unto all.

582 The lover's response to his beloved is in passionate words that are practically all taken from the Canticles. But an important psychological change is apparent at this point: for the first time the anima figure is addressed directly. Till now either she herself was speaking, or the author was speaking to a human audience and telling them of Wisdom's "glory." He was quite literally "seized" or "possessed" by her, but was unable to turn that experience inwards and confront it actively. Now he has passionately turned to the bride herself—which means, psychologically, an emotional acceptance of the unconscious, a joyous affirmation of the anima. The author turns away from his fellow human beings, and though they will be invited to share the bliss of the lovers, his earlier didactic intentions have largely disappeared. The archetypal image of a divine pair and of their hierosgamos fills the text from now on, god and goddess consummate the mystic marriage, and a pagan *joie de vivre* breaks through in words that border on the heretical. At the same time the text conveys a feeling of inner liberation, as if the

388

prison of conventional religious ideas and human narrow-mindedness had finally burst open, and the author had left his previous mental world behind him like an empty shell.

583   In his paean of praise the bridegroom describes the bride in symbolic images that show her as the essence of wholeness. "Thy navel is as a round bowl never wanting cups" (Cant. 7 : 2) was interpreted by Honorius of Autun [134] as signifying "temperance," [135] which has its seat in the middle of the body, and the cups are the seven gifts of the Holy Spirit. Temperance, he says, is "round by reason of its circumspection, and fruitful by reason of its wisdom." Rhabanus Maurus interprets the navel as the contemplative Order.[136] In the text there is probably a subsidiary allusion on the one hand to the ecclesiastical view of Mary as the *vas devotionis* and of the Church as the vessel of "true doctrine" and of the human body as the vessel of the spirit,[137] and on the other hand to the alchemical *vas* symbolism with its complex meanings.[138] The vessel had to be round because it was an image of the cosmos and of the heavenly spheres,[139] as well as of the human head as the seat of the *anima rationalis*.[140] In the *Corpus Hermeticum* the cosmos is described as a vessel or sphere, and this sphere was also the Nous, which moved like a head; everything connected with this head was immortal.[141] To this "cosmic reason" or "soul" the Harranites erected hemispherical temples.[142] The *krater* (mixing bowl) also has a hylic significance; in the *Corpus Hermeticum*, matter (and

134 Migne, *P.L.*, vol. 172, cols. 457 and 465.

135 See "temperance" in Parable V, supra, p. 336.

136 Or as *luxuria* (Migne, *P.L.*, vol. 112, col. 1085).

137 Lactantius, "Divinae institutiones," 2. 12. 11 (*Works*, I, p. 122).

138 *Psychology and Alchemy*, Index, s.v. "vas."

139 Senior, p. 122. Cf. the "spherical apparatus" of the Greeks (*Alch. grecs*, IV, vii) and the Zosimos quotation in Olympiodorus (ibid., II, iv): "And he points to the house of the souls of the philosophers, saying: The house was spherical or egg-shaped, looking to the west . . . and it had the form of a snail's shell."

140 Cf. "The Visions of Zosimos," par. 113, and "Transformation Symbolism in the Mass," pp. 239ff. Also *Turba*, p. 254, n. 3. According to the *Fihrist*, alchemists are those who are "famed for the production of the head and of the perfect elixir." In "Cons. coniug.," *Ars chemica*, p. 66, the water is called the "caput mundi." Cf. Berthelot, *Moyen âge*, III, pp. 140f., and Lippmann, I, pp. 97f.

141 Scott, *Hermetica*, I, p. 194.

142 Chwolsohn, *Die Ssabier und der Ssabismus*, II, pp. 367, 376, 382. Cf. the round "barba" (pyramid) in Senior, *De chemia*, p. 80.

in Plutarch, time) [143] is called the vessel of genesis and decay, and in Neoplatonism the cosmos is a hollow or cave.[144] Plato and, later, certain Orphic sects held that the world-creator mixed the cosmos in a huge *krater*,[145] and Zosimos in his vision [146] saw the elements being transformed in a "bowl-shaped" altar which embraced the entire cosmos.[147] Such is the context of the bride's designation as a *crater tornalis*.

584   Come forth, daughters of Jerusalem, and see, and tell and declare what ye have seen; say, what shall we do for our sister, who is little and hath no breasts, in the day when she shall be wooed? I will set my strength upon her and will take hold of her fruits, and her breasts shall be as the clusters of the vine.

585   This passage, based on Canticles 8 : 8–9 and 7 : 8, shows that the *soror mystica* is still too young for marriage and will only be matured by the man's wooing. In patristic literature it was interpreted as referring to the "young Church" which is ripened by Christ,[148] or to Mary, who lacked the "breasts of concupiscence." As applied to alchemy it suggests that the bride still lacks something, namely the "strength" of the male. The Song of Songs continues: "If she be a wall, let us build upon it bulwarks of silver" (8 : 9). A final *fixatio* through the "body" or "spirit-body" is still missing. This implies that only an individual realization of the anima gives her her specific form and quality. Only when God—and the bride *is* God—is realized in a human being does he become actual. Therefore, compared with man, he quite logically appears as a "woman" lacking strength, and even as an undeveloped girl. This image is almost an over-accentuation of God's helplessness—to compensate the dogmatic image of a father-deity alien to man and removed to the realm of metaphysics.

586   A striking parallel is furnished by the Persian idea that

143 Scott, I, p. 422, and III, p. 396; Plutarch, *De Ei*, 392 (Loeb edn., V, p. 243).

144 Porphyry, *De antro nympharum*, 5 and 21 (ed. Nauck, pp. 59, 70f.).

145 *Timaeus*, 41D; Lucian, *Bis accusatus*, 34, 834 (*The Double Indictment*, IV, p. 58); Servius, *Grammatici*, II, p. 93; Macrobius, *Somn. Scip.*, I. 12. 8. Cf. Scott, II, pp. 141 and 151, and Leisegang, *Gnosis*, pp. 126, 336.

146 "The Visions of Zosimos," pars. 86f.

147 See *Psychology and Alchemy*, pars. 408ff., and Scott, I, p. 148, for the interpretation of the *krater*.

148 Honorius, *Expos. in Cant.* (Migne, *P.L.*, vol. 172, col. 480).

when a man dies, he meets his soul in the form of a beautiful young girl of about fifteen, who is also an old sage.[149] So this motif of the "little sister" again has associations with ideas that are linked with the experience of death.

587 Come, my beloved, and let us go into thy field, let us abide in the villages, let us go up early to the vineyard, for the night is past and the day is at hand; let us see if thy vineyard flourisheth, if thy flowers have brought forth fruits. There shalt thou give thy breasts to my mouth, and I have kept for thee all fruits new and old;

588 The bridegroom summons his beloved to go out into the country and celebrate a feast of joy with men, "for the night is past and the day is at hand." [150] After the night of the moon and the dawn, when the "woman" ruled, there now breaks the day of the sun, when the lapis is perfected. "Going into thy field" and "abiding in the villages" suggests expansion and liberation from cramped humanity, and ecstatic union with nature. But it might also mean relinquishing the sick body at death—death breaks like a new morning, and in its light everything is transformed: it brings an entirely new state of consciousness. In this new light the lovers enjoy their bliss.

589 let us therefore enjoy them and use the good things speedily as in youth, let us fill ourselves with costly wine and ointments, and let no flower pass by us save we crown ourselves therewith, first with lilies, then with roses, before they be withered. Let no meadow escape our riot. Let none of us go without his part in our luxury,

590 This passage has no ecclesiastical parallel, for the words which the author puts into the mouth of the bridegroom are those spoken by the "ungodly" (*luxuriantes*) in Wisdom 2 : 5ff. Either he suffered a lapse of memory or else he was consciously alluding to a non-Christian mystery. At any rate it is a break-through of the classical or pagan feeling for nature, or—to speak with Heraclitus—a "phallic hymn" sung in honour of Dionysus

---

149 Reitzenstein, *Erlösungsmysterium*, p. 31.
150 Cf. St. Ambrose, *Hexaemeron*, IV. 8. 32 (Migne, *P.L.*, vol. 14, col. 204), according to whom these words are addressed to men by the Church (Luna), "who enlightens the darkness of our temporal world," the word "day" signifying the appearance of Christ (Sol).

and Hades.[151] Liberation from the prison of the body seems also to be a liberation from the narrowness of spiritual prejudice; the natural man is set free and celebrates his oneness with nature.

591   The lovers invite all men to pick flowers (lilies and roses = *albedo* and *rubedo*) and to crown themselves with them.[152] The burgeoning of the earth has already been mentioned in the sixth parable, where it was said that there was a "germinating water" in the earth which produces "fruits and bread and wine and herb for the service of men." This water is like the *quinta essentia,* which the "Expositio epistulae Alexandri Regis" [153] says is a "spirit, which quickeneth and changeth all things, and maketh every seed to sprout, and kindleth every light, and bringeth all fruits to bear." [154] According to the *Turba,*[155] flowers are the "virtue" which proceeds from the divine water, and in Senior golden flowers are equated with the tinctures.[156] Pseudo-Democritos says that the "house of the mystery" is surrounded by "pools and gardens." [157] In Greek alchemy flowers and blossoms are an image for spirits or souls; [158] the lapis is a "terrestrial sun" or "blossom of metal," [159] or a "well-formed flower sprouting from four branches." [160] Flowers

151 Heraclitus in Freeman, *Ancilla,* p. 25, No. 15: "If it were not in honour of Dionysus that they conducted the procession and sang the phallic hymn, their activity would be completely shameless. But Hades is the same as Dionysus, in whose honour they rave and perform the Bacchic revels."

152 Flowers correspond to the stars, with which they are connected through the medium of the air: ". . . as heaven is married to earth, having for a bridesman Mercury, or the aforesaid aerial spirit" (Mennens, *Theatr. chem.,* V, p. 379). Cf. the herbs used in Dorn's alchemical procedure, *Mysterium,* pp. 479f.

153 *Art. aurif.,* I, p. 247. *

154 The "germinating water" is the *aqua divina* which contains the spirit of God. Cf. "Psychology and Religion," pp. 100f. For the alchemical significance of the spring rain see *Carmina Heliodori* (p. 37, Carmen II, verses 93–97): "It rains, and fruits are brought forth in all the earth . . . spring enters the warm and moist ground, and the earth sprouts forth every kind of flowers."

155 P. 145.   156 *De chemia,* pp. 11, 57, and 108.   157 *Alch. grecs,* II, iv.

158 Synesios, ibid., II, iii: "By the word flower he (Democritus) means the subliming of souls, i.e., pneumata."

159 "The Book of Sophe," ibid., III, xlii, 1. Zosimos calls the sublimation (ἄρσις) the "rising of the flowers" (ibid., III, ii, 3; III, xv). For Democritus the most important flowers are "sea blossom" and the "Italic rose" (II, i); for Synesios they are the Cilician crocus and "anagillis," which signifies the "ascent of souls" (II, iii).

160 *Carmina Heliodori,* pp. 30f.

also play a role in the hierosgamos described in Komarios: [161] "The waters run along and waken the sleeping bodies and the spirits languishing in prison . . . and they rise up and clothe themselves with many beautiful colours, like the flowers in the spring . . ." "Behold the fulfilment of the art: the union of bride and bridegroom. . . . Behold the plants and their variations—behold, I tell you the whole truth! See and understand, how the clouds rise up from the sea, bearing the blessed waters with them, and they water the earth, and seeds and flowers come forth. . . . Take care to water your earth and nourish your seeds, that you may reap ripe fruit." [162] This sowing of the seed in Komarios refers to the "vegetal resurrection" of Osiris, that is, to the Egyptian ritual for the dead, at which seeds and bulbs were placed on the mummy, their germination signifying its resurrection. In the non-alchemical Hermetic text "Isis to Horus" (named "Kore Kosmou"), [163] the demiurge by a magic spell creates the world out of pneuma, fire, and other ingredients, and when the mixture is stirred a volatile, transparent substance, which only God can see, rises to the surface, which he calls *psychosis*—soul-stuff. This is the "efflorescence" (τὸ ἐπανθοῦν), and from it the souls are formed.

592   Flowers also play a role in ecclesiastical symbolism. Ephraem Syrus says that, when Christ was united with his bride, the Church, in the Easter month of Nisan, [164] the earth was filled with flowers. [165] St. Ambrose interprets the passage "the winter is past . . . the flowers appear on the earth," etc. (Cant. 2 : 11f.), to which allusion is made in the text, as referring to the Church in her final glory. [166] Elsewhere in patristic literature flowers are

---

[161] *Alch. grecs*, IV, xx.

[162] Komarios goes on to say: "Fire has been subordinated to water, and earth to air. Also air has been subordinated to fire, and earth to water, fire and water to earth, and earth to air, and they have become one. From the plants and vapours the One is formed."   [163] Scott, I, pp. 464ff.

[164] Nisan (March-April) is the month of the opus in the Syrian alchemical texts. In Egypt it was Pharmouthi. Cf. Lippmann, I, pp. 48 and 58.

[165] "De resurrectione Christi," XX, in *Hymni et sermones*, II, cols. 756f.: "Nisan, the month of victory, brought forth the spouse of the King, disturbed the earth with its outpourings and filled it with scattered flowers . . . the pure nuptials being effected in the desert." • Hymn XXI: "Nisan also filled the earth with a garment woven of colours of all kinds, the earth put on a tunic and garment of flowers." •

[166] *Hexaemeron*, 4. 5. 22 (Migne, *P.L.*, vol. 14, cols. 198f.).

an image for the transience of human life,[167] or they are blossoms of the mind bedewed by the Holy Spirit and warmed by the sun of the Logos.[168] They appear in the works of the martyrs and also in the *typi*, the symbols of Christ.[169] According to Origen,[170] flowers symbolize the burgeoning of the "seed of spiritual understanding" and a "living meaning" which the spirit infuses into the Scriptures. In general, flowers symbolize feeling and emotion, and it is noticeable how in the text of *Aurora* the feeling of ecstasy breaks through more and more strongly and sweeps away all didactic and rational aspects. Perhaps the nearest thing to this part of the text is a curious fragment which Lacinius ascribes to Albertus Magnus,[171] though I was unable to trace it in the extant Albertus treatises (or in those of Pseudo-Albertus). It runs: "Pluck divers kinds of flowers filled with the odour of all good things. In them is the odour of sweetness and the light of beauty, the splendour and glory of the world. This is the flower of flowers, the rose of roses, and the lily in the valley. Rejoice therefore in thy youth, O youth, and learn to pluck the flowers; for I have led thee into the garden of paradise.[172] Weave

---

[167] Ephraem Syrus, II, col. 318. The same view is found in Simon Magus (Leisegang, *Gnosis*, p. 69).

[168] Ibid., II, col. 752: "Who hath seen flowers bursting forth from books as from the hills? Chaste maidens have filled with them the wide spaces of the mind. Lo, a voice like the sun scattered flowers over the crowds." Col. 754: "Children have scattered fair and reasonable flowers before the king. The little one is crowned with them; . . . let each gather all flowers and mix them with the flowers which have grown in his land. . . . Let them offer to our Lord a crown of flowers; the bishop his sermons, the priests their praises, the deacons their readings . . . Let us invite . . . the martyrs, apostles, and prophets, their flowers are like to him: their roses are copious, their lilies have a sweet smell: from the garden of delights they gather most beauteous flowers, and bring them to the crown of our most beauteous feast. Glory to thee from the blessed. The crowns of kings are poor in comparison to the riches of thy crown. Purity is woven into it; faith triumphs in it; humility is resplendent in it; many-hued sanctity shines in it; great charity gleams in it, the queen of all flowers. Lo, thy crown is perfect. Blessed be he who granted us to weave it." • Honorius, *Expos. in Cant.* (Migne, col. 392): "Flowers are men who flourish in faith" (the flower of the vine = the faith of Christ).

[169] Ephraem Syrus, I, pp. 112 and 148–56; II, p. 756.

[170] *In Cant. hom.*, Lib. III.

[171] Collectanea Lacinii ex Alberto Magno, in *Pret. marg. nov.*, fol. 180ʳ.

[172] Cf. Albertus, "Mariale," CLXIV (Borgnet, XXXVII, p. 245), with reference to Mary: ". . . fulness of flowers, herbs, and fruits, signifying perfection of manners, virtues, and divers operations." •

thyself a wreath for thy head and enjoy the delights of this world, praising God and succouring thy neighbour in distress. Now will I reveal to thee the science and disclose the secret and give thee understanding of the hidden things of the art, and that which hath long been concealed shall be brought to light." A commentator explains that this passage refers to the "purification of the spirits."

593   The flower motif recalls the peculiar role which certain flowers and herbs play in Paracelsus and Dorn, discussed at considerable length in Jung.[173] Flowers are, so to speak, ingredients of the "lower heaven," equivalents of the stars—in other words, they represent components of our psychic totality, the self. Since the soul "can live only in and from human relationships," [174] these flowers in *Aurora,* which blossom during the coniunctio, indicate a blossoming of psychic relationship. This relationship means being filled with the spirit of Wisdom, who even cleanses the joy of the "ungodly" of its sinfulness and herself shares it; [175] for, as we have said, it is the words of the sinners that are here put into the mouth of the bridegroom. Whether the author was conscious of this fact is impossible to say. Since the coniunctio was presumably experienced in a transconscious state in the preliminary stages of death, all equivocal interpretations of this passage are beside the point—*ubi spiritus, ibi libertas.*

594   let us leave everywhere tokens of joy, for this is our portion, that we should live in the union of love with joy and merriment, saying: Behold how good and pleasant it is for two to dwell together in unity. Let us make therefore three tabernacles, one for thee, a second for me, and a third for our sons, for a threefold cord is not easily broken.

595   The words of Psalm 132 : 1, "Behold how good and how pleasant it is for brethren to dwell together in unity," are here

[173] "Paracelsus as a Spiritual Phenomenon," pars. 171, 190ff., and *Mysterium,* pp. 479ff.
[174] "The Psychology of the Transference," par. 444.
[175] Nevertheless, I have not ventured to read "pecum/pĉtum" of the MSS as "peccatum" instead of the Biblical "pratum" (meadow) of the printed text. (The meadows in the Song of Songs were interpreted as the heavenly mysteries and the herbs as the words of the Gospel. Cf. Honorius, *Quaest. et Resp.,* Migne, *P.L.,* vol. 172, col. 327.) For all that, it might easily have been a psychologically significant parapraxis on the part of an early copyist, unconsciously adapted to the meaning of the context.

referred to the alchemical coniunctio, but out of the dwelling of two-in-one is made a dwelling of three-in-one—the image of the three tabernacles and the threefold cord which "is not easily broken." [176] From the Biblical original (Eccles. 4 : 11–12) it is difficult to see how the saying about the threefold cord joins up with the praise of marriage, of "two lying together." We have to suppose a third, unifying power which acts as a link between the two.[177] Three, the ternarius, was a "sign of concord and conjunction" in medieval number symbolism.[178] In alchemy we often come across the image of a pair linked together by a third, for instance by *Mercurius senex,* who clearly stands for the Holy Spirit.[179]

596   The motif of the cord is a widespread archetypal idea. Alike in the initiations of the shamans and in the Tibetan religious texts we find that the initiate has to climb up a rope into the other world. In Tibet the dead ruler was given a certain rope so that he could climb back to the place from which the first ruler once came down on a similar rope.[180] The rope thus represents a continuity of experience or meaning through which consciousness is connected with its substrate, the collective unconscious. On the other hand, ropes, nooses, snares, etc. signify magical "bonds," [181] generally with demons or gods—that is, alliance with or subjection to an archetype. The point of many shamanistic initiations is to establish contact with the other side, the lost paradise.[182] In this case the rope is a variant of the fairy-

[176] Honorius (Migne, col. 339) interprets the threefold cord as the Trinity.

[177] Richard of St. Victor, *Explic. in Cant.* (Migne, *P.L.,* vol. 196, col. 478): "For he exhorts not merely with twofold, but with threefold voice, that she may come, declaring the vastness of the love and desire which he has for her, since a threefold repetition is an attestation of greatness and strength, for a threefold cord is not easily broken." •

[178] Helinandus of Froidmont, *De cognitione sui* (Migne, *P.L.,* vol. 212, col. 728): "The binarius, which has no middle term, is without a link, and signifies division. But the ternarius, which has a middle term, is the sign of concord and conjunction. For it is the first of the odd numbers, and the first wholly unequal, whence as it were all is concord. . . . And when the singer of Mantua [Virgil] said, 'God rejoices in odd numbers,' it is as if he had said: God loves peace and love, for he is himself peace and love." •

[179] Cf. *The Book of Lambspringk* (Waite, *Mus. Herm.,* I, fig. xi, p. 297), where the pair is replaced by a father-son group.

[180] Eliade, *Shamanism,* pp. 430ff.

[181] Ibid., p. 419.   [182] P. 484. Examples on pp. 490, 492, 311, 117.

tale motif of the world-tree ("Jack and the Beanstalk," etc.) or world-axis. In an American Indian tale, a man follows his dead wife by means of a magic string. Here the rope has the significance of a fated union that lasts beyond death. It is indeed very remarkable to see how, in this last parable, more and more mythological motifs turn up which are connected with the idea of life after death or with experiences during which the body lies there in sickness or trance. It is a revelation of psychic contents that border on the extreme limit of conscious experience.

597   The three tabernacles are an allusion to the transfiguration of Christ (Matt. 17:4: "Let us make here three tabernacles, one for thee, and one for Moses, and one for Elias"). This again stresses the death aspect and the parallel of the lapis with the risen Christ, but we have also to think of Apocalypse 21:3, where it is said of the new Jerusalem coming down from heaven that "the tabernacle of God is with men, and he will dwell with them, and they shall be his people." This association is suggested by the text because the third tabernacle is intended for the "sons" of the pair. In the language of alchemy "sons" mean the alchemists themselves. They, therefore, are mysteriously implicated in the conjunction and resurrection of the pair, and unexpectedly take the place of the mediator, the Holy Spirit, or *Mercurius senex*.[183] Petrus Bonus, writing a little later than the author of *Aurora*, described the resurrection mystery as follows: "And in the reunion of the resurrection the body becomes wholly spiritual like to the soul herself, and they are made one like water mixed with water, and they are not separated any more for ever, since there is no diversity in them, but rather unity and identity of all three, spirit, soul, and body, without separation for ever. So likewise it is manifest of the identity and unity of the most holy Trinity in God, that is, of Father and Son and Holy Spirit, which in the same God are one and the same with distinction of persons but without difference in substance. From which words we can see directly that the old philosophers of this art were truly prophets through this divine art, namely of the resurrection of the soul with her body

---

[183] As a parallel we might mention that in Cabalistic interpretation Moses, symbolizing the children of Israel, becomes one with the "higher queen," the Sefira Binah, and is thus united with God. This is the "mysterium of the kisses." (Knorr von Rosenroth, *Kabbala denudata*, II, part 3, p. 149.)

and its glorification, of the appearing of God in human flesh, that is Christ, and of his identity with God by the mediating infusion and emanation of the Holy Spirit, although they told of these things very indistinctly and confusedly. . . . For in this stone is truly assigned the Trinity in unity and the converse, with distinction but without diversity, as is clear to him who considers it subtly and with knowledge." [184]

598   In alchemy the mediator who unites the pair in place of the Holy Spirit is the spirit Mercurius, who like him manifests himself in many individuals. This means that God becomes manifest in the individual man, for the "sons" in the *Aurora* text are individuals who, through the opus, have themselves become "gods and sons of the Highest"—they even restore to unity and wholeness the "oppositeness" in God's nature. Man becomes God's redeemer, uniting in him his two aspects as man and woman.

599   By his allusion to the transfiguration, the author plainly tells us that he feels identical with the bridegroom. For in *Aurora* it is the bridegroom who invites his bride to make three tabernacles, whereas in the Bible it is Peter, "not knowing what he said" (Luke 9 : 33). Peter represents the ordinary man, who beheld the transfiguration as in a vision, just after having been "heavy with sleep" (9 : 32). Similarly, the author of *Aurora* must have been in a state of rapture, in which he not only beheld the mysterium coniunctionis but became one with the bridegroom. Therefore his concern is not, like Peter's, for the divine figures of Moses and Elias, but for the "sons," who, spiritually begotten out of the coniunctio, will later accomplish the same work.

600   The quotation shows, further, that the author was alluding to something inconceivable, which Christ forbade his disciples to speak of "until the Son of man be risen again from the dead" (Matt. 17 : 9). This is another indication that it was an experience which anticipated a post-mortal state.

601   He that hath ears to hear, let him hear what the spirit of the doctrine saith to the sons of the discipline concerning the espousal of the lover to the beloved. For he had sowed his seed, that there might ripen thereof threefold fruit, which the author of the *Three Words*

184 *Pret. marg. nov.*, pp. 120ff. *

saith to be three precious words, wherein is hidden all the science, which is to be given to the pious, that is to the poor, from the first man even unto the last.

602   These concluding words of the text return to the recurrent motif of the seed and the ripening of threefold fruit. They seem to me to contain an allusion to that "unitary world" (*unus mundus*) whose significance is discussed in Jung's commentary on Dorn's text.[185] In that potential, unitary world, we are told, all the "pious" will be united outside time, for the *unus mundus* does not exist within the space-time continuum.

603   The image of the seed seems to go back to Gnostic sources. Thus in the system of Basilides the "threefold sonship of God" is likened to a grain of seed: "[God] did not create the cosmos as it later came to exist in its full extension and proportion, rather he created a seed of the cosmos. The cosmic seed contains everything within it, as the grain of mustard-seed contains everything at once within the smallest space: the roots, the stem, the branches, innumerable leaves, seeds of seeds which are produced by the plant itself, and hence a multitude of ever other seeds and other plants. Thus did the non-existent God create a not-yet-existing cosmos, by letting a single seed fall in its place, which contained the whole germ of the cosmos. But I will make what they mean even plainer: Just as the egg of a very variegated and multi-coloured bird, say of a peacock, or of another bird still more variegated and more multi-coloured, contains within it many kinds of beings of many shapes, many colours, and composed of many things, even though it be but a single egg— so the non-existent seed which the non-existent God let fall contained the whole germ of the cosmos, with all its many shapes and many natures." [186] In this unformed creation the third sonship lies as a germ, corresponding to the alchemical *filius macrocosmi*.[187]

604   We find the same cosmogonic aspect of the seed in the *Corpus Hermeticum*, Tract XIV, where Hermes explains the creation of the world to Asclepius: [188] ". . . and how God makes things, and how the things made come into being, you may see an image of it. . . . Look at a husbandman sowing seed, here

185 *Mysterium*, pp. 533ff.   186 Leisegang, *Gnosis*, pp. 215f.
187 *Aion*, p. 66.   188 Scott, *Hermetica*, I, p. 260.

wheat, there barley, and elsewhere some other kind of seed. Look at him planting now a vine, and now an apple-tree, and trees of other kinds; the same man plants them all. And even so God sows immortality in heaven, and change on earth, and in all the universe life and movement." [189] In this connection we might mention a prayer to the Agathodaimon in a Magic Papyrus: [190] "Come to me, good countryman, Agathodaimon, Knouphi . . . come to me, holy Orion,[191] that dwellest in the north and rollest along the floods of the Nile,[192] uniting with the sea and working change through the life process, even as a man . . .[193] the seed of the union of love, who sets the cosmos on a firm foundation." [194] The conception of the alchemical opus as the sowing and flowering of a grain of seed is an important one and is derived from the most ancient sources. Zosimos quotes a treatise of Hermes: "Go to the peasant Achaab, and you will learn that whoever sows wheat brings forth wheat. . . . For the treatise says, the colours do not decompose into anything but the corporeal and the incorporeal." [195] This probably means that the divine ideas (the incorporeal) entering into a body produce the created world. A variant of this passage occurs in "Isis to Horus": "Come and watch and question the peasant Acharantos, and learn from him what is sown and harvested; learn that whoever sows barley harvests barley, and whoever sows wheat harvests the same. When you have heard this as an introduction, my son, think afterwards upon the whole of creation and the genesis of things, and know that a man can

---

189 In other treatises the cosmos is a receptacle of God's ideas, the ἀγγεῖον γενέσεως (vessel of genesis), which receives the seed of becoming (ibid., p. 288). Cf. "Hermes to Ammon" (p. 438) and the teachings of Hermes Trismegistus in Stobaeus, 1. 11. 2 (pp. 422–24). Or the cosmos is called the "second God" or demiurge, the "sower of life," who by casting the seed grants renewal to creatures (pp. 179ff.).

190 Berlin Papyrus 5025 (Preisendanz, *Papyri Graecae Magicae*, I, p. 4).

191 In ancient Egypt Orion was considered to be the *ba* of Osiris.

192 The water of the Nile is the alchemical "spermatic water."

193 Lacuna in text.

194 Here we might mention the classical Janus-Aion conception of God as the *sator mundi*, "planter of the world" (Martial, X, 28), and Philo's commentary on Gen. 9 : 20 (*De plantatione*, Loeb edn., III, pp. 212ff.): "It is the Lord of all things that is the greatest of planters and most perfect master of his art. It is this world that is a plant." This idea goes back to Plato (*Republic*, 597D), who calls God φυτουργόν, 'planter.'

195 *Alch. grecs*, II, iv, 32.

beget only a man, a lion a lion, and a dog a dog. . . . For as I have said that barley begets barley and man a man, so also only gold can harvest gold, and like like. Thus is the mystery revealed." [196]

605   These passages probably refer to the Egyptian rites of mummification. Professor Helmut Jacobsohn informs me that the name "Acharantos" may be derived from the Egyptian god Aker, who played an important part in the cult of the dead. He was represented as a double-headed lion or dog, and in his arms the sun-god is renewed, and together with him the dead man. The sowing of wheat in the earth is an alchemical motif that dates back to the Osiris mysteries. It points to a post-mortal process of resurrection or regeneration in which many are produced from one and there is a secret identity of things that are "like." The potential unity of the cosmos is indicated in the seed motif, but it also has an intrapsychic meaning as the germ of conscious realization of the self. Thus the Marcosians celebrated a hierosgamos of which Irenaeus [197] reports that Marcos said to the women with whom he had intercourse: "May that Charis [grace] who is before all things, and who transcends all knowledge and speech, fill thine inner man, and multiply in thee her own knowledge, by sowing the grain of mustard seed in thee as in good soil." And again: [198] "Adorn thyself as a bride. . . . Receive the seed of light into thy nuptial chamber. . . . Behold Charis hath descended upon thee. . . ." [199]

606   Many of these images in their ancient connotations are preserved in the language of the Church Fathers. There the "corn," especially the "corn of wheat" in John 12 : 24, which dying "bringeth forth much fruit," refers to Christ. Ephraem Syrus in his hymns for the feast of the Epiphany [200] calls Christ a

---

[196] Ibid., I, xiii, 6. This passage occurs as the saying of a "very ancient writer" (ἀρχαιότατος) in Pelagios, ibid., IV, i, 9.

[197] Adv. haer., 1. 13. 2 (Writings, I, p. 52).

[198] Ibid., p. 53.

[199] The Valentinians seem to have had a similar ceremony. Cf. Irenaeus, 1. 13. 4, and Tertullian, Adv. Valentinianos, cap. 1. The Corpus Hermeticum says, likewise, that God "sows" virtue, reason, and gnosis in the human mind, and the 13th treatise describes the inner rebirth of man from the intelligible wisdom and seed of goodness, which comes from God (Scott, Hermetica, I, pp. 179f. and 238).

[200] I, cols. 21f.* Cf. John 15 : 1: "I am the true vine, and my Father is the husbandman."

"spiritual husbandman," who "committed his body as seed to the sterile field. That body was the grain, which breaking through all things is now arisen and hath brought the new bread." [201] "Like a grain of wheat falling into the earth, Christ fell into the underworld and rose up like a sheaf and as the new bread—blessed be his sacrifice." [202] "Christ was plunged into the depths by his murderers, like a grain of wheat by the peasant, whence he rose again and wakened many with him." [203] Here the crop is the multitude of believers, an image that occurs again among the Manichaeans and Mandaeans: the righteous are "pearls of the invisible" which were sown by the "son of life" in the earth torn open by the plough. They are the "living crop" which, coming from the realm of life, light, and spirit, was sown in the "land of fire and water." [204] Honorius of Autun says in his *Elucidarium:* [205] "And as bread is made up of many grains, so is the body of Christ gathered together from many elect ones. . . . And wine is composed of many grapes, and is trodden out in the wine-press; so is the body of Christ put together out of many just men, which is tormented on the scaffold of the cross; and this wine is turned into the blood of Christ, that our soul, which is in the blood, may through it be quickened." Here the body of Christ is the Church [206] or, to be more accurate, the *ecclesia spiritualis.*[207]

607   The archetypal idea underlying all these symbols is that of the self as a multiple unity, a "conglomerate soul"—an image that crops up again and again in the text and now reappears at the end. Rapt in the otherworldliness of an inner archetypal

201 Mary is the "field which knew not the furrow of the husbandman" and yet "brought forth fruit." "The Lord poured out his living dew and rain upon Mary, the thirsting earth." II, col. 526. Cf. cols. 546 and 554.

202 II, col. 744. Cf. col. 360.

203 I, col. 166. In other parables Ephraem says that Wisdom scatters the "seed of truth" (I, col. 574) and that Christ is the "planter of the vineyard of his Church" (I, col. 388).

204 Reitzenstein, *Erlösungsmysterium*, p. x, and Usener, "Die Perle."

205 Migne, *P.L.*, vol. 172, col. 1129. * Cf. cols. 457 and 463.

206 Cf. Anastasius the Sinaite, *Hexaemeron, P.L.*, vol. 89, col. 1067.

207 For Joachim of Flora gold was a symbol of the perfect, spiritual monastic orders in contrast to lead, which represented the corrupt clergy. *Concordia,* IV, p. 25: "For that order which on account of the brightness of wisdom could be called gold is now darkened and is again like to black lead" * (Hahn, *Geschichte der Ketzer im Mittelalter*, III, p. 101).

event, the author experiences a mystic oneness with all those of like mind, outside space and time.

608   The fact that he concludes with Calid's "three precious words" shows that he understood the *ecclesia spiritualis* specifically as a community of all those who were enlightened by the Holy Spirit and took part in the alchemical transformation and union of opposites—the "sons of the discipline," with whom the "tabernacle of God dwells." [208]

609   His allusion to the transfiguration of Christ, and the hint that the community of the pious and the poor lives on in secret, emphasize that this final solution was essentially an inner and spiritual realization. All earthly elements have dropped away, extinguished in the overwhelming image of the *unio mystica*. In many respects this ending reminds us of the final scene in *Faust*, where man, become a child again, is rapt into the other world and beholds the mysteries of Sophia. The Luciferian aspect of the spirit Mercurius has, like Mephistopheles, no more part in it; he has vanished into the depths from which he came: the "corrupting humidity," the world and the black earth are distilled away. Therefore the text ends with an avowal of a trinitarian symbol of totality—the three precious words of Calid.

610   In conclusion, we may say that the final parable presents the following picture: two transcendent, archetypal figures celebrate a hierosgamos, and the author is somehow included in their mystic union. What had been hinted in the parable of the treasure-house of Wisdom, that this union was the God-image par excellence, is now revealed in all clarity: God is made manifest in the two-in-oneness of lover and beloved. Unlike other mystical texts, such as Hugh of St. Victor's colloquy with his soul, where the soul, personified as a woman, turns to her bridegroom Christ,[209] the author's ego no longer exists as a separate figure; as a man he is only one of the "poor" or one of the "sons" of the divine lovers—an anonymous particle of humanity —and elsewhere in the text he seems to feel himself identical with the bridegroom. Such a state amounts to an extinction of individual consciousness and its dissolution in the collective unconscious. It might very well be an abnormal psychic state,

---

[208] A close parallel would be Joachim of Flora's doctrine of the "three ages of the world." *Concordia*, II, Tract. 1 (Hahn, III, pp. 108ff.).
[209] Cf. Hannah, "Hugh de St. Victor's Conversation with His Anima," pp. 23ff.

but the accumulation of motifs which in other realms of thought are connected with death suggests rather that it was an ecstatic or delirious state experienced *in conspectu mortis*. Indeed, the individuation process, which is here reflected in the alchemical symbolism, is in a sense a preparation for death as the natural end of a process whose goal is the fullest possible development of all the potentialities inherent in the personality.

IV

WAS ST. THOMAS AQUINAS
THE AUTHOR OF
A URORA   CONSURGENS?

611   Before I discuss the authorship of *Aurora,* it seems to me necessary to recapitulate some of the conclusions which have resulted
from the foregoing commentary.

612   Although *Aurora* consists of a mosaic of quotations drawn
on the one hand from the Bible and other ecclesiastical texts
and from the "classical," or early medieval, alchemical texts on
the other, it nevertheless has the effect of a homogeneous work
cast in a single mould. From the very first chapters in praise of
Wisdom and of the mystic science unknown to the ignorant,
and all through the seven parables describing the transformation process, the impassioned elation of the author strikes one
with a force one has seldom encountered before.[1] In the last
parable, which is largely a paraphrase of the Canticles, it rises
to the point of ecstasy. It is difficult to withstand the impression
that the whole treatise was composed in an abnormal psychic
state. Moreover, minor inaccuracies in the quotations make it
evident that these were reproduced on the spot and written
down quickly. We can therefore conclude that the treatise must
have been composed under unusual circumstances. The abnormal state of mind seems to consist mainly in the steady flow
of imagery, which guided the author's pen in a way that is
ordinarily observed only during periods of intense excitement
bordering on rapture or possession, when unconscious contents
overwhelm the conscious mind. The loss of conscious control
would explain the extraordinary manner of speech and expres-

[1] The nearest comparison might be some of the quotations in Hippolytus from
Gnostic writings, where there is a similar associative chain of archetypal images
whose meaning can be elicited only by psychological interpretation. The chain of
associations in *Aurora* is not unlike the chain of Biblical quotations found, for
instance, in the Sermons of St. Bernard (as my critics have pointed out). There
the associations follow in a known, i.e., conscious pattern, while in our case the
context can be reconstructed only if one considers the unconscious background.

sion to which the author had involuntarily to submit. *Aurora* is unique, not only with respect to the mystical literature of the time, but also among the authentic alchemical treatises of whatever period. One is forced to the conclusion that it cannot have been written by an alchemist who lived entirely in the world of "chemical" ideas. Evidence for this is the fact that only about a dozen of the "classics" of alchemy are quoted, and only the most general sayings at that, while all evidence of any detailed knowledge of the material, as well as chemical recipes and technical instructions, together with the word "alchemia" itself, are lacking. In the case of a man who was only an alchemist mention of these things would be almost obligatory. On the other hand, we have to postulate for our author a fairly good knowledge of the alchemical literature and an intimate acquaintance with the Bible and the liturgy. These facts combine to suggest that he was, above all, a cleric. His praise of the "parvuli" and "pauperes" might be an indication that he was a member of the Dominican or Franciscan Order.

613 In the Paris, Vienna, and Venice versions, and also in the "Rosarium," *Aurora* has no attribution (the incipit is missing in the Zurich codex), but in the Bologna and Leiden manuscripts and in the printing of Rhenanus it is stated to be a work of St. Thomas Aquinas.[2]

614 At first this attribution seems rather shocking,[3] since in

[2] Bologna: "Aurora . . . vel Liber trinitatis compositus a S. Thoma de Aquino." Leiden: "Tractatus, qui dicitur Thomae Aquinatis De Alchemia modus extrahendi quintam essentiam. Liber Alchemiae qui a non nullis dicitur Aurora consurgens latine cum figuris." Printed edition of Rhenanus: "Beati Thomae de Aquino Aurora sive Aurea hora."

[3] In Quetif and Echard, *Scriptores Ordinis Praedicatorum*, I, p. 345 and II, p. 818, *Aurora* is listed as a forgery, as are also the "opera chemica falso illi tributa" in *Theatrum chemicum*. These are: "Tractatus . . . de lapide philosophico" or "Secreta alchimiae" (*Theatr. chem.*, III, 1659, pp. 267ff.), "Tractatus . . . datus fratri Reinaldo in arte Alchemiae" (ibid., pp. 278ff.), and "Tractatus sextus de esse et essentia mineralium" (ibid., V, 1660, pp. 806ff.). The last is undoubtedly a false attribution, as it was written by the Dominican Thomas of Bologna, who dedicated the treatise to Robert of Naples, born 1275 (!). (Cf. Grabmann, "Die echten Schriften des heiligen Thomas von Aquin," p. 104.) Meyrink, on the other hand, endeavours to prove the genuineness of "De lapide philosophico," and states that a MS with the Incipit: "Sicut lilium inter spinas" is equally genuine (*Thomas von Aquino: Abhandlung über den Stein der Weisen*, p. xxiii). The MS "Sicut lilium" was printed as "Liber lilii benedicti" in *Theatr. chem.*, IV (1659), pp. 959ff. Schmieder (*Geschichte der Alchemie*, p. 139) also thinks these alchemical

style and content *Aurora* offers the strongest possible contrast to the known writings of St. Thomas. We have, however, to consider that *Aurora*, as we have said, was written under the impact of an encounter with the unconscious, so that, in content and form, such a composition would compensate or complement a totally different level of consciousness and mode of expression. It could, for instance, compensate a hyper-intellectual attitude caught in the limitations of logic—an attitude that afforded but little outlet to feeling, emotion, and mystic paradoxes. In that case *Aurora* would represent the discharge of energies that had been dammed up behind the narrowness and rigidity of the conscious attitude of the author.[4]

615 It may be worth while, therefore, to scrutinize the life and career of St. Thomas from a psychological point of view.[5] He was born about 1225 in Rocca Secca, near Naples, the son of Count Landulfo of Aquino, of Lombard origin, and of Teodora, Countess of Teano,[6] and the youngest of four brothers

---

treatises of Thomas are genuine. Waite (*Lives of Alchemystical Philosophers*, pp. 61f.) considers the "Secreta alchimiae" genuine, but all the other treatises not. Ruska (*Turba*, pp. 93, 339) mentions a "Commentum Beati Thomae de Aquino super codicem veritatis qui et Turba dicitur phylosoforum," and a second commentary, "In Turbam breviorem." The former begins like *Aurora* with a quotation from Wisdom. Unfortunately I could not get hold of a copy of these writings. One of them may perhaps be identical with the "Compendium" of St. Thomas cited in "Clangor buccinae" (*Artis auriferae*, I, p. 329). (Cf. Lippmann, II, p. 28.) In none of these writings, whose genuineness cannot be discussed here, can any positive connections with *Aurora* be inferred. Both in style and content *Aurora* is entirely unique. Only in the "Secreta alchimiae" (*Theatr. chem.*, III, 1659, pp. 278ff.) which is dedicated to Frater Reinaldus do we find the same quotations as in *Aurora* concerning the need for patience and deliberation, but as quotations from Avicenna and Geber, whereas in *Aurora* they are attributed to Morienus and Calid. Further, the author of "Secreta alchimiae" speaks of his "teacher Albertus," contrary to Thomas's usual habit of not mentioning him. On p. 279 the passage about rising early to see if the vineyard flourishes (Cant. 7 : 11f.) is meaningless in that context, whereas in *Aurora* it fits as an organic part of the text. I do not know whether it is meant as an allusion to *Aurora*, but think it likely.
[4] Scholastic thinking in general and the *Summa* in particular, with its rigid division into questions and answers in accordance with the laws of medieval logic, are perfect examples of such an attitude of consciousness.
[5] Cf. Walz, *St. Thomas Aquinas* (trans. Bullough) and the literature there mentioned (especially the writings of Grabmann); Bourke, *Thomistic Bibliography 1920–1940*; Wyser, "Thomas von Aquin"; Pruemmer, *Fontes Vitae S. Thomae*, Parts I–III.
[6] Or Teate (Chieti) of the Neapolitan nobility, originally Norman.

and four or five sisters.[7] He was the grandchild of Franziska of Swabia,[8] a sister of Barbarossa.

When still a small boy of about five he was sent to a monastery and placed under the care of his uncle Sinibaldo, who was then (1227–36) the abbot of Monte Cassino.[9] From the beginning everyone was struck by the boy's quiet and taciturn manner.[10] About 1235–37, around the age of twelve,[11] he had to leave Monte Cassino because of political unrest, and a year or two later went to Naples to continue his studies. There the teaching of the natural sciences was particularly well advanced, thanks to the protection of the emperor Frederick II;[12] in 1231, Michael Scotus had begun his translations of Aristotle.[13] His most important teacher there was Peter of Spain (Petrus Hispanus), and it was probably he who induced Thomas to enter the Dominican Order.[14] He was invested about 1240–41 or more probably 1244–45.[15] His mother did not want him lost to the family's political ambitions, and desired him to take up a worldly career;[16] at her instigation, and probably with the connivance of Frederick II, the young man's brothers abducted him and held him prisoner in the castle of Acquapendente,[17]

---

[7] Cf. also Sertillanges, *Der heilige Thomas von Aquin*, p. 23, and Chénu, *Introduction à l'étude de S. Thomas d'Aquin*, passim, esp. pp. 11ff. Unfortunately I was unable to obtain Petitot's more recent *La Vie intégrale de Saint Thomas d'Aquin*, so I had to use instead his *Saint Thomas d'Aquin: La vocation, l'œuvre, la vie spirituelle*. Grabmann's *The Interior Life of St. Thomas* (trans. Ashenbrener) was less useful, as it contains few facts and is more a panegyric. But cf. the literature there mentioned.

[8] Petitot, p. 17. His grandfather, the Count of Sommacle, was one of Barbarossa's generals.

[9] Walz, p. 8; Sertillanges, p. 25; Chénu, p. 11; Petitot, p. 16; Tocco, *Vita S. Thomae* (in Pruemmer, *Fontes Vitae*), II, p. 69.

[10] Walz, p. 16.   [11] Petitot, p. 19.   [12] Walz, p. 21.

[13] Haskins, "Michael Scot and Frederick II"; Walz, p. 21. Cf. Grabmann, "Methoden und Hilfsmittel des Aristotelesstudiums im Mittelalter," pp. 64f.

[14] As Monte Cassino belongs to the Benedictines, one might have expected Thomas to join that Order.

[15] Walz, p. 33. His novitiate lasted from 6 to 12 months. Cf. Petitot, p. 24.

[16] According to certain sources (e.g., Petitot), she wanted him to be a Benedictine, so that later he would become abbot of Monte Cassino.

[17] His superiors, in expectation of what was to come, had sent Thomas to Rome, with the intention of bringing him to Paris from there. He was ambushed near Acquapendente (Walz, pp. 34f.). Cf. Thomas of Cantimpré, *Bonum universale de apibus*, I, 20, pp. 81ff.

on his father's domains.[18] The family sent beautiful courtesans to visit him in his prison, in the hope of luring him back to the world, but he chased them away with a burning brand from his fire,[19] and the following night had a vision in which two angels gave him a chastity belt, so that he awoke with a shout of pain.[20] Thereafter he abhorred the sight of women.[21] Meanwhile his superior had gone to Bologna to intervene with the Chapter General. On July 25, 1243, a new pope, Innocent IV, had been elected, and in July 1245 he deposed Frederick II. About the same time the family relented, and Thomas was set free,[22] whereupon he returned to Naples. His mother, who seems to have been a hard woman, never forgave him for his intransigeance.[23]

617   Soon afterwards (ca. 1245) he went to Paris, and later (ca. 1248) to Cologne to study under Albertus Magnus.[24] His meeting with this formidable personage seems to have been an incisive experience for young Thomas. It is related that during his time in Cologne he was so tongue-tied and abstracted that his fellow students called him the "dumb ox" (bos mutus). Only Albertus recognized his gifts, and prophesied that this "dumb ox" would one day fill the whole earth with his doctrinal bellowings.[25] Albertus inducted him into all the burning intellectual and spiritual problems of that age, and made him more closely

18 Petitot, p. 27.   19 Ibid., p. 31; Tocco (*Fontes*), p. 75.
20 Walz, pp. 34, 37f.; Petitot, p. 32; Petrus Calo (in Pruemmer, *Fontes Vitae*), I, pp. 23f. Cf. Pelster, *Kritische Studien*, pp. 63f. and 71.
21 Tocco (*Fontes*), p. 75.• This was probably because he, like Aristotle, regarded woman as a mistake on the part of nature, who really wanted to produce males: "Woman is a misbegotten male, produced as it were unintentionally by nature." • (Gabriel of Barletta, *Sermones* I, fol. 165ᵛ.) Cf. *Summa*, I, q. 99, art. 2, obj. 2 and ad 1; q. 92, art. 1 obj. 1 and ad 1 (Eng. edn., I, pp. 495f.); q. 92, art. 1 obj. 1 and ad 1 (Eng., p. 466); also 2 *Sent.* 20, 2, 1, obj. 1, and 3 *Sent.* 11, 1, 1c. (*Opera*, ed. Fretté and Maré, XXX, pp. 345, 455.)
22 Walz, pp. 38f. In other versions he escaped. Petitot, p. 34; Tocco (*Fontes*), p. 77.
23 Petitot, p. 28.
24 Walz, pp. 44f. For the dates, see pp. 45f. Possibly he was in Cologne in 1245, in Paris in 1245–48, and then again in Cologne; or (according to Pelster) he studied under Albertus in 1245 and again from 1248 to 1252. Cf. Sertillanges, p. 23; Chénu, p. 12.
25 Tocco (*Fontes*), pp. 77f.: "He began to be marvellously silent and taciturn. . . . The brethren began to call him the Dumb Ox." • (Cf. Pelster, *Kritische Studien*, p. 14.) Henry of Herford (*Chronicon*, p. 201): "There will come a time when all the world will marvel at the lowing of this ox." • Cf. Petrus Calo (*Fontes*), pp. 26f.

acquainted with the writings of Aristotle, the scientific literature of the Arabic peripatetics, and—not least—the writings of
Avicenna and Arabic alchemical philosophy.

618   It was during the years 1245–50, the time of his first meeting
with Thomas, that Albertus was making an intensive study of
alchemy and occult problems.[26] One can imagine what an impression the personality and ideas of this temperamental, free-
thinking scholar must have made on Thomas. Albertus seems
to have belonged psychologically to the extraverted type, his
interest being directed to the outer object and to experimental
science.[27] For instance, he even took the trouble to travel about
visiting alchemists in their laboratories.[28] Theologically, he
justified his interest in nature by arguing that God works
through the natural processes, and that, as one could not search
out God's will directly, it was valuable to investigate the natural
processes which were God's instrument. Again and again he
states in his writings that he had observed this or that for himself, or had tested it by experiment.[29] In his "Mineralia" (III. i.
1, and IV. i. 6; Borgnet, V, pp. 59f., 90) he admits that he had
personally attended alchemical experiments in Paris, Cologne,
and other cities.[30] He also conducted experiments in the occult
and magic arts,[31] as we know not only from "Liber aggrega-

26 Practically all the important writings of Albertus on this theme are cited in
Vincent of Beauvais, and hence were written between 1240 and 1245, except for
"Mineralia," though this is relatively early too. (Thorndike, *History of Magic,*
II, pp. 524ff.) Even Mandonnet ("Albert le Grand," in *Dictionnaire de théologie
catholique*), who gives the lifetime of Albertus a later date (b. 1206 instead of
1193), thinks these writings must belong to those years. Albert wanted to popu-
larize Aristotle: "to make all these parts intelligible to Latin readers," as he puts it.
27 As Thorndike points out (II, pp. 530f.), Albertus was at his most original in
his scientific writings.
28 In "De causis et proprietatibus elementorum," I. 2. 9 (Borgnet, IX, p. 619), he
says: "It is not enough to know in general, but we seek to know everything according to its own proper nature, for this is the best and most perfect kind of
knowledge." *
29 Thorndike, II, pp. 538ff.
30 "Mineralia," IV. i. 6 (Borgnet, V, p. 90): ". . . but those who work much in
copper in our parts, that is at Paris and Cologne and other places where I have
been and seen and experimented . . ." *
31 In "De somno et vigilia," III. ii. 6 (Borgnet, IX, p. 20 3)he explains—following
Avicenna and Algazel—that man's power to fascinate and exert magical influence
(what we would call hypnosis and suggestion) comes from the soul. "Mineralia,"
II. i. 1 (Borgnet, V, p. 24): ". . . and in this wise, they say, the soul of one man or

tionis" (whose authenticity is doubted), but from "De vegetabilibus et plantis" (VI. ii. 1),[32] where he says he had proved by
experiment and found it true that a toad could make an emerald explode or, again, would die at the sight of it![33] He declares that many of these occult things could not be proved
"along physical principles"[34] and emphasizes, on the authority
of Avicenna, that alchemy properly appertains to magic,[35] since
it depends on the occult powers of the human soul,[36] which in
turn are moved by the "heavenly powers."[37] The stars are the
instruments of God *par excellence*, by which he governs the
sublunar world.[38] He held with Avicenna that it was possible

animal will enter into and go out of another, and bewitch it and interfere with
its workings." • This is in striking agreement with the views in the *Liber aggregationis*, and reinforces the assumption that it is genuine.

[32] Borgnet, X, pp. 218f.

[33] He believed in the magical effects of stones, plants, etc., in love potions, and the
making of seals (ibid., pp. 555f.). *De veg. et plant.*, VI. i. 30–34, ii *passim;* Borgnet,
X, pp. 199ff., 223ff.

[34] "Mineralia," II. iii. 5 (Borgnet, V, p. 55); Thorndike, p. 557.

[35] Cf. ibid., II. i. 9 (Borgnet, V, p. 24).   [36] Thorndike, pp. 558–62.

[37] "Mineralia," II. i. 1 (Borgnet, V, pp. 30ff.); cf. "De causis elementorum," I. ii. 7
(Borgnet, IX, p. 615), Thorndike, II, pp. 557ff. Also "Mineralia," II. i. 2 (Borgnet,
V, pp. 23ff.): "And the art brings this about with great labour and many errors,
but nature does so without difficulty or trouble: the reason for which is that the
powers existing in the matter of stones and metals are moved by sure and effi-
cacious heavenly powers when the matter works: and those powers are the operations of intelligences which do not err unless it be by accident or through the
inequality of the material." • Quoted in part in Ruska, *Tabula Smaragdina*, p. 187.
Cf. also p. 188: "In Lib. III, which treats of metals in general, Albertus again
enters the sphere of alchemical ideas: 'Concerning the transmutation of these
bodies and the changing of them one into another it is not for the physicist to
determine, but rather for the art that is called Alchemy.' " • Ibid.: "According to
the teachings of Hermes and his pupils, the powers of all earthly things are
dependent above all on the stars and constellations. Through the circle 'alaur'
they are transferred to the lower world." Ruska rightly emphasizes that Albertus
was greatly influenced by the Arabian astrologers and alchemists, particularly
Avicenna. Certain quotations from Albertus show that he was interested in the
details of alchemical recipes (examples in Ruska, *passim*).

[38] Thorndike, II, p. 583 and Albertus, "Mineralia," II. i. 2 (Borgnet, V, p. 26):
"But all powers are infused into the lower things by the first circle of celestial
images." • That is the reason "why precious stones have wonderful powers exceeding those of others, namely because they are more like in substance to the
higher things . . . , wherefore precious stones are called by some, elemental
stars." • According to "Mineralia," II. i. 4 (Borgnet, V, p. 28f.), the heavenly
powers are infused "according to the merits of the material."

to purify metals in a natural way and reduce them to their prima materia—sulphur or mercury—but afterwards they could be turned into the desired metal only "magically," by taking account of the elemental or heavenly powers.[39] In other words, the chemical analysis was physical, but the synthesis could be achieved only psychologically. Most alchemists, Albertus continues, proceed in the wrong way and get only superficial colorations of the metal. We find the same attitude towards alchemy in his (possibly genuine) work "De alchemia," where he relates that he had long travelled around "exul" (banished? in a foreign country?) and attended numerous experiments which were all fruitless; but finally, through the grace of the Holy Spirit, he found the thing that conquers nature. What this is he does not say, true to tradition, but only hints at it in symbol.

619   Albertus was an impressive and vital personality, with a highly receptive mind. Probably he was an intuitive, setting less store by systematic clarity of thought [40] but having an innate sense for anything new and of value for the future.[41] It may well have been his intuition that enabled him to spot so quickly the importance of young Thomas.[42]

620   The biographical data suggest that Thomas Aquinas, on the other hand, belonged to the introverted type. We have seen

[39] III. i. 4 (Borgnet, V, pp. 63f.).

[40] Thorndike, II, pp. 530f. Cf. the rather sharp judgment of Sertillanges, p. 39, who accuses him of superficiality. Chénu, p. 97, speaks of his "faconde presque désordonnée."

[41] Jung describes this type as follows: "The intuitive never finds himself where generally accepted reality values are found, but always where there are possibilities. He has a fine nose for future developments. . . . He grasps new objects and new ways with great intensity. . . . The intuitive's morality is neither intellectual nor emotional; he has a morality of his own, consisting in fidelity to his own views." (*Psychological Types*, 1923 edn., p. 464.) His unconscious, inferior sensation function expresses itself in compulsive ties to people or objects, imaginary illnesses, a neurotic proneness to hypochondriac obsessional ideas, phobias, and absurd body sensations (ibid., p. 467). This might explain Albertus's melancholia in old age and his almost exaggerated grief at the death of Thomas.

[42] Mandonnet ("Albert le Grand," *Dictionnaire de théologie catholique*, I, col. 671) says of Albertus: "il joua un véritable rôle de révélateur intellectuel." Walz ("De Alberti Magni et S. Thomae Personali Relatione," p. 311): "As formerly by *divination* he commended the wonderfully increasing intellect of Brother Thomas, so afterwards he was a *prophet* of the everlasting victory of Master Thomas's teaching." * (My italics.)

that even as a boy he was reserved and taciturn.[43] So we know very little of what was going on in him. His biographers extol his quiet gravity, his equable and humble acceptance of the religious rule, and his precocious knowledge. At thirteen he knew the greater part of the Psalms, gospels, and epistles of Paul by heart, and had translated among other things the *Moralia* of Gregory the Great.[44] His resistance to the attempts of his family to lure him back into the world has something almost timorous about it; it betrays his sensitivity,[45] perhaps also a certain weakness in regard to the sphere of sexuality, which he shunned as menacing and diabolical. His reluctance to appear before the public is further evidence of an introverted disposition. For instance, he was overcome by nervousness when he had to deliver his inaugural lecture (*prolusio*) as Magister in Paris.[46] Then an old friar of the Order appeared to him in a dream, saying: "Behold, thou art heard, accept the Master's office, for God is with thee; but for thy beginning take this text: 'Thou waterest the hills from thy upper rooms, the earth is sated with the fruit of thy works' " (Psalm 103 : 13).[47] Thomas obeyed the dream's command and gave an address on this passage (to which allusion is made in *Aurora*).[48] From a psychological point of view, the dream figure [49] was admonishing him to place more reliance on the inspiration of the unconscious. Obviously in his conscious life he was inclined to lose himself in reflection and intellectual speculation.

621   If the typology we have hazarded is correct, the friendship uniting Albertus and Thomas would be readily understandable since their attitude-types [50] complemented one another. As function-types [51] they cannot have been direct contrasts, for both inclined to the side of thinking and intuition, though with Albertus the irrational function (intuition) predominated, and with Thomas the rational (thinking), so that they stimulated

---

[43] Tocco (*Fontes*), p. 69: "For the aforesaid child was not talkative and garrulous, but already beginning to be taciturn and given to inward meditation." •
[44] Petitot, p. 18.
[45] Ibid., p. 39: "We see that the Saint was extremely, even astonishingly sensitive; his tougher companions and disciples found this surprising. This very Italian, almost feminine delicacy . . ."   [46] Ca. 1256. Cf. Sertillanges, p. 24.
[47] Tocco (*Fontes*), p. 85. •   [48] Supra, pp. 348, 350.
[49] A personification of the archetype of the wise old man.
[50] Extravert, introvert.   [51] Thinking, feeling, sensation, intuition.

and complemented one another that way too. The fact that Albertus felt the death of his friend telepathically shows that there was a *participation mystique* between them, as often happens in the case of an intense relationship with mutual projection.

622   Albertus is described as being small in stature, of delicate build, nimble, vivacious, and extremely amiable;[52] Thomas, on the other hand, as a large, lumbering, coarse-boned man, with an elongated face, low forehead, and a great round head inclining to baldness.[53] He is said to have suffered from stomach trouble,[54] which may perhaps have been of nervous origin. If this was a psychogenic symptom, it would show that there was something he found hard to "digest" or could not "stomach." Because of their bad psychological digestion, introversion in the cases of such persons usually leads to one-sidedness.

623   Once, at a court dinner with Louis IX, the story goes, Thomas so lost the use of his senses as to forget himself, and, overcome by the force of his contemplation, he smote the table with his fist, and exclaimed in a loud voice that he had found a final and compelling argument against the Manichaeans.[55] By this he probably meant the neo-Manichaean heresy, which was very influential at that time.[56]

624   This story shows that his intense introvertedness was not the result of lack of temperament or evidence of inner tranquillity. Rather, behind his outward composure violent psychic conflicts were going on, and it is clear that he was personally affected in the strongest way by the religious problems of that restless age.

625   Further proof of passionate inner struggles and doubts is afforded by various reports of dreams and visions in which the Mother of God, Christ, or St. Paul appeared to him. Characteristically, the first thing he asked these persons was whether what he had written was right or not.[57] With a man who was

---

52 Petitot, p. 51.   53 Tocco (*Fontes*), pp. 111f. Cf. Petitot, pp. 39 and 73f.

54 It is reported that he was suddenly unable to eat and died of the resulting weakness. Tocco (*Fontes*), pp. 129f.

55 *Acta Bollandiana*, p. 673: "He came to the king, and being by him at table, suddenly, inspired with the truth of the faith, he smote the table and said: 'That finishes with the heresy of the Manichaeans!'" • Cf. Calo (*Fontes*), p. 42.

56 Hahn, *Geschichte der Ketzer*, I, pp. 55ff.

57 Tocco, in *Acta Sanctorum Martii*, I, p. 670; *Fontes*, pp. 106f.

not tormented by doubts about his own work (but rather about the object of belief), one would expect a gesture of adoration and reverence—anything rather than this anxious question. Obviously it was not so much the metaphysical reality of these persons which he doubted as the form in which he himself had attempted to give intellectual definitions of their nature.

626   His writings, too, display a marked dichotomy in his creative powers, for his main works were written in the dry, logical, scholastic style of the period ("he always spoke formally"),[58] but on the side he composed hymns and sermons of great poetic beauty.[59] Gulielmo de Tocco even declares that he wrote many of them in a kind of ecstasy ("in raptu mentis").[60] None of the known poems, however, comes anywhere near *Aurora* in intensity of feeling. In my view, Thomas must have been a man in whom there was the greatest tension between feeling and intellect. Presumably, as I have said, he was an introverted thinking type. His thinking was not related to the object but was founded on ideas. He was more interested in the principles of the Aristotelian system than in questions of detail.[61] One can imagine what a shock it must have been for him to find himself caught up in the whirlwind of an extraverted intuitive like Albertus, who actually carried out practical experiments in mineralogy, zoology, and botany, and was specially interested in alchemical and parapsychological questions.[62]

[58] Said of him by Cajetan, cited in Chénu, p. 93.

[59] Petitot (p. 143) says of the sermon he preached before the Consistory for the institution of the feast of Corpus Christi: "It was wholly lyrical, exclamatory, and formless, without heads or divisions."

[60] Vita di S. Thomaso, *Acta Bollandiana*, p. 665: He even speaks of a "continuous mental rapture" (*Fontes*, p. 122). Cf. Walz, "De Alberti Magni et S. Thomae Personali Relatione, "p. 316, n. 44.

[61] Gilson, "Pourquoi Saint Thomas a critiqué Saint Augustin," pp. 124f.: "St. Thomas has left to us neither a 'Discourse on Method' nor a 'Confessions,'and we have no evidence to show the course of the evolution of his philosophical principles. . . . This Minerva sprang fully armed from the head of Jupiter."

[62] For which reason his contemporary Engelbert of Strassburg named him an "expert in magic." Cf. Peter of Prussia, *Vita B. Alberti Magni*, p. 126. Albertus thought magic was due to demonic influences (ibid., p. 551), the demons having the support of the stars. There was a "right" or positive magic. Its "magistri" were people who philosophized about the stars and nature. Cf. *In Evang. Matth.*, II. 1 (Borgnet, XX, p. 61), where he calls the wise men from the East such "magistri," and *In Daniel*, I. 20 (Borgnet, XVIII, p. 465): "They are called Magi . . . from being magisters who philosophize about all things." •

627   From that time on, under the influence of Albertus, Thomas accepted in principle the possible existence of occult phenomena. He says in the *Summa* that in the physical order things have certain occult powers, the reason for which cannot be assigned by man.[63] Like Albertus, he believed in the occult powers of precious stones,[64] and that alchemy was a "true art, but difficult on account of the occult influences of the celestial powers." [65] In his *In quatuor libros Sententiarum Petri Lombardi,* an early work, he emphasizes that in principle he believed in the transmutation of metals, but that "the alchemists make something that is similar to gold so far as its outward accidents are concerned: yet they do not make real gold, for the substantial form of gold does not come into being through the heat of the fire which the alchemists use, but through the heat of the sun in a definite place where the mineral virtue operates, and therefore their gold has not a power in accordance with its appearance, and so likewise with the other things that come into being through their work." [66] For him, therefore, the most important thing in alchemy seems to have been these astrological and magical powers.[67] His convictions in this matter seem to have grown even stronger with age.[68] Such assevera-

[63] II-II, q. 96, art. 2 (Eng. edn., II, p. 1609). •
[64] He thought they could have astrological and demonic effects. Cf. Thorndike, II, p. 603.
[65] *Meteorol.,* III. 9. "Whence also the Alchemists themselves by the true art of alchemy, difficult though it be because of the hidden operations of celestial power. . . ." • Cf. Thorndike, II, pp. 607ff., and the evidence for his belief in astrology: There was an "imprinting of forms from above," i.e., by the stars, which acts "as the magnet attracts iron" (Codex Vat. Urb. 1491, fols. 76f.). Thomas also had the same views as Albertus concerning fascination and hypnosis (*Contra Gentiles,* III, 103, and *Summa theol.,* I, 117, 3). The stars were moved by the angels (Thorndike, II, pp. 608f.). God used them to guide the lower world (Boll, *Sternglaube und Sterndeutung,* pp. 39 and 102). Man's "humours" were also influenced by the stars (*De veritate,* XII.10, and *Summa,* II-II, q. 95, art. 5 ad 1).
[66] •
[67] Similar views are found in the doubtfully authentic "De lapide philosophico" (cf. Meyrink, *Thomas von Aquino: Abhandlung über den Stein der Weisen,* p. 3) and in Bacon, *De speculis comburentibus* (cited by Little, *Roger Bacon Essays*), p. 394. A common source in all these cases may have been Witelo.
[68] The treatise "De occultis operibus naturae ad quendam militem" (*Opera,* 1871-80, XXVII, pp. 504-07) is relatively late, and the still later *Summa* is more favourably disposed towards alchemy than the earlier Commentary on the *Sentences* (Thorndike, II, 607ff.).

tions, coming from authenticated works of his, demand to be taken seriously.

628   What we miss, however, is the emotional factor: to what extent did these alleged facts impress themselves on his feelings? The "dumb ox" anecdote seems to indicate that impressions went much deeper than one would have supposed, but that he kept them locked away in himself. His later thinking, cramped by formal logic, could well be a defence-reaction against these and similar impressions, for the attempt to gain control over the menacing world of objects by conceptual means is characteristic of introverted thinking, and "occult" objects must have exerted a particularly numinous effect on a scholastic. Thomas's own uncertainty, when in his dreams and visions he tormented himself with doubts as to whether he had formulated everything correctly, betrays the typical dependence of the introvert on the "subjective factor," [69] and on the other hand shows that formal thinking was extraordinarily important to him, perhaps because it served as a defence against impulses and interpretations of quite another kind.[70]

629   If Thomas was an introvert, it must have been all the more exasperating for him that his success as a university teacher involved him more and more in external duties and activities which he could not escape because of his vow of obedience. After he had functioned as Bachelor and then as Master in Paris from about 1254 to 1260,[71] the Chapter General in Naples nominated him "Preacher General." Even before that he had had to attend many congresses in different cities, where occasionally he met Albertus.[72] In the autumn of 1265 he stayed for a while in Rome, and in 1267 at the Chapter General in Bologna. At that time he was active in some capacity (perhaps as lector?) at the Papal Court.[73] Besides that, all through this period he was engaged on a monumental literary task: in

---

[69] *Psychological Types* (1923 edn.), pp. 473ff.

[70] Thomas's brother Raynaldus was a well-known writer of love poems and piquant romances. His own handwriting seems to have been very "pâteuse" (thick) (Petitot, pp. 31 and 42). It is conceivable that he had a sensuous temperament which was held well in check.

[71] Walz, p. 89.

[72] For instance, at Anagni in 1256 (Walz, pp. 81ff.) and Valenciennes in 1259 (p. 85).

[73] Walz, pp. 89f.

1266 he had begun the *Summa*[74] and the *De anima* commentary.[75] In 1268–72 he stayed for a second time in Paris. He was in contact with numerous distinguished personalities connected with the Church: Vincent of Beauvais, St. Bonaventure, Witelo, William of Moerbeke, to name but a few. The famous Averroist controversy occurred during his second stay in Paris, and on December 10, 1270, certain of Thomas's theses were officially condemned. It is possible that the incident at the Court dinner with Louis IX took place about this time,[76] for it is then that he became more and more the official defender of the Catholic faith against the contemporary heresies.

630   The Dominican Order to which Thomas belonged, as well as the Franciscan Order, which together are usually known as the mendicant orders, had been called into being by a profound crisis within the Church.[77] Externally it was caused by the pressure of Islam and the Tartars,[78] but internally by the decay of the nobility and the growth of towns. The mendicant orders considered it their task to reform the Church and to bring back into the fold the masses of the people, who were slipping into sectarianism and paganism. The Franciscans took over the practical cure of souls, while the Dominicans considered it their main task to combat heresies scientifically, styling themselves "Domini canes"—God's watchdogs. Since no serious encounter with an opponent is possible without partial approximation to his point of view, it is understandable that a party of Franciscans found themselves slipping into an heretical popular religious movement. They called themselves the "Tertiaries," and they later merged almost indistinguishably with the Beguines and Beghards, *Fratres pauperes,* Brethren of the Free Spirit, and other sects.[79] The Dominicans too, including Thomas and his teacher Albertus, came into conflict with bigoted representatives of the Church such as William of Saint-Amour, because they were alleged to have taken over too much Arabic Aristotelianism into their theological views[80] and to have given too much protection to the Left Wing of the mendi-

---

[74] Ibid., p. 100.   [75] Pp. 104f.   [76] Pp. 128f.

[77] Chénu, p. 34.   [78] Ibid., pp. 11 and 35ff.

[79] Cf. Tocco, in *Acta SS. Martii,* I, p. 666, concerning the "Poor Men of Lyons," and Kroenlein, *Amalrich von Bena und David von Dinant,* pp. 279ff.

[80] Mandonnet, *Siger de Brabant et l'Averroïsme latin au XIIe siècle.*

cant orders. Thomas alone composed three treatises in their defence, and he and Albertus went on several occasions to Rome to defend them.[81] There is even an important document from Albertus in existence concerning the Beguines and Beghards, which he had obviously written to protect this movement, whose centre was in Cologne, against the Inquisition.[82] Both he and Thomas display an astonishing knowledge of the contemporary philosophical sects, such as those of Amalric of Bene, David of Dinant, etc.[83] Thomas refers to them as "certain modern philosophers." [84] It is also important to note that he protested when William of Saint-Amour wanted to brand the teaching of Joachim of Flora as the teaching of Antichrist.[85] He knew the so-called "Liber Introductorius," a summary of Joachim's teaching, and said that though some things in it were to be "held in reprobation," to call it the teaching of Antichrist was false.[86] Thomas, therefore, not only was acquainted with this movement but took a fair and not entirely negative view of it.[87]

631   In 1272 he left Paris and travelled to Naples, where a "studium generale" was to be instituted, and there became chief

---

81 Thorndike, II, p. 525.

82 Preger, *Geschichte der Mystik*, I, p. 466, and Haupt, "Zwei Tractate gegen Beginen und Begharden," p. 85. Cf. Hahn, II, p. 472, and Doellinger, *Beiträge zur Sektengeschichte des Mittelalters*, II, pp. 403 and 702.

83 *Summa*, I, q. 3, art. 8 (Eng. edn., I, pp. 19f.). Cf. Kroenlein, p. 282. David of Dinant seems to have been influenced by Scotus Erigena and his pantheistic doctrine (ibid., pp. 284 and 303). Cf. also Thery, *Autour du décret de 1210*.

84 *In Sent.*, II, 17, q. 1, a. 1, solutio. For Amalric of Bene see Kroenlein, pp. 282 and 284. David of Dinant was probably known to Albertus through Baldwin of Canterbury (Albertus's *Summa*, I, Tr. 4, q. 20, memb. 2, and II, 12, 72, 4, 2, in Borgnet, XXXI). Cf. Kroenlein, pp. 302f., 311ff.

85 Petitot, pp. 71f.

86 Thomas Aquinas, *Contra impugnantes Dei cultum et religionem*, p. 110: "Wherefore when certain men try to change the gospel of Christ into a certain Gospel which they call eternal, it is clear that they are declaring the times of Antichrist to be at hand. But this gospel of which they speak is an introduction to the books of Joachim, which is condemned by the Church, or rather the teaching itself by Joachim, by which as they say the Gospel is changed. Hence when the said teaching, which they call the law of Antichrist, is set forth at Paris, it is a sign that the time of Antichrist is at hand. But that the teaching of Joachim or of that Introduction, although it contains certain things that are to be held in reprobation, is the teaching which Antichrist will preach, is false." •

87 Chénu (pp. 39ff.) calls Joachim "un écho sonore des aspirations de son temps."

lecturer. Gulielmo de Tocco reports that he did not work only in the academic world, but "with closed eyes" preached ecstatic sermons which were attended by great throngs of people.[88] Fits of absent-mindedness, like the one recorded in the story of his clinching argument against the Manichaeans, became more and more frequent,[89] and on one occasion he even had a *raptus mentis* in the presence of a Roman cardinal, and repeatedly during the celebration of the Mass. At Mass he would often burst into tears over the sufferings of Christ. There are even reports of levitations.[90] The following report from Gulielmo de Tocco points to an inner conflict with the shadow:

632   Once when a Neapolitan judge was visiting Thomas, and the two were pacing up and down a terrace by the sea, the judge saw the figure of a black-clad Ethiopian approaching the saint. But Thomas shook his fist at him and cried out: "Do you dare to tempt me again?" Whereupon the "noonday devil" fled.[91] (One thinks of the Ethiopian as a symbol of the *nigredo* in *Aurora*!)

633   Reports of this kind, partly historical, partly legendary, may be taken as the psychological ambiance of a formidable and highly strung personality whose depths were unsuspected and still less understood by the ordinary man. The superb one-sidedness of his conscious thinking alone is enough to guarantee the existence of a totally different inner world, whose task it was to maintain the balance of the personality as a whole. Reports of ecstasies and other unusual biographical data are indicative of this invisible background. They belong to the phenomenology of an imposing personality, filling out the picture on the unconscious side, which generally expresses itself only indirectly. The predominance of rationality in St. Thomas would evoke an equally powerful counterposition in the unconscious psyche, which, to compensate his "universalist" thinking, would reach down to the depths of the psychic past and activate the corresponding archetypal contents. Since everything that is activated in the unconscious strives for conscious realization, manifest signs of the conflict will not be lacking. At all events, the conscious mind cannot shake off the feeling of

88 Walz, p. 150.   89 Ibid., p. 151.
90 Petitot, p. 133; Petrus Calo (*Fontes*), pp. 36f.; Tocco (*Fontes*), pp. 107f.
91 Petitot, pp. 146f.; Tocco (*Fontes*), p. 128.

inner foreboding but will feel obliged to parry the counter-thrust of the unconscious by rational means—in the case of Thomas, with scholastic-theological formulations. This attempt is doomed to failure, in view of the necessary presence of the counterthrust and its balancing function. At any rate, the opposition between the two halves of the psyche was not equalized in the life of St. Thomas, but became if possible even stronger. Petitot goes so far as to speak of his capacity for "dédoublement." [92] For instance, through mental concentration he could render himself insensitive to pain, and in his trancelike states he could still talk to the people around him, and even dictate to them, "as if in a hypnotic state." An English witness declares that he took down Thomas's dictation while the saint slept.[93]

634 After middle life, this tension led to a severe crisis which was reported by his friend Reginald of Piperno. It is even possible that his early death was the direct or indirect consequence of psychic overstrain.[94] Since Thomas was probably one of those people whose highly differentiated thinking and intellectual concentration had suppressed the natural man and the demands of feeling, his feeling would come more and more into conflict with his spiritual attitude and build up a powerful counterposition. His conscious convictions would then be under continual attack and would eventually be undermined. This would produce a "sentiment d'insuffisance," of which clear traces can be found in Thomas. But the counterposition is always personified by the anima, and this would explain his horror of women.

635 Such, we may suppose, are the psychological facts which—perhaps in conjunction with a physical illness of some kind [95]

[92] Petitot, p. 130; Tocco (*Fontes*), pp. 107f., 121.

[93] Tocco (*Fontes*), p. 89.

[94] This is a point of dispute between Walz, "De S. Thomae Aquinatis e Vita discessu," pp. 41–55, and Petitot, "La Mort de Saint Thomas d'Aquin," pp. 312–36. (Cf. also the discussion in the *Bulletin Thomiste*, Nov. 1925, p. [17].) Walz and others see no causal connection between the vision of December 6, 1273, and the death of the saint, whereas Petitot supposes that the vision ushered in a state of physical and mental exhaustion which was causally connected with the death. On a psychological view and also in the light of the lesser visions mentioned below, a psychological connection seems to me plausible.

[95] According to Calo (*Fontes*, p. 47f.), he lost appetite, could not eat, and died of the resulting weakness. After his death the rumour arose that he had been poisoned (Petitot, p. 152).

—caused those fits of absent-mindedness or trancelike states and, later, the depression of which we shall speak below. Gradually, premonitions of death appeared. A short while before the depression set in his dead sister Marotta appeared to him in a vision and told him that she would soon see him again in the other world.[96] When, in 1273, he received an invitation to the Chapter General at Lyons for the following year, the premonition of approaching death grew stronger, although he had not yet reached his fiftieth year. The dead Pater Romano da Roma appeared to him in a vision and informed him that he had obtained the "true knowledge of divine things" after a journey through purgatory. Thomas thereupon asked him whether the knowledge which a man acquires in this life is preserved in the other world. Romano did not answer directly ("in forma"), but referred him to the fact of the "Visio Dei." Thomas then asked: "How can a man see God without a medium or intermediate species?" [97] And Romano answered him in the words of Psalm 47 : 9: "As we have heard, so we have seen, in the city of the Lord of hosts. . . ." [98] This vision brought Thomas joy and consolation. But then, in the middle of his *Summa,* while working on the section on penance, that celebrated experience befell him which put an end to his literary activity and, a month later, to his life. The report of it is contained in the *Acta Bollandiana* and rests on the testimony of Bartholomew of Capua,[99] who in turn had it direct from Reginald of Piperno, Thomas's best friend and confidant.[100]

636   "Moreover the same witness [Bartholomew of Capua] said that, when the said Brother Thomas was saying Mass in the said chapel of St. Nicholas at Naples, he was smitten with a wonderful change, and after that Mass he neither wrote nor dictated anything more, but suspended his writing in the third part of the *Summa,* in the treatise on Penance. And when the same Br. Reginald saw that Br. Thomas had ceased to write, he said to him: Father, why have you put aside so great a work, which you began for the praise of God and the enlightenment of the

96 Walz, p. 108, Tocco (*Fontes*), p. 118.

97 "Sine media vel mediante similitudine."

98 Walz, p. 155, Tocco (*Fontes*), pp. 118f.

99 Mandonnet, *Des Écrits authentiques de St. Thomas d'Aquin,* p. 32.

100 *Acta Bollandiana,* pp. 712f.*

world? And the said Br. Thomas replied: I cannot go on. But the said Br. Reginald, fearing that he had fallen into madness as a result of too much study, kept on pressing the said Br. Thomas to go on with his writing, and likewise Br. Thomas replied: I cannot do it, Reginald, everything I have written seems as worthless as straw.[101] Then Br. Reginald, overcome with surprise, so arranged matters that the said Br. Thomas went to visit his sister, the Countess of San Severino, of whom he was very fond; he hastened to her with great difficulty, and when he arrived, and the Countess came to meet him, he hardly spoke to her. Then the Countess, in a state of great fear, said to Br. Reginald: What is all this? Why is Br. Thomas all struck with a stupor, and hardly speaks to me? And Br. Reginald answered: He has been like this since about St. Nicholas's day, and since then he has not written anything.[102] And the said Br. Reginald began to press the said Br. Thomas to tell him for what reason he refused to write and why he was stupefied like this. And after a great many pressing questions from Br. Reginald, Br. Thomas replied to the said Br. Reginald: I adjure you by the living God Almighty and by your duty to our Order and by the love you have for me, that so long as I am alive you will never tell anyone what I am going to tell you. And he went on: Everything that I have written seems to me worthless in comparison with the things I have seen and which have been revealed to me. And as the aforesaid Countess continued to be very taken aback, Br. Thomas departed and returned to Naples, and then resumed his journey to the Council according to the invitation he had received, writing nothing whatever. And on the road, in the village of Magentia in Campania, he was attacked by the illness from which he afterwards died." [103]

637   This was in January 1274, on the journey to Rome, from where he wanted to go and attend the council of Lyons at the request of Gregory X. Riding along absent-mindedly on a mule,

101 Cf. "Processus Canonizationis S. Thomae Aquinatis Neapoli," in Pruemmer, *Fontes,* p. 377; Tocco (*Fontes*), p. 120; Walz, p. 157. He also said a little later: "This is the end of my literary activity, so I hope I shall soon reach the end of this life." Sertillanges, p. 27, and Petitot, "La Mort de St. Thomas," p. 329f.

102 Cf. Walz, p. 158. Reginald said to the Countess (Tocco [*Fontes*], p. 120): "He is often rapt in spirit when in contemplation, but I have never seen him so taken out of his senses as he is now." • Cf. *Bulletin Thomiste,* p. [18].

103 Cf. Walz, pp. 155, 160.

he struck his head on a branch and fell unconscious. In Maenza,[104] where he stayed for a while with his niece Francisca of Aquino, he asked to be taken to the Cistercian monastery of St. Mary at Fossanova.[105] There he spent his last month. The report continues: [106]

638   "And the said witness said moreover, that when the said Br. Thomas began to be overcome with sickness in the said village of Magentia, he besought with great devotion that he might be borne to the monastery of St. Mary at Fossanova: and so it was done. And when the said Br. Thomas entered the monastery, weak and ill, he held on to a door-post with his hand and said: This is my rest for ever and ever. . . .[107] And he remained for several days in that monastery in his ill state with great patience and humility, and desired to receive the Body of our Saviour.[108] And when that Body was brought to him, he genuflected, and with words of wondrous and long-drawn-out adoration and glorification he saluted and worshipped it, and before receiving the Body he said: I receive thee, price of my soul's redemption, I receive thee, viaticum of my pilgrimage, for love of whom I have studied and watched and laboured and preached and taught; never have I said aught against thee unless it were in ignorance: nor am I obstinate in my opinion, but if I have said aught ill, I leave it all to the correction of the Roman Church. And then he died, and was buried near the high altar of the church of that monastery, in a marshy place close to the garden of the said monastery, where there is a stream, from which a water-wheel takes up water, by which all that place is watered, as the witness himself has often and carefully observed." [109]

639   As there are no authenticated reports to inform us of the content of that last, evidently overwhelming vision, we cannot explain why he broke off his work (he was at most forty-eight

---

104 Or Faenza (Petitot).

105 Though he had lost all appetite, he still read the Mass amid many tears. At the urgent request of Br. Reginald he ate some herrings, of which he was very fond. (Petitot, p. 323.)

106 *Acta Bollandiana*, p. 713.*

107 Cf. Walz, p. 165; Tocco (*Fontes*), p. 130.

108 This was on the 4th or 5th of March, 1274 (Walz, p. 164).

109 Cf. "Thou waterest the hills from thy upper rooms, the earth is sated with the fruit of thy works"! (Psalm 103 : 13.)

or forty-nine at the time of his death).[110] But his reaction in regard to the *Summa,* that it seemed to him "worthless as straw," suggests that this last vision (an immediate experience of the unconscious) struck a layer of his being in comparison with which his scholastic thinking seemed totally inadequate.[111] Also, his words on receiving the viaticum are rather strange, for he tells Christ that he has never said anything against him— which suggests that the psychological possibility did exist of his saying something unorthodox.

640   The very fact that the biographers state that he interpreted the Canticles to the monks of the monastery on his deathbed [112] may give us a clue to the inner events of those last days: it is possible that the Canticles came closest to the vision, or lent it adequate expression. The Canticles have always fascinated the mystics of the Church (Honorius of Autun, Gregory the Great, Teresa, John of the Cross, the Victorines, to name but a few),[118] and it is no accident, either, that medieval alchemy, beginning with *Aurora,* made particular use of their symbolism. Through it, the archetype of the hierosgamos found the easiest means of access to the formalized conceptual world of Christianity and also enabled the alchemists to amalgamate Christian ideas with their conceptions of the alchemical coniunctio. Nor can one help being struck by the fact that the witnesses are remarkably silent about the content of this interpretation of the Canticles.[114] Petitot observes: "He agreed to make a last mental effort, and to expound to the religious the most mystical of Old Testament writings. Is there not good reason to think that the last moments of a Saint who dies fully conscious are always suggestive? On his deathbed St. Thomas, even though he had left his *Summa* unfinished, undertook to commentate the Canticles. . . . It has not been sufficiently appreciated that St. Thomas

---

110 Sertillanges, p. 27. Later, in the presence of Reginald of Piperno, the head and a thumb were severed from the corpse, boiled in wine *more Teutonico* ("after the German fashion"), and handed over to the Countess of San Severino (*Bulletin Thomiste,* p. [20]).

111 Sertillanges (p. 27) speaks of "profound discouragement."

112 Grabmann, "Die echten Schriften," pp. 189ff.

113 Honorius, Migne, *P.L.,* vol. 172, cols. 347–518; Richard of St. Victor, *P.L.,* vol. 196, cols. 405–524; Gregory the Great, *P.L.,* vol. 79, cols. 471–548.

114 Petitot ("La Mort de St. Thomas," p. 325) is understandably astonished at this silence of the witnesses.

Aquinas died from having contemplated God in an ecstatic vision."[115] I agree with Petitot that this last interpretation is connected in some way with the vision of December 6, 1273 and also with the death of the saint.

641   It is the more probable that Thomas's preoccupation with the Canticles on his deathbed was connected with this vision in that the latter was a prodromal symptom of death, while on the other hand the coniunctio symbolism mirrored suprapersonal, archetypal processes transcending space and time, such as are experienced more particularly in the presence of death. In the Cabala, for instance, death is described as a mystic marriage. At the burial of Rabbi Simeon ben Yochai his disciples heard a voice saying: "Up and come to the marriage of Rabbi Simeon! Let there be peace, let them rest upon their couches."[116] Christ's death on the cross was interpreted as a "marriage" by St. Augustine: "Like a bridegroom Christ went forth from his chamber, he went out with a presage of his nuptials into the field of the world. He ran like a giant exulting on his way and came to the marriage-bed of the cross, and there in mounting it he consummated his marriage. And when he perceived the sighs of the creature, he lovingly gave himself up to the torment in place of his bride, and he joined himself to the woman for ever."[117] Honorius of Autun says the crucifixion was a deadly wound of love which Christ received for the Church in order to make her his bride at death.[118] Interpretations like these were undoubtedly known to Thomas, yet underlying them is a primordial experience which may be repeated at any time, and this, in my view, is what caused him to return to the Canticles on his deathbed. The motif of the death-marriage is found in many variations in folklore: the unconscious psyche often represents death as a union of opposites, as the achievement of an inner wholeness.[119] It therefore seems to me possible that the long-repressed anima appeared to Thomas, in that vision shortly before his death, in the guise of Wisdom and the bride. A report

115 Petitot, *Saint Thomas d'Aquin*, p. 154.
116 *Der Sohar* (ed. Mueller), p. 390; cf. p. 113.
117 *Sermo suppositus*, 120, 8 (*In Natali Domini*, IV). I am indebted to Professor Jung for this reference.
118 *Expos. in Cant.* (Migne, P.L., vol. 172, col. 419).
119 In the ancient Persian religion, his soul appears to the pious man at the moment of death in the form of a beautiful girl.

of Sixtus of Siena [120] says that Thomas died in a state of ecstasy at the words: "Venite, dilecti filii, egredimini in hortum . . ." [121] He passed away as dawn was breaking.[122]

642 Albertus, who outlived his pupil, is supposed to have felt the moment of his death telepathically.[123] When the death was later confirmed, he wept with great emotion, and whenever afterwards Thomas's name was mentioned he burst into tears so violently that people thought he had succumbed to senile decay ("senilis hebetudo").[124]

643 These biographical data lead me to believe that in the treatise "Beati Thomae de Aquino Aurora sive Aurea hora" we have before us a document that really does stem from St. Thomas and reveals to us the "other side" of the great Doctor Angelicus, since it was composed during an invasion from the unconscious.[125] In that case it would naturally not agree stylistically with his other works.[126] Nevertheless, one point of

[120] *Bibliotheca sancta* (1575), p. 331. Cf. Grabmann, "Die echten Schriften," p. 189. Cf. also Walz, *St. Thomas Aquinas: A Biographical Study.*

[121] According to Touron (*La Vie de St. Thomas*, p. 686), what he said was taken down by the monks. Grabmann states that the commentaries on the Canticles hitherto circulated under the name of St. Thomas are not genuine ("Die echten Schriften," pp. 178ff.). Unfortunately I was unable to examine the only unpublished MS mentioned by him (p. 191) in the library at Salins (France), with the Incipit: "Donum sapiens poscens. . . . Explicit postilla super Cantica ed. a S. Thoma de Aquina quadruplici sensu exposita Scripta per manum fratris J. Berlueti Turoniae 1393." Cf. Vrede, *Die beiden dem Hl. Thomas zugeschriebenen Commentare zum Hohenlied*. Cf. also Schumpp, "Hat der hl. Thomas einen Kommentar zu dem Hohenlied geschrieben?," pp. 47ff. Schumpp asserts that Thomas never wrote such a commentary.

[122] Tocco, *Acta SS. Martii* 7, p. 679: ". . . that at the hour when morning dawns the saint should attain the climax of his vision and enter upon the day of the full light of glory." •

[123] Pelster, *Kritische Studien*, pp. 18, 39.

[124] Walz, "De Alberti et Thomae Personali Relatione," pp. 299ff. Cf. Ptolemy of Lucca, *Historia ecclesiastica*, XXII, 19 (Muratori, *Rerum Italicarum Scriptores*, XI, col. 1151), and Thorndike, II, p. 523. Albertus died at about the age of 80.

[125] Grabmann has shown in his thorough investigation of the writings of the saint (*Thomas Aquinas: His Personality and Thought*, pp. 18ff.; "Die echten Schriften" [1920], p. 13) that the lists of writings considered definitive by Mandonnet are not complete, and, moreover, that they do not cite all his scientific writings, such as the undoubtedly genuine "De natura materiae" and "De dimensionibus interminatis."

[126] Grabmann emphasizes that no definitive stylistic criteria exist for distinguishing between genuine and spurious writings and that contradictions sometimes

textual criticism needs stressing: with regard to the fourth parable, "Of the Philosophic Faith," I came to the conclusion (for psychological reasons implicit in the text) that in this one chapter the author was struggling to regain his conscious standpoint, and that he partially succeeded with the help of the concept of the Holy Spirit. His exposition of the "workings" of the Holy Spirit is, both in style and content, in complete agreement with St. Thomas's discussion of the Holy Spirit in the *Expositio in symbolum Apostolorum*,[127] where he even uses the recurrent formula in *Aurora* from Apocalypse 2 : 7: "He that hath ears to hear, let him hear what the spirit . . ." When the author expresses himself more or less consciously, he does in fact write in the style of St. Thomas. But when, swallowed up in the unconscious, he speaks of his inner experiences, he employs a compensatory, excited language which is not in agreement with St. Thomas's usual style. Since we know that St. Thomas died talking in an ecstasy, *Aurora* might very well be a transcript of his last words (perhaps elaborated later by another hand). Or was it written in a similar ecstasy at an earlier phase of his life? If, as I believe, *Aurora* is his last "seminar," he himself could hardly have written it down—he was far too weak for that. As far back as 1737 Antoine Touron[128] thought that this last interpretation of the Canticles on the deathbed could only have been preserved in a text taken down by another hand.[129] My personal conjecture is that *Aurora* is indeed this last seminar, and that the last precious words of St. Thomas were

---

occur in the work of the saint ("Die echten Schriften" [1920], pp. 6f., 18). The fact that we have no canon for his writings is also emphasized by Pelster ("Zur Forschung nach den echten Schriften des hl. Thomas," pp. 36ff.). Thus we have to rely in the end on documentary and psychological criteria in attributing or disallowing a work to St. Thomas. Transcripts and notes of his lectures also exist. For instance, the first book of the *De anima* commentary is a lecture taken down by Reginald of Piperno (Sertillanges, p. 26).

127 *Sanctorum Patrum Opuscula Selecta* (ed. Hurter), VI, pp. 227ff. Concerning the genuineness of this treatise see Grabmann, *Die Werke des hl. Thomas*, p. 288. According to Bartholomew of Capua, it is part of the "Reportata," and would therefore reproduce the spoken style of St. Thomas's lectures. The stylistic agreement is all the more illuminating since I maintain that *Aurora* might also be an "opus reportatum."

128 *La Vie de St. Thomas d'Aquin*, p. 686.

129 Sertillanges (p. 27) also refers to the fact that St. Thomas dictated on his deathbed.

not preserved officially,[130] as one would certainly have expected, but were transmitted as an "apocryphon" for the very good reason that they reveal the other, unconscious personality of the saint,[131] which had overpowered him on several occasions before in his trancelike states and now manifested itself again in the mystic marriage at the moment of death. I would not venture to advance this as a conclusive result, but the facts nevertheless seem to me significant enough to warrant my submitting them to the judgment of my reader.

[130] It may make the reader sceptical that the MSS of *Aurora* that have so far been found are few and all relatively late. But it must be borne in mind that this is a document which was probably composed under very unusual conditions and that its content was opposed to the spirit of the age and of the secular and ecclesiastical authorities. It is therefore to be regretted that persons with scientific interests are not permitted to examine the written material at the Vatican.

[131] There are on the one hand reliable reports that St. Thomas wrote a commentary on the Canticles (Grabmann, "Die echten Schriften" [1920], p. 190), while on the other hand it seems proved that the two commentaries that have been preserved, with the Incipits "Salomon inspiratus" and "Sonet vox tua," are not by St. Thomas. Grabmann says (p. 191): "The genuine commentary of St. Thomas is therefore not known to us, and there is little prospect of our being able to establish it." The Bull for the canonization of the saint does not mention this episode of the dictation, although all the other details of the death scene are recorded. (Cf. "Die Kanonisationsbulle des hl. Thomas von Aquin," pp. 210ff.) This affords a cogent argument from silence. Petitot, too ("La Mort de St. Thomas," p. 325), rightly emphasizes the peculiarity of the fact that on the one hand the commentary on the Canticles is an established tradition, but that on the other hand the precious last words of the saint have not been preserved. He explains this by saying (following Tocco) that St. Thomas on his deathbed spoke only "breviter" and to only a few persons. If, as I conjecture, these last words were uttered in a delirious state and were interspersed with alchemical sayings, as in *Aurora*, this conspiracy of silence is hardly surprising.

APPENDIXES

I. LATIN AND GREEK TEXTS

The asterisks (*) in the footnotes refer to the following passages quoted by the author in Latin or Greek. In general, only translations are given in the body of the book. Unless otherwise stated, the translations are by A. S. B. Glover. The entries below carry the pertinent footnote numbers. Errors in the Swiss edition have been corrected.

I, 2. *The Transmission of the Text*

1. Derisio scientiae est causa ignorantiae.

I, 3. *The Sources*

13. Illud igitur quod est causa determinationis magnitudinis et augmenti est principalis causa augmenti. Hoc autem non est ignis. Manifestum est enim quod ignis augmentum non est usque ad determinatam quantitatem sed in infinitum extenditur si in infinitum materia combustibilis inveniatur. Manifestum est igitur quod ignis non est principale agens in augmento et alimento sed magis anima. Et hoc rationabiliter accidit quia determinatio quantitatis in rebus naturalibus est ex forma quae est principium speciei, magis quam ex materia. Anima autem cooperatur ad elementa quae sunt in corpore vivente sicut forma ad materiam. Magis igitur terminus et ratio magnitudinis et augmenti est ab anima quam ab igne.

23. . . . prout dicit Hermes: sufficiet homini per mille millia annorum et si quotidie duo millia hominum pasceres non egeres; tingit enim in infinitum.

37. . . . ergo ipsa vis animae habet alias vires . . . quae omnes operantur ad hoc ut perveniat aptitudo instrumentorum ad perfectiones secundas ipsius animae . . .

40. Et maxime sapientem timere aliquod non decet. Nam si timuerit cito desperabit. Quod si desperaverit eius animus vacillabit. . . . Ad haec subrisit rex [Calid] et ait: Nunc vere scio quod nisi homini praestat Deus patientiam crudeliter confunditur. Festinatio enim ex parte Diaboli est.

42. Qui patientiam non habet manus ab opere suspendat, quia impediet eum festinantem credulitas . . . Ad hanc tria necessaria sunt, patientia, mora, et instrumentorum aptatio.

53. Quicumque animam dealbaverit, et eam rursum ascendere fecerit, et corpus bene custodierit, et ab eo omnem obscuritatem abstulerit, etc., ipsam in corpus infundere poterit. Et in hora coniunctionis maxima miracula apparebunt. / Quicumque animam dealbaverit et eam rursum ascendere fecerit et corpus a combustione bene custodierit . . . animam poterit a corpore extrahere et ipsum corpus obscurum relinquitur et in hora coniunctionis maximum apparebit miraculum.

57. Unde Alphidius in Clav. Phil.: Hanc scientiam habere non potes quousque mentem tuam Deo purifices et Deus sciat te mentem habere contritam. . . . Si humilis fueris eius Sophia et Sapientia perficietur. / Et Alphidius in Clav. Phil. cum dicit lapis noster ex vilis re est in oculis hominum pretio carente fastidita quam homines pedibus conculcant in viis.

70. . . . qui vere dicitur carbunculus: et ideo ille qui vere speciem suam attingit, lucet in tenebris sicut noctiluca.

72. De tertio scribitur, quod lapides in gemmas pretiosas transmutat, ut superius allegatum est in libro sextario, ubi dicitur, quod lapides Jacincti, Coralli rubei et albi, Smaragdi, Chrysoliti, Saphyri, ex ipsa materia formari possunt. Et in charta sacerdotum traditur, quod ex christallo, carbunculus, sive rubinus, aut topazius per eam fieri potest, qui in colore et substantia excellunt naturales.

76. Secundum illud quoque de quo semel in vita Crassum ait risisse Lucilius "similem habent labra lactucam asino carduos comedente."

77. . . . igitur proposui levissima, quae nemini licet ignorare, sciens quod asino, cardones edenti, dignam habent labra lactucam.

82. . . . in quo etiam dicit [Gellius] stultum est asino praebere lactucas cum ei sufficiant cardui.

83. Atque ipsemet Aristoteles enim dicit in libro secretorum quod esset fractor sigilli coelestis qui communicaret secreta naturae et artis. . . . Caeterum in hoc casu dicit A. Gellius in libro Noctium Atticarum de collatione Sapientium quod stultum est asino praebere lactucas cum ei sufficiant cardui.

87. Frater Hermannus de Mynda Saxo genere . . . in libro historiarum, qui De mirabilibus mundi inscribitur, libro quarto de vita domini Alberti sub brevi, verborum compendio multa comprehendit, quae suis in locis nostro opusculo inserta sunt.

436

I, 4. *The Problem of Dating*

9. Et ideo scientiam quam sine fictione didici, sine invidia communico, qua invidia labescente deficit, quoniam talis homo non erit particeps amicitiae Dei. Omnis sapientia et scientia a Domino Deo est, sed hoc quocumque modo dicitur semper a Spiritu Sancto est. . . . Itaque qui habet aures audiendi tantam gratiam deificam, audiat secretum, quod mihi desponsatum gratia Dei et indignis nullatenus revelat . . .

14. Magister Degenhardus Augustini Ordinis monachus, verus lapidis possessor, in suo libro de Via Universali ait . . . Est Spiritus Sancti donum. In ipso latet mysterium perveniendi ad thesaurum sapientum. Et hoc est plumbum Philosophorum, quod plumbum aeris appellant, in quo splendida columba alba inest, quae sal metallorum vocatur, in quo magisterium operis consistit. Haec est casta sapiens et dives illa regina ex Saba velo albo induta, quae nulli nisi Regi Salomoni se subicere volebat. Nullius hominis cor haec omnia satis scrutari potest.

III, 1. *Here Beginneth the Treatise . . .*

2. Sapientia foris praedicat—Christus Jesus qui est Dei virtus et Dei sapientia . . . in foribus portarum urbis sanctae Ecclesiae, etc.

3. primordiales causae se ipsas sapiunt, quoniam in sapientia creatae sunt aeternaliterque in ea subsistunt. / Simul enim Pater et sapientiam suam genuit et in ipsa omnia fecit.

4. Unde et a Sapientia Dei omnis et vitam et esse habent . . . quia juxta sapientiam Dei, quae vita omnium est, factum est omne quod factum est. Hoc enim exemplar Dei fuit, ad cuius exemplaris similitudinem totus mundus factus est, et est hic ille archetypus mundus, ad cuius similitudinem mundus iste sensibilis factus est.

5. . . . ad similitudinem Dei et Patris, qui de se ipso Filium suum, qui est sapientia sua, gignit, qui se ipsum sapit.

6. In verbo autem Dei ab aeterno exstiterunt non solum rationes rerum corporalium, sed etiam rationes omnium spiritualium creaturarum. / Sapientia quae a philosopho ponitur virtus intellectualis, considerat divina secundum quod sunt investigabilia ratione humana. / Et primo quidem, quantum ad intellectum,

adduntur homini principia supernaturalia, quae divino lumine capiuntur: et haec sunt credibilia, de quibus est fides.

10. Omnis sapientia a Domino Deo est: et cum illo fuit semper et est ante aevum (Ecclus. 1 : 1). Quicumque ergo diligit Sapientiam apud ipsum quaerat et ab ipso petat, quia ipse dat omnibus affluenter et non improperat (Jac. 1 : 6). Ipse enim est altitudo et profunditas omnis scientiae et thesaurus totius sapientiae: quoniam ex ipso et in ipso et per ipsum sunt omnia (Rom. 11 :36). Et sine eius voluntate nihil potest fieri. Ipsi honor et gloria in saecula saeculorum. Amen. Unde in principio mei sermonis invoco eius auxilium, qui est fons et origo omnium bonorum, ut ipse per suam bonitatem et pietatem dignetur parvitatem scientiae meae supplere per gratiam sui Spiritus sancti, ut per meam doctrinam lumen quod in tenebris latet manifestare valeam et errantes ad semitam veritatis perducere. . . . Cum in multas regiones et plurimas provincias nec non civitates et castella causa scientiae, quae vocatur Alchimia, maximo labore perlustraverim et a litteratis viris et sapienti- bus de ipsa arte ab ipsis diligenter inquisierim, ut ipsam plenius investigarem; et cum scripta omnia perscriberem, et in operi- bus ipsorum saepissime persudarem, non inveni tamen verum in his, quae libri eorum affirmabant. . . . Ego vero non des- peravi . . . quousque, quod quaerebam, inveni, non ex mea scientia, sed ex Spiritus sancti gratia. Unde cum saperem et intelligerem quod naturam superaret, diligentius vigilare coepi in decoctionibus . . .

20. Per Austrum vero calidum scil. ventum Spiritus sanctus figura- tur, qui dum mentes electorum tangit ab omni torpore relaxat et ferventes facit, ut bona, quaeque desiderant, operentur.

22. Filia namque regis austri (qui in coelis regnat et in calidis amore spiritibus). / [non] desinit nos igne charitatis accendere ad amandum et . . . [ut] in calore Spiritus sancti operari va- leamus.

23. Interiora ergo austri sunt occulti illi angelorum ordines et sec- retissimi patriae coelestis sinus, quos implet calor Spiritūs sancti. Ibi per diem quasi in meridiano tempore ardentius solis ignis accenditur, quia conditoris claritas mortalitatis nostrae iam pressa caligine manifestius videtur et velut sphaerae radius ad spatia altiora se elevat: quia de semetipsa veritas subtilius illus- trat. Ibi lumen intimae contemplationis sine interveniente cernitur umbra mutabilitatis. / Meridies est Chesed, unde Maiores nostri: Quicumque vult sapiens fieri convertat se ad meridiem.

26. Verbum enim Dei et sermo scientiae non in publico et palam positus neque conculcandus pedibus apparet, sed cum quaesitus fuerit invenitur . . .

28. . . . et hoc fit, per adiectionem lapidis occulti, qui sensu non comprehenditur, sed intellectu solum per inspirationem, vel revelationem divinam, aut per doctrinam scientis . . . et dixit Alexander: duo sunt in hac arte ordines, scilicet aspectus oculo, intellectusque corde. Et hic lapis occultus est, qui proprie dicitur donum Dei, . . . et hic est lapis divinus occultus, sine cuius commixtione lapis parenti annihilatur alchemia, cum ipse sit ipsa alchemia. . . . Et hic lapis divinus est cor et tinctura auri, quaesita a philosophis.

29. res . . . quae ubique invenitur, quae lapis est et non lapis, vilis et pretiosa, obscura celata et a quolibet nota. / Quam mira est philosophorum diversitas . . . et eorum conventus in hac paula re vilissima, qua regitur pretiosum. Et si vulgus . . . istud paulum et vilissimum scirent, mendacium putarent; cuius vim si scirent, non vilipenderent. / Et dixerunt alii quod ipsum arsenicum est lapis gentium, vilis pretii, et repudiatus et deiectus per fora et per stercora et balnea.

30. Si recumbis capite super petram, dividunt et rapiunt eam; si dormis in sterquilinio, illud fit Ecclesia ad fundendas preces.

31. Figuris vestitur, typos portat . . . thesaurus eius absconditus et vilis est, ubi autem aperitur mirum visu . . .

34. Creaturae possunt considerari ut res vel ut signa. / Crediderunt [Christum] non Deum esse, et qui fuit aurum mundissimum crediderunt esse cuprum.

35. Clara est et quae nunquam marcescit sapientia, sicut scriptum est (Sap. 6 : 13–17) et facile videtur ab his qui diligunt eam et invenitur ab his qui quaerunt illam. Praeoccupat qui se concupiscunt, ut illis se prior ostendat. Qui de luce vigilaverit ad illam non laborabit, assidentem enim illam foribus suis inveniet. Cogitare ergo de illa sensus est consummatus, et qui vigilaverit propter illam cito securus erit. Quoniam dignos se ipsa circuit quaerens, et in viis se ostendit illis hilariter, et in omni providentia occurrit illis. Item scriptum est (Ecclus. 24 : 29 et seq.) : Qui edunt me adhuc esurient et qui bibunt me adhuc sitient. Qui audit me non confundetur, et qui operantur in me non peccabunt. Qui elucidant me vitam aeternam habebunt.

36. ψυχὴ δ'ἀνθρώποισιν ἀπ' αἰθέρος ἐρρίζωται. / Maria et arbor unum sunt. Agnus in ramis pendebat . . .

43. Anima autem cooperatur ad elementa, quae sunt in corpore vivente, sicut forma ad materiam. / Nihil autem potest per se

operari nisi quod per se subsistit. Non enim est operari nisi entis in actu . . . Relinquitur enim animam humanam, quae dicitur intellectus vel mens, esse aliquid incorporeum et subsistens. / Sic ergo ex ipsa operatione intellectus apparet quod intellectivum principium unitur corpori et forma.

44. Et ideo ad hoc unitur [anima] corpori ut sit et operetur secundum naturam suam. / Dicemus igitur nunc: quod anima potest dici vis vel potentia comparatione affectionum quae emanant ab ea . . . potest etiam dici perfectio hac comparatione scl. quod perficitur genus per illam et habet esse species per illam, etc. / ergo ipsa est vis animae habentis alias vires, quarum una haec est, quae omnes operantur ad hoc ut perveniat aptitudo instrumentorum ad perfectiones secundas ipsius animae. / Motus igitur ratione qua motus est, et magnitudo sive dimensio, utpote prior forma in materia, ut optime ait Commentator De substantia orbis [Averroes], infinita sunt, et ob hoc omni mobili potest esse mobilius. Deus igitur cum sit infinitus, non receptus in aliquo, omni motu et operacione potest operari seu movere velocius. Volens igitur Sapiens ostendere occulte et subtiliter Dei infinitatem et ipsius Sapientiae, ait optime: "Omnibus mobilibus mobilior est Sapientia." . . . Rursus etiam imaginatio quae circa magnitudinem versatur potest imaginari quolibet magno maius, etiam coelo. Unde per hoc Augustinus, libro De quantitate animae, probat animam esse maiorem toto mundo.

46. Esse autem divinum, super quod ratio divinae potentiae fundatur, est esse infinitum non limitatum ad aliquod genus entis, sed praehabens in se totius esse perfectionem.

47. . . . quia ignis solus inter omnia corpora et alitur virtute propria et augmentatur . . . per appositionem cremabilium.

57. Quintus modus [cognoscendi] est cognoscere rem per elevationem et abstractionem ipsius animae. Et de hoc modo elevationis nusquam loquitur Philosophus, sed Avicenna de hoc modo loquitur in suo libro de anima, ubi dicit, quod intellectus duae sunt facies. Una est, quam habet intellectus ad virtutes inferiores, secundum quod intellectus agens recipit a possibili. Alia est, quam habet intellectus per abstractionem et elevationem ab omnibus condicionibus materialibus, et hanc habet per relationem ad Intelligentiam influentem. Et quando anima sic est elevata, intelligentia ei multa detegit. Unde dicit Avicenna, quod recolit praeterita et praedicit futura et potest precipere pluviis et tonitruo, ut cadant, et potest nocere per malum oculum suum. Unde dicit Avicenna quod oculus fascinatus facit cadere caniculam in foveam, et sic elevantur illi, qui sunt in

ecstasi, ut religiosi contemplativi et maniatici et phrenetici, et hoc modo anima cognoscit Primum et se ipsam per essentiam per reflexionem sui ipsius supra se.

62. Nam omnes moderni dicunt quod intellectus agens in animas nostras, et illuminans eas, est pars animae, ita quod in anima sunt duae partes, agens scilicet et possibilis; et intellectus possibilis vocatur qui est in potentia ad scientiam, et non habet eam de se, sed quando recipit species rerum, et agens influit et illuminat ipsum, tunc nascitur scientia in eo; . . . Et omnes sapientes antiqui, et qui adhuc remanserunt usque ad tempora nostra, dixerunt quod fuit Deus.

66. Tertio idem apparet ex hoc quod in vita contemplativa homo communicat cum superioribus scilicet cum Deo et angelis, quibus per beatitudinem assimilatur. . . . Assimilatio intellectus speculativi ad Deum est secundum unionem vel informationem.

68. Anima humana cognoscit in rationibus aeternis, per quarum participationem omnia cognoscimus. Ipsum enim lumen intellectuale, quod est in nobis, nihil est aliud quam quaedam participata similitudo luminis increati, in quo continentur rationes aeternae.

69. Prophetica revelatio se extendit . . . et ad quantum ad ea, quae proponuntur omnibus credenda, quae pertinent ad fidem et quantum ad altiora mysteria, quae sunt perfectorum, quae pertinent ad Sapientiam.

70. Cum ergo aliquis cognoscit se moveri Spiritu Sancto—hoc proprie ad prophetiam pertinet, cum autem movetur sed non cognoscit, non est perfecta prophetia sed quidam instinctus propheticus. / . . . per quendam instinctum occultissimum quem nescientes humanae mentes patiuntur.

71. Duplex est cognitio veritatis, una quidem quae habetur per gratiam, alia vero quae habetur per naturam. Et ista quae habetur per gratiam est duplex: una quae est speculativa tantum, sicut cum alicui aliqua secreta divinorum revelantur, alia vero, quae est affectiva, producens amorem Dei, et haec proprie pertinet ad donum Sapientiae.

72. Virtus intellectiva non habet finem in operatione, non habet finem in tempore. / Quod si dixerit quis, quia intellectus omnino non est forma nec habens formam, et ideo impossibile est ipsum agere: respondemus, quia intellectus in se ipso, in esse suo et in specie sua, forma est. Quemadmodum humor crystallinus aut spiritus visibilis in esse suo formatum est, et tamen ad lucem et colores quodammodo materiale: sic et intellectus

ad omnia intelligibilia, quae sunt extra se. Neque agit, in quantum est materiale, hoc modo, scilicet ex essentia sua, sed per formam . . .

83. . . . actus primus ordinatus ad actum secundum.

88. Praeterea ex causis naturalibus non potest accipi significatio super ea, quae naturaliter non fiunt, sed astrologi accipiunt significationes super prophetiam ex motibus corporum coelestium, ergo prophetia est naturalis. Praeterea philosophi in scientia naturali non determinaverunt nisi de his quae naturaliter possunt accidere. Determinavit autem Avicenna in libro sexto de Naturalibus de prophetia etc. Praeterea ad prophetiam non requiruntur nisi tria, scilicet claritas intelligentiae et perfectio virtutis imaginativae et potestas animae, ut ei materia exterior oboediat, ut Avicenna ponit in sexto de Naturalibus, sed haec tria possunt accidere naturaliter. / Primum Ens est actus purus, omnia vero alia entia constant ex potentia et actu. . . . Solus Deus est suum esse, in omnibus autem aliis differt essentia rei et esse eius. / Nihil enim dat esse nisi inquantum est ens in actu. Deus autem conservat res in esse per suam providentiam. / Neque est superfluum, si Deus per se ipsum potest omnes effectus naturales producere quod per quasdam alias causas producantur. Non enim hoc est ex insufficientia divinae virtutis sed ex immensitate bonitatis ipsius, per quam suam similitudinem rebus communicare voluit, non solum quantum ad hoc quod essent sed etiam quantum ad hoc quod aliorum causae essent. / Nihil autem est causa essendi nisi inquantum agit in virtute divina. / Deus est causa operandi omnibus operantibus.

90. quando ipsa fertur in magnum amoris excessum aut odii aut alicuius talium. . . . fertur in grandem excessum alicuius passionis invenitur experimento manifesto quod ipse ligat res et alterat ad idem quod desiderat et diu non credidi illud. . . . inveni quod affectio animae hominis est radix maxima omnium harum rerum seu propter grandem affectionem alteret corpus suum et altera, quae intendit sive propter dignitatem eius oboediant ei res aliae viliores seu cum tali affectione exterminata concurrat hora conveniens aut ordo caelestis aut alia virtus, quae quodvis faciat, illud reputavimus tunc animam facere. . . . Qui ergo vult scire huius rei secretum ut operetur illud et dissolvat, sciat quod ligare potest omnis omnia quando venit in grandem excessum . . . et debet facere hoc in illa hora, in qua invadit eum ille excessus et cum illis rebus quas sibi dictat tunc anima. . . . Ipsa enim anima cum sic est avida rei

quam ipsa vult operari, arripit ex se horam maiorem et meliorem quae est et super res magis convenientes ad illud. . . . Et
sic anima, quae est magis desiderans rem, ipsa facit eas magis
efficaces et magis habentes similitudinem eius quod venit; nam
scientia est factio caracterum . . . Similiter enim est operatio
in omnibus quae desiderat anima forti desiderio. Omnia enim
quae tunc agit illud intendens, movent et efficaciam habent ad
id, quod anima desiderat.

94. Ipsa est congregans principia et materias sui corporis . . . serv-
ans corpus etc. / Scientia enim de anima maius adminiculum est
ad cognoscendas dispositiones corporales, etc. / Dicemus igitur
nunc: quod anima potest dici vis vel potentia comparatione
affectionum quae emanant ab ea. Similiter potest dici vis ex alio
intellectu: comparatione scilicet formarum sensibilium et intelligibilium, quas recipit: potest dici etiam forma comparatione materiae in qua existit: ex quibus utriusque constituitur
substantia vegetabilis aut animalis etc.

97. Non autem dicimus ad summam, quod ex anima solet con-
tingere in materia corporali permutatio complexionis quae
acquiritur sine actione et passione corporali ita quod calor acci-
dat non ex calore et frigiditas non ex frigido. Cum enim imagi-
natur anima aliquam imaginationem et corroboratur in ea,
statim materia corporalis recipit formam habentem comparationem ad illam aut qualitatem . . . plerumque autem non
permutantur (scil. principia) nisi per contraria quae subsistunt
in eis. . . . Attende dispositionem infirmi cum credit se con-
valescere aut sani cum credit se aegrotare, multoties contingit ex
hoc, ut cum corroboratur forma in anima eius, patiatur ex ea
ipsius materia et proveniant ex hac sanitas aut infirmitas et est
actio haec efficacior et quam id, quod agit medicus instrumentis
suis et mediis. . . . Ergo cum esse formarum impressum fuerit
in anima et constat animae quod habent esse, continget saepe
materiam pati, ex eis quae solent pati, ex eis, et ut habeant esse
. . . Multoties autem anima operatur in corpore alieno sicut in
proprio quemadmodum est opus oculi fascinantis et aestima-
tionis operantis. Immo cum anima fuerit constans, nobilis, similis principiis, oboediet ei materia, quae est in mundo et patitur
ex ea et invenitur in materia quidquid formabitur in illa, quod
fit propter hoc, quod anima humana, sicut postea ostendemus,
non est impressa in materia sua, sed est providens ei, et quoniam
quidem propter hunc modum colligationis potest ipsa permu-
tare materiam corporalem, ab eo quod expetebat materia eius.
Tunc non est mirum, si anima nobilis et fortissima transcendat

443

operationem suam in corpore proprio ut cum non fuerit demersa in affectum illius corporis vehementer et propter hoc fuerit naturae praevalentis constantis in habitu suo, sanet infirmos et debilitet pravos et contingat pronari naturas et permutari sibi elementa ita ut, quod non est ignis fiat ei ignis, et quod non est terra, fiat ei terra, et pro voluntate eius contingant pluviae et fertilitas sicut contingit absorbitio a terra et mortalitas, et hoc totum perveniat secundum virtutem intelligibilem, omnino enim possibile est ut comitetur eius velle esse id, quod pendet ex permutatione materiae in contraria. Nam materia oboedit ei naturaliter etc.

106. omnis animus sequens concupiscentiam, i.e. opinionem suam vanam, fluit, i.e. fluctuat et divagatur per diversas vias erroneas.

107. Amor vel delectatio naturaliter . . . antecedit cognitionem. Nisi enim esset aliquis appetitus substantiae cognoscentis ad ipsum cognoscibile, nunquam esset ordinatio huius ad hoc neque perficeretur unum ad alio. / Quia carnales sumus et de carnis concupiscentia nascimur, necesse est ut cupiditas vel amor noster a carne incipiat; quae si recto ordine dirigitur, quibusdam suis gradibus duce gratia proficiens, spiritu tandem consummabitur.

108. Unumquodque tendens in suam perfectionem tendit in divinam similitudinem. Ultima autem perfectio ad quam homo ordinatur consistit in perfecta Dei cognitione.

110. Amor . . . est prima passionum concupiscibilis. . . . Amor est appetitus ad bonum . . . Motus autem ad bonum est desiderium vel concupiscentia, quies autem in bono est gaudium et delectatio. / Sed quia concupiscentia vel cupiditas est primus effectus amoris quo maximo delectamur ut supra dictum est. Ideo frequenter Augustinus cupiditatem vel concupiscentiam pro amore ponit . . .

111. Contemplatio spiritualis pulchritudinis vel bonitatis principium amoris spiritualis. Sic igitur cognitio est causa amoris ea ratione qua est bonum, quod non potest amari nisi cognitum.

112. Appetitivus motus circulo agitur ut dicitur in tertio de anima. . . . Unde et Dionysius dicit (De div. nom. cap. 4) quod amor est virtus unitiva, et Philosophus dicit in II. Polit. quod unio est opus amoris.

113. Nec ista hyle malum dicenda est. / Et unaquaeque creatura intendit consequi suam perfectionem, quae est similitudo perfectionis et bonitatis divinae. Sic ergo divina bonitas est finis omnium rerum. / Id vero quod desiderat omnis res, est esse et

perfectio esse, inquantum est esse. Privacio vero inquantum est privacio non desideratur.

120. Ipsae autem res sunt causa et mensura scientiae nostrae, unde sicut et scientia nostra refertur ad res realiter et non e contrario, ita res referuntur realiter ad scientiam Dei et non e contrario. / Res dicuntur verae per comparationem ad intellectum divinum.

121. Ut ostendam quod philosophia inutilis sit et vana, nisi prout ad sapientiam Dei elevatur.

122. Eo itaque modo quo forma huius in mente huiusmodi architectoris esset forma domus, est ars, sive sapientia, sive Verbum omnipotentis Dei forma omnium creaturarum. Ipsa enim simul et exemplar est et efficiens et formans est in forma data conservans est, dum ad ipsam applicantur et revocantur creaturae.

123. Veritas enim uniuscuiusque rei non est, nisi substantia, vel essentia, sive esse ipsius.

124. Sapientia est veritas scientiae rerum primarum sempiternarum.

125. Et quia veritas nihil aliud est quam adaequatio intellectus ad rem.

126. Et ars eodem modo ut natura operatur.

127. Et natura ipso artifice ministrante operatur. / Et illuminat omnia corpora, quoniam est lumen et tinctura illuminans et perficiens omne corpus. Et si artifex huius magisterii hoc lumen non cognoscit, tamquam in tenebris ambulans multipliciter per devia errat, propter elongationem eius a veritate, et unitate huius scientiae.

128. Intellectus noster, id est vis intellectiva, vis est generativa et velut matrix quaedam scientiae vel sapientiae.

130. ἔκστρεψον τὴν φύσιν καὶ εὑρήσεις τὸ ζητούμενον. / ἐκφέρεις ἔξω τὴν ἔνδον κεκρυμμένην.

159. Arcanum in quo est veritatis tinctura. / Regite igitur ipsum coquendo humore, donec natura abscondita appareat.

166. Virtus intrinseca est lumen luminum, tinctura illustrans . . .

III, ii. *What Wisdom Is*

1. Quemadmodum ars poetica per fictas fabulas allegoricasque similitudines moralem doctrinam seu physicam componit . . ita theologica veluti quaedam poetria sanctam scripturam fictis imaginationibus ad consultum nostri animi et reductionem corporalibus sensibus exterioribus, veluti ex quandam imperfecta pueritia, in rerum intelligibilium perfectam cognitionem

445

conformat etc. Propter humanum animum sancta Scriptura in diversis symbolis atque doctrinis contexta [est] etc.

2. [Naphtali] quia ergo quidquid scriptum reperit, ad spiritualem intelligentiam convertit.

3. quaedam cognitio obumbrata et obscuratis admixta.

4. Lapis et non lapis quod multis nuncupatur nominibus, ne quis ipsum agnoscat insipiens. / Quemadmodum inquam terrenus philosophicusque hicce lapis una cum sua materia multa diversimodaque immo mille paene, uti dictum est, nomina habet, inde quoque mirabilis appellatur, ita etiam hi et id genus alii supra commemorati tituli atque nomina multo potius immo in summo gradu a Deo omnipotente et Summo Bono praedicari possunt.

15. Patet etiam quomodo omnes cogitationes famulantur theologiae.

III, III. *Of Them Who Know Not and Deny This Science*

3. Non est [in]conveniens ut eveniat hoc stultis cum sapientibus et vulgo cum electis. / Honor Dei est abscondere rem.

III, IV. *Of the Name and Title of This Book*

1. Baptismo et intellectu unio fit duorum luminum. Ista lumina ditissimos emittunt radios et caligo a mente removetur. Tunc anima nitida contemplatur absconditum gloriae Christum . . .

5. Pater . . . hominem sola intellegentia mentis inluminans; qui, discussis ab animo errorum tenebris, et veritatis claritate percepta, toto se sensu intellegentiae divinae commiscet.

7. Aurora quippe ecclesia dicitur quae a peccatorum suorum tenebris ad lucem iustitiae permutatur. . . . Quae est ista etc. quasi aurora electorum surgit Ecclesia quae pravitatis pristinae tenebras deserit et sese in novi luminis fulgorem convertit. / Ortus vero aurorae est illa nova nativitas resurrectionis, qua sancta Ecclesia etiam carne suscitata oritur ad contemplandum lumen aeternitatis.

8. Quid est enim locus aurorae nisi perfecta claritas visionis internae?

10. Si enim sapientia a sapore dicta est, sapor autem rei non sentitur, nisi cum ipsa res gustatur, gustatur autem cum ad horam gustu tangitur, profecto sola intellegentia sapientia perficitur,

quia ea sola et rara hora et parva mora Deus utique sentitur.
. . . Ita sola intelligentia Deus gustari dicitur, quia ex omnibus
viribus animae ea sola in praesenti et in futuro quasi nullo
mediante tangitur. Hic tamen proprie gustamus ubi ad horam
intelligendo raptim de Deo aliquid sentimus. Ibi vero satia-
bimur ubi eo sine fine perfruemur.

11. Quoniam scientia creaturae in comparatione scientiae Creatoris
quodammodo vesperascit: itemque lucescit et mane fit, cum et
ipsa refertur ad laudem dilectionemque Creatoris nec in noctem
vergitur, ubi non Creator creaturae dilectione relinquitur. . . .
Cognitio quippe creaturae in se ipsa decoloratior est, ut ita
dicam, quam cum in Dei sapientia cognoscitur, velut in arte in
qua facta est. Ideo vespera congruentius quam nox dici potest,
quae tamen, ut dixi, cum ad laudandum et amandum refertur
Creatorem, recurrit in mane. Et hoc cum facit in cognitione sui
ipsius, dies unus est: cum in cognitione firmamenti . . . dies
secundus . . . terrae ac maris omniumque gignentium, quae
radicibus continuata sunt terrae, tertius . . . atque ipsius
hominis dies sextus.

20. Oriens cum suis astris figura fuit Mariae, e cuius sinu ortus est
nobis Dominus astrorum. Ille sua nativitate tenebras a mundo
fugavit.

23. Sicut in mundo maiori firmamentum movetur ab oriente in
occidentem et revertitur in orientem, sic ratio in homine
movetur a contemplatione orientalium, id est coelestium, primo
considerando Deum et divina, consequenter descendit ad occi-
dentalia, id est ad considerationem terrenorum, ut per visibilia
contemplatur invisibilia, deinde revertitur ad orientem iterum
considerando coelestia.

24. Sicut enim aurora surgens tenebras noctis depellit, solem mundo
inducit, sic Ecclesia nascens tenebras ignorantiae reppulit, et
solem mundo dictis et exemplis induxit.

III, v. *Of the Provocation of the Foolish*

3. Omnis enim locus sub coelo lunari locus est generationis et cor-
ruptionis, quoniam locus est conflictus et actionis et passionis,
ex quibus sunt generatio et corruptio universaliter.

12.   Pax, amor, virtus, regimen, potestas,
          Ordo, lex, finis, via, dux, origo,
          Vita, lux, splendor, species, figura,
            Regula mundi.

447

26. Et hoc voluerunt (philosophi) quod typice protulerunt, memo-
rando Planetas septem, et signa duodecim, et naturas eorum,
et colores, et quidquid in eis est.

28.   Septem sunt Urbes, septem pro more metalla,
        suntque dies septem, septimus est numerus.
        septem litterulae, septem sunt ordine verba.
        Tempora sunt septem, sunt totidemque loca.
        Herbae septem, artes septem, septemque lapilli.
        hoc in numero cuncta quiete valent.

29. Loquetur Spiritus sapientiae utrique populo omnem veritatem
et ostendet se esse unum de septem angelis . . . albugo litterae
ab oculis mentis suae. / justitia religiosorum quae major est et
pretiosior illa est vilescet in diebus illis respectu spiritualis iustitiae quae signatur in auro. / Septenarius numerus pertinet ad
Spiritum sanctum, propter septem munera gratiarum. / Erit
dies una, quae nota est Domino. Non dies neque nox et in
tempore vesperae erit lux. Et erit in die illa exibunt aquae vivae
de Hierusalem medium earum ad mare orientale et medium
earum ad mare novissimum. / Novam Hierusalem quae fundata
est Romae, lapides autem pretiosos apostolos, martyres, confes-
sores et virgines.

III, vi. *The First Parable: Of the Black Earth . . .*

14. Nocte quippe mortis et miseriae, quae a peccato Adae in-
choans cunctos suae caligine involvit, haec sacra nox (scil.
resurrectionis) finem imposuit.

16. Occulta Dei iudicia quaedam tenebrae sunt. / Aer caliginosus
est quasi carcer daemonibus usque ad tempus iudicii.

22. Effodiatur igitur sepulchrum illi Draconi, et sepeliatur illa
mulier cum eo, qui cum illa fortiter vinctus muliere, . . .
muliebribus armis . . . in partes secatur . . . et totus vertitur
in sanguinem.

28. itemque est bonorum morum imaginari concupiscentias turpes,
non tum vult illas, alius autem vult; et hae duae dispositiones
non sunt solius hominis sed etiam omnium animalium.

33. Et cavete ignis intensionem, quoniam si intendatis ignem ante
terminum rubeum fit, quod nihil vobis prodest, eo quod in
initio regendi vultis albedinem.

42. Umbram siquidem Christi, carnem reor esse ipsius, de qua
obumbratum est et Maria, ut eius obiectu fervor splendorque
spiritus illi temperaretur. /

448

Hac in domo Deus homo
fieri disposuit.
Hic absconsus pius Sponsus
Vestem suam induit.

45. Obscoenae inquinatae obsoletaeque quidem vestes illius sunt, purgabo tamen illos et ex corde illam amabo. Sitque mea soror, sponsa mea cum uno oculorum meorum.

52. Cathedra significat locum operationis, et formam vasorum, quod est intus.

53. Ex his igitur quatuor elementis omnia creata sunt, coelum, thronus, angeli, sol, luna, stellae, terra.

56. Notandum est quod omnis actio efficientis gravis est et molesta, nisi ipsi passo conferatur vis aliqua et imprimatur, qua vi cooperetur, formaliter inhaerente, ipsi suo agenti sive efficienti. "Violentum enim est, cuius agens est extra, non conferente vim passo." Sic ait Philosophus III Ethic. . . . et haec est ratio propter quam motus violentus in fine remittitur, naturalis vero in fine intenditur. Natura enim vis est insita rebus.

57. Felle caret, quo spiritualiter quoque sponsa Christi carere debet ut secundum Apostolum: Omnis amaritudo et ira et clamor et blasphemia tollatur . . . cum omni malitia (Eph. 4).

59. Bonum ut bonum semper dulce est. . . . Fex amaritudo est. / Omne agens intendit se alterum; et quousque ad hoc attingat, labor est; et gravis et amara omnis dissimilitudo et imperfectio, quam dat. Si daret se ipsum alterum primo, omnium actio esset suavis hinc inde, agenti scilicet et patienti, nec esset inter ipsos pugnae amaritudo, sed dulcedo et suavitas.

66. [Christus] exinanivit eam ut repleat, qui etiam se exinanivit, ut omnia impleret, exinanivit se ut descenderet nobis . . . ergo annuntiavit Luna mysterium Christi.

80. Et quid per byssum nisi candens decore munditiae corporalis castitas designatur?

89. Et illud est quod nominaverunt Regem de terra prodeuntem, et de coelo descendentem. Et simile est huic quod dicit quidam in ista aqua.

91. Recte [plane] lunae comparatur Ecclesia et ipsa nos lavacri rore perfundit et terram corporis nostri baptismatis rore vivificat.

96. Vestes vestrae, fratres, candidae sunt ut nix, et nitor vester refulget ut nitor Angelorum.

106. Labia tua stillant pharmacum vitae, balsamum fluit e digitis tuis, pulchri sunt oculi tui . . . Omnes filii Ecclesiae te ardentissime appetunt.

107. Dominus Lapidum . . . et rex . . . et sic est aurum inter cor-

449

pora sicut sol inter sidera, quia sol est rex siderum et lumen et cum eo complentur res terrarum et vegetabilium . . .

109. Dicet aliquis: quomodo influentiae praedictae metallorum . . . parentes montes penetrabunt? Respondet Propheta regius: Montes sicut cera fluxerunt a facie Domini.

110. Eptacephalus draco, princeps tenebrarum, traxit de coelo cauda sua partem stellarum et nebula peccatorum eas obtexit atque mortis tenebris obduxit. Unde sol aeternus iubar suae claritatis nube carnis operuit. In occasu mortis pro stellis occubuit; de caligine productas ipse de nocte mortis oriens sereno coelo restituit.

112. verum masculus est coelum feminae et foemina terra masculi.

III, vii. *The Second Parable: Of the Flood of Waters . . .*

2. recte significari aquas populos intelligimus. . . . Aquae terrestres sunt trepidae, terrenae, tenebrosae, absorbere nos volentes, animis in ira concitatis, et toto diabolici furoris impetu commotis.

10. Ipsa caritas occidit quod fuimus, ut simus quod non eramus; facit nobis quandam mortem dilectio.

11. Amor ergo boni convenientis est perfectivus et meliorativus amantis: Amor autem boni, quod non est conveniens amanti, est laesivus et deteriorativus amantis: unde maxime homo perficitur et melioratur per amorem Dei, laeditur autem et deterioratur per amorem peccati . . . liquefactio importat quandam mollificationem cordis qua exhibet se cor habile ut amatum in ipsum subintret. / Quia amans a se ipso separatur in amatum tendens et secundum hoc dicitur amor extasin facere et fervere, quia quod fervet extra se bullit et exhalat. . . .

16. Quia usque ad albedinem humiditatis corruptio et foeminae viget dominium.

26. Similiter nominant hanc aquam Nubem vivificantem, mundum inferiorem, et per haec omnia intelligunt Aquam foliatam, quae est aurum philosophorum.

27. [Maria] est nebula refrigerans, pluens, et donans. / nubes umbrationis et ductionis.

28. Lapis huius generis undique est: conceptio eius sit in inferno, partus in terra, vita in coelo, moritur in tempore et demum beatitudinem aeternam impetrat.

31. Christus multis locis in sanctis Scripturis allegorice Sol est appellatus.

52. ἡ δημιουργικὴ δεκὰς νοῦς ἐλλάμπουσα ταῖς ψυχαῖς.

54. Deinde ingreditur salsatura secundo in eo recens, quae est femina secunda, et facta sunt universa quatuor, scilicet duo masculi et duae feminae, ex quibus exierunt quatuor colores, et hi sunt numerus eius. Intellige hoc principium numeri, primum et secundum, et dicis duo, et illa sunt tria in numero, deinde dicis tria, quae sunt in numero sex, deinde dicis quatuor, et fiunt in numero decem numeri manifesti, occulti autem ipsorum quatuor. His autem numeris perficis Magnesia, quae est Abarnahas, existens ex quatuor. Decem vero sunt quatuor, et ex eis extrahuntur, et quatuor ex eis sunt decem. Haec sunt quatuor naturae, scilicet terra, aqua, aer et ignis, ex quibus consistit omnis creatura, Intellige autem hoc.

58. Per Aquilas substantiam volatilem intelligas.

61. Eva mater omnium viventium fons mortis effecta est omnibus viventibus.

67. Eva interpretatur vita. Vita autem est etiam Ecclesia, exhibens perpetuam baptismatis regenerationem et vitam, quae est per aquam et Spiritum.

69. Mors per Evam facta est, vita per Mariam reddita est. Illa a diabolo victa est, haec diabolum ligavit et vicit.

87. Et ideo dicendum quod cum generatio unius semper sit corruptio alterius, necesse est dicere quod tam in homine quam in animalibus aliis, quando perfectior forma advenit, fit corruptio prioris, ita tamen quod sequens forma habet quidquid habebat prima et adhuc amplius; et sic per multas generationes et corruptiones pervenitur ad ultimam formam substantialem tam in homine quam in aliis animalibus. Sic igitur dicendum est, quod anima intellectiva creatur a Deo in fine generationis humanae, quae simul est et sensitiva et nutritiva, corruptis formis praeexistentibus.

III, VIII. *The Third Parable: Of the Gate of Brass*

4.　　　　　　　Christe, Rex mundi, Creator,
　　　　　　　Dira claustra diruens,
　　　　　　Ferrea vincla resolvens
　　　　　　　Es, retrusos eximens.

6. Et dicitur Ecclesia candelabrum aureum, quia lucens scientia, gratia pretiosa, patientia solida, oboedientia ductilis, praedicatione sonora, perseverantia longa, fide Trinitatis fundata, quae est repleta septemplici Spiritus sancti gratia.

451

7. Maria est candelabrum illuminationis . . .

12. Ex his igitur apparet tibi quam deiecta et depressa sit ab altitudine luminositatis, et nobilitatis suae naturalis, virtus intellectiva, sive anima humana quantum ad illam.

13. . . . et qui me habentem Lunarem et Mercurialem materiam de loco meo, id est de corpore aeris, abstulerit, id est sublimare fecerit, vi, id est per vim putrefactionis et solutionis, ac dilectum meum, id est pinguedinem solarem mecum, id est cum humiditate Lunari vinculaverit . . . regenerabunt nos in vitam, per quam non erit ultra mors.

17. Et tamen qui credit et timet sed non intellegit quasi ad solius patris notitiam perductus est . . . qui autem credunt et intellegunt quasi ad Patris et Filii notitiam perducuntur, quia Filius Patris sapientia est . . . sed et qui credunt, intellegunt et delectantur, habentes notitiam Patris et Filii usque ad Spiritus sancti intelligentiam pervenisse noscuntur, quia ipse est delectatio et amor Dei, ipse mel de petra oleumque de saxo durissimo. Ipse est, inquam, mel de petra, ipse laetitia spiritualis etc.

23. ut nos per ipsam [Ecclesiam] generemur et regeneremur donec praeterierit nox huius saeculi et rursus exortus fuerit Christus sol justitiae. / Luna vero habente gubernationem et administrationem auctoritatis aquae et Spiritus sancti . . . ut nos per ipsum generemur et regeneremur.

25. Cum ergo interius diaboli sit de natura ignis, manifestum est, ipsum contrariari et inimicari ipsius animae naturae, quae est natura aequalitatis.

28. Vult per oleum animam . . . Et hoc genitum est pinguedo quam vocant animam et ovum.

31. Dixit autem Hermes: Omne subtile ingreditur in omne grossum.

36. Retribue etiam iis, qui adduxerunt populum in lacum inferiorem, i.e. in Babylonem.

39. Per mare saeculum insinuatur, quod voluminibus adversitatum iugiter elevatur. In hoc diabolus circumnatat ut Leviathan, multitudinem animarum devorat.

56. De Sion veniet Salvator. . . . Sion . . . spiritualis et collis visionum seu revelationum Ecclesia est. / Significat etiam mysterium ecclesiae, quae liberata est per crucem a manu diaboli. / Filiae quoque Syon, id est animae in Christo renatae, in Rege suo hodie exultent.

58. Sterilis sum et solitaria. . . . Haec Ecclesiam respiciunt sive enim eam revereantur sive persequantur valde magnificant et multiplicant eam. / Ecclesia autem, diu sterilis, fidelem filium

scilicet Christianum populum ad speciales observantias gener-
avit.

61. Christus ascendit . . . sicut radix de terra sitienti de Maria
virgine.

63. Christus Redemptor autem noster in carne veniens [septem]
pleiadas iunxit.

70. Hac de causa videntur ad coniugatos pertinere . . . denarius
numerus, ad clericos vigenarius . . . ad monachos trigenarius
hoc est denarii simul tres.

III, ix. *The Fourth Parable: Of the Philosophic Faith . . .*

2. . . . sub nomine Davidis ibidem Christum celebrando, qui
dicit: Ego vici mundum, et alibi: Iam Princeps huius mundi
eiectus est foras.

16. Creavit omnia in pondere etc., id est in se ipso, qui est numerus
sine numero, mensura sine mensura, pondus sine pondere. Vel
aliter exponitur: Creavit Deus omnia in numero, id est numerus
omnis apud eum certus, similiter omnium mensura certa est et
quicquid ponderis habet aliquid apud eum est certissimum. Vel
aliter: His tribus, numero mensura pondere voluit ostendere
scriptura nil Deo esse aequale. Numerus enim simplicitatem,
mensura immensitatem, pondus felicitatem et stabilitatem ex-
cludit. Creavit omnia in numero, id est nihil creavit summae
simplicitatis. In mensura, id est nihil creavit immensum. In
pondere quia nihil creavit quod ex se deficere vel sua felicitate
cadere possit.

17. In unitate itaque puncto atque centro, quae tria sunt principia
numeri, mensurae, atque ponderis (quam etiam nihil eorum
sint), cuncta creata sunt, et cum nihil videantur nobis, sunt
tamen apud Deum vel in Deum omnia; et idcirco dicitur Deus
ex nihilo creasse cuncta in principio, quod est mysterium magnum, videlicet sacrosancta Trinitas, ipsaque Sapientia; centro
enim cuncta sustinet, puncto adimplet, unitate denique per-
ficit.

21. . . . videtur tamen aliquod opus pertinere ad Patrem, lectio ad
Filium, iubilatio ad Spiritum sanctum, quia et timor Dei veram
sibi exigit servitutem et Christi magisterium subiectionem doctrinae et gaudium Spiritus sancti iubilationis tripudium. . . .
Tria igitur sunt quibus nobis Deus trinus et unus appropin-
quare dicitur: timor sapientia caritas, et tria per quae manent in
nobis tria ista: labor lectio et iubilatio.

23. [Tertius ordo] qui procedit ex utroque electus est ad libertatem contemplationis, scriptura attestante, quae ait: Ubi Spiritus Domini, ubi libertas. / Sanctus Spiritus exhibet libertatem, quia amor est.

24. Coniungetur gentilis populus cum Hebraeo et fiet unum ovile et unus pastor, quae coniunctio recte viris spiritualibus attribuenda est.

31. . . . Aquis perfunderis sapientiae, donec informeris, et gladio Verbi Dei vitiorum spinis carere valeas, ac insulsa doctrina tui pectoris ab antro exclusa, nostram doctrinam a Spiritu sancto traditam, mentis puritate possis excipere . . . iamiam suae nequitiae sentinam verbis divinorum librorum antea coopertam securi aperiunt . . . procul dubio in charybdi falsae opinionis hactenus cum indoctis iacuisti: nunc vero erectus in culmine totius veritatis, integrae mentis oculos ad lumen verae fidei aperire coepisti . . . atque sancti Spiritus dono repleberis, qui scripturarum omnium profunditatem, ac veram dignitatem, absque scrupulo te docebit. / Tunc autem crucifigitur Filius Dei et flagellatur . . . tunc moritur Filius quatenus aliquis ipsorum cadit in mortale peccatum vel redit a secta; resurgit autem per poenitentiam.

33. Item, spiritus hominis, ex quo bonus est, si moritur, est idem quod spiritus Dei, et ipse Deus. / Item, haec est Trinitas, quam vel in qua credunt, ut sit Pater, qui alium in bonum convertit, qui convertitur, Filius; id per quod convertit, et in quo convertitur, Spiritus sanctus.

34. Si aliquis in spiritu est aiebant et faciat fornicationem, vel aliqua alia pollutione polluatur, non est ei peccatum, quia ille Spiritus qui est Deus omnino separatus a carne non potest peccare.

45. Nonnulli . . . Patri attribuerunt potentiam, . . . sapientiam Filio, . . . voluntatem vel amorem Spiritui sancto. / Spiritus sanctus accendit nos igne caritatis. / Est illa lux quae illuminat omnem hominem venientem in hunc mundum et procedit ille calor qui vivificat omnia.

49. ἐὰν μὴ τὰ σώματα ἀσωματώσῃς καὶ τὰ ἀσώματα σωματώσῃς καὶ ποιήσῃς τὰ δύο ἕν, οὐδὲν τῶν προσδοκουμένων ἔσται.

57. Et in fine illorum dierum Deus infundit benedictionem generis humani, animam scilicet seu vitam.

77. Significant ergo per mediatorem aerem . . . quod natus sapientiae in aere nascitur, quando sublimatur ad alembicum. Propter quod fit aqua vivificans terram illorum, et embrionem, qui est terra, qui est anima ex corpore eorum.

97. Nomen itaque Dei quadriliterum, sanctissimam Trinitatem designare videtur, et materiam, quae etiam triplex existit, ut ante tradidimus, quae et umbra eius dicitur et a Moyse Dei posteriora.

98. Quod illud, quod est materia prima, est in se multa et plures et secundum numerum quaternarium in ordine ad quatuor elementa.

105. Urticae iunctae vepribus,
 Vulnus curant vulneribus,
 Flammata mens divinitus
 Ignem extinguit ignibus. /
Bene ergo in igne apparuit Spiritus, quia ab omni corde quod replet torporem frigoris excutit.

110. Hoc est sulphur rubeum luminosum in tenebris et est hyacinthus rubeus . . . et leo victor.

112. Rex clarus ut carbunculus. / Radius . . . in terris, qui lucet in tenebris instar carbunculi in se collectus. / Inveni quendam lapidem rubeum, clarissimum, diaphanum et lucidum, et in eo conspexi omnes formas elementorum et etiam eorum contrarietates.

113. Et quod dixit Rubinus, per hoc vult Animam tingentem, propter quod acquisivit virtutem ex igne.

114. Anima tingens latet in aqua . . . alba.

115. Haec est avis noctu volans absque alis, quam coeli ros primus continuata decoctione, sursum atque deorsum ascensione descensioneque in caput corvi convertit, ac tandem in caudam pavonis, et postea candidissimas et olorinas plumas, ac postremo summam rubedinem acquirit indicium igneae suae naturae.

122. Sal enim filius Dei est. Quod cum misisset illud sal fontem aquarum, quod factum est in annunciatione, ait: Haec dicit Dominus: Sanavi has aquas, id est, humanam naturam fluidam et pestiferam, et non erit in eis ultra mors neque sterilitas, sed vita et foecunditas.

123. Verus mercurii spiritus et sulphuris anima una cum sale spirituali simul unita.

124. Qui Paraclitus diceris,
 Donum Dei altissimi,
 Fons vivus, ignis, caritas,
 Et spiritalis unctio. /
[Addis adhuc ut quaeras, quid mihi causae videtur cur] potentia Patri in scripturis sanctis specialius attribuitur, sapientia Filio, caritas vel bonitas Spiritui sancto.

125. Hic lapis triangulus est in esse, quadrangulus in qualitate.

129. Ex hoc . . . lapide cum confringitur, varii vobis colores apparebunt. / Imbuite ipsum, quousque extrahat vobis Deus colores et appareant. / Cumque apparuerint colores, vel tincturae, erit hoc sicut cum apparet . . . pullus.

131. Ἐὰν μὴ τὰ πάντα τῷ πυρὶ ἐκλεπτυνθῇ καὶ ἡ αἰθάλη πνευματωθεῖσα βασταχθῇ, οὐδὲν εἰς πέρας ἀχθήσεται.

133. Ideo dicit Philosophus, portavit eum ventus in ventre suo. Planum est ergo quod ventus est aer, et aer est vita, et vita est anima; id est oleum et aqua.

134. Tunc omnia vapor facta sunt . . . hoc autem et spiritum et animam philosophi vaporem appellaverunt . . . sic opus nostrum . . . nihil aliud est quam vapor et aqua.

136. Esse illum Spiritum Domini, qui terrarum orbem impleat et ab initio aquis supernatavit. Spiritum veritatis quoque illum appellant qui mundo absconditus absque inspiratione Spiritus Dei . . . comprehendi nequeat. Qui quidem in quovis loco, ex re quavis potentialiter, in unico vero hoc subiecto perfecte ac plenarie tantum reperiatur. In Summa esse spiritualem substantiam quae neque coelestis neque infernalis sit sed aereum purum . . .

138. Septem Elisaei purificationes figura sunt septem spirituum per baptismum expellendorum.

140. Aquas naturales consecravit Elisaeus, invocato Abscondito, in illas immersit se leprosus notus, sed vis occulta purificavit eum. Dissipata est lepra in aquis et iniquitas in baptismo.

142. [210], qui est numerus vocis Naaman, id est Naemani Syri principis militiae Regis Aram 2. Reg. 5:1 per quem allegorice intelligitur materia medicinae metallicae septies per Jordanum purificanda, quam multi metallicae rei studiosi Gur vocant.

III, x. *The Fifth Parable: Of the Treasure-House* . . .

4. Nota de domo thesaurorum de qua dixit author in primo. Assiduus loquitur de ea sic: Ergo fili locum huius lapidis tibi ostendam. . . . Hanc [scientia] autem quodam est in loco qui est ubique [*I read* est ubique *for* in utique]; locus est 4 elementa et sunt 4 januae, quas si nosse vis dico primo 4 esse stationes, 4 angulos, 4 terminos et 4 parietes . . . Haec autem domus est thesauraria in qua omnia thesaurizantur sublimia de scientiis sive sapientiis vel rebus gloriosissimis quae haberi non possunt ⟨et⟩ in hac domo thesaurizantur. Domus in qua hi thesauri sunt 4 januis clauduntur quae 4 clavibus reserantur. . . . Scito ergo

456

fili . . . quod qui scit clavem unam et ignorat residuas, domus ianuas sua clave aperiet, sed ea quae sunt in domo non aspiciet quoniam domus superficiem habet ad infinitum [*I read* infinitum *for* infimum] visum tendentem. Ergo oportet ut singulae ianuae singulis clavibus aperiantur quousque domus tota adimpleatur lumine, tunc ingrediatur quivis de thesauro accipiens . . .

8. Ecce facturus sum lapides tuos beryllos et fundamenta tua firmaturus sum lapidibus saphyri. Et parietes tuos constructurus sum lapidibus iaspidis, et portas tuas lapidibus crystalli. Et omnes qui recesserunt e manibus meis ingredientur ad te. . . . Haec spiritualia sunt et ad Ecclesiam hodie pertinent et antea per res terrae pretiosas figurata sunt.

11. [Maria] est domus et vestiaria ex qua indutus fuit Filius Dei carne.

13. Per eius vinum unio fit.

17. In ignea igitur substantia intellige Patrem, in splendore Filium, in calore Spiritum sanctum.

18. . . . potest aliter dici quod habet lucem caelum empyraeum non condensatam ut radios emittat sicut corpus solis sed magis subtilem vel habet claritatem gloriae, quae non est conformis claritati naturali.

30. Oportebat sponsam quam Pater desponsaverat in thalamis caelestibus habitare. — intima Mariae cum Filio coniunctio. — Pari modo, hac de re agentes Reginam describunt in regiam coelorum aulam per triumphum ingredientem ac dextero Divini Redemptoris assidentem lateris: itemque Canticorum Sponsam inducunt "quae ascendit per desertum sicut virgula fumi ex aromatibus myrrhae et thuris" ut corona redimiatur. Quae quidem ab iisdem veluti imagines proponuntur caelestis illius Reginae, caelestisque Sponsae, quae una cum Divino Sponso ad caelorum aulam evehitur.

38. Qui vult esse adamas, hircino sanguine tingui luxuriae caveat, ne frangat malleus illum.

50. Ex te undique vita fluit. — Tibi gloria, qui induisti corpus hominis mortalis, illudque fontem vitae effecisti omnibus mortalibus.

74. Vicit sol et quibus ascendit gradibus signavit mysterium. Duodecim ecce dies ex quo ascendit . . . symbolum . . . duodecim eius apostoli.

75. Et in illo lumine, quod in singulis gradibus est, revelatur quidquid revelatur . . . Et propterea omnia in unum gradum ascendunt et omnia una eademque re coronantur . . . Lumen

illud quod manifestatur vocatur vestimentum. Nam ipse rex est
Lumen omnium intimum . . . Et omnes lucernae et omnia
lumina lucent a Sene Sanctissimo.

77. Nam Christus est lapis angularis, tamquam punctus in quo
componuntur duodecim apostoli; et alias 24 seniores in Apocalypsi; et oportet quod de uno numero vel alio spiritualiter sit,
quilibet qui Christo Domino debeat uniri et super Christum
fundari.

78. 24 Seniores: hic [numerus] constat ex duodecim et duodecim,
qui item constat ex tribus et quattuor; sancti vero praedicatores
nomen sanctae Trinitatis per quattuor mundi partes annun-
tiant.

84. et praedictum Alphabetum sive corona illa caelestis licet causas
possideat rerum varias verum tamen coniunctissimas et quae in
unam hominis speciem productionemque eorum, quae in usum
eiusdem veniunt, conspirent.

96. Oportet [Alchemistam] . . . arrogantiae vitium a se repellere
et pium esse . . . Sed doctrinae filius ⟨sit⟩ vir subtilissimo ingenio decoratus, . . . sanus, firmus in proposito et constans etc.

105. ratione candoris signatur claritas, ratione soliditatis impassi-
bilitas, ratione modicitatis subtilitas, ratione rotunditatis
agilitas.

106. Vel sic: Dabo illi calculum. Id est Christum, qui per calculum
signatur; quia calculus lapis pretiosus, qui et carbunculus
dicitur, et dicitur sic a carbone, quia ab eo similitudinem ducit;
lucet enim positus in tenebris. Sic Christus in mundi tenebris
refulsit, quando Verbum caro factum est et habitavit in nobis.

107. quia fides est de his quae non videntur et spes de his, quae non
habentur.

108. Charitas, quae comparatur auro propter valorem, colorem,
pretiositatem.

112. Pertinet ad monachos quasi trigenarius numerus in eo quod
scientes et venerantes literam veteris testamenti et novi in patri-
archis et apostolis, quos electos esse sciunt, intellectui spirituali
qui ex utraque litera procedit, adhaerent etc.

III, xi. *The Sixth Parable: Of Heaven and Earth* . . .

4. Hermes quoque ait: Terra est mater elementorum: de terra
procedunt et ad terram revertuntur. / Hermes: terra est elementum et de terra omnia facta sunt et ad terram convertuntur.
Moyses: terra est mater elementorum, omnia de terra procedunt

et ad terram convertuntur. Sic recitat Morienus: Haec autem terra est corpus et fermentum . . .

7. Secundum hoc ergo dicitur terra inanis et vacua vel invisibilis et incomposita, quia materia per formam cognoscitur . . . Materia autem secundum id quod est, est ens in potentia.

12. Mundus inferior est corpus et cinis combustus ad quem reducunt Animam honoratam. Et cinis combustus et anima, sunt aurum sapientum, quod seminant in terra sua alba. . . .

13. Seminate aurum vestrum in terram albam foliatam, quae per calcinationem facta est ignea, subtilis, aerea. / Seminate ergo animam in terram albam foliatam, quoniam ipsa retinet eam quoniam cum ascenderit a terra in coelum iterumque descenderit in terram recipiet vim inferiorum et superiorum . . .

14. Et Malchuth erit Foemina Metallica et Luna sapientum, agerque in quem conicienda sunt semina minerarum secretarum, nempe Aqua auri, prout hoc nomen occurrit Gen. 36 : 39; sed scito fili mi in his talia latere mysteria, quae nulla hominum lingua effari poterit.

16. Quam pretiosus est cinis . . . et quam pretiosum est, quod ex eo fit. Miscentes igitur cinerem aquae, iterum coquite . . .

18. Cinerem, qui est in fundo vasis, ne vilipendatis; est quidem in inferiori loco, sed est terra corporis tui, quae est permanentium cinis. / Cinerem ne vilipendas; nam ipse est diadema cordis tui.

28. Cum autem coagulatum fuerit totum, tunc nominatur mare sapientum. Et haec terra est mater mirabilium, et mater coelorum. . . . et est totum et ex ipsa trahitur totum.

30. Ascendit a terra in coelum, iterumque descendit in terram, et recipit vim superiorum et inferiorum. Sic habebis gloriam totius mundi.

32. In principio spiritus foecunditatis incubavit aquis; et illae conceperunt pepereruntque dracones, pisces et aves. Spiritus sanctus incubavit aquis baptismi, quae pepererunt mysticas aquilas, nempe virgines et Ecclesiae rectores.

36. Lux caelestium corporum causat formas substantiales in istis inferioribus. Dat etiam esse spirituale coloribus quia facit eos visibiles actu. Ergo lux non est aliqua qualitas sensibilis sed magis substantialis forma aut spiritualis . . . : lumen agit quasi instrumentaliter in virtute corporum caelestium ad producendas formas substantiales etc.

38. Ἡ μὲν γῆ ἐστερέωται ἐπάνω τῶν ὑδάτων, τὰ δὲ ὕδατα ἐν ταῖς κορυφαῖς τῶν ὀρέων κτλ.

42. Dixit Hermes quod secretum uniuscuiusque rei in una est aqua et principium generationis hominis est aqua.

48. Fecit lunam in tempora . . . Intelligimus spiritualiter Ecclesiam crescentem de minimo et ista mortalitate vitae quodammodo senescentem: sed ut propinquet ad Solem!

50. Quartus enim numerus perfectus est atque omnem numerum sive multitudinem in se complectitur, unum enim duo tria quatuor simul iuncta denarium constituunt ultra quem progredi non datur absque regressu ad unitatem.

57. Erit autem nox illa nox tribulationis et angustiae, nox in qua pertransibunt omnes bestiae silvae.

62. Virga Moysi petram aperuit et fluxerunt aquae . . . Ecce a latere Christi fluxit fons vitae.

64. Maria est virga aurea, signum vitae aeternae.

66. cum per donum Spiritus sancti fortiter inundans scripturae Sapientia sanctam ecclesiam, vel cuiuslibet capientis mentem, infusione sua exhilarat.

69. Deus enim permittit mala fieri ut inde melius eliciat aliquid. Unde dicitur Rom. 5 : 20: Ubi abundavit iniquitas, superabundavit gratia. Unde in benedictione cerei paschalis dicitur: O felix culpa, quae talem ac tantum meruit habere Redemptorem!

71. Et quemadmodum protoplastus ille Adam de rudi terra et de adhuc virgine (nondum enim pluerat Deus et homo non erat operatus in terram) habuit substantiam et plasmatus est manu Dei id est Verbo Dei . . . ita recapitulans in se Adam ipse Verbum existens a Maria, quae adhuc erat virgo recte accipiebat generationem Adae recapitulationis.

72. Quid est Verbum nisi sapientia? Idem enim qui Verbum Dei a Joanne dicitur ipse sapientia Dei a Paulo nominatur. Christum enim, inquit Paulus apostolus, Dei virtutem et Dei sapientiam (I Cor. 1). Christus igitur ipse et Verbum et iste est Sapientia. Verbum Sapientia, et Sapientia Verbum. Verbum Sapientis, quia "Etructavit cor meum verbum bonum" (Ps. 44). Sapientia Verbum, quia "Ego Sapientia ex ore Altissimi . . ." (Ecclus. 24). Sapientia igitur Verbum cordis etc. . . . . Itaque si Verbum illuminat Sapientia illuminat. / quia Filius Patris Sapientia est. / Sapientiam Dei Patris . . . et causam creatricem omnium esse et in omnibus, quae creat, creari et fieri et omnia in quibus creatur et fit, continere. / [Deus] qui de se ipso Filium suum, qui est sapientia sua, gignit. / ut ipsae primordiales rerum causae a Graecis prototypa, hoc est primordialia exemplaria vel proorismata vocantur.

76. Θείαν οὖσαν τὴν ψυχὴν ἄνωθεν, ἐπιθυμίᾳ θηλυνθεῖσαν δεῦρο ἥκειν εἰς γένεσιν καὶ φθοράν.

78. Convivium laudet te, quia multiplicasti vina eius . . . Inter invitatos gratias agam, quod potu me refecit. Invitavi sponsum coelestem, qui se demisit, ut omnes invitaret. Ad convivium eius purissimum conviva ingrediar, inter iuvenes gratias agam, quia ipse sponsus est et non est qui ad thalamum eius frustra pulset.

79. Ipsa [scilicet Maria] est cellaria totius Trinitatis, quae de vino Spiritus sancti dat, et propinat, cui vult et quantum vult.

81. Virtus retentiva foeminina est frigida et sicca, et est terra. Virtus digestiva seu alterativa est masculina, calida et humida, et est aer. . . . Quinta essentia vero est vita, quae est propria, nec est calida, nec humida; nec frigida nec sicca; nec masculina nec foeminina.

III, xii. *The Seventh Parable: Of the Confabulation*

11. Quia vero necdum omnium peccatorum sorde purgata, necdum lota est in salute, nigra dicitur, sed in atro colore non permanet. Itaque candida quando ad maiora consurgit . . . diciturque de ea: Quae est ista quae ascendit dealbata?

14. Unde Propheta exclamat: Quis dabit mihi pennas ut columbae, videlicet cogitationes contemplationesque immaculatas ac simplices, et volabo et requiescam? Quis nisi Pater caelestis? Quare inquit Christus: Nemo venit ad me nisi Pater meus traxerit eum, et tum videlicet cum perfecerit integrum circulum, et erit Deus omnia in omnibus ut semper fuit.

19. Videndum est quod in magisterio et termino operationis, cum oritur anima ipsa, quaerit corpus suum, ut uniatur cum eo et recipiat vitam et operationem; et unio ista et compositio fit mediante spiritu; et cum coniuncta fuerit corpori vivit in aeternum cum suo corpore; haec autem coniunctio fit in ortu et resurrectione animae, quia quamvis prius creata esset, cum suo corpore tamen propter inquinationem corporis et corruptibilitatem, non poterat anima suas proprias et incorruptibiles ostendere operationes, immo tamquam mortua et inutilis iacebat et quasi cum corpore tumulata et quando per magisterium ipsa purificatur et candidatur, resurgit a suo corpore separata et tunc suum corpus est etiam purificatum et ipsa quaerit suum corpus et desiderat coniungi sibi ut in aeternum vivat nec potest coniungi cum corpore alieno . . . quod anima nostra orta est in Orizonte aeternitatis antequam suo corpori uniatur . . . et in hac coniunctione resurrectionis fit corpus totum spirituale ut ipsa anima, et fiunt sic unum sicut aqua mixta aquae et non

separantur de caetero in aeternum cum in eis nulla sit diversitas, immo unitas et identitas omnium trium, scilicet spiritus, animae et corporis absque separatione in aeternum.

25. et quoniam post adunationem hominis, hoc est, duplicis sexus in pristinam naturae unitatem, in qua neque masculus neque foemina, sed simpliciter homo erat, confestim orbis terrarum adunatio ad paradisum sequetur.

31. ὁ λίθος ὁ ἀκρογωνιαῖος, ὁ ἐκλεκτός, ὁ ἔντιμος, ἐνδοτέρῳ λίθου κεῖμαι πρὸς ὀλίγον χρόνον, λίθος προσκόμματος Ἰουδαίοις, καὶ σωτήριος τοῖς πιστεύουσιν. ἐνεφυτεύθη τοίνυν τὸ ξύλον τῆς ζωῆς ἐν τῇ γῇ, ἵνα ἀπολαύῃ τῆς εὐλογίας ἡ καταραθεῖσα γῆ καὶ ἵνα λυθῶσιν οἱ νεκροί.

43. Et istud occultum est de natura Solis et ignis, et est pretiosissimum oleum omnium occultorum, et tinctura viva, et aqua permanens, quae semper vivit et permanet, et acetum Philosophorum et spiritus penetrativus; et est occultum tingitivum, aggregativum et revivificativum: quod rectificat et illuminat omnes mortuos et surgere eos facit.

44. Tunc apparebit justorum gloria quasi sol in regno patris eorum consummatisque ad integrum muris Hierusalem et universo numero electorum Dei apparebit gloriosa et felix sedens quasi regina a dextris Dei in vestitu deaurato circumamicta varietate. Dabit autem illi Dominus Deus partem gloriae suae et regnabit cum illa usque in aeternum et regni eius non erit finis. Amen.

45. Nisi [Christus] Deus erat, quomodo per aurem intrare potuit? Per aurem enim spiritus intravit et ex ventre caro egressa est. / Ac conceptio quidem per auditum facta est. / Verbum intravit per aurem Virginis et exivit per auream portam.

46. Ingressus est per aurem et secretum uterum inhabitavit.

47.

Hac in domo Deus homo
fieri disposuit.
Hic absconsus pius Sponsus
vestem suam induit.

54. Quod ex sulphure sulphuri mixto pretiosissimus fit color, qui non variatur nec ab igne fugit, quando anima in corporis intima infertur ac corpus continet et colorat.

56. Anima . . . quae est spiritualis natura ex qua colores apparuerunt.

58. Deinde fiunt corpora spiritus et animas habentes tingentes eo, quod invicem germinant.

67. Lux coram eis effulsit, Jesus ut sponsus e thalamo suo exsiliit, remansit sepulcrum cum angelis in medio.

69. Exultat Ecclesia in Deo suo, quia induit me vestimento salutis, id est stola gloriae baptismi; illa quippe est verum salutis vesti-

462

mentum et candida gloriae stola. Et fecit me tamquam sponsum gloriosum per absolutionem. Et tamquam sponsam ornatam. Sponsa ecclesia est, quae exornata est pulchritudine omnium populorum. / E coelo divina eius natura et e terra eius vestimentum carnis. Omnis qui sua exuit vestimenta ea commiscet cum vestimento Christi in aeternum. Ab eo in aquis acquirite vestimentum quod non teritur nec amittitur, vestimentum quod ipso indutos semper obtegit.

71.
> Flos campi convallium,
> Singulare lilium,
>> Christus ex te prodiit.
> Tu caelestis paradisus . .
> Tu thronus es Salomonis,
> Cui nullus par in thronis
>> Arte vel materia.

76. Maria est lilium totius castitatis. Sicus spina rosam genuit Judaea Mariam.

82. Floruit autem Maria, nova vitis prae vite antiqua Heva, habitavitque in ea vita nova Christus.

83. Simeon botrum vitae e vite virginali decerptum portavit in ulnis suis . . . / Vitis virginalis uvam dedit cuius dulce vinum flentibus solamen attulit. / Ipsa [Maria] quippe erat paradysus malorum, fons hortorum, quia in ea surrexit lignum vitae, atque de ea profluxit fons sapientiae, omnibusque deliciis affluebat, in qua omnes thesauri sapientiae et scientiae absconditi erant.

87. Ita mentis pax et tranquillitas lectulus est in quo sponsa quiescit.

101. Absque eo quod intrinsecus latet, hoc nobis beatus Job intimat cum Austri interiora commendat.

106. Stat Maria mater tua, soror tua, sponsa tua, ancilla tua. . . . Magister matris, Deus matris, Domine matris, matre iunior et senior.

107. Rex qui nuptias filio fecit, est Deus Pater, qui Iesu Christo, Filio suo, sponsam Ecclesiam coniunxit. Huius nuptialis thalamus erat sacrae Virginis uterus. / De his nuptiis texuit rex Salomon dulce epithalamium dum in laude Sponsi et Sponsae per Spiritum concinuit Cantica Canticorum.

109. Mater me genuit et per me gignitur ipsa.

112. Vult per oleum animam, . . . quae non ingreditur per ignem, sed aqua extrahit eam. / Et hoc genitum est pinguedo quam vocant animam et ovum.

114. Funda [David] quippe erat circumdata Christi humanitas, pas-

sionibus circumrotata, Lapis qui frontem Goliae penetravit erat divinitas quae maxillam Leviathan perforavit.

122. Solvunt enim hanc tincturam cum humiditate, quae est ex ipso in principio et in fine cum igne, sicut vides granum Hospho seu Offoto in gramine suo, cum aqua et igne naturaliter augmentari et nutriri et generatur in eo tinctura. . . . Vertite aurum in folia. / Tinctura, . . . quam etiam vocavit Hermes aurum, cum dixit Seminare aurum in terram albam foliatam, significavit hanc tincturam . . . et nominaverunt eam crocum et Effer. / Tinctura vera, Kalid, id est fixa incombustibilis, cum granum eius prius fuerat combustibile.

124. Ego sum frumentum seminatum in terram puram, quod nascens crescit et multiplicatur et adfert fructum seminanti: quia omne quod generatur genere suo [generatur] et quodlibet individuum multiplicat formam suae speciei, et non alterius. . . .

130. Denarius est Christus, ut in Apocalypsi (6 : 6) "quod qui . . . in fidem et operationem tenent, ad Christum pertinent."

153. Quinta essentia spiritus est, qui omnia vivificat et alterat, et omne germen germinat, et omne lumen accendit, et omnes fructus floret.

165. Nisan, mensis victoriae eduxit Sponsam Regis, suis effusionibus turbavit terram eamque sparsis suis floribus implevit . . . factae nuptiae purae in deserto./ Nisan etiam terram induit vestimento coloribus omnis generis texto, induitur tellus tunica pallioque florum.

168. Quis vidit flores e libris veluti e montibus erumpentes? Castae puellae iis impleverunt spatiosos mentis sinus. Ecce vox ut sol super turbas flores sparsit. . . . Flores pulchros et rationales sparserunt pueri coram rege. Pullus illis coronatus est. . . . Unusquisque colligat cunctos flores et hos misceat floribus qui creverunt in terra sua. . . . Offerunt Domino nostro in coronam florum; pontifex suas homilias, presbiteri sua encomia, diaconi suas lectiones. . . . Invitemus . . . martyres, apostolos et prophetas. Ipsi similes sunt eorum flores . . . ditissimae sunt eorum rosae, suave olent eorum lilia; ex horto deliciarum colligunt pulcherrimos flores, eosque adducunt ad coronam festi nostri pulcherrimi. Gloria tibi a beatis. Coronae regum pauperes sunt in conspectu divitiarum tuae coronae. Inserta est in ea puritas; triumphat in ea fides; splendet in ea humilitas; fulget in ea multicolor sanctitas; nitet in ea charitas magna, omnium florum regina. Ecce corona tua perfecta est. Benedictus qui dedit nobis ut plecteremus eam. / Flores sunt homines fide florentes etc.

172. Quam plenitudinem florum, herbarum, et fructuum, significantem perfectionem morum, virtutum, et operationum diversarum.

177. Quod autem non solum duplicata voce, sed etiam triplicata hortatur, ut veniat, immensitatem desiderii et amoris, quem habet ad eam, insinuat, et ut trina repetitio immensitatis et firmitatis est attestatio, funiculus triplex difficile rumpitur.

178. Binarius, qui sine medio est, sine vinculo est, et ipse divisionem significat. Ternarius autem, qui medium habet, concordiae et coniunctionis est signum. Est enim primus imparium numerorum, et primus totus impar, unde quasi totus concordia est. . . . vatem Mantuanam, cum dixit: Numero Deus impare gaudet, quod idem est ac si diceret: Deus pacem diligit ac dilectionem, quia ipse pax et dilectio est.

184. . . . et in . . . coniunctione resurrectionis fit corpus totum spirituale ut ipsa anima, et fiunt sic unum sicut aqua mixta aquae et non separantur de caetero in aeternum, cum in eis nulla sit diversitas, immo unitas et identitas omnium trium scilicet spiritus, animae et corporis absque separatione in aeternum. Sicut vere patet de identitate et unitate sanctissimae Trinitatis in Deo scilicet Patris et Filii et Spiritus sancti, quae sunt in ipso Deo unum et idem cum distinctione personarum absque diversitate in substantia. Ex quibus verbis coniicere possumus directe quod philosophi antiqui huius artis fuerunt vates vere per hanc divinam artem, scilicet de resurrectione animae cum suo corpore et eius glorificatione, de apparitione Dei in humana carne scilicet Christi et identitate ipsius cum Deo mediante influxu et manatione Spiritus sancti, quamvis indistincte valde haec noverunt et confuse. . . . Nam in hoc lapide vere assignatur trinitas in unitate et e converso, cum distinctione et absque diversitate, ut patet subtiliter intuenti et scienti.

200. Ad annum decimum sextum laudet granum frumenti spiritualem agricolam, qui corpus suum agro sterili ut semen commisit. Corpus illud granum fuit, quod omnia praerumpens mox ortum est et panem novum praebuit.

205. Et sicut panis ex multis granis conficitur, ita Christi corpus ex multis electis colligitur. . . . Vinum etiam ex multis acinis eliquatur, et in torculari exprimitur; ita corpus Christi ex multis iustis compaginatur, quod in praelo crucis torquetur; quod vinum in sanguinem Christi vertitur, ut anima nostra quae in sanguine est, per hoc vivificetur.

207. Etenim ordo ille qui pro claritate sapientiae dici poterat aurum modo obscuratum est et rursum velut in nigrum plumbum.

IV. *Was St. Thomas the Author of*
"Aurora Consurgens?"

21. Mulierum aspectum semper abhorruit. / Femina est mas occa-
sionatus, quasi praeter intentionem naturae proveniens.

25. Coepit miro modo taciturnus esse silentio. . . . coeperunt eum
fratres vocare bovem mutum. / Tempus erit in quo mugitum
bovis istius totus mundus admirabitur.

28. Non autem sufficit scire in universali sed quaerimus scire unumquodque secundum quod in propria natura se habet, hoc
enim optimum et perfectum est genus sciendi.

30. Hi autem qui in cupro multum operantur in nostris partibus,
Parisiis videlicet ac Coloniae et in aliis locis in quibus fui et
vidi experiri . . .

31. et hoc modo dicunt animam unius hominis vel alterius animalis egredi et ingredi in alterum et fascinare ipsum et impedire
operationes ipsius.

37. Et hoc quidem operatur ars cum labore et erroribus multis,
natura vero sine difficultate et labore; cuius causa est, quia
virtutibus caelestibus certis et efficacibus moventur virtutes
in materia lapidum et metallorum existentes, quando materia
operatur; et illae virtutes sunt intelligentiarum operationes,
quae non errant nisi per accidens et inaequalitate scilicet materiae. / De transmutatione autem horum corporum et mutatione unius in aliud non est physici determinare, sed artis quae
vocatur Alchemia.

38. Omnes autem virtutes infundi in inferioribus omnibus per circulum imaginum caelestium. / quoniam lapides pretiosi prae
aliis habent mirabiles virtutes quia videlicet in substantia magis
simulantur superioribus propter quod a quibusdam eorum
stellae elementales esse dicuntur.

42. Sicut divinans quondam ingenium splendide increscens fratris
Thomae commendavit, ita postea propheta fuit de magistri
Thomae doctrinae victoria perenni.

43. Erat autem praedictus puer non verbis garrulus sed meditari
intra se iam incipiens taciturnus.

47. Ecce exauditus es, suscipe onus magisterii, quia Deus tecum est,
et pro tuo autem principio nihil aliud proponas nisi hoc:
Rigans montes, etc.

55. . . . accessit ad regem, juxta quem existens in mensa subito
veritate fidei inspirata mensam percussit et dixit: Modo con-
clusum est contra haeresim Manichaei!

62. Magi dicuntur . . . quasi magistri qui de universis philosophantur.

63. Res autem naturales habent quasdam virtutes occultas quarum ratio ab homine assignari non potest.

65. Unde etiam ipsi Alchemistae per veram artem alchimiae sed tamen difficilem, propter occultas operationes virtutis coelestis . . .

66. Alchimistae faciunt aliquid simile auro quantum ad accidentias exteriores; sed tamen non faciunt verum aurum, quia forma substantialis auri non est per calorem ignis quo utuntur alchimistae, sed per calorem solis in loco determinato ubi viget virtus mineralis, et ideo tale aurum non habet operationem consequentem speciem, et similiter in aliis quae per eorum operationem fiunt.

86. Unde cum quidam iam Christi evangelium mutari conentur, in quoddam aliud evangelium, quod dicunt aeternum, manifeste dicunt instare tempora Antichristi. Hoc autem evangelium de quo loquuntur est quoddam introductorium in libro Joachim compositum, quod est ab Ecclesia reprobatum, vel etiam ipsa doctrina Joachim, per quam ut dicunt Evangelium Christi mutatur . . . Unde cum doctrina praedicta, quam legem Antichristi dicunt, sit Parisius exposita, signum est tempus Antichristi instare. Sed doctrinam Joachim vel illius Introductorii quamvis alia reprobanda contineat, esse doctrinam, quam praedicabit Antichristus, falsum est.

100. Item dixit idem testis quod, cum dictus Frater Thomas celebraret Missam in dicta capella S. Nicolai Neapoli, fuit mira mutatione commotus, et post ipsam Missam non scripsit, neque dictavit aliquid, imo suspendit organa scriptionis in tertia parte Summae in tractatu de Poenitentia. Et dum idem Fr. Raynaldus videret, quod ipse Fr. Thomas cessaverat scribere, dixit ei: Pater, quomodo dimisistis opus tam grande, quod ad laudem Dei et illuminationem mundi coepistis? Cui respondit dictus Fr. Thomas: Non possum. Idem vero Fr. Raynaldus timens ne propter multum studium aliquam incurrisset amentiam, instabat semper, quod idem Fr. Thomas continuaret scripta, et similiter ipse Fr. Thomas respondit: Raynalde, non possum, quia omnia quae scripsi videntur mihi paleae. Tunc Fr. Raynaldus stupefactus . . . [effecit] quod dictus Fr. Thomas iret ad Comitissam S. Severini sororem suam, quam caritative diligebat: quo properavit magna cum difficultate, et cum illuc accederet, ipsi Comitissae sibi occurrenti vix locutus est. Tunc Comitissa dixit dicto Fr. Raynaldo cum magno timore: Quid

467

est hoc, quod Fr. Thomas totus est stupefactus et vix mihi locutus est? Respondens idem Fr. Raynaldus ait: A festo B. Nicolai circa fuit in isto statu et ex tunc nihil scripsit. Et idem Fr. Raynaldus coepit instare apud dictum Fr. Thomam, ut diceret illi, qua de causa scribere recusaverat, et quare ita stupefactus erat. Et post multas interrogationes omni importunitate factas per ipsum Fr. Raynaldum, respondit Fr. Thomas eidem Fr. Raynaldo: Ego adiuro te per Deum vivum omnipotentem et per fidem quam tenetis ordini nostro et per caritatem qua modo stringeris, quod ea, quae tibi dixero, nulli reveles in vita mea. Et subiunxit illi: Omnia quae scripsi videntur mihi paleae respectu eorum quae vidi et revelata sunt mihi. Praedicta vero Comitissa remanente multum desolata, recessit Fr. Thomas et rediit Neapolim et deinde assumpsit iter eundi ad Concilium iuxta vocationem sibi factam penitus nihil scribens. Et in itinere invasit eum infirmitas in castro Magentiae de Campania, de qua post modum decessit.

102. Frequenter in spiritu rapitur, cum aliqua contemplatur, sed ex toto tempore, sicut nunc, nunquam vidi ipsum sic a sensibus alienum.

106. Item dixit dictus testis, quod, quando idem Fr. Thomas incepit gravari infirmitate in eodem castro Magentiae, petiit cum multa devotione quod portaretur ad monasterium S. Mariae de Fossanova, sicque factum est. Et cum dictus Fr. Thomas intrasset monasterium infirmus et debilis, adhaesit per manum posti et dixit: Haec est requies mea in saeculum saeculi etc. ... Et stetit in eodem monasterio pluribus diebus infirmus cum patientia et humilitate multa, et voluit sumere Corpus Salvatoris nostri. Et cum Corpus ipsum fuit illi portatum genuflexit et cum verbis mirae et longae adorationis et glorificationis salutavit et adoravit ipsum et ante sumptionem Corporis dixit: Sumo te pretium redemptionis animae meae, sumo te viaticum peregrinationis meae, pro cuius amore studui, vigilavi et laboravi et praedicavi et docui, nihil unquam contra te dixi, sed si quid dixi ignorans; nec sum pertinax in sensu meo, sed si quid male dixi, totum reliquo correctioni Ecclesiae Romanae. Et subsequenter mortuus est et sepultus prope altare magnum ecclesiae ipsius monasterii in loco palustri prope quoddam viridarium ipsius monasterii, ubi est fluvius, ex quo perducitur aqua per rotam, per quam totus locus ille humectatur, sicut ipse testis frequenter et diligenter inspexit.

117. Procedit Christus quasi sponsus de thalamo suo, praesagio nuptiarum exiit ad campum saeculi, cucurrit sicut gigas exultando

per viam usque venit ad crucis torum et ibi firmavit ascendendo coniugium . . . commercio pietatis se pro coniuge dedit . . . et copulavit sibi perpetuo iure matronam.

122. . . . ut . . . hora matutinali diluculum aenigmatice visionis finem acciperet et plenae lucis sanctus diem gloriae inchoaret.

II. SUPPLEMENT TO THE APPARATUS

The following variants and omissions were not mentioned:

1. The chapter headings, which in D are missing throughout.

2. All omissions in the MSS at the stereotyped concluding sentence of the parables: *Qui habet aures audiendi*, etc. Mostly either *doctrinae* or *disciplinae* is missing, or both; the Vienna MS (V) has throughout: *quid dicat spiritus filiis doctrinae.*

3. One source is given in D as *Liber quintae essentiae*, in the other MSS as σ͞χto or σ͞ēe (*sexto? secreto? secretorum?*) and in V as lϕᵉ, with *sexagesimae* written alongside. These variants will be explained only when the sources come to light.

4. In D and V Morienus always occurs as Morigenes; in BLRh, as Morienes; in MP, as Morienus.

5. Occasionally, obvious mistakes, such as *absturimus* for *abstulimus* L (IX.85) or *igno* P (IX.90), and variants such as *aministratio* for *administratio* P (IX.98), were not mentioned.

6. The large lacunae in B, which can hardly be considered a usable MS. These omissions are: I.10. me / 12–13. a iumentis ~ Et / 18. exigua / 24. operationes pulchrae et / 25. neque deformes / 27. quia scientia ~ peribit / 29. ait enim / 36. Hoc idem vult / 37. cum dicit / II.4–7. vobis enim ~ conversabitur / 8–9. et non abscondam. Et namque / 10. a sapientum / 12. neque cum invidia ~ habebo / 18. homo, et, illius / III.10. mittendus est ~ manducandum / 18. ait / IV.1. De nomine / 4. aureum / 14. summa / 16. De illa ~ est: ut dicit n9 / V.10. sapientiam hanc / 19. ingeniose et constanter, *etc.* / VI.8. mei / 9. a facie iniquitatis meae / 14. mecum / 19. quod est valde, non / 20. supra omnia ~ quae est / 21–22. tota pulchra ~ laeserit / 23. sapore convalesco / 25. cuius ~ exinanitur / 26–28. sapiens qui ~ aeternum / 31. non apponet illi / 32–33. nivis. Omnibus ~ erit / 35. quia ~ comedit / 40–43. condemnabitur ~ Talis / 44. filius / 44–45. speciosum ~ mirantur / 47. autem / VII.9. meus a tactu

dilecti mei / 9–10. mei, postquam / 12. omnes, et / 13. et sol ~ apparuerit / 14–15. sicut ~ est / 16. olim / 17. ab oriente ~ pretiosa / 19. quia / 20. Hodie / 23. amplius / 24–26. inventa ~ integratus / 28. ullus dolor: luctus, *cetera om.* / 30–31. philosophi innuunt, *cetera om.* / **VIII.**4. meos / 14. meis / 22–25. extento ~ filiarum Syon / 29–30. est ~ Jerusalem / 31. nostrorum / 32–34. qui scriptus ~ intellectus / 39. innuunt / **IX.**6. et super ~ Israel / 8–9. in veritate / 13–14. talis ~ sunt / 19–20. sunt ~ iudicia / 20–21. attribuitur ipse ~ id / 22–24. qui ~ restauravit / 26. vegetando / 27–28. sicut ~ Nam / 29. cum / 30. descendit / 33. quoniam ~ terram / 90–91. Igne ~ idem / 124–27. Et ~ testantur / **X.**10–11. illum ~ mecum / 12. domum hanc / 20–21. et iuvenescentem / 23. si autem / 30. ierit, est / 35. (corde) et / 37. de / 38–39. ecce ~ generationes / 42–44. et iterum ~ eius. Et / 60. quod ~ nominavit / 61. autem / 67. anima / 74. sic, Et (Propheta) / 96. et fovet / 98. autem / 108. vestrae / 111. utrum ~ deficiens / 112–15. O quam ~ laborem / 116. scribitur: dicitur / 118. et dictis / 119. et proveniunt, Domino / 126. quam / **XI.**4. terra / 6. cum / 21. fatuorum / 28–29. per ~ mundum / 32. testante / 33. non ~ saeculi / 58–59. Ubi ~ victoria, ibi ~ gratia / 60–62. vivificabuntur ~ advenit / 67. Ut / 72–73. aeternum est / 76. Adam / **XII.**12. vocavi ~ nemo / 15. pulcherrimam veste / 17. tunc / 21. toto ~ desiderio / 22–24. quid ~ mihi, omnes / 29. et laetitiae / 32. me (nec) / 38. quia audit ~ tuus / 42. et agnitionis ~ spei / 43–44. et flores ~ honestatis / 46–47. respiciens ~ mei / 49. aromatizans / 50. et myrrha electa / 51–52. progrediens ~ latet / 54. et laetitiae quia / 56–57. et ~ abstulit / 62. et (faciens) / 73. namque / 73–75. et laudabunt ~ saeculum / 78–79. quod siccum ~ illud / 81. tota / 81–82. lex ~ propheta et, Ego / 82–83. Ego ~ eruere / 85. et nemo / 87–90. quae dulcis ~ Esebon / 91. venter ~ poculis / 97–98. et erunt ~ vineae / 98. mi / 102. tua, servavi / 103. et utamur ~ celeriter / 104–9. et nos impleamus ~ amore / 112. quia / 117. danda /

7. Further isolated and unimportant omissions in the other MSS are as follows: I.12. in viis *V, corr. V*₂ / 14. et (Deus) *L* / 14. eam *L* / 19. et sine causa non est *L* / 21. illius *V* / 26. vitae *L* / 29. eius *V* / 31. milia *L* / 38. et augmenti *P* / 41. in *D* / II.17. infinitus omnibus *L* / III.11. sunt *L* / 12–13. hic enim ~ scientia *V* / 13. esset *L* / 17. cum dormiente loquitur *V* / 19. ultra *L* / IV.5. in *P* / 8. in *P* / 12. et ultimo *D* / V.3. et *V* / 4. Intelligite *M* / 5. parabolam et *L* / VI.1. nigra *L* / 12. me *L* / 22. mihi *V* / 26. et ipse ~ laetificat patrem hunc *D* / 29. meam *L* / VII.23. drachma *L* / 27. erit *D* / VIII.10. me *L* / 14. meis *B* / 23. suis *L* / 29. est *L* / 35. et *P* / IX.4. et eiecerit *M* / 10. et *P*, est *M* / 25. et (flammis) *M* / 36. est (in) *P* / 37. in aqua

P / 40–42. quia ignis ~ vitae *P* / 57. unius *P* / 58–59. alterius. Et ~ frigidum *L* / 78. Et *L* / 79. et (ignis) *D* / 80. nam *D* / 83. scribitur *P* / 99. et *Rh* / 102. hanc *L* / 104–5. infima ~ visceribus, *transposed V* / 106. de quo ~ vinctos *V* / 113. et in ipso *L* / 118. Et *D* / 122. et *D* / 124–25. dictum est *Rh* / 126. in *L* / **X**.2. quam *L* / 6. hac *M* / 29. ipsi *L* / 40–41. cum isto ~ Si *M* / 52. dicitur *L* / 53. est *L* / 54. sua *P* / 88. pro bono *Rh* / 88–89. sed bonitas ~ pro parvo *P* / 91. Et *D* / 96. et *L* / 100. ne *L* / 111. an deficiens *L* / **XI**.3. est *M* / 4. etiam *D* / 7. sit *L* / 11. sacro eloquio *L* / 14. auri *V* / 23–24. prohiberet ~ vult *V* / 25. terrae *L* / 40. producens *L* / 47. anni *M* / 52. in *D* / 58. ubi est ~ victoria *L* / 65. homo *L* / **XII**.4–5. decoloravit ~ operuerunt *L* / 5. est *D* / 10. me *D* / 11. quaesivi *L* / 16. mihi *L* / 22. et *P* / 24. mea *L* / 25. te *L* / 26. meam *P*, et *P* / 40. meus *L*, locutus *V* / 51. valde *L* / 65. et granum ipsorum *L* / 73. pane *L* / 76. non (paveo) *M*, meo *L*, sum *M* / 78. est *L* / 79–80. et illud ~ viceversa *M* / 88–90. O quam ~ Esebon *M* / 91. non *M* / 92. nive, nitidiores *L* / 93. est *L* / 93–94. atque desiderabile *D* / 97. eius *P* / 100. et *D* / 110. quam (iucundum) *D* / 118. homine *L* /

8. Variants which are of importance for textual criticism but which were nevertheless discounted in our text: **I.**5. illa: prima *D* / 9. confundantur *D* / concupiscite *D* / 10. sapientiam *B* / Domini *DL* / 11. et *om. MPVF, corr. V²* / dixit *P* / homines: omnes *L* / 14. etiam eam: ex causa *M* / 15. Salomonem *M* / composuit *B* / posuit et omnem pulchritudinem *L cetera om.* / 17. illi: huic *L*, illo *M* / comperavit *M* / 18. existimabitur *M* / 20. negacione *L* / 21. huius *om. BL* / modi *M* / 23. dextra *DV* / vero *om. BL* / 24. pulchra et laudabilis *P* / 25. difformes *L* / moderata *L* / 27. iis *D* / illam *B* / 28. quia: quare *M* / 31. quod: quia *L* / viveret homo: unus *L* / mille *L* / 35. cui quantum et quando vult *L* / et *om. BD* / 36. libro *om. BL* / 37. cum: tantum *M* / 38. terminus: unius *VD* / 39. cessit in finitum *M* / invenit *PB* / 41. viis: vicis *M* / ipsam *M* / gressos *L*, egressus *B* / 42. dicit: docet *DL*, ait *B* / autem: enim *L*, autem *L*2, *om. B* / 43. quando: quoniam *D* / fuerunt *D*, fuerit *M* / 44. anima *L* / sequitur: servat *D* / 47. Sapientia *M* / providentiam *D* / 48. namque: numquam *L*, enim inquam quod *M* / est: et *L* / naturale et subtile *M* / 49. proficiens *P* / vigilaverit *MD* / 50. securi: secum *D*, cum *L* / illum *M*, illa *D* / 51. nec: et *BL* / iis *D* / **II**.3. regnetur *M* / omnes: eius *D* / 4. qui: quae *M* / librorum natura est infinita *M* / estis infiniti *VP*, imbuti *B* / scientiam *D*, sapientia *M* / 5. prophetiis *DL* / 6. parabolorum *MP* / interibit *D* / exquirat *MP* / discutit *DL* / 7. abscondite *M* / parabolorum *MP*, enigmatum *L* / conversatur *MP* / 9. res: vos *P* / 10. a: ad *MPV* / est: et *P*, est et *D*, *om. L* / trip-

licis M / occulta LV, obcultata M / 11. pone in luce P / eius *om.* DL /
12. iterum MPV / habeo ML / 14. est MP / Et *om.* MPV / 15. in
mirabiles D, in minerales M / mihi: me D / fixione P, ex fine fixione
M / 17. quam MP / 18. cum homo invenerit DL / dicit: debet D /
18–19. laetari velim et D / 21. didicit B / qui: quoniam L / 23. illud
D / post: praeter L / (homo) certissime (habet), *add.* L / **III.**1. negan-
tibus: refutantibus BL / 3. sanctorum: secretorum D / 5. ignorant
MPL / volunt D / 6. discet imperitus M / qui est *om.* LD / 8. enim:
omnium D / sapientiae et (scientiae) *add.* B / causa: eam V / 9. eis:
illis L / 10. neque: nam M / 11. margaritas P / 12. scientiae: sapientiae L / 13. archanum D / huius: illius L / 14. intrabit D / huius:
illius L / 15. carpere D, capere BL / 16. insipientibus: nisi sapientibus L / qui enim: quia qui B / 17. insipiente: eo B / 18. haberent L,
habet V / 19. ultra *om.* L / locutus M / 20. neque: et B / globulo M /
moralium B / 21. noverci M / medias modicis L / augustas P / deflent
P, defloret L / **IV.**1. De titulo huius libri cap. quart. Aurora consurgens L / 2. volumine M / baptisatus L / 3. haec M / 5. diem ac
noctem D / 6. rubee et citrine MP / 7. album: rubeum L / 8. in:
ut V / 10. laborantes LV / inficientem MPV / 11. ut philosophus
ait D, propheta B, in Psalmo PMV / 12. (ultimo) modo *add.* L /
13. nostra: vero MP, *om.* B / 15. eam MP, cum mea V / 16. offenditur
P / 17. eructas P / **V.**1. fatuorum B, et stultorum *add.* L / 3. librum
MPV / clamat V / 5. interpretationis D / 6. enim: vero MP / usi:
visi MP / 7. super L / globolo luminari M / 9. autem: igitur D,
om. L / (autem) hanc *add.* B / intellegit L / intelligemus M / 12. nec
non: et BV / videmus M / 13. manum D / et (virtus) *add.* P / 17.
regnans: regnanter D / 18. me *om.* BL / 19. et: ac L / **VI.**2. qua P /
3. magnam: nigram L / 5. putruerant D / 6. inferiorum L / 6–7. et
quia umbra (L: umbrae) mortis et tempestas dimiserunt me DL /
7. procedent MP / 8. Ideo *om.* DL / 9. et *om.* DL / 10. Ergo: ego
DL / 12. meam *om.* MP / inferni MP, de Inferno L / 15. offenderit
V / acquisiverit DL, *om.* B / 16. turbavit L / vestimentum quoque
L / 17. amiserit DL, arserit M / poculum B / 18. vitiaverit et (foedaverit) *add.* L / 20. super L / 21. et *add.* L / 22. mihi *om.* V / 25. cum
dormitione P, condormitatione M / 26. ipsi P / in patre M / in
filium: filius BL / 27. in excelsum P, in excelsis D / 30. custodiverint
L / 31. opponet D / illi: ei L / 32. ambulaverint L / 35. comedet D /
36. illius: illis M / 37. habent M / 38–39. crediderunt ~ bene fuerunt
baptizati D / 39. fuerint M / 39–41. salvus erit ~ sunt haec *om.* M /
47. habent L, audient L / 48. dicit D / 52. videntur P / **VII.**1. Particula M / 3. et (femina) *add.* L / 4. fuit / maris: avari M / 5. sagipte
M / 7. horreum meum L / 9. et postea venter meus a tactu dilecti
mei intumuerit *om.* LVB / 10. pessulio M / 16. olim *om.* B, aliquando

V / 17. tria: tanta *D* / 18. illo *D* / 19. aspexit *L* / 20. regnatio *D*, re-
generaturus *L* / 21. feminam intulit *M* / 22. mors enim: ores eius *M* /
nec: et *B* / 23. eam: vos (eos?) *L* / 27. Quia non ~ clamor *P* / 31.
anima *M* / 31.–32. quia corruptio: corruptio autem *DL*, om. *B* /
VIII.1. parabola: particula *M* / 2. et vecte: perfecte *M* / 5. quocumque *P* / movit *B* / 10. congregabant *PV* / 11. terrae *M* / effundant: efficiant *M* / me om. *L* / 14. Ideoque *DL* / 16. ut: ne *D* / habi-
tet *V* / 18. et praeterit ~ mittendus est qui om. *LD* / iugum: Migrum
L / 20. nostrae: meae *D* / sedabamus *P* / septem *L* / 22. quia elevati
L / ambularunt *D* / 23. suis om. *L* / composita *M*, incomposito *D*, in
composito *L*, recomposito *V* / 24. decalundabit *M*, et calvabit *V*, om.
L / ergo om. *MLVP* / ergo ~ Sion om. *M.* / 28. cooperimus *BD*, non
cooperimus *L* / defundimus *M* / 30. recepit *L* / 31. impleatur *L* /
32. quo scriptum *P* / 33. (salvabitur) et salvus vocabitur add. *DL* /
sordum *L* / 34. tum *D* / 36. in aeternum om *DL* / 38. septem *L* / 39.
annis *L* / philosophus insinuat *L* / **IX.**1. Parabola: Particula *M* /
2. trinario *V* / 4. eieceritque *L* / et eiecerit om. *M* / 7. cognoscunt *L* /
10. Spiritum sanctum: in spiritum *M* / 12. aequalitatis *L* / 17–18. est
procedens: procedit *B* / 20. (iudicia) eius add. *D* / 21. ex: ab *L* /
23. et (peccato) add. *M* / deperditum *D* / 25. flumen *L* / 26. quando:
quoniam *D* / 27. alluit *M* / 31. imminenti *V* / ad haec *M* / 32. haec
est aqua *M* / 33. spirat *M* / 34. cum: quando *D* / 35. portavit *L* /
38–39. (in qua) sibi (consistit) add. *MVP* / 39. autem: vult *V* / 42.
prius: mihi *M* / qui prius om. *L* / erat om. *DL* / 44. fructum *V* /
46. praeteribit onus *D* / 47. et om. *MP* / ipse: is *B*, om. *L* / 49. suis *M* /
munere *MP*, numeris *D* / 50. operandi *L*, operandam *M* / terra *L* /
51. prophetam *M* / 52. calcavit *P*, conculcavit *L* / operationem meam
P / 60. adusionem *M* / quo *DL* / 61. terram *L* / 62. et (in aestu) add.
M / 63. Et: unde *D*, om. *L* / 64. Res est in qua *D*, rex in qua *M* /
adusio *M* / 65. quae: quo *V* / et dignior: est indignior et *V* / 66. virtus
V / id est: et *M* / 68. sancti: seu *D*, sanctus *B* / liquefaciat *M* / 71.
quia: quod *D* / 73. haec *M* / 74. (mollificat) id add. *D* / et: ac *L* /
spiritus *L* / 75. quo canitur: coquando *M* / horrendas *L*, arridas *M* /
76. purgat *P* / tenebrosas *M* / attende *P* / (sensibus) infunde add.
L / 77. nocte om. *L* / in om. *LM* / 78. omnem *M* / 79. rubeus *L* /
81. propter hoc: propterea *D* / 82. Et: Unde *L* / 83. in Turba *RhL* /
85. dealbuntur *L* / Et: unde *D* / 87. quinto: eruto *D* / quando:
quoniam *D* / 88. sic *D* / 89. erogenia *P* / 90. ob hoc: quoniam *B* /
igno *P* / 92. et (eduxisti) add. *V* / et: in *D* / 93. subtilia *B* / liquescit
P / et om. *M* / 94–96. aqua liquescit ~ glorificatam om. *BL* / 96.
quod: tunc *L* / 96–97. postremae operationis operationem *D* /
97. praecedit: percipit *MP* / 97–98. purificabit *L* / 98. quae a: quo
L / vel mundificatio om. *B* / 99. (rectificatio) nuncupatur add. *L* /

99–100. a quibusdam ~ nuncupatur *om. BD* / 101. muneris *D* / 105.
quando: quoniam *D* / 106. (propheta) dicit *add. L* / ducit *L* / victos
M / 109. fecit *DL* / noverit *Rh* / 112. Nisi: ubi *D* / ascendit *BD* /
114. opus: corpus *L* / quando: quoniam *D* / qua *PD* / 116. esse:
omnes *D* / 117. Unde (et propheta) *add. D* / 118. nimime minimum
L / levia *L* / nisi: cum *D* / 119. nisi: cum *D* / 120. detendi *D* / in non
corporea *B* / 122. adimplicatur *M* / quia: quare *M* / potest facere:
facit *D* / 124. ananiam *P*, naminam *M* / 125. lava te *L* / Jordano
LD / et *om. MP* / 127. prophetae *L* / testatur *P* / Qui: Quia *L*,
qui *L₂* / 129. quo: quia *P* / adimpletur *L* / 130. destilla *D* / **X**.1. Particula *M* / 3. introiverit *L* / 4. inebriabunt *L* / 5. atriis: domo *L* /
6. eam *M* / 8. Nam: ut *B* / 9. audiverit *M* / 10. intrabo *L* / satiebor
L / 13. hominum *D* / 14. quae decet: quam docet *B*, quam decet
VP, om. D / 17. ut: et *D* / 18. ac: et *D* / 19. sitiant *B* / 20. inveniat
L / 22. procul dolore *M* / pauci: praerumper *D* / 23. reservant *M* /
qui: quia *V* / ut (parvuli): ita p. *B* / sapiunt: sentiunt *D*, et sapiunt
M / 24. Seniorem *M* / ipsius *M* / 27. lunae: lucem *D* / 28. enim
om. MP / habet *D* / 29. ligaverit et solverit *D* / fiat *L* / 31. inenar-
rabiles *P* / 33–34. potentiales *D* / 34. quo *RhDL* / 40. (Alex.) dicit
add. M / isto: ipso *P* / 42. quo *DL* / prophetae *V* / 43. (eris) etc.
add. L / 46. delĕs *Rh* / volutates *MP* / 47–48. qua noiam *M*, quam
veram *B*, vocavi *V* / 51. Unde *om. RhL* / dicit: ait *L* / 52. Quidam:
quid *D* / 53. Et: item *L* / 54. superiorem *P* / inferiorem *P* / 55. pene-
trativum *M* / 56. sufficissem *D*, suffecisset *P* / 57. quo *D* / 62. et *om.*
MVB / 65. loquitur *L* Et (fides) *add. L* / 68–69. terram et aquam
M / 69. scilicet *om. MDV*, videlicet *L* / scilicet aer: puta aer *RhL* /
70. confunditur *M* / credit *D* / 73. beatificat *P* / 74. consequere *M* /
75. eo *D* / 79. Aldephonsus *BDRh*, Adelphonsus *L* / verus *D*, vero
M / 80. desinit *MPV* / Gregorius: allegorico *P*, allegorice *MV* /
81. Et Job *om. MPBD LRh* / Et (omnia) *add. MPB* / 83. isto *om.*
MP / et: etiam *D* / 86. benignus: benignitas *M* / 87. reddat *L* /
88. parvum: maximum *L* / 91. scripturae *L* / habemus *D* / 93. necessaria: noia *M* / 95. temperantia vero bñ est temperantia *M* / 96.
quod: quia *L* / et (in): id est (in) *D* / conservet *P* / 97. anima:
nam *M* / 98. cum: quando *D* / 100. temperantur *M* / 101. excedit
L / 102. cave *L* / 103. convertatur *L* / cave *P* / 104. supra: per *L* /
105. temperanter *D* / posite *M* / 106. tredecima *Rh* / seu *DRh* /
107. qua *L* / dicitur (Apostolus) *add. L* / 109. spirituale *D* / 111. proficiens *L* / 112–13. intelligent *M* / 113. ii *D* / 115. propter *D* /
quo *P* / 117. factus *om. BM* / oboediens *om. P* / 118. oboediatis *V* /
119. perveniunt *V* / 123. regnum *P* / 127. reserare *L* / (elementa) etc.
add. Rh / **XI**.1. Particula *M* / 5. vero: ubi *L* / notantur *L* / 7. (aliorum) omnium *add. B* / et mater: terre materia *M* / 8. Initio ~ id

est *om. MB* / 9. a terra: cetera *P* / 10. separando *L* / 11. sancto *D* /
13. commiscere *D* / promanente *L* / 14. aurum: anima *B* / 17. ascendet
D / 19. quae est (aqua) *D* / 21. Et: ut *M* / 22. ire in aliquo loco ne
D, (ne) hoc *add. B* / vel (scriptotenus) *add. B* / ponantur *D*, pro-
ponerent *L* / lucidae *D* / 23. gloriam *M* / 25. terrae: reñe (?) *P* / advenit *P* / 26. id est: et *D* / 28. destillaverunt *D* / 29. ut enarrat gloria
D / 30. solum *L* / 34. stabant *M* / 35. rigantis *P* / 36. de fructu: defectu *P* / 37. (virtutes) terrae *add. M* / ibi: coeli *L* / 38. germina *D* /
coelorum *D* / 39. et fructum educens *D* / et: in *P* / 41. inquit *B* /
42. artum *P* / 45. egrediemur *D* / 46. serviant *L* / 47. eius: ipsius *B* /
septem *L* / 49. Turba *L* / 50. sustinet *L* / 51. quia *L* / 52. rubeo *L* /
53. et: est *L*, corr. *L₂* / sicca *L* / 57. fiat *L* / 58. dilectum *M* / 59.
ibi: ubi *P* / 63. sumpserat *V* / 64. conceptum *D* / 66. transivit *D*,
infundavit *M*, transiverunt *L* / 68. moritur: mortuum *D* / 69. fuit
L / 71. dicet *D* / 72. possidete *B* / 78. habuerit *M* / 79. tum *D* /
habemus *D* / **XII**.1. Particula *M* / 2. ad dilectam *Rh*, ad dilectum
L / 7. fimo *P* / 10. in manum suam *D* / 11. in: cum *M* / 12. nemo:
non *L* / 13. Surgam: Q꜕ℑ *L* / (ergo) ego *add. L* / 15. pulcherrima *L* /
17. eo *M* / coelum *L* / 18. quiescam *L* / 19. varietate: veritate *L* /
ergo: quaeso *D* / 21. toto: te *L* / et *M* / 25. in regionem *V* / 26. pur-
purata *M* / 30. signo: sum *P* / 33. faciat *M* / 36. sponsa: speciosa *V* /
tuo: meo *L* / 37. vel: et *D* / 38. quiesces *D* / 39. habitate Jerusalem
M / 40. Ego: et *L* / 41. floris *M* / 44–45. abierunt *MB* / 46. nocturnos vel (nocturnales) *add. L* / 47. perspiciens *L* / vulneratum *D* /
49. odorem *M* / 50. Ego: et *L*, ergo *M* / 51. electa: coruscans *D* /
52. Et (ego) *add. L* / 54. sponsationis *V* / 55. Ego: Et *D* / 57. quae
DL / 59. inmissit *P* / secunda *om. RhL* / (tertia) et (sexta) *add. D* /
64. seminat *P* / eorum *D* / 66. illud: id *V* / 67. aufert *D*, afferat *L* /
68. quidem: quod *L* / terra bona *L* / 69. quia: quare *D* / filiorum
D / 70. in decem millium *D* / 71. granis et fructibus *D* / 75. reficio
L / 78. illud: id *D* / 82. sermo: primus *V* / 82–83. occidam quod
vivere *D* / 84. ipsius: impius *P* / ipsa *P* / 85. separabat *M* / 86. quia:
quare *P* / dilectio nostra: dilecto meo *L* / nostra: mea *M* / 87. sonat
L / 90. pisc̃m ei neschebon *P* / aureae *P* / 91. poculo *V* / 92. tuas M /
93. dilectabile *M* / 94. Israel *B* / (dicite) *add. M* / faciam consorori
D / 98. electa *D* / 101. parrutuerunt *D* / ori meo: mods me *P* / 102.
ubera: verba *M* / poña P, ponam *M* / 103. ergo: et *B* / 104. et (vino)
add. D / praeteriat *Rh*, praetereat nos flos temporis *cetera om. V* /
105. quin: quoniam *L* / 107–8. relinquimus *L* / 108. hac *D* /
109. coitu et amore *D*, amoris *M* / 110. duobus: fratres *L* / 111.
secundum: unum *L* / 113. dicat: loquitur *L* / 114. ad filios *L* / dis-
ponsatione *M*, dispositione *D* / desp. ubi dil. ad dil. semen suum *V* /
115. marcescat *M*, maturescit *B* / eam *D* /

BIBLIOGRAPHY

BIBLIOGRAPHY

The items are arranged alphabetically under two headings: *A*. Ancient volumes containing collections of alchemical tracts by various authors; *B*. General bibliography, including cross-references to the material in section *A*. Short titles of the volumes in *A* are printed in capital letters.

A. ANCIENT VOLUMES CONTAINING COLLECTIONS OF ALCHEMICAL TRACTS BY VARIOUS AUTHORS

ARS CHEMICA, quod sit licita recte exercentibus, probationes doctissimorum iurisconsultorum. . . . Argentorati [Strasbourg], 1566.

Contents quoted in this volume:

  i Septem tractatus seu capitula Hermetis Trismegisti aurei [pp. 7–31; usually referred to as "Tractatus aureus"]
 ii Tabula smaragdina [pp. 32–33]
iii Studium Consilii coniugii de massa solis et lunae [pp. 48–263; usually referred to as "Consilium coniugii"]

ARTIS AURIFERAE quam chemiam vocant. . . . Basileae [Basel], [1593]. 3 vols. (For later edition see below.)

Contents quoted in this volume:

VOLUME I

  i Turba philosophorum, first version [pp. 1–65]
 ii Turba philosophorum, second version [pp. 66–139]
iii Aenigmata ex visione Arislei et allegoriis sapientum [pp. 146–54; usually referred to as "Visio Arislei"]
 iv In Turbam philosophorum exercitationes [pp. 154–82]
  v Aurora consurgens [Part II only; pp. 185–246]
 vi Rosinus ad Sarratantam episcopum [pp. 277–319]

VOLUME II

vii Rosarium philosophorum [pp. 284–384]

479

Another edition. Basileae [Basel], 1610. 3 vols.

Contents quoted in this volume:

VOLUME I

   i   Allegoriae super librum Turbae [pp. 89–93]
  ii   In Turbam philosophorum exercitationes [pp. 99–117]
 iii   Aurora consurgens [Part II only; pp. 119–58]
  iv   Rosinus ad Euthiciam [pp. 158–78]
   v   Rosinus ad Sarratantam episcopum [pp. 178–202]
  vi   Liber trium verborum Calidis [pp. 226–31]
 vii   Aristoteles de lapide philosophorum tractatulus [pp. 232–39]
viii   Avicenna de conglutinatione lapidis [pp. 240–45]
  ix   Expositio epistolae Alexandri regis [pp. 245–49]
   x   Opusculum autoris ignoti de secretis lapidis [pp. 249–51]
  xi   Clangor buccinae [pp. 288–349]
 xii   Incertus autor de arte chymica [pp. 369–405]

VOLUME II

 xiii   Morienus Romanus de compositione alchimiae (De transmutatione metallorum) [pp. 7–37]
  xiv   Scala philosophorum [pp. 71–111]
   xv   Rosarium philosophorum [pp. 133–252]
  xvi   Rosarium Arnaldi [pp. 258–98]
 xvii   Arnaldus [Arnold of Villanova]: Flos florum ad regem Aragonum [pp. 311–22]
xviii   Rogerius Bacho Anglus [Roger Bacon]: De mirabili potestate artis et naturae [pp. 327–46]

In hoc volumine DE ALCHEMIA continentur haec. Gebri Arabis . . . Norimbergae [Nuremberg], 1541.

Contents quoted in this volume:

   i   Geber: Summa perfectionis metallorum [pp. 20–205]
  ii   Tabula smaragdina [p. 363]

MANGET(US), JOANNES JACOBUS (ed.). *BIBLIOTHECA CHEMICA CURIOSA, seu Rerum ad alchemiam pertinentium thesaurus instructissimus.* . . . Coloniae Allobrogum [Geneva], 1702. 2 vols.

Contents quoted in this volume:

VOLUME I

   i   Hoghelande: De alchimiae difficultatibus [pp. 336–68]
  ii   Artefius: Clavis majoris sapientiae [pp. 503–08]

   iii Calid: Liber de compositione alchimiae quam edidit Mori-
        enus Romanus [pp. 509–19]
    iv Geber: Summa perfectionis [pp. 519–58]
     v Geber: Liber investigationis magisterii [pp. 558–62]
    vi Geber: Testamentum [p. 562]
   vii Joannes Braceschius: De Alchemia dialogus [pp. 565–98]
  viii Bacon: De alchemia (Speculum alchemiae) [pp. 613–16]
    ix Aristotle: De perfecto magisterio [pp. 638–59]
     x Arnoldus: Thesaurus thesaurorum et Rosarium philoso-
        phorum [pp. 662–76]
    xi Arnoldus: De perfecto magisterio [pp. 679–83]

                        VOLUME II

   xii Rosarium philosophorum [pp. 87–119]
  xiii Rosarium philosophorum [second version; pp. 119–33]
   xiv Scala philosophorum [pp. 134–47]
    xv Ficino: Liber de arte chemica [pp. 172–83]
   xvi Calid: Liber trium verborum [pp. 189–91]
  xvii Senior: De chemia [pp. 216–35]
 xviii Consilium coniugii [pp. 235–66]
   xix Ripley: Liber duodecim portarum [pp. 275–85]
    xx Bernardus Trevisanus: De secretissimo philosophorum opere
        chemico [pp. 388–408]
   xxi Grasseus: Arca arcani [pp. 585–619]

*MUSAEUM HERMETICUM reformatum et amplificatum . . .
continens tractatus chimicos XXI praestantissimos . . .* Franco-
furti [Frankfort], 1678. For translation, see: ARTHUR EDWARD
WAITE (trans.). *The Hermetic Museum restored and enlarged.*
London, 1893. 2 vols. (Repr., 1953.)

                Contents quoted in this volume: *

     i [Hermes Trismegistus:] Tractatus aureus de lapide philoso-
        phorum [pp. 1–52] (The Golden Tract: I, 7–50)
    ii Henricus Madathanus: Aureum saeculum redivivum [pp.
        53–72] (The Golden Age Restored: I, 51–67)
   iii [Siebmacher:] Hydrolithus sophicus, seu Aquarium sapien-
        tum [pp. 73–144] (The Sophic Hydrolith: I, 71–120)
    iv Joannes de Meung: Demonstratio naturae [pp. 145–71] (A
        Demonstration of Nature: I, 121–41)

* The titles and page numbers within parentheses refer to the English translation.

v   Liber Alze [pp. 325–35] (The Book of Alze: I, 259–70)

vi Lambspringk: De lapide philosophico et emblemata [pp. 337–72] (The Book of Lambspring: I, 271–306)

vii Michael Sendivogius: Novum lumen chemicum [pp. 545–600] (The New Chemical Light: II, 79–158)

THEATRUM CHEMICUM, praecipuos selectorum auctorum tractatus . . . continens. 6 vols. Vols. I–III, Ursellis [Ursel], 1602; Vol. IV, Argentorati [Strasbourg], 1613; Vol. V, Argentorati, 1622; Vol. VI, Argentorati, 1661. Later edition, as quoted in this volume: Vols. I–IV, Strasbourg, 1659; Vol. V, Strasbourg, 1660; Vol. VI, Strasbourg, 1661. In the following references for Vols. I–V, the former set of page numbers refers to the earlier, the latter to the later, edition of the respective volumes.

Contents quoted in this volume:

VOLUME I

i   Hoghelande: De alchemiae difficultatibus [pp. 121–206; 109–91]

ii Dorn: Speculativae philosophiae, gradus septem vel decem continens [pp. 259–310; 228–76]

iii Dorn: Congeries Paracelsicae chemicae de transmutationibus metallorum [pp. 563–646; 491–568]

iv Flamel: Excerpta ex Democrito [p. 881; 776]

VOLUME II

v   Albertus: Scriptum super arborem Aristotelis [pp. 524–27; 456–58]

VOLUME III

vi   De magni lapidis compositione et operatione liber (De Alchemia, incerti auctoris) [pp. 5–76; 1–56]

vii Aristotle: De perfecto magisterio [pp. 56–118; 76–127]

viii Arnaldus de Villanova: Liber perfecti magisterii, qui Lumen luminum nuncupatur. Vocatur etiam Flos florum [pp. 118–28; 128–43]

ix   Thomas Aquinas: Secreta alchimiae magnalia (Tractatus de lapide philosophico) [pp. 277–88; 267–77]

x   Thomas Aquinas: Thesaurus alchimiae secretissimus (Tractatus . . . datus fratri Reinaldo in arte alchemiae) [pp. 290–97; 278–83]

xi   Melchior Cibinensis: Addam et processum sub forma missae [pp. 853–60; 758–61]

VOLUME IV

xii   Artefius: Clavis majoris sapientiae [pp. 220–40; 198–214]

xiii   Hermes Trismegistus: Tractatus aureus de lapidis physici secreto [pp. 672–797; 587–718]

xiv   Albertus Magnus: Compositum de compositis [pp. 929–47; 825–41]

xv   Albertus: Liber octo capitulorum de lapide philosophico [pp. 948–71; 841–63]

xvi   Avicenna: De re recta ad Hasen [pp. 972–85; 863–74]

xvii   Avicenna: Declaratio lapidis physici filio suo Aboali [pp. 986–94; 875–82]

xviii   Avicenna: De congelatione et conglutinatione lapidis [pp. 995–99; 883–87]

xix   Thomas Aquinas: Liber lilii benedicti [pp. 1082–99; 959–74]

VOLUME V

xx   Turba philosophorum [pp. 1–57; 1–52]

xxi   Platonis Liber Quartorum [pp. 114–208; 101–85]

xxii   Senior: De chemia [pp. 219–66; 191–240]

xxiii   Mennens: Aurei velleris . . . libri tres [pp. 267–470; 245–428]

xxiv   Consilium coniugii [pp. 479–566; 429–507]

xxv   Bonus: Pretiosa margarita novella [pp. 589–794; 511–713]

xxvi   Thomas Aquinas: Tractatus sextus de esse et essentia mineralium [pp. 901–10; 806–14]

xxvii   Bacon: Epistola de secretis operibus artis et naturae [pp. 943–62; 844–61]

VOLUME VI

xxviii   Grasseus: Arca arcani [pp. 294–381]

B. GENERAL BIBLIOGRAPHY

ABU AFLAH. *Sefer ha-Tamar: Das Buch von der Palme.* Edited and translated by Gerhard G. Scholem. Jerusalem, 1926; Hanover, 1927. 2 vols.

ABU 'L-QĀSIM MUHAMMAD IBN AHMAD AL-'IRĀQĪ. *Kitāb al-'ilm al-muktasab fī zirā'at adh-dhahab.* (Book of Knowledge acquired concerning the Cultivation of Gold.) Edited and translated by Eric John Holmyard. Paris, 1923.

Acta Archelai. See HEGEMONIUS.

Acta Bollandiana. See BOLLANDUS.

Acts of Philip. See JAMES.

Acts of Thomas. See JAMES.

[ADAM OF ST. VICTOR.] *The Liturgical Poetry of Adam of St. Victor.* Translated by Digby S. Wrangham. London, 1881. 3 vols.

ADAMSON, ROBERT. See *Encyclopaedia Britannica.*

Adumbratio Kabbalae Christianae. See KNORR VON ROSENROTH.

AESCHYLUS. [*Works.*] With an English translation by Herbert Weir Smith. (Loeb Classical Library.) London and New York, 1922–26. 2 vols.

AETIUS. *De Placitis reliquiae.* In DIELS, *Doxographi Graeci* (q.v., below), pp. 273–444.

AGOBARDUS, BISHOP OF LYONS. *Liber de correctione Antiphonarii.* In MIGNE, *P.L.,* vol. 104, cols. 329–40.

AGRIPPA VON NETTESHEIM, HENRICUS CORNELIUS. *De occulta philosophia libri tres.* Strasbourg, 1531.

ALANUS DE INSULIS (Alan of Lille). *De planctu naturae.* In MIGNE, *P.L.,* vol. 210, cols. 431–82.

———. *Distinctiones dictionum theologicalium.* In MIGNE, *P.L.,* vol. 210, cols. 849–902.

ALBERTUS MAGNUS, SAINT (Albert the Great). *Beati Albert Magni Opera Omnia.* Edited by Auguste and Emil Borgnet. Paris, 1890–99. 38 vols.

———. "Biblia Mariana." In *Opera,* vol. 37, pp. 365–443.

———. *Commentarii in Danielem.* In *Opera,* vol. 18, pp. 449–642.

———. "Compositum de compositis." See *(A) Theatrum chemicum,* xiv.

———. "De adhaerendo Deo libellus." In *Opera,* vol. 37, pp. 523–42. Another edition, with a Life of Albert, compiled by Peter of Prussia. Antwerp, 1621.

———. "De anima." In *Opera*, vol. 5, pp. 117–420.

———. "De causis et proprietatibus elementorum." In *Opera*, vol. 9, pp. 585–653.

———. "De mineralibus et rebus metallicis." Cologne, 1569. Also, under the title "Mineralium libri quinque," in *Opera*, vol. 5, pp. 1–103.

———. "De mirabilibus mundi." Incunabulum in Zentralbibliothek, Zurich.

———. "De proprietatibus originalium et lapidum." Lyons (?), 1528.

———. "De rebus metallicis." See "De mineralibus . . ." above.

———. "De secretis mulierum libellus . . . de virtutibus herbarum, lapidum, et animalium quorundam . . . item de mirabilibus mundi." Strasbourg, 1615.

———. "De somno et vigilia." In *Opera*, vol. 9, pp. 121–207.

———. "De vegetabilibus et plantis." In *Opera*, vol. 10, pp. 1–305.

———. *Enarrationes in Apocalypsim beati Joannis.* In *Opera*, vol. 38, pp. 465–792.

———. *Enarrationes in Evangelium sancti Matthaei.* In *Opera*, vols. 20–21.

———. "Libellus de Alchemia." In *Opera*, vol. 37, pp. 545–73. For translation, see: *Libellus de Alchemia.* Ascribed to Albertus Magnus. Translated . . . by Sister Virginia Heines, S.C.N. With a foreword by Pearl Kibre. Berkeley and Los Angeles, 1958.

———. *Liber aggregationis.* Edited by H. Quentell. Cologne, *ca.* 1485.

———. "Liber octo capitulorum de lapide philosophico." See (*A*) *Theatrum chemicum,* xv.

———. *Mariale, sive CCXXX quaestiones super Evangelium Missus Est.* In *Opera*, vol. 37, pp. 5–321.

———. "Mineralium libri quinque." See "De mineralibus . " above.

———. "Paradisus animae." In *Opera*, vol. 37, pp. 447–511.

———. "Scriptum super arborem Aristotelis." See (*A*) *Theatrum chemicum,* v. See also *Opera*, vol. 37, pp. 574–76.

——. *Sermones de Sanctis.* In *Opera,* vol. 13, pp. 408–634.

——. *Summa Theologiae.* In *Opera,* vols. 31–35.

——. "Tractatus de mettallis et Alcimia." See PANETH, "Über eine alchemistische Handschrift des 14. Jahrhunderts. . . ."

ALCUIN. *Epistola 83.* In MIGNE, *P.L.,* vol. 100, cols. 270–74.

——. *Grammatica.* In MIGNE, *P.L.,* vol. 101, cols. 849–902.

ALEXANDER OF APHRODISIAS. *De anima (Peri psyches).* Edited by Ivo Bruns. (Supplementum Aristotelicum II : 1.) Berlin, 1887–92.

ALEXANDER OF LYCOPOLIS. "On the Tenets of the Manichaeans." In *The Writings of Methodius, Alexander of Lycopolis, etc.* Translated by William R. Clark, James B. H. Hawkins, and others. (Ante-Nicene Christian Library, XIV.) Edinburgh, 1869. (Pp. 236–66.)

ALFARABI. *Das Buch der Ringsteine.* With the Commentary of Emir Isma'il el-Hoseini el-Farani. Edited and translated (into German) by Max Horten. (Beiträge zur Geschichte der Philosophie des Mittelalters, V : 3.) Münster, 1906.

"Allegoriae super librum Turbae." See *(A) Artis auriferae* (1610), i.

ALLENDY, RENÉ. *Le Symbolisme des nombres.* Paris, 1948.

[ALPHIDIUS.] "Liber Alphidii." See Codices and MSS., iii, vi.

AMBROSE, SAINT. *Hexaemeron libri sex.* In MIGNE, *P.L.,* vol. 14, cols. 123–274.

ANASTASIUS SINAITA (the Sinaite). *Anagogicarum Contemplationum in Hexaemeron libri duodecim.* In MIGNE, *P.G.,* vol. 89, cols. 851–1078.

ANRICH, ERNST. *Moderne Physik und Tiefenpsychologie.* Stuttgart, 1963.

ANSELM OF LAON. *Enarrationes in Apocalypsim.* In MIGNE, *P.L.,* vol. 162, cols. 1499–1586.

APTOWITZER, VIKTOR (Avigdor). "Arabisch-jüdisch Schöpfungstheorien," *Hebrew Union College Annual* (Cincinnati), VI (1929), 205–46.

APULEIUS, LUCIUS. *The Golden Ass [Metamorphoses].* With an English translation by W. Adlington. Revised by Stephen Gaselee. (Loeb Classical Library.) London and Cambridge, Mass., 1947.

"Aquarium sapientum." See (A) *Musaeum hermeticum*, iii.

ARCHELAUS. *Carmen*. See HELIODORUS.

[ARISLEUS.] "Aenigmata ex visione Arislei." See (A) *Artis auriferae* (1593), iii.

ARISTOTLE. *De anima*. In the version of William of Moerbeke, and the Commentary of St. Thomas Aquinas. Translated by Kenelm Foster and Silvester Humphries. (Rare Masterpieces of Philosophy and Science.) London, 1951. See also Codices and MSS., ix, xi.

———. *Ethics*. With English text by H. Rackham. (Loeb Classical Library.) London and New York, 1926.

———. See also LACOMBE.

ARISTOTLE, pseudo-. "De perfecto magisterio." See (A) MANGET, *Bibliotheca chemica curiosa*, ix; (A) *Theatrum chemicum*, vii.

———. "De proprietatibus originalium et lapidum" (otherwise called "Secreta secretorum"). Lyons (?), 1528.

———. "Liber de causis." See BARDENHEWER.

———. "De lapide philosophico tractatulus." See (A) *Artis auriferae* (1610), vii.

ARIUS DIDYMUS (Areios Didymos). *Epitomes Fragmenta Physica*. In DIELS, *Doxographi Graeci* (q.v., below), pp. 447–72.

ARNOLD OF (ARNALDUS DE) VILLANOVA. "De perfecto magisterio" (otherwise "Flos Florum" or "Lumen luminum"). See (A) *Theatrum chemicum*, viii; (A) *Artis auriferae* (1610), xvii; (A) MANGET, *Bibliotheca chemica curiosa*, xi.

———. "Rosarium." See (A) *Artis auriferae* (1610), xvi.

ARTEFIUS. "Clavis majoris sapientiae." See (A) MANGET, *Bibliotheca chemica curiosa*, ii; (A) *Theatrum chemicum*, xii.

[*Ascensio Isaiae*.] *The Ascension of Isaiah*. Translated and edited by R. H. Charles. (Translations of Early Documents, I.) London, 1917.

ATHANASIUS, SAINT. *Expositio in Psalmum LXXXVIII*. In MIGNE, *P.G.*, vol. 27, cols. 383–96.

AUGUSTINE, SAINT. *De civitate Dei (The City of God)*. In MIGNE, *P.L.*, vol. 41. For translation, see: *The City of God*. Translated by John Healey. London and Toronto, 1931. 3 parts in 1 vol.

——. *De Genesi ad litteram.* In MIGNE, *P.L.,* vol. 34, cols. 245–486.

——. *De quantitate animae.* In MIGNE, *P.L.,* vol. 32, cols. 1035–80.

——. *De vera religione.* In MIGNE, *P.L.,* vol. 34, cols. 121–72. For translation, see: "Of True Religion." In *Augustine: Earlier Writings.* Translated by John H. S. Burleigh. (Library of Christian Classics, VI.) London, 1953. (Pp. 225–83.)

——. *Enarrationes in Psalmos.* In MIGNE, *P.L.,* vols. 36, 37. For translation, see: *Expositions of the Book of Psalms.* Translated by J. Tweed, T. Scratton, and others. (Library of the Fathers of the Holy Catholic Church.) Oxford, 1847–57. 6 vols.

——. *Sermo CLII.* In MIGNE, *P.L.,* vol. 38, cols. 819–25.

——. *Sermo CCCLXVI.* In MIGNE, *P.L.,* vol. 39, cols. 1646–50.

——. *Sermo Suppositus CXX (In Natali Domini IV).* In MIGNE, *P.L.,* vol. 39, cols. 1984–87.

"Aureum saeculum redivivum." See MADATHANUS.

"Aurora consurgens" (Part I). See RHENANUS.

——. (Part II). See *(A) Artis auriferae* (1593), v, or (1610), iii.

——. With reference to both parts, see Codices and MSS., **ii, iv, x, xv–xvii.**

AVERROES (Muhammad ibn Ahmad, called ibn Rushd). *Destructio destructionis.* In *Aristotelis Opera latina.* Venice, 1510.

——. *Sermo de Substantia orbis.* In *Aristotelis . . . omnia . . . opera,* vol. 9. Venice, 1508.

AVICENNA (Husain ibn 'abd Allah). *Avicennae perhypatetici philosophi . . . opera . . .* Venice, 1508.

——. "De anima." In *Avicennae perhypatetici . . . ,* folios 1ʳ–28ᵛ.

——. "De conglutinatione lapidis." See *(A) Artis auriferae* (1610), viii, or (under the title "De congelatione et conglutinatione lapidum") in *(A) Theatrum chemicum,* **xviii.**

——. "De re recta ad Hasen." See *(A) Theatrum chemicum,* **xvi.**

——. "Declaratio lapidis physici filio suo Aboali." See *(A) Theatrum chemicum,* **xvii.**

——. "Liber sextus naturalium." Identical with "De anima" (above).

——. *Metaphysica.* In *Avicennae perhypatetici* . . . , folios 70ʳ–110ᵛ.

BACON, ROGER. *Fr. Rogeri Bacon Opera quaedam hactenus inedita.* Edited by J. S. Brewer. (Rerum Britannicarum medii aevi scriptores.) London, 1859. 1 vol. only published.

——. *Compendium studii philosophiae.* In *Opera . . . inedita,* pp. 393–519.

——. "De alchemia (Speculum alchimiae)." See *(A)* MANGET, *Bibliotheca chemica curiosa,* viii.

——. "De mirabili potestate artis et naturae." See *(A) Artis auriferae* (1610), xviii, or (under the title "De secretis operibus artis et naturae") *(A) Theatrum chemicum,* xxvii. Also, as "Epistola de secretis operibus artis et naturae," in *Opera . . . inedita,* pp. 523–51.

——. "De speculis comburentibus." See COMBACH(IUS).

——. *Opus majus.* Edited by John Henry Bridges. Oxford, 1897. 2 vols.

——. *Opus minus.* In *Opera . . . inedita,* pp. 313–89.

——. *Opus tertium.* In *Opera . . . inedita,* pp. 3–310.

——. *Sanioris medicinae magistri D. Rogerii Baconis Angli de arte chymiae scripta.* Frankfort, 1603.

BAEUMKER, CLEMENS. *Der Platonismus im Mittelalter.* Munich, 1916.

BALDWIN, ARCHBISHOP OF CANTERBURY. *Tractatus XIV.* In MIGNE, *P.L.,* vol. 204, cols. 539–46.

BARDENHEWER, OTTO (ed.). *Die pseudo-aristotelische Schrift über das reine Gute: Liber de causis.* Freiburg im Breisgau, 1882.

BERNARD (OF CLAIRVAUX), SAINT. *De diligendo Deo ad Haimericum.* In MIGNE, *P.L.,* vol. 182, cols. 973–1000.

——. *Sermones in Cantica Canticorum.* In MIGNE, *P.L.,* vol. 183, cols. 785–1198. For translation, see: *Sermons on the Canticle of Canticles.* Translated by a Priest of Mount Melleray [Ailbe J. Luddy]. Dublin, 1920. 2 vols.

BERNARD, JOHN HENRY. See *Solomon, Odes of.*

BERNARDUS TREVISANUS (Bernard of Treviso). "De secretissimo philosophorum opere chemico." See *(A)* MANGET, *Bibliotheca chemica curiosa,* **xx.**

BERTHELOT, MARCELLIN. *La Chimie au moyen âge.* (Histoire des sciences.) Paris, 1893. 3 vols.

———. *Collection des anciens alchimistes grecs.* Paris, 1887–88. 3 vols.

BLOCHET, EDGARD. "Études sur le gnosticisme musulman," *Revista degli studi orientali* (Rome), II–VI (1908–15). (II, 717–56; III, 177–203; IV, 47–79, 267–300; VI, 5–67.)

BLUME, CLEMENS, and DREVES, GUIDO M. *Analecta hymnica medii aevi.* Leipzig, 1886–1922. 55 vols.

BOEHME, JAKOB. *Aurora.* Translated by John Sparrow. Edited by C. J. B[arker] and D. S. H[ahner]. London, 1914.

———. "On the Earthly and Heavenly Mystery." In *Six Theosophic Points and other writings.* Translated by John Rolleston Earle. London, 1919. (Pp. 141–62.) (Original: "Vom irdischen und himmlischen Mysterium.")

———. *The Signature of All Things.* With an Introduction by Clifford Bax. (Everyman's Library.) London and New York, 1913.

BOEHMER, F. *Der Neoplatonismus.* (Klassische philosophische Studien, edited by E. Bickel, 7.) Leipzig, 1936.

BOLL, FRANZ. *Aus der Offenbarung Johannis. Hellenistische Studien zum Weltbild der Apokalypse.* Leipzig, 1914.

———. *Sphaera.* Leipzig, 1903.

———. *Sternglaube und Sterndeutung.* 2nd edn., Leipzig, 1919.

BOLLANDUS, JOANNES, and HENSCHENIUS, GODEFRIDUS. *Acta Sanctorum.* New edn., Paris and Brussels, 1863– . 64 vols. published.

BONAVENTURE, SAINT. *Opera omnia.* Quaracchi, 1882–1902. 10 vols.

———. *Commentaria in quatuor libros Sententiarum Petri Lombardi.* In *Opera,* vols. 1–4.

———. *De reductione artium ad theologiam.* In *Opera,* vol. 5, pp. 319–25.

BONUS, PETRUS. *Pretiosa margarita novella.* Edited by James Lacinius. Venice, 1546. See also *(A) Theatrum chemicum,* **xxv.**

BOURKE, VERNON JOSEPH. *Thomistic Bibliography, 1920-40.* St. Louis, 1945.

BOUSSET, WILHELM. *The Antichrist Legend.* Translated by A. H. Keane. London, 1896. (Original: *Der Antichrist.* Göttingen, 1895.)

———. *Hauptprobleme der Gnosis.* (Forschungen zur Religion und Literatur des Alten und Neuen Testaments, X.) Göttingen, 1907.

BRACESCHIUS, JOANNES. "De alchemia dialogus." See *(A)* MANGET, *Bibliotheca chemica curiosa,* vii.

BRANDT, AUGUST JOHANN HEINRICH WILHELM. *Die mandäische Religion.* Leipzig, 1899.

BREWER, J. S. See BACON.

BRUNO OF ASTI, BISHOP OF SEGNI. *Sententiae.* In MIGNE, *P.L.,* vol. 165, cols. 875-1078.

Buch der Alaune und Salze. See RUSKA.

BUDGE, E. A. WALLIS. See SOLOMON, BISHOP OF BASRA.

CAESARIUS OF HEISTERBACH. *Dialogus miraculorum.* Edited by Joseph Strange. Brussels, 1851.

CALID. "Liber de compositione alchimiae quam edidit Morienus Romanus" ("De transmutatione metallica"). See *(A)* MANGET, *Bibliotheca chemica curiosa,* iii.

———. "Liber trium verborum." See *(A) Artis auriferae* (1610), vi; *(A)* MANGET, *Bibliotheca chemica curiosa,* xvi.

———. "Quaestiones Calid regis ad Morienum Romanum." See Codices and MSS., vii.

CALO, PETRUS. See PRUEMMER.

CARINI, ISIDORO. "Sulle scienze occulte nel medio evo," *Revista sicula* (Palermo), VII (1872), 138-82.

CHARLES, ÉMILE A. *Roger Bacon: sa vie, ses ouvrages, ses doctrines.* Paris, 1861.

CHARLES, ROBERT HENRY (ed.). *The Apocrypha and Pseudepigrapha of the Old Testament in English.* Oxford, 1913. 2 vols. ("[Ethiopic] Book of Enoch," II, 163-281; "Book of the Secrets of Enoch," II, 425-69; "Fourth Book of Esdras," II, 542-64.)

Chénu, M.-D. *Introduction à l'étude de Saint Thomas d'Aquin.* (Université de Montréal, Publications de l'Institut d'Études Médiévales, XI.) Montreal and Paris, 1950.

Chollet, A. "Concupiscence." In A. Vacant and E. Mangenot (eds.). *Dictionnaire de théologie catholique.* Paris, 1903–50. 15 vols. (Vol. 3, cols. 803–14.)

Chrysologus. See Peter Chrysologus.

Chwolsohn, D. *Die Ssabier und der Ssabismus.* St. Petersburg, 1856. 2 vols.

"Clangor buccinae." See *(A) Artis auriferae* (1610), xi.

"Clavis maioris sapientiae." See Artefius.

Clement of Alexandria. *Stromata.* In Otto Stählin (ed.). [*Works of*] *Clement of Alexandria,* vols. 2 and 3. Leipzig, 1906–9. For translation, see: *The Writings of Clement of Alexandria.* Translated by William Wilson. (Ante-Nicene Christian Library, IV, XII.) Edinburgh, 1867–69. 2 vols. (I, 349–470, and II.)

[Clement of Rome, pseudo-.] *The Clementine Homilies and the Apostolical Constitutions.* Translated by Thomas Smith, Peter Peterson, and James Donaldson. (Ante-Nicene Christian Library, XVII.) Edinburgh, 1870.

Cleomedes. *De motu circulari corporum celestium libri II.* Edited by Hermann Ziegler. Leipzig, 1891.

Codices and Manuscripts.

 i Bologna, University Library. MS. 138. 15th cent. Contains three alchemical treatises ascribed to Albertus Magnus: "Semita recta," "Speculum secretorum," and "Liber xii aquarum."

 ii Bologna, University Library. MS. 747. 1492. Contains "Aurora consurgens" (folios 97^v–120^r).

 iii Florence. Codex Riccardianus 1165. 15th cent. Contains "Liber Alphidii" (folios 163^r–166^v).

 iv Leiden. University Library. Codex Vossianus Chemicus 520 (29). Contains "Aurora consurgens."

 v London. British Museum. MS. Additional 5025. 1588. "Four Rolls Drawn in Lübeck" (The "Ripley Scrowle").

vi Oxford. Bodleian Library. MS. Ashmole 1420. Contains "Liber Alphidii."

vii Oxford. Bodleian Library. MS. Ashmole 1450. 15th cent. Contains "Quaestiones Calid ad Morienum Romanum" (folios 49^r–55^v).

viii Oxford. Bodleian Library. MS. Digby 164. Contains "Alphidius de Lapide philosophico" or "Liber metheaurorum."

ix Paris. Bibliothèque Nationale. MS. 6296. 13th cent. Contains William of Moerbeke's translation of Aristotle's *De anima*.

x Paris. Bibliothèque Nationale. MS. 14006. 15th cent. Contains "Aurora consurgens" (folios 1^v–12^v).

xi Paris. Bibliothèque Mazarine. MS. 3462. 13th cent. Contains the "old translation" of Aristotle's *De anima*.

xii Paris. Bibliothèque Nationale. MS. 2578. Contains "Le Livre d'Hermès."

xiii St. Gall. Codex N. Vadiana 390. Contains "Turba philosophorum."

xiv Vatican Library. MS. Urbanus 1491. Contains Thomas Aquinas, "Meteorologica."

xv Venice. Codex Marcianus 1475. Contains "Aurora consurgens" (folios 65^r–161^r).

xvi Vienna. National Library. MS. 5230. 15th–16th cent. Contains "Aurora consurgens" (folios 239^r–248^v).

xvii Zurich. Codex Rhenoviensis 172. 15th cent. Contains part of "Aurora consurgens" (beginning at 4th parable).

COMBACH(IUS), JOANNES (ed.). *Rogerii Baconis Specula Mathematica.* Frankfort, 1614. ("De speculis comburentibus," pp. 168–204.)

"Consilium coniugii." See *(A) Ars chemica*, iii; *(A)* MANGET, *Bibliotheca chemica curiosa*, xviii; *(A) Theatrum chemicum*, xxiv.

CORBETT, JAMES. *Catalogue des MSS alchimistiques latins.* Brussels, 1939–51. 2 vols.

Corpus Hermeticum. See SCOTT, *Hermetica*.

COSTA DE BEAUREGARD, COMTE OLIVIER MARIE JEAN STANISLAS. *Le Second Principe de la science du temps.* Paris, 1963.

CROUS, ERNST (ed.). *Gesamtkatalog der Wiegendrucke.* Leipzig, 1925– . 7 vols. published.

CYRIL OF ALEXANDRIA, SAINT. *Glaphyrorum in Genesim libri septem.* In MIGNE, *P.G.,* vol. 69, cols. 13–386.

———. *In Isaiam prophetam commentarium.* In MIGNE, *P.G.,* vol. 70, cols. 9–1450.

CYRIL OF JERUSALEM, SAINT. *Opera.* Edited by Wilhelm Karl Reischl and Joseph Rupp. Munich, 1848–60. ("Katechesis," I, 89–II, 343.)

[CYRILLUS, BISHOP.] See GRAESSE.

D'ACHERY, LUC. *Spicilegium.* Paris, 1723. 3 vols.

DAEHNERT, ULRICH. *Die Erkenntnislehre des Albertus Magnus.* (Studien und Bibliographien zur Gegenwartsphilosophie, IV.) Leipzig, 1934.

DANIEL, HERMANN ADALBERT. *Thesaurus hymnologicus.* Halle and Leipzig, 1841–56. 5 vols.

DARMSTAEDTER, ERNST. *Die Alchimie des Geber.* Berlin, 1922.

"De aluminibus et salibus." See RUSKA, *Buch der Alaune und Salze.*

"De arte chymica." In *(A) Artis auriferae* (1610), xii.

"De chemia." See ZADITH SENIOR.

"De magni lapidis compositione et operatione." See *(A) Theatrum chemicum,* vi.

"De perfecto magisterio." See ARISTOTLE, pseudo-; ARNOLD OF VILLANOVA.

"De secretis lapidis." See *(A) Artis auriferae* (1610), x.

DELATTE, LOUIS (ed.). *Textes latins et vieux français relatifs aux Cyranides.* (Bibliothèque de la Faculté de Philosophie et des Lettres de l'Université de Liège, 93.) Liège and Paris, 1942.

DELISLE, LÉOPOLD. *Inventaire des manuscrits de Saint-Germain des Prés conservés à la Bibliothèque impériale, sous les numéros 11504–14231 du fonds latin.* Paris, 1868.

DIDYMUS OF ALEXANDRIA. *De Trinitate libri tres.* In MIGNE, *P.G.,* vol. 39, cols. 269–992.

DIELS, HERMANN (ed.). *Doxographi graeci.* Berlin, 1879.

DIETERICH, ALBRECHT. *Eine Mithrasliturgie.* Leipzig, 1903.

———. *Mutter Erde.* 2nd edn., Leipzig and Berlin, 1913.

DIETRICH, MEISTER. See KREBS.

DIOGENES LAERTIUS. *Lives of Eminent Philosophers.* With an English translation by R. D. Hicks. (Loeb Classical Library.) London and New York, 1928–31. 2 vols.

DIONYSIUS THE AREOPAGITE, pseudo-. *De divinis nominibus.* See MIGNE, *P.G.,* vol. 3, cols. 585–996. For translation, see: *The Divine Names.* Translated by the Editors of the Shrine of Wisdom. Fintry, Surrey (The Shrine of Wisdom), 1957.

DOELGER, FRANZ JOSEPH. *Antike und Christentum.* Münster, 1929–36. 5 vols.

———. *Die Sonne der Gerechtigkeit und der Schwarze.* (Liturgiegeschichtliche Forschungen, II.) Münster, 1918.

DOELLINGER, JOHANN JOSEPH IGNAZ VON. *Beiträge zur Sektengeschichte des Mittelalters. Munich,* 1890. 2 parts.

[Dominican Breviary.] *Breviarium juxta ritum S. Ordinis Praedicatorum.* Rome, n.d. [1947]. 2 vols.

DONAHOE, DANIEL JOSEPH. *Early Christian Hymns.* London, [1909].

DORN, GERHARD. "Congeries Paracelsicae chemicae de transmutatione metallorum." See *(A) Theatrum chemicum,* iii.

———. "Speculativae philosophiae." See *(A) Theatrum chemicum,* ii.

[ECKHART, MEISTER.] [*Works of*] *Meister Eckhart.* Translated by C. de B. Evans. London, 1924–52. 2 vols.

EISLER, ROBERT. "Angelos," *Archiv für neutestamentliche Zeitgeschichte* (Leipzig), 1930.

ELIADE, MIRCEA. *Shamanism: Archaic Techniques of Ecstasy.* Translated by Willard R. Trask. New York (Bollingen Series LXXVI) and London, 1964.

Encyclopaedia Britannica. 11th edn., Cambridge, 1910–11. 29 vols. ("Bacon, Roger," by Robert Adamson, III, 153–56.)

"Enoch, Ethiopic Book of." See "Book of Enoch" in CHARLES, R. H.

"Enoch, Slavonic Book of." See "Book of the Secrets of Enoch" in CHARLES, R. H.

EPHRAEM SYRUS, SAINT. *Hymni et sermones.* Edited by Thomas Joseph Lamy. Mechlin, 1882–1902. 4 vols. (References are to cols., not to pp.)

EPIPHANIUS. *Ancoratus and Panarium.* Edited by Karl Holl. (Griechische christliche Schriftsteller.) Leipzig, 1915–33. 3 vols.

ERIGENA, JOANNES SCOTUS. *Commentarius in sanctum Evangelium secundum Joannem.* In MIGNE, *P.L.,* vol. 122, cols. 297–348.

———. *De divisione naturae.* In MIGNE, *P.L.,* vol. 122, cols. 439–1022.

———. *Expositiones super ierarchiam caelestem Sancti Dionysii.* In MIGNE, *P.L.,* vol. 122, cols. 125–268.

Esdras, Fourth Book of. See CHARLES, R. H.

EUSEBIUS PAMPHILUS. *Praeparatio evangelica.* MIGNE, *P.G.,* vol. 3.

EUTHYMIUS ZIGABENOS. *Panoplia Dogmatica.* MIGNE, *P.G.,* vol. 130.

EVANS, C. DE B. See ECKHART.

EVANS-WENTZ, W. Y. (ed.). *The Tibetan Book of the Great Liberation.* With a psychological commentary by C. G. Jung. Oxford, 1954. (For Jung's commentary, see also Vol. 11 of his *Collected Works.*)

"Exercitationes in Turbam." See *(A) Artis auriferae* (1593), **iv**; (1610), **ii**.

"Expositio epistolae Alexandri regis." See *(A) Artis auriferae* (1610), **ix**.

FERCKEL, CHRISTOPH. "Thomas von Chantimpré über die Metalle." In J. RUSKA (ed.). *Studien zur Geschichte der Chemie.* Festgabe Edmund O. von Lippmann. Berlin, 1927. (pp. 75–79.)

FERGUSON, JOHN. *Bibliotheca Chemica.* Catalogue of the Alchemical Books in the Collection of James Young. Glasgow, 1906. 2 vols.

FICINO, MARSILIO. "Liber de arte chemica." See *(A)* MANGET, *Bibliotheca chemica curiosa,* **xv**.

FIERZ-DAVID, LINDA (ed.). *The Dream of Poliphilo.* Translated by Mary Hottinger. (Bollingen Series XXV.) New York, 1950.

FLAMEL, NICHOLAS. "Excerpta ex Democrito." See *(A) Theatrum chemicum,* **iv**.

"Flos florum." See ARNOLD OF VILLANOVA.

FLÜGEL, GUSTAV. *Mani, seine Lehre und seine Schriften.* Leipzig, 1862.

FOREST, AIMÉ. *La Structure métaphysique du concret selon saint Thomas d'Aquin.* (Études de philosophie médiévale, XIV.) Paris, 1931.

FÖRSTER, RICHARD. *De Aristotelis quae feruntur Secreta secretorum commentatio.* Kiel, 1888.

——. "Handschriften und Ausgaben des pseudo-Aristotelischen Secretum Secretorum," *Centralblatt für Bibliotheken* (Leipzig), VI (1889), 1–22, 57–76, 218.

FRANZ, MARIE-LOUISE VON. "Die Passio Perpetuae." In C. G. JUNG. *Aion.* (Psychologische Abhandlungen, VIII.) Zurich, 1951. (Pp. 389–496.)

FREEMAN, KATHLEEN. *Ancilla to the Pre-Socratic Philosophers.* Oxford, 1948.

GABRIEL OF BARLETTA. *Sermones.* Venice, 1571. 2 vols.

GALEN, CLAUDIUS. *De placitis Hippocratis et Platonis libri novem.* Edited by Ivan Mueller. Leipzig, 1874. (1 vol. only published.)

GEBER (Jabir ibn Hayyan). "Liber investigationis." See *(A)* MANGET, *Bibliotheca chemica curiosa,* v. For translation, see next entry.

——. "Summa perfectionis." See *(A) De alchemia,* i; *(A)* MANGET, *Bibliotheca chemica curiosa,* iv. For translation, see: *The Works of Geber.* Englished by Richard Russell, 1678. New edn., with introduction by E. J. Holmyard. London, Toronto, and New York, 1928. ("The Sum of Perfection, or Of the Perfect Magistery," pp. 23–297; "Of the Investigation or Search of Perfection," pp. 3–19.)

——. "Testamentum." See *(A)* MANGET, *Bibliotheca chemica curiosa,* vi.

GELLIUS, AULUS. *Noctes Atticae.* Edited by Martin Hertz. Berlin, 1883–85. 2 vols.

Gesamtkatalog der Wiegendrucke. See CROUS.

GILBERT OF HOYLAND (Gillebertus de Hoilandia). *Sermones in Cantica XLVI.* In MIGNE, *P.L.,* vol. 184, cols. 11–252.

GILSON, ÉTIENNE. *L'Esprit de la philosophie médiévale.* Paris, 1932. 2 vols. For translation, see: *The Spirit of Medieval Philosophy.* Translated by A. H. C. Downes. London, 1936.

———. "Pourquoi Saint Thomas a critiqué Saint Augustin," *Archives d'histoire doctrinale et littéraire du moyen-âge* (Paris), I (1926), 5–127.

———. "Les Sources gréco-arabes de l'augustinisme avicennisant," *Archives d'histoire doctrinale et littéraire du moyen-âge* (Paris), IV (1929), 5–149.

GLAUBER, JOHANN RUDOLPH. *Tractatus de natura salium.* Amsterdam, 1658.

GOLDBRUNNER, JOSEF. *Individuation: A Study of the Depth-Psychology of Jung.* Translated by Stanley Godman. London and New York, 1955.

GOLDSCHMIDT. See HELIODORUS.

GRABMANN, MARTIN. *Die echten Schriften des heiligen Thomas von Aquin.* (Beiträge zur Geschichte der Philosophie des Mittelalters, ed. Baeumker, XXII.) Münster, 1920; 2nd edn., 1931.

———. *Forschungen über die lateinischen Aristotelesübersetzungen des 13. Jahrhunderts.* (Beiträge zur Geschichte der Philosophie des Mittelalters, XVII : 5–6.) Münster, 1916.

———. "Guglielmo di Moerbeke, O.P., il traduttore delle opere di Aristotele," *Miscellanea Historiae Pontificiae* (Rome), XI (1946), 41ff.

———. *The Interior Life of St. Thomas Aquinas.* Translated by Nicholas Ashenbrener. Milwaukee, 1953. (Original: *Das Seelenleben des heiligen Thomas von Aquin.*)

———. *Methoden und Hilfsmittel des Aristotelesstudiums im Mittelalter.* (Sitzungsberichte der bayrischen Akademie der Wissenschaften, Philosophisch-philologische und historische Klasse, 1939, part 5.) Munich, 1939.

———. *Mittelalterliche Deutung und Umbildung der aristotelischen Lehre vom νοῦς ποιητικός.* (Sitzungsberichte der bayrischen Akademie der Wissenschaften, Philosophisch-philologische und historische Klasse, 1936, part 4.) Munich, 1936.

———. *Mittelalterliche lateinische Aristotelesübersetzungen und Aristoteleskommentare in Handschriften spanischer Bibliotheken.* (Sitzungsberichte der bayrischen Akademie der Wissenschaften, Philosophisch-philologische und historische Klasse, 1928, part 5.) Munich, 1928.

———. *Thomas Aquinas: His Personality and Thought.* Translated by Virgil Michel. New York and London, 1928. (Original: *Thomas von Aquin.*)

———. *Die Werke des heiligen Thomas von Aquin.* (Beiträge zur Geschichte der Philosophie und Theologie des Mittelalters, XXII : 1 and 2). Münster, 1931.

GRAESSE, J. G. T. *Die beiden altesten lateinischen Fabelbücher des Mittelalters: das Bischofs Cyrillus Speculum Sapientiae und das Nicolaus Pergamenus Dialogus Creaturarum.* (Stuttgart Literarische Vereins Bibliothek, 148.) Tübingen, 1880. ("Speculum sapientiae," pp. 1–124.)

GRASSEUS, JOHANNES. "Arca arcani." See *(A) Theatrum chemicum,* **xxviii;** *(A)* MANGET, *Bibliotheca chemica curiosa,* **xxi.**

[GRASSHOFF, JOHANN.] *Ein philosophischer und chemischer Tractat genannt Der kleine Baur.* With commentaries by Johann Walch. Strasbourg, 1658.

GREGORY THE GREAT, SAINT. *Epistolae.* In MIGNE, *P.L.,* vol. 77, cols. 441–1328.

———. *Homiliae in Evangelia.* In MIGNE, *P.L.,* vol. 76, cols. 1075–1312.

———. *Homiliarum in Ezechielem Libri II.* In MIGNE, *P.L.,* vol. 76, cols. 786–1072.

———. *Moralia, seu Expositio in Librum beati Job.* In MIGNE, *P.L.,* vol. 75, col. 509–vol. 76, col. 782. For translation, see: *Morals on the Book of Job. . . .* Translated [by James Bliss]. (Library of the Fathers.) Oxford, 1844–59. 3 vols.

———. *Super Cantica Canticorum Expositio.* In MIGNE, *P.L.,* vol. 79, cols. 471–548.

GRESSMANN, HUGO. *Tod und Auferstehung des Osiris.* (Der alte Orient, XXIII : 3.) Leipzig, 1923.

GRIMM, JACOB and WILHELM. *Fairy Tales.* Translated by Margaret Hunt and James Stern. New York, 1944. ("The Golden Bird," pp. 272–79.)

GUNDISSALINUS (Dominicus Gundisalvus). *De divisione philosophiae.* Edited by Ludwig Baur. (Beiträge zur Geschichte der Philosophie des Mittelalters, edited by Clemens Baeumker and Georg von Hertling, IV : 2–3.) Münster, 1903.

———. *De immortalitate animae*. See: *Der Dominicus Gundissalinus Schrift von der Unsterblichkeit der Seele (De immortalitate animae)*. Edited by George Bülow. (Beiträge zur Geschichte der Philosophie des Mittelalters, edited by Clemens Baeumker and Georg von Hertling, II : 3.) Münster, 1897.

HAHN, CHRISTOPH ULRICH. *Geschichte der Ketzer im Mittelalter*. Stuttgart, 1845–50. 3 vols.

HANEBERG, B. "Zur Erkenntnislehre von Ibn Sina und Albertus Magnus." *Abhandlungen der königlich bayrischen Akademie der Wissenschaften*, Philosophisch-philologische Klasse (Munich), XI : 1 (1886), 189–267.

HANNAH, BARBARA. "Hugh de St. Victor's Conversation with his Anima," *Harvest* (privately printed for the Analytical Psychology Club, London), I (1954).

Harmoniae inperscrutabilis . . . See RHENANUS.

HASKINS, CHARLES HOMER. "A List of Textbooks from the Close of the Twelfth Century." *Harvard Studies in Classical Philology* (Cambridge, Mass.), XX (1909), 75–94.

———. "Michael Scot and Frederick II," *Isis* (Brussels), IV (1922), 250–75.

———, and LOCKWOOD, DEAN PUTNAM. "The Sicilian Translators of the Twelfth Century and the First Latin Version of Ptolemy's Almagest," *Harvard Studies in Classical Philology* (Cambridge, Mass.), XXI (1910), 75–102.

HAUPT, HERMAN. "Beiträge zur Geschichte der Sekte vom Freien Geiste und des 'Beghardentums'," *Zeitschrift für Kirchengeschichte* (Gotha), VII : 4 (1885), 503–76.

———. "Zur Geschichte des Joachimismus," *Zeitschrift für Kirchengeschichte* (Gotha), VII : 3 (1885), 372–425.

———. "Zwei Tractate gegen Beginen und Begharden," *Zeitschrift für Kirchengeschichte* (Gotha), XII : 1 (1891), 85–90.

HEGEMONIUS. *Acta Archelai*. Edited by Charles Henry Beeson. (Griechische christliche Schriftsteller.) Leipzig, 1906.

HELINANDUS OF FROIDMONT. *De cognitione sui*. In MIGNE, *P.L.*, vol. 212, cols. 721–36.

HELIODORUS. *Carmina quattuor, ad fidem Codicis Casselani*. Edited by Günther Goldschmidt. (Religionsgeschichtliche Versuche und Vorarbeiten, XIX : 2.) Giessen, 1923.

HENRY OF HERFORD (Henricus de Hervordia). *Liber de rebus memorabilioribus seu Chronicon*. Edited by A. Potthast. Göttingen, 1859.

HERMES TRISMEGISTUS. "Tabula smaragdina." See *(A) Ars chemica*, ii; *(A) De alchemia*, ii.

——. "Tractatus aureus de lapidis physici secreto." See *(A) Ars chemica*, i; *Musaeum hermeticum*, i; *Theatrum chemicum*, xiii.

HERRAD OF LANDSBERG. See A. STRAUB and G. KELLER. *Herrad von Landsberg Hortus deliciarum*. Strasbourg, 1879–99. 2 vols.

HILARIUS (Saint Hilary). *Tractatus super Psalmos*. In MIGNE, *P.L.*, vol. 9, cols. 231–908.

HIME, HENRY WILLIAM LOVETT. *Gunpowder and Ammunition: Their Origin and Progress*. London, 1904.

HIPPOLYTUS. *Elenchos (Refutatio Omnium Haeresium)*. In: *Werke*, vol. 3. (Die griechische christliche Schriftsteller.) Edited by Paul Wendland. Leipzig, 1916. For translation, see: *Philosophumena: or, The Refutation of All Heresies*. Translated by Francis Legge. London and New York, 1921. 2 vols.

——. *Kommentar zum Hohenlied (Commentarium in Cantica Canticorum)*. Edited by Nathaniel Bonwetsch. (Texte und Untersuchungen zur Geschichte der altchristlichen Literatur, new series, VIII : 2.) Leipzig, 1902.

HOGHELANDE, THEOBALDUS DE. "De alchemiae difficultatibus." See *(A) Theatrum chemicum*, i; *(A)* MANGET, *Bibliotheca chemica curiosa*, i.

HOLMYARD, ERIC JOHN. " 'Abu 'l-Qāsim al-'Irāqī," *Isis* (Bruges), VIII (1926), 403–26.

——. "A Romance of Chemistry," *Chemistry and Industry, Journal of the Society of Chemical Industry* (London), XLIV (1925), 75–77, 106–8, 136–37, 272–76, 300–1, 327–28.

——. See also ABU 'L-QĀSIM.

HONORIUS OF AUTUN. *De philosophia mundi*. In MIGNE, *P.L.*, vol. 172, cols. 41–102.

————. *Elucidarium*. In MIGNE, *P.L.*, vol. 172, cols. 1109–1176.

————. *Expositio in Cantica Canticorum*. In MIGNE, *P.L.*, vol. 172, cols. 347–496.

————. *Quaestiones et Responsiones in Proverbia et Ecclesiasten*. In MIGNE, *P.L.*, vol. 172, cols. 313–48.

————. *Speculum Ecclesiae*. In MIGNE, *P.L.*, vol. 172, cols. 813–1108.

HORTEN, MAX. See ALFARABI.

HUGH OF ST. VICTOR. *Allegoriae in Novum Testamentum*. In MIGNE, *P.L.*, vol. 175, cols. 751–924.

————. "Annotationes elucidariae in Evangelium Joannis." In *Allegoriae*, cols. 827–80.

————. *De Bestiis et aliis rebus . . . ad Raynerum conversum*. In MIGNE, *P.L.*, vol. 177, cols. 15–164.

————. *De Sapientia animae Christi*. In MIGNE, *P.L.*, vol. 176, cols. 845–56.

————. *De Unione corporis et spiritus*. In MIGNE, *P.L.*, vol. 177, cols. 285–94.

————. *Eruditionis Didascaliae libri septem*. In MIGNE, *P.L.*, vol. 176, cols. 741–838.

HURTER, H. (ed.). *Augustini Opuscula . . . addidit S. Thomae Aquinatis in Symbolum Apostolorum Expositio*. (Sanctorum Patrum Opuscula Selecta, VI.) 2nd edn., Innsbruck, 1887. ("Expositio," pp. 164–254.)

HURWITZ, SIGMUND. "Archetypische Motive in der chassidischen Mystik." In *Zeitlose Dokumente der Seele*. (Studien aus dem C. G. Jung-Institut, III.) Zurich, 1952.

IAMBLICHUS. *De anima*. See STOBAEUS, vol. I, pp. 362ff.

————. *De Vita Pythagorae*. Edited by Ludwig Deubner. Leipzig, 1937.

"In Turbam Philosophorum Exercitationes." See *(A) Artis auriferae* (1593), iv; (1610), ii.

IRENAEUS, SAINT. *Contra [or Adversus] Haereses libri quinque*. See MIGNE, *P.G.*, vol. 7, cols. 423–1224. For translation, see: *The Writings of Irenaeus*. Translated by Alexander Roberts and W. H.

Rambaut. (Ante-Nicene Christian Library, V, IX.) Edinburgh, 1868–69. 2 vols.

ISAAC OF ANTIOCH. *Opera omnia*. Edited by Gustav Bickell. Giessen, 1873–77. 2 vols.

ISIDORE OF SEVILLE, SAINT. *De natura rerum*. Edited by Gustav Becker. Berlin, 1857.

JACOBSOHN, HELMUTH. *Die dogmatische Stellung des Königs in der Theologie der alten Ägypter*. (Aegyptologische Forschungen, edited by Alexander Scharff, VIII.) Gluckstadt, Hamburg, and New York, 1939.

JAMES, MONTAGUE RHODES (ed. and trans.). *The Apocryphal New Testament*. Oxford, 1924. ("Acts of Philip," pp. 439–53; "Acts of Thomas," pp. 364–438.)

JEROME, SAINT. *Selected Letters*, with an English Translation by F. A. Wright. (Loeb Classical Library.) London and New York, 1933.

Jeû, Books of. *Die beiden Bucher des Jeû*. In *Koptische-Gnostische Schriften*, edited by Karl Schmidt. (Die Griechische christliche Schriftsteller.) Vol. I. 2nd edn., Berlin, 1954. (Pp. 257–329.)

JOACHIM OF FLORA. See HAHN.

JOANNES DE MEUNG. "Demonstratio naturae." See *(A) Musaeum hermeticum*, iv.

JOHN CHRYSOSTOM, SAINT. *In Genesim Homiliae*. In MIGNE, *P.G.*, vols. 53 and 54.

JOHN DAMASCENE, SAINT. *De fide orthodoxa*. In MIGNE, *P.G.*, vol. 94, cols. 790–1228.

——. *Homilia II in Dormitionem Beatae Mariae Virginis*. In MIGNE, *P.G.*, vol. 96, cols. 721–54.

JOHN THE DEACON (Joannes Diaconus). *Vita sancti Gregorii Magni*. In MIGNE, *P.L.*, vol. 75, cols. 59–242.

JOURDAIN, AMABLE. *Recherches critiques sur l'âge et l'origine des traductions latines d'Aristote*. Paris, 1819.

JUNDT, AUGUSTE. *Essai sur le mysticisme spéculatif de Maître Eckhardt*. Strasbourg, 1871.

JUNG, CARL GUSTAV. *Collected Works.* New York (Bollingen Series XX) and London. Translated by R. F. C. Hull. 1953– . 18 vols. published.

——. *Aion. Collected Works,* vol. 9, part ii.

——. "Answer to Job." In *Collected Works,* vol. 11.

——. *Mysterium Coniunctionis. Collected Works,* vol. 14.

——. *Memories, Dreams, Reflections.* Recorded and edited by Aniela Jaffé. Translated by Richard and Clara Winston. London and New York, 1963. (Differently paginated.)

——. "On the Nature of the Psyche." In *Collected Works,* vol. 8.

——. "On Psychic Energy." In *Collected Works,* vol. 8.

——. "Paracelsus as a Spiritual Phenomenon." In *Collected Works,* vol. 13. Alternative source: "Paracelsus als geistige Erscheinung," in *Paracelsica.* Zurich, 1942.

——. "The Phenomenology of the Spirit in Fairytales." In *Collected Works,* vol. 9, part i.

——. "The Philosophical Tree." In *Collected Works,* vol. 13. Alternative source: "Der philosophische Baum," in *Von den Wurzeln des Bewusstseins.* Zurich, 1954.

——. *The Practice of Psychotherapy. Collected Works,* vol. 16.

——. "A Psychological Approach to the Dogma of the Trinity." In *Collected Works,* vol. 11.

——. "Psychological Commentary on the Tibetan Book of the Great Liberation." In *Collected Works,* vol. 11.

——. *Psychological Types. Collected Works,* vol. 6. Alternative source: Translation by H. G. Baynes. London and New York, 1923.

——. *Psychology and Alchemy. Collected Works,* vol. 12, 2nd edn.

——. "The Psychology of the Child Archetype." In *Collected Works,* vol. 9, part i.

——. "Psychology and Religion." In *Collected Works,* vol. 11.

——. "The Psychology of the Transference." In *Collected Works,* vol. 16, 2nd edn.

——. *The Secret of the Golden Flower.* See WILHELM and JUNG.

———. "The Spirit Mercurius." In *Collected Works*, vol. 13. Alternative sources: *The Spirit Mercury*. Translated by Gladys Phelan and Hildegard Nagel. New York, 1948; or "Der Geist Mercurius," in *Symbolik des Geistes*. Zurich, 1953.

———. "A Study in the Process of Individuation." In *Collected Works*, vol. 11.

———. *Symbols of Transformation. Collected Works*, vol. 5.

———. "Synchronicity: An Acausal Connecting Principle." In *Collected Works*. vol. 8.

———. "Transformation Symbolism in the Mass." In *Collected Works*, vol. 11.

———. "The Visions of Zosimos." In *Collected Works*, vol. 13. Alternative source: "Die Visionen des Zosimos," in *Von den Wurzeln des Bewusstseins*. Zurich, 1954.

———, and KERÉNYI, C. *Essays on a Science of Mythology*. Translated by R. F. C. Hull. (Bollingen Series XXII.) New York, 1949. (Also published as: *Introduction to a Science of Mythology*. London, 1950.) (For Jung's essays, see *Coll. Works*, vol. 9, i.)

JUNKER, HERMANN. *Die Stundenwachen in den Osiris-Mysterien.* (Denkschriften der kaiserlichen Akademie der Wissenschaften, Philosophisch-historische Klasse, LIV : 1.) Vienna, 1911.

"Kanonisationsbulle der heiligen Thomas von Aquin, Der." *Divus Thomas* (Fribourg), I (1923), 109–217.

KELLY, WILLIAM L. *Die neuscholastische und die empirische Psychologie*. Mannheim, 1961.

KERN, OTTO (ed.). *Orphicorum fragmenta*. Berlin, 1922.

KHUNRATH, HENRICUS (Heinrich). *Von hylealischen, das ist, primaterialischen catholischen, oder algemeinem natürlichen Chaos.* Magdeburg, 1597.

KLINGSEIS, RUPERT. "Moderne Theorien über das Unterbewusstsein und die Thomistische Psychologie," *Divus Thomas* (Fribourg), VII (1929), 147–83, 279–300; VIII (1930), 40–59, 192–206, 381–405.

KNORR VON ROSENROTH, CHRISTIAN. *Kabbala denudata seu Doctrina Hebraeorum*. Sulzbach and Frankfort, 1677/8–1684. 2 vols. (*Adumbratio Kabbalae Christianae* is an appendix to vol. 2.)

Koran, The. Translated by N. J. Dawood. (Penguin Classics.) Harmondsworth and Baltimore, 1956.

"Kore Kosmou." See Scott, *Hermetica* (vol. 1, pp. 457–95.)

Krebs, Engelbert. *Die Schriften Meister Dietrichs: Theodorus Teutonicus de Vriberg.* (Beiträge zur Geschichte der Philosophie des Mittelalters, edited by Clemens Baeumker, V : 6.) Münster, 1906. ("De miscibilibus in mixto," pp. 45*–51*.)

Kroenlein, J. H. "Amalrich von Bena und David von Dinant." *Theologische Studien und Kritiken* (Hamburg), 1847, pp. 271–330.

Lacinius, Janus. "Collectanea Lacinii ex Alberto Magno atque divo Thoma aliisque autoribus non vulgaribus." In Bonus, *Pretiosa margarita novella,* q.v. (folios 180ʳ–194ᵛ).

Lacombe, George. *Corpus Philosophorum Medii Aevi: Aristoteles latinus.* Part I, Rome, 1939; Part II, Cambridge, 1955. 2 vols.

Lactantius, L. Caelius Firmianus. *Opera omnia.* Edited by Samuel Brandt and Georg Laubmann. (Corpus scriptorum ecclesiasticorum Latinorum, XIX, XXVII.) Vienna, 1890–93, 2 vols. ("Divinae institutiones," vol. I.) For translation, see: *The Works of Lactantius.* Translated by William Fletcher. (Ante-Nicene Christian Library, XXI, XXII.) Edinburgh, 1871. 2 vols.

[Lambspringk.] "The Book of Lambspring." See *(A) Musaeum hermeticum,* vi.

Lavaud, Benoît. *La Vie profonde de Nicolas de Flue.* Fribourg, 1942.

Leisegang, Hans. *Die Gnosis.* Leipzig, 1924.

———. *Der heilige Geist.* Book I, part i (no more published). Leipzig and Berlin, 1919.

"Liber Alze." See *(A) Musaeum hermeticum,* v.

"Liber de magni lapidis compositione." See *(A) Theatrum chemicum,* vi.

"Liber lilii benedicti." See *(A) Theatrum chemicum,* xix.

"Liber metheaurorum." See Codices and MSS., viii.

"Liber trium verborum Calidis." See Calid.

Lippmann, Edmund O. von. *Entstehung und Ausbreitung der Alchemie.* Berlin, 1919–54. 3 vols.

LITTLE, ANDREW GEORGE. *Initia operum latinorum quae saeculis XIII, XIV, XV attribuuntur.* (Publications of the University of Manchester, Historical Series, II.) Manchester, 1904.

—— (ed.). *Roger Bacon Essays.* Contributed by various writers on the occasion of the commemoration of the seventh centenary of his birth. Oxford, 1914.

LOEWENTHAL, A. *Pseudo-Aristoteles über die Seele. Eine psychologische Schrift des 11. Jahrhunderts und ihre Beziehungen zu Salomo ibn Gabirol (Avicebron).* Berlin, 1891.

LOHMEYER, ERNST. *Vom göttlichen Wohlgeruch.* (Sitzungsberichte der Heidelberger Akademie der Wissenschaften, Philosophisch-historische Klasse, IX.) Heidelberg, 1919.

LUCIAN. "Bis accusatus" (The Double Indictment). In *The Works.* Translated from the Greek by several eminent hands [Walter Moyle and others]. London, 1711. 4 vols. (IV, 34–58.)

LUCRETIUS (Titus Lucretius Carus). *De rerum natura.* With an English translation by W. H. D. Rouse. (Loeb Classical Library.) London and New York, 1924.

"Lumen luminum." See ARISTOTLE, pseudo-; ARNOLD OF VILLANOVA.

LYDGATE, JOHN, and BURGH, BENEDICT. *Secrees of Old Philosoffres.* Edited by Robert Steele. (Early English Text Society Series, LXVI.) London, 1894.

LYDUS, JOHANNES LAURENTIUS. *De mensibus.* Edited by Richard Wuensch. Leipzig, 1898.

McCONNELL, J. V. See *Worm Runner's Digest.*

MACROBIUS. *Commentary on the Dream of Scipio.* Translated by William Harris Stahl. (Records of Civilization, Sources and Studies, XLVIII.) New York, 1952.

MADATHANUS, HENRICUS. "Aureum saeculum redivivum." See *(A) Musaeum hermeticum,* ii.

MAIER, MICHAEL. *Symbola aureae mensae duodecim nationum.* Frankfort, 1617.

MANDONNET, PIERRE. "Albert le Grand." In A. VACANT and E. MANGENOT (eds.). *Dictionnaire de théologie catholique.* Paris, 1903–50. 15 vols. (Vol. I, cols. 666–74.)

———. *Des Écrits authentiques de Saint Thomas d'Aquin.* 2nd edn., Fribourg, 1910.

———. *Siger de Brabant et l'Averroïsme latin au XII⁰ siècle.* 2nd edn., Louvain, 1908–11. 2 parts.

MANSI, GIOVANNI DOMENICO. *Sacrorum conciliorum nova et amplissima collectio.* Venice, 1759–1927. 54 vols.

MAP, WALTER. *De nugis curialium.* Edited by Thomas Wright. (Camden Society.) London, 1850. For translation, see *De Nugis Curialium.* Translated by Montagu R. James. (Cymmrodorion Record Series, IX.) London, 1923.

MARTIAL (Marcus Valerius Martialis). *Epigrams.* With an English translation by Walter C. A. Ker. (Loeb Classical Library.) London and New York, 1910–25. 2 vols.

MAXIMUS OF TURIN. *Homilia 101.* In MIGNE, *P.L.,* vol. 57, cols. 487–90.

MAXIMUS OF TYRE. *Dissertations.* Translated by Thomas Taylor. London, 1804. 2 vols.

MEIER, MATTHIAS. *Die Lehre des Thomas von Aquino "De passionibus animae" in quellenanalytischer Darstellung.* (Beiträge zur Geschichte der Philosophie des Mittelalters, XI : 2.) Münster, 1912.

MELCHIOR CIBINENSIS, NICOLAUS. "Addam et processum sub forma missae." See *(A) Theatrum chemicum,* xi.

MENNENS, GULIELMUS. *Aurei velleris libri tres [Aureum vellus].* Antwerp, 1604. See also *(A) Theatrum chemicum,* xxiii.

MESEGUER IRLES, PEDRO. *The Secret of Dreams.* Translated by Paul Burns. London, 1960.

METHODIUS OF PHILIPPI [OF OLYMPUS]. *Symposion,* or *Convivium decem virginum sive De castimonia.* In MIGNE, *P.G.,* vol. 18, cols. 27–220.

MEYRINK, GUSTAV. *Thomas von Aquino: Abhandlung über den Stein der Weisen.* Leipzig, Zurich, Vienna, and Munich, 1925.

MIGNE, JACQUES PAUL (ed.). *Patrologiae cursus completus.*

    [*P.L.*] Latin series. Paris, 1844–64. 221 vols.

    [*P.G.*] Greek series. Paris, 1857–66. 166 vols.

[These works are cited as "MIGNE, *P.L.*" and "MIGNE, *P.G.*" respectively. References are to columns, not to pages.]

MILO. *De sobrietate*. See TRAUBE.

MOHLBERG, LEO CUNIBERT. *Katalog der Handschriften der Zentral-bibliothek in Zurich*. Vol. I: *Mittelalterliche Handschriften*. Zurich, 1952.

MORET, ALEXANDRE. *Mystères Égyptiens*. Paris, 1922.

MORIENUS ROMANUS. "De transmutatione metallorum." See *(A) Artis auriferae* (1610), xiii.

———. See also CALID.

MUELLER, ERNST. *Der Sohar und seine Lehre*. Vienna and Berlin, 1920.

[MUHAMMAD IBN UMAIL.] "Three Arabic Treatises on Alchemy, by Muhammad ibn Umail," edited by H. E. Stapleton and M. Hidayat Husain, *Memoirs of the Asiatic Society of Bengal* (Calcutta), XII (1933), 1–213.

———. See also ZADITH SENIOR.

MURATORI, LODOVICO ANTONIO (ed.). *Rerum Italicarum Scriptores*. Milan, 1723–51. 25 vols. (Ptolemy of Lucca, *Historia Ecclesiastica*, in vol. XI, cols. 743–1242.)

MYLIUS, JOHANN DANIEL. *Philosophia reformata*. Frankfort, 1622.

NEALE, JOHN MASON. *Collected Hymns, Sequences, and Carols*. London, 1914.

NEMESIUS. *De natura hominis* (On the Nature of Man). Edited by William Telfer. (Library of Christian Classics, IV: Cyril of Jerusalem and Nemesius of Emesa.) London, 1955.

NEUMANN, ERICH. *Amor and Psyche: The Psychic Development of the Feminine*. Translated by Ralph Manheim. New York (Bollingen Series LIV) and London, 1956.

———. *The Origins and History of Consciousness*. Translated by R. F. C. Hull. New York (Bollingen Series XLII) and London, 1954.

Neurose und Religion. See RUDIN.

NINCK, MARTIN. *Wodan und germanischer Schicksalsglaube*. Jena, 1935.

Nolan, Paul. *Saint Thomas and the Unconscious Mind.* Abstract of a dissertation. (Catholic University of America: Philosophical Series.) Washington, 1953.

Norden, Eduard. *Die Geburt des Kindes.* (Studien der Bibliothek Warburg, III.) Leipzig, 1924.

Notker Balbulus. *Liber sequentiarum.* In Migne, *P.L.,* vol. 131, cols. 1005–26.

"Novum lumen chemicum." See Sendivogius.

Numenius. See Proclus.

"Opusculum autoris ignoti de secretis lapidis." See *(A) Artis auriferae* (1610), x.

Origen. *Commentaria in Joannis Evangelium.* In Migne, *P.G.,* vol. 14, cols. 21–830.

——. *Commentarium in Epistolam ad Romanos.* In Migne, *P.G.,* vol. 14, cols. 837–1292.

——. *Contra Celsum.* Translated by Henry Chadwick. Cambridge, 1953. (Original text in Migne, *P.G.,* vol. 11, cols. 657–1632.)

——. *In Cantica Canticorum Homiliae.* In Migne, *P.G.* vol. 13, cols. 37–58.

——. *In Jeremiam Homiliae.* In Migne, *P.G.,* vol. 13, cols. 255–514.

——. *In Numeros Homiliae.* In Migne, *P.G.,* vol. 12, cols. 585–806.

Paneth, Fritz. "Über die Schrift Alberts des Grossen 'De Alchemia'," *Archiv für Geschichte der Mathematik, der Naturwissenschaften und der Technik* (Leipzig), XII (new series, 4), (1929–30), 408–13.

——. "Über eine alchemistische Handschrift des 14. Jahrhunderts und ihr Verhältnis zu Alberts Magnus' Buch 'De Mineralibus'," *Archiv für Geschichte der Mathematik, der Naturwissenschaften und der Technik* (Leipzig), XII (new series, 3), (1929–30), 33–45. (The text of "Tractatus de mettallis et Alcimia" is given on pages 34–39.)

Partington, J. R. "Albertus Magnus on Alchemy," *Ambix* (London), I (1937), 3–20.

Pegis, Antoine Charles. "St. Thomas and the Nicomachaean Ethics," *Medieval Studies* (Toronto), XXV (1963), 73.

PELSTER, FRANZ. *Kritische Studien zum Leben und zu den Schriften Alberts des Grossen.* (Ergänzungshefte zu den Stimmen der Zeit, series 2, part 4.) Freiburg im Breisgau, 1920.

——. "Die Übersetzungen der Aristotelischen Metaphysik in den Werken des hl. Thomas von Aquin," *Gregorianum* (Rome), XVII (1936), 377–406.

——. "Zur Forschung nach den echten Schriften des heiligen Thomas von Aquin," *Philosophisches Jahrbuch* (Fulda), XXXVI (1923), 36–49.

PETER CHRYSOLOGUS, SAINT. *Sermones.* In MIGNE, *P.L.,* vol. 52, cols. 183–666.

PETER DAMIAN. See BLUME and DREVES.

PETER OF PRUSSIA (Petrus de Prussia). *Vita beati Alberti Magni.* See ALBERTUS MAGNUS, 'De adhaerendo Deo."

PETITOT, HENRI. "La Mort de Saint Thomas d'Aquin," *La Vie Spirituelle* (Paris), X (1924), 312–36.

——. *Saint Thomas d'Aquin: La Vocation — l'œuvre — la vie spiri-tuelle.* Paris, 1923.

PHILO. [*Works.*] Translated by F. H. Colson and G. H. Whitaker. (Loeb Classical Library.) London and New York, 1929–   . 12 vols. ("Allegorical Interpretation of Genesis II, III" [Legum Allegoriae], I, 146–473; "Concerning Noah's Work as a Planter" [De planta-tione], III, 212–305; "The Eternity of the World" [De aeternitate mundi], IX, 184–291; "On the Account of the World's Creation Given by Moses" [De opificio mundi], I, 6–137; "On the Birth of Abel and the Sacrifices Offered by him and his Brother Cain" [De sacrificiis Abelis et Caini], II, 94–195; "On Drunkenness'" [De ebrietate], III, 318–435; "On Husbandry" [De agricultura], III, 108–203; "On the Life of Moses" [De vita Mosis], VI, 276–595; "That the Worse is Wont to Attack the Better" [Quod de-terius potiori insidiari solet], II, 202–319; "Who is the Heir of Divine Things?" [Quis rerum divinarum heres?], IV, 284–447.)

——. *Quaestiones in Genesim (Questions and Answers on Genesis).* Translated by Ralph Marcus. (Loeb Classical Library.) London and Cambridge, Mass., 1953. 2 vols.

PHILOSTRATUS. *Vita Apollonii* (Life of Apollonius of Tyana). With a translation by F. C. Conybeare. (Loeb Classical Library.) London and New York, 1912. 2 vols.

Picinellus, Philippus (Filippo Picinelli). *Mundus Symbolicus.* Cologne, 1687. 2 vols.

Pistis Sophia. Edited and translated by G. R. S. Mead. London, 1955.

Pius XII, Pope. *The Assumption of Our Blessed Lady: Munificentissimus Deus.* An anonymous translation. Dublin, 1950. For original, see: *Acta Apostolicae Sedis* (Vatican City), XXXXII (2nd series, XVII), (1950), 753–73.

——. *Mary, Queen of All Creation.* Encyclical Letter, Ad Caeli Reginam, on the Royal Dignity of the Blessed Virgin Mary. [Translated by Philip Wroe.] London, [1955]. For original, see: *Acta Apostolicae Sedis* (Vatican City), XXXXVI (2nd series, XXI), (1954), 625–40.

Plato. *The Dialogues.* Translated by Benjamin Jowett. New York, 1937. 2 vols. (*Republic*, I, 591–879; *Timaeus*, II, 3–68.)

"Platonis Liber Quartorum." See *(A) Theatrum chemicum*, **xxi.**

Plotinus. *The Enneads.* Translated by Stephen Mackenna. 2nd edn., revised by B. S. Page. London, 1956.

Plutarch. *Moralia.* With an English translation by Frank Cole Babbitt and others. (Loeb Classical Library.) London and New York, 1927– . 14 vols. ("De Ei" [The E at Delphi], V, 198–253; "De facie in orbe lunae" [The Face of the Moon], XII, 34–223.)

——. *Moralia.* Edited by Gregorius N. Bernardakis. Leipzig, 1888–96. 8 vols. ("Adversus Coloten," VI, 422–78.)

Pontificale Romanum. Editio secunda post typicam. Ratisbon (Regensburg), 1908.

Porphyry (Porphyrius). *Opuscula selecta.* Edited by August Nauck. Leipzig, 1886. ("De antro nympharum," pp. 55–81.)

Prado, N. del. *De veritate fundamentali philosophiae Christianae.* Fribourg, 1911.

Preger, Wilhelm. *Geschichte der deutschen Mystik im Mittelalter.* Leipzig, 1874. 3 vols.

PREISENDANZ, KARL. *Papyri Graecae Magicae: Die Griechischen Zauberpapyri.* Berlin, 1928–31. 2 vols.

Pretiosa margarita novella. See BONUS.

PROCLUS. *In Platonis Timaeum Commentaria.* Edited by Ernst Diehl. Leipzig, 1903–6. 3 vols. For translation, see: TAYLOR, THOMAS (trans.). *The Commentaries of Proklos on the Timaeus of Plato.* London, 1820. 2 vols.

PRUEMMER, DOMINIK M. *Fontes Vitae S. Thomae Aquinatis.* Toulouse, 1912–37. 6 parts. (Petrus Calo, *Vita S. Thomae Aquinatis,* 17–55; Gulielmus de Tocco, *Vita S. Thomae Aquinatis,* 57–160.)

PTOLEMY OF LUCCA (Ptolemaeus Lucensis). *Historia Ecclesiastica.* See MURATORI.

QUERFELD, ARTHUR HEINRICH. *Michael Scotus und seine Schrift De Secretis Naturae.* (Dissertation.) Leipzig, 1919.

QUETIF, JACQUES, and ECHARD, JACQUES. *Scriptores Ordinis Praedicatorum.* Paris, 1719–21. 2 vols.

QUISPEL, GILLES. *Gnosis als Weltreligion.* Zurich, 1951.

RAHNER, HUGO. "Antenna Crucis II: Das Meer der Welt," *Zeitschrift für katholische Theologie* (Innsbruck and Leipzig), LXVI (1942), 112ff.

——. "Flumina de ventre Christi," *Biblica* (Rome), XXII (1941), 269–302, 367–403.

——. "Mysterium lunae," *Zeitschrift für katholische Theologie* (Innsbruck and Leipzig), LXIII (1939), 311–49, 428–42, and LXIV (1940), 61–80, 121–31.

——. "Die seelenheilende Blume. Moly und Mandragore in antiker und christlicher Symbolik," *Eranos-Jahrbuch XII,* Festgabe für C. G. Jung (Zurich, 1945), 117–239.

REITZENSTEIN, RICHARD. "Alchemistische Lehrschriften und Märchen bei den Arabern," *Religionsgeschichtliche Versuche und Vorarbeiten* (Giessen), XIX : 2 (1923), 63–86.

——. "Zur Geschichte der Alchemie und des Mystizismus," *Nachrichten von der Gesellschaft der Wissenschaften zu Göttingen,* Philologisch-historische Klasse (Göttingen, 1919), 1–37.

——. *Die hellenistischen Mysterienreligionen.* 3rd edn., Leipzig and Berlin, 1927.

——. *Das iranische Erlösungsmysterium.* Bonn, 1921.

——. *Poimandres.* Leipzig, 1904.

REUTER, HERMANN. *Geschichte der religiösen Aufklärung im Mittelalter.* Berlin, 1875–77. 2 vols.

RHABANUS MAURUS. *Allegoriae in sacram scripturam.* In MIGNE, *P.L.*, vol. 112, cols. 849–1088.

RHENANUS, JOHANNES (ed.). *Harmoniae inperscrutabilis chymico-philosophicae sive Philosophorum antiquorum consentientium decades duae.* Frankfort, 1625. ("Aurora sive Aurea hora," Decas II, pp. 175–242.)

RHINE, J. B. *The Reach of the Mind.* New York, 1947; London, 1948.

RICHARD OF ST. VICTOR. *Explicatio in Cantica Canticorum.* In MIGNE, *P.L.*, vol. 196, cols. 405–524.

——. *De tribus appropriatis personis in Trinitate.* In MIGNE, *P.L.*, vol. 196, cols. 991–94.

RIPLEY, GEORGE. *Opera omnia chemica.* Cassel, 1649.

——. "Cantilena." See *Opera omnia chemica,* pp. 421ff. For translation, see JUNG, *Mysterium Coniunctionis,* pp. 274ff.

——. "Liber duodecim portarum." See *Omnia opera chemica,* above (pp. 1–100); also *(A)* MANGET, *Bibliotheca chemica curiosa,* xix.

——. "Verses belonging to an Emblematicall Scrowle." In ELIAS ASHMOLE (ed.). *Theatrum Chemicum Britannicum.* London, 1652. (Pp. 375–79.)

——. ["The Ripley Scrowle."] See Codices and MSS., v.

ROBERT DE GROSSETESTE. "De unica forma omnium." In LUDWIG BAUR (ed.). *Die philosophischen Werke des Robert Grosseteste.* (Beiträge zur Geschichte der Philosophie im Mittelalters, IX.) Münster, 1912.

[Roman Breviary.] *Breviarium Romanum . . .* Editio quinta post typicam. Vatican City, 1956.

[Roman Missal.] *Missale Romanum . . .* Editio VI juxta typicam Vaticanam amplificata III. New York (Benziger Brothers), 1947.

"Rosarium Arnaldi." See *(A) Artis auriferae* (1610), xvi.

"Rosarium philosophorum." See *(A) Artis auriferae* (1593), **vii**, and (1610), **xv**; *(A)* MANGET, *Bibliotheca chemica curiosa*, **xii**.

ROSE, VALENTIN. *De Aristotelis librorum ordine et auctoritate*. Berlin, 1854.

ROSENCREUTZ, CHRISTIAN (Johann Valentin Andreae). *Chymische Hochzeit*. Strasbourg, 1616. (There are two editions of this place and date: the one cited in this volume bears the imprint "In Verlägung Lazari Zetzners S. Erben," and at the end the colophon "Bei Conrad Scher.")

"Rosinus ad Euthiciam." See *(A) Artis auriferae* (1610), **iv**.

"Rosinus ad Sarratantam." See *(A) Artis auriferae* (1593), **vi**; (1610), **v**.

RUDIN, JOSEF (ed.). *Neurose und Religion: Krankheitsbilder und ihre Problematik*. Olten and Freiburg im Breisgau, 1964.

——. *Psychotherapie und Religion: Seele, Person, Gott*. Olten, 1960.

RUDOLF OF NYMWEGEN. *Legenda litteralis Beati Alberti Magni*. Cologne, 1490.

RULAND, MARTIN. *Lexicon alchemiae, sive Dictionarium alchemisticum*. Frankfort, 1612. For translation, see: *A Lexicon of Alchemy or Alchemical Dictionary*. [London, 1892.]

RUSKA, JULIUS. "Die Alchemie des Avicenna," *Isis* (Bruges), XXI (1934), 14–51.

——. "Arabische Alchemisten: I. Chālid ibn Jazīd ibn Mu'āwija. II: Ga'far Alṣādiq, der Sechste Imam," *Heidelberger Akten der von-Portheim-Stiftung*, VI (1924). (The two articles are separately paginated.)

—— (ed.). *Buch der Alaune und Salze* ("De aluminibus et salibus"). Berlin, 1935.

——. "Studien zu Muhammad ibn Umail," *Isis* (Bruges), XXIV (1935–36), 310–42.

——. *Tabula Smaragdina; ein Beitrag zur Geschichte der hermetischen Literatur*. Heidelberg, 1926.

—— (ed.). *Turba Philosophorum*. Berlin, 1931.

—— (trans.). "Übersetzung und Bearbeitungen von Al-Razis Buch Geheimnis der Geheimnisse," *Quellen und Studien zur Geschichte der Naturwissenschaften und der Medizin* (Berlin), IV (1935).

——. See also FERCKEL.

SALVATORE, F. *Due sermone inediti di San Tommaso.* Rome, 1912.

SARTON, GEORGE. *Introduction to the History of Science.* Washington, 1927–48. 3 vols. in 5 parts.

"Scala philosophorum." See *(A) Artis auriferae* (1610), **xiv**; *(A)* MANGET, *Bibliotheca chemica curiosa,* **xiv.**

SCHMIDT, CARL. "Ein voriraenisches gnostisches Originalwerk in koptischer Sprache" [Gospel according to Mary], *Sitzungsberichte der königlich Preussischen Akademie der Wissenschaften zu Berlin* (1896), 839–46.

SCHOLEM, G. G. See ABU AFLAḤ.

SCHUMPP, M. "Hat der hl. Thomas einen Kommentar zu dem Hohenlied geschrieben?" *Divus Thomas* (Fribourg), VIII (1921), 47–58.

SCOTT, WALTER (ed.). *Hermetica.* Oxford, 1924–36. 4 vols.

"Secreta secretorum." See ARISTOTLE, pseudo-.

SELLIN, ERNST. *Introduction to the Old Testament.* Translated by W. Montgomery. London, 1923.

SENDIVOGIUS, MICHAEL. "Novum lumen chemicum." See *(A) Musaeum hermeticum,* vii.

SENIOR. See ZADITH SENIOR.

"Septem tractatus Hermetis." See HERMES TRISMEGISTUS, "Tractatus aureus."

SERTILLANGES, A. D. *Der heilige Thomas von Aquin.* Hellerau, 1928.

[SERVIUS.] *Servii Grammatici qui feruntur in Vergilii Carmina commentarii.* Edited by Georg Thilo and Hermann Hagen. Leipzig, 1878–1902. 3 vols.

SIEBMACHER, JOHANN AMBROSIUS. "Hydrolithus sophicus" [Aquarium sapientum"]. See *(A) Musaeum hermeticum,* iii.

SIEWERTH, GUSTAV. "Die Apriorität der menschlichen Erkenntnis nach Thomas von Aquin," *Symposion* (Freiburg and Munich), I (1948; pub. 1949), 89–167.

SILBERER, HERBERT. *Problems of Mysticism and Its Symbolism.* Translated by Smith Ely Jelliffe. New York and London, 1917.

SINGER, DOROTHEA WALEY. *Catalogue of Latin and Vernacular Alchemical MSS. in Great Britain and Ireland dating from before the 16th Century.* Brussels, 1928–31. 3 vols.

SIXTUS OF SIENA. *Bibliotheca sancta.* Venice, 1566. 2nd edn., Frankfort, 1575.

SOLOMON, BISHOP OF BASRA. *The Book of the Bee.* Edited and translated by E. A. Wallis Budge. (Anecdota Oxoniensia, Semitic Series, I : 2.) Oxford, 1886.

Solomon, Odes of. Edited with Introduction and Notes by John Henry Bernard. (Texts and Studies, VIII : 3.) Cambridge, 1912.

SOLOMON. See also *Testament of Solomon.*

STANGHETTI, G. "Da San Tommaso a Max Planck." (Acta Pontificia Academiae Romanae S. Thomae Aquinatis et Religionis Catholicae, IX.) Rome and Turin, 1944.

STAPLETON, H. E., and M. HIDĀYAT HUSAIN. "Muhammad bin Umail: His Date, Writings, and Place in Alchemical History," *Memoirs of the Asiatic Society of Bengal* (Calcutta), XII (1933), 117–43.

STEELE, ROBERT. See LYDGATE, JOHN.

STEINBUECHEL, THEODOR. *Der Zweckgedanke in der Philosophie des Thomas von Aquino.* (Beiträge zur Geschichte der Philosophie des Mittelalters, XI : 1.) Münster, 1913.

STEINSCHNEIDER, MORITZ. *Die europäischen Übersetzungen aus dem Arabischen bis Mitte des 17. Jahrhunderts* (Sitzungsberichte der kaiserlichen Akademie der Wissenschaften in Wien, Philosophisch-historisch Klasse, 149, 151). Vienna, 1904–5. 2 parts.

——. *Die hebräischen Übersetzungen des Mittelalters und die Juden als Dolmetscher.* Berlin, 1893.

——. "Zur pseudepigraphischen Literatur insbesondere der geheimen Wissenschaften des Mittelalters," *Wissenschaftlichen Blätter aus der Veitel Heine Ephraimischen Lehranstalt in Berlin,* Sammlung I, no. 3 (1862).

STEUER, ROBERT O. *Über das wohlriechende Natron bei den alten Ägyptern.* Leiden, 1937.

[STOBAEUS, JOHN.] *Ioannis Stobaei Anthologium.* Edited by Kurt Wachsmuth and Otto Hense. Berlin, 1884–94. 5 vols.

"Tabula smaragdina." See HERMES TRISMEGISTUS; RUSKA.

Tabulae Codicum manu Scriptorum in Bibliotheca Palatina Vindo-bonensi asservatorum. (Österreichische Akademie der Wissen-schaften.) Vienna, 1864–99. 10 vols.

TERTULLIAN. *De anima.* In MIGNE, *P.L.,* vol. 2, cols. 641–752. For translation, see: *The Writings of Tertullian,* vol. II. Translated by Peter Holmes. (Ante-Nicene Christian Library, XV.) Edinburgh, 1870.

——. *Adversus Hermogenem.* In MIGNE, *P.L.,* vol. 2, cols. 195–238.

——. *Adversus Valentinianos.* In MIGNE, *P.L.,* vol. 2, cols. 538–94.

Testament of Solomon, The. Edited with an introduction by Chester Charlton McCown. (Untersuchungen zum neuen Testament, IX.) Leipzig and New York, 1922.

THEODORET OF CYRUS. *Explanatio in Canticum Canticorum.* In MIGNE, *P.G.,* vol. 81, cols. 27–214.

——. *Interpretatio in Isaiam.* In MIGNE, *P.G.,* vol. 81, cols. 215–494.

THERY, G. *Autour du décret de 1210.* (Bibliothèque Thomiste, VI and VII.) Kain (Belgium), 1925–26. 2 vols.

——. "Le Commentaire de Maître Eckhart sur le livre de la Sagesse," *Archives d'histoire doctrinale et littéraire du moyen-âge* (Paris), III, 321–443; IV, 233–392 (1928–29.)

THOMAS AQUINAS. *Opera.* Edited by E. Fretté and P. Maré. Paris, 1871–80. 34 vols.

——. *Commentarium in Epistolam ad Hebraeos.* In *Opera,* vol. 21, pp. 561–734.

——. *Commentarium in Libros IV Sententiarum Petri Lombardi.* In *Opera,* vols. 7–11, 30.

——. *Compendium of Theology.* Translated by Cyril Vollert. St. Louis and London, 1952. (Original: *Compendium theologiae,* in *Opera,* vol. 27, pp. 1–12.)

——. *Contra impugnantes Dei cultum et religionem.* In *Opera,* vol. 19, pp. 1–116.

——. *De anima.* See ARISTOTLE, *De anima.*

——. *De coelo et mundo.* In *Opera,* vol. 23, pp. 1–266.

——. *De ente et essentia.* In *Opera*, vol. 27, pp. 468–79. For translation, see: *Concerning Being and Essence.* Translated by George G. Leckie. New York and London, [1937].

——. *De malo.* In *Opera*, vol. 13, pp. 320–618. Alternative source: *Quaestiones disputatae* (see below), vol. 2, pp. 370–719.

——. *De occultis operibus naturae ad quendam militem.* In *Opera*, vol. 27, pp. 504–7.

——. *De potentia.* In *Opera*, vol. 13, pp. 1–319. Alternative source: *Quaestiones disputatae* (see below), vol. 2, pp. 1–370.

——. *De veritate.* In *Opera*, vol. 14, pp. 315–640. For translation, see: *Truth.* Translated by Robert W. Mulligan. Chicago, 1952–54. 3 vols.

——. *Expositio in Symbolum apostolorum.* In *Opera*, vol. 27, pp. 203–29. See also HURTER.

——. *Expositio super librum Boethii De Trinitate.* Edited by Bruno Decker. (Studien und Texte zur Geistesgeschichte des Mittelalters, IV.) Leiden, 1955.

——. *Meteorologica.* In *Opera*, vol. 23, pp. 387–571. See also Codices and MSS., **xiv**.

——. *Quaestiones disputatae.* Paris, 1925. 2 vols.

——. *Quaestiones quodlibetales.* Paris, 1926.

——. "Liber lilii benedicti." See *(A) Theatrum chemicum*, **xix**.

——. "Secreta alchimiae magnalia." See *(A) Theatrum chemicum*, **ix**.

——. *Summa contra Gentiles.* In *Opera*, vol. 12. For translation, see: *Summa contra Gentiles.* Translated by the English Dominican Fathers. London, 1924–29. 4 vols.

——. *Summa theologica.* In *Opera*, vols. 1–6. For translation, see: *Summa theologica.* Translated by the English Dominican Fathers. New York, 1947–48. 3 vols.

——. "Thesaurus alchimiae." See *(A) Theatrum chemicum*, **x**.

——. "Tractatus sextus de esse et essentia mineralium." See *(A) Theatrum chemicum*, **xxvi**.

THOMAS OF CANTIMPRÉ (Thomas Cantipretanus). *Bonum universale de apibus.* Douai, 1627.

THORNDIKE, LYNN. "Additional Incipits of Medieval Scientific Writings in Latin," *Speculum* (Cambridge, Mass.), XIV (1939), 93–105.

——. "Alchemical Writings in Vatican Palatine Manuscripts," *Speculum* (Cambridge, Mass.), XI (1936), 370–83.

——. *A History of Magic and Experimental Science.* New York, 1923–58. 8 vols.

——. "More Incipits of Medieval Scientific Writings in Latin," *Speculum* (Cambridge, Mass.), XVII (1942), 342–66.

——, and KIBRE, PEARL. *A Catalogue of Incipits of Medieval Scientific Writings in Latin.* (Medieval Academy of America Publications, XXIX.) Cambridge, Mass., 1937.

TITUS OF BOSTRA. *Adversus Manichaeos libri tres.* In MIGNE, *P.G.,* vol. 18, cols. 1069–1260.

TOCCO, GULIELMO DE. *Vita sancti Thomae Aquinatis.* See PRUEMMER. Alternative source: BOLLANDUS, *Acta Sanctorum Martii,* I, 657–85.

TOURON, ANTOINE. *La Vie de Saint Thomas d'Aquin.* Paris, 1737.

"Tractatus aureus de lapide." See HERMES TRISMEGISTUS.

TRAUBE, LUDWIG (ed.). *Poetae Latini aevi Carolini.* (Monumenta Germaniae historica.) Berlin, 1880–1914. 4 vols. (MILO, *De sobrietate,* III, 615–75.)

TRISMOSIN, SOLOMON. *Splendor solis.* With introduction and explanatory notes by J. K. London, 1920.

"Turba philosophorum." See RUSKA; also *(A) Artis auriferae* (1593), i, ii; *Theatrum chemicum,* xx; Codices and MSS., xiii.

UEBERWEG, FRIEDRICH, and BAUMGARTNER, MATTHIAS. *Grundriss der Geschichte der Philosophie.* Part II: Die mittlere oder die patristische und scholastische Zeit. 10th edn., Berlin, 1915.

USENER, HERMANN. "Die Perle." In *Theologische Abhandlungen, Carl von Weizsäcker zu seinem 70.sten Geburtstage gewidmet, von A. Harnack usw.* Freiburg im Breisgau, 1892. (Pp. 203–13.)

VACANT, JEAN MICHEL ALFRED, and MANGENOT, EUGÈNE (eds.). *Dictionnaire de Théologie catholique.* Paris, 1899–1950. 15 vols.

VALENTINELLI, GIUSEPPE. *Bibliotheca Manuscripta ad S. Marci Venetiarum.* 1868–73. 6 vols.

VANDIER, JACQUES. *La Religion égyptienne.* (Introduction à l'histoire des religions, I.) 2nd edn., Paris, 1949.

VERBEKE, GÉRARD. *Thémistius: Commentaire sur le traité de l'âme d'Aristote, traduction de Guillaume de Moerbeke.* (Corpus latinum commentariorum in Aristotelem graecorum, I.) Louvain and Paris, 1957.

VICTORINUS AFER, MARIUS. *In Epistolam Pauli ad Galatas libri duo.* In MIGNE, *P.L.*, vol. 8, cols. 1145–98.

VINCENT OF BEAUVAIS. *Speculum maius.* Venice, 1591.

VIRGIL (Publius Virgilius Maro). [*Works.*] With an English translation by H. Rushton Fairclough. (Loeb Classical Library.) London and New York, 1916–18. 2 vols.

"Visio Arislei." See *(A) Artis auriferae* (1593), iii.

VREDE, WILHELM. *Die beiden dem heiligen Thomas von Aquino zugeschriebenen Commentare zum Hohenlied.* Berlin, 1913.

WAITE, ARTHUR EDWARD. *Lives of Alchemystical Philosophers.* London, 1888.

——. See also *(A) Musaeum hermeticum.*

WALZ, ANGELO. "De Alberti Magni et S. Thomae personali relatione," *Angelicum* (Rome), II : 3 (1925), 299–319.

——. "De Aquinatis et Vita Discessu." *Xenia Thomistica* (Rome), III (1925), 41–55.

——. *St. Thomas Aquinas: A Biographical Study.* Translated by Sebastian Bullough. Westminster, Maryland, 1951. (Original: *San Tommaso d'Aquino*, Rome, 1944.)

WENZL, ALOYS. *Die philosophischen Grenzfragen der modernen Naturwissenschaft.* 3rd edn., Stuttgart, 1960.

WHITE, VICTOR. *God and the Unconscious.* London, 1952.

——. "St. Thomas's Conception of Revelation," *Dominican Studies* (Oxford), I (1948), 3–34.

WILHELM, RICHARD, and JUNG, C. G. *The Secret of the Golden Flower.* Translated by Cary F. Baynes. London and New York, 1931; rev. edn., 1962. (For Jung's commentary, see also Vol. 13 of his *Collected Works.*)

WILLIAM OF AUVERGNE (Gulielmus Alvernus). *Opera Omnia.* Paris, 1674. 2 vols. ("De anima," vol. II Suppl., 65–228; "De legibus," vol. I, 18–102; "De trinitate," vol. II Suppl., 1–64; "De universo," vol. I, 593–1074.)

WILLIAM OF THIERRY. *Expositio altera super Cantica Canticorum.* In MIGNE, *P.L.,* vol. 180, cols. 473–546.

WITELO. *Liber de intelligentiis.* Edited by Clemens Baeumker. (Beiträge zur Geschichte der Philosophie des Mittelalters, III : 2.) Münster, 1908.

WITTEKINDT, W. *Das Hohe Lied und seine Beziehungen zum Istarkult.* Hanover, 1925.

WOLBERO, ABBOT OF ST. PANTALEON, COLOGNE. *Commentaria super Canticum Canticorum.* In MIGNE, *P.L.,* vol. 195, cols. 1001–1278.

Worm Runner's Digest, The. Edited by J. V. McConnell and published irregularly at the University of Michigan, Ann Arbor, 1959– .

WUESTENFELD, HEINRICH FERDINAND. "Die Übersetzungen arabischer Werke in das Lateinische seit dem 11. Jahrhundert," *Abhandlungen der königlichen Gesellschaft der Wissenschaften zu Göttingen,* Historisch-philologische Klasse (Göttingen), XXII : 2 (1877).

WUNDERLICH, EVA. *Die Bedeutung der roten Farbe im Kultus der Griechen und Römer, . . . mit Berücksichtigung entsprechender Bräuche bei anderen Völkern.* (Religionsgeschichtliche Versuche und Vorarbeiten, XX : 1.) Giessen, 1925.

WYSER, PAUL. *Thomas von Aquin.* (Bibliographische Einführungen in das Studium der Philosophie, edited by I. M. Bochenski, 13/14.) Bern, 1950.

ZADITH SENIOR (Zadith ben Hamuel). *De chemia Senioris antiquissimi philosophi libellus.* Strasbourg, 1566. See also *(A) Theatrum chemicum,* xxii; *(A)* MANGET, *Bibliotheca chemica curiosa,* xvii.

Zohar, The. Translated by Harry Sperling and Maurice Simon. London, 1931–34. 5 vols. See also MUELLER.

INDEXES

INDEX OF BIBLICAL REFERENCES
AND PARALLELS

The Books of the Old Testament, Apocrypha, and New Testament are here arranged in the order of the Protestant Bible (e.g., Authorized or King James version); that of the Vulgate in some cases differs. In the text and notes of this volume, the chapter and verse references follow the Vulgate (and Douay version). In this index, the Vulgate numeration is followed; but, for convenience, references (in parentheses) are given to the Protestant (King James) version also, where its numeration differs from the Vulgate. (N.B. In Psalms, the numbering of the two versions seldom coincides.)

GENERAL INDEX

For references to "separate treatises" composing alchemical compilations, see the Bibliography, above, pp. 479*ff*, where the names are listed.

matter: divinization of, 385; and form, 164, 346; redemption of, 272; *see also* soul
Maximus of Turin, 236n
Maximus of Tyre, 346n
Maya, 242
meaning, 284
"measure, number, and weight," 279
mediator, 397, 398
medicine, 199
Meier, M., 246n
Melchior Cibinensis, 222n
memory, species, xn
mendicant orders, 327, 420
Mennens, Gulielmus (William), 23, 241n, 277n, 280, 299, 330n, 352n, 365n, 382n, 383n, 385n, 392n
Mephistopheles, 403
Mercurius, 142fn, 163n, 259, 324, 334, 343f, 354, 381, 384, 398; chthonic, 221; and long life, 11; Luciferian aspect, 403; senex, 396, 397
mercury, evaporated, 217
meretrix, 182n
Mersad el-ibad, 339n
Meseguer Irles, P., xiin
Mesopotamia, 269
metals; imprisonment of, 269; and planets, 350; as servants, 235; seven, 214n, 215, 240, 273; transmutation of, 418
"Metaphora Belini," 384n
Metatron, 263
Methodius of Philippi, 204n, 211n
Meyrink, G., 408n, 418n
Michael Scotus, 8, 410
microcosm, as house, 325, 332, 339n
midday, 189
Milo, 324
Minkowski-Einstein world, x
miracles, 177
Miriam, 363
Mithras / Mithraic mysteries, 320, 329, 374
Moerbeke, *see* William
Mohammed, light of, 305n
Mohlberg, C., 26

moisture, lunar, 263
moly, 376
monad, 254
Monte Cassino, 410
Montfort, heretical sects at, 283n
mouths, twelve, 214n, 215
moon, 211, 320, 351, 384n; Church as, 203, 236; full, 380; new, 363; *see also* Luna
moon-plant, 376
Moret, A., 329n, 331n
Morienus, 7, 8, 12ff, 21, 34fn, 92fn, 114fn, 120fn, 202, 310, 341n, 345n; cited in *Aurora,* 48f, 92f, 94f, 112f, 114f, 201, 306, 309, 335, 336
Moses, 363, 397n; rod of, 323, 326, 354f; Song of, 312
mother / Mother: divine, need for, 212; Great, 248; Holy Spirit as, 359n
"Mother of All Living" / "Mother of All Things," 188, 189, 257, 258n; *see also* All-Mother
Mother of God, 321
mountains, 349
mud, abyssal, 258
Muhammad ibn Umail at-Tamimi, 10, 16
multiplicatio, 385f
multitude of the faithful, 385, 402
mummification, 401
mundus: archetypus, 155, 242; *potentialis,* 351
Munificentissimus Deus (Papal encyclical), 322n
Muratori, L. A., 429n
Musaeum hermeticum, see titles of separate treatises
Mylius, J. D., 173n, 305n
mysteries: change of clothing in, 374; Eleusinian, 241n, 333n; Mithraic, 329; of Osiris, 401
mysterium coniunctionis, 213, 321, 359, 398
mystery religions, 241n, 329, 373
mysticism, Islamic, 173
myths, 178

W

Waite, A. E., 409*n*

Waldensians, 18, 283*n*

Waldkirch, Conrad, 6

Walz, A., 409*n*, 410*n*, 411*n*, 414*n*, 417*n*, 419*n*, 420*n*, 422*n*, 423*n*, 424*n*, 425*n*, 426*n*, 429*n*

water: divine, 199, 243, 258*f*, 288, 323, 348; figure of life and death, 258; of Holy Spirit, 287*f*; Uroboros as, 268

Wenzl, Aloys, ix

wheat, sowing of, 401

White, Victor, x*f*, xi*fn*, 162*n*, 170*n*, 196*n*

whitening, 306, 312; see also *albedo*

wholeness, 237; bride as, 389; preconscious, 274; psychic, 232; threeness and, 294

William of Auvergne, 18*n*, 167, 174*n*, 182, 183*n*, 184*n*, 185*n*, 246*n*, 263

William of Moerbeke, 420; translation of *De anima*, xi*n*, 8, 9*n*

William of Saint-Amour, 420

William of Thierry, 246*n*

window, 379

wine, 350

Wisdom, *passim;* as anima figure, 166; as Aurora, 204; black earth as, 300; in centre of earth, 368; chthonic aspect, 293; as concrete substance, 194; desire for rejuvenation, 230; earth and, 341; emergence from matter, 243; as father of alchemist, 232; feminine pneuma, 159; God as, 319; Holy Spirit and, 286; identity with filius, 238; images of, 162*ff*; imperfection of, 224; as lapis, 160; Mercurius and, 221; personal form of, 192; prima materia as, 224; as Second Adam, 358; sunk in matter, 224; transpersonal, 170; treasure-house of, 214; Yahweh's playmate, 242; *see also* Sapientia

wise old man, 358, 365, 415*n*

Witelo, 180*n*, 420

Wittekindt, W., 362*n*

Wolbero, 228*n*

wolf, 352

woman: black, 363; great, of the Apocalypse, 211, 212*ff*, 221, 321; unconscious as, 218; white, 365

women: St. Thomas and, 411, 423; seven, 270*ff*

Word, the, and Wisdom, 357*n*

world, unitary, see *unus mundus*

world-axis, 397

world-soul, 358, 373; see also *anima mundi*

world-tree, 397

Wunderlich, E., 274*n*

Wyser, P., 409*n*

Y

Yahweh, 242; antinomy of, 230; light side of, 233

Yesod, 322

Z

Zadith, *see* Senior

zodiac, 214, 215, 254*n*, 329

Zohar, 226, 322, 325*n*

Zosimos, 16, 161, 163*n*, 173*n*, 185*n*, 196*n*, 217, 218*n*, 243*n*, 258, 259*n*, 278, 289*n*, 290, 320, 323*n*, 324, 330, 333*n*, 345, 346, 347, 352*n*, 365*n*, 369, 374, 377, 389*n*, 390, 392*n*, 400